MW00781091

INDIVIDUAL CREATIVITY
IN THE WORKPLACE

Explorations in Creativity Research

Series Editor

James C. Kaufman

INDIVIDUAL CREATIVITY IN THE WORKPLACE

Edited by

RONI REITER-PALMON
University of Nebraska, Omaha, NE, USA

VICTORIA L. KENNEL
University of Nebraska Medical Center, Omaha, NE, USA

JAMES C. KAUFMAN
University of Connecticut, Storrs, CT, USA

ACADEMIC PRESS

An imprint of Elsevier

Academic Press is an imprint of Elsevier
125 London Wall, London EC2Y 5AS, United Kingdom
525 B Street, Suite 1650, San Diego, CA 92101, United States
50 Hampshire Street, 5th Floor, Cambridge, MA 02139, United States
The Boulevard, Langford Lane, Kidlington, Oxford OX5 1GB, United Kingdom

Library of Congress Cataloging-in-Publication Data
A catalog record for this book is available from the Library of Congress

British Library Cataloguing-in-Publication Data
A catalogue record for this book is available from the British Library

ISBN: 978-0-12-813238-8

For information on all Academic Press publications
visit our website at https://www.elsevier.com/books-and-journals

  Working together
to grow libraries in
developing countries

www.elsevier.com • www.bookaid.org

Publisher: Nikki Levy
Editorial Project Manager: Barbara Makinster
Production Project Manager: Mohana Natarajan
Designer: Matthew Limbert

Typeset by SPi Global, India

Dedication

To Ophir, who loved me, encouraged me, supported me, cheered me on, every step of the way

Roni

To Isabella

Vicki

For Adam S. Bristol,
One of my dearest friends,
An amazing father and husband to Indre,
A trusted colleague and collaborator,
And always the actor I envision as the lead role in all my plays
With love,

James

Contents

1

CREATIVITY AND INNOVATION: LARGER CONCEPTS

1. Moving From Creativity to Innovation
ERIC F. RIETZSCHEL, SIMONE M. RITTER

2. The Fuzzy Front-End? How Creativity Drives Organizational Innovation
DAVID H CROPLEY, MICHELLE L. OPPERT

3. An Integrated Model of Dynamic Problem Solving Within Organizational Constraints
JOHNATHAN R. CROMWELL, TERESA M. AMABILE, JEAN-FRANÇOIS HARVEY

4. Conceptualization of Emergent Constructs in a Multilevel Approach to Understanding Individual Creativity in Organizations

SOONMOOK LEE, JAE YOON CHANG, ROSEMARY HYEJIN MOON

2

INTELLIGENCE AND COGNITION

5. Interruptions and Multitasking: Advantages and Disadvantages for Creativity at Work

FRANCESCA MOCHI, NORA MADJAR

6. The Skills Needed to Think Creatively: Within-Process and Cross-Process Skills

MICHAEL D. MUMFORD, ERIN MICHELLE TODD, CORY HIGGS, SAMANTHA ELLIOTT

3

MOTIVATION/AFFECT/PREFERENCES

4

LEADERSHIP AND TEAMS

14. The Role of Individual Differences in Group and Team Creativity

LAUREN E. COURSEY, PAUL B. PAULUS, BELINDA C. WILLIAMS, JARED B. KENWORTHY

15 Constructing an Evidence-Based Model for Managing Creative Performance

BEN WIGERT

16. The Role of Creative Capacity in the 21st Century Army

GREGORY A. RUARK, NIKKI BLACKSMITH, LEE SPENCER WALLACE

Contributors

Julian B. Allen   Penn State University, University Park, PA, United States

Teresa M. Amabile   Entrepreneurial Management Unit, Harvard Business School, Boston, MA, United States

Nikki Blacksmith   Consortium Research Fellows Program, Alexandria, VA, United States

Sabina Bogilović   Faculty of Administration, University of Ljubljana, Ljubljana, Slovenia

Matej Černe   Faculty of Economics, University of Ljubljana, Ljubljana, Slovenia

Jae Yoon Chang   Sogang University, Seoul, Republic of Korea

Bo T. Christensen   Copenhagen Business School, Frederiksberg C, Denmark

Lauren E. Coursey   University of Texas at Arlington, Arlington, TX, United States

Johnathan R. Cromwell   Department of Entrepreneurship, Innovation, and Strategy, University of San Francisco, San Francisco, CA, United States

David H. Cropley   University of South Australia, Adelaide, SA, Australia

Lily Cushenbery   Stony Brook University, Stony Brook, NY, United States

Samantha Elliott   The University of Oklahoma, Norman, OK, United States

Peter V.W. Hartmann   Performance, Analytics & HRIS, Getinge, Copenhagen, Denmark

Jean-François Harvey   Department of Entrepreneurship and Innovation, HEC Montréal, Montréal, QC, Canada

Rachel Heinen   Penn State University, University Park, PA, United States

Cory Higgs   The University of Oklahoma, Norman, OK, United States

Matt C. Howard   University of South Alabama, Mobile, AL, United States

Samuel Hunter   Penn State University, University Park, PA, United States

James C. Kaufman   University of Connecticut, Storrs, CT, United States

Victoria Kennel   University of Nebraska Medical Center, Omaha, NE, United States

Jared B. Kenworthy   University of Texas at Arlington, Arlington, TX, United States

Soonmook Lee   Sungkyunkwan University, Seoul, Republic of Korea

Jeffrey B. Lovelace   University of Virginia, Charlottesville, VA, United States

Nora Madjar   University of Connecticut, Storrs, CT, United States

Hector P. Madrid   School of Management, Pontificia Universidad Católica de Chile, Santiago, Chile

Alexander S. McKay   Virginia Commonwealth University, Richmond, VA, United States

Francesca Mochi   Università Cattolica del Sacro Cuore, Milano, Italy

Rosemary Hyejin Moon   Sogang University, Seoul, Republic of Korea

Michael D. Mumford   The University of Oklahoma, Norman, OK, United States

Michelle L. Oppert   University of South Australia, Adelaide, SA, Australia

Malcolm G. Patterson   Institute of Work Psychology, Management School, University of Sheffield, Sheffield, United Kingdom

Paul B. Paulus   University of Texas at Arlington, Arlington, TX, United States

Thomas Hedegaard Rasmussen   National Australia Bank, Melbourne, VIC, Australia

Roni Reiter-Palmon   University of Nebraska at Omaha, Omaha, NE, United States

Eric F. Rietzschel   Department of Psychology, University of Groningen, Groningen, Netherlands

Simone M. Ritter   Radboud University Nijmegen, Behavioural Science Institute, Nijmegen, Netherlands

Gregory A. Ruark   United States Army Research Institute for the Behavioral and Social Sciences, Fort Belvoir, VA, United States

Erin Michelle Todd   The University of Oklahoma, Norman, OK, United States

Lee Spencer Wallace   United States Army, The Pentagon, Washington, DC, United States

Ben Wigert   The Gallup Organization, Omaha, NE, United States

Belinda C. Williams   University of Texas at Arlington, Arlington, TX, United States

Individual Creativity in the Workplace: An Introduction

Roni Reiter-Palmon*, *Victoria Kennel*[†],
James C. Kaufman[‡]

*University of Nebraska at Omaha, Omaha, NE, United States [†]University of Nebraska Medical Center, Omaha, NE, United States [‡]University of Connecticut, Storrs, CT, United States

For the past two decades, interest in creativity and innovation in organizations has increased dramatically (Cummings & Oldham, 1997; Ford, 1996; Woodman, Sawyer, & Griffin, 1993). Changes in technology, globalization, and increased competition have all created an environment in which creativity and innovation are needed to cope with situational demands, economic pressures, and frequent changes (Mumford, Scott, Gaddis, & Strange, 2002; Shalley, Zhou, & Oldham, 2004; West, Hirst, Richter, & Shipton, 2004; Woodman et al., 1993). Whereas early research in organizational creativity has focused on occupations such as scientists and Research and Development (R & D), current thinking is that employees can exhibit creativity in almost any job or occupation (Mumford, Whetzel, & Reiter-Palmon, 1997). Therefore, scholars have sought to identify those factors that facilitate or inhibit creativity in a variety of organizational settings in an effort to improve organizational creativity (Reiter-Palmon, Mitchell, and Royston, in press). A recent survey by IBM (2010) indicated that addressing rapid changes and uncertainty is viewed as commonplace for managers; therefore one of the most important skills for managers is that of creative thinking. Consequently, it is not surprising that organizational researchers have increasingly been interested in understanding the antecedents of creativity in organizations and, more specifically, studying individual creativity in the workplace.

The purpose of the book is to provide a deeper understanding of the various factors that may influence individual creativity in the workplace and how individuals can exhibit creativity in the workplace. Understanding how individual creativity is fostered or inhibited in the workplace is critical to our ability to improve organizational creativity overall. Analyzing how individual creativity is part of the larger, multilevel context, of the team and wider organization is critical. Organizational creativity does not occur in a vacuum; it is not enough to study creativity at the individual, team, leader, or organizational level; the way that these different levels of creativity interact and intersect is equally important (Agars, Kaufman, Deane, & Smith, 2012).

The first section, *Creativity and Innovation: Larger Concepts,* includes four chapters focusing on broader issues of creativity and innovation, linking the individual to the organization. Rietzschel and Ritter's chapter, *Moving from Creativity to Innovation,* addresses the evaluation and selection of creative ideas. Idea evaluation and selection activities occur after the generation of ideas but before their implementation and are an important but underemphasized element of creative problem solving. This chapter offers an overview of current research on the creative evaluation and selection process and its outcomes. Rietzschel and Ritter describe several individual and contextual factors that affect the evaluation of creative ideas, such as expertise, personality characteristics, and evaluation instructions. Variables that affect idea selection performance include selection criteria, preferences for feasible (rather than original) ideas, and unconscious thought processes. They explore factors that affect the likelihood of creative idea implementation in organizations, such as the ability to pitch and sell ideas, as well as being able to garner acceptance of and support for new ideas from coworkers and supervisors. Finally, they conclude the chapter with practical recommendations to support the successful evaluation and selection of creative ideas by individuals in organizations. Idea selection outcomes may be improved through loosening implicit constraints about usefulness and originality, using instructions for idea evaluation and selection that encourage choosing creative ideas, inducing specific psychological conditions that may have a positive influence on creative idea evaluation and selection, and training employees in idea evaluation and selection skills. The successful "selling" of a highly creative idea may be improved through stressing feasibility and effectiveness, preparing for resistance to the idea, showing confidence and enthusiasm for the idea, focusing on the long-term implications of the idea, and engaging commitment from multiple stakeholders.

The next paper in this section, by Cropley and Oppert, continues the theme of creativity and its relation to innovation. In the chapter *The Fuzzy Front-End? How Creativity Drives Organizational Innovation,* the authors propose that creativity serves as a "fuzzy front-end" to the innovation process. They argue that change serves as the key driver of innovation because change necessitates the generation of new solutions. Organizations engage in innovation when they capitalize on such change through incrementation and disruption. Cropley and Oppert illustrate various models and stages of the innovation process and portray creativity as a well-defined, understood, and manageable essential "front-end" of innovation. They conclude by presenting their Innovation Phase Model, which explains how key elements of creativity serve as drivers of innovation.

Cromwell, Amabile, and Harvey suggest in their chapter *An Integrated Model of Dynamic Problem Solving Within Organizational Constraints* that creativity can occur using two different pathways. One, the more typical pathway studied, is a problem-focused approach, where ideas are generated in response to a problem. However, an alternative exists in which ideas are developed and then the search begins for the problem the ideas can solve. Cromwell et al. suggest that the contradiction between these two approaches can be resolved by evaluating the role that constraints play in the creative process. Specifically, they suggest that the level and type of constraint that people face at different times during the creative process differentiates between the problem-first and the idea-first models. Cromwell et al. provide a review of these two different models and develop a typology of constraints based on two dimensions: type of constraints (resource or problem constraints) and source of constraints (internal or external). Using this typology as well as the two models, Cromwell et al. develop a model to synthesize these elements—the dynamic problem solving process model.

The final chapter in this section, *Conceptualization of Emergent Constructs in a Multi-level Approach to Understanding Individual Creativity in Organizations* by Lee, Chang, and Moon, provides a multilevel perspective on creativity in organizations. Much of the study of organizational creativity has focused on how creativity can flow from the bottom up, from individual creativity to team and organizational creativity. Yet there is some research focused on how creativity can flow from the top down, that is, from emergent and general properties at the organization and team level to the individual. However, to truly understand creativity in organizations from a multilevel perspective, both frameworks need to be employed simultaneously. This chapter provides researchers interested in such an approach a typology of categories of emergence to facilitate the conceptualization and measurement of such multilevel phenomena.

The second section in the book focuses on *Intelligence and Cognition* and includes three chapters. In their chapter, *Interruptions and Multitasking: Advantages and Disadvantages for Creativity at Work*, Mochi and Madjar theorize and review evidence regarding how different types of interruptions and multitasking may influence creativity. They describe five types of interruptions: intrusions, breaks, distractions, information technology, and multitasking and task switching. They propose that these types of interruptions influence the creative process and its outcomes through both cognitive and affective mechanisms via the provision or depletion of cognitive resources and through their effect on positive and negative affect. Mochi and Madjar further suggest various conditions that may influence these effects, such as the timing and frequency of interruptions, personal discretion to initiate interruptions, the nature of the intervening activity or break as it relates to creative activity, and individual preferences for involvement in any number of tasks. Mochi and Madjar conclude with recommendations for future research and practical tips for organizations regarding how interruptions may enhance and hinder creative performance.

The next chapter is *The Skills Needed to Think Creatively: Within-Process and Cross-Process Skills,* by Mumford, Todd, Higgs and Elliot. It focuses on the cognitive processes necessary to think creatively. Mumford et al. conceptualize creativity in the context of problem solving. The chapter provides a review examining the processes people must execute to produce creative problem solutions. Processes such as problem construction and identification, conceptual combination, and idea evaluation are reviewed. Next, the authors examine the strategies used in process execution that contribute to creative performance, focusing on the question of what skills must people possess to execute each of these processes? Mumford et al. discuss both process specific skills as well as cross-process skills. Cross-process skills are those skills that generalize across multiple processes. Five cross-process skills were identified by Mumford et al.: (1) causal analysis, (2) forecasting, (3) error analysis, (4) applications analysis, and (5) wisdom. Mumford et al. conclude by discussing some ways in which the study of these cross-process skills can contribute to our understanding of creativity such as providing new ways of measuring creative potential.

The third and final chapter in this section takes a different direction. Here, the authors Bogilović and Cerne evaluate the field of creativity research. Their chapter, *The Intellectual Structure and Outlooks for Individual Creativity Research: A Document Cocitation Analysis 1950–2015,* provides a detailed and nuanced look into the growth and development of the field of creativity research. Using bibliometric analysis based on cocitation and bibliographic coupling techniques, Bogilović and Cerne provide a discussion of the key articles and authors, and how constructs and theory have evolved over time. Their chapter suggests a growing interest in the field of individual creativity, indicated by a significant growth of publications over time. Their analysis suggests that early research (up to 1970) focused on a number of topics: (1) creative processes and intelligence, (2) creative talent and talent development, (3) measurement of creativity, and (4) brainstorming. The next time period (1971–85) shows the following topics (1) creative problem solving, (2) individual differences related to creativity including personality and intelligence, and (3) stimulating and measuring creativity. From 1986 to 2000, the interest and publications on creative problem solving and intelligence continued and remained very strong, as well as work on personality and creativity. New research topics emerge focusing on creativity in the workplace and the social psychology of creativity. From 2001 to 2010, we see a continuation of publications on individual differences, personality, and creative problem solving, and a stronger and more detailed set of publications on creativity in the workplace. Finally, since 2011 we see the additional emergence of team creativity, leadership and leading for creativity, and more attention to methodology and measurement. The chapter concludes with suggestions for future research based on this bibliographic analysis.

The third section in the book focuses on *Motivational, Affect and Preferences* aspects of individuals that relate to creativity and includes four chapters. Reiter-Palmon and Kaufman's chapter, *Creative Styles in the Workplace: New* vs. *Different*, explores the theoretical development and application of creative styles in the workplace. They synthesize existing theory and research to propose a model of "New" and "Different" creative styles that indicate *how* people choose to be creative. The foundational elements of the New and Different model derive from key distinguishing features of divergent and convergent thinking, radical and incremental creative contributions, and opportunities and constraints. Individuals with the New creative style are more likely to focus on radically novel ideas, seek a larger variety of ideas, and perceive potential constraints as opportunities; whereas, those with a Different creative style may desire to adapt and improve existing concepts, seek optimal ideas, and work to operate within constraints. Reiter-Palmon and Kaufman propose that both styles play a role in organizational creativity among individuals and teams: The New style benefits idea development, and the Different style identifies and addresses obstacles to idea development and implementation. They introduce a new creativity assessment, the *Creative Response Evaluation at Work (CRE-W)*, used to evaluate the New and Different creative styles. Finally, they describe the CRE-W's potential to support organizational initiatives to improve creativity through team composition, training, coaching, and development.

The section continues with a chapter by Rietzschel, *Freedom, Structure, and Creativity,* which address the tension between freedom and autonomy versus constraints and structure. Rietzschel argues that creativity is typically viewed as requiring freedom and that constraints and structure have a negative effect on creativity. In this chapter, Rietzschel suggests that this point of view is limited and ignore the creative potential of structure and constraints. Rietaschel reviews the literature on autonomy, freedom, and creativity, and explores the role that individual differences may play in the effect that freedom has on creativity. He suggests that freedom, although important for motivation and creativity, also implies complexity and cognitive load, and that this may diminish creative performance. As a result, constraints and structure at times have benefits for creativity depending on the situation and the individual. The chapter continues with a review of theory and empirical findings on individual difference variables that allow for creativity when constraints and structure are present. The chapter concludes with a discussion about the optimal balance between freedom and structure, with recommendations to organizations.

McKay, Lovelace, and Howard's chapter, *The Heart of Innovation: Antecedents and Consequences of Creative Self-Efficacy in Organizations*, offers a current review of the literature on creative self-efficacy in organizational settings. They review the existing theoretical background and conceptualization of creative self-efficacy, and discuss the results of previously published and new meta-analytic reviews on the construct. They describe several antecedents of creative self-efficacy including personal (job self-efficacy, job knowledge, and personality), contextual (leadership, job complexity, job autonomy, and job requirements), and social sources (social network characteristics), and report that job type and culture may moderate these relationships. McKay and colleagues explore creativity as the key outcome of studies on creative self-efficacy and suggest that culture, job type, and methodological factors (e.g., self- vs. other-report, cross-sectional vs. time-lagged design, measure type, and type of creativity) may moderate this relationship. They describe various measures of creative self-efficacy and conclude with directions for future research.

The section concludes with a chapter by Madrid andPatterson, *Affect and Creativity*. The authors conclude from a review of relevant literature that studies on creativity applied in organizational environments indicate that positive affect is a positive predictor of creativity, while the relationship between negative affect and creativity is less clear. Madrid and Peterson further discuss a number of theoretical approaches that have been used to address these findings such as the dual tuning and the affective shift process theories. However, they suggest that it is important to move beyond positive and negative affect. Therefore, accounting for both affective valence and activation offers the opportunity to study how a more diverse array of feelings might, or might not, be directly relevant to understanding creativity. In order to more fully address the role of affect in creativity, Madrid and Peterson adopt an affective valence and activation approach, specifically the Theory of Core Affect, to discuss and delineate a finer-grained understanding to the affective experience and creativity.

The final section focuses on individual creativity within the context of *teams and leadership* and includes five chapters. Hunter, Allen, Heinen, and Cushenbery's chapter, *Proposing a Multiple Pathway Approach to Leading Innovation: Single and Dual Leader Approaches*, suggests two general approaches to leading for innovation. They describe how the complexities of innovation create role conflict for those charged with leading innovation, and describe how such conflict directly and indirectly affects innovation outcomes. Under this lens, they propose a multiple pathway approach to leading for innovation. The first pathway employs a single leader capable of ambidexterity to engage in the wide variety of behaviors associated with successful innovation. The second utilizes a dual-leadership approach where two leaders engage in shared leadership to manage the responsibilities of leading innovation. Hunter and colleagues present the advantages and challenges of each leadership pathway and offer three key considerations to determine the appropriate approach, including rapid decision-making demands, clarity of leadership roles, and the diversity of innovation demands inherent in the organization.

Christensen, Hartmann, and Rasmussen's chapter, *Creative Leaders in Bureaucratic Organizations: Are Leaders More Innovative at Higher Levels of the Organizational Hierarchy?*, explores the associations between innovativeness and intelligence of leaders and their respective level of leadership in the organizational hierarchy. They tested these relationships in a sample of leaders from a large international corporation. Their results indicated that personal intelligence and innovativeness both independently predicted the leader's level of leadership in the organization. Trends in their results indicated that the relationship of intelligence and innovativeness with leadership level became stronger as leaders demonstrated greater tenure with the organization. Christensen and colleagues conclude with recommendations to help bureaucratic organizations engage in creative efforts.

Coursey, Paulus, Williams, and Kenworthy review the extensive literature on team creativity in their chapter The Role of *Individual Differences in Group and Team Creativity*. Although there is a tremendous amount of research on factors that facilitate and inhibit team creativity, Coursey et al. note that the research on individual differences and their effect on team creativity is more limited. The chapter reviews the literature on the factors that influence the role of individual differences on team creativity. Coursey et al. discuss the role of various factors that impede or facilitate individual contribution to team creativity and argue that when these factors are not present individual differences may have a stronger effect. The role of group composition and individual difference such as personality variables, motivation, and cognitive orientation, and their effect on overall creativity and the creative processes, is also considered in this chapter. Coursey et al. note that different individual differences may come into play and be more important for groups and teams engaging divergent vs. convergent aspects of creative problem solving. The chapter concludes with a proposed model to predict the effects of group composition on creativity.

Wigert, in his chapter on *Managing creativity in organizations*, addresses the issue of how organizations can manage creativity and innovation. His chapter provides a summary of data collected from a representative sample of employees in the United States regarding how employees are experiencing these key elements of the creative process in relation to best practices for driving creativity. The chapter then proceeds to cover cultivating the creativity of individual employees through improved management strategies and organizational performance strategies.

The final chapter in this section, by Ruark, Blacksmith, and Wallace, *The role of creative Capacity in the 21st Century Army*, focuses on a specific instance of creativity, in an area that seems somewhat less conducive to creativity—the military. Ruark and his colleagues discuss the role that creativity has in the military in the 21st century. Specifically, they suggest that although the hierarchical structure and focus on structured processes may be viewed as an antithetical to the Army, that is not the case. Rather, successful military operations require creativity. However, soldiers must balance the need for creative thinking and compliance with processes and procedure. In this chapter, they provide a discussion of the individual difference characteristics that the Army values that are central to creativity. Ruark et al. further acknowledge the difficulty inherent in enacting creativity in an organization that thrives on rules and doctrine and discuss way in which the Army can balance these through selection and developing creative soldiers.

Creativity and innovation are complex, multifaceted constructs. We hope that this book helps the streams of research seem more manageable. The relevant literature reviews will help readers catch up on areas in which they may be less familiar. The theories and models will help sort and organize complicated and nuanced concepts. The frequent connections to real-world situations will highlight how theory and studies can be applied in organizations. Finally, the suggestions and tips will offer specific ways that both scholars and organizational leaders can team up to direct the way toward the best possible future.

References

Agars, M. D., Kaufman, J. C., Deane, A., & Smith, B. (2012). Fostering individual creativity through organizational context: a review of recent research and recommendations for organizational leaders. In M. D. Mumford (Ed.), *Handbook of organizational creativity* (pp. 271–294). New York: Elsevier.

Cummings, A., & Oldham, G. R. (1997). Enhancing creativity: managing work contexts for the high potential employee. *California Management Review, 40*, 22–38.

Ford, C. M. (1996). A theory of individual creative action in multiple social domains. *Academy of Management Review*, (4), 1112–1142.

IBM. (2010). IBM 2010 Global CEO Study: Creativity selected as most crucial factor for future success [press release]. Retrieved from https://www-03.ibm.com/press/us/en/pressrelease/31670.wss.

Mumford, M. D., Scott, G. M., Gaddis, B., & Strange, J. M. (2002). Leading creative people: orchestrating expertise and relationships. *The Leadership Quarterly, 13*, 705–750. https://doi.org/10.1016/S1048-9843(02)00158-3.

Mumford, M. D., Whetzel, D. L., & Reiter-Palmon, R. (1997). Thinking creatively at work: organization influences on creative problem solving. *Journal of Creative Behaviour, 31*, 7–17.

Reiter-Palmon, R., Mitchell, K. S., & Royston, R. P. (in press). Improving creativity in organizational settings: applying research on creativity to organizations. To appear in J. C. Kaufman & R. J. Sternberg (Eds.), *Cambridge Handbook of creativity*.

Shalley, C. E., Zhou, J., & Oldham, G. R. (2004). The effects of personal and contextual characteristics on creativity: where should we go from here? *Journal of Management, 30*(2), 933–958. https://doi.org/10.1016/j.jm.2004.06.007.

West, M. A., Hirst, G., Richter, A., & Shipton, H. (2004). Twelve steps to heaven: successfully managing change through developing innovative teams. *European Journal of Work and Organizational Psychology, 13*(2), 269–299. https://doi.org/10.1080/13594320444000092.

Woodman, R., Sawyer, J., & Griffin, R. (1993). Toward a theory of organizational creativity. *The Academy of Management Review, 18*(2), 293–321. https://doi.org/10.2307/258761.

CREATIVITY AND INNOVATION: LARGER CONCEPTS

1

Moving From Creativity to Innovation

Eric F. Rietzschel*, *Simone M. Ritter*†

*Department of Psychology, University of Groningen, Groningen, Netherlands, †Radboud University Nijmegen, Behavioural Science Institute, Nijmegen, Netherlands

Creativity is one of our most important abilities, having led to humans exploring and colonizing the entire planet (as well as parts of extraterrestrial space), the invention of agriculture, medicine, and astounding levels of technological advances, not to mention science, philosophy, and art—it is no exaggeration to state that the world would look completely differently (for better or for worse) without human creativity. However, creativity's potential to change the world relies on something that has traditionally been overlooked in the field of creativity research: the ability to get creative ideas implemented and adopted. This requires more than idea generation: creative ideas need to be recognized and selected, resources need to be harvested, and relevant stakeholders need to be convinced of the value of a creative idea before implementation can successfully take place. In this chapter, we summarize much of the literature on the evaluation and selection of creative ideas, discuss what we think are some of the main challenges in moving from creativity to innovation and, finally, provide practical advice for successful idea evaluation and selection and for "selling" a highly creative idea.

DEFINING CREATIVITY AND INNOVATION

Creativity is commonly defined as the ability to generate ideas, solutions, or products that are both novel and appropriate (e.g., Amabile, 1996; Sternberg & Lubart, 1999; also see Litchfield, Gilson, & Gilson, 2015, for a discussion of different quality dimensions of "creative" ideas). Thus ideas that are merely good solutions to a problem without any element of novelty or surprise would be considered mundane, and ideas that are only novel without being somehow feasible or appropriate in a given domain would be considered eccentric or "weird," but neither would be considered creative contributions. Note, however, that mundane ideas are not necessarily worthless: Often the most important thing, especially in organizations, is that an idea *works*. However, there are many situations in which organizations are specifically looking for novel ideas, for example, when conventional solutions are known to be ineffective, or when searching for a way to gain a competitive advantage through innovation.

The relation between creativity and innovation is best described by stating that creativity is a *necessary, yet insufficient condition* for innovation (e.g., Baer, 2012; Rietzschel, Nijstad, & Stroebe, 2006; West, 2002a, 2002b). While the common definition of creativity revolves around idea generation, innovation is usually defined as "the intentional introduction and application within a job, work team or organization of ideas, processes, products or procedures which are new to that job, work team or organization and which are designed to benefit the job, the work team or the organization" (West & Farr, 1990, p. 9). Thus innovation centers around the *implementation* of creative ideas in an organizational context.

The Importance of Distinguishing Creativity From Innovation

The difference between creativity and innovation is important for several reasons. Firstly, the terms "creativity" and "innovation" describe different behaviors, and as such should also be distinguished conceptually. In fact, the two are not always strongly or even positively related, nor are they necessarily predicted by the same (dispositional or contextual) variables (e.g., Oldham & Cummings, 1996; Perry-Smith & Coff, 2011; Somech & Drach-Zahavy, 2013; West, 2002a, 2002b). Thus, factors that contribute to idea generation may not lead to better idea implementation, and sometimes the factors that enhance the one seem to actually hinder the other. This has serious implications for organizations interested in increasing their innovative output. Distinguishing between creativity and innovation is, therefore, important from both a theoretical and a practical perspective.

Secondly, we currently know far more about idea generation than about idea implementation. Although a substantial amount of research has looked at innovation in organizations, this research has rarely explicitly distinguished between idea generation and idea implementation (but see, e.g., Baer, 2012; Oldham & Cummings, 1996; Somech & Drach-Zahavy, 2013, for exceptions)—the two are often measured together in a global assessment of innovative job performance. In contrast, there is a large body of literature that has looked specifically at creativity (see, e.g., Zhou & Shalley, 2008, for overviews of organizational creativity research), addressing issues such as individual differences, group interaction, contextual influences, and so on. The consequence is that we know quite a lot about the factors that contribute to successful idea generation, but—given the lack of research on idea implementation and the weak and complicated relation between idea generation and implementation—relatively little about the factors that contribute to idea implementation specifically.

Thirdly, innovation research suggests that it is precisely in the *transition* from idea generation to implementation that individuals and groups run into difficulties: getting to successful implementation simply seems to be the bigger challenge. As West (2002a, 2002b) famously stated, "ideas are ten a penny" (p. 411): There usually is no shortage of creative ideas, but rather a lack of *willingness*, *support*, or the necessary *resources* (either tangible or intangible) to get these ideas implemented. Thus, research on the conditions for a successful transition from creativity to idea implementation is sorely needed.

Moving From Creativity to Innovation in the Organizational Context

Several scholars have addressed the creative or innovative process as a series of stages, although in reality the process is more likely to be iterative. An influential example is the model by Mumford, Lonergan, and Scott (2002), who proposed a process where (a) ideas are generated, and (b) possible outcomes and implications are forecasted, after which (c) the viability of the idea within the intended implementation context is assessed. This can then lead to (d) a decision to either drop the idea altogether, or begin planning for implementation, or—more likely—move into a revision process, after which the idea gets implemented or might still be dropped. What this and similar models suggest is that idea implementation is difficult because ideas encounter multiple challenges along the way, such as *evaluation* (creative ideas need to be recognized), *selection* (only a limited number of ideas can be chosen for further development), *selling or promotion* (other stakeholders need to be convinced of the value of an idea), and *further revision and implementation*.

Organizational creativity and innovation is a multilevel phenomenon influenced by many stakeholders (e.g., Woodman, Sawyer, & Griffin, 1993). Idea generation can happen in many ways, such as during brainstorming sessions (e.g., Osborn, 1953; Sutton & Hargadon, 1996), suggestions entered into an internal suggestions system (e.g., Frese, Teng, & Wijnen, 1999; Verworn, 2009), or ideas generated and pursued as part of one's regular work duties (e.g., Shalley, Gilson, & Blum, 2000). Similarly, the screening, selection, and further development of ideas can happen in a variety of ways and settings, such as workgroup meetings (where workgroup members collectively decide which ideas or options to pursue) or board meetings (where the management may decide on the allocation of funds), but also individually, when employees or supervisors decide on their own which ideas or options seem most promising. Regardless of how ideas are generated and selected, however, organizational reality requires the involvement of other stakeholders at some point; apart from small, self-owned businesses, employees are rarely if ever in the position to generate, select, and implement creative ideas at work themselves (apart from those ideas that only concern people's own work processes, such as adopting a new way of organizing one's own work tasks). Thus, although innovation requires that the person who came up with an idea sees the value of her idea and is able to select it as a promising option to develop and implement, this is by no means enough: even if individual creators would score perfectly on recognizing and selecting their most creative ideas (which, as we will see, they do not), this would be no guarantee for the idea to get implemented. The other stakeholders within the organization will need to be convinced that the idea is worthwhile (also see Litchfield, Ford, & Gentry, 2015). Thus, key to our analysis is the proposition that moving from creativity to innovation requires looking beyond individual creative abilities or behavior.

In the following, we first summarize and discuss much of the literature in the area of idea evaluation (including creative forecasting) and idea selection. Then, we focus on the question of whether there are other factors that can aid or hinder the transition from idea selection to idea implementation. Finally, we reflect on the research discussed thus far to provide some practical suggestions for successfully "selling" a highly creative idea.

IDEA EVALUATION AND CREATIVE FORECASTING

The first challenge in moving from creativity to innovation is to recognize whether the available ideas have creative potential. Thus, once ideas have been generated, the next step involves *idea evaluation*—the assessment of the available options against certain standards (e.g., originality, usefulness, popularity, potential, impact, risk and cost; e.g., Frederiksen & Knudsen, 2017).

Most creativity theories recognize idea evaluation as an important component of the creative process. For example, an evaluation operation was included in Guilford's (1968) structure of intellect and in Vygotsky's theory of imagination (Ayman-Nolley, 1992; Smolucha, 1992), and Amabile's (1996) Componential Theory of creativity includes "response validation" as a part of the creative process. Moreover, it has been suggested that creative ideas only earn social acceptance after they were critically scrutinized

(Simonton, 1988), and that evaluation and criticism are important aspects of imaginative invention (Csikszentmihalyi, 1999).

Several researchers have stated that idea evaluation begins with *forecasting*—the prediction of likely outcomes or the consequences of implementing an idea within a particular setting. People's evaluations of an idea will therefore strongly depend on their expectations regarding the success of an idea (Besemer & O'Quin, 1999; Christiaans, 2002; Dörner & Schaub, 1994; Lonergan, Scott, & Mumford, 2004; Mumford et al., 2002). Forecasts can be subject to several kinds of errors (Pant & Starbuck, 1990). For example, people may tend to underestimate the resources that would be needed, and to overestimate the outcomes, especially positively valued outcomes (Schwenk & Thomas, 1983). The latter, also called "optimistic bias," appears to arise from different sources, such as the failure to consider base rate information, and a predisposition to discount obstacles (Buehler, Griffin, & Ross, 1994; Francis-Smythe & Robertson, 1999; Mumford, Schultz, & Van Doorn, 2001; Schwenk & Thomas, 1983).

Only a limited number of studies have so far investigated how idea evaluation and forecasting operate (although idea evaluation appears to have been studied more extensively than idea selection). In the following section, we review the available literature on idea evaluation and forecasting to shed light on the question *whether* and *when* people can accurately evaluate and forecast ideas.

One important question is whether the creativity of an idea can be objectively assessed (i.e., whether some ideas are "actually" more creative than others). If not, this might be taken to mean that the creativity or quality of an idea is merely "in the eye of the beholder" and that no judgment of any idea is better than another. Most creativity researchers take the perspective that, although all creativity ratings or judgments are inherently subjective, this does not mean that all judgments are equally valid (also see Silvia, 2008). For example, the operational definition of creativity underlying Amabile's (1982, 1996) Consensual Assessment Technique is that "A product or response is creative to the extent that appropriate observers independently agree it is creative. Appropriate observers are those familiar with the domain in which the product was created or the response articulated" (Amabile, 1996, p. 33). In fact, ratings of creativity provided by experts or trained raters show good interrater reliability for different kinds of creative ideas and products, including drawings (e.g., Dollinger & Shafran, 2005), stories (e.g., Baer, Kaufman, & Gentile, 2004), and ideas in divergent thinking tasks (e.g., Amabile, 1982; Diehl & Stroebe, 1987; Rietzschel et al., 2006; Ritter, van Baaren, & Dijksterhuis, 2012; Silvia, 2008). The agreement between judges indicates that creativity is generally an identifiable and quantifiable characteristic of ideas and products (Benedek et al., 2016).

Interestingly, earlier research on idea evaluation has shown a moderate association (36% shared variance) between people's evaluation of their *own* ideas (i.e., intrapersonal evaluation) and their evaluation of *others'* ideas (i.e., interpersonal evaluation; Runco & Smith, 1992). In other words, people's evaluation of ideas strongly depends on the source of the ideas. This may possibly be explained by one's role in the evaluation process: One can either be "actor" (during intrapersonal evaluation) or "observer" (during interpersonal evaluation) (also see Berg, 2016). Both roles may have advantages and disadvantages for the evaluation process. For example, having generated an idea may provide relevant information regarding idea development, but may also lead to biased perceptions due to feelings of loss when having to let go of the idea; this is also sometimes called the "ownership bias" (e.g., Kahneman, Knetsch, & Thaler, 1991; Onarheim & Christensen, 2012). Directly addressing these different roles and their effect on idea evaluation, Berg (2016) studied the conditions for accurate creative forecasting in a field study and a lab experiment. In the field study, creators (i.e., professionals in the circus arts industry) and managers forecasted the success of new circus acts with audiences. Forecasting accuracy was assessed using data from >10,000 audience members, and revealed that both managers and creators underestimated the success of new acts. However, creators were more accurate than managers in forecasting the success of other people's ideas (but not their own).

As evaluating one's own ideas clearly differs from evaluating others' ideas, we discuss research on these two activities separately.

Interpersonal Evaluation

In an extensive research program, Runco and colleagues (Basadur, Runco, & Vega, 2000; Runco, 1993; Runco & Basadur, 1993; Runco & Chand, 1994, 1995; Runco, McCarthy, & Svenson, 1994; Runco & Smith, 1992; Runco & Vega, 1990) have established that, as mentioned previously, people are generally able to accurately evaluate others' ideas (i.e., their evaluations tend to be substantially positively correlated with those of experts). Nevertheless, there is room for improvement. Recently, for example, Benedek et al. (2016) found that people tended to underestimate the creativity of ideas. Specifically, although people recognized the novelty of highly creative ideas, they tended to underestimate the appropriateness of these ideas. Moreover, results showed a positive relationship between participants' divergent thinking skills and their interpersonal evaluation skill: participants who were better at generating creative ideas were also better at recognizing other people's creative ideas. Dailey and Mumford (2006) and Runco and Vega (1990) found similar positive relationships between interpersonal evaluation and idea generation skills, suggesting a common ability or trait underlying both behaviors.

Expertise

In addition to the roles that different evaluators may have (cf. Berg, 2016), they may also differ in their expertise regarding the ideas being judged, and such differences in expertise could influence idea evaluation. For example, Kaufman, Baer, Cole, and Sexton (2008) asked experts (published poets) and novices (college students) to evaluate poems on their creativity. The results revealed moderate correlations between the evaluations of experts and novices, with experts evaluating the poems as less creative than novices. Moreover, experts showed a much higher interrater agreement than novices. In line with these results, Onarheim and Christensen (2012) found that more experienced engineers agreed more strongly with executives in the evaluation of engineering design ideas. Furthermore, although employee evaluations were likely to be biased by the visual complexity of the ideas, this bias was less strong among experienced employees. Further, Dailey and Mumford (2006) investigated the accuracy of undergraduate students in predicting the resources needed for, and consequences of, implementation of creative ideas. Although participants on the whole underestimated resource requirements, and overestimated outcomes, participants with high domain knowledge were more accurate in forecasting some important aspects, such as the likely impact of an idea on organizations, the difficulties involved in idea implementation, and the novelty of the idea. In line with these findings, Önkal, Yates, Simga-Mugan, and Öztin (2003) found that as people acquire experience, forecasts become more accurate.

Such findings strongly suggest that expertise positively affects the evaluation and forecasting of creative ideas. This raises the question *how much* expertise really is necessary. For example, Kaufman, Baer, Cropley, Reiter-Palmon, and Sinnett (2013) compared the evaluation performance of experts, quasiexperts (i.e., more domain experience than novices, but no professional experience), and novices. In line with the findings from Kaufman et al. (2008), experts outperformed novices. The results for quasiexperts, however, were less consistent, showing that quasiexperts sometimes, but not always performed as accurately as experts. Boundary conditions for the accuracy of quasiexperts might be the domain or field of the ideas (Kaufman et al., 2013), or the degree to which the ideas are radical versus incremental (Moreau, Lehmann, & Markman, 2001).

Intrapersonal Evaluation

Thus far, only a few studies have been conducted on the evaluation and forecasting of one's own ideas (i.e., on *intrapersonal* evaluation and forecasting). Several of these studies have looked at the relation between idea generation skills and evaluation skills (also see previously). For example, Runco and colleagues (Runco & Dow, 2004; Runco & Smith, 1992) asked their participants to first generate ideas and then to rate their own ideas on creativity, and found that participants who generated many original ideas were also the most accurate in their idea ratings. Similar results were obtained by Basadur et al. (2000) and by Grohman, Wodniecka, and Kłusak (2006).

Silvia (2008) conducted a study on "discernment," that is, the degree to which people are able to recognize their most creative ideas. In his study, participants first generated ideas in several divergent thinking tasks, and then were asked to identify their most creative responses.[1] Results showed that, on the whole, people were able to identify their most creative ideas (i.e., their choice was highly correlated with that of experts). Moreover, people who scored high on the personality trait openness to experience (a classic predictor of creative performance) were significantly more discerning than those scoring low on openness. As Silvia (2008) noted, these results suggest that "generation skills and evaluation skills are distinct but correlated traits—people high in one tend to be high in the other" (p. 144).

While effective idea evaluation is of course important for the innovative process as such, engaging in evaluation itself may also benefit the creative process. For example, Byrne, Shipman, and Mumford (2010) asked undergraduates to generate advertising campaigns for a new product. Prior to formulating the campaigns, the students had to forecast the implications of their ideas. It was found that the extensiveness of forecasting was related to the quality, originality, and elegance of the advertising campaigns. Thus, the more participants thought about what might be the implications of their ideas, the better and more creative their final products. These results fit with a more recent study by Hao et al. (2016), who found that participants generated more original ideas when they were asked to reflect on the originality of their ideas halfway through the task. Thus, reflection on the quality of one's ideas may not merely be a matter of separating the wheat from the chaff, but could also enhance subsequent idea generation.

Other Factors Influencing Idea Evaluation and Forecasting

The research discussed so far suggests that people are generally able to recognize creative ideas. Moreover, people who are able to generate many (original) ideas tend to be the most accurate in evaluating and forecasting their own ideas, and at least a moderate degree of expertise seems to be necessary for accurate forecasting and evaluation, although this may be different for highly novel ideas. The finding by, for example, Silvia (2008) that openness to experience predicts evaluation accuracy raises the

[1] Although participants in this study made a selection from their own ideas, we discuss this study under "Evaluation" because the research question focused on people's ability to *recognize* their most creative ideas.

question whether other known predictors of idea generation might also relate to evaluation accuracy. Recent research has therefore focused on the effects of several factors (e.g., regulatory focus, construal level, mood) that were previously found to influence the ability of individuals and groups to generate creative ideas.

Regulatory Focus

Regulatory focus theory describes how people engage in self-regulation, the process of bringing oneself into alignment with one's standards and goals (Higgins, 1997). According to regulatory focus theory, people may adopt a *promotion focus* (a focus on growth, attaining desired outcomes, and realizing ambitions), or a *prevention focus* (a focus on safety and security, avoiding undesirable outcomes, and fulfilling one's responsibilities).

Regulatory focus has been linked to creative idea generation (e.g., Friedman & Förster, 2001), people's willingness to make risky decisions (Crowe & Higgins, 1997), and the degree to which organizational teams engage in the promotion and selling of their creative ideas (Rietzschel, 2011). Therefore, it might plausibly be related to idea evaluation as well. This indeed appears to be the case. In a recent study on interpersonal idea evaluation, for example, Zhou, Wang, Song, and Wu (2017) showed that people's regulatory focus affected their novelty perception as well as their interpersonal evaluation accuracy: on the whole, people with a strong promotion focus, as compared to people with either a weak promotion focus or a strong prevention focus, were better able to recognize the novelty and creativity of an idea. Similar effects have been found with regard to intrapersonal idea evaluation. Herman and Reiter-Palmon (2011) found that participants with a strong promotion focus were better able to assess the originality of self-generated ideas, whereas participants in a prevention focus were more accurate in assessing idea "quality" (i.e., how coherent and "workable" the idea was). In line with these results, Fürst, Ghisletta, and Lubart (2016) found that convergence and conscientiousness—both associated with a prevention focus, although this was not directly assessed in this study—were related to individuals' tendency to critically evaluate and correct their own ideas.

Uncertainty Tolerance

People vary in their ability to tolerate uncertainty and ambiguity (see Furnham & Ribchester, 1995, for an overview), and these differences predict creativity (e.g., Kornilova & Kornilov, 2010; Zenasni, Besançon, & Lubart, 2008). Original ideas, by definition, are relatively new and untested and the more original an idea, the higher the uncertainty (Amabile, 1996). Hence, the degree to which people are willing or able to tolerate such uncertainty might be related to their evaluation of creative ideas as well. Mueller, Melwani, and Goncalo (2012) proposed that although people say that they value creativity, they may have an unconscious bias against originality, especially when they feel the need to reduce uncertainty. Across two studies on interpersonal idea evaluation, Mueller et al. (2012) demonstrated that when individuals' motivation to diminish uncertainty was high, they exhibited a stronger implicit bias against originality, but not a stronger explicit bias. Importantly, the implicit bias negatively predicted people's ability to recognize creativity, suggesting that certain circumstances may make people less open to creative ideas without their being aware of it. Such results also fit with those by, for example, Silvia (2008) on the relation between openness to experience and discernment.

Construal Level

Construal level theory describes the relation between psychological distance (e.g., temporal, spatial, social) and the extent to which people's representations of events, situations, or decisions are abstract or concrete (Trope & Liberman, 2010). The general idea is that with high psychological distance people hold a more abstract (high-level construal), while with low psychological distance people hold a concrete (low-level) mind-set. Construal level has been linked to creative performance, the underlying rationale being that high-level construals are associated with flexibility and remote associations (e.g., Förster, Friedman, & Liberman, 2004; Jia, Hirt, & Karpen, 2009; Polman & Emich, 2011). Because a high construal level is associated with a stronger focus on high-level considerations, such as desirability, than on low-level considerations, such as feasibility, it might also predict people's evaluation performance. Mueller, Wakslak, and Krishnan (2014) manipulated participant's construal level mind-set, and found that when a high-level construal mind-set was induced, as compared to a low-level construal mind-set, people evaluated a creative idea higher on creativity. Interestingly, the relationship between construal level priming and idea evaluation was sometimes mediated by uncertainty. Specifically, participants with a low-level "how" mind-set (Study 3) reported higher uncertainty about a creative idea than participants with a high-level "why" mind-set, and this uncertainty in turn negatively predicted creativity ratings.

Evaluation Criteria and Evaluation Instructions

Although creativity is sometimes seen as necessarily spontaneous and "inspired" (Baas, Koch, Nijstad, & De Dreu, 2015; Ritter & Rietzschel, 2017; Sternberg & Lubart, 1999), giving people-specific goals or instructions can significantly enhance creative performance (Litchfield, 2008; O'Hara & Sternberg, 2001; Runco, Illies, & Reiter-Palmon, 2005). Similar effects might exist for idea evaluation, because evaluation performance also depends on the salience of particular dimensions or aspects of ideas (e.g., Herman & Reiter-Palmon, 2011). For example, in a study on interpersonal idea evaluation, Blair and Mumford (2007) found that participants were more likely to prefer original ideas when evaluation criteria were loose and when time pressure was high. Lonergan et al. (2004) found that the use of different appraisal and revision standards affected students' creative revision of previously generated ideas for an advertisement campaign. Specifically, applying implementation efficiency criteria to original ideas, and innovative criteria to less original ideas, respectively, led to the best results.

RESEARCH ON IDEA SELECTION

All in all, it appears that people are generally able to distinguish between creative and less creative ideas, but not always to the same degree: individual and contextual factors can significantly affect the recognition of creative contributions. More important than mere evaluation and forecasting, however, are people's actual *decisions* regarding the possible development and implementation of an idea. These decisions are usually dichotomous in nature: ideas are either selected for further development or implementation or not (also see Rietzschel, Nijstad, & Stroebe, 2018). Of course, a decision can be changed during the development or implementation process, and ideas that were initially rejected may get a second chance later on. Nevertheless, selection is a crucial stage in moving from creativity to innovation, and unfortunately, as we will see in the following sections, research shows that people tend not to do it very well.

Idea Selection After Brainstorming

Relatively many of the existing idea selection studies have been done in the field of brainstorming research. Originally proposed by Osborn (1953), brainstorming is a creativity technique aimed at the generation of as many ideas as possible. It is often done in groups, although research unambiguously shows that group brainstorming leads to lower productivity than brainstorming in nominal groups (i.e., people working individually, whose nonredundant ideas are then pooled; see e.g., Diehl & Stroebe, 1987; Stroebe, Nijstad, & Rietzschel, 2010; Taylor, Berry, & Block, 1958). The main question in research on idea selection after brainstorming has been whether higher productivity (and hence higher availability of high-quality ideas) also carries over into better idea selection, and whether group interaction would offer benefits for idea selection (groups might be able to overcome their productivity loss by making a more effective selection).

Faure (2004) looked at differences in idea generation and selection performance between interactive and nominal groups. These groups first generated ideas in a brainstorming task, and then selected ideas from their own production (i.e., intrapersonal idea selection). All group members first made an individual preselection, after which the group collectively made their final selection. Although interactive groups—as in earlier research—outperformed nominal groups in terms of productivity, this did not carry over into idea selection performance: members of nominal and interactive groups selected ideas of equal quality.

Similar results were obtained in subsequent studies, such as Rietzschel et al. (2006), who also found that interactive and nominal groups selected ideas of equal quality, despite the substantial differences in initial productivity. Although this might seem to suggest a highly effective selection by the interactive groups, selection performance was abysmal in all conditions: the quality of the selected ideas was not significantly different from that of the generated ideas; in other words, neither interactive nor nominal groups appeared to perform above chance level. Putman and Paulus (2009) also found that interactive and nominal groups performed suboptimally in making their selection (no significant difference between the quality of generated and selected ideas). Nominal groups did select ideas that were more original, but this was due to the fact that they generated more original ideas in the first place.

Causes of Suboptimal Selection After Brainstorming

Following up on these results, Rietzschel, Nijstad, and Stroebe (2010) hypothesized that effective idea selection might be too cognitively demanding when there are many ideas to choose from, and that people might therefore benefit from the opportunity to first prescreen their ideas before making the final selection. This also fits with the notion of idea evaluation or creative forecasting as an important stage in the journey from idea to innovation (e.g., Mumford et al., 2002; however, also see Kennel, Reiter-Palmon, De Vreede, & de Vreede, 2013). Additionally, they noted that participants might have used different selection criteria than those used by researchers, and that it would, in a way, be unfair to speak of "suboptimal" selection performance if people simply used different criteria. In two studies, they found that prescreening instructions did not affect selection performance, but selection criteria did. Interestingly, the effect of selection criteria depended on the kinds of criteria given. Instructing participants to select ideas that were both original and feasible (in line with the common definition of creativity) did not lead to better selection as compared with the default instruction to "select the best ideas." In contrast, instructions to simply select "creative" ideas led to participants choosing ideas of higher originality, but lower effectiveness.

These results suggest that at least part of the low selection performance in earlier studies was due to the kind of selection criteria that participants used. In line with this interpretation, Rietzschel et al. (2010) found that participants were more likely to base their selection on considerations of feasibility and desirability in the absence of specific selection instructions (also see Blair & Mumford, 2007). Providing them with selection criteria increased their focus on originality, but at the cost of lower satisfaction with the selection they made (see Rietzschel, Nijstad, & Stroebe, 2014, for similar results). Moreover, participants seemed to make a trade-off between different criteria (focusing either on originality and creativity, or on feasibility and desirability), and their self-reported tendency to select "the best" idea was most strongly and positively correlated with their tendency to select feasible and desirable ideas.

Other Idea Selection Research

Research on idea selection has not been limited to brainstorming research. Results of other studies are more or less in line with the previously discussed results: people generally perform suboptimally when it comes to selecting creative ideas, and they tend to prefer feasible ideas over original ones.

Suboptimal Selection Performance

Several studies have yielded additional evidence for the poor selection performance found in the brainstorming studies discussed previously. For example, Girotra, Terwiesch, and Ulrich (2010) conducted a study on different kinds of group interaction in idea generation and selection, finding that groups in all conditions made a suboptimal selection from their own ideas, but that a "hybrid" structure, alternating between individual and group work, worked better than other configurations. Toh and Miller (2016a, 2016b) studied idea generation and selection in teams of design students, and found that teams generally failed to select their most creative ideas, "even though creativity is regarded as an important element of successful engineering design" (p. 82). Kennel et al. (2013) had teams generate and select solutions to a problem, finding that, although most teams selected ideas that they themselves rated as original and/or feasible, expert ratings showed lower scores for the selected ideas, with almost half of the teams selecting ideas that were rated as neither original nor feasible. Moreover, teams performed suboptimally on idea selection even after having evaluated the ideas on creativity-relevant criteria, suggesting that, important as idea evaluation may be, it is not enough in itself to lead to accurate selection. Further, Reiter-Palmon and Arreola (2015) compared the effects of two different creative strategies on the quality of the final idea. Participants were either instructed to generate many ideas and then select their best idea or were instructed to generate a single best idea. Results showed that, although participants in the "generate many ideas" condition came up with idea sets that were more likely to contain at least one very original idea, they selected ideas of lower quality (feasibility, originality, and elaboration) than participants in the "single idea" condition.

Preference for Feasibility Over Originality

In an experiment where participants were instructed to rate and select ideas in a project funding task, Blair and Mumford (2007) found that participants tended to reject highly original or risky ideas, and were more likely to select ideas that were consistent with social norms, easy to understand, and likely to quickly lead to desirable outcomes, especially under high time pressure. These results are in line with those discussed previously by Rietzschel et al. (2010, 2014), and with the findings on regulatory focus and construal level described previously: circumstances or traits that lead people to focus less on feasibility and more on originality tend to enhance the recognition of creative ideas, as well as their selection. Recently, De Buisonjé, Ritter, De Bruin, Ter Horst, and Meeldijk (2017) conducted a field study where participants had to select the most creative ideas from an idea pool. Participants who had been brought into a promotion-focused state with positive affect selected more creative ideas than did participants in the control condition (also see Perry-Smith & Coff, 2011).

On the whole, then, the strong preference for feasibility seems to be one of the major causes (if not the single most important cause) for people's poor selection performance (also see Rietzschel et al., 2018). Generally, originality and feasibility tend to be negatively correlated (Nijstad, De Dreu, Rietzschel, & Baas, 2010), which makes it challenging to find those rare ideas that are high on both. The research discussed so far strongly suggests a sort of trade-off, where people—depending on circumstances or the traits and preferences they bring to the task—will focus on either of the two dimensions, at the cost of the other dimension. Thus one of the challenges for effective idea selection may be to get people to *not* make a trade-off, but select ideas that are high on both dimensions.

The Role of Unconscious Thought

Idea selection can be considered a form of *convergent* creativity, in that one goes from several possible options (generated in the *divergent* stages of the process) to one or a couple of ideas that will be developed further and possibly will be implemented. In this regard, idea selection may be similar to such tasks as solving insight problems, in that one attempts to find or identify the idea or solution that best fulfills a certain set of criteria, which may be or seem to be incompatible, such as high originality and high feasibility (also see Reiter-Palmon & Arreola, 2015). Several researchers (see Sternberg & Davidson, 1995, for a collection of overviews) have pointed out that creative problem-solving may critically depend on the relaxation of implicit constraints: often our assumptions about what an acceptable solution or solution strategy should be are not fully articulated, or inappropriate in the given situation (cf. Luchins & Luchins, 1969). The Duncker candle problem (Duncker, 1945) is a classic example. In this problem-solving task, participants are provided with a candle, a box of tacks, and a set of matches, and have to come up with a way to attach the candle to a wall in such a way that it can be lighted without dripping wax on the floor. Participants will only manage to find the correct solution if they realize that the box containing the tacks can be a platform as well as a container, and could be attached to the wall using the tacks. Idea selection may suffer from similar problems. For example, if people assume that ideas tend to be either original or feasible (see previously), this constraint will make it very difficult to select an idea that scores high on both dimensions. Thus if idea selection is psychologically similar to these kinds of insight tasks, circumstances that help people to relax implicit constraints (such as the implicit assumption that original ideas are not feasible) might help them select more creative ideas.

This question was studied, for example, by Ritter, Van Baaren, et al. (2012), who studied the effects of unconscious thought in the creative process. Previous research had shown that engaging in a certain amount of unconscious thought could be beneficial for problem-solving (Dijksterhuis & Meurs, 2006; Zhong, Dijksterhuis, & Galinsky, 2008), in line with the classic notion of "incubation" as a common stage in the creative process (e.g., Wallas, 1926). Ritter et al. applied this reasoning to idea selection. In their studies, participants first generated and then selected ideas. Before the creative task, participants were either asked to consciously think about the problem at hand, or were asked to do another task, which was assumed to allow for unconscious task-related thought. In a third condition, participants proceeded immediately to the creative task. Results across two studies showed that idea generation and idea selection were differently affected by the manipulation. While the results on idea generation differed between the studies, selection performance was consistently higher in the "unconscious thought" condition than in the other two conditions; in fact, only in this condition did a majority of participants manage to select their best ideas as rated by external judges (suggesting poor selection performance in the absence of unconscious thought).

In another study, Ritter, Strick, Bos, Van Baaren, and Dijksterhuis (2012) tested the effects of diffused odor during sleep on creative performance. Participants were presented with a problem in the evening, and then literally "slept on it" through the night. During the sleep period an odor was diffused in the room—either the odor that had been present during the presentation of the problem (and hence was assumed to be associated with the topic, stimulating task-related cognition during sleep), or a different odor; in the control condition, no odor was diffused during sleep.

The authors found that participants in the "conditioned odor" condition generated and selected more creative ideas after waking up than participants in the other condition. Specifically, in the "conditioned odor" condition, approximately 75% of participants selected their most creative idea (as judged by raters), as compared to around 40% in the other two conditions.

These findings suggest that unconscious processes can indeed contribute to the selection of more creative ideas, and that more extensive deliberation is not necessarily the best way to attain creative outcomes—possibly because deliberation does not help us relax implicit constraints or overcome cognitive biases. In line with this perspective, Zhu, Ritter, Müller, and Dijksterhuis (2017) investigated the role of intuitive and deliberative processing modes in creative idea selection, and found that participants who had been instructed to make their selection intuitively selected ideas that were more creative, more original (and equally useful) than the ideas selected by participants who had been instructed to make their selection deliberatively. In fact, only participants in the intuitive condition performed above chance level in their selection.

GETTING IDEAS IMPLEMENTED IN THE ORGANIZATIONAL CONTEXT

Thus far, the research discussed suggests that (a) people are able to *recognize* creative ideas, but not always to the same extent, and (b) people have a hard time actually *selecting* creative ideas (i.e., performance is not better than chance level), although selection performance is better under certain circumstances. Moreover, the selection of creative ideas (as well as their recognition) seems to be particularly difficult when people strongly focus on feasibility and are motivated to reduce uncertainty or avoid risks. However, even if individuals or groups succeed in selecting the most creative idea(s), this does not guarantee actual innovation. Ideas need to be implemented, and this usually requires involvement of more stakeholders than only the idea creator(s) and selector(s). In fact, Csikszentmihalyi's (1999) systems theory of creativity explicitly argues that it is in the interplay between creators and the field they work in that creativity comes into existence. According to this perspective, the creativity of a contribution is not so much (exclusively) a function of properties of the contribution, but rather of the way in which the field, or gatekeepers in the field, respond to it.

In short, some individuals or teams may be excellent at generating, evaluating, and selecting their best ideas, and still fail to get these ideas implemented. In this section, we will discuss some individual factors that have been found to contribute to or hinder the implementation of creative ideas.

Getting Ideas Accepted by Coworkers

Although creativity is often highly valued, this does not necessarily mean that creative ideas are always appreciated (cf. Mueller et al., 2012). In the organizational context, creative ideas can also be considered disruptive or threatening. For example, Janssen (2003) argues that innovative ideas are likely to be seen as a challenge to the status quo and hence may lead to conflict, especially among highly involved employees. In a field study, Janssen indeed found that employees who showed high levels of innovative job performance (as rated by their supervisors) experienced more conflict and less satisfactory relations with their coworkers, but only when they had high levels of job involvement.

Along similar lines, Baer (2012) noted that highly creative ideas are more likely to lead to controversy and differences of opinion than mundane ones (cf. Moreau et al., 2001). Highly creative ideas might therefore be at a disadvantage as compared to less creative ideas when it comes to implementation, because it is more difficult to gather sufficient support for these ideas. However, Baer also argued that the move toward implementation is especially open to social-political maneuvering, "because a decision to allocate or redirect resources often involves multiple constituents who are likely to disagree about the value of an idea, especially one that is novel and inherently ambiguous" (p. 1105). In line with this perspective, a field study showed that the more radical employees' ideas were, the less likely these were to get implemented, unless the employee had strong networking skills, a large number of "buy-in ties" (interested stakeholders in his/her network), or experienced strong implementation instrumentality (expected to benefit from implementation of the idea). Further, Perry-Smith and Mannucci (2017) present an extensive analysis of the way in which different stages of the "idea journey" from creativity to innovation may require different kinds of network activation, not all of which are mutually compatible—in other words, what is required for, say, idea generation may not be helpful for idea championing or idea implementation.

Pitching and Selling Ideas

The success of an idea will not only depend on the networks that people have, but also on their ability to convince the people in and outside their network that an idea is valuable and creative. Some people simply might be better at presenting or pitching their idea and thereby garnering support (also see Rietzschel, 2011). This was shown, for example, by Goncalo, Flynn, and Kim (2010), who addressed the relation between narcissism and creativity in a series of three studies. Their results showed that narcissists were not actually more creative, but that the ideas they pitched were rated as more creative. Moreover, the observed relation between narcissism and perceived creativity was mediated by the perceived enthusiasm of the pitcher. Goncalo et al. conclude that "narcissists may be effective at convincing others that their ideas are creative, in part because they convey traits that are closely associated with a creative personality prototype" (p. 1490).

Another illustration of how personal characteristics (as opposed to characteristics of one's ideas) may affect other people's perceptions and evaluations of creativity comes from Proudfoot, Kay, and Koval (2015), who make the case that the creativity stereotype of divergence and independence fits with a classic and stereotypical representation of masculinity, with its emphasis on independence, agency, adventurousness, and self-reliance. This could also lead to a gender bias in the attribution of creativity. Across five studies, they show that creativity is indeed associated more strongly with "masculine" attributes than "feminine" ones, that men are ascribed more creativity than women even when the creative product is the same, and that female executives (in organizations) and speakers (on TED.com) are rated as less innovative. Thus, and in line with the results found by Goncalo et al. (2010), individual characteristics other than the creativity of one's ideas may nevertheless affect other people's evaluations of these ideas.

In line with this perspective, Litchfield, Ford, et al. (2015) point out that convincing others (such as coworkers) of the potential value of an idea may require the ability to take other people's perspective, for example to understand or predict which kinds of ideas will be likely to be appreciated or supported by which stakeholders. Thus, perspective-taking may help creators sell their ideas more effectively by enabling them to identify whom the idea should or could be sold to, as well as the best way to do so. In a field study among employees, their coworkers, and their supervisors, Litchfield, Ford, et al. (2015) found that organizational innovation was highest when high individual creativity was accompanied by a strong creative team environment and high levels of individual perspective-taking, again demonstrating that success in selling an idea not only depends on the quality of the idea itself.

Getting Ideas Accepted by a Supervisor

It is not just the characteristics of the creator that affect other people's reactions. Often, employees come up with an idea (e.g., to improve work processes) and communicate this to their direct supervisor, who is in a position to support the idea, to assign resources to further development, or to champion the idea to higher management. In such cases, acceptance of the idea by the supervisor is of course essential, but not all supervisors are equally likely to recognize or support their subordinates' creative ideas. Recognizing subordinates' creative ideas can be considered a special case of interpersonal idea evaluation, and in line with the research discussed earlier, Basadur et al. (2000) found that managers' ability to accurately evaluate highly original ideas was positively predicted by their own ability to generate creative ideas. Beside the ability to recognize creative ideas, research also suggests that a supervisor's *achievement goals* may affect his or her willingness to support creative ideas. In the achievement goal literature, a distinction is often made between performance (wanting to outperform others) and mastery (wanting to outperform oneself) goals (Elliot, 2005). In several studies, Sijbom, Janssen, and Van Yperen (2015a, 2015b, 2016) found that leaders with a mastery orientation were more likely to adopt a creative idea, whereas leaders with a performance orientation were more likely to oppose the idea. Sijbom et al. (2015a, 2015b) also found that this effect depended on, among others, the presence (vs absence) of a problem identification in the idea. When the idea contained an explicit problem identification, Sijbom et al. argue, performance-oriented leaders saw the creative idea as an implicit evaluation of their leadership skills, which threatened them and hence made them less receptive. When the idea was presented without an explicit problem statement, performance-oriented leaders were as receptive as mastery-oriented leaders. Moreover, Sijbom et al. (2016) showed that the effects of achievement goals were specific to leaders evaluating ideas proposed by subordinates—the effects did not occur when a superior rather than a subordinate proposed the ideas.

Supervisory Support

Clearly, supervisors play an important role in the transition from creativity to innovation. Receiving support from supervisors has long been known to be an important precondition for employees to display creative behavior at work (see, e.g., Tierney, 2008; Zhou, 2008, for overviews), and several studies and conceptual analyses have focused on the important role of leaders in facilitating or stimulating employees' innovative performance (e.g., De Jong & Den Hartog, 2007; Stenmark, Shipman, & Mumford, 2011; also see Zhou & Shalley, 2008, for several relevant overviews). Recently, more specific attention has been begun to be paid to the effects of support on successfully selling and implementing creative ideas. For example, Axtell et al. (2000) found that the relation between employees' contribution of ideas for improvements on the workfloor and implementation of these ideas depended on managerial support: when employees experienced little managerial support, the relation was quite weak. Only when employees felt supported by management, a clear positive relation between idea generation and idea implementation was observed. In a recent paper, Škerlavaj, Černe, and Dysvik (2014) found evidence (both in a field study and a lab experiment) for a *curvilinear* relation between idea generation and idea implementation. Škerlavaj et al. argue that employees who spend an inordinate amount of time or resources on the generation of ideas may be less effective at selling those ideas to coworkers and management, because time and resources are limited. Thus, they hypothesized and found an inverse U-shaped relation between idea generation and idea implementation. Importantly, this curve was moderated by supervisory support, such that when employees perceived high support, the relation between idea generation and implementation was positive and linear.

What these results show is that a focus on the properties of creative ideas and people's ability to recognize or select these ideas is too narrow. Even if employees have generated and selected the best of all possible ideas, the idea needs to be sold to the other stakeholders in the organization, who may or may not be motivated or able to recognize an idea's value.

PRACTICAL RECOMMENDATIONS FOR THE ORGANIZATIONAL CONTEXT

Whereas various techniques, strategies, and trainings have been developed and tested to enhance the ability of individuals and groups to generate ideas, research on *facilitating* idea evaluation and idea selection skills is scarce. However, based on the research discussed so far, several recommendations and practical solutions can be tentatively formulated to help individuals and organizations to successfully evaluate and select creative ideas. We discuss two classes of recommendations: (a) suggestions on how to improve idea selection in organizations, and (b) suggestions on how to improve one's success in selling creative ideas to coworkers and supervisors.

Improving Idea Selection

Loosen Implicit Constraints About Originality and Usefulness

As explained before, an idea has to be original (i.e., novel) and useful (i.e., feasible, effective) in order to be considered creative. Nevertheless, people tend to perceive an incompatibility between the originality and the usefulness/feasibility dimension (Rietzschel et al., 2010, 2014). Moreover, Blair and Mumford (2007) found that people tended to reject highly original ideas and were more likely to select ideas that are consistent with social norms. Generally, the implicit assumption that original ideas cannot be feasible seems to strongly hinder effective idea selection. In line with the aforementioned work on insight and unconscious thought, a possible approach to diminish this "either-originality-or-usefulness" constraint could be to enhance the opportunity for unconscious thought (Ritter, Strick, et al., 2012; Ritter, van Baaren, & Dijksterhuis, 2012) or to rely on a more intuitive processing style. Research by Magnusson, Netz, and Wästlund (2014) also suggests that intuition can be used as a successful means for evaluating ideas, and Zhu et al. (2017) found that an intuitive (as opposed to a deliberative) thinking style led to better idea selection. Thus, creating circumstances that make it easier for people to move beyond the heuristic trade-off between originality and feasibility are likely to be helpful for idea selection (also see Litchfield, Gilson, et al., 2015). Of course this is all the more important in the organizational context, where feasibility is highly salient (e.g., because of limited resources or a competitive market). However, it may be difficult to justify these kinds of intuitive decisions to stakeholders; other, more explicit interventions such as the use of selection criteria will perhaps be received more favorably.

Use Instructions for Idea Evaluation and Selection

Overcoming the trade-off between originality and feasibility can also be stimulated by the use of explicit selection criteria. As we have seen, people tend to prefer and select highly feasible ideas over highly original ones. While changing people's preferences may not always be immediately possible (however, see later), the initial selection of creative ideas can benefit from explicitly using originality as a selection criterion (e.g., Rietzschel et al., 2010, 2014), or from loosening the selection criteria and allowing people to select multiple ideas (so as to allow for the selection of at least some highly original ideas; e.g., Blair & Mumford, 2007). The criteria used may also have to be contingent on the quality of the available ideas. For example, Lonergan et al. (2004) found that better advertising campaigns were obtained when innovative criteria instructions were applied to less original ideas, and when implementation efficiency criteria instructions were applied to more original ideas. Thus, being more explicit about the importance of selecting original ideas may be helpful. However, since—as discussed previously—this may come at the cost of lower satisfaction (Rietzschel et al., 2010, 2014), it remains to be seen whether people will be willing to actually support these ideas or invest resources in them. This may require something more than selection criteria.

Induce Specific Psychological Conditions

Research discussed previously has shown that specific psychological conditions, such as regulatory focus (i.e., promotion focus), construal level (i.e., abstract mind-set), and uncertainty tolerance, can positively influence idea evaluation and idea selection. The underlying mechanism seems to be that these conditions make people more open to original ideas and more willing to take risks. Thus, idea selection and implementation in organizations are likely to benefit from contexts that instill or enhance such psychological conditions. For example, organizations could consider explicitly framing innovation projects in terms of potential gains rather than potential losses (and hence avoid an innovation imperative based on, for example, the fear of being outcompeted), and stakeholders might be encouraged to focus more strongly on abstract "why"-considerations and long-term considerations. Rather than directly changing the selection process by providing people with different criteria, then, these kinds of interventions are aimed at changing people's preferences, or at least their willingness to take certain ideas into consideration.

Train Evaluation and Selection Skills

Most of the studies described in this chapter focused on the question whether activating a specific psychological condition (i.e., changes on state level) right before the idea evaluating and/or idea selecting process leads to temporarily enhanced evaluation and selection performance. Another means could be to *train* people's evaluation and selection skills and hence make them chronically more open to original ideas. Runco and Basadur (1993) provided managers with a 20h intensive multiphase creative problem solving training, and found that the training increased managers' evaluative accuracy as compared to a premeasurement. Licuanan, Dailey, and Mumford (2007) found that errors in evaluating the originality of highly novel ideas can be reduced by having participants engage in active analysis of product originality. Reiter-Palmon, Ligon, Schoenbeck, and McFeely (2017) trained undergraduates in evaluating and rating creativity, manipulating the availability of practice ratings and feedback, as well as the quality of the rating rubrics the trainee received. To assess rating accuracy, trainee's ratings of creative solutions were compared with expert ratings. Rating practice and more descriptive rating rubrics increased the quality rating accuracy, but not the originality rating accuracy.

Successful selling of a highly creative idea

Based on the research discussed thus far, some global practical suggestions can be formulated for employees who would like to increase their chance of moving their ideas closer toward implementation.

Stress Feasibility and Effectiveness, Not Originality

Paradoxically, although originality is considered to be the hallmark of creative ideas (e.g., Runco & Charles, 1993), originality may also be what causes an idea to be rejected. Research discussed so far shows that people may be strongly biased against original ideas (e.g., Blair & Mumford, 2007; Mueller et al., 2012; Rietzschel et al., 2010, 2014). Since people prefer highly feasible ideas, and appear to believe that highly original ideas cannot be feasible, selling a creative idea will likely go better if one manages to convince the other party that an idea is easy to implement and likely to work. Of course, usually this is exactly what is wanted. But in situations where innovation explicitly is the goal, or where common and routine solutions are known to no longer be effective, getting highly original ideas accepted is critically important, and in those situations it can be important to resist the temptation to emphasize how novel and radical an idea is (except when it is clear that novelty really is what is sought, for example when looking for radical new advertisement concepts). In fact, Goldenberg, Horowitz, Levav, and Mazursky's (2003) notion of the "innovation sweetspot" suggests that it may even be worthwhile to actively *downplay* the novelty of an idea somewhat.

Prepare for Resistance

We have discussed several studies showing that people generally cannot be expected to respond positively to creative ideas immediately. Examples are the work by Mueller et al. (2012) on the implicit bias against creativity, a field study by Janssen (2003) showing that employees who contribute innovative ideas can easily run into conflict with their coworkers, and studies by Sijbom et al. (2015a, 2015b, 2016) who found that competitive leaders were more likely to reject subordinates' creative ideas, especially if the idea was voiced in an aggressive (as opposed to considerate) manner. Creative ideas may be more likely to get supported if they are presented or pitched in such a way that they do not elicit uncertainty (Mueller et al., 2012) or a sense of competitive threat (Sijbom et al., 2015b), but it is easy to fall into the pitfall of getting carried away with one's own idea (see later) and to assume that everybody will like it.

Show Confidence and Enthusiasm

Generating creative ideas strongly depends on intrinsic motivation and task engagement, and employees may be very much committed to their ideas. If the goal is to convince somebody (e.g., a supervisor) that one's idea is highly creative, this can be useful. Goncalo et al. (2010) found that the perceived enthusiasm of narcissistic participants mediated the higher creativity rating these participants received. Enthusiasm and charisma are considered part of the "creativity stereotype" (Elsbach & Kramer, 2003; Goncalo et al., 2010); displaying these kinds of behaviors may therefore lead to more positive creativity perceptions. Following up on research showing that an abstract mind-set may lead to better recognition of creativity (Mueller et al., 2014), and research linking positive, high-arousal emotions to the adoption of an abstract mind-set (De Dreu, Baas, & Nijstad, 2008), one might speculate that a process of *emotional contagion* (e.g., Hatfield, Cacioppo, & Rapson, 1993) could in part be responsible for this effect: presenting an idea with enthusiasm may make the audience enthusiastic as well, and therefore better able to recognize the idea's creativity. However, whether or not this will also mean that the idea is received more favorably is another issue (see previously).

Focus on the Long Term

As mentioned before, people's responses are often mostly driven by their expectations regarding the feasibility and effectiveness of an idea. This will be especially the case if short-term considerations (e.g., thoughts of imminent implementation) guide the evaluation or selection process (also see Rietzschel et al., 2018). Thus, presenting an idea in such a way that the long term becomes more salient than the short term could increase acceptance by reducing the focus on feasibility. Moreover, as shown by Mueller et al. (2014), when people are focused more on the long term and hence adopt an abstract mind-set, they are better at recognizing creative ideas, and tend to evaluate these ideas more positively.

Don't Do It All Alone

One of the things we have stressed in this chapter is that idea implementation in organizations is not an individual endeavor, but requires support and commitment from multiple stakeholders. The stereotype of the creative "lone genius" notwithstanding, creative success strongly depends on the ability to muster the necessary support from others. Investing in one's professional network within and outside of the organization is therefore important (also see Perry-Smith & Mannucci, 2017). While several studies have found that network ties can contribute significantly to creative output (especially so-called "weak ties"; see e.g., Perry-Smith & Shalley, 2003), research such as that by Baer (2012) shows that networking success also increases the chance of getting one's ideas implemented. Further, Škerlavaj et al. (2014) found that high levels of supervisory support were associated with a more positive relationship between creativity and idea implementation, and Somech and Drach-Zahavy (2013) found that a favorable team climate, rather than individual abilities, was crucial in getting creative ideas implemented.

CONCLUDING REMARKS

In a world characterized by fast technological and social change, and facing the pressures of climate change and the need for a more sustainable society, few things are as important and urgent as successful innovation. Optimizing the creative process is of critical importance for both public and private organizations. The success of this process usually depends on the quality of the idea that is identified as the most creative idea. Thus, in addition to being able to generate creative ideas, one also has to succeed in recognizing and selecting ones most creative idea. Moreover, recent developments in the World Wide Web, crowd-sourcing, and open innovation have opened the floodgates for idea generation in many domains, making it increasingly important to recognize and select the most creative idea from a pool of available ideas (i.e., interindividual idea evaluation and selection). Thus far, idea evaluation and, to a greater extent, idea selection are far from optimal. This implies that, unless more attention is paid to the idea evaluation and selection process, creativity and innovation will remain at suboptimal levels. Practitioners and researchers alike should not merely focus on idea generation, but should take a different track than they have done so far—spending serious effort on understanding and improving idea evaluation and selection.

References

Amabile, T. M. (1982). Social psychology of creativity: a consensual assessment technique. *Journal of Personality and Social Psychology*, 43, 997–1013. https://doi.org/10.1037/0022-3514.43.5.997.

Amabile, T. M. (1996). *Creativity in context: Update to "the social psychology of creativity"*. Boulder, CO: Westview Press.

Axtell, C. M., Holman, D. J., Unsworth, K. L., Wall, T. D., Waterson, P. E., & Harrington, E. (2000). Shopfloor innovation: facilitating the suggestion and implementation of ideas. *Journal of Occupational and Organizational Psychology*, 73, 265–285. https://doi.org/10.1348/096317900167029.

Ayman-Nolley, S. (1992). Vygotsky's perspective on the development of imagination and creativity. *Creativity Research Journal*, 5, 77–85. https://doi.org/10.1080/10400419209534424.

Baas, M., Koch, S., Nijstad, B. A., & De Dreu, C. W. (2015). Conceiving creativity: the nature and consequences of laypeople's beliefs about the realization of creativity. *Psychology of Aesthetics, Creativity, and the Arts*, 9, 340–354. https://doi.org/10.1037/a0039420.

Baer, M. (2012). Putting creativity to work: the implementation of creative ideas in organizations. *Academy of Management Journal*, 55, 1102–1119. https://doi.org/10.5465/amj.2009.0470.

Baer, J., Kaufman, J. C., & Gentile, C. A. (2004). Extension of the consensual assessment technique to nonparallel creative products. *Creativity Research Journal*, 16, 113–117. https://doi.org/10.1207/s15326934crj1601_11.

Basadur, M., Runco, M. A., & Vega, L. A. (2000). Understanding how creative thinking skills, attitudes and behaviors work together: a causal process model. *The Journal of Creative Behavior*, 34, 77–100. https://doi.org/10.1002/j.2162-6057.2000.tb01203.x.

Benedek, M., Nordtvedt, N., Jauk, E., Koschmieder, C., Pretsch, J., Krammer, G., et al. (2016). Assessment of creativity evaluation skills: a psychometric investigation in prospective teachers. *Thinking Skills and Creativity*, 21, 75–84.

Berg, J. M. (2016). Balancing on the creative highwire: forecasting the success of novel ideas in organizations. *Administrative Science Quarterly*, 61, 433–468. https://doi.org/10.1177/0001839216642211.

Besemer, S. P., & O'Quin, K. (1999). Confirming the three-factor creative product analysis matrix model in an American sample. *Creativity Research Journal*, 12, 287–296. https://doi.org/10.1207/s15326934crj1204_6.

Blair, C. S., & Mumford, M. D. (2007). Errors in idea evaluation: preference for the unoriginal? *The Journal of Creative Behavior*, 41, 197–222. https://doi.org/10.1002/j.2162-6057.2007.tb01288.x.

Buehler, R., Griffin, D., & Ross, M. (1994). Exploring the 'planning fallacy': why people underestimate their task completion times. *Journal of Personality and Social Psychology*, 67, 366–381. https://doi.org/10.1037/0022-3514.67.3.366.

Byrne, C. L., Shipman, A. S., & Mumford, M. D. (2010). The effects of forecasting on creative problem-solving: an experimental study. *Creativity Research Journal, 22*, 119–138. https://doi.org/10.1080/10400419.2010.481482.

Christiaans, H. M. (2002). Creativity as a design criterion. *Creativity Research Journal, 14*, 41–54. https://doi.org/10.1207/S15326934CRJ1401_4.

Crowe, E., & Higgins, E. T. (1997). Regulatory focus and strategic inclinations: promotion and prevention in decision-making. *Organizational Behavior and Human Decision Processes, 69*, 117–132. https://doi.org/10.1006/obhd.1996.2675.

Csikszentmihalyi, M. (1999). Implications of a systems perspective for the study of creativity. In R. J. Sternberg & R. J. Sternberg (Eds.), *Handbook of creativity* (pp. 313–335). New York, NY: Cambridge University Press.

Dailey, L., & Mumford, M. D. (2006). Evaluative aspects of creative thought: errors in appraising the implications of new ideas. *Creativity Research Journal, 18*, 367–384. https://doi.org/10.1207/s15326934crj1803_11.

De Buisonjé, D. R., Ritter, S. M., de Bruin, S., ter Horst, J.M.-L., & Meeldijk, A. (2017). Facilitating creative idea selection: the combined effects of self-affirmation, promotion focus and positive affect. *Creativity Research Journal, 9*, 1–8. https://doi.org/10.1080/10400419.2017.1303308.

De Dreu, C. W., Baas, M., & Nijstad, B. A. (2008). Hedonic tone and activation level in the mood-creativity link: toward a dual pathway to creativity model. *Journal of Personality and Social Psychology, 94*, 739–756. https://doi.org/10.1037/0022-3514.94.5.739.

De Jong, J. P., & Den Hartog, D. N. (2007). How leaders influence employees' innovative behaviour. *European Journal of Innovation Management, 10*, 41–64. https://doi.org/10.1108/14601060710720546.

Diehl, M., & Stroebe, W. (1987). Productivity loss in brainstorming groups: toward the solution of a riddle. *Journal of Personality and Social Psychology, 53*, 497–509. https://doi.org/10.1037/0022-3514.53.3.497.

Dijksterhuis, A., & Meurs, T. (2006). Where creativity resides: the generative power of unconscious thought. *Consciousness and Cognition, 15*, 135–146. https://doi.org/10.1016/j.concog.2005.04.007.

Dollinger, S. J., & Shafran, M. (2005). Note on consensual assessment technique in creativity research. *Perceptual and Motor Skills, 100*, 592–598. https://doi.org/10.2466/PMS.100.3.592-598.

Dörner, D., & Schaub, H. (1994). Errors in planning and decision-making and the nature of human information processing. *Applied Psychology: An International Review, 43*, 433–453. https://doi.org/10.1111/j.1464-0597.1994.tb00839.x.

Duncker, K. (1945). *On problem-solving. (psychological monographs, No. 270.).* Washington, DC: American Psychological Association.

Elliot, A. J. (2005). A conceptual history of the achievement goal construct. In A. J. Elliot, C. S. Dweck, A. J. Elliot, & C. S. Dweck (Eds.), *Handbook of competence and motivation* (pp. 52–72). New York, NY: Guilford Publications.

Elsbach, K. D., & Kramer, R. M. (2003). Assessing creativity in hollywood pitch meetings: evidence for a dual-process model of creativity judgments. *Academy of Management Journal, 46*, 283–301. https://doi.org/10.2307/30040623.

Faure, C. (2004). Beyond brainstorming: effects of different group procedures on selection of ideas and satisfaction with the process. *Journal of Creative Behavior, 38*, 13–34.

Förster, J., Friedman, R. S., & Liberman, N. (2004). Temporal construal effects on abstract and concrete thinking: consequences for insight and creative cognition. *Journal of Personality and Social Psychology, 87*, 177–189. https://doi.org/10.1037/0022-3514.87.2.177.

Francis-Smythe, J. A., & Robertson, I. T. (1999). On the relationship between time management and time estimation. *British Journal of Psychology, 90*, 333–347. https://doi.org/10.1348/000712699161459.

Frederiksen, M. H., & Knudsen, M. P. (2017). From creative ideas to innovation performance: the role of assessment criteria. *Creativity and Innovation Management, 26,* 60–74. https://doi.org/10.1111/caim.12204.

Frese, M., Teng, E., & Wijnen, C. D. (1999). Helping to improve suggestion systems: predictors of making suggestions in companies. *Journal of Organizational Behavior, 20,* 1139–1155. https://doi.org/10.1002/(SICI)1099-1379(199912)20:7<1139::AID-JOB946>3.0.CO;2-I.

Friedman, R. S., & Förster, J. (2001). The effects of promotion and prevention cues on creativity. *Journal of Personality and Social Psychology, 81,* 1001–1013. https://doi.org/10.1037/0022-3514.81.6.1001.

Furnham, A., & Ribchester, T. (1995). Tolerance of ambiguity: a review of the concept, its measurement and applications. *Current Psychology: A Journal for Diverse Perspectives on Diverse Psychological Issues, 14,* 179–199. https://doi.org/10.1007/BF02686907.

Fürst, G., Ghisletta, P., & Lubart, T. (2016). Toward an integrative model of creativity and personality: theoretical suggestions and preliminary empirical testing. *The Journal of Creative Behavior, 50,* 87–108. https://doi.org/10.1002/jocb.71.

Girotra, K., Terwiesch, C., & Ulrich, K. T. (2010). Idea generation and the quality of the best idea. *Management Science, 56,* 591–605. https://doi.org/10.1287/mnsc.1090.1144.

Goldenberg, J., Horowitz, R., Levav, A., & Mazursky, D. (2003). Finding your innovation sweet spot. *Harvard Business Review, 81,* 120–129.

Goncalo, J. A., Flynn, F. J., & Kim, S. H. (2010). Are two narcissists better than one? The link between narcissism, perceived creativity, and creative performance. *Personality and Social Psychology Bulletin, 36*(11), 1484–1495. https://doi.org/10.1177/0146167210385109.

Grohman, M., Wodniecka, Z., & Kłusak, M. (2006). Divergent thinking and evaluation skills: do they always go together? *The Journal of Creative Behavior, 40,* 125–145. https://doi.org/10.1002/j.2162-6057.2006.tb01269.x.

Guilford, J. P. (1968). Intelligence has three facets. *Science, 160*(3828), 615–620. https://doi.org/10.1126/science.160.3828.615.

Hao, N., Ku, Y., Liu, M., Hu, Y., Bodner, M., Grabner, R. H., et al. (2016). Reflection enhances creativity: beneficial effects of idea evaluation on idea generation. *Brain and Cognition,* 10330–10337. https://doi.org/10.1016/j.bandc.2016.01.005.

Hatfield, E., Cacioppo, J. T., & Rapson, R. L. (1993). Emotional contagion. *Current Directions in Psychological Science, 2,* 96–99. https://doi.org/10.1111/1467-8721.ep10770953.

Herman, A., & Reiter-Palmon, R. (2011). The effect of regulatory focus on idea generation and idea evaluation. *Psychology of Aesthetics, Creativity, and the Arts, 5,* 13–20. https://doi.org/10.1037/a0018587.

Higgins, E. T. (1997). Beyond pleasure and pain. *American Psychologist, 52*(12), 1280–1300. https://doi.org/10.1037/0003-066X.52.12.1280.

Janssen, O. (2003). Innovative behaviour and job involvement at the price of conflict and less satisfactory relations with co-workers. *Journal of Occupational and Organizational Psychology, 76,* 347–364. https://doi.org/10.1348/096317903769647210.

Jia, L., Hirt, E. R., & Karpen, S. C. (2009). Lessons from a faraway land: the effect of spatial distance on creative cognition. *Journal of Experimental Social Psychology, 45,* 1127–1131. https://doi.org/10.1016/j.jesp.2009.05.015.

Kahneman, D., Knetsch, J., & Thaler, R. (1991). Anomalies: the endowment effect, loss aversion, and status quo bias. *Journal of Economic Perspectives, 5,* 193–206.

Kaufman, J. C., Baer, J., Cole, J. C., & Sexton, J. D. (2008). A comparison of expert and non-expert raters using the consensual assessment technique. *Creativity Research Journal, 20,* 171–178. https://doi.org/10.1080/10400410802059929.

Kaufman, J. C., Baer, J., Cropley, D. H., Reiter-Palmon, R., & Sinnett, S. (2013). Furious activity vs. understanding: how much expertise is needed to evaluate creative work? *Psychology of Aesthetics, Creativity, and the Arts, 7,* 332–340. https://doi.org/10.1037/a0034809.

Kennel, V., Reiter-Palmon, R., De Vreede, T., & de Vreede, G. J. (2013). In *Creativity in teams: an examination of team accuracy in the idea evaluation and selection process System Sciences (HICSS), 2013 46th Hawaii International Conference* (pp. 630–639): IEEE.

Kornilova, T. V., & Kornilov, S. A. (2010). Intelligence and tolerance/intolerance for uncertainty as predictors of creativity. *Psychology In Russia: State of the Art, 32*, 40–256. https://doi.org/10.11621/pir.2010.0012.

Licuanan, B. F., Dailey, L. R., & Mumford, M. D. (2007). Idea evaluation: error in evaluating highly original ideas. *The Journal of Creative Behavior, 41*, 1–27. https://doi.org/10.1002/j.2162-6057.2007.tb01279.x.

Litchfield, R. C. (2008). Brainstorming reconsidered: a goal-based view. *The Academy of Management Review, 33*, 649–668. https://doi.org/10.2307/20159429.

Litchfield, R. C., Ford, C. M., & Gentry, R. J. (2015). Linking individual creativity to organizational innovation. *The Journal of Creative Behavior, 49*, 279–294. https://doi.org/10.1002/jocb.65.

Litchfield, R. C., Gilson, L. L., & Gilson, P. W. (2015). Defining creative ideas: toward a more nuanced approach. *Group & Organization Management, 40*, 238–265. https://doi.org/10.1177/1059601115574945.

Lonergan, D. C., Scott, G. M., & Mumford, M. D. (2004). Evaluative aspects of creative thought: effects of appraisal and revision standards. *Creativity Research Journal, 16*(2–3), 231–246. https://doi.org/10.1207/s15326934crj1602&3_7.

Luchins, A. S., & Luchins, E. H. (1969). Einstellung effect and group problem solving. *The Journal of Social Psychology, 77*, 78–89. https://doi.org/10.1080/00224545.1969.9919848.

Magnusson, P. R., Netz, J., & Wästlund, E. (2014). Exploring holistic intuitive idea screening in the light of formal criteria. *Technovation, 34*, 315–326.

Moreau, C. P., Lehmann, D. R., & Markman, A. B. (2001). Entrenched knowledge structures and consumer responses to new products. *Journal of Marketing Research, 38*, 14–29. https://doi.org/10.1509/jmkr.38.1.14.18836.

Mueller, J. S., Melwani, S., & Goncalo, J. A. (2012). The bias against creativity: why people desire but reject creative ideas. *Psychological Science, 23*, 13–17. https://doi.org/10.1177/0956797611421018.

Mueller, J. S., Wakslak, C. J., & Krishnan, V. (2014). Construing creativity: the how and why of recognizing creative ideas. *Journal of Experimental Social Psychology, 5181*–5187. https://doi.org/10.1016/j.jesp.2013.11.007.

Mumford, M. D., Lonergan, D. C., & Scott, G. (2002). Evaluating creative ideas: processes, standards, and context. *Inquiry: Critical Thinking Across the Disciplines, 22*, 21–30. https://doi.org/10.5840/inquiryctnews20022213.

Mumford, M. D., Schultz, R. A., & Van Doorn, J. R. (2001). Performance in planning: processes, requirements, and errors. *Review of General Psychology, 5*, 213–240. https://doi.org/10.1037/1089-2680.5.3.213.

Nijstad, B. A., De Dreu, C. W., Rietzschel, E. F., & Baas, M. (2010). The dual pathway to creativity model: creative ideation as a function of flexibility and persistence. *European Review of Social Psychology, 21*, 34–77. https://doi.org/10.1080/10463281003765323.

O'Hara, L. A., & Sternberg, R. J. (2001). It doesn't hurt to ask: effects of instructions to be creative, practical, or analytical on essay-writing performance and their interaction with students' thinking styles. *Creativity Research Journal, 13*, 197–210. https://doi.org/10.1207/S15326934CRJ1302_7.

Oldham, G. R., & Cummings, A. (1996). Employee creativity: personal and contextual factors at work. *Academy of Management Journal, 39*, 607–634. https://doi.org/10.2307/256657.

Onarheim, B., & Christensen, B. T. (2012). Distributed idea screening in stage-gate development processes. *Journal of Engineering Design, 23*, 660–673. https://doi.org/10.1080/09544828.2011.649426.

Önkal, D., Yates, J. F., Simga-Mugan, C., & Öztin, Ş. (2003). Professional vs. amateur judgment accuracy: the case of foreign exchange rates. *Organizational Behavior and Human Decision Processes*, *91*, 169–185. https://doi.org/10.1016/S0749-5978(03)00058-X.

Osborn, A. F. (1953). *Applied imagination*. Oxford: Scribner and Sons.

Pant, P. N., & Starbuck, W. H. (1990). Innocents in the forest: forecasting and research methods. *Journal of Management*, *16*, 433–460. https://doi.org/10.1177/014920639001600209.

Perry-Smith, J. E., & Coff, R. W. (2011). In the mood for entrepreneurial creativity? How optimal group affect differs for generating and selecting ideas for new ventures. *Strategic Entrepreneurship Journal*, *5*, 247–268. https://doi.org/10.1002/sej.116.

Perry-Smith, J. E., & Mannucci, P. V. (2017). From creativity to innovation: the social network drivers of the four phases of the idea journey. *Academy of Management Review*, *42*, 53–79. https://doi.org/10.5465/amr.2014.0462.

Perry-Smith, J. E., & Shalley, C. E. (2003). The social side of creativity: a static and dynamic social network perspective. *The Academy of Management Review*, *28*, 89–106. https://doi.org/10.2307/30040691.

Polman, E., & Emich, K. J. (2011). Decisions for others are more creative than decisions for the self. *Personality and Social Psychology Bulletin*, *37*, 492–501. https://doi.org/10.1177/0146167211398362.

Proudfoot, D., Kay, A. C., & Koval, C. Z. (2015). A gender bias in the attribution of creativity: Archival and experimental evidence for the perceived association between masculinity and creative thinking. *Psychological Science*, *26*(11), 1751–1761. https://doi.org/10.1177/0956797615598739.

Putman, V. L., & Paulus, P. B. (2009). Brainstorming, brainstorming rules and decision making. *The Journal of Creative Behavior*, *43*, 23–39. https://doi.org/10.1002/j.2162-6057.2009.tb01304.x.

Reiter-Palmon, R., & Arreola, N. J. (2015). Does generating multiple ideas lead to increased creativity? A comparison of generating one idea vs. many. *Creativity Research Journal*, *27*, 369–374. https://doi.org/10.1080/10400419.2015.1087274.

Reiter-Palmon, R., Ligon, G., Schoenbeck, M., & McFeely, S. (2017). In *Training to understand creativity: can training facilitate recognition of creative ideas? Paper presented at the UPCE Conference, March 31st 2017*.

Rietzschel, E. F. (2011). Collective regulatory focus predicts specific aspects of team innovation. *Group Processes & Intergroup Relations*, *14*, 337–345. https://doi.org/10.1177/1368430210392396.

Rietzschel, E. F., Nijstad, B. A., & Stroebe, W. (2006). Productivity is not enough: a comparison of interactive and nominal brainstorming groups on idea generation and selection. *Journal of Experimental Social Psychology*, *42*, 244–251. https://doi.org/10.1016/j.jesp.2005.04.005.

Rietzschel, E. F., Nijstad, B. A., & Stroebe, W. (2010). The selection of creative ideas after individual idea generation: choosing between creativity and impact. *British Journal of Psychology*, *101*, 47–68. https://doi.org/10.1348/000712609X414204.

Rietzschel, E. F., Nijstad, B. A., & Stroebe, W. (2014). Effects of problem scope and creativity instructions on idea generation and selection. *Creativity Research Journal*, *26*, 185–191. https://doi.org/10.1080/10400419.2014.901084.

Rietzschel, E. F., Nijstad, B. A., & Stroebe, W. (2018). Idea evaluation and selection. In P. B. Paulus & B. A. Nijstad (Eds.), *The oxford handbook of group creativity*. Oxford: Oxford University Press. [in press].

Ritter, S. M., & Rietzschel, E. F. (2017). Lay theories of creativity. In C. M. Zedelius, B. N. Müller, J. W. Schooler, C. M. Zedelius, B. N. Müller, & J. W. Schooler (Eds.), *The science of lay theories: How beliefs shape our cognition, behavior, and health* (pp. 95–126). Cham: Springer International Publishing. https://doi.org/10.1007/978-3-319-57306-9_5.

Ritter, S. M., Strick, M., Bos, M. W., Van Baaren, R. B., & Dijksterhuis, A. P. (2012). Good morning creativity: task reactivation during sleep enhances beneficial effect of sleep on creative performance. *Journal of Sleep Research, 21*, 643–647. https://doi.org/10.1111/j.1365-2869.2012.01006.x.

Ritter, S. M., van Baaren, R. B., & Dijksterhuis, A. (2012). Creativity: the role of unconscious processes in idea generation and idea selection. *Thinking Skills and Creativity, 7*, 21–27. https://doi.org/10.1016/j.tsc.2011.12.002.

Runco, M. A. (1993). Divergent thinking, creativity, and giftedness. *Gifted Child Quarterly, 37*, 16–22. https://doi.org/10.1177/001698629303700103.

Runco, M. A., & Basadur, M. (1993). Assessing ideational and evaluative skills and creative styles and attitudes. *Creativity and Innovation Management, 2*, 166–173. https://doi.org/10.1111/j.1467-8691.1993.tb00088.x.

Runco, M. A., & Chand, I. (1994). Problem finding, evaluative thinking, and creativity. In M. A. Runco & M. A. Runco (Eds.), *Problem finding, problem solving, and creativity* (pp. 40–76). Westport, CT: Ablex Publishing.

Runco, M. A., & Chand, I. (1995). Cognition and creativity. *Educational Psychology Review, 7*, 243–267. https://doi.org/10.1007/BF02213373.

Runco, M. A., & Charles, R. E. (1993). Judgments of originality and appropriateness as predictors of creativity. *Personality and Individual Differences, 15*, 537–546.

Runco, M. A., & Dow, G. T. (2004). Assessing the accuracy of judgments of originality on three divergent thinking tests. *Korean Journal of Thinking & Problem Solving, 14*, 5–14.

Runco, M. A., Illies, J. J., & Reiter-Palmon, R. (2005). Explicit instructions to be creative and original: a comparison of strategies and criteria as targets with three types of divergent thinking tests. *Korean Journal of Thinking & Problem Solving, 15*, 5–15.

Runco, M. A., McCarthy, K. A., & Svenson, E. (1994). Judgments of the creativity of artwork from students and professional artists. *The Journal of Psychology, 128*, 23–31.

Runco, M. A., & Smith, W. R. (1992). Interpersonal and intrapersonal evaluations of creative ideas. *Personality and Individual Differences, 13*, 295–302. https://doi.org/10.1016/0191-8869(92)90105-X.

Runco, M. A., & Vega, L. (1990). Evaluating the creativity of children's ideas. *Journal of Social Behavior & Personality, 5*, 439–452.

Schwenk, C., & Thomas, H. (1983). Formulating the mess: the role of decision aids in problem formulation. *Omega, 11*, 239–252.

Shalley, C. E., Gilson, L. L., & Blum, T. C. (2000). Matching creativity requirements and the work environment: effects on satisfaction and intentions to leave. *Academy of Management Journal, 43*, 215–223. https://doi.org/10.2307/1556378.

Sijbom, R. L., Janssen, O., & Van Yperen, N. W. (2015a). Leaders' receptivity to subordinates' creative input: the role of achievement goals and composition of creative input. *European Journal of Work and Organizational Psychology, 24*, 462–478. https://doi.org/10.1080/1359432X.2014.964215.

Sijbom, R. L., Janssen, O., & Van Yperen, N. W. (2015b). How to get radical creative ideas into a leader's mind? Leader's achievement goals and subordinates' voice of creative ideas. *European Journal of Work and Organizational Psychology, 24*, 279–296. https://doi.org/10.1080/1359432X.2014.892480.

Sijbom, R. L., Janssen, O., & Van Yperen, N. W. (2016). Leaders' achievement goals and their integrative management of creative ideas voiced by subordinates or superiors. *European Journal of Social Psychology, 46*, 732–745. https://doi.org/10.1002/ejsp.2223.

Silvia, P. J. (2008). Discernment and creativity: how well can people identify their most creative ideas? *Psychology of Aesthetics, Creativity, and the Arts, 2*, 139–146. https://doi.org/10.1037/1931-3896.2.3.139.

Simonton, D. K. (1988). *Scientific genius*. Cambridge: Cambridge University Press.

Škerlavaj, M., Černe, M., & Dysvik, A. (2014). I get by with a little help from my supervisor: Creative-idea generation, idea implementation, and perceived supervisor support. *The Leadership Quarterly, 25*, 987–1000. https://doi.org/10.1016/j.leaqua.2014.05.003.

Smolucha, F. C. (1992). A reconstruction of Vygotsky's theory of creativity. *Creativity Research Journal, 5,* 49–67. https://doi.org/10.1080/10400419209534422.

Somech, A., & Drach-Zahavy, A. (2013). Translating team creativity to innovation implementation: the role of team composition and climate for innovation. *Journal of Management, 39,* 684–708. https://doi.org/10.1177/0149206310394187.

Stenmark, C. K., Shipman, A. S., & Mumford, M. D. (2011). Managing the innovative process: the dynamic role of leaders. *Psychology of Aesthetics, Creativity, and the Arts, 5,* 67–80. https://doi.org/10.1037/a0018588.

Sternberg, R. J., & Davidson, J. E. (1995). *The nature of insight.* Cambridge, MA: The MIT Press.

Sternberg, R. J., & Lubart, T. I. (1999). The concept of creativity: prospects and paradigms. In R. J. Sternberg & J. Robert (Eds.), *Handbook of creativity* (pp. 3–15). New York, NY: Cambridge University Press.

Stroebe, W., Nijstad, B. A., & Rietzschel, E. F. (2010). Beyond productivity loss in brainstorming groups: the evolution of a question. In M. P. Zanna, J. M. Olson, M. P. Zanna, & J. M. Olson (Eds.), Vol. 43. *Advances in Experimental Social Psychology.* (pp. 157–203). San Diego, CA: Academic Press. https://doi.org/10.1016/S0065-2601(10)43004-X.

Sutton, R. I., & Hargadon, A. (1996). Brainstorming groups in context: effectiveness in a product design firm. *Administrative Science Quarterly, 41,* 685–718.

Taylor, D. W., Berry, P. C., & Block, C. H. (1958). Does group participation when using brainstorming facilitate or inhibit creative thinking. *Administrative Science Quarterly,* 323–347. https://doi.org/10.2307/2390603.

Tierney, P. (2008). Leadership and employee creativity. In J. Zhou & C. Shalley (Eds.), *Handbook of organizational creativity* (pp. 95–124). New York: Erlbaum.

Toh, C. A., & Miller, S. R. (2016a). Creativity in design teams: the influence of personality traits and risk attitudes on creative concept selection. *Research in Engineering Design, 27,* 73–89.

Toh, C. A., & Miller, S. R. (2016b). Choosing creativity: the role of individual risk and ambiguity aversion on creative concept selection in engineering design. *Research in Engineering Design, 27,* 195–219.

Trope, Y., & Liberman, N. (2010). Construal-level theory of psychological distance. *Psychological Review, 117,* 440–463. https://doi.org/10.1037/a0018963.

Verworn, B. (2009). Does age have an impact on having ideas? An analysis of the quantity and quality of ideas submitted to a suggestion system. *Creativity and Innovation Management, 18,* 326–334. https://doi.org/10.1111/j.1467-8691.2009.00537.x.

Wallas, G. (1926). *The art of thought.* London: J. Cape.

West, M. A. (2002a). Sparkling fountains or stagnant ponds: an integrative model of creativity and innovation implementation in work groups. *Applied Psychology: An International Review, 51,* 355–387. https://doi.org/10.1111/1464-0597.00951.

West, M. A. (2002b). Ideas are ten a penny: it's team implementation not idea generation that counts. *Applied Psychology: An International Review, 51,* 411–424. https://doi.org/10.1111/1464-0597.01006.

West, M. A., & Farr, J. L. (1990). Innovation at work. In M. A. West, J. L. Farr, M. A. West, & J. L. Farr (Eds.), *Innovation and creativity at work: Psychological and organizational strategies* (pp. 3–13). Oxford: John Wiley & Sons.

Woodman, R. W., Sawyer, J. E., & Griffin, R. W. (1993). Toward a theory of organizational creativity. *The Academy of Management Review, 18,* 293–321. https://doi.org/10.2307/258761.

Zenasni, F., Besançon, M., & Lubart, T. (2008). Creativity and tolerance of ambiguity: an empirical study. *The Journal of Creative Behavior, 42,* 61–73. https://doi.org/10.1002/j.2162-6057.2008.tb01080.x.

Zhong, C. B., Dijksterhuis, A., & Galinsky, A. D. (2008). The merits of unconscious thought in creativity. *Psychological Science, 19,* 912–918. https://doi.org/10.1111/j.1467-9280.2008.02176.x.

Zhou, J. (2008). Promoting creativity through feedback. In J. Zhou & C. Shalley (Eds.), *Handbook of organizational creativity* (pp. 125–146). New York: Erlbaum.

Zhou, J. & Shalley, C. E. (Eds.), (2008). *Handbook of organizational creativity*. New York: Erlbaum.

Zhou, J., Wang, X. M., Song, L. J., & Wu, J. (2017). Is it new? Personal and contextual influences on perceptions of novelty and creativity. *Journal of Applied Psychology, 102*, 180–202. https://doi.org/10.1037/apl0000166.

Zhu, Y., Ritter, S. M., Müller, B. C. N., & Dijksterhuis, A. (2017). Creativity: intuitive processing outperforms deliberative processing in creative idea selection. *Journal of Experimental Social Psychology, 73*, 180–188. https://doi.org/10.1016/j.jesp.2017.06.009.

Further Reading

Amabile, T. M. (1983). *The social psychology of creativity*. New York: Springer.

Basadur, M. (1995). Optimal ideation-evaluation ratios. *Creativity Research Journal, 8*, 63–75. https://doi.org/10.1207/s15326934crj0801_5.

Mumford, M. D., Mobley, M. I., Uhlman, C. E., Reiter-Palmon, R., & Doares, L. M. (1991). Process analytic models of creative capacities. *Creativity Research Journal, 4*, 91–122. https://doi.org/10.1080/10400419109534380.

Nijstad, B. A., & Stroebe, W. (2006). How the group affects the mind: a cognitive model of idea generation in groups. *Personality and Social Psychology Review, 10*, 186–213. https://doi.org/10.1207/s15327957pspr1003_1.

2

The Fuzzy Front-End? How Creativity Drives Organizational Innovation

David H. Cropley, Michelle L. Oppert

University of South Australia, Adelaide, SA, Australia

INTRODUCTION—CHANGE AND UNCERTAINTY

> Cause people often talk about being scared of change, but for me I'm more afraid of things staying the same. Cause the game is never won by standing in any one place for too long. *Nick Cave and The Bad Seeds—Jesus of the Moon, 2008*

Attempting to define creativity in a short and succinct sentence has often been considered difficult; however, this is no longer the case. The notion that the definition of creativity was elusive was likely driven by the fact that different people, working in diverse domains, experience the generation and realization of new ideas in very dissimilar ways. When speaking about creativity and the artist, for example, the term may evoke ideas of colors and materials, and how a story can be shared, whereas creativity for the educator may elicit ideas of group concepts and methods of engaging student attention, while for the engineer, creativity represents the development of a concrete solution to an expressed need.

The concept of creativity, in fact, is well understood and thoroughly researched, with a widely accepted definition of creativity highlighting the method by which ideas can lead to new and valuable products (Florida, 2002). *Products*, in the very broadest sense, are the outcome of creativity and the examples of the artist, educator, and engineer demonstrate that these are found across diverse domains, in the form of both tangible objects and intangible concepts. Innovation, in contrast, refers to a broader process incorporating creativity, and including stages in which ideas are developed and implemented toward a goal of both improved, and wholly new, products, processes, and services (e.g., Anderson, Potocnik, & Zhou, 2014). Innovation is required for people, ideas, and organizations to remain relevant and competitive in a developing world, where the ability to adapt to constant change is vital for survival. Buzan (2007) expresses the imperative for innovation very clearly: *"right now any individual, company or country wishing to survive the twenty-first-century must… innovate"* (p vii). No organization is immune to change and the ability of organizations to respond to consumers' constantly evolving needs and requirements is paramount for a competitive edge and success in an expanding and fast-paced global market place. While the idea of change can be daunting, it is an unavoidable reality, and a characteristic of business. Given the right tools and processes to facilitate creativity, and thus innovation, change can be anticipated, absorbed, and even embraced within the organizational context.

Organizations engaging in creativity and innovation are faced with a range of internal and external drivers and constraints. These factors vary depending on the organization itself. The biggest threats disturbing the status quo for many organizations are global; prominent among these are climate change, health-related issues, financial shocks, and local and national demographics. For example, a recent overview and projection of climate change impacts in Cyprus (Zachariadis, 2016) noted that there are still areas of uncertainty in how to cope with climate change and make a positive difference. These uncertainties are due, in part, to a long-standing failure by governments, enterprises, and individuals to recognize the problem, and acknowledge the impacts likely to occur in the absence of any attempt to find a solution. The consequences of climate change reach every corner of the planet and affect all aspects of human activity including, but not limited to, ecosystems, biodiversity, coastal zones, agriculture, human health, water sources, and energy supply and demand. While there are factors that cannot be controlled, such as a lack of rain in established agricultural regions, there are factors that remain subject to human intervention, such as the use of innovative and environmentally friendly energy sources. In some cases, policy change is being enforced by government: an example being the taxing of organizations that emit excessive levels of carbon. Climate change is a prime example of how organizations need to reconsider their practices to fit around new policy and environmental change in order to remain competitive and productive.

Demographic factors injecting change into global systems include, but again are not limited to, fertility rates, population size, growth and density, and life expectancy. A poignant example of organizations and governments needing to be creative and innovative in their adaptation to change is the aging of the population in many Western countries. In Australia, for example, in 1975 the ratio of people between the ages of 15 and 64 to people aged over 65 was 7.3:1. In 2015, this ratio had fallen to 4.5:1, and it is expected to drop further to only 2.7:1 by 2055. While on the one hand a significant achievement for humankind, the phenomenon of an aging population also brings with it factors that have not been experienced before on a national or global scale, affecting productivity, healthcare, taxation, and a range of other economic and social factors. In Australia, it has been recognized that policy measures must be enacted to ensure that the economy grows faster than the population, in order to meet the increasing demands of the aging population (Uddin, Alam, & Gow, 2016). This economic growth must occur as a response to change: to address the problems arising from such a fundamental demographic shift, including the need for a larger skilled healthcare workforce, and the more extensive use of technology and artificial intelligence as the proportion of the population engaged in employment shrinks.

An emerging theme linking organizations and the pressure to innovate is the concept of *consumer consciousness*. Consumer consciousness is the theory that individuals buy and invest in products and services that are ethical, environmentally focused, and which subscribe to fair trade principles. An example is the reaction of a growing proportion of the population to the environmental burden of meat production and associated factors. A recent study (Pohjolainen, Tapio, Vinnari, Jokinen, & Räsänen, 2016) revealed that there is a need for a wide range of social and political solutions, for example, to guide and even regulate meat consumption. There is a further need for tools and policies to assist groups and individuals in making sustainable and environmentally friendly dietary changes. A Neilson study (The Neilson Company, 2015) revealed that 66% of consumers, mostly Millennials, are willing to pay more for a product or brand if they know it is sustainably produced. Additionally, this study found that consumer goods derived from brands that demonstrate a commitment to sustainability grew by 4% whereas those that did not grew by less than 1%. Adapting to this social change—the growth of consumer consciousness—offers organizations both opportunities and challenges. For example, in the short term, production costs may increase; however, evidence suggests that there are longer term benefits to be gained, not least in the form of increased revenue.

The central theme of the problems described previously, both negative and positive, is that they require the generation of *new solutions*. Globalization is forcing organizations to compete on a level playing field because the world, from an economic perspective, is now flat (Friedman, 2007). For organizations to remain competitive players in this "flat world" they need to learn continuously, adapt and improve their capabilities to remain relevant and successful (Dyer, Nobeoka, Gulati, Nohria, & Zaheer, 2000). If change generates new problems and if innovation is the organizational process that connects new problems to new solutions, then what is the underlying process that drives innovation?

The core driver of innovation is often represented as a *fuzzy front-end* of creativity, that is, the generation of novel and effective ideas. The following sections will explore the relationship between creativity and innovation, while outlining the psychological and organizational factors and stages that connect new problems to exploitable, novel, and effective solutions. This chapter will explain the importance of the capacity of organizations to find new and effective solutions, while explaining how an organization's capacity to innovate is driven by creative antecedents—the so-called fuzzy front-end.

WHAT IS INNOVATION?

Organizations of all types—for example, for-profit businesses, not-for-profit charities, government departments, and even schools—sustain themselves, in large part, through the application of tried and tested solutions to established, *precedented* problems. This may be understood through the concept of *product lifecycles* whereby products and services go through distinct phases with respect to factors such as investment cost and return on investment (e.g., Christensen, 1999). The key role that the *growth* and *maturity* lifecycle phases play in delivering sustainable activity for organizations of all types cannot be underestimated. Thus the Coca-Cola Company continues to sell its eponymous beverage as the foundation (approximately 80%) of its global soft drink business, while the largest slice of Microsoft's revenue continues to be derived from its traditional strengths in the *Office* software suite and the *Windows* operating system (41%)[1]. Even Google, often held up as a paragon of innovation, derives a healthy majority (68.3%) of its total revenue from advertising on Google-owned websites (e.g., Google Search, YouTube)[2]. In more general terms, these core business activities may be described as a form of *replication*—in essence, doing the same thing over and over again, and expecting the *same* result (to misquote Einstein). Replication may also be understood as a process of connecting existing solutions to existing problems (see Fig. 1, quadrant A). While replication is not just necessary, but vital, to sustaining any organization, alone it cannot address situations where change occurs.

---

[1] The *Office* software suite individually comprised 25.2% of revenue, while the Windows operating system comprised 15.8% of FY2015 revenue, see: https://revenuesandprofits.com/how-microsoft-makes-money-understanding-microsoft-business-model/

[2] Revenue figures for Google, for FY2014, include US$45 billion (68.3%) for advertising on Google websites; US$14 billion (21.2%) for advertising on Google Network Member websites, and; US$7 billion (10.5%) from other sources—see: https://revenuesandprofits.com/how-google-makes-money/

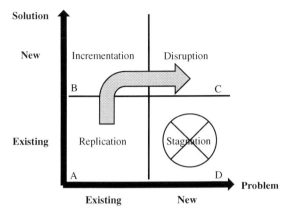

FIG. 1   Innovation: connecting solutions to problems.

Imagine, for example, a for-profit business suddenly faced with a new competitive pressure; a rival company introduces a substantially cheaper product, or customers demand improvements to an existing product line. These changes to the status quo create pressure to do things better, faster, or cheaper. In other words, such changes create pressure to find new solutions to existing problems. In such a situation, an organization has two simple choices. Either the organization innovates incrementally (Fig. 1, quadrant B)—finding improved solutions to the existing problem—or it remains anchored in replication, now doing the same thing over and over again, but expecting a different result (to correctly paraphrase Einstein[3]).

The status quo of replication can also be disturbed by a different type of change. Frequently customers demand not merely *improvements* to existing products or services, but express demands that are wholly new. Similarly, competitors may introduce a new product or service that shifts the prevailing paradigm to the point that incremental responses are inadequate. A good example is seen in the fate of US typewriter and mechanical calculator manufacturer Smith Corona. The company was a successful, and indeed incrementally innovative, organization in both markets for many decades. However, the introduction of the electronic calculator in the 1960s wiped out the mechanical calculator, while the introduction of the digital word processor in the early 1980s was the death knell for typewriters. In both cases, Smith Corona responded with incremental innovation—ever better mechanical calculators and typewriters—however, the world no longer wanted either product, no matter how good they were. When change so disturbs the status quo that incremental innovation is insufficient as a response, organizations must react with disruptive, or

---

[3] Albert Einstein is frequently attributed as the source of the saying that "The definition of insanity is doing the same thing over and over again, but expecting different results."

radical, innovation (Fig. 1, quadrant C). Buhl (1960) captured the essence of this pressure for change, noting that "Industries are continually being supplanted, not by modifications, but by innovations. Locomotives were not displaced by modified locomotives but by a new approach to transportation needs – the car" (p. 10). When change disturbs the status quo, organizations must respond either incrementally or through disruption. Innovation is how organizations respond to ubiquitous change.

WHY IS INNOVATION IMPORTANT TO ORGANIZATIONS?

Innovation is a response to change, and change injects novelty into an organization's activities, either through a pressure for new solutions to existing problems (incremental innovation), or through new solutions to wholly new problems (disruptive innovation)—see Fig. 1. Regardless of the driving force behind innovation, one thing is clear: responding to the novelty that accompanies change by ignoring it at best delays an organization's demise, and at worst, actively accelerates it. Organizations that respond to new problems with existing solutions drive themselves toward *stagnation* (Fig. 1, quadrant D). Imagine, for example, a government responding to the challenges of climate change and greenhouse gas emissions by building *more* coal-fired power stations. Not only would this represent a failure to respond to change through incrementation (e.g., converting existing stations to clean-coal technology) or disruption (e.g., replacing coal-fired stations with solar-thermal power generation), but the persistence with an outmoded solution concept would actually make the problem worse—no matter how *clean*, coal-fired stations still emit carbon, and therefore add to the problem!

A simple and complementary representation of the value of innovation to organizations can be seen through the framework of *diminishing returns*. Most, if not all, systems are subject to the Law of Diminishing Returns[4], such that incremental improvements have a finite limit. A classic example is found in agriculture. Adding fertilizer to a crop will increase the yield of that crop (Fig. 2). However, as more fertilizer is added, at some point (the point of diminishing returns), the increase in yield begins to tail off as the crop is saturated with fertilizer. Furthermore, if fertilizer continues to be added to the crop, the yield may actually go into decline. Prior to the point of diminishing returns, fertilizer represents an incremental solution to the problem of how to increase crop yield.

[4]Created by economists in the 19th century, it is used here as a metaphor for the drivers of incremental and disruptive innovation. In economics The Law of Diminishing Returns indicates that the relative increase in yield in a productive process declines as the input is increased (see, e.g., Cannan, 1892).

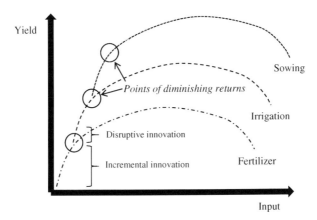

FIG. 2   Diminishing returns and types of innovation.

Once the point of diminishing returns is reached, the relative value of the incremental innovation begins to decline. Some organizations will persist with this incremental approach, seeking to extract as much additional value from the innovation as possible, but with less and less impact. Persisting with an incremental innovation beyond the point of *negative* returns flips the problem-solving paradigm from incrementation to stagnation (Fig. 1). Therefore it is at the point of diminishing returns that organizations must supplement their incremental efforts with disruptive innovation—finding wholly new solutions to the problem.

In the agricultural example, this is represented by the incorporation of new solutions into the system—for example, artificial irrigation and/or improved methods for sowing seeds—as means for further increasing crop yield (Fig. 2). Once introduced, those solutions may be incrementally improved, at least until new points of diminishing returns are reached. In this manner, the growth in yield can be kept strong and positive, but only through the judicious application of a combination of incremental innovation (to improve existing solutions) and disruptive innovation (wholly new solutions).

The *direct* organizational benefits of innovation are therefore growth, competitiveness, profitability, a sustained ability to solve problems, and to meet the needs of stakeholders (e.g., Anderson et al., 2014; Cohen, 2010; Kleinknecht & Mohnen, 2001). In addition to these benefits, the capacity for innovation is also known to underpin *indirect* organizational benefits such as increased productivity, improved teamwork, better staff motivation and collaboration (e.g., Mumford, Bedell-Avers, & Hunter, 2008; Mumford, Hester, & Robledo, 2012; Rosenbusch, Brinkmann, & Bausch, 2011).

Innovation—both incremental and disruptive—therefore is not only a response to change, but is a prerequisite for sustained growth. Innovation is how organizations *prosper* in response to ubiquitous change.

CHANGE AS THE DRIVER OF INNOVATION

We have suggested, somewhat obliquely so far, that *change* is a key factor in innovation. Knapper and Cropley (2000) were more direct, suggesting that change is a fundamental problem confronting societies as a whole, while Tidd and Bessant (2013) make change explicit to organizations, arguing that a common characteristic of successful organizations of all types and sizes is an ability to manage change. What are these changes and where do they come from?

Cropley and Cropley (2015) explained that change is discontinuous, making it nonlinear and unpredictable. It is found in many domains and is not limited only to technological variations and transformations. In fact, change is found across many areas: climate, demographic, social, regulatory, governmental, and economic, to name just a few. The problems that accompany change are, for example: how to deal with excessive carbon emissions, how to feed a growing world population, how to solve inequality, how to meet the needs of an aging population, how to educate people, and so forth. Change also generates problems related to the means of production, distribution, and marketing in organizations. It drives customer demands, competition, and, through factors such as globalization, destabilizes economic conditions and related business activities. Barreto (2012) described both *exogenous* (i.e., externally imposed) and *endogenous* (i.e., internally driven) shocks that result from change, impacting on organizations of all types.

Change therefore is a constant, across many, if not all, domains. It is the antecedent—the cause—of innovation (Fig. 3).

THE STAGES OF INNOVATION

To understand innovation, and ultimately, to manage it, requires a deeper exploration of the stages that comprise the generation of solutions to the problems stemming from change. A variety of *process* models of innovation have been defined, starting with a simple distinction between *invention* and *exploitation* (reported by Roberts, 1988, and derived from a roundtable discussion of the Industrial Research Institute in 1970). Invention implies "…the generation of an idea," while exploitation addresses "…the conversion of that invention into a business or other useful

FIG. 3   Change as the antecedent of innovation.

application" (p.12). Bledow, Frese, Anderson, Erez, and Farr (2009) made a similar distinction, further emphasizing the association between invention and creativity. Cropley and Cropley (2015) also reinforce the association between creativity and the stages of innovation, referring to both the generation, and the exploitation, of *effective novelty*.

Guilford (1959), although writing about creativity and problem solving, describes stages that are entirely consistent with the concept of innovation (see Table 1). More recent models (e.g., Cropley & Cropley, 2008a, 2008b; Luecke & Katz, 2003; Mumford, Mobley, Reiter-Palmon, Uhlman, & Doares, 1991) reflect a similar blend of elements of invention, or creativity, coupled with the development and practical exploitation of ideas. What each of these models, and many others, make clear is that the first step in the process of innovation—and the stage that immediately follows the causal change—is *creativity*.

Koen et al. (2002) provide us with one more complementary view of the innovation process, and one that employs a term that is becoming synonymous with creativity as a driver of the innovation process. They describe three stages of innovation: the *Fuzzy Front-End* (FFE), New Product Development (NPD), and Commercialization. As Koen et al. noted (p. 5), "The first part – the FFE – is generally regarded as one of the greatest opportunities for improvement of the overall innovation process." Therefore change drives and stimulates creativity (the fuzzy front-end), which leads to exploitable solutions, resulting in the overall process of innovation (Fig. 4).

The creative, fuzzy, front-end of the innovation process—those stages that define "invention" (see Table 1)—is therefore critical to the success of organizations seeking to prosper in response to change. Koen et al. (2002), however, correctly note that the term *fuzzy* carries an implication that "…the FFE is mysterious, lacks accountability, and cannot be critically evaluated, (p. 30)." In fact, as creativity researchers know, this is far from the truth, and, while sometimes hindered by myths and misconceptions (e.g., Cropley, 2017; Hong, Part, & Rowell, 2017), creativity is well defined, and well understood, measurable and manageable. The following section outlines, and demystifies, the key elements of the creative, fuzzy, front-end of innovation.

CREATIVITY: THE FUZZY FRONT-END OF INNOVATION?

Four factors are commonly understood to characterize creativity, widely referred to as the *4Ps* (see, e.g., Barron, 1969; Cropley & Cropley, 2015; Kaufman, 2016; Kozbelt, Beghetto, & Runco, 2010; Rhodes, 1961). *Person* describes the psychological resources (Rauch, Wiklund, Lumpkin,

TABLE 1 Models of the Stages of Innovation

Model	Stages				
Roberts (1988)	Invention				Exploitation
Guilford (1959)	Problem recognition	Idea generation	Idea evaluation		Solution validation
Luecke and Katz (2003)	Opportunity recognition	Idea generation	Idea evaluation		Development and commercialization
Cropley and Cropley (2008a, 2008b)	Preparation	Activation	Generation	Illumination	Verification	Communication	Validation

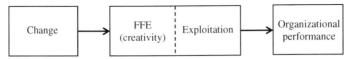

FIG. 4   The fuzzy front-end of innovation.

& Frese, 2009) that the individual brings to the process of generating effective and novel ideas, and which function as "antecedents of proactive behavior" (Parker, Williams, & Turner, 2006, p. 636) for creativity and innovation. These psychological resources typically include: personal properties (e.g., openness to experience), motivational states (e.g., intrinsic motivation), and emotional or affective states (e.g., excitement).

Process describes the cognitive, or thinking, processes that underpin the generation and exploitation of novel ideas. Although frequently treated as synonymous with creativity, divergent thinking—generating many *possible* solutions to a problem—in fact, is only one of two core cognitive processes employed in the front-end of innovation, and indeed in the latter stages as well. Guilford (1950) first noted the importance of convergent thinking—the ability to derive the single best, or correct, answer to a problem—as an essential complement to divergent thinking. Cropley (1999, 2006) explored both forms of thinking in the context of fully effective creativity, similarly stressing the role of convergent thinking as a complement to divergent thinking.

Press describes the environment in which the fuzzy front-end activity sits. In fact, two *environments* define and characterize the press. In a more general sense, there is a social environment surrounding innovation processes, defining societal norms and rules. More specifically, there is also an organizational environment that has a more immediate, day-to-day impact on creativity and innovation. Puccio and Cabra (2010) describe an environment outside of the organization, and an environment inside the organization, highlighting also the interaction between the two.

The last of the 4Ps is *Product*. This describes the outcomes, or solutions, that result from the fuzzy, creative, front-end of innovation. There is broad agreement in creativity research that, as a minimum, a creative product (whether tangible artifact, or intangible idea) must be both *novel*—that is, new, original, or surprising—and in some way *relevant*, or *appropriate*, to the task at hand. Taylor (1975), for example, described these as originality and relevance, while Besemer and O'Quin (1987) described novelty, resolution, elaboration, and synthesis as key qualities associated with newness and relevance. Cropley and Cropley (2005) developed four criteria of a creative product: novelty, relevance and effectiveness, elegance, and genesis, in addition arguing that these exist in a hierarchy, whereby the first two are prerequisites for creativity, while the latter two add further value to a creative product. Most recently, Cropley, Kaufman, and Cropley (2011), as well as Cropley and Kaufman (2012), developed a five-factor model of product creativity defining: (a) relevance and effectiveness (the product does what it is supposed to do), (b) problematization (the product helps to define the problem at hand), (c) propulsion (the product sheds new light on the problem at hand), (d) elegance (the product is well-executed), and (e) genesis (the product changes how the problem is understood).

The 4Ps help to dispel the notion that creativity—on its own, or as the front-end of innovation—is fuzzy, ill defined, and by extension, unmanageable. However, the 4Ps framework remains a rather static description of creativity. It implies a uniform, stable set of conditions and qualities that favor the generation of novel and effective ideas. The notion of fuzziness may arise from an apparent mismatch between the static world of creativity, and dynamic world of innovation and problem solving. To resolve this mismatch, and debunk the fuzziness of the creative front-end of innovation, requires a dynamic representation of the impact of Person, Process, Press, and Product across the stages of innovation—from initial problem identification and formulation, through the implementation of a solution. Equipped with such a model, we have the means to manage the innovation process much more effectively, and a tool that makes it possible to render the front-end of innovation accountable and subject to critical evaluation.

MANAGING CREATIVITY IN THE PROCESS OF INNOVATION

Cropley and Cropley (2008a, 2008b) first proposed a combination of the 4Ps of creativity across seven stages of the innovation process to construct an extended phase model of innovation. The resulting *Innovation Phase Model* sought to resolve the *paradoxes* that have frequently been noted as a feature of innovation (e.g., Bledow et al., 2009; Cropley & Cropley, 2012; Miron-Spektor, Erez, & Naveh, 2011), and which may be the reason why creativity has been characterized as the *fuzzy* front-end of innovation.

The essence of the Innovation Phase Model (Table 2) states that the factors that define and characterize creativity—for example, motivation, cognitive process, organizational culture—do so not in a static, one-size-fits-all sense, but in different ways according to the stage of innovation that is active at any given point in time. Divergent thinking, often exclusively equated with creativity, is thus both vital for innovation, for example, when seeking to generate a wide range of solution ideas, but may inhibit innovation in a stage that requires the selection of one single idea for implementation (and therefore Convergent Thinking). The Innovation Phase Model defines a continuum for each element of the 4Ps—in fact, expanding to a total of six dimensions, to give adequate weight to elements

TABLE 2 The Innovation Phase Model

Building blocks		Invention					Exploitation	
Phase	**Poles**	Preparation	Activation	Generation	Illumination	Verification	Communication	Validation
		Knowledge, problem recognition	Problem definition, refinement	Many candidate solutions	A few promising solutions	A single optimal solution	A working prototype	A successful "product"
Process	Convergent vs divergent	Convergent	Divergent	Divergent	Convergent	Convergent	Mixed	Convergent
Person (motivation)	Reactive vs proactive	Mixed	Proactive	Proactive	Proactive	Mixed	Reactive	Reactive
Person (properties)	Adaptive vs innovative	Adaptive	Innovative	Innovative	Innovative	Adaptive	Adaptive	Adaptive
Person (feelings)	Conserving vs generative	Conserving	Generative	Generative	Generative	Conserving	Conserving	Conserving
Product	Routine vs creative	Routine	Creative	Creative	Creative	Routine	Routine	Routine
Press	High demand vs low demand	High	Low	Low	Low	High	High	High

Based on Cropley, D. H., & Cropley, A. J. (2015). The psychology of innovation in organizations. New York, NY: Cambridge University Press.

1. CREATIVITY AND INNOVATION: LARGER CONCEPTS

of the Person—with contrasting *poles* defining the state that is most active in any given stage (Table 2). In this manner, the state of Process (Convergent or Divergent Thinking) that facilitates innovation in the stage of Generation is contrasted with the state that is necessary in the stage of Verification. Through this combination of dimensions and stages, creativity is no longer merely an opaque front-end to innovation, but provides structure and clarity about the role of each of the 4Ps as the process of innovation unfolds.

The Innovation Phase Model helps organizations make sense of the alignment of their own human capital to the requirements of the fuzzy front-end of innovation. If creativity requires, for example, both the ability to generate possible solutions to a problem (in the Generation phase), and the ability to analyses those solutions, selecting the best for the current problem (in the Illumination phase), then the model makes it clear that this will be facilitated by not only the ability to think divergently, and to think convergently, but also the ability of individuals to switch between these two modes of thinking at the appropriate time. The Innovation Phase Model serves as a roadmap for innovation in organizations.

The Innovation Phase Model serves not only as a framework to *explain* the interaction of creativity with the stages of innovation. Because it defines the ideal state for each of the 4Ps at each stage of the innovation process, the model becomes a tool for guiding and managing the innovation process. To aid in this process, Cropley, Cropley, Chiera, and Kaufman (2013) constructed and tested a survey instrument—the Innovation Phase Assessment Instrument—designed to diagnose an organization's alignment to the ideal states defined in the model, at each stage of the innovation process. Using this instrument, organizations are able to assess areas of misalignment—or weakness—and take remedial action to improve their overall capacity for innovation (see, e.g., Cropley, 2016; Cropley & Cropley, 2017). This makes it possible for organizations to target remedial actions far more precisely.

CONCLUDING THOUGHTS

Innovation begins with change—for example, climate, demographic, regulatory, and financial change—and change defines novel problems that must be solved. While some organizations tackle this by applying existing, known solutions, this approach ultimately leads to stagnation. New problems require *new* solutions—either incrementally or radically new—if organizations and societies hope to grow and prosper. This requirement for novelty means that the first step in the innovative process is one of creativity. While creativity has often been characterized as a *fuzzy* process, implying a lack of rigor, clarity, and understanding, in fact, creativity is well understood. The mechanisms by which individuals generate novel ideas, and the circumstances which support this, have been the subject of scientific research for more than 60 years. However, to break the association between creativity and *fuzziness* that persists in some literature, it is necessary to show how the 4Ps of creativity are more than a static model of creativity. Combined with a stage model of innovation, it is possible to show how creativity defines a *dynamic* framework of states of the Person, Process, Product, and Press. In doing so, this dynamic model resolves long-standing paradoxes of innovation. Divergent thinking, for example, may be good for innovation in one stage, but may inhibit innovation in another stage. The dynamic Innovation Phase Model provides a framework for applying the psychological knowledge base of creativity to innovation, removing the notion of fuzziness, and giving clarity that allows innovation processes to be measured, managed, and optimized.

References

Anderson, N., Potocnik, K., & Zhou, J. (2014). Innovation and creativity in organizations: a state-of-the-science review and prospective commentary. *Journal of Management, 40*, 1297–1333.

Barreto, I. (2012). Solving the innovative puzzle: the role of innovative interpretation in opportunity formation and related processes. *Journal of Management Studies, 49*, 356–380.

Barron, F. X. (1969). *Creative person and creative process*. New York, NY: Holt, Rinehart & Winston.

Besemer, S. P., & O'Quin, K. (1987). Creative product analysis: testing a model by developing a judging instrument. In S. G. Isaksen (Ed.), *Frontiers of creativity research: Beyond the basics* (pp. 367–389). Buffalo: Brady.

Bledow, R., Frese, M., Anderson, N., Erez, M., & Farr, J. (2009). A dialectic perspective on innovation: conflicting demands, multiple pathways, and ambidexterity. *Industrial and Organizational Psychology, 2*(3), 305–337.

Buhl, H. R. (1960). *Creative engineering design*. Ames, IA: Iowa State University Press.

Buzan, A. (2007). Foreword. In S. C. Lundin & J. Tan (Eds.), *CATS: The nine lives of innovation* (pp. iv–viii). Spring Hill: Management Press.

Cannan, E. (1892). The origin of the law of diminishing returns, 1813-15. *The Economic Journal, 2*(5), 53–69.

Christensen, C. M. (1999). *Innovation and the general manager*. Boston, MA: Irwin/McGraw-Hill.

Cohen, L. Y. (2010). *10 reasons why we need innovation* Retrieved from http://www.amcreativityassoc.org/Articles/CohenTOP%2010%20Reasons%20Why%20We%20Need%20INNOVATION.pdf.

Cropley, A. J. (1999). Creativity and cognition: producing effective novelty. *Roeper Review, 21*(4), 253–260.

Cropley, A. J. (2006). In praise of convergent thinking. *Creativity Research Journal, 18*(3), 391–404.

Cropley, D. H. (2016). Measuring capacity for innovation in local government organisations. *Journal of Creativity and Business Innovation, 2*(1), 31–45.

Cropley, D. H. (2017). Creative products: defining and measuring novel solutions. In J. A. Plucker (Ed.), *Creativity and innovation: Theory, research, and practice* (pp. 61–74). Waco, TX: Prufrock Press Inc.

Cropley, D. H., & Cropley, A. J. (2005). Engineering creativity: a systems concept of functional creativity. In J. C. Kaufman & J. Baer (Eds.), *Creativity across domains: Faces of the muse* (pp. 169–185). Mahwah, NJ: Lawrence Erlbaum Associates Publishers.

Cropley, A. J., & Cropley, D. H. (2008a). Resolving the paradoxes of creativity: an extended phase model. *Cambridge Journal of Education, 38*(3), 355–373.

Cropley, D. H., & Cropley, A. J. (2008b). Elements of a universal aesthetic of creativity. *Psychology of Aesthetics, Creativity, and the Arts, 2*(3), 155–161.

Cropley, D. H., & Cropley, A. J. (2012). A psychological taxonomy of organizational innovation: resolving the paradoxes. *Creativity Research Journal, 24*(1), 29–40.

Cropley, D. H., & Cropley, A. J. (2015). *The psychology of innovation in organizations*. New York, NY: Cambridge University Press.

Cropley, D. H., & Cropley, A. J. (2017). Innovation capacity, organisational culture and gender. *European Journal of Innovation Management, 20*(3), 493–510.

Cropley, D. H., Cropley, A. J., Chiera, B. A., & Kaufman, J. C. (2013). Diagnosing organizational innovation: measuring the capacity for innovation. *Creativity Research Journal, 25*(4), 388–396.

Cropley, D. H., & Kaufman, J. C. (2012). Measuring functional creativity: non-expert raters and the creative solution diagnosis scale. *The Journal of Creative Behavior, 46*(2), 119–137.

Cropley, D. H., Kaufman, J. C., & Cropley, A. J. (2011). Measuring creativity for innovation management. *Journal of Technology Management & Innovation, 6*(3), 13–30.

Dyer, J. H., Nobeoka, K., Gulati, R., Nohria, N., & Zaheer, A. (2000). Creating and managing a high-performance knowledge-sharing network: the Toyota case. *Strategic Management Journal, 21*(3), 345–367. https://doi.org/10.1002/(SICI)1097-0266(200003)21: 3<345::AID-SMJ96>3.0.CO;2-N.

Florida, R. (2002). *The rise of the creative class*. New York, NY: Basic Books.

Friedman, T. L. (2007). *The world is flat : A brief history of the twenty-first century* (1st ed.). New York, NY: Farrar, Straus and Giroux.

Guilford, J. P. (1950). Creativity. *American Psychologist, 5,* 444–454.

Guilford, J. P. (1959). Traits of creativity. In H. H. Anderson (Ed.), *Creativity and its cultivation* (pp. 142–161). New York, NY: Harper.

Hong, E., Part, R., & Rowell, L. (2017). Children's and teachers' conceptions of creativity: contradictions and implications in classroom instruction. In R. A. Beghetto & B. Sriraman (Eds.), *Creative contradictions in education: Cross disciplinary paradoxes and perspectives* (pp. 303–331). Switzerland: Springer International Publishing.

Kaufman, J. C. (2016). *Creativity 101* (2nd ed.). New York, NY: Springer Publishing Company.

Kleinknecht, A. & Mohnen, P. A. (Eds.), (2001). *Innovation and firm performance*. London: Palgrave Macmillan.

Knapper, C., & Cropley, A. J. (2000). *Lifelong learning and higher education*. London: Kogan Page.

Koen, P. A., Ajamian, G. M., Boyce, S., Clamen, A., Fisher, E., Fountoulakis, S., et al. (2002). *Fuzzy front end: Effective methods, tools, and techniques*. New York, NY: Wiley.

Kozbelt, A., Beghetto, R. A., & Runco, M. A. (2010). Theories of creativity. In J. C. Kaufman & R. J. Sternberg (Eds.), *The Cambridge handbook of creativity* (pp. 20–47). New York, NY: Cambridge University Press.

Luecke, R., & Katz, R. (2003). *Managing creativity and innovation*. Boston, MA: Harvard Business School Press.

Miron-Spektor, E., Erez, M., & Naveh, E. (2011). The effect of conformist and attentive-to-detail members on team innovation: reconciling the innovation paradox. *Academy of Management Journal, 54*(4), 740–760.

Mumford, M. D., Bedell-Avers, K. E., & Hunter, S. T. (2008). Planning for innovation: a multi-level perspective. In M. D. Mumford, S. T. Hunter, & K. E. Bedell (Eds.), *Innovation in organizations: A multi-level perspective* (pp. 107–154). Oxford: Elsevier.

Mumford, M. D., Hester, K. S., & Robledo, I. C. (2012). Creativity in organizations: Importance and approaches. In M. D. Mumford (Ed.), *Handbook of organizational creativity*. London, UK: Academic Press.

Mumford, M. D., Mobley, M. I., Reiter-Palmon, R., Uhlman, C. E., & Doares, L. M. (1991). Process analytic models of creative capacities. *Creativity Research Journal, 4*(2), 91–122.

Neilson. (2015). *The sustainability imprative. New insights on consumer expectations* Retrieved from www.nielsen.com/au/en/insights/reports/2015/the-sustainability-imperative.html.

Parker, S. K., Williams, H. M., & Turner, N. (2006). Modeling the antecedents of proactive behavior at work. *Journal of Applied Psychology, 91*(3), 636–652.

Pohjolainen, P., Tapio, P., Vinnari, M., Jokinen, P., & Räsänen, P. (2016). Consumer consciousness on meat and the environment–exploring differences. *Appetite, 101*, 37–45.

Puccio, G. J., & Cabra, J. F. (2010). Organizational creativity: a systems approach. In J. C. Kaufman & R. J. Sternberg (Eds.), *The Cambridge handbook of creativity* (pp. 145–173). New York, NY: Cambridge University Press.

Rauch, A., Wiklund, J., Lumpkin, G. T., & Frese, M. (2009). Entrepreneurial orientation and business performance: an assessment of past research and suggestions for the future. *Entrepreneurship Theory and Practice, 33*(3), 761–787.

Rhodes, M. (1961). An analysis of creativity. *The Phi Delta Kappan, 42*(7), 305–310.

Roberts, E. B. (1988). Managing invention & innovation. *Research Technology Management, 33*, 1–19.

Rosenbusch, N., Brinckmann, J., & Bausch, A. (2011). Is innovation always beneficial? A meta-analysis of the relationship between innovation and performance in SMEs. *Journal of Business Venturing, 26*(4), 441–457.

Taylor, I. A. (1975). An emerging view of creative actions. In I. A. Taylor & J. W. Getzels (Eds.), *Perspectives in creativity* (pp. 297–325). Chicago, IL: Aldine.

Tidd, J., & Bessant, J. R. (2013). *Managing innovation: Integrating technological, market and organizational change* (5th ed.). Chichester: John Wiley and Sons.

Uddin, G. A., Alam, K., & Gow, J. (2016). Population age structure and savings rate impacts on economic growth: evidence from Australia. *Economic Analysis and Policy, 52*, 23–33.

Zachariadis, T. (2016). *Climate change in Cyprus : Review of the impacts and outline of an adaptation strategy.* New York, NY: Springer International Publishing.

An Integrated Model of Dynamic Problem Solving Within Organizational Constraints

Johnathan R. Cromwell*, Teresa M. Amabile[†], Jean-François Harvey[‡]

*Department of Entrepreneurship, Innovation, and Strategy, University of San Francisco, San Francisco, CA, United States, [†]Entrepreneurial Management Unit, Harvard Business School, Boston, MA, United States, [‡]Department of Entrepreneurship and Innovation, HEC Montréal, Montréal, QC, Canada

INTRODUCTION

The journey that people take to produce creative ideas is often a winding path that involves several twists, turns, detours, and reversals of direction. At many points throughout the process, people are confronted with questions of whether they should keep investing resources into an existing idea, start searching for a new idea, or change the problem they are working on altogether. The result is that creative projects often take seemingly unique paths to success, making it difficult to predict the circumstances of creative success. Consider, for example, the creation of the commercial light bulb and the Nintendo Wii, two technological inventions that took quite different paths to development.

In 1878, more than 75 years after the electric light bulb was invented, Thomas Edison began a research program with the goal of developing a commercially viable light bulb, which needed to satisfy the criteria of being long-lasting, cheap to produce, and energy efficient (Israel, 1998). Throughout the course of development, Edison and his team conducted thousands of experiments using different combinations of designs and materials. After more than a year of experimentation, in October 1879, they developed a viable solution that went on to revolutionize the energy industry. By contrast, the Nintendo Wii was created in 2006 based on a technology that was developed nearly 30 years earlier by people working in a completely different industry (Verganti, 2009). In the late 1970s, a company called STMicroelectronics developed a new semiconductor that could detect three-dimensional movement. After creating the technology, engineers searched for commercial applications across a broad range of industries, but found limited success with applications in computers, home appliances, and automobiles. It was not until 2005, after meeting with game developers at Nintendo, that they learned how their technology could be used to create a highly novel gaming experience. Shortly thereafter, the Nintendo Wii debuted on the market and went on to transform the gaming industry.

Both of these stories illustrate creative invention, but they differ in two important ways. First, the creative process seemed to take two different paths to success. In the case of the light bulb, Edison and his team began with a well-defined problem and then searched broadly for materials and technology that could solve the problem, generating thousands of different idea combinations until they finally developed a viable solution. This creative process resembles the "problem-solving" model of creativity that is commonly described in the organizational creativity literature. According to this model, an inventor first finds, defines, or formulates a problem (e.g., Getzels & Csikszentmihalyi, 1976; Mumford, Reiter-Palmon, & Redmond, 1994), and then engages in a dynamic process of gathering information, generating ideas, elaborating ideas, evaluating ideas, and selecting ideas until a solution has been created (Amabile, 1983; Amabile & Pratt, 2016; Mumford, Mobley, Reiter-Palmon, Uhlman, & Doares, 1991).

In the case of the Nintendo Wii, however, engineers started with a well-defined technology and then searched broadly for commercial applications across different industries, eventually discovering a problem in the gaming industry that could be solved with their technology. This process resembles the "Geneplore" model of creativity (Finke, Ward, & Smith, 1992), in which an inventor first generates a potentially useful idea—what is known as a "preinventive structure"—and then explores how it may solve problems across a wide variety of problem domains until a problem and solution emerge together. While the problem-solving model begins with the definition of a problem and is followed by a search for solutions, the Geneplore model begins with the creation of a preinventive idea and is followed by a search for problems. At first blush, these *problem-first* and *idea-first* models seem to describe entirely different creative processes.

The second way in which these two examples differ is that the conditions of constraint for each group of inventors appear to have been quite different. Edison and his team were heavily constrained by the problem they were trying to solve, but they had great flexibility when searching for a solution to that problem. The semiconductor engineers, on the other hand, were heavily constrained by the technology they were working with, but had great flexibility when searching for a problem that could be solved with that particular preinventive idea.

In each case, inventors experienced a different confluence of constraints and engaged in a different creative process. We argue that this is no mere coincidence. Indeed, these examples suggest that constraints might systematically influence the creative process—an idea that has received little attention in the creativity literature (see Caniëls & Rietzschel, 2015 for a review). While prior literature has developed extensive theory on how constraints can influence *creative outcomes* (e.g., Amabile, Conti, Coon, Lazenby, & Herron, 1996; Baer & Oldham, 2006; Byron, Khazanchi, & Nazarian, 2010; Finke et al., 1992; Hunter, Bedell, & Mumford, 2007), it has developed little theory on how they might shape the *creative process*.

Taken as a whole, prior literature presents two competing models of the creative process, each of which is compelling. But it is unclear when and why people are likely to engage in one process over the other. In this chapter, we address this puzzle by first reviewing the theoretical foundations of each model, showing that they originate from the same underlying cognitive framework of problem solving. However, we find that a clear differentiator between the two models is based on the level and type of constraint that people face at different times during the creative process. We use this observation—that constraints can shape the creative process—as the underlying premise for our own model, and we expand upon these arguments to account for more recent findings on creativity and constraint.

We build our model by first developing a typology of constraints that is based on two fundamental dimensions of constraint—types of constraint (*resource constraints* vs *problem constraints*) and sources of constraint (*internal constraints* vs *external constraints*). We then synthesize the problem-first and idea-first models of the creative process into a new *dynamic problem-solving* model. The result is an integrated model in which different creative processes unfold depending on the confluence of constraints that people face on a creative project. The model is dynamic, in that it allows for dynamic iteration between these two models, so that as constraints shift over time, inventors may shift from one creative process to the other.

THE CREATIVE PROCESS: TWO PATHS OR ONE?

Creativity in organizations is the creation of novel and useful (or appropriate) products, processes, services, or ideas (Amabile, 1983, 1988; Oldham & Cummings, 1996; Shalley & Zhou, 2008; Woodman, Sawyer, & Griffin, 1993). To produce these outcomes, people engage in a messy and unpredictable process that includes a wide range of activities such as defining problems, generating ideas, and evaluating ideas against criteria—among others. While many of these activities are often necessary for creativity, the order and sequence by which they produce creative outcomes can vary widely. Scholars have broadly codified these activities into one of two general models, which we refer to as the *problem-first* and *idea-first* models of the creative process. We summarize these models in Fig. 1, showing how each model theorizes the set of activities and sequence of activities that characterize the creative process.

A majority of organizational creativity research has adopted the problem-first model of the creative process (Amabile, 1983, 1988; Amabile & Pratt, 2016; Mumford et al., 1991; Wallas, 1926). According to this model, organizational creativity begins when a problem is defined, which is often considered the most important step of the process. As Einstein described it, "The formulation of a problem is often more essential than its solution, which may be merely a matter of mathematical or experimental skill. To raise new questions, new possibilities, to regard old problems from a new angle, requires creative imagination and marks real advance in science" (Einstein & Infeld, 1938). In organizations, problems are usually defined when a higher-level manager presents a problem to an employee, but it can also occur when employees define their own problem to solve

Problem-first model of the creative process

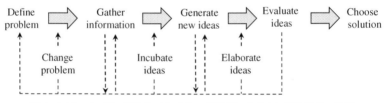

(Abstracted from Amabile, 1983; Amabile & Pratt, 2016; Mumford et al., 1991; Wallas, 1926)

Idea-first model of the creative process

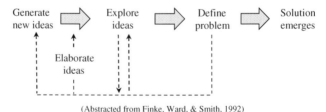

(Abstracted from Finke, Ward, & Smith, 1992)

Notes: Dotted lines refer to feedback loops in which individuals can return to earlier activities of the creative process. According to the theorists cited, the activities in each creative process need not occur in the exact sequence shown.

FIG. 1   Summary of two general models of the creative process.

(Getzels & Csikszentmihalyi, 1976; Unsworth, 2001). Once a problem has been defined, people engage in a sequence of activities—such as gathering information, generating ideas, and evaluating ideas against criteria—until a viable solution has been reached. Gathering information involves the collection of data and materials that will help individuals solve a problem. Generating ideas involves drawing on resources to develop a set of ideas that can potentially solve the problem. And evaluating ideas involves taking a subset of promising ideas and evaluating them against the problem criteria.

When an idea satisfies all the criteria, it becomes a viable solution to the problem and can be selected for implementation, thereby ending the creative process. But if an idea fails to satisfy all the criteria, people must revert back to earlier stages of the process. For instance, they may need to generate a new set of ideas or elaborate upon existing ideas (Perry-Smith & Mannucci, 2017). They may need to gather additional information about the problem, or they can set the problem aside and not consciously work on it for a time—a process known as incubation that can sometimes result in a breakthrough idea (Guilford, 1950; Kounios & Beeman, 2015; Wallas, 1926). They may also need to change the problem they are working on by applying existing resources to new problems (e.g., Baker & Nelson, 2005; Sonenshein, 2014). In most versions of the problem-first model (e.g., Amabile & Pratt, 2016), people can return to an earlier point from any later point in the process, resulting in a cyclical process until (ideally) a viable solution is created that satisfies all the problem criteria.

By contrast, a growing body of literature draws from an idea-first model of the creative process (Finke et al., 1992). According to this model, the creative process begins when people generate a new idea that has the potential to be useful, but the problem has not yet been defined. These ideas are called "preinventive structures" because they do not reflect fully formed solutions, but rather, reflect ideas that are precursors to solutions that will eventually emerge from the creative process. For example, the STM engineers began their creative process by developing a semiconductor that could detect movement in three-dimensional space. While this initial technology represented a potentially useful idea, they did not know specifically what problems could be solved with it (Verganti, 2009), and thus it was only a preinventive idea.

Once a preinventive idea has been created, people can explore whether it can solve a specific problem within a problem domain. If a problem cannot be defined, then people must return to an earlier activity in the process, either generating a new preinventive idea, elaborating an idea that they already generated, or exploring their idea in the context of a different problem domain. If a problem can be defined, a viable solution emerges to become a creative outcome. For example, the STM engineers explored whether their new semiconductor could solve a problem within a broad range of industries, but they struggled to develop creative solutions in many of them. Once they came across the gaming industry, however, they discovered a specific problem that could be solved with their technology, and a solution emerged in the form of a new videogame system.

Theoretical Origins of the Problem-First and Idea-First Models of the Creative Process

An initial comparison of these two models suggests that they reflect entirely different creative processes. However, both models are actually built on a cognitive framework of problem solving (Newell, Shaw, & Simon, 1962; Newell & Simon, 1972), and they differ in their assumptions about individuals who are engaged in this problem-solving process. According to the cognitive framework, problem solving occurs within a problem space, which consists of (a) an initial state, (b) a desired goal state, and (c) all intermediate states in between. The process begins when an individual reads a problem statement, which triggers a variety of memories, concepts, or other cognitive elements that are relevant to the problem at hand. Then, drawing from these cognitive elements, the individual generates ideas that could solve the problem. For example, imagine a movie producer who is presented with the problem of creating her 10th film. When presented with this problem, she will draw on all her prior expertise and knowledge from developing her previous nine films (as well as her formal and informal training), which could then be applied to developing her 10th film.

After generating a potential pool of ideas, the individual evaluates these ideas against the criteria of the goal state. If an idea satisfies all the criteria, it is considered a viable solution to the problem and the process can end. But if it fails to satisfy the criteria, the individual must revert back to earlier stages of the process. She can generate new ideas based on cognitive elements she already possesses, or gather new information from the environment to build a larger base of cognitive elements to use for generating ideas. The particular set of ideas and the sequence in which they are produced define the intermediate states of the problem space.

A key feature of this process is that problems exist along a continuum, ranging from being "well-structured," in which all three parts of the problem space are well known, to being "ill-structured," in which at least one part of the problem space is unknown (Reitman, 1965; Simon, 1973). When a problem is well structured, it can be solved algorithmically: That is, an individual can apply her existing knowledge to the new problem, and problem solving will be fairly linear. For example, a movie producer who has extensive experience creating *Spider-Man* movies will be able to develop much of a new *Spider-Man* movie by relying on her existing knowledge.

Although audience tastes may change and resources or equipment can evolve, developing the film will follow a fairly linear and predictable sequence of steps.

Problems become ill structured when aspects of the problem space are unknown. The simplest form of ill-structured problems occurs when the goal state is known and the initial state and intermediate states are unknown. Under these conditions, a problem must be solved heuristically: That is, an individual must use their intuition to develop ideas that might solve the problem, but there is more uncertainty because they are operating with incomplete information. For example, if the movie producer who specializes in *Spider-Man* movies tries to develop a movie for a different superhero—such as Superman—much of her knowledge might still be relevant, but she may need to spend more time gathering new information, elaborating ideas, and evaluating ideas against criteria throughout the process. If she were creating a film in an entirely different genre—such as a comedy—she would need to spend even more time engaging in these activities, resulting in an even more cyclical creative process. Generally speaking, the degree to which problems are ill structured determines the degree to which the creative process is cyclical.

The most complex form of ill-structured problems occurs when all three aspects of the problem space are unknown, including the initial state, intermediate states, and final goal state. These problems have been described as "open problems," whereas situations in which the goal state is known are called "closed problems" (Unsworth, 2001). When problems are open, problem statements are vague and poorly defined, and they fail to trigger specific cognitive elements that can be used to solve the problem at hand. For example, a movie producer may be given the problem statement, "develop a new breakthrough movie," but this can be so vague—even for an experienced movie producer—that it does not trigger any specific cognitive elements that can be used to produce a viable solution. This was the situation that movie producers at Pixar found themselves in when they were developing the world's first feature-length computer-generated film in the late 1990s (Catmull, 2014). Aided with new computer technology that gave them the ability to create any plotline, character, or setting they could imagine, they experienced extreme levels of ambiguity and struggled to develop ideas that could solve their problem. It was not until they focused their efforts on developing a compelling storyline that their idea for *Toy Story* began to take shape.

It is under these open-problem conditions that the two models of the creative process begin to diverge. According to problem-solving scholars, people can approach open problems by engaging in a multitiered version of the problem-first model (Simon, 1973). First, they read the vague problem statement, which triggers several vague cognitive elements that are relevant to the problem. For example, the movie producer who is asked to "develop a new breakthrough movie" will think of several vague cognitive elements such as "genre, plotline, cast, characters, and break-through movies." Each of these vague cognitive elements then becomes a new subproblem to solve, which triggers a new set of cognitive elements. For example, addressing the "genre" subproblem might trigger cognitive elements such as "action, adventure, comedy, etc.," which in turn could trigger a new set of cognitive elements that become new subproblems. With each tier of the process, problem statements and cognitive elements become more specific; eventually, the open problem is adapted into a net-work of smaller, more specific, and closed subproblems.

An important consequence of this process is that the various subprob-lems become interdependent, meaning that solving one subproblem changes the problem space for other subproblems. For example, the movie producer may develop a solution to the "character" subproblem, which in turn may change the initial state of the "genre" subproblem; and devel-oping a solution to the "genre" subproblem may change the initial state of the "plotline" subproblem, and so on. Each time the problem space for one subproblem changes as a result of progress made on other subprob-lems, the problem solver has to reassess whether the goal states across all subproblems are aligned. If there is any misalignment, she must modify some of the goal states of the subproblems. Therefore when people are working on open problems, a new activity emerges that does not exist for closed problems: They must constantly redefine problems during the problem-solving process. Eventually, open problems become closed prob-lems, and people can then adopt the problem-first model to developing solutions.

By contrast, the idea-first model proposes an alternative set of activ-ities when working on open problems (Finke et al., 1992). Rather than adapting open problems into a network of smaller, closed subproblems, the opposite can be done, that is, the problem statement can be removed altogether, allowing people to generate ideas in the absence of thinking about a specific problem at all. To demonstrate this point, Finke (1990) conducted an experiment in which subjects were given a subset of 3 out of 15 materials (e.g., hook, ball, and spring, etc.) to develop inventions in 1 out of 8 problem domains (e.g., furniture, toys, or appliances, etc.). In the first condition, subjects received both the materials and problem domain at the beginning of the task, and they were given 2 min to develop an idea for an invention. In the second condition, subjects received the materials at the beginning of the task, and they were given 1 min to generate a "po-tentially useful" idea; then, they received the problem domain and were given an additional minute to explore their ideas within that problem domain. Results showed that subjects in the second condition produced more creative ideas than those in the first condition, revealing that people can be highly creative when they first generate an idea and then explore that idea in the context of a problem domain.

Two Paths or One? The Role of Constraint

Finke and colleagues argue that while the problem-first model is a useful tool to understand the creative process for closed problems, it is ultimately limited, because in the real world, few meaningful problems are truly closed: "[Problem-solving] approaches detail specific processes, but they apply to highly restricted domains rather than to creative functioning in general. We believe that in order to understand the true nature of creativity, cognitive processes must be considered in a much broader perspective, where the *problems and solutions are not necessarily restricted or known*" (Finke et al., 1992, p. 5; emphasis added). They go on to argue that the key difference between their framework and the problem-first model comes down to a difference in when constraint appears in the problem-solving process: "[Our] approach can complement the more usual [problem-solving] approach... whether one approach or the other should be used depends on how early in the creative process product constraints would need to be imposed" (Finke et al., 1992, p. 191). Therefore, according to these scholars, when constraints are applied early in the process, the problem-first model unfolds, and when constraints are applied late in the process, the idea-first model unfolds.

While we agree with this general notion, we also believe that these scholars have defined constraints too narrowly as they focus on constraints related to the problem definition. When considering more recent research on creativity and constraint, a much broader range of constraints have been shown to influence the creative process. For instance, constraints on resources such as time, finances, materials, or knowledge can limit creativity by undermining a person's engagement in the creative process (e.g., Amabile et al., 1996; Byron et al., 2010; Hunter et al., 2007). Therefore we believe the picture is more complex than what has been previously theorized.

In the following sections, we aim to develop a more complete theoretical model that presents a more complex view of constraint and encompasses both the problem-first and idea-first models of the creative process. First, we draw on research in organizational creativity to derive two dimensions of constraint that we use to build a typology of constraints that affect creative problem solving in organizational settings. Then, we synthesize the creative activities that make up the problem-first and idea-first models into a new model that we call the *dynamic problem-solving* process. Finally, building on Finke's assertion about the timing of constraint, we develop a set of propositions that describe when particular confluences of constraint influence the dynamic problem-solving process to result in different creative processes.

DYNAMIC PROBLEM SOLVING WITHIN ORGANIZATIONAL CONSTRAINTS

Prior researchers have defined constraint in one of two ways: as any element that influences problem solving (e.g., Finke et al., 1992; Reitman, 1965), or as any external factor that in some way limits—or could be perceived as limiting—the way that a problem solver completes a task (e.g., Amabile, 1979; Amabile & Gitomer, 1984; Deci & Ryan, 1985). To encompass these somewhat different views, we define constraint quite broadly as *any factor that places limits or boundaries on creative problem solving*. With this definition in mind, we derive two dimensions of constraint that we believe to be important in all problem-solving situations.

The first dimension is *type of constraint*, which is based on Rosso's finding that there are two fundamentally different types of constraint that influence the creative process (Rosso, 2014). First, he identified "process constraints," which include limitations on time, materials, finances, and equipment that restrict people's ability to engage in the creative process. Second, he identified "product constraints," which include product requirements, customer preferences, and organizational needs that structure the goals that people pursue during the creative process. He argued that while process constraints usually place detrimental limits on creative problem solving, product constraints can provide structure to problems that improve the creative process.

Viewing process constraints and product constraints through the lens of the cognitive framework on problem solving (Newell & Simon, 1972), we reason that these two types of constraint are related to different factors that structure the problem space. Process constraints place limits on the resources that people use when generating ideas as they navigate through the problem space; and product constraints establish how the problem is defined by the goal state. Therefore we differentiate between *resource constraints* (what Rosso calls "process constraints") and *problem constraints* (what Rosso calls "product constraints") to reflect the qualitatively different effects that constraints can have on problem solving.

The second dimension of constraint is the *source of constraint* (Deci & Ryan, 1985; Ryan & Deci, 2000), which influences the degree to which people perceive themselves to be constrained during the problem-solving process. According to Deci and Ryan, an individual's autonomy is determined by the extent to which they feel like they have control over the factors that influence their behavior. When an individual feels like they have a high degree of self-determination of their own behavior, they perceive higher levels of autonomy; when they feel like external factors determine their behaviors, they perceive lower levels of autonomy.

In the context of creative problem solving, resource constraints and problem constraints determine the behaviors that people can engage in during the problem-solving process. Therefore the degree to which people feel like they have control over the resources and problems that structure their problem space determines how constrained they feel during the creative process. For the sake of simplicity, we dichotomize this dimension, differentiating between internal constraints and external constraints, but we acknowledge that this dimension can be more accurately depicted as a bipolar continuum, such that constraints can range from being completely internally controlled to completely externally controlled (e.g., Ryan & Deci, 2000). *Internal constraints* refer to resource or problem constraints that are self-imposed on creative problem solving; *external constraints* refer to resource or problem constraints that are imposed by an external source—for instance, by a higher-level manager or supervisor.

Typology of Constraints

Together, these two dimensions of constraint form a typology of constraints that serves as the foundation of our model. In the typology, each dimension has two categories, creating four quadrants of constraint: (a) *internal resource constraints*, (b) *external resource constraints*, (c) *internal problem constraints*, and (d) *external problem constraints*. Before describing the specific list of constraints that occupy each quadrant in more detail, we note two caveats. First, we tried to include constraints that we believe to be relevant in organizational settings, but we recognize that our list may not be entirely exhaustive. We expect that the four quadrants of constraint will generalize across all problem-solving situations, but specific constraints may differ according to the particular setting. Second, we categorized constraints based on what we believe to be typical in most organizational settings, that is, when an individual employee is working on a creative project under a manager in an organization. However, we understand that constraints can also be categorized differently, depending on the situation.

Internal Resource Constraints

This quadrant includes resource constraints that are implicitly "imposed" on the creative process by the individual who is engaged in creative problem solving. These resources include the individual's *creativity skills*, which reflect the person's ability to combine ideas in novel ways, and *domain-relevant skills*, which include knowledge and technical expertise that is necessary for navigating the problem space and generating ideas (Amabile, 1983). People who have more diverse sets of knowledge and greater skills can represent a problem in multiple ways, giving them a greater capacity to generate ideas through conceptual combination and analogic thinking (Finke et al., 1992; Newell & Simon, 1972). Such knowledge and skills are also valuable for defining or formulating problems (Mumford et al., 1994; Runco, 1994), which can also result in more creative outcomes (Getzels & Csikszentmihalyi, 1976; Reiter-Palmon, Mumford, O'Connor Boes, & Runco, 1997). These resources are constrained based on the extent to which the individual lacks creativity and domain-relevant skills; therefore it can be difficult and time consuming for people to decrease these constraints over time. Although an individual can acquire new knowledge or learn how to think more creatively, each of these resources can take a long time to develop and may not be readily applied to solving an immediate problem.

External Resource Constraints

This quadrant includes resource constraints that are imposed on the creative process by external forces such as managers or supervisors. These constraints include limitations on resources such as *time, materials,* or *finances,* all of which help people generate ideas (e.g., Amabile et al., 1996; Baer & Oldham, 2006; Weiss, Hoegl, & Gibbert, 2011). We also include a resource that we call *extrinsic knowledge,* which is different from domain-relevant knowledge in that it exists in the external world and can be acquired by the individual problem solver through search activities (Fleming, 2001; Taylor & Greve, 2006). For example, designers at IDEO regularly solved problems by taking ideas from one industry and applying them as solutions to problems in another industry (Hargadon & Sutton, 1997). Similarly, individuals may communicate with people inside or outside their organization to search for ideas that can help them solve a problem they are working on (Hargadon & Bechky, 2006; Lingo and O'Mahony, 2010; Perry-Smith & Shalley, 2003).

Internal Problem Constraints

All creative problems are defined by at least two primary criteria: *novelty* and *usefulness* (or appropriateness) (Amabile, 1982, 1983; Shalley & Zhou, 2008; Woodman et al., 1993). Novelty is based on the extent to which an idea is original or different from previous ideas that solve a problem; and usefulness is based on the extent to which an idea provides some objective or useful value to a designated audience, which in organizational settings, is typically a customer. Prior research shows that managers have a fairly strong bias against novelty and a preference for usefulness (Berg, 2016; Ford & Gioia, 2000; Mueller, Melwani, & Goncalo, 2012; Rietzschel, Nijstad, & Stroebe, 2006, 2010). Therefore we reason that in most organizational settings, novelty is determined primarily by an individual's desire to generate novel ideas (i.e., is an internal constraint), and usefulness is determined primarily by a manager's preferences or customer demands (i.e., is an external constraint). Other internal problem constraints include *domain-relevant goals*, which are goals that are motivated by a person's desire to have an impact in a particular domain of expertise, but may seem superfluous in the eyes of other stakeholders. For example, circus performers who are creating new performances may be motivated to create new acts that showcase their particular talent or skill (and thus impress other circus professionals), but managers primarily care about how much a paying audience likes the act, and may therefore discount ideas that do not appeal to a mass audience (Berg, 2016).

External Problem Constraints

Finally, this quadrant includes constraints that place external limits or boundaries on the problem definition. In most organizational settings, problems are largely defined by other stakeholders such as managers, organizational leaders, teammates, customers, colleagues, or collaborators from other organizations. These various *stakeholder demands* represent criteria that an individual must satisfy that are beyond the scope of the problem that they would otherwise try to meet. For example, an engineer who developed the world's first digital camera at Kodak created a product that was novel and potentially useful for customers, but failed to meet the criterion of aligning with the organization's strategy, which was imposed by senior managers, and therefore the product was rejected (Lucas & Goh, 2009). Similarly, a problem may be constrained by *broader contextual factors* such as an organization's culture, societal values, or institutional norms coming from the environment. For example, when Edison developed the commercial light bulb, he was constrained by customers' expectations about gas-lighting technology, so he artificially reduced the power of his light bulbs to conform to external institutional pressures (Hargadon & Douglas, 2001). Finally, there are other *situational factors* that are viewed as inherent to the task itself that may also constrain the problem. For example, during the *Apollo 13* space mission to the moon, an unexpected explosion damaged the air filtration system within the space capsule. NASA engineers in Houston were confronted with the problem of needing to change the oxygen-to-carbon dioxide ratio to a certain level within a certain period of time, or else the astronauts would die.

The Dynamic Problem-Solving Process

The four types of constraint described previously are always operating on people as they engage in the creative process, but they are not always operating in equal strength. It is possible for people to experience high levels of one type of constraint and low levels of another type of constraint, which can influence the overall creative process differently. For instance,

Edison and his colleagues were operating under low levels of internal and external resource constraint, as they had ample amounts of time, materials, finances, and expertise to use for experimentation; but they also had a high level of external problem constraint, because the specific criteria that had to be satisfied to develop a commercially viable light bulb were determined primarily by factors outside of their control—such as customer expectations about the technology and scientific limitations inherent in the problem itself. Alternatively, the STM engineers experienced a different confluence of constraints, in which they experienced high levels of external resource constraints—in the form of a restricted technology—and low levels of internal and external problem constraints.

We visually depict how various constraints relate to the creative process in Fig. 2. The horizontal dimension of constraint depicts the two types of constraint, with the left half representing resource constraints and the right half representing problem constraints. The vertical dimension depicts the two sources of constraint, with the lower half representing internal constraints and the upper half representing external constraints. In the center of Fig. 2 lies the *dynamic problem-solving* process, which synthesizes all the activities from the problem-first and idea-first models of

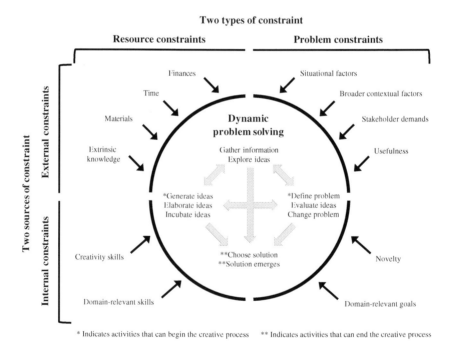

FIG. 2   Typology of constraints on the dynamic problem-solving process of individuals in organizational settings.

the creative process into a more unified, comprehensive model. We call it "dynamic" specifically because it accounts for both prior models while also allowing for dynamic iteration between them.

Creative activities such as generating ideas, elaborating ideas, and incubating ideas are represented together on the left side of the figure, because they are all directly influenced by the level of resources available during the creative process. By contrast, activities such as defining problems, evaluating ideas, and changing problems are represented together on the right side of the figure, because they are all directly influenced by the problem constraints that people face during the process. Gathering information and exploring ideas are represented near the top of the figure because they are directly influenced by constraints that are external to the problem solver. Finally, the activities of choosing a solution or a solution emerging are represented near the bottom of the figure because they are directly influenced by constraints that are internal to the problem solver.

One important difference between our model and prior models is that, rather than linking creative activities together through cyclical feedback loops, as shown in Fig. 1, we connect different sets of activities with double- or single-headed arrows. This allows for a dynamic model that can account for both models that are depicted in Fig. 1. On one hand, individuals can begin the dynamic process by defining the problem and then moving through an iterative process of gathering information, evaluating ideas against criteria, and elaborating ideas until a solution is chosen—as depicted by the problem-first model in Fig. 1 (Amabile, 1983; Amabile & Pratt, 2016; Mumford et al., 1991). On the other hand, individuals can begin the dynamic process by generating new ideas and then exploring them in the context of different problem domains until a problem and solution emerge together—as depicted by the idea-first model in Fig. 1 (Finke et al., 1992).

Our model also allows for alternative paths that involve a dynamic iteration between the problem-first and idea-first models. We believe that such flexibility is important to capture a broad range of creative processes that might occur in real organizational settings. For example, problem solvers may begin the creative process by trying to develop a solution to a well-defined problem, thereby following the problem-first model. But they may confront an obstacle that forces them to pivot their efforts to pursue a new problem (e.g., Baker & Nelson, 2005), at which point they may need to transition from a problem-first model to an idea-first model. Once they discover a new problem to solve, they can transition back to a problem-first model. Although there are many possible paths that individuals can take to produce creative outcomes, the dynamic problem-solving process begins either when people define a problem or generate ideas, and it ends either when people choose a viable solution to a problem or a solution emerges by discovering a problem that can be solved with a previously created preinventive idea.

HOW CONSTRAINTS SHAPE THE DYNAMIC PROBLEM-SOLVING PROCESS

The degree to which constraints shape the problem-solving process is primarily a function of the *level* of each type of constraint. Prior research has focused on how levels of constraint influence creative outcomes, but it presents a confusing picture. For instance, research has shown that people can be more creative when they experience lower levels of resource constraint (e.g., Amabile et al., 1996; Hunter et al., 2007), higher levels of resource constraint (e.g., Hoegl, Gibbert, & Mazursky, 2008; Moreau & Dahl, 2005), lower levels of problem constraint (e.g., Getzels & Csikszentmihalyi, 1976; Unsworth, 2001), and higher levels of problem constraint (e.g., Finke, 1990; Ward, 1994). In an effort to bring more clarity to this picture, we develop theory that explains how different confluences of constraint shape the creative process. For the sake of simplicity, we theorize about very high or very low levels of each type of constraint, while acknowledging that each type of constraint can be depicted as a continuum (similar to sources of constraint). By dichotomizing this dimension into extreme levels of constraint, we outline the boundary conditions for which our theory explains creative phenomena in organizations.

We also consider how the source of constraint can have a moderating influence on the relationship between the levels of each type of constraint and the dynamic problem-solving process. Many constraints are based on concrete limitations to problem solving such as the amount of time, finances, materials, or knowledge that are available for generating ideas. However, the source of these constraints can have a strong influence on the *perceived* level of constraint (e.g., Amabile & Gitomer, 1984; Byron et al., 2010; Deci & Ryan, 1985). Thus we develop theory that also explains how the source of constraint interacts with the levels of each type of constraint to influence the creative process.

We summarize our theory in Fig. 3, which shows how two particular confluences of constraint can shape the activities that people engage in during the dynamic problem-solving process, which yield two effective modes of problem solving. When people perceive a low level of resource constraint and a high level of problem constraint (depicted on the left side of Fig. 3), they feel like they are working on a well-defined problem and have the flexibility to engage in a wide range of creative activities in the pursuit of developing a solution to the problem. We call the mode of problem solving under this particular confluence of constraints *deliberate problem solving*, because it reflects the experience of deliberately generating ideas with the intent of solving a well-defined problem (e.g., Amabile & Pratt, 2016).

Alternatively, when people perceive a high level of resource constraint and a low level of problem constraint (depicted on the right side of Fig. 3),

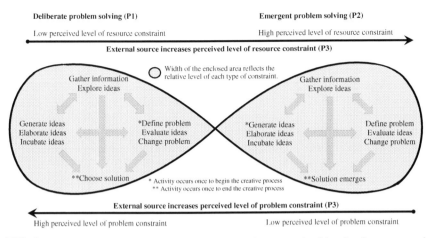

FIG. 3 Two types of problem solving as emergent from perceived levels of two types of constraint.

they might feel limited when generating ideas, but they have the flexibility to explore their ideas across several problem domains as they try to discover a problem that can be solved by one of their ideas. Sometimes, a solution never emerges, and other times—as in the case of the Nintendo Wii—a breakthrough solution emerges. Therefore we call this mode of problem solving *emergent problem solving*, because it reflects the experience of generating an idea and then exploring that idea in the context of a problem domain until a problem and solution emerge together (e.g., Finke et al., 1992). Together, our model shows how two seemingly different creative processes—as shown in Fig. 1—can transpire from the same underlying dynamic problem-solving process.

The Dynamic Problem-Solving Process as Shaped by Two Confluences of Constraint

As defined earlier, resource constraints place limits on the time, finances, materials, and knowledge that people use when generating ideas during the problem-solving process. Generating new ideas involves the conceptual combination of existing ideas (Guilford, 1950; Koestler, 1964), and consequently, increasing the amount of resources available (i.e., reducing the level of resource constraint) exponentially increases the number of ideas that can be generated during problem solving. For example, when participants in Finke's (1990) problem-solving experiment were given a subset of 3 out of 15 materials, they had the potential to create 455 unique material combinations, which could then be used to develop thousands of new conceptual ideas. If they were given just one additional material (for a total of four), they would have been able to create 1365 unique material combinations or three times as many.

Therefore when people perceive low levels of resource constraint, they have a high degree of flexibility when generating ideas, elaborating ideas, and incubating ideas. For example, Edison and his colleagues had access to a large number of financial and material resources, in addition to great expertise, enabling them to generate and elaborate upon thousands of ideas in their quest to develop a commercially viable light bulb. As the level of resource constraint increases, flexibility decreases, and people suffer from a reduced capacity to engage in these activities. At the most extreme levels of resource constraint, they can only generate one initial idea, which can make it difficult to solve problems, but not impossible. For example, the STM engineers took a single new idea—the semiconductor technology that detected three-dimensional motion—and explored broadly for commercial applications across several industries.

Problem constraints, on the other hand, refer to the internal and external demands that define the goal state. When there are low levels of problem constraint, problem statements are vague or poorly defined, meaning that people have a high degree of flexibility when engaging in activities such as defining problems, evaluating ideas against criteria, and changing problems. For example, the STM engineers were not confined to using their technology within a particular industry, and each time they explored their technology in the context of a new industry, they defined new problems or changed problems in their quest to discover a commercial application of their technology. As the level of problem constraint increases, flexibility decreases, and people become more restricted when defining or changing problems. At the most extreme levels of problem constraint, problems are clearly defined and highly rigid, meaning that the problem is defined once during the problem-solving process and cannot be changed. For example, Edison and his colleagues identified several criteria that needed to be met in order to produce a commercially viable light bulb; once defined, the problem did not change over the course of the entire project.

Levels of these two types of constraint work together to produce two stylized versions of the dynamic problem-solving process. First, people may perceive a low level of resource constraint and a high level of problem constraint, which creates conditions for deliberate problem solving to unfold—as depicted on the left side of Fig. 3. Under these conditions, the problem-solving process begins when an individual defines a problem (or is presented with a well-defined problem). It continues as the individual engages in a wide range of activities that include gathering information, generating ideas, elaborating ideas, incubating ideas, exploring ideas, and evaluating ideas against criteria. The process ends when an idea that fully satisfies all the problem criteria is selected as a viable solution. Note that this process closely resembles the problem-first model of the creative process (e.g., Amabile, 1983; Amabile & Pratt, 2016; Mumford et al., 1991; Wallas, 1926). Therefore we propose the following:

> Proposition 1: When people perceive a low level of resource constraint in combination with a high level of problem constraint, they are likely to engage in a deliberate problem-solving process that resembles the problem-first model: The problem will be defined once at the beginning of the process, and then people will engage in a variety of creative activities until they choose a solution to end the process.

By contrast, people may perceive a high level of resource constraint and a low level of problem constraint, which creates conditions for emergent problem solving to unfold—as depicted on the right side of Fig. 3. Under these conditions, problem solving begins when an individual generates an idea, which is followed by a series of activities such as exploring ideas in the context of numerous problem domains, defining problems that could be solved by that idea, and elaborating on the original idea until a solution emerges to a discovered problem. Note that this process resembles the idea-first model of the creative process (e.g., Finke et al., 1992), but our synthesized model also includes a broader range of activities. Many of these activities—such as gathering information, evaluating ideas, and changing criteria—were actually discussed by Finke and his colleagues in their original work, but were only implicitly included in the model. Therefore our model provides a more complete, explicit version of activities that can take place during emergent problem solving.

One notable change that we make to the idea-first model is that we also include incubating ideas, which Finke and colleagues specifically rejected. They developed their model under the assumption that creative thinking is a purposeful cognitive activity rather than a passive, unconscious one. While we agree that much creativity occurs through purposeful cognitive thought, recent research has provided physiological evidence that people can indeed produce creative breakthroughs that arise into consciousness seemingly out of nowhere (Kounios & Beeman, 2015). Therefore we include idea incubation to complement the purposeful creative activity that Finke and colleagues described. Therefore we propose the following:

> Proposition 2: When people perceive a high level of resource constraint in combination with a low level of problem constraint, they are likely to engage in an emergent problem-solving process that resembles the idea-first model: An idea will be generated once to begin the process, and then people will engage in a variety of creative activities until a solution emerges to end the process.

The source of constraint can also shape dynamic problem solving—specifically by changing the individual's perception of the level of constraint during the process (Deci & Ryan, 1985). Amabile and Gitomer (1984) conducted an experiment to demonstrate this effect for resource constraints. In their experiment, they asked subjects to create a collage using various materials. In the first, "choice" condition, subjects were presented with 10 closed boxes of materials and were told to choose 5 of the 10 boxes to use for the task. In the second, "no choice" condition, the experimenter presented all 10 boxes and then chose 5 boxes for the subjects to use. Results showed that subjects in the "choice" condition produced more creative outcomes than subjects in the "no choice" condition, despite using an identical set of materials and spending an equal amount of time on the task. These results are consistent with a broad range of research showing that externally controlled resource constraints can decrease the feeling of autonomy, which in turn can inhibit creativity by increasing the perceived level of constraint (Amabile et al., 1996; Deci & Ryan, 1985; Hunter et al., 2007).

These effects can also be applied to problem constraints. Ryan and Deci (2000) argue that any factor that reduces the feeling of having control over one's own behaviors can increase the perception of constraint. According to problem-solving scholars (Newell & Simon, 1972), the problem definition is the primary driver of behavior during the creative process. Therefore when people have control over the problem, they should also feel like they have control over their behaviors during problem solving, and thus perceive a lower level of constraint. When external forces control the problem, people feel like they have less control over their behaviors, and thus perceive a higher level of constraint. Altogether, we reason that the extent to which resources or problems are external determines the degree to which people perceive themselves to be constrained. Internal constraints decrease the perceived level of constraint, whereas external constraints increase the perceived level of constraint. We summarize these possibilities in the following proposition:

> Proposition 3: The source of constraint will moderate the perceived levels of resource or problem constraints, such that external constraints will be perceived as more constraining than internal constraints.

Ineffective Problem Solving as Shaped by Two Other Confluences of Constraint

The two forms of problem solving described in the previous section, each arising from a different confluence of constraint, can be highly effective in leading to creative outcomes. However, two other confluences of constraint are also possible, which result in ineffective modes of problem solving. First, when people perceive high levels of both resource and problem constraints, they feel like they are working on a well-defined and highly rigid problem, but they do not have the flexibility to generate, elaborate, or incubate ideas as they try developing a solution to the problem. When working on a well-defined problem, people need flexibility to generate a wide variety of ideas to increase their chances of developing a viable solution. Without that flexibility, people are likely to feel that their problem-solving efforts are futile, which will inhibit their capacity to produce viable solutions.

Second, when people perceive low levels of both resource and problem constraints, they feel like they can develop a large number of potential solutions to a large number of potential problems. While these conditions may seem favorable because they provide people with a high level of flexibility throughout the entire problem-solving process, research shows that people can actually struggle to think creatively under these conditions (Goldenberg, Mazursky, & Solomon, 1999; Moreau & Dahl, 2005; Ward, 1994). People may have little direction on which idea to pursue, resulting in a feeling of ambiguity that increases levels of stress, anxiety, and frustration (Schwartz, 2000). These negative feelings can reduce a person's engagement in the problem-solving process (Iyengar & Lepper, 2000), which can subsequently inhibit creativity (Chua & Iyengar, 2006, 2008). In summary, then, our model describes the confluences of constraints that are most likely to result in successful creative problem-solving efforts, and it also points to confluences of constraints that are likely to undermine the problem-solving process.

DISCUSSION AND CONCLUSION

Creativity is a challenging endeavor in which people must navigate through a complex confluence of constraints on their journey to discovery and creation. Most research in organizational creativity has been conducted under the assumption that problems are closed (or clearly defined at the outset) (Unsworth, 2001), and that people can be creative when they have a high degree of flexibility to develop a wide range of ideas during the creative process. According to this view, the most important tools that organizations have at their disposal to foster a more creative workforce are to give people a well-defined problem and provide them with enough resources to solve it creatively (Amabile et al., 1996; Anderson, Potocnik, & Zhou, 2014; Shalley, Zhou, & Oldham, 2004). Within this paradigm, resources play an important role in facilitating the creative process, but perhaps the most important step is defining the right problem to solve in the first place (Amabile, 1983; Getzels & Csikszentmihalyi, 1976; Mumford et al., 1994).

However, these approaches overlook an alternative model of problem solving that may be more appropriate when people are working on open, ill-defined problems. Under such circumstances, rather than focusing on adapting a vague, poorly defined problem into several well-defined subproblems (Simon, 1973), it may be wiser to start the process by generating ideas in the absence of a clear problem definition altogether (Finke et al., 1992).

We believe that the main contribution of this chapter is the synthesis of these two previously disparate views on the creative process. We show how they emerge from the same underlying dynamic problem-solving model, but differ as a function of the confluence of constraints that people perceive as operating on them during the process. Understanding these dynamics can be important for organizational creativity scholars, because creativity in the workplace is often subject to a shifting set of demands from numerous stakeholders (Drazin, Glynn, & Kazanjian, 1999; Kanter, 1988), resulting in an ever-evolving set of constraints. Problems in real organizations are also considerably more open than what prior theory on organizational creativity has assumed (Unsworth, 2001), and our theory provides guidance on how to better understand and explain creativity under these challenging conditions.

Implications for Theory and Research

In this chapter, we developed an integrated model of dynamic problem solving, which makes theoretical contributions to both prior models. We contribute to literature citing the problem-first model by allowing for a more dynamic sequence of activities during the creative process, which helps account for a broader range of phenomena in organizations that the problem-first model could not previously explain. Most importantly, it could not explain creative processes that begin with generating ideas and end when a solution emerges to a discovered problem (e.g., Finke et al., 1992; von Hippel & von Krogh, 2016).

We also contribute to literature citing the idea-first model by expanding the scope of activities that take place during the creative process and providing a clearer structure to explain how various activities are affected by constraints. For example, Finke and colleagues built their model on the assumption that constraints play a fundamental role in shaping the generation and exploration of ideas, but they failed to recognize that different types of constraints can have a stronger effect on different parts of the process. Building on more recent research that studies creativity and constraint (e.g., Rosso, 2014; Ryan & Deci, 2000), we develop a more detailed model that explains how different types of constraint can systematically shape different parts of the creative process.

Our second contribution is that we develop theory that explains how seemingly different models of the creative process are derived from the same underlying problem-solving process. Previous researchers have described two unique paths in developing creative outcomes—summarized as the problem-first and idea-first models of the creative process—but for the most part, literature citing each model has remained isolated from each other. The majority of organizational creativity literature draws from the problem-first model to frame research (e.g., Amabile & Pratt, 2016;

Anderson et al., 2014; Perry-Smith & Mannucci, 2017; Shalley & Zhou, 2008), overlooking the apparent contradiction with the idea-first model. By contrast, literature drawing from the idea-first model addresses the contradictory nature that constraints can have on creative outcomes (e.g., Caniëls & Rietzschel, 2015; Chua & Iyengar, 2008; Hoegl et al., 2008; Moreau & Dahl, 2005; Roskes, 2015), but has not explicitly addressed how constraints might influence the creative process. We take a broad view to show how various constraints work together to shape the problem-solving process, thereby providing a more comprehensive picture of the relationship between creative problem solving and constraint.

By integrating these two disparate views of the creative process into a coherent model, we also raise several new questions that can be investigated in future research. Primarily, we describe two modes of problem solving that are optimal under two confluences of extreme levels of constraint: deliberate problem solving (low resource constraint, high problem constraint) and emergent problem solving (high resource constraint, low problem constraint). Yet, in organizational settings, the process of creating new products, ideas, processes, or services is highly dynamic, and the levels of resource and problem constraints are constantly shifting over time. While recent research has provided glimpses into how people can engage in different creative processes to deal with different confluences of constraint (e.g., Frishammar, Dahlskog, Krumlinde, & Yazgan, 2016; Harrison & Rouse, 2014; Harvey & Kou, 2013; Sonenshein, 2014), it is still unclear how people might transition between deliberate and emergent modes of problem solving over time. How might people impose or relax constraints on themselves to facilitate the problem-solving process? How might they react to unexpected shifts in their constraint environment? What role do organizations and managers play in facilitating these dynamics? These reflect only a few of the numerous questions that can be addressed in future research.

Another possibility is to investigate the degree to which individuals with different characteristics thrive under different confluences of constraint. For example, one of the earliest streams of creativity research focused on explaining creative outcomes through individual traits and abilities (Guilford, 1950; Koestler, 1964; Nicholls, 1972; Rothenberg & Greenberg, 1976). One useful distinction that came from this research was that people have different problem-solving styles. For example, Kirton (1976) differentiated between *adaptors*, or people who excel at "doing things better"; and *innovators*, or people who excel at "doing things differently." Similarly, Jabri (1991) differentiated between *logical* problem solvers, or people who prefer to solve problems in a logical sequence of steps, and *intuitive* problem solvers, or people who prefer to solve problems by making unexpected connections between ideas and embracing the uncertainty associated with creative thinking.

In light of our theory, it may be possible that individuals with different problem-solving styles may be better suited to different modes of problem solving. For example, logical problem solvers (or adaptors) may thrive when they are engaged in deliberate problem solving, but struggle when they are engaged in emergent problem solving. Alternatively, intuitive problem solvers (or innovators) may thrive when they are engaged in emergent problem solving, but struggle when they are engaged in deliberate problem solving. This reflects only one of many opportunities to investigate how individual characteristics and traits may influence an individual's ability to engage in different modes of problem solving.

Similar research can also be developed at the team level of analysis, which may offer even more opportunities to develop novel insights given the relative lack of research on team creativity compared to individual creativity (Anderson et al., 2014; Shalley & Zhou, 2008). For instance, prior research shows that teams can benefit from both broad search and local search during creative problem solving (Perretti & Negro, 2006; Taylor & Greve, 2006). In the context of our theory, it is possible that broad or local search can apply to either searching for solutions or searching for problems, and teams may be most successful when engaging in a combined process of broad search for solutions and local search for problems or vice versa. Rather than viewing search as a single continuum, different combinations of search may be optimal based on different confluences of constraint. Such distinctions have neither been theorized nor empirically tested, providing rich opportunities for future research.

Managerial Implications

Organizations are complex environments in which problems are often ill structured and open, and our theory offers insights that could help managers better understand how to manage the creative process under these difficult conditions. One dilemma that managers face is how to give workers enough flexibility to solve problems creatively while also asserting enough control so that workers produce solutions that are aligned with the organization's goals. Perhaps the most powerful application of our model is that it provides managers with a tool to understand how they can manipulate constraints to strike this flexibility-control balance more effectively.

One approach is that managers can adopt a deliberate mode of problem solving, in which they give people a well-defined problem that aligns with the organization's goals, but also give people enough resources so that they can develop an optimal solution to the problem. The search for solutions can be done within the organization's boundaries, where workers draw on the available skills and resources to solve the problems themselves (for a review, see Shalley & Zhou, 2008), or it can be expanded beyond the organization's boundaries, allowing people to gather and evaluate solutions developed by a crowd of problem solvers (e.g., Lifshitz-Assaf, 2017). This mode of problem solving can help managers simultaneously maintain control over the outcomes of the problem-solving process while providing flexibility to workers so that they may determine the best way to solve the problem.

Another approach would be to adopt an emergent mode of problem solving, which might be particularly useful when organizations experience greater ambiguity in their mission and goals. For example, any organization that is trying to develop a breakthrough technology is operating under conditions of high ambiguity (Kaplan & Tripsas, 2008), and startup organizations are often trying to identify target market needs while simultaneously trying to develop the product (e.g., Navis & Glynn, 2010). In these conditions, organizations can maintain control by restricting the set of resources that they are committing to a new project, but also provide flexibility by allowing workers to search broadly for problems that could be solved with those resources. This approach could help organizations shorten product development cycles (Ries, 2011) or foster the creative use of resources (Sonenshein, 2014), which may be particularly valuable when organizations are operating in highly dynamic markets that are changing quickly (e.g., Brown & Eisenhardt, 1997; Eisenhardt & Tabrizi, 1995).

CONCLUSION

Creativity is an essential source of new ideas, products, processes, or services that help organizations gain a competitive advantage against rivals and flourish, but creativity is a challenging endeavor because people must work within a complex confluence of constraints that are constantly changing over time. Prior research has described two fundamentally different models of creativity, but each model provides contradicting views on the creative process, raising questions about how people can successfully navigate through these complex environments to achieve highly creative outcomes. This chapter reconciles these contradictions by synthesizing these models into a coherent model, revealing that different modes of problem solving emerge from different confluences of constraints. In so doing, we advance a new integrated model of dynamic problem solving within organizational constraints, which offers guidance to both scholars and practitioners who are interested in understanding and facilitating creativity in organizational settings.

Acknowledgments

This work was supported by the Harvard Business School Division of Research and the Social Sciences and Humanities Research Council of Canada [430-2017-00527]. An earlier version of this chapter was presented at the Academy of Management meeting in Atlanta, GA. We also gratefully acknowledge the help of several colleagues for their insightful comments and feedback in preparing this manuscript, including Matthew Cronin, Spencer Harrison, Jennifer Mueller, and Ryan Raffaelli.

References

Amabile, T. M. (1979). Effects of external evaluation on artistic creativity. *Journal of Personality and Social Psychology, 37*(2), 221–233.

Amabile, T. M. (1982). Social psychology of creativity: A consensual assessment technique. *Journal of Personality and Social Psychology, 43*(5), 997–1013.

Amabile, T. M. (1983). The social psychology of creativity: A componential conceptualization. *Journal of Personality and Social Psychology, 45*(2), 357–376.

Amabile, T. M. (1988). A model of creativity and innovation in organizations. In B. M. Staw & L. L. Cummings (Eds.), Vol. 10. *Research in organizational behavior* (pp. 123–167). Greenwich, CT: JAI Press.

Amabile, T. M., Conti, R., Coon, H., Lazenby, J., & Herron, M. (1996). Assessing the work environment for creativity. *Academy of Management Journal, 39*(5), 1154–1184. https://doi.org/10.2307/256995.

Amabile, T. M., & Gitomer, J. (1984). Children's artistic creativity effects of choice in task materials. *Personality and Social Psychology Bulletin, 10*(2), 209–215.

Amabile, T. M., & Pratt, M. G. (2016). The dynamic componential model of creativity and innovation in organizations: Making progress, making meaning. *Research in Organizational Behavior, 36*, 157–183. https://doi.org/10.1016/j.riob.2016.10.001.

Anderson, N., Potocnik, K., & Zhou, J. (2014). Innovation and creativity in organizations: A state-of-the-science review, prospective commentary, and guiding framework. *Journal of Management, 40*(5), 1297–1333. https://doi.org/10.1177/0149206314527128.

Baer, M., & Oldham, G. R. (2006). The curvilinear relation between experienced creative time pressure and creativity: Moderating effects of openness to experience and support for creativity. *Journal of Applied Psychology, 91*(4), 963–970. https://doi.org/10.1037/0021-9010.91.4.963.

Baker, T., & Nelson, R. E. (2005). Creating something from nothing: Resource construction through entrepreneurial bricolage. *Administrative Science Quarterly, 50*(3), 329–366. https://doi.org/10.2189/asqu.2005.50.3.329.

Berg, J. M. (2016). Balancing on the creative high-wire: Forecasting the success of novel ideas in organizations. *Administrative Science Quarterly, 61*(3), 433–468.

Brown, S. L., & Eisenhardt, K. M. (1997). The art of continuous change: Linking complexity theory and time-paced evolution in relentlessly shifting organizations. *Administrative Science Quarterly, 42*(1), 1–34.

Byron, K., Khazanchi, S., & Nazarian, D. (2010). The relationship between stressors and creativity: a meta-analysis examining competing theoretical models. *Journal of Applied Psychology, 95*(1), 201–212. https://doi.org/10.1037/a0017868.

Caniëls, M. C. J., & Rietzschel, E. F. (2015). Organizing creativity: creativity and innovation under constraints. *Creativity and Innovation Management, 24*(2), 184–196. https://doi.org/10.1111/caim.12123.

Catmull, E. (2014). *Creativity Inc.*. New York: Random House.

Chua, R. Y. J., & Iyengar, S. S. (2006). Empowerment through choice? A critical analysis of the effects of choice in organizations. *Research in Organizational Behavior, 27*, 41–79. https://doi.org/10.1016/s0191-3085(06)27002-3.

Chua, R. Y. J., & Iyengar, S. S. (2008). Creativity as a matter of choice: Prior experience and task instruction as boundary conditions for the positive effect of choice on creativity. *Journal of Creative Behavior, 42*(3), 164–180.

Deci, E. L., & Ryan, R. M. (1985). The general causality orientations scale: Self-determination in personality. *Journal of Research in Personality*, 19(2), 109–134.

Drazin, R., Glynn, M. A., & Kazanjian, R. K. (1999). Multilevel theorizing about creativity in organizations: A sensemaking perspective. *Academy of Management Review*, 24(2), 286–307. https://doi.org/10.2307/259083.

Einstein, A., & Infeld, L. (1938). *The evolution of physics*. New York: Simon & Schuster.

Eisenhardt, K. M., & Tabrizi, B. N. (1995). Accelerating adaptive processes: Product innovation in the global computer industry. *Administrative Science Quarterly*, 40(1), 84–110.

Finke, R. A. (1990). *Creative imagery: Discoveries and inventions in visualization*. Hoboken, NJ: Erlbaum.

Finke, R. A., Ward, T. B., & Smith, S. M. (1992). *Creative cognition: Theory, research, and applications*. Cambridge, MA: MIT Press.

Fleming, L. (2001). Recombinant uncertainty in technological search. *Management Science*, 47(1), 117–132.

Ford, C. M., & Gioia, D. A. (2000). Factors influencing creativity in the domain of managerial decision making. *Journal of Management*, 26(4), 705–732.

Frishammar, J., Dahlskog, E., Krumlinde, C., & Yazgan, K. (2016). The front end of radical innovation: A case study of idea and concept development at prime group. *Creativity and Innovation Management*, 25(2), 179–198.

Getzels, J. W., & Csikszentmihalyi, M. (1976). *The creative vision: A longitudinal study of problem finding in art*. New York: Wiley.

Goldenberg, J., Mazursky, D., & Solomon, S. (1999). Toward identifying the inventive templates of new products: A channeled ideation approach. *Journal of Marketing Research*, 36(2), 200–210.

Guilford, J. P. (1950). Creativity. *American Psychologist*, 5, 444–454.

Hargadon, A. B., & Bechky, B. A. (2006). When collections of creatives become creative collectives: A field study of problem solving at work. *Organization Science*, 17(4), 484–500.

Hargadon, A. B., & Douglas, Y. (2001). When innovations meet institutions: Edison and the design of the electric light. *Administrative Science Quarterly*, 46(3), 476–501.

Hargadon, A. B., & Sutton, R. L. (1997). Technology brokering and innovation in a product development firm. *Administrative Science Quarterly*, 42(4), 716–749.

Harrison, S. H., & Rouse, E. D. (2014). Let's dance! Elastic coordination in creative group work: A qualitative study of modern dancers. *Academy of Management Journal*, 57(5), 1256–1283. https://doi.org/10.5465/amj.2012.0343.

Harvey, S., & Kou, C. Y. (2013). Collective engagement in creative tasks the role of evaluation in the creative process in groups. *Administrative Science Quarterly*, 58(3), 346–386.

Hoegl, M., Gibbert, M., & Mazursky, D. (2008). Financial constraints in innovation projects: When is less more? *Research Policy*, 37(8), 1382–1391. https://doi.org/10.1016/j.respol.2008.04.018.

Hunter, S. T., Bedell, K. E., & Mumford, M. D. (2007). Climate for creativity: A quantitative review. *Creativity Research Journal*, 19(1), 69–90.

Israel, P. (1998). *Edison: A life of invention*. New York: John Wiley & Sons.

Iyengar, S. S., & Lepper, M. R. (2000). When choice is demotivating: Can one desire too much of a good thing? *Journal of Personality and Social Psychology*, 79(6), 995–1006. https://doi.org/10.1037//0022-3514.79.6.995.

Jabri, M. M. (1991). The development of conceptually independent subscales in the measurement of modes of problem solving. *Educational and Psychological Measurement*, 51(4), 975–983.

Kanter, R. M. (1988). When a thousand flowers bloom: Structural, collective and social conditions for innovation in organization. In B. M. Staw & L. L. Cummings (Eds.), Vol. 10. *Research in organizational behavior* (pp. 169–211). Greenwich, CT: JAI Press.

Kaplan, S., & Tripsas, M. (2008). Thinking about technology: Applying a cognitive lens to technical change. *Research Policy*, 37(5), 790–805. https://doi.org/10.1016/j.respol.2008.02.002.

Kirton, M. (1976). Adaptors and innovators: A description and measure. *Journal of Applied Psychology*, 61(5), 622.

Koestler, A. (1964). The act of creation. New York: Dell.

Kounios, J., & Beeman, M. (2015). *The eureka factor: Aha moments, creative insight, and the brain.* New York: Random House.

Lifshitz-Assaf, H. (2017). Dismantling knowledge boundaries at NASA: From problem solvers to solution seekers. *Administrative Science Quarterly.* forthcoming.

Lingo, E. L., & O'Mahony, S. (2010). Nexus work: Brokerage on creative projects. *Administrative Science Quarterly*, 55(1), 47–81.

Lucas, H. C., & Goh, J. M. (2009). Disruptive technology: How Kodak missed the digital photography revolution. *The Journal of Strategic Information Systems*, 18(1), 46–55. https://doi.org/10.1016/j.jsis.2009.01.002.

Moreau, C. P., & Dahl, D. W. (2005). Designing the solution: The impact of constraints on consumers' creativity. *Journal of Consumer Research*, 32(1), 13–22.

Mueller, J. S., Melwani, S., & Goncalo, J. A. (2012). The bias against creativity: Why people desire but reject creative ideas. *Psychological Science*, 23(1), 13–17. https://doi.org/10.1177/0956797611421018.

Mumford, M. D., Mobley, M. I., Reiter-Palmon, R., Uhlman, C. E., & Doares, L. M. (1991). Process analytic models of creative capacities. *Creativity Research Journal*, 4(2), 91–122.

Mumford, M. D., Reiter-Palmon, R., & Redmond, M. R. (1994). Problem construction and cognition: Applying problem representations in ill-defined domains. In M. A. Runco (Ed.), *Problem finding, problem solving, and creativity* (pp. 5–39). Norwood, NJ: Ablex Publishing.

Navis, C., & Glynn, M. A. (2010). How new market categories emerge: Temporal dynamics of legitimacy, identity, and entrepreneurship in satellite radio, 1990-2005. *Administrative Science Quarterly*, 55, 439–471.

Newell, A., Shaw, J., & Simon, H. (1962). The processes of creative thinking. In H. Gruber, G. Terrell, & M. Wertheimer (Eds.), *Contemporary approaches to creative thinking.* New York: Atherton Press.

Newell, A., & Simon, H. A. (1972). *Human problem solving.* Englewood Cliffs, NJ: Prentice-Hall.

Nicholls, J. (1972). Creativity in the person who will never produce anything original and useful: The concept of creativity as a normally distributed trait. *American Psychologist*, 27, 517–527.

Oldham, G. R., & Cummings, A. (1996). Employee creativity: Personal and contextual factors at work. *Academy of Management Journal*, 39(3), 607–634.

Perretti, F., & Negro, G. (2006). Filling empty seats: How status and organizational hierarchies affect exploration versus exploitation in team design. *Academy of Management Journal*, 49(4), 759–777.

Perry-Smith, J. E., & Mannucci, P. V. (2017). From creativity to innovation: The social network drivers of the four phases of the idea journey. *Academy of Management Review*, 42(1), 53–79. https://doi.org/10.5465/amr.2014.0462.

Perry-Smith, J. E., & Shalley, C. E. (2003). The social side of creativity: A static and dynamic social network perspective. *Academy of Management Review*, 28(1), 89–106.

Reiter-Palmon, R., Mumford, M. D., O'Connor Boes, J., & Runco, M. A. (1997). Problem construction and creativity: The role of ability, cue consistency, and active processing. *Creativity Research Journal*, 10(1), 9–23.

Reitman, W. R. (1965). *Cognition and thought: An information processing approach.* Oxford: Wiley.

Ries, E. (2011). *The lean startup: How today's entrepreneurs use continuous innovation to create radically successful businesses.* New York: Crown Business.

Rietzschel, E. F., Nijstad, B. A., & Stroebe, W. (2006). Productivity is not enough: A comparison of interactive and nominal brainstorming groups on idea generation and selection. *Journal of Experimental Social Psychology*, 42(2), 244–251. https://doi.org/10.1016/j.jesp.2005.04.005.

Rietzschel, E. F., Nijstad, B. A., & Stroebe, W. (2010). The selection of creative ideas after individual idea generation: Choosing between creativity and impact. *British Journal of Psychology, 101,* 47–68. https://doi.org/10.1348/000712609x414204.

Roskes, M. (2015). Constraints that help or hinder creative performance: A motivational approach. *Creativity and Innovation Management, 24*(2), 197–206.

Rosso, B. D. (2014). Creativity and constraints: Exploring the role of constraints in the creative processes of research and development teams. *Organization Studies, 35*(4), 551–585. https://doi.org/10.1177/0170840613517600.

Rothenberg, A., & Greenberg, B. (1976). *The index of scientific writings on creativity: General* (1566–1974). Hamden, CT: Archon Books.

Runco, M. A. (1994). *Problem finding, problem solving, and creativity.* Greenwood Publishing Group.

Ryan, R. M., & Deci, E. L. (2000). Self-determination theory and the facilitation of intrinsic motivation, social development, and well-being. *American Psychologist, 55*(1), 68–78.

Schwartz, B. (2000). Self-determination: The tyrany of freedom. *American Psychologist, 55*(1), 79–88.

Shalley, C. E., & Zhou, J. (2008). Organizational creativity research: A historical overview. In J. Zhou & C. E. Shalley (Eds.), *Handbook of organizational creativity* (pp. 3–31). Abingdon, UK: Taylor & Francis.

Shalley, C. E., Zhou, J., & Oldham, G. R. (2004). The effects of personal and contextual characteristics on creativity: Where should we go from here? *Journal of Management, 30*(6), 933–958. https://doi.org/10.1016/j.jm.2004.06.007.

Simon, H. A. (1973). The structure of ill structured problems. *Artificial Intelligence, 4*(4), 181–201.

Sonenshein, S. (2014). How organizations foster the creative use of resources. *Academy of Management Journal, 57*(3), 814–848. https://doi.org/10.5465/amj.2012.0048.

Taylor, A., & Greve, H. R. (2006). Superman or the fantastic four? Knowledge combination and experience in innovative teams. *Academy of Management Journal, 49*(4), 723–740.

Unsworth, K. (2001). Unpacking creativity. *Academy of Management Review, 26*(2), 289–297.

Verganti, R. (2009). *Design driven innovation: Changing the rules of competition by radically innovating what things mean.* Boston: Harvard Business Press.

von Hippel, E., & von Krogh, G. (2016). CROSSROADS—Identifying viable "need–solution pairs": Problem solving without problem formulation. *Organization Science, 27*(1), 207–221. https://doi.org/10.1287/orsc.2015.1023.

Wallas, G. (1926). *The art of thought.* New York: Harcourt Brace.

Ward, T. B. (1994). Structured imagination: The role of category structure in exemplar generation. *Cognitive Psychology, 27*(1), 1–40.

Weiss, M., Hoegl, M., & Gibbert, M. (2011). Making virtue of necessity: The role of team climate for innovation in resource-constrained innovation projects. *Journal of Product Innovation Management, 28,* 196–207. https://doi.org/10.1111/j.1540-5885.2011.00870.x.

Woodman, R. W., Sawyer, J. E., & Griffin, R. W. (1993). Toward a theory of organizational creativity. *Academy of Management Review, 18*(2), 293–321.

Conceptualization of Emergent Constructs in a Multilevel Approach to Understanding Individual Creativity in Organizations

Soonmook Lee*, Jae Yoon Chang[†], Rosemary Hyejin Moon[†]

*Sungkyunkwan University, Seoul, Republic of Korea, [†]Sogang University, Seoul, Republic of Korea

DUAL PROPERTIES OF INDIVIDUAL CREATIVITY IN ORGANIZATIONS

As Agars, Kaufman, and Locke (2008) mentioned, a multilevel perspective is necessary for understanding organizational creativity. Although organizations have been considered in the form of "press" or environment in models of creativity, it has not been fully incorporated into empirical investigations. Moreover, what the general organizational creativity literature mostly lacks is a thorough understanding of the dual properties of creativity-relevant constructs including individual creativity: bottom-up and top-down processes (Kozlowski & Klein, 2000; Morgeson & Hofmann, 1999). The bottom-up processes refer to the emergent processes through which unit-level constructs (e.g., team creativity, organizational climate for creativity) are emergent at individual levels and manifest at unit levels including teams and other intermediate (e.g., dyad, department) levels in organizations. On the other hand, the top-down processes refer to downward processes through which contextual effect impinges upon individu-

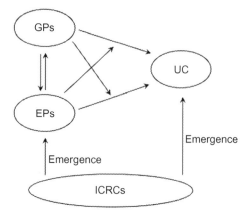

FIG. 1 Emergence process in a cross-level model: *ICRCs*, individual creativity-relevant constructs; *GPs*, global properties; *EPs*, emergent properties; *UC*, unit creativity.

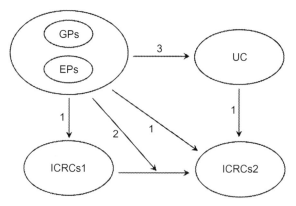

FIG. 2 Top-down process in a cross-level model: 1,3, direct effect; 2, moderator effect; *ICRCs*, individual creativity-relevant constructs; *GPs*, global properties; *EPs*, emergent properties; *UC*, unit creativity.

als. The emergence and top-down processes are presented in Figs. 1 and 2 in the context of creativity research in organizations.

Fig. 1 shows that individual creativity-relevant constructs (ICRCs) are the elementary resources based on which unit creativity-relevant constructs (UCRCs) are formed at higher levels in organizations. The major concepts for UCRCs are global properties (GPs), emergent properties (EPs), and unit creativity (UC). In terms of resources for conceptualization at unit levels, multilevel theorists have already addressed the distinction between global unit-level properties and emergent unit-level properties, with the latter defined as the emergent properties from lower- to higher- levels in organization levels (Kozlowski & Klein, 2000). Global properties at the organization level might be the responses of human resource managers (or organizational leaders) to questions regarding the unit-level information such as the number of patents, unit sizes, major technologies, and CEOs' capabilities. The unit creativity may include creativity at different unit levels related to creative performance in organizations. However, the present study focuses on emergent properties at the unit levels since they represent a more complex aspect related to and contributed by individual creativity.

Fig. 2 shows that once UCRCs come to form, they can exert downward contextual influence impinging on individuals, as a result leading to revision of ICRCs. Line 1s posit direct effects of global properties, emergent properties, and unit creativity on ICRCs. ICRCs can be ICRCs1 for predictors (e.g., climate for creativity perceived at individuals) and ICRCs2 for criteria (e.g., individual creativity). Line 2 posits the moderator effect that global and/or emergent properties can have on the relations between two ICRCs. Line 3 posits the direct effect of global and emergent properties on unit creativity at a unit level. The global and emergent properties may have two indirect effects on ICRCs2: (GPs and EPs) → UC→ ICRCs2; (GPs and EPs) → ICRCs1 → ICRCs2.

In empirical research on individual creativity in organizations, it is the utmost challenge to understand that the bottom-up and top-down processes are not separate single-level phenomena. Although these two processes are not separate, they are distinct and composed of dual processes that are well discoursed in organizational literature (e.g., Kozlowski, Chao, Grand, Braun, & Kuljanin, 2013; Kozlowski & Klein, 2000; Morgeson & Hofmann, 1999; Rousseau, 1985).

Once the UCRCs come to form, they can subsequently have an influence on the individuals who were the original resources in developing the UCRCs. Drawing on Giddens (1993), Morgeson and Hofmann (1999) call this two-way influence as duality of structure that is partly independent of the interaction that gave rise to it. This interwoven dual nature is totally missing in the current research of individual creativity in organizations. Due to this problem, there is no creativity study in organizations that takes the true sense of multilevel perspective. Even the most recent literature in individual creativity research can be characterized as single-level studies despite that many of the authors describe their studies as cross-level or multilevel studies. In studies of bottom-up processes, ICRCs were not modeled or analyzed when emergent constructs (e.g., team/group/organization level creativity defined as an aggregate variable of individual creativity) were analyzed at unit levels (e.g., Bechtoldt, Choi, & Nijstad, 2012; Gong, Kim, Lee, & Zhu, 2013; Gumusluoglu & Ilsev, 2009). In studies of top-down processes, UCRCs were not analyzed while studies were conducted at individual levels in organizations (e.g., George & Zhou, 2002; Taggar, 2002; Zhang & Bartol, 2010).

Although both individual- and unit-level analyses are required together in consideration of the dual properties of individual creativity in organizations, research has just begun to consider creativity at cross- or multilevels of systems (a total of 52 studies out of 452 creativity studies in organizations published from 1995 to 2009), with fewer studies connecting individuals and higher levels in organizations (James & Drown, 2012). Among the limited number of cross- and multilevel studies on creativity in organizations, top-down contextual influence, whereby higher-level phenomena influence lower-level phenomena, is "perhaps the only type of creative feedback that is really receiving much attention (James & Drown, 2012, p.28)." Even with these studies of top-down processes, parallelism is pervasive in analyzing the contextual effect of UCRCs on ICRCs, assuming that theoretical concepts defined at individual levels exist at unit levels with the same content as in the original levels and taking the aggregate of individual-level measures as the measures at unit levels. This parallelism is no less apparent in bottom-up studies. Overall it is a dominant practice to consider aggregate measures of individual creativity as measures of team or organizational creativity without theoretical and empirical justification of the parallelism as lamented by Sacramento, Dawson, and West (2008).

There are two difficulties in conducting cross- and multilevel studies involving emergent constructs originated from individual creativity. The first is the challenge of conceptualization of creativity-relevant constructs at unit levels over and above individual levels. The other is the operationalization following such conceptualization for empirical research. It is apparent that research effort of individual creativity in organizational settings suffers the poor general conceptualization, in which presumed parallelism is dominant or implicitly assumed across levels and dual properties of individual creativity are not incorporated into empirical research.

In order to guide creativity researchers regarding conceptualization of emergent constructs we adopted Kozlowski and Klein's (2000) canonical work on emergence processes and modified to make them fit to creativity research in organizations. We expect the modified version of conceptualization to be helpful for researchers understanding the dynamics of individual creativity in organizations. Although issues related to operationalization are no less important than conceptualization, they will only be mentioned in the conclusion in passing due to space limitations.

CATEGORIES OF EMERGENCE

Drawing on general systems theory (Boulding, 1956; von Bertalanffy, 1951) and other studies on the nature of collective constructs (Chan, 1998; Morgeson & Hofmann, 1999; Rousseau, 1985), Kozlowski and Klein (2000) provided a typology of six different conceptualizations of emergent properties on a continuum of isomorphic composition and discontinuous compilation (e.g., Kozlowski & Klein, 2000, pp. 65–73). In their framework, any emergent construct may be construed as a combination of composition and compilation. The former is characterized by isomorphism and the latter by discontinuity between constructs across levels in organizations. Moreover, the proportional degree of isomorphism and discontinuity determines where an emergent property would be located on a continuum of composition and compilation. However, instead of conceptualizing emergence on a continuum, the following considers the limitations in Kozlowski and Klein's typology and proposes a "categorization" of emergence.

KOZLOWSKI AND KLEIN'S TYPOLOGY

Kozlowski and Klein (2000) used three assumptions to distinguish ideal forms of composition and compilation on a continuum: (1) elemental contributions to higher-level phenomena (similarities vs. dissimilarities), (2) interaction processes and dynamics (incremental/stable/low dispersions vs. irregular/high dispersions), and (3) representations (linear convergences vs. nonlinear configurations). These three assumptions consider the nature of social-psychological interactions among individuals in a unit (Sacramento et al., 2008) and can be utilized as exemplars to delineate six types of emergence. However, variations between composition and compilation cannot be illuminated through social-psychological interactions alone as levels go up to organizations. Organizations have diverse components (e.g., culture, technology, structure, and management systems) in which control systems are required to coordinate the subunits and align them in order to achieve certain goals and missions. Such control systems are a unique nature of the emergence process that transforms complicated dissimilarities or differences within units into emergent constructs manifest at higher levels (Massaro, Bardy, & Pitts, 2012).

Overall, Kozlowski and Klein's (2000) three assumptions are close to dimensions in appearance but do not clearly coincide with the continua, thus making their distinction between the emergence types less effective. Regarding the assumption of elemental contributions to higher-level phenomena, "similarity and dissimilarity" do not effectively explain the types and amounts of contributions. Moreover, "variance," as an exemplar of emergence, is characterized by variable types and amounts of elemental contributions, which are not clearly mapped on the continuum of "similar vs dissimilar" (see Kozlowski & Klein, 2000, p. 67, Fig. 1.3, "variance" column). Regarding the assumption of interaction processes, "minimum/maximum" (another exemplar of emergence) is not described by low vs. high dispersion while low vs. high dispersion is used on a dimensional scheme (see Kozlowski & Klein, 2000, p. 67, Fig. 1.3, "Min/Max" column). Regarding the assumption of representation, linear convergence and nonlinear configuration are used to map different exemplars of composition and compilation on a continuum. However, nonlinearity is hardly accommodated on the same continuum as linearity, since linearity and nonlinearity are qualitatively different.

Furthermore, Kozlowski and Klein's (2000) typology is biased, judging from our viewpoint of examining creativity in organizations; that is, "creativity" and "diversity" in their scheme are the two exemplar constructs that directly represent creativity. However, despite its relative importance in the field of creativity, "variance" (the emergence exemplar of these two constructs) is only considered as one of the six exemplars, thus making the coverage of creativity too narrow. Considering the theoretical gap between what Kozlowski and Klein (2000) meant by "exemplars of emergence" and what can be construed using their three dimension-like assumptions, their typology can be reconsidered for theoretical consistency and our purpose of studying creativity-relevant constructs in organizations. For this purpose, we take the Roschian approach to categorization drawing upon the concepts of prototypes and exemplars in cognitive psychology. Table 1 presents the categories of emergence for creativity-relevant constructs as a modification of Kozlowski and Klein's (2000) typology of emergence.

ROSCHIAN APPROACH TO CONCEPTUALIZATION

A classic view of "concept" had been based on necessary and sufficient attributes for definition until the middle of 1970s when Rosch and her colleagues (Rosch, 1973; Rosch, Mervis, Gray, Johnson, & Boyes-Braem, 1976) developed a categorization approach to conceptualization of natural and conceptual types including objects, behaviors, psychological concepts, and situations. However, in this approach, a focal construct is not defined by necessary and sufficient attributes, but by prototypes which are hypothetical cases that best represent a focal construct. That is, instead of a definition-based model (e.g., a bird may be defined by features such as feathers, beak, and ability to fly), Roschian prototype theory would consider a category like bird as consisting of different elements which have unequal status (e.g., a *sparrow* is more prototypical of a *bird* than, say an *ostrich*).

As shown in Table 1, there are three categories of focal constructs: (1) composition emergence, (2) complementarity emergence, and (3) compilation emergence. Categories are specified in terms of their features (Cantor, Smith, French, & Mezzich, 1980) and prototypes are an ideal type described by the features. For example, in Table 1, each category of emergence includes three features (i.e., problem type, individual contributions, and outcome of interactions) and the likelihood of a construct's classification into a category is based on its typicality, which is generally determined by its similarity or resemblance (Rosch et al., 1976) to the prototype. The prototypes for these three different categories of emergence are or-

TABLE 1 Categories of Emergence for Creativity-Relevant Constructs

Conceptualization	Emergence	Composition	Complementarity	Compilation
	Prototypes	Organizational climate for creativity	Diversity-based group creativity	Integrational innovation
	Exemplars	Team ideational fluency Shared belief, climate, efficacy, motivation, and attitude Performance of a focus group solving an assigned problem	Culture strength Norm crystallization Diversity of unit (team, organizational) personality Leader-member exchange Competence of a team solving an unprecedented problem	Knowledge spirals Team productivity Organizational performance Other types of innovations
	Problem type	Closed problem Well-defined problem	Closed/open problem Mixed problem	Open problem Ill-defined problem
	Individual contributions	<Similarity> Within-unit similarity among individuals Type: similar contents Amount: similar Functional equivalence	<Variability> Within-unit variability and interrole dependence among individuals Type: variable, but related contents Amount: variable Functional equivalence	<Dissimilarity> Within-unit dissimilarity among individuals Type: dissimilar contents Amount: dissimilar Functional equivalence
	Outcome of interactions within unit and with environment	Sharedness of cognitive processes	Sharedness of cognitive processes and knowledge of one another	Controlled pattern of coordinating goals and directions

ganizational climate for creativity (Amabile, 1996), diversity-based group creativity (Bechtoldt et al., 2012; Goncalo & Staw, 2006; Kozlowski & Klein, 2000), and integrational innovation (Massaro et al., 2012; Sternberg, Pretz, & Kaufman, 2003), respectively. We chose these three prototypes based on three criteria: (1) they should connote levels higher than individual levels as prototypes of emergence are constructs manifested over and above individual levels; (2) they should be directly related to creativity; (3) the mechanisms embedded in the prototypes should reflect the meanings of corresponding emergence. They are closer to some features and less close to or farther from other features specifying the category. Any construct can be on the borderline or in between two categories, especially if it fails to include significant features of the prototype (Cantor et al., 1980). Given the prototype and exemplars, it is possible to construe which emergent constructs belong to which categories of emergence. Thus the following section discusses each emergence category in detail.

CONCEPTUALIZATION OF COMPOSITION EMERGENCE

Features of Composition Emergence

In terms of problem type, composition emergence may be observed in closed or well-defined problems. A closed problem is well defined in terms of methods to get to solutions before participants begin creative work. This contrasts with an open problem, in which the participants are required to find, invent, or discover any problem (Unsworth, 2001). When faced with well-defined problems, individuals are likely to constrain alternative choices, thus yielding high sharedness of cognition in a given unit. Conversely, as the openness of a problem increases, variability in a unit also increases, which, in turn, causes dissimilarities in individuals' behaviors and activities.

Regarding individual contributions, similarity (isomorphism) is the main theme characterizing within-unit similarity and functional equivalence. A within-unit similarity has been described as a "similarity in the type and amount of elemental content" (Kozlowski & Klein, 2000, p. 62). It has also been referred to as a "structural similarity" (Morgeson & Hofmann, 1999) or "structural equivalence" (Kozlowski & Klein, 2000), that is, the consensual quality of individual contributions within a unit. This feature constrains the structure of collective constructs, allowing researchers to treat the focal phenomena isomorphic across levels. Functional equivalence refers to the same theoretical function between higher- and lower- level constructs, meaning that constructs at more than one level hold the same positions or roles in multilevel models

(Kozlowski & Klein, 2000; Morgeson & Hofmann, 1999; Rousseau, 1985). For all categories of emergence, functional equivalence is expected to be held across levels since constructs at unit and individual levels do not function differently.

Regarding the outcome of interactions within the unit and with the environment, composition emergence is described in such a way that individuals in a unit are seen as individual cognitive systems that "have specific roles and functions that contribute to creative and noncreative thinking, and ... play the roles of these cognitive components in such a way that the group [unit] works as if it had an overall mind" (Sacramento et al., 2008, p. 278). Within-unit similarity and functional equivalence across levels gear similarity among individuals toward the sharedness of cognitive processes. Moreover, such similarities induce attraction just like birds of a feather flocking together (Forsyth, 2010), whereby members share psychological meanings that render same constructs across levels. Through these isomorphic cognitive processes, UCRCs emerge as shared (unit) properties (Kozlowski & Klein, 2000); that is, similarity-based attraction promotes the sharedness of beliefs, climate, efficacy, motivation, and attitude within a unit.

Prototypes and Exemplars of Composition Emergence

In this section, prototypes and exemplars are described in accordance with the features of composition emergence. The prototype is "organizational climate for creativity" (Amabile, 1996). When an individual's job in a unit has well-defined guides and rules, shared perceptions of some types of climate such as climate for unit creativity will develop. Regarding individual contributions, if unit members share the same job guided by rules and regulations (similar contents), their personal investments in terms of quantity would be similar. As the outcome of interactions, individuals eventually have common cognitive processes, including information, perspective, knowledge, and finally interpretation. Based on these shared cognitive processes among participants, we derive the collective construct of "organizational climate for creativity," which is a suitable prototype for composition emergence.

As an extreme example, the performance of a focus group (i.e., a team) to solve a well-defined problem (like climbing as a team) is considered. In this case, the problem is a conjunctive one (Steiner, 1972) since the slowest member's performance becomes the team's performance. More specifically, as the team members are given a clear definition of their task describing how to solve the problem, the best way to solve the problem is to follow the given method as quickly as possible. Although the type of behaviors may be similar or identical, the amount of individual contribution is never similar because every member does her best to shorten her working time.

Only the slowest member's time is considered in the emergence process of the team's performance, while the longest time taken by the last member will be the collective performance. This may make the emergent construct look atypical in the category of composition emergence. However, it is still closer to composition, in comparison to complementarity or compilation.

In order to utilize composition models for conceptualizing UCRCs as emergent properties, researchers should provide theoretical underpinnings on how a conceptual definition for UCRCs is related to an individual-level counterpart. For example, suppose that organizational climate for creativity is used as a construct for organization levels and psychological climate for creativity is used as a construct for individual ones. Then, UCRCs, following James's (1982) composition theory for climate, may be viewed as a shared "understanding of how individuals in general impute meaning to environments [units], and especially, how individuals in general will respond to environments [units]" (James, 1982, p. 220). The sharedness of psychological climate for creativity among individuals within the unit will emerge as a collective construct (UCRCs) based on the social interactions between individuals and contexts (Morgeson & Hofmann, 1999). This category of composition emergence is consistent with parallelism, which is assumed in many cross-level studies on creativity in organizations (Chen, Bliese, & Mathieu, 2005; Sacramento et al., 2008). However, the remaining two categories do not entail parallelism across levels.

CONCEPTUALIZATION OF COMPLEMENTARITY EMERGENCE

Features of Complementarity Emergence

In terms of problem type, complementarity emergence may be observed in closed problems that are not entirely closed or open problems that are not fully open. These problems are well described elsewhere (cf., Unsworth, 2001). The present study refers to such problems as "mixed problems." To the extent that methods of solving a problem are well defined, the problem is closed, as in the emergence of culture strength and norm crystallization with sharedness of cognitive processes emphasized. To the extent that methods of solving a problem are ill defined, the problems are open, as seen in the emergence of unit creativity, diversity of unit personality, and leader-member exchange with knowledge of each other emphasized. While the shared cognition in composition emergence is individual cognition, it is extended to interpersonal construction of cognition in complementarity emergence. Moreover, in contrast to within-group variance being treated as error variance in composition emergence, within-group variance can serve as another conceptualization of a focal construct in complementarity emergence.

In mixed problems, individual contributions are characterized by variability which ranges from high to low in the types and amounts of individual contributions (Kozlowski & Klein, 2000) and role interdependence among individuals. Role interdependence is observed when outcomes of each member's work are dependent on those of other members in the unit, subsequently leading to shared knowledge of one another's role, strength/weakness, etc. The addition of such knowledge within a unit makes a qualitative difference between composition and complementarity emergence at the unit level. This knowledge also increases as members become more aware of others' preferences, strengths, and weaknesses, especially in terms of their functional roles and responsibilities within the unit (Cannon-Bowers & Salas, 2001). This distributed cognition can maximize the overall performance of a unit when encountered with open (ill-defined) problems. Moreover, as the problem expands from closed to open, the need for complementarity among the members for coping with various environmental challenges increases as the knowledge of other members constructed through social interactions is emphasized. However, the variability of individual contributions is limited (to some extent) since problems are not fully open and individuals are related in roles. Hence, functional equivalence holds across levels, as is necessary in the nature of emergence.

Finally, the outcome of interactions is characterized by the knowledge of other members, in addition to the sharedness of cognitive processes in composition emergence. Faced with "not entirely closed" problems, individuals tend to seek role interdependence in order to reduce uncertainty. Moreover, the need of complementarity induced by role interdependence increases acceptance for variability among the members when dealing with open problems. At the same time, individuals are attracted to one another, thus leading them to share information and to thus have single mode in the distribution of individual contribution (Kozlowski & Klein, 2000).

Prototype and Exemplars of Complementarity Emergence

This section considers the group creativity taking advantage of diversity (Kozlowski & Klein, 2000) in dealing with closed/open problems as the prototype of complementarity emergence. Researchers (e.g., Bechtoldt et al., 2012; Goncalo & Staw, 2006) report studies on relationships between creativity and individualism-collectivism. As groups encounter more open and challenging problems, individual uniqueness and group diversity tend to conduce to creativity than group harmony or cooperation does. In such group settings, "competition, lack of comfort, and individualism are supposed to stimulate creativity because they lead to differentiation and unique … contributions" (Bechtoldt et al., 2012, p. 838). This type of creativity converges on Kozlowski and Klein's (2000) group creativity exploiting diversity. Diversity in groups is utilized to encourage different perspectives and to complement each other's lacking knowledge and skills. The benefit of diversity is maximized when an individual knows where his or her colleagues are stuck and exchanges experience of failure to complement each other's deficiency.

Regarding individual contributions, diversity-based group creativity typically emerges through variability in the types and amounts of individual contents as well as through interrole dependence among individuals, which are typical characteristics of individuals working on challenging tasks that need diverse thinking and skills. As unhealthy differences among individuals tend to be limited, individuals working on mixed problems share a process flow; in other words, one's role-based performance becomes input for others (interrole dependence), promoting a single mode of distribution (Chan, 1998). For example, in customer satisfaction teams of a home-shopping company, there are many professional counselors trained to respond to customers' complaints. In this case, the counselors largely benefit from sharing one another's knowledge regarding products, types of complaints, actions, and outcomes. Furthermore, function of their actions is equivalent in terms of dealing with customers' complaints either individually or as a collective across levels.

Regarding the outcome of interactions, the counselors should know who is specialized in which product, in addition to sharing their knowledge, experiences, and outcomes in dealing with customers. The importance of knowledge of each other increases as the nature of the problem becomes more open.

Finally, exemplars of complementarity emergence include culture strength, norm crystallization, and diversity of unit personality, which Kozlowski and Klein (2000) categorized into a "variance" exemplar between composition emergence and compilation emergence. However, it is notable that in our modified categorization, interpersonal construction of emergent constructs is predicated on low-to-high variability in complementarity emergence. In this regard, low diversity in individual contributions with emphasis on the sharedness of cognitive process predicates culture strength and norm crystallization, while high diversity with emphasis on interrole dependence develops diversity of unit personality or competence to solve unprecedented problems.

CONCEPTUALIZATION OF COMPILATION EMERGENCE

Features of Compilation Emergence

In terms of problem type, compilation emergence may be observed in open or ill-defined problems. Voluntary artistic or scientific endeavors that are classified into proactive creativity (Unsworth, 2001) generally represent open problems. Moreover, in organizations, organizational productivity/performance, knowledge spirals, or innovations represent the constructs related to open problems, since there are no clear methods for obtaining solutions to certain problems.

In open problems, individual contributions are characterized by dissimilar but patterned processes of describing "episodes of changes in behaviors exhibited by an individual or by a ... [unit] rather than the specific behavioral acts or perceptions" (Chan, 1998, p. 241). In addition, the types and amounts are dissimilar across individuals, while functional equivalence holds across levels. For example, a process characterized by dissimilar types and amounts of individual contributions can be in the form of knowledge representation, which has prevailed in the field of semantic memory (e.g., Goldsmith, Johnson, & Acton, 1991; Schvaneveldt, Durso, & Dearholt, 1985). The process can also be in the form of networks of individual contributions, by which performance is configured at the unit level (Kozlowski & Klein, 2000).

With compilation emergence, control systems regulate the outcome of interactions, especially regarding dissimilarity or discontinuity in individual contributions for coordinating goals and directions. Control systems are routines and procedures that are formally used for altering or maintaining configurational patterns of diverse behaviors and activities emergent at the unit level. The addition of control system defines unique qualitative difference from previous two emergence processes at the unit level. Patterns of competing or conflicting behaviors are also compiled into complex constructs at higher levels through some type of control in the higher units (Massaro et al., 2012). Thus control system is necessary (in addition to the sharedness of cognitive processes and the knowledge of other members) for describing the mechanism of composition and/or complementarity emergence.

Prototype and Exemplars of Compilation Emergence

This section considers integrational innovation (Massaro et al., 2012; Sternberg et al., 2003) as the prototype of compilation emergence. Organizational differentiations (Lawrence & Lorsch, 1967) into dissimilar subunits generate rivalry/incongruence in goals as well as dissimilarities in contributions of individuals or subunits. Faced with this hard-to-coordinate situation, organizations must integrate within-organization processes to keep individuals or subunits aligned toward increasing profits and decreasing losses. In this case, control systems are necessary for coordinating dissimilar goals and directions as well as integrating knowledge across subunits (Massaro et al., 2012). Sternberg et al. (2003) referred to this integration as "a type of innovation." For example, management control systems are formal and information-based systems used to maintain/alter patterns in organizational behaviors and activities (Massaro et al., 2012). Through such systems, ideas from distinct types are integrated to yield innovations for organizations (Sternberg et al., 2003).

Regarding individual contributions, organizational specialization and differentiation bring about within-unit dissimilarity in terms of the types and amounts of individuals devoted to the emergence of higher-level constructs. In this case, individuals or the subunits are in disagreement, rather than agreement, regarding the sharedness of knowledge and experiences. However, through the integration process, behaviors, activities, and relations among the dissimilar individuals are coordinated and transformed into controlled patterns that can contribute to innovations. As a result, controlled patterns are obtained as the outcome of this compilatory interaction. In the same way, such exemplars as patterns of the association or relationship among individuals come into emergence of knowledge spirals, team productivity, organizational performance, or the seven types of innovations mentioned in Sternberg et al. (2003).

Finally, the relationships among the three categories of emergence are not clearly distinct, since the categorization is based on fuzzy sets that blur the boundaries between the categories. In addition to the emergence of composition and compilation, Kozlowski and Klein (2000) showed several fuzzy composition processes between the two ends (Tay, Woo, & Vermunt, 2014). For example, early notions of mental models that assume the sharedness of knowledge among team members (e.g., Cannon-Bowers, Salas, & Converse, 1993; Klimoski & Mohammed, 1995, recited from Kozlowski & Klein, 2000) are exemplar constructs of composition emergence. However, Kozlowski, Gully, Salas, and Cannon-Bowers (1996) indicated that the knowledge of different members in a unit complement one another in the unit, which makes the team's mental model an exemplar construct of complementarity emergence. Moreover, if the team members assume different roles and compete with one another, then a control system is necessary to achieve team performance. In this case, the team's mental model is an exemplar construct of compilation emergence.

CONCLUSION

Through the history of creativity research in organizational settings, vast knowledge about creativity has been accumulated at the individual and unit levels, mostly in manners of single-level studies. A multilevel modeling approach to research on individual creativity is still in its infancy since the dual property of individual creativity has not been thoroughly understood and practiced. On one hand, individuals become resources as ICRCs operate at individual levels above all, and the individuals give rise to UCRCs as they interact with others and units. Many concepts describing behaviors and activities at different unit levels are derived from the emergence processes although there are global properties at the unit level that tend to exist without emergence processes (Kozlowski & Klein, 2000).

On the other hand, individuals are affected by unit-level phenomena that are in part formed by individuals' interactions. Once the emergent constructs or global properties at the unit level are established, they exert influence over the ICRCs. This duality of process and structure (Morgeson & Hofmann, 1999) raise questions about the validity of single-level studies on individual creativity in organizations. Therefore it is compelling that a multilevel approach be accepted as a norm in creativity research in organizations.

Even among a handful of cross-level or multilevel studies on creativity in organizational settings, we found that bottom-up emergent processes have been largely neglected, in comparison to top-down contextual processes (James & Drown, 2012; Kozlowski et al., 2013). A critical reason for such negligence is that the conceptualization of emergent constructs has not yet been established. In relation to this problem, we noticed a fuzziness in Kozlowski and Klein's (2000) conceptualization of the different types of emergence. Hence, the present study introduced the Roschian approach, which utilized a fuzzy set-theoretic classification scheme. This attempt led to a framework that applied three categories of emergence, which were more parsimonious and efficient in categorizing the different exemplars of emergent constructs for creativity research.

We also introduced the mechanism of system control in organizations, which coordinates dissimilar types and amounts of individual contributions, and ensures functional equivalence across organizational levels, especially in situations where unit-level constructs emerge through compilation. The introduction of system control as emergence mechanisms enhances the meaning of compilation over and above social-psychological interactions, which is considered the key explanatory mechanism in Kozlowski and Klein's (2000) discourse.

Regarding operationalization part of UCRCs given the current status of conceptualization, there has been some advance for composition emergence. As models that can be used to operationalize emergent constructs in empirical research, consensus models are dominantly used, assuming the validity of parallelism in conceptualization. Consensus models specify that the simple mean of ICRCs is interpreted as a valid measure of relevant UCRCs. Although researchers are responsible for demonstration of validity, they had been forced to draw a parallel between similar unit- and individual-level constructs and to employ models for operationalization of UCRCs, even though such parallelism has not yet been proved. Chen et al. (2005) recognized this problem of unjustified parallelism in multilevel research and suggested advanced conceptual framework and statistical procedures for delineating and testing parallelism. However, the other two categories of emergence have not garnered so much attention as composition emergence in terms of models to operationalize UCRCs and measures to unit levels (Chan, 1998; Kozlowski et al., 2013; Kozlowski & Klein, 2000). This lack of advance in empirical research is not an isolated problem from the issue of conceptualization. As Kozlowski and Klein (2000) lamented, "the dominance of composition models ... has tended to limit consideration to shared models of emergence" (Kozlowski & Klein, 2000, p. 61).

The present study supports Kozlowski and Klein's statement since some important emergent constructs such as organizational creativity and innovation are the prototypes or exemplars of the other two neglected types of emergence: complementarity and compilation emergence. These two categories represent the bottom-up emergence in which increasingly open problems lead to a more dynamic emergence of constructs in contrast to composition emergence. More importantly, empirical studies currently practiced have encountered a major limitation (i.e., indirect access to emergence processes through survey questionnaires). Kozlowski et al. (2013) argued that computation modeling or agent-based simulations provide a direct access to the dynamics of emergence, which can open a new approach to investigating more complicated emergence phenomena, especially compilation emergence.

Although typical composition models based on the sharedness of cognitive processes will increase even more in the near future, they should not be unconditionally endorsed in multilevel theoretical research. Moreover, in very recent studies employing composition emergence that assumed parallelism of constructs across levels, the authors did not clarify the underlying rationale regarding why they chose the specific category of emergence. Consequently, this insufficient rationale brought about the critique arguing that parallelism across levels has been adopted without justification (Sacramento et al., 2008).

Finally, our focus on emergent constructs at the unit level might have created a bias for emergent constructs, excluding the importance of global properties. In order to avoid such a misperception, a warning is in order to emphasize the utility of global indices at the unit level. In addition, researchers are encouraged to collect global properties that are relevant to organizational creativity. As problems change from closed to open types, environmental demands are not limited to human behaviors/activities. Instead, organizational variables such as strategies, structures, technologies, sales volumes, amount of investments, returns on investments, and new product developments may be required as predictors or outcomes of creativity at unit levels as UCRCs are related to ICRCs. Researchers who wish to avoid uncertainties embedded in the aggregate data collected at individual levels may believe that they could gain access to UCRCs through unit-level data (Rousseau, 1985), while others may argue that using global-unit measures only hinders researchers from looking into ecology at individual levels, thus causing ecological fallacies (Robinson, 1950). Of course, using only individual-level data or ICRCs to infer upper-level phenomena or UCRCs can be equally dangerous causing an atomic fallacy (Kozlowski & Klein, 2000).

References

Agars, M. D., Kaufman, J. C., & Locke, T. R. (2008). Social influences and creativity in organizations: a multi-level lens for theory, research, and practice. In M. D. Mumford, S. T. Hunter, & K. E. Bedell-Avers (Eds.), *Vol. 7. Multi-level issues in creativity and innovation* (pp. 3–62). New York: JAI Press.

Amabile, T. M. (1996). *Creativity in contexts: update to the social psychology of creativity.* Boulder, CO: Westview Press.

Bechtoldt, M. N., Choi, H. S., & Nijstad, B. A. (2012). Individuals in mind, mates by heart: individualistic self-construal and collective value orientation as predictors of group creativity. *Journal of Experimental Social Psychology, 48*, 838–844.

Boulding, K. E. (1956). General system theory skeleton of science. *Management Science, 2*, 197–208.

Cannon-Bowers, J. A., & Salas, E. (2001). Reflections on shared cognition. *Journal of Organizational Behavior, 22*, 195–210.

Cannon-Bowers, J. A., Salas, E., & Converse, S. A. (1993). Shared mental models in expert team decision-making. In N. J. Castellan Jr. (Eds.), *Current issues in individual and group decision making* (pp. 221–246). Mahwah, NJ: Erlbaum.

Cantor, N., Smith, E. E., French, R. D., & Mezzich, J. (1980). Psychiatric diagnosis as prototype categorization. *Journal of Abnormal Psychology, 89*, 181–193.

Chan, D. (1998). Functional relations among constraints in the same content domain at different levels of analysis: a typology of compositional models. *Journal of Applied Psychology, 83*, 234–246.

Chen, G., Bliese, P. D., & Mathieu, J. E. (2005). Conceptual framework and statistical procedures for delineating and testing multilevel theories of homology. *Organizational Research Methods, 8*, 375–409.

Forsyth, D. R. (2010). *Group dynamics.* Stamford, CA: Cengage Learning.

George, J. M., & Zhou, J. (2002). Understanding when bad moods foster creativity and good ones don't: the role of context and clarity of feelings. *Journal of Applied Psychology, 87*, 687–697.

Giddens, A. (1993). *New rules of sociological method: A positive critique of interpretive sociologies* (2nd ed.). Stanford, CA: Stanford University Press.

Goldsmith, T. E., Johnson, P. J., & Acton, W. H. (1991). Assessing structural knowledge. *Journal of Educational Psychology, 83*, 88–96.

Goncalo, J. A., & Staw, B. M. (2006). Individualism-collectivism and group creativity. *Organizational Behavior and Human Decision Processes, 100*, 96–109.

Gong, Y., Kim, T.-Y., Lee, D.-R., & Zhu, J. (2013). A multilevel model of team goal orientation, information exchange, and creativity. *Academy of Management Journal, 56*, 827–851.

Gumusluoglu, L., & Ilsev, A. (2009). Transformational leadership, creativity, and organizational innovation. *Journal of Business Research, 62*, 461–473.

James, L. R. (1982). Aggregation bias in estimates of perceptual agreement. *Journal of Applied Psychology, 67*, 219–229.

James, K., & Drown, D. (2012). Organizations and creativity: trends in research, status of education and practice, agenda for the future. In M. Mumford (Ed.), *Handbook of organizational creativity.* New York: Academic Press.

Klimoski, R., & Mohammed, S. (1995). Team mental model: construct or metaphor? *Journal of Management, 20*, 403–437.

Kozlowski, S. W. J., Chao, G. T., Grand, J. A., Braun, M. T., & Kuljanin, G. (2013). Advancing multilevel research design: capturing the dynamics of emergence. *Organizational Research Methods, 16*, 581–615.

Kozlowski, S. W. J., Gully, S. M., Salas, E., & Cannon-Bowers, J. A. (1996). Team leadership and development: theory, principles, and guidelines for training leaders and teams. In M. Beyerlein, D. Johnson, & S. Beyerlein (Eds.), *Vol. 3. Advances in interdisciplinary studies of work teams: Tea leadership* (pp. 251–284). Greenwich, CT: JAI Press.

Kozlowski, S. W. J., & Klein, K. J. (2000). A multilevel approach to theory and research in organizations: contextual, temporal, and emergent processes. In K. J. Klein & S. W. J. Kozlowski (Eds.), *Multilevel theory, research, and methods in organizations*. San Francisco: Jossey-Bass.

Lawrence, P., & Lorsch, J. (1967). Differentiation and integration in complex organizations. *Administrative Science Quarterly, 12*, 1–30.

Massaro, M., Bardy, R., & Pitts, M. (2012). Supporting creativity through knowledge integration during the creative processes: a management control system perspective. *Electronic Journal of Knowledge Management, 10*, 258–267.

Morgeson, F. P., & Hofmann, D. A. (1999). The structure and function of collective constructs: implications for multilevel research and theory development. *Academy of Management Review, 24*, 249–265.

Robinson, W. S. (1950). Ecological correlations and the behavior of individuals. *American Sociological Review, 15*, 351–357.

Rosch, E. (1973). On the internal structure of perceptual and semantic categories. In T. E. Moore (Ed.), *Cognitive development and acquisition of language*. New York: Academic Press.

Rosch, R., Mervis, C., Gray, W., Johnson, D., & Boyes-Braem, P. (1976). Basic objects in natural categories. *Cognitive Psychology, 8*, 382–439.

Rousseau, D. M. (1985). Issues of level in organizational research: multi-level and cross-level perspectives. In B. M. Staw & L. L. Cummings (Eds.), *Research in organization behavior* (pp. 1–37). Greenwich, CT: JAI Press.

Sacramento, C. A., Dawson, J. A., & West, M. A. (2008). Team creativity: more than the sum of its parts? In M. D. Mumford, S. T. Hunter, & K. E. Bedell-Avers (Eds.), *Vol. 7. Multi-level issues in creativity and innovation* (pp. 3–62). New York: JAI Press.

Schvaneveldt, R. W., Durso, F. T., & Dearholt, D. W. (1985). *Pathfinder: Scaling with network structures (Memorandum in Computer and Cognitive Science, MCCS-85-9, Computing Research Laboratory)*. Las Cruces: New Mexico State University.

Steiner, I. D. (1972). *Group process and productivity*. New York: Academic Press.

Sternberg, R. J., Pretz, J. E., & Kaufman, J. C. (2003). Types of innovations. In L. Shavinina (Ed.), *The international handbook of innovation* (pp. 158–169). Mahwah, NJ: Elsevier Science.

Taggar, S. (2002). Individual creativity and group ability to utilize individual creative resources: a multilevel model. *Academy of Management Journal, 45*, 315–330.

Tay, L., Woo, S. E., & Vermunt, J. K. (2014). A conceptual and methodological framework for psychometric isomorphism: validation of multilevel construct measures. *Organizational Research Methods, 17*, 77–106.

Unsworth, K. (2001). Unpacking creativity. *Academy of Management Review, 26*, 289–297.

Von Bertalanffy, L. (1951). General system theory: a new approach to unity of science. *Human Biology, 23*, 303–361.

Zhang, X., & Bartol, K. M. (2010). Linking empowering leadership and employee creativity: the influence of psychological empowerment, intrinsic motivation, and creative process engagement. *Academy of Management Journal, 53*, 107–128.

INTELLIGENCE
AND COGNITION

5

Interruptions and Multitasking: Advantages and Disadvantages for Creativity at Work

Francesca Mochi[*], *Nora Madjar*[†]

[*]Università Cattolica del Sacro Cuore, Milano, Italy, [†]University of Connecticut, Storrs, CT, United States

INTRODUCTION

The topic of creativity and innovation has been gaining a great deal of traction in management research and practice (Lu, Akinola, & Mason, 2017; Madjar, Shalley, & Herndon, in press; Zhou & Hoever, 2014). Creativity, in particular, has been described as both the starting point for a lot of new ventures and initiatives, as well as a necessity for solving problems and resolving issues at work (Amabile, 1996). However, with few exceptions (e.g., Beeftink, van Eerde, & Rutte, 2008; Madjar & Oldham, 2006; Madjar & Shalley, 2008), the current research on creativity has examined work on a creative task in isolation, without any consideration of how it fits in the overall job, as if individuals have only one creative task to do and they always accomplish it from start to finish without interruptions. But planning and scheduling one's creative work can prove particularly challenging, and when creative ideas do not come, we can continue working or stop and do something else. Moreover, the current work environment sometimes requires work on multiple tasks simultaneously and information technologies often expose employees to constant interruptions that may disrupt thinking processes and tasks (Carr, 2010; Conley, 2011). While for noncreative tasks it is better to complete one task before moving to another (Leroy, 2009), research on creative tasks suggests that incubation (Wallas, 1926), or taking time away from the problem to work on something else, may be a more effective approach (Elsbach & Hargadon, 2006). Multitasking, doing multiple tasks at the same time (Adler & Benbunan-Fich, 2013, p. 1441; Rubinstein, Meyer, & Evans, 2001), in most of its different forms (e.g., sequential multitasking, simultaneous multitasking, task switching, and task rotation) involves the interruption of the main or primary task and the engagement in another one (subsequent task), thus we consider multitasking as a type of interruption. These additional tasks, breaks, and interruptions may be beneficial for creativity in terms of time for incubation and reduction of cognitive fixation (Lu et al., 2017), but they may be detrimental as well by creating distractions (Leroy, 2009; Ophir, Nass, & Wagner, 2009), increasing anxiety (Becker, Alzahabi, & Hopwood, 2013), and heightening the propensity to forget (Einstein, McDaniel, Williford, Pagan, & Dismukes, 2003) among others.

Moreover, while some organizations may want to limit the amount of interruptions and multitasking to facilitate creativity and allow individuals to focus, others, like Google and 3 M for instance, have encouraged their employees to switch tasks and spend 20% of their time on so-called choice projects to foster creativity and innovation (Coget, Shani, & Solari, 2014; Mainemelis & Ronson, 2006). While the job and work design literatures have identified the importance of particular factors in the work and job design for achieving higher level of performance (Garg & Rastogi, 2006; Parker, Morgeson, & Johns, 2017), we still do not know enough about how job design and task and break scheduling affect creativity.

Thus as described in the following figure, the goal of this chapter is to theorize and systematically review the evidence about how interruptions due to intrusions, breaks, multitasking, or other distractions may influence creativity. We first identify the cognitive and affective mechanisms through which multitasking and interruptions may facilitate or hinder creativity. We then review what we know about the effects of interruptions, breaks, and multitasking as job design factors that may facilitate or hinder creativity via these cognitive and affective mechanisms. Based on our review and theorizing, we provide important implications for how individuals can maximize their creativity in contexts with interruptions and multitasking.

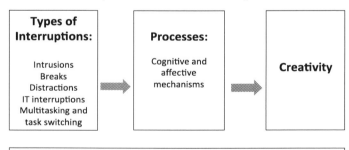

INTERRUPTIONS AND MULTITASKING

We live in an "Interruption age" (Tams, Thatcher, Grover, & Pak, 2015) consisting of a dramatic increase of interruptions at work due to both the physical and psychological work environment (Jett & George, 2003). Interruptions are generally defined as "incidents or occurrences that impede or delay organizational members as they attempt to make progress on work tasks" (Jett & George, 2003, p. 494). Open space offices, telecommuting, and the pursuit of flexibility increase the chance of interruptions (Oldham, Kulik, & Stepina, 1991; Perlow, 1999). Moreover, the proliferation of information technologies (ITs) such as emails, instant messaging, smartphones with notifications, and constant connectivity exponentially increase the number and typology of interruptions in the contemporary work environment, consuming employees' time and cognitive resources (Addas & Pinsonneault, 2015; Gupta, Sharda, & Greve, 2011; Jett & George, 2003; Lin, Kain, & Fritz, 2013; Spira & Feintuch, 2005; Tams et al., 2015). Lin et al. (2013) summarized the results of a technical report by Basex that found that interruptions at work consumed 2.1 h per day with a productivity loss for the U.S. economy due to lost time of $588 billion. In a similar way, Wajcman and Rose (2011), investigating the way knowledge workers interact with information technologies, found that during a working day employees faced an average of nine interruptions per day due to ITs and 12 interruptions per day due to face-to-face interaction, resulting in approximately three interruptions per hour throughout the workday. Given the relevance of the topic and the widespread presence of interruptions in different working environment, it is very important to understand the effects of these interruptions on creativity. Jett and George (2003), in their seminal work about interruptions distinguished four types of interruptions: intrusions, breaks, distractions, and discrepancies. We examine some of these suggested interruption types and their potential effect on creativity. We focus on the types that have an objective element of interruption and exclude from this review discrepancies, that is, perceived inconsistencies between the individual's expectation and external environment that catch the individual's attention, as a type of interruption, as well as all kinds of psychological interruptions that do not have an objective task transition as their effects depend too much on the individual involved and not so much on the job design, task, or context (Jett & George, 2003) .

In addition or in conjunction with the increase of interruption in the workplace, another element of the job design that may have a strong impact on creativity is multitasking, or how multiple tasks are scheduled in the context of a job. Multitasking is becoming more and more pervasive both at work and in everyday life due to the changing demands in the workplace, the presence of multiple duties, the requirement of flexibility, and the widespread availability of ITs (Kirchberg, Roe, & Van Eerde,

2015). When individuals have to attend to multiple tasks and deadlines or responsibilities, they often have to interrupt their work on one task to attend to another. Thus we look at multitasking and task scheduling as another type of interruption that comes from the nature of the work or job. We explore the effects of this type of interruption as well.

THE EFFECT OF INTERRUPTIONS AND MULTITASKING ON CREATIVE PERFORMANCE

Before we review the different types of interruptions, in order to understand their impact on creative performance, it is important to understand their positive and negative effects on cognitive and affective processes, and subsequently on creativity. To do that, we believe that it is essential to focus on what we know about the creative process and the cognitive and affective mechanisms that may affect it. The creative process has been described as involving several stages (Wallas, 1926), including preparation, incubation, illumination, and verification. We believe that the most critical stage that interruptions and task switching may affect is incubation. Incubation is commonly associated with the "aha" factor, when individuals are faced with a problem and time away from the problem (e.g., working on another task, break, or interruption) may lead to a breakthrough. That is, incubation occurs when the individual is no longer consciously working on the task, but may be unconsciously still processing information that may lead to new combinations of ideas (Csikszentmihalyi & Sawyer, 1995; Segal, 2004; Smith & Dodds, 1999). Alternatively, incubation may serve as a break that may represent time away from the task to rejuvenate and potentially come back to the problem with a fresh lens (Jett & George, 2003). This suggests that one mechanism through which interruptions and multitasking can positively influence creativity may be through providing additional cognitive (different perspectives) and informational (new knowledge) resources and an opportunity to incubate.

Another alternative mechanism may be the affective influence and the impact of tasks and interruptions on individuals' emotions that may hinder or stimulate creativity. Interruptions may affect individuals' emotions, for example, breaks can alleviate stress, while intrusions may increase it (Jett & George, 2003; Lin et al., 2013), and previous research has found that positive and negative moods can both increase or diminish creativity (To, Fisher, Ashkanasy, & Rowe, 2012). Moreover, individuals can experience both positive and negative affect almost simultaneously during the switching from task to task, for example, they can be relieved by a task and stressed by the subsequent one, and previous research highlights that triggering two independent emotions, that is, having emotional ambivalence, may develop the ability to make unusual idea associations and increased creativity (Kapadia, 2016). Thus we explore the impact of job design and interruptions on the affective influences for creativity as well.

INTERRUPTIONS, MULTITASKING, AND COGNITIVE RESOURCES FOR CREATIVITY

How could interruptions and multitasking affect the creative process and incubation, in particular, by influencing the cognitive resources for creativity? Several hypotheses have been proposed to explain the potential effects of incubation on creativity (e.g., Seifert, Meyer, Davidson, Patalano, & Yaniv, 1995; Zhong, Dijksterhuis, & Galinsky, 2008), such as selective forgetting or recovering from cognitive exhaustion (Sio & Ormerod, 2009). Opportunistic assimilation theory has received significantly more empirical support than competing perspectives (for a review see Sio & Ormerod, 2009) for explaining the effect of incubation or time away from a task on creativity (Seifert et al., 1995). We believe that certain interruptions, if happening at an opportune moment, will stimulate incubation and advocate an opportunistic assimilation focus for explaining their potential cognitive effects on creativity. According to this perspective, unsolved problems stay in our memory and when switching to engage in something else, are open to chance connections between emergent ideas, leading to remote associations (Patalano & Seifert, 1994) and to the combination of disparate ideas that triggers new connections, ideas, and solutions (Christensen & Schunn, 2005; Reiter-Palmon, Mumford, Boes, & Runco, 1997; Seifert et al., 1995). By itself, however, this effect will not enhance creativity. Incubation is conceptualized as a two-step process (Zhong et al., 2008), in that, after experiencing these chance encounters working on another task or during an interruption, in the critical second step, these new associations have to be transferred back and integrated into the creative task, which may make the effects of different types of interruptions more complex. When people approach a task, they extend their search to previously unexplored areas of knowledge, and incubation (through interruptions) may help to widen this search of available knowledge to identify as many relevant connections as possible, which potentially lead to higher creativity (Sio & Ormerod, 2009). Incubation likely occurs when participants engage in an intervening activity versus doing nothing or just taking a break, and is especially likely to result in more significant positive effects for creativity when the intervening activity demands full attention (Segal, 2004) and high engagement (Madjar & Shalley, 2008). In addition to considering the effect of breaks and interruptions on incubation, Beeftink et al. (2008) investigated the effect of interruptions on the feeling of being "cognitively" stuck. The psychological state of impasse occurs when individuals reach a state of fixation and negative feelings, including frustration and confusion build up to a level that individuals decide to give up on the task. The two scholars found support for the hypothesis that individuals who are interrupted or who have the discretion to take a break, report fewer psychological states of impasse than those who work continuously on an insight problem, thus pointing out that interruptions are beneficial for creative problem solving in cases of impasse. Beeftink et al. (2008) also found that individuals who can take a break at their own discretion perceived fewer impasses than those who are interrupted. Thus we believe that one way through which interruptions and multitasking (as a particular type of multitasking) may stimulate creativity is by providing additional cognitive resources, new information, and different perspectives for creativity through the reduction of impasses and the very serendipitous process of opportunistic assimilation (Seifert et al., 1995). But in addition to these positive cognitive effects of interruptions and multitasking on creativity for stimulating incubation through opportunistic assimilation, we are aware of many other more mixed or negative effects. Recalling Wallas' (1926) creative problem-solving model in which the incubation time is a time away from a problem or task that is beneficial for creative problem solving, Beeftink et al. (2008) investigated directly whether interruptions affect creativity. Their hypothesis that individuals who are interrupted solve more insight problems than individuals who work continuously on them without interruptions was not supported. Research on routine performance, focusing on errors for example, has shown that interruptions lead to a reduction of accuracy in task performance and an increase of errors (Eyrolle & Cellier, 2000; Ratwani, Trafton, & Myers, 2006). Foroughi, Werner, Nelson, and Boehm-Davis (2014) were interested in the effect of interruptions on overall quality tasks and in whether the timing of the interruption matters. In an experimental design, the authors administered a creative thought task in which participants had to outline and write an essay. The treatment group faced three interruptions scheduled by the researchers at different phases of the experiment, either when the participants were engaged in the outlining or in the writing part of the task. Results indicated that interruptions during the execution phase—writing—lead to a lower amount of content, and the amount of content was positively correlated with the final score of the essay, thus suggesting that interruptions during a creative complex task in some cases may reduce performance quality. To further corroborate the results, Foroughi et al. (2014) ran a second experiment in which they changed the overall time that participants had to complete the essay and they randomized the three interruptions in order to reduce their possible predictability. However, the results remained the same, demonstrating that interruptions decrease the quality of the creative task, especially if they occur during the execution phase. Thus while interruptions might improve perceptions of impasses, they are not always beneficial for creativity. The cognitive effects of interruptions on creativity are mixed and we may need to examine specifically how different types of interruptions may affect the creative process.

Moreover, these potential cognitive resources and incubation boosters that result from interruptions and multitasking may come at a cost. Previous research on task completion has demonstrated that an unfinished task leads to attention residue on the preliminary task that persists while working on a subsequent task, thus inducing individuals to work under cognitive load that eventually hurts performance (Johnson, Chang, & Lord, 2006; Kanfer & Ackerman, 1989). Leroy's research (2009) is a milestone study on multitasking. She compared the effect of task switching and sequential multitasking on attention residue—the persistence of cognitive activity related to a task A when working on a task B. First, her results demonstrated that individuals who do not finish a preliminary task before switching to a subsequent task experience more attention residue than individuals who finish the preliminary task before the switching. Secondly, she also indicated that individuals who do not finish task A before switching to task B exhibit lower performance on task B than people who finish task A prior to switching to task B. These results are in line with previous research that highlighted that performance suffers when individuals dedicate only part of their attention to the task (Beal, Weiss, Barros, & MacDermid, 2005; Kahn, 1992). Although, these results referred to mostly routine performance and not necessarily creativity, they suggest that attention residue on a preliminary unfinished task may decrease cognitive resources on the subsequent one and thus decrease creative performance. Moreover, finishing a task does not guarantee the absence of attention residue as task completion is usually followed by the evaluation of the task that keeps individuals to process information about the preliminary task (Gollwitzer, 1990; Mayseless & Kruglanski, 1987), thus cognitive closure is needed. These results paint a more complex picture for the effect of interruptions on incubation and creativity. They show that while interruptions are part of the incubation process, they do not always provide the cognitive resources necessary for increased creativity and a nuanced review of the cognitive processes through which different types of interruptions will affect the creative process is warranted.

INTERRUPTIONS, MULTITASKING, AND THEIR AFFECTIVE INFLUENCES ON CREATIVITY

Another potential mechanism through which job design, and in particular interruptions and multitasking may influence creativity is through their effects on individual's affect. There are some theoretical perspectives that argue that contextual conditions influence individuals' moods, which, in turn, affect their creative responses to later tasks and activities (Baron, 1994; George & Brief, 1992). Moods refer to pervasive generalized affective states that are not necessarily directed at any particular object or behavior. Rather, moods capture an individual's affective experience over short periods (George, 1991; Watson & Pennebaker, 1989). They provide affective coloring for day-to-day events and activities (George & Brief, 1992) and may fluctuate across situations and longer periods.

Moreover, previous work has suggested that mood consists of two separate and independent dimensions: positive (characterized by emotions ranging from high to low levels of excitation and elatedness) and negative (characterized by emotions ranging from high to low levels of distress and fear; Brief & Roberson, 1989; Burke, Brief, George, Roberson, & Webster, 1989; Watson & Tellegen, 1985). Some work has suggested that construing and measuring mood in terms of four (vs. two) dimensions adds even more precision to the description of mood states (Burke et al., 1989; Huelsman, Nemanick, & Munz, 1998; Oldham, Cummings, Mischel, Schmidtke, & Zhou, 1995; Saavedra & Kwun, 2000). The four dimensions and the experiences that characterize them are enthusiasm (positive arousal), fatigue (low arousal), nervousness (negative activation), and relaxation (low activation). Positive and low arousal are considered positive mood states, whereas the other two dimensions are associated with negative moods (Burke et al., 1989; Madjar & Oldham, 2002).

Most of the theoretical work concerned with creativity and affect has argued for the beneficial effects of the positive affective state for creativity, while the effects of negative affect are rather mixed (Davis, 2009; Watson & Tellegen, 1985). Some work has suggested the effects of interruptions and multitasking on mood and emotions as one mechanism for influencing creativity and George and Zhou (2002) have examined the motivational effects of these mood states for creativity, They found that negative moods are positively related to creative performance when perceived recognition and rewards for creative performance and clarity of feelings are high, while on the contrary, positive moods are negatively related to creative performance in the same conditions. We believe that in addition to their cognitive effects, the different types of interruptions and multitasking may have a large impact on creativity through their effect on affective states; the combination of these cognitive and affective influences will determine their impact on the creative process and outcomes. Thus next, we explore the different types of interruptions and multitasking and their potential cognitive and affective effects on creativity.

TYPES OF INTERRUPTIONS AND MULTITASKING AND THEIR COGNITIVE AND AFFECTIVE INFLUENCES ON CREATIVITY

Intrusions

Intrusions occur when unexpectedly something interrupts an individual's workflow and continuity and temporarily stops his or her work. Examples of intrusions are an unexpected visit, an unscheduled phone call, an email; and often those intrusions are not instrumental for the primary task that the individual is performing (Jett & George, 2003). Because intrusions are unexpected, frequent, and often unrelated to the task currently performed, they are considered disruptive for individual's routine performance. The literature has focused attention mainly on the negative effects of intrusions, such as the frustration of individuals trying to finish their primary task, the difficulty of being in a state of total involvement in the job, and the perceived anxiety and stress, especially when intrusions occur with scarce time for completing the main task (Jett & George, 2003). Lin et al. (2013) approached the topic of intrusions with a resourced-based framework and found that intrusions threaten valued resources like time, self-regulatory and cognitive resources, and lead to strains. They also ascertained that intrusions are associated with increased emotional exhaustion, that is, the result of prolonged affective, cognitive and physical exertion (Demerouti, Bakker, Nachreiner, & Schaufeli, 2001), physical complaints, and increased anxiety. However, intrusions could be beneficial too, for example, when the result is an exchange of information that is relevant for the task completion or informal feedback and information sharing (Jett & George, 2003).

While intrusions have the potential for opportunistic assimilation and the introduction of new perspectives or a new, refreshed view of the task at hand, as well as an opportunity to boost positive affect with some exciting positive news, we believe that their negative effects on the emotional side and the accompanied need to refocus attention later will counteract and negate these possible benefits. In effect, Shalley, Zhou, and Oldham (2004) stated that intrusions, especially present in dense settings, distract individuals' attention from the work, thus lowering their intrinsic motivation and diminishing creativity. In addition, most intrusions will not be able to induce incubation and their effects on stress and frustrations will make them more detrimental and less beneficial by draining cognitive resources for creativity.

Breaks

Unlike intrusions, breaks are planned or unscheduled recesses from work that again interrupt task flow and continuity. Similar to intrusions they stop an individual's work, but unlike intrusions they can be self-induced in order to accommodate personal needs, prescheduled by the individuals or the organization, or naturally and spontaneously occurring when individuals are bored, frustrated, or tired (Jett & George, 2003). Previous research has categorized breaks in different types, and differentiated between physical and psychological activities that permit to relax the body and mind, such as a short walk, listening to music, mind wandering; or social activities such as chatting with coworkers about trivial matters or contacting friends and family through texts, phone calls, or social media.

Both Effort-Recovery Theory (Meijman & Mulder, 1998) and Conservation of Resources Theory (Hobfoll, 1989) consider the importance of breaks during the workday. The first theory posits that sufficient time of recovery is necessary to prevent strain due to negative load reactions, accumulated throughout the workday, in other words the purpose of breaks and recovery time includes the prevention and repair of the negative effects of work stressors. The Conservation of Resources Theory asserts that individuals use various resources for completing work tasks such as time, cognitive attention, physical energy, but they have to replenish those resources during breaks in order to avoid stress (Kim, Park, & Niu, 2017). Thus like intrusions, breaks have both cognitive and affective, and positive and negative effects. Concerning the cognitive effects of breaks, the individual interrupted by a break could lose available time and focus and be disengaged from the task. If the break lasts for a long time it could enhance procrastination (Jett & George, 2003) or reduce activation. Regarding the implications of breaks on affect, Kim et al. (2017) found that relaxation and social activities reduce the effects of work demands on negative affect at the end of the working day, while cognitive activities worsen the effects of work demands on negative affect. The breaks that they considered in the research are spontaneously taken by the employees, because there is not enough evidence to guide organizations and employees for specific or predetermined types of break activities, helpful for momentary recovery (Kim et al., 2017). Despite the negative effects, breaks are usually perceived as beneficial interruptions and they can lead to positive outcomes. They can enhance cognitive stimulation, job satisfaction, emotional well-being, high levels of work performance, and creative output (Csikszentmihalyi, 1975; Jett & George, 2003).

Previous research has found that undemanding tasks that maximize mind wandering may be perceived and experienced as a break and serve to enhance incubation and hence creativity (Baird et al., 2012; Dijksterhuis & Meurs, 2006; Sio & Ormerod, 2009). Similarly, breaks filled with "mindless work" that requires limited amount of cognitive resources and attention permit the subconscious mind to have time for incubation and elaboration of ideas, thus increasing the chance to have a higher creative performance (Csikszentmihalyi & Sawyer, 1995; Elsbach & Hargadon,

2006; Jett & George, 2003). Madjar and Shalley (2008) demonstrated that individuals who can take a break at their own discretion solve more insight problems than those who work continuously on them or those who are interrupted, thus suggesting that breaks could be beneficial for creative problem solving if they are taken discretionally by the individual himself and not imposed by others (Madjar & Shalley, 2008). Eliav and Miron-Spektor (2015) asserted that interruptions force individuals to restart the ideation process thus preventing cognitive exhaustion and triggering a "recovery effect" useful to generate new ideas. They also demonstrated that there is a temporary increase in the number of generated ideas after the occurrence of an interruption. Breaks are usually associated with more positive emotions that may encourage broader categorization and creativity (Beeftink et al., 2008). They also provide many chances for opportunistic assimilation that may cognitively facilitate creativity, thus we believe that when an interruption is perceived as a break, it will facilitate creativity both affectively (through reduced stress and induction of positive emotions) as well as cognitively (through the introduction of new perspectives and information).

Distractions

Distractions, another type of interruption, are "psychological reactions triggered by external stimuli or secondary activities that interrupt focused concentration on a primary task" (Jett & George, 2003, p. 500). Distractions (e.g., background noises) are irrelevant for the primary task and affect individual's concentration. The construct is related to the studies of cognitive interference (i.e., studies on the functioning of memory and attention) and has the peculiar characteristic to be perceived differently between individuals. The same event may be more or less distracting, depending on the task a person is working on and a person's temperament, for example, music can be very distracting for some people or help with concentration for others (Jett & George, 2003; Oldham et al., 1995). In effect, when a person is engaged in a new or unfamiliar task he may be more vulnerable to distractions (Gillie & Broadbent, 1989; Jett & George, 2003). As distractions are tied with individual personality and the characteristic of the task (Jett & George, 2003), their effects are bonded to those circumstances too. For example, impatient individuals are more sensitive to the negative effects of distractions than patient individuals (Kirmeyer, 1988). The negative effects of distractions are stronger also for individuals that are lacking in stimulus-screening capabilities as they are more prone to pay attention to distractions. Negative consequences of distractions arise when the task is complex, demanding, and requires individuals' full attention (Jett & George, 2003; Speier, Valacich, & Vessey, 1999). However, when the task is perceived as boring, simple, routine, or unchallenging, distractions could lead to a quicker information processing without decreasing decision accuracy and the quality of the output (Jett & George, 2003; Speier et al., 1999; Zijlstra, Roe, Leonora, & Krediet, 1999). Concerning the affective side, distractions lead to stress due to difficulty to concentrate, and a negative perception of the work regardless of the actual performance (Jett & George, 2003).

Thus distractions have an equal chance to have both positive and negative effects on creativity, depending on the nature of the task, as well as the personality of the individual involved. Some individuals may need the additional cognitive stimuli from distractions to be creative, while others may struggle with attention focus in their presence. While distractions can minimize the frustrating feeling of being "stuck" and limit the experience of an impasse, we believe that due to the heightened stress and time pressure associated with them, as well as their negative effect on focus of attention and the low potential to bring useful new information and insights, distractions lead mainly to negative effects both cognitively and affectively.

IT Interruptions

For their relevance and frequency during the workday, information technology interruptions deserve special attention. IT interruptions result in a loss of 10 min per hour for managers and stop office workers 70 times per day with a task resumption time between 1 min and 24 min for each interruption (Addas & Pinsonneault, 2015; Hemp, 2009; Jackson, Dawson, & Wilson, 2003). Research examining this type of interruption relied on Distraction Conflict Theory, which considered all interruptions as competing with the primary task (Addas & Pinsonneault, 2015). Combining content relevance and content structure Addas and Pinsonneault (2015) distinguished five different IT interruption subtypes with their benefits and drawbacks on primary task performance. They found that some IT interruptions (informational intrusions, actionable intrusions, and system intrusions) decreased individual's efficiency because they diverted attention and consumed time that could be used for the primary task. Others (informational interventions and actionable interventions) improved performance outcomes by revealing information about a discrepancy between expected and actual task performance and providing additional cognitive resources, although they still consumed additional project time.

Wang, Ye, and Teo (2014) focused their attention on IT interruptions and the effect on individuals' creative thinking. When external interruptions occur, the individual puts a halt to the primary task and responds to the interruption, resulting in a fragmentation of thoughts and in processing the focal task in a disfluent manner that can lead to abstract thinking and creative cognition (Liu, 2008; Mehta, Zhu, & Cheema, 2012). However, creative tasks require a great deal of cognitive resources, and when the resources are exhausted the information processing is undermined, thus resulting in a decrease of creative performance. Given these premises, Wang et al. (2014) ascertained that IT interruptions with low cognitive resource requirements enhanced creative thinking, while IT interruptions with high cognitive resource requirements impaired creative thinking. The results indicated that individual's creative thinking could benefit from IT interruptions of low cognitive resource requirements; however, when the interruptions consume excessive cognitive resources (complex thoughts) they have a detrimental effect on creative thinking. We believe that IT interruptions influence creativity mainly through the cognitive resources they provide or consume, and less through affect. However, previous research highlights the negative effects of IT interruptions on affect as well. According to the Control Theory of Interruptions, large numbers of IT interruptions limit individuals to establish a continuous relationship with their task (Mullarkey, Jackson, Wall, Wilson, & Grey-Taylor, 1997), decreasing the expectations of making progress on the main task, thus producing feelings of stress (Carver & Scheier, 1990). Studies also referred to this mechanism as perceptions of overload that arise when there is a high quantity of IT interruption, which induce individuals' strain (Galluch, Grover, & Thatcher, 2015). Furthermore, when an IT message is off-task (i.e., the content of the message conflicts with the task), also referred to perceptual conflict, it imposes greater demands on individual's cognitive load as compared to on-task messages, thus inducing pressure and strain. However, on-task messages limit perceptual message ambiguity and perceptual conflict, and do not lead to as much stress and strain as the off-task ones (Galluch et al., 2015). Based on this evidence we believe that the cognitive and affective influences of IT interruptions on creativity are rather mixed and their effects will depend on some other factors from the context and the individuals involved such as the content relevance of the interruption, or its cognitive resource requirements as well as the susceptibility to distractions of the individuals involved.

Multitasking and Task Switching as Interruptions

Multitasking is usually defined as "undertaking multiple tasks at the same time" (Adler & Benbunan-Fich, 2013, p. 1441; Rubinstein et al., 2001). We believe that multitasking and switching to work on a different task or any task transition is also a type of interruption. Whether an individual works on multiple tasks by switching back and forth between them, or interrupts a main task to attend to another task, in both cases the person experiences an interruption in the continuous work and in the creative process on the main task. In addition, in today's organizations, employees are expected to engage in multiple tasks simultaneously (Morgan et al., 2013).

For example, they may need to analyze and report on the market research data for one client while creating a new marketing campaign for another, to solve multiple problems, often report to multiple bosses and manage multiple deadlines. Unlike distractions, IT interruptions, or breaks, multitasking and being interrupted or interrupting oneself to work on a different task requires a more complete transfer of attention to the new intervening task. In addition, the intervening task may be somewhat related to the main task or job it is interrupting or in the same domain. While working on two tasks simultaneously, task switching or interrupting one task to work on another may have similar effects to other interruptions, complex tasks require employees to dedicate their full attention to each task and avoid distractions. That is, individuals must frequently stop or interrupt their work on one task, finished or unfinished, and switch to and fully focus on another, or sometimes to continuously jump back and forth between two or more tasks (Leroy, 2009) and the multitasking literature can help us understand the effects of these actions on creativity. People may multitask because doing multiple tasks in the same timeframe gives them a sense of productivity; however, many studies suggest that when attention is divided between multiple tasks, performance decreases, especially in the case of difficult tasks (Adler & Benbunan-Fich, 2013; Bailey & Konstan, 2006; Speier, Vessey, & Valacich, 2003).

Benbunan-Fich, Adler, and Mavlanova (2011) used two principles to define multitasking: (1) task independence (i.e., tasks are self-contained), and (2) performance concurrency (i.e., tasks are at least in part performed in an overlapping timeframe). Depending on the amount of overlapping time, three strategies can be used to organize multiple tasks: sequential strategy, parallel strategy (i.e., simultaneous multitasking), and interleaved strategy (i.e., task switching and task rotation).

Sequential Multitasking

Sequential multitasking occurs when each task starts after the accomplishment of another (Bluedorn, Kaufman, & Lane, 1992). Although this is not multitasking per se and does not involve interruptions, because of the absence of time overlap, the multitasking literature usually considers the sequential task strategy as a baseline for comparing with other multitasking approaches (Adler & Benbunan-Fich, 2013). Which task is performed first and what is the nature of the next, subsequent task; task order or duration of working on each task before switching to the next may have important implications for both routine performance and creativity (Madjar & Oldham, 2002). Few research studies have investigated the effect of the nature of the preliminary (first) task on subsequent (following) task performance (Amabile, 1996; Conti, Amabile, & Pollak, 1995; Maddi, Charlens, Maddi, & Smith, 1962; Sobel & Rothenberg, 1980). Complex and challenging preliminary tasks have been shown to induce positive mood states—excitement, enthusiasm, enjoyment—and low fatigue (Madjar & Oldham, 2002; Saavedra & Kwun, 2000), which enhance cognitive and motivation processes and subsequent task performance and creativity (Isen, 1999; Vosburg, 1998). The duration of the preliminary tasks is also relevant here as simple and routine tasks induce a sense of boredom and fatigue, and may negatively influence creative performance on subsequent tasks if performed for long periods of time (Madjar & Oldham, 2002). Madjar and Oldham (2002) found that individuals engaged in a simple preliminary task for a long period or in a complex preliminary task for a brief period show higher subsequent task creativity than individuals engaged in other task and time interval, and this relationship was partially mediated by positive mood. Research has found that individuals respond more positively if they work on challenging tasks for a short period (Andrews, 1967; Katz, 1978). Thus the nature and the duration of the preliminary task may significantly influence the creativity of the subsequent task, even when we have fully sequential multitasking, through the motivational effect of engagement in the subsequent task as well as the mood created by the preliminary task as well as the cognitive resources left for the execution of the subsequent task. As the tasks are not interrupted, we do not believe this strategy will have an effect on opportunistic assimilation and incubation.

Simultaneous Multitasking, Task Switching, and Task Rotation

Parallel strategy or simultaneous multitasking happens when tasks occur at the same time or there is a perfect time overlap (Bluedorn et al., 1992). True parallel multitasking is difficult to achieve because of the difficulty of paying attention to two or more activities at the same time, and it is more frequently a continuous switching of attention between different tasks. Nevertheless, the definition of simultaneous multitasking depends on the time window considered; if the time window is the workday or the workweek, then all the tasks occurring during this time frame are considered simultaneous (Kirchberg et al., 2015).

Task switching or task interleaving occurs when a task is voluntarily or involuntarily interrupted in order to pay attention to another task (Payne, Duggan, & Neth, 2007). Task switching is often considered as a continuum where at one extreme tasks are continuously switched (e.g., every second or more often than usual), and this kind of frequent switching is similar to parallel multitasking; then we may have task rotation when individuals switch tasks intermittently to attend and work on a different task and on the other extreme of the continuum the tasks are switched after a very long span of time, similarly to what happens in sequential multitasking, although in sequential multitasking individuals finish the preliminary task and then switch to the subsequent one (Adler & Benbunan-Fich, 2013).

Multitasking in all its forms, especially the task switching type, is related to interruptions and thus presents similar beneficial and detrimental effects to what we have discussed previously. Prior works have mainly revealed negative consequences of multitasking such as a lower level of attention, increase of distractions (Leroy, 2009; Ophir et al., 2009), anxiety (Becker et al., 2013), decrease of learning (Hembrooke & Gay, 2003), and a propensity of forgetting (Einstein et al., 2003). However, Lu et al. (2017) found also a positive effect of task switching on the reduction of cognitive fixation, and in turn a positive effect on creativity. We do not know much about the influence of multitasking on affect but we expect a very mixed impact, with increase in negative affect that may be due to time pressure and experienced stress of switching tasks but also an increase in positive affect from the fresh perspective available from switching tasks often.

Important Factors Determining the Positive or Negative Influence of Interruptions and Multitasking on Creativity

So far we reviewed two theoretical mechanisms through which job design and in particular interruptions and multitasking may influence creativity and the creative process—first, through the provision or depletion of cognitive resources, and second, through their effect on positive and negative affect. The evidence so far though is inconclusive and we believe that there are certain important factors, both as personality characteristics and as part of the job design and context that may change these relationships.

Time and Frequency of Interruptions

All of the previous examples of multitasking and interruptions involve different frequency and timing of the interruption/switching and we believe that the timing of the interruption may have critical effects on creativity. Madjar et al. (in press) considered the timing of switching between tasks (earlier vs later) and found that switching later in the work on a creative task was more beneficial for creativity than interrupting the work earlier. Lu et al. (2017) also investigated the effect of timing and frequency and found that individuals who continually rotate tasks by switching back and forth between two creativity tasks, showed a higher level of performance than individuals who switched tasks at their discretion, and than individuals who engaged in a single task for half of the allotted time and then switched to the other task for the remaining time. These results revealed the relevance of encouraging continuous task switching in order to have a higher creative performance; however, people are usually not aware of the benefits of continuous task switching, and do not choose the right switching strategy or fail to adopt a continual-switching approach, unaware of the positive outcomes for creativity (Lu et al., 2017).

Discretion to Multitask/Interrupt

If interruptions and multitasking potentially can produce both positive and negative effects, to understand better their impact it may be critical to pay attention also to the autonomy or discretion individuals have for structuring their work or the choice to switch tasks or take a break as part of the task context. The choice to interrupt a task and switch to another one could be the result of negative triggers such as frustration, obstruction, and exhaustion that induce individuals to stop in order to replenish the cognitive resources. It could also be the result of positive triggers that encourage individuals to interrupt the task in order to engage in exploratory behavior or allow incubation to occur (Adler & Benbunan-Fich, 2013). Thus having the control and autonomy to stop working on a task and take a break or switch, when you feel that it may be beneficial, may be the critical factor for increasing creativity. Madjar and Shalley (2008) investigated the effect of discretion in task switching on creative performance, and found that discretion was important for creativity for cognitive replenishment, particularly under high goal conditions. Moreover, having a goal on the intervening task, as well as on the creative tasks, helped individuals to have higher levels of focus of attention and to experience incubation when they had discretion to switch tasks.

Domain and Nature of Intervening Activity/Break

One of the benefits of interruptions and multitasking is to reduce stress and exhaustion and facilitate incubation, but this does not happen in a vacuum. While the intervening activity or alternate task may provide enough opportunities for cognitive stimulation and opportunistic assimilation, the individual needs to be able to identify these additional cognitive resources and link them back (associate them) with ideas and solutions for the creative task. If the activity during the break or the alternative task is too removed from the domain of the main task, it may be hard to bring the new resources back to the creative task. In this respect Madjar et al. (in press) highlighted the importance of intervening tasks that are in the same domain as the main creative task to facilitate remote associations and creativity after interruptions of work on the main task.

In addition, if in multitasking both tasks are equally complex and cognitively exhausting and using the same cognitive resources, it may be hard to replenish one's cognitive assets by just switching to another hard-creative task, and an intervening task that is not cognitively taxing and requires a different kind of cognitive resources may be more appropriate (Madjar et al., in press; Madjar & Shalley, 2008). Eliav and Miron-Spektor (2015) also found that the effect of interruptions on creativity is stronger when the primary task is a divergent thinking task instead of a convergent thinking one.

Polychronicity and Other Personality Characteristics

While we note so far certain conditions that may make interruptions and multitasking more beneficial or detrimental for creativity, another important factor, together with the context, is the individual involved and his personality characteristics. For example, polychronicity—or the number of tasks and conditions an individual prefers to be involved at one time (Bluedorn, Kalliath, Strube, & Martin, 1999)—may be a critical factor in determining whether an individual will benefit from interruptions and multitasking. Madjar and Oldham (2006), for example, found that individuals who prefer involvement in multiple tasks benefit from multitasking and task rotation for creativity, while individuals low on polychronicity do not, as they experience the task switching as higher level of task pressure. The same applies to individuals who can easily refocus their attention after switching tasks. Some other personality dimensions, like openness to experience, introversion and extroversion, abstractedness, emotional stability and sensitivity (Guastello, Guastello, & Guastello, 2014), or different affective states may also play a role. For example, individuals high on openness to experience may benefit more from the opportunistic assimilation and the additional cognitive resources encountered through interruptions and multitasking and be able to take advantage of them, while individuals with low openness to experience may not be able to appreciate them.

CONCLUSIONS, IMPLICATIONS, AND FUTURE DIRECTIONS

In this chapter, we have sought to theorize the cognitive and affective mechanisms through which different types of job design and in particular, interruptions and different multitasking configurations, can influence individual creativity. We review the research and evidence on how different types of interruptions and multitasking can have differential effects, both positive and negative, on cognitive resources and affect and through these mechanisms on creativity. We also review and suggest some conditions and factors, such as time and frequency of interruptions, discretion to multitask, nature of intervening task, and polychronicity that may influence the relation between interruptions and creativity.

Although different types of interruptions have been considered previously (Jett & George, 2003), research is still lacking in differentiating their effects on creative performance. Based on our review, it is important to better understand which type of interruptions could be beneficial for creativity and organizations should encourage and which ones should be suppressed. Our review suggests that organizations can structure tasks and interruptions in a way to facilitate incubation by using the interruptions to replenish cognitive resources and influence affective states. For example, to avoid some of the detrimental effects of interruptions on creativity, organizations could provide interruption-free work time (no IT interruptions) or facilitate interruption anticipation by scheduling or grouping them (Carton & Aiello, 2009; Foroughi, Werner, Barragán, & Boehm-Davis, 2015). Supervisors can also use interruptions wisely as tools to prevent the psychological state of impasse, avoid cognitive fixation, and trigger a refreshment of ideas and problem-solving ability (Beeftink et al., 2008; Eliav & Miron-Spektor, 2015). Breaks seem to be more beneficial than intrusions or IT interruptions and in this respect organizations may be able to manage some interruptions and incorporate them as breaks or make employees aware of their effects, so individuals are able to manage and control the amount of interruptions, for example, IT interruptions, they receive during the creative process.

Multitasking configurations, like interruptions, seem to present both positive and negative consequences, like attention residue, absence of cognitive closure, increase in distractions (Leroy, 2009), and time pressure (Madjar & Oldham, 2006). However, they could also enhance creativity by increasing energetic activation (Kapadia, 2016), exploratory behavior, and incubation time (Adler & Benbunan-Fich, 2013). Thus more research is needed to clarify when multitasking could be beneficial, in which organizational setting and for which tasks. The literature also shows that the combination of goal setting and discretion to switch tasks is beneficial for task creativity (Madjar & Shalley, 2008), therefore suggesting to supervisors to set goals for each task but also to let employees autonomously decide when to change tasks. As Madjar et al. (in press), the timing of switching between tasks (later rather than earlier) and switching to a task in the same domain (rather than a completely unrelated task or activity) can also facilitate creative performance. However, future studies should investigate further the right task-switching time or scheduling, as well as the influence of the individuals' pacing patterns to reach a deadline (Baird et al., 2012).

As the multitasking literature indicates, the effect of interruptions and multitasking may be related to individual characteristics such as polychronicity, openness to experience, stress toleration, working memory capacity (Courage, Bakhtiar, Fitzpatrick, Kenny, & Brandeau, 2015; Morgan et al., 2013). Organizations that value multitasking could try to match employees' personality to particular multitasking configurations. Similarly, individuals who present high levels of traits like polychronicity could be assigned to task rotation and multitasking jobs or in teams that have to work on multiple projects.

We believe that one of the biggest implications of our review is that managers and individuals need to be aware of the differential effects of interruptions and multitasking on creativity as well as the conditions that may make them more valuable. The evidence suggests that breaks associated with individual discretion to take them as well as switching tasks to other tasks that are engaging but not cognitively exhausting or task configurations that facilitate positive emotions and relieve stress may provide more cognitive and affective benefits than costs for creativity. In this respect, breaks, which are anticipated, and switching to cognitively different tasks as well as having the discretion to take a break or switch tasks may be very important. In addition, the frequency or the number of breaks may play a critical role as well as the personality of the individuals involved. While one or two interruptions or distractions may provide some cognitive benefits and facilitate new idea cues and different perspectives, many breaks may lead to cognitive exhaustion and require a lot of attention resources to refocus on the task and be perceived as a detriment rather than a benefit. These are just some ways in which interruptions and multitasking configurations can facilitate creativity and they raise a multitude of interesting opportunities for future research.

References

Addas, S., & Pinsonneault, A. (2015). The many faces of information technology interruptions: a taxonomy and preliminary investigation of their performance effects. *Information Systems Journal*, 25(3), 231–273.

Adler, R. F., & Benbunan-Fich, R. (2013). Self-interruptions in discretionary multitasking. *Computers in Human Behavior*, 29(4), 1441–1449.

Amabile, T. M. (1996). *Creativity in context*. Boulder, CO: Westview.

Andrews, F. M. (1967). Creative ability, the laboratory environment, and scientific performance. *IEEE Transactions on Engineering Management*, 14, 76–83.

Bailey, B. P., & Konstan, J. A. (2006). On the need for attention-aware systems: measuring effects of interruption on task performance, error rate, and affective state. *Computers in Human Behavior*, 22(4), 685–708.

Baird, B., Smallwood, J., Mrazek, M. D., Kam, J. W., Franklin, M. S., & Schooler, J. W. (2012). Inspired by distraction mind wandering facilitates creative incubation. *Psychological Science*, 23(10), 1117–1122.

Baron, R. A. (1994). The physical environment of work settings: effects on task performance, interpersonal relations, and job satisfaction. In B. Staw & L. Cummings (Eds.), Vol. 16. *Research in organizational behavior* (pp. 1–46). Greenwich, CT: JAI.

Beal, D. J., Weiss, H. M., Barros, E., & MacDermid, S. M. (2005). An episodic process model of affective influences on performance. *Journal of Applied Psychology*, 90(6), 1054–1068.

Becker, M. W., Alzahabi, R., & Hopwood, C. J. (2013). Media multitasking is associated with symptoms of depression and social anxiety. *Cyberpsychology, Behavior, and Social Networking*, 16(2), 132–135.

Beeftink, F., Van Eerde, W., & Rutte, C. G. (2008). The effect of interruptions and breaks on insight and impasses: do you need a break right now? *Creativity Research Journal*, 20(4), 358–364.

Benbunan-Fich, R., Adler, R. F., & Mavlanova, T. (2011). Measuring multi-tasking behavior with activity-based metrics. *ACM Transactions on Computer–Human Interaction*, 18(2), 1–22.

Bluedorn, A. C., Kalliath, T. J., Strube, M. J., & Martin, G. D. (1999). Polychronicity and the inventory of Polychronic values (IPV) the development of an instrument to measure a fundamental dimension of organizational culture. *Journal of Managerial Psychology*, 14(3/4), 205–231.

Bluedorn, A. C., Kaufman, C. F., & Lane, P. M. (1992). How many things do you like to do at once? An introduction to monochronic and polychronic time. *The Executive, 6,* 17–26.

Brief, A. P., & Roberson, L. (1989). Job attitude organization: an exploratory study. *Journal of Applied Social Psychology, 19*(9), 717–727.

Burke, M. J., Brief, A. P., George, J. M., Roberson, L., & Webster, J. (1989). Measuring affect at work: confirmatory analyses of competing mood structures with conceptual linkage to cortical regulatory systems. *Journal of Personality and Social Psychology, 57*(6), 1091–1102.

Carr, N. (2010). *The shallows: What the internet is doing to our brains.* New York: W.W. North & Company.

Carton, A. M., & Aiello, J. R. (2009). Control and anticipation of social interruptions: reduced stress and improved task Performance1. *Journal of Applied Social Psychology, 39*(1), 169–185.

Carver, C. S., & Scheier, M. F. (1990). Origins and functions of positive and negative affect: a control-process view. *Psychological Review, 97,* 19–35.

Christensen, B. T., & Schunn, C. D. (2005). Spontaneous access and analogical incubation effects. *Creativity Research Journal, 17*(2–3), 207–220.

Coget, J. F., Shani, A. B. R., & Solari, L. (2014). The lone genius, or leaders who tyrannize their creative teams. *Organizational Dynamics, 43*(2), 105–113.

Conley, D. (2011). Wired for distraction: kids and social media. *Time Magazine, 19,* 44–46.

Conti, R., Amabile, T. M., & Pollak, S. (1995). The positive impact of creative activity: effects of creative task engagement and motivational focus on college students' learning. *Personality and Social Psychology Bulletin, 21,* 1107–1116.

Courage, M. L., Bakhtiar, A., Fitzpatrick, C., Kenny, S., & Brandeau, K. (2015). Growing up multitasking: the costs and benefits for cognitive development. *Developmental Review, 35,* 5–41.

Csikszentmihalyi, M. (1975). *Beyond boredom and anxiety.* San Francisco: Jossey-Bass.

Csikszentmihalyi, M., & Sawyer, K. (1995). Creative insight: the social dimension of a solitary moment. In R. J. Sternberg & J. E. Davidson (Eds.), *The nature of insight* (pp. 329–363). Cambridge, MA: MIT Press.

Davis, M. A. (2009). Understanding the relationship between mood and creativity: a meta-analysis. *Organizational Behavior and Human Decision Processes, 108,* 25–38.

Demerouti, E., Bakker, A. B., Nachreiner, F., & Schaufeli, W. B. (2001). The job demands-resources model of burnout. *Journal of Applied Psychology, 86*(3), 499–512.

Dijksterhuis, A., & Meurs, T. (2006). Where creativity resides: the generative power of unconscious thought. *Consciousness and Cognition, 15,* 135–146.

Einstein, G. O., McDaniel, M. A., Williford, C. L., Pagan, J. L., & Dismukes, R. (2003). Forgetting of intentions in demanding situations is rapid. *Journal of Experimental Psychology: Applied, 9*(3), 147–162.

Eliav, E., & Miron-Spektor, E. (2015). In *The recovery effect: the creative potential of frequent interruptions Academy of management proceedings (Vol. 2015, No. 1, p. 18083)*: Academy of Management.

Elsbach, K. D., & Hargadon, A. B. (2006). Enhancing creativity through "mindless" work: a framework of workday design. *Organization Science, 17*(4), 470–483.

Eyrolle, H., & Cellier, J. M. (2000). The effects of interruptions in work activity: field and laboratory results. *Applied Ergonomics, 31,* 537–543.

Foroughi, C. K., Werner, N. E., Barragán, D., & Boehm-Davis, D. A. (2015). Interruptions disrupt reading comprehension. *Journal of Experimental Psychology: General, 144*(3), 704–709.

Foroughi, C. K., Werner, N. E., Nelson, E. T., & Boehm-Davis, D. A. (2014). Do interruptions affect quality of work? *Human Factors, 56*(7), 1262–1271.

Galluch, P. S., Grover, V., & Thatcher, J. B. (2015). Interrupting the workplace: examining stressors in an information technology context. *Journal of the Association for Information Systems, 16*(1), 1–47.

Garg, P., & Rastogi, R. (2006). New model of job design: motivating employees' performance. *Journal of Management Development, 25*(6), 572–587.

George, J. M. (1991). State or trait: effects of positive mood on prosocial behaviors at work. *Journal of Applied Psychology, 76*(2), 299–307.

George, J. M., & Brief, A. P. (1992). Feeling good-doing good: a conceptual analysis of the mood at work-organizational spontaneity relationship. *Psychological Bulletin, 112*(2), 310–329.

George, J. M., & Zhou, J. (2002). Understanding when bad moods foster creativity and good ones don't: the role of context and clarity of feelings. *Journal of Applied Psychology, 87*(4), 687–697.

Gillie, T., & Broadbent, D. (1989). What makes interruptions disruptive? A study of length, similarity, and complexity. *Psychological Research, 50*(4), 243–250.

Gollwitzer, P. M. (1990). Action phases and mind-sets. In E. T. Higgins & R. M. Sorrentino (Eds.), Vol. 2. *Handbook of motivation and cognition* (pp. 53–92). New York: Guilford Press.

Guastello, A. D., Guastello, S. J., & Guastello, D. D. (2014). Personality trait theory and multitasking performance: implications for ergonomic design. *Theoretical Issues in Ergonomics Science, 15*(5), 432–450.

Gupta, A., Sharda, R., & Greve, R. A. (2011). You've got email! Does it really matter to process emails now or later? *Information Systems Frontiers, 13*(5), 637–653.

Hembrooke, H., & Gay, G. (2003). The laptop and the lecture: the effects of multitasking in learning environments. *Journal of Computing in Higher Education, 15*(1), 46–64.

Hemp, P. (2009). Death by information overload. *Harvard Business Review, 87*(9), 83–89.

Hobfoll, S. E. (1989). Conservation of resources: a new attempt at conceptualizing stress. *American Psychologist, 44*(3), 513–524.

Huelsman, T. J., Nemanick, R.C.J.R., & Munz, D. C. (1998). Scales to measure four dimensions of dispositional mood: positive energy, tiredness, negative activation, and relaxation. *Educational and Psychological Measurement, 58*(5), 804–819.

Isen, A. M. (1999). On the relationship between affect and creative problem solving. In S. Russ (Ed.), *Affect, creative experience, and psychological adjustment* (pp. 3–17). Philadelphia: Brunner/Mazel.

Jackson, T., Dawson, R., & Wilson, D. (2003). Reducing the effect of email interruptions on employees. *International Journal of Information Management, 23*(1), 55–65.

Jett, Q. R., & George, J. M. (2003). Work interrupted: a closer look at the role of interruptions in organizational life. *Academy of Management Review, 28*(3), 494–507.

Johnson, R. E., Chang, C. H., & Lord, R. G. (2006). Moving from cognition to behavior: what the research says. *Psychological Bulletin, 132*(3), 381–415.

Kahn, W. A. (1992). To be fully there: psychological presence at work. *Human Relations, 45*(4), 321–349.

Kanfer, R., & Ackerman, P. L. (1989). Motivation and cognitive abilities: an integrative/aptitude-treatment interaction approach to skill acquisition. *Journal of Applied Psychology, 74*(4), 657–690.

Kapadia, C. (2016). In *Doing more in less time: how multitasking increases creativity Academy of management proceedings (Vol. 2016, No. 1, p. 17543)*: Academy of Management.

Katz, R. (1978). Job longevity as a situational factor in job satisfaction. *Administrative Science Quarterly, 23*, 204–223.

Kim, S., Park, Y., & Niu, Q. (2017). Micro-break activities at work to recover from daily work demands. *Journal of Organizational Behavior, 38*(1), 28–44.

Kirchberg, D. M., Roe, R. A., & Van Eerde, W. (2015). Polychronicity and multitasking: a diary study at work. *Human Performance, 28*(2), 112–136.

Kirmeyer, S. L. (1988). Coping with competing demands—interruption and the type-a pattern. *Journal of Applied Psychology, 73*, 621–629.

Leroy, S. (2009). Why is it so hard to do my work? The challenge of attention residue when switching between work tasks. *Organizational Behavior and Human Decision Processes, 109*(2), 168–181.

Lin, B. C., Kain, J. M., & Fritz, C. (2013). Don't interrupt me! An examination of the relationship between intrusions at work and employee strain. *International Journal of Stress Management, 20*(2), 77–94.

Liu, W. (2008). Focusing on desirability: the effect of decision interruption and suspension on preferences. *Journal of Consumer Research, 35*(4), 640–652.

Lu, J. G., Akinola, M., & Mason, M. F. (2017). "Switching on" creativity: task switching can increase creativity by reducing cognitive fixation. *Organizational Behavior and Human Decision Processes, 139*, 63–75.

Maddi, S. R., Charlens, A. M., Maddi, D. A., & Smith, A. J. (1962). Effects of monotony and novelty on imaginative productions. *Journal of Personality, 30*, 513–527.

Madjar, N., & Oldham, G. R. (2002). Preliminary tasks and creative performance on a subsequent task: effects of time on preliminary tasks and amount of information about the subsequent task. *Creativity Research Journal, 14*(2), 239–251.

Madjar, N., & Oldham, G. R. (2006). Task rotation and polychronicity: effects on individuals' creativity. *Human Performance, 19*(2), 117–131.

Madjar, N., & Shalley, C. E. (2008). Multiple tasks' and multiple goals' effect on creativity: forced incubation or just a distraction? *Journal of Management, 34*(4), 786–805.

Madjar N., Shalley C. E. & Herndon B. (in press). Taking time to incubate: the moderating role of 'what you do' and 'when you do it' on creative performance, *Journal of Creative Behavior*.

Mainemelis, C., & Ronson, S. (2006). Ideas are born in fields of play: towards a theory of play and creativity in organizational settings. *Research in Organizational Behavior, 27*, 81–131.

Mayseless, O., & Kruglanski, A. W. (1987). What makes you so sure? Effects of epistemic motivations on judgmental confidence. *Organizational Behavior and Human Decision Processes, 39*(2), 162–183.

Mehta, R., Zhu, R., & Cheema, A. (2012). Is noise always bad? Exploring the effects of ambient noise on creative cognition. *Journal of Consumer Research, 39*(4), 784–799.

Meijman, T. F., & Mulder, G. (1998). Psychological aspects of workload. In P. J. D. Drenth & H. Thierry (Eds.), Vol. 2. *Handbook of work and organizational psychology* (pp. 5–33). Hove: Psychology Press.

Morgan, B., D'Mello, S., Abbott, R., Radvansky, G., Haass, M., & Tamplin, A. (2013). Individual differences in multitasking ability and adaptability. *Human Factors, 55*, 776–788.

Mullarkey, S., Jackson, P. R., Wall, T. D., Wilson, J. R., & Grey-Taylor, S. M. (1997). The impact of technology characteristics and job control on worker mental health. *Journal of Organizational Behavior, 18*(5), 471–489.

Oldham, G. R., Cummings, A., Mischel, L. J., Schmidtke, J. M., & Zhou, J. (1995). Listen while you work? Quasi-experimental relations between personal-stereo headset use and employee work responses. *Journal of Applied Psychology, 80*(5), 547–563.

Oldham, G. R., Kulik, C. T., & Stepina, L. P. (1991). Physical environments and employee reactions: effects of stimulus-screening skills and job complexity. *Academy of Management Journal, 34*(4), 929–938.

Ophir, E., Nass, C., & Wagner, A. D. (2009). *Proceedings of the National Academy of Sciences, 106*(37), 15583–15587.

Parker, S. K., Morgeson, F. P., & Johns, G. (2017). One hundred years of work design research: looking back and looking forward. *Journal of Applied Psychology, 102*(3), 403–420.

Patalano, A. L., & Seifert, C. M. (1994). Memory for impasses during problem solving. *Memory & Cognition, 22*, 234–242.

Payne, S. J., Duggan, G. B., & Neth, H. (2007). Discretionary task interleaving: heuristics for time allocation in cognitive foraging. *Journal of Experimental Psychology: General, 136*(3), 370–388.

Perlow, L. A. (1999). The time famine: toward a sociology of work time. *Administrative Science Quarterly, 44*(1), 57–81.

Ratwani, R. M., Trafton, J. G., & Myers, C. (2006). In *Helpful or harmful? Examining the effects of interruptions on task performance Proceedings of the human factors and ergonomics society annual meeting (Vol. 50, No. 3, pp. 372–375)*: Sage Publications.

Reiter-Palmon, R., Mumford, M. D., Boes, O. J., & Runco, M. A. (1997). Problem construction and creativity: the role of ability, cue consistency, and active processing. *Creativity Research Journal, 10*, 9–24.

Rubinstein, J. S., Meyer, D. E., & Evans, J. E. (2001). Executive control of cognitive processes in task switching. *Journal of Experimental Psychology: Human Perception and Performance, 27*(4), 763–797.

Saavedra, R., & Kwun, S. K. (2000). Affective states in job characteristics theory. *Journal of Organizational Behavior, 21*, 131–146.

Segal, E. (2004). Incubation in insight problem solving. *Creativity Research Journal, 16*(1), 141–148.

Seifert, C. M., Meyer, D. E., Davidson, N., Patalano, A. L., & Yaniv, I. (1995). Demystification of cognitive insight: opportunistic assimilation and the prepared-mind perspective. In R. J. Sternberg & J. E. Davidson (Eds.), *The nature of insight* (pp. 65–124). Cambridge, MA: MIT Press.

Shalley, C. E., Zhou, J., & Oldham, G. R. (2004). The effects of personal and contextual characteristics on creativity: where should we go from here? *Journal of Management, 30*, 933–958.

Sio, U. N., & Ormerod, T. C. (2009). Does incubation enhance problem solving? A meta-analytic review. *Psychological Bulletin, 135*, 94–120.

Smith, S. M., & Dodds, R. A. (1999). Incubation. In M. A. Runco & S. R. Pritzker (Eds.), *Encyclopedia of creativity* (pp. 39–43). London: Academic Press.

Sobel, R. S., & Rothenberg, A. (1980). Artistic creation as stimulated by superimposed versus separated visual images. *Journal of Personality and Social Psychology, 39*, 953–961.

Speier, C., Valacich, J. S., & Vessey, I. (1999). The influence of task interruption on individual decision making: an information overload perspective. *Decision Sciences, 30*(2), 337–360.

Speier, C., Vessey, I., & Valacich, J. S. (2003). The effects of interruptions, task complexity, and information presentation on computer-supported decision-making performance. *Decision Sciences, 34*(4), 771–797.

Spira, J. B., & Feintuch, J. B. (2005). *The cost of not paying attention: how interruptions impact knowledge worker productivity*. New York, NY: Basex, Inc.

Tams, S., Thatcher, J., Grover, V., & Pak, R. (2015). Selective attention as a protagonist in contemporary workplace stress: implications for the interruption age. *Anxiety, Stress, & Coping, 28*(6), 663–686.

To, M. L., Fisher, C. D., Ashkanasy, N. M., & Rowe, P. A. (2012). Within-person relationships between mood and creativity. *Journal of Applied Psychology, 97*(3), 599–612.

Vosburg, S. K. (1998). The effects of positive and negative mood on divergent-thinking performance. *Creativity Research Journal, 11*, 165–172.

Wajcman, J., & Rose, E. (2011). Constant connectivity: rethinking interruptions at work. *Organization Studies, 32*(7), 941–961.

Wallas, G. (1926). *The art of thought*. New York: Harcourt.

Wang, X., Ye, S., & Teo, H. H. (2014). In *Effects of interruptions on creative thinking. Proceedings of the 35th international conference on information systems.*Auckland: New Zealand.

Watson, D., & Pennebaker, J. W. (1989). Health complaints, stress, and distress: exploring the central role of negative affectivity. *Psychological Review, 96*(2), 234–254.

Watson, D., & Tellegen, A. (1985). Toward a consensual structure of mood. *Psychological Bulletin, 98*(2), 219–235.

Zhong, C. B., Dijksterhuis, A., & Galinsky, A. D. (2008). The merits of unconscious thought in creativity. *Psychological Science, 19*(9), 912–918.

Zhou, J., & Hoever, I. J. (2014). Research on workplace creativity: a review and redirection. *Annual Reviews of Organizational Psychology and Organizational Behavior, 1*(1), 333–359.

Zijlstra, F. R., Roe, R. A., Leonora, A. B., & Krediet, I. (1999). Temporal factors in mental work: effects of interrupted activities. *Journal of Occupational and Organizational Psychology, 72*(2), 163–185.

Further Reading

Altmann, E. M., & Trafton, J. G. (2004). Task interruption: Resumption lag and the role of cues. *Proceedings of the 26th annual conference of the cognitive science society,* 42–47.

Monk, C. A. (2004). In *The effect of frequent versus infrequent interruptions on primary task resumption Proceedings of the human factors and ergonomics society annual meeting (Vol. 48, No. 3, pp. 295–299)*: SAGE Publications.

The Skills Needed to Think Creatively: Within-Process and Cross-Process Skills

Michael D. Mumford, Erin Michelle Todd,
Cory Higgs, Samantha Elliott
The University of Oklahoma, Norman, OK, United States

Although creativity has been defined in many ways, in recent years a consensus has emerged as to what we mean when we use the term creativity (Mumford, 2003). Creativity is held to require the production of high quality, original, and elegant solutions (Besemer & O'Quin, 1999; Christiaans, 2002) to complex, novel, ill defined, or poorly structured, problems (Mumford & Gustafson, 2007). Of course, many variables influence peoples' ability to produce creative solutions to the kinds of problems that call for creative thought, including intelligence (Vincent, Decker, & Mumford, 2002), divergent thinking (Acar & Runco, 2012), and personality attributes, such as openness (Feist & Gorman, 1998), as well as interest and intrinsic motivation (Zhang & Bartol, 2010).

We do not wish to dispute the importance of these, and a number of other variables, that influence peoples' performance in solving the kind of problems that call for creative thought. However, creativity ultimately requires the production of problem solutions. As a result, it seems plausible to argue, in keeping with Weisberg (2011), that creative thinking requires domain-specific knowledge or expertise (Baer, 1998; Weisberg, 2011). However, it is not sufficient simply to have expertise—if this was the case all experts would be creative. Rather, what appears to be critical is the way people work with knowledge to generate creative problem solutions (Mumford, Medeiros, & Partlow, 2012).

In the present effort, we will examine the ways, or strategies, people use to generate creative problem solutions. To provide a background for this discussion, we will begin by examining the processes people must execute to produce creative problem solutions. Subsequently, we will examine the strategies used in process execution that contribute to creative performance. After examining these process-specific skills, we will then examine a set of creative thinking skills—for example, causal analysis, error analysis, and forecasting—that appear to contribute to the effective execution of multiple creative thinking processes. In addition, the implications of our observations with respect to these within and cross-process creative thinking skills for the assessment and development of creative potential will be discussed.

CREATIVE THINKING PROCESSES

For many years it has been recognized that the production of high quality, original, and elegant solutions to novel, complex, and ill-defined problems depended on the ways people work with domain-relevant knowledge. Put somewhat differently, to produce creative problem solutions people must work with available knowledge in new, or unique, ways. Accordingly, for many years, students of creativity have sought to identify the key processing activities contributing to creative problem-solving (e.g., Dewey, 1910; Finke, Ward, & Smith, 1992; Parnes & Noller, 1972; Sternberg & O'Hara, 1999; Wallas, 1928). A review of the various attempts to define critical creative thinking processes, conducted by Mumford, Mobley, Uhlman, Reiter-Palmon, and Doares (1991), led to the identification of eight core processes involved in most incidents of creative problem-solving: (1) problem definition or problem construction (Mumford, Reiter-Palmon, & Redmond, 1994), (2) information gathering (Mumford, Baughman, Supinski, & Maher, 1996), (3) concept selection (Mumford, Baughman, Supinski, & Anderson, 1998), (4) conceptual combination and reorganization (Baughman & Mumford, 1995), (5) idea generation (Eubanks, Murphy, & Mumford, 2010), (6) idea evaluation (Lonergan, Scott, & Mumford, 2004), (7) implementation planning (Osburn & Mumford, 2006), and (8) adaptive solution monitoring (Mumford & Hunter, 2005). Fig. 1 presents an illustration of the model of the key processing activities held to contribute to creative problem-solving (Mumford et al., 1991).

The model begins with the assumption that creative problem-solving starts with identification of a problem and a search for information, either internal or external searches, which is then understood in terms of relevant, conceptual, case based, and experiential knowledge structures (Hunter, Bedell-Avers, Hunsicker, Mumford, & Ligon, 2008). Critical to creative problem-solving, however, is the combination and/or reorganization of the knowledge which provides a basis for the generation of

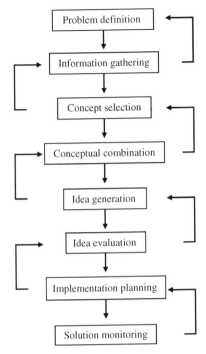

FIG. 1   Creative problem-solving processes.

new ideas (Estes & Ward, 2002; Mobley, Doares, & Mumford, 1992). Plans for problem-solving using these ideas are formulated and plan execution monitored (Caughron & Mumford, 2008). These processes are held to operate sequentially with people cycling back to an earlier process (e.g., problem definition) if execution of a given process (e.g., information gathering) proves inadequate. Moreover, errors are held to carry through all processes. Thus errors in problem definition will lead to inadequate information gathering.

Mumford and his colleagues have conducted an ongoing set of studies intended to assess key propositions arising from the model. For example, Redmond, Mumford, and Teach (1993) asked undergraduates to formulate advertising campaigns for a new product, the 3D holographic television, where plans were evaluated by marketing executives for quality and originality. A manipulation intended to encourage problem construction was found to result in solutions of higher quality and originality. Scott, Lonergan, and Mumford (2005) presented participants with multiple concepts of cases reflecting the same concepts and asked participants to formulate plans for leading an experimental secondary school. When participants engaged in activities contributing to successful combination and organization efforts, plans of greater quality and originality were obtained. Osburn and Mumford (2006) provided participants with training to influence their implementation planning and found that better implementation planning resulted in production of higher quality and more original creative problem solutions.

Other studies have served to demonstrate the relevance of each of these eight processes to the production of creative problem solutions using different creative problem-solving tasks and different methods (Dailey & Mumford, 2006; Licuanan, Dailey, & Mumford, 2007; Lonergan et al., 2004; Mumford, Baughman, Maher, Costanza, & Supinski, 1997; Mumford, Baughman, Supinski, & Maher, 1996; Reiter-Palmon, Mumford, O'Connor Boes, & Runco, 1997). Therefore evidence is available for the relevance of each process to creative problem-solving. Moreover, Mumford, Supinski, Baughman, Costanza, and Threlfall (1997) have shown that effective execution of *each* of these processes makes a unique contribution to the production of creative problem-solving performance. Still other work by Mumford, Antes, Caughron, Connelly, and Beeler (2010) has shown that effective execution of all of these processes are positively related to creative problem-solving across different domains of creative activity—although the significance of a particular process may vary as a function of the domain.

In still another study seeking to provide evidence for this model, Friedrich and Mumford (2009) asked undergraduates to solve a marketing problem calling for creative thought. At various points during execution of certain processes (e.g., problem definition, conceptual combination), errors were induced by presenting participants with conflicting information as they worked through a given processing activity. Performance in the processing activity was assessed based on judges' appraisals of responses to a sequence of "prompt" questions. In accordance with this model, it was found that errors flowed through the various processing activities. Other more recent work by Medeiros (2016) has provided confirmation for this conclusion based on imposition of constraints rather than imposition of conflicting information. Thus not only does performance in executing each of these processes contribute to creative problem-solving, the model of process relationships proposed also seems to hold.

SKILLS IN PROCESS EXECUTION

Having provided some evidence for Mumford et al.'s (1991) model of creative problem-solving processes, a new question comes to fore: What skills must people possess to execute each of these processes? Process execution skills are often subsumed under the rubric strategies. And, research on the strategies contributing to effective execution of each of these processes has allowed us to begin to formulate some understanding of requisite process execution skills.

Problem Construction

In a study of problem construction, Mumford, Baughman, Threlfall, Supinski, and Costanza (1996) asked 124 undergraduates to provide solutions to both marketing problems and public policy problems calling for creative thought. Judges appraised problem solutions for quality and originality. Prior to working on these problems, however, participants were presented with a measure intended to assess preferences for working with different types of information in problem definition. Here participants were asked to read through descriptions of complex problems and select from a list of sixteen redefinitions the four they believed to be most useful to work with. These redefinitions reflected goal restatements, procedures to be employed, key information, and restrictions or constraints. It was found that highest quality and most original solutions were obtained when people redefined problems with respect to solution procedures and constraints. Thus skill in working with key procedures and skill in the analysis of constraints contributes to problem definition.

Medeiros (2016) examined constraint analysis skill vis-à-vis multiple processes involved in creative thought: conceptual combination and idea generation. She found that constraint analysis skills were most important for creative problem-solving when applied during problem construction. In this regard, however, it is important to bear in mind the findings of Medeiros, Partlow, and Mumford (2014), which indicated that creative problem-solving is disrupted if too few, or too many, constraints are considered in problem definition. Based on this research, it seems plausible to argue constraint analysis skills must focus on critical constraints, especially constraints which might be modified, or acted on, in subsequent problem-solving activities.

Information Gathering

Mumford, Baughman, Supinski, and Maher (1996) examined information gathering skills in a study of 137 undergraduates. In this study, participants were asked to prepare marketing campaigns for a new product, a 3D holographic television, where the resulting marketing plans were appraised by judges for quality and originality. Prior to starting work on this creative task, participants were presented with four other creative problems and a series of cards reflecting information bearing on these problems. The cards presented, however, varied with respect to the type of information on them: (1) key factual data, (2) incongruent or anomalous information, (3) principles that might help solve the problem, (4) information bearing on additional goals, (5) information bearing on restrictions, and (6) diverse information. The time participants spent reading each card was recorded to measure intensity of processing. It was found that those producing the highest quality and most original solutions were those who spent more time processing key facts and anomalies. Apparently, skill in search for both critical information *and* information inconsistent with other facts appears to contribute to creative problem-solving.

Of course, expertise contributes to peoples' ability to recognize and work with key facts and anomalies in problem-solving (Ericsson, 2009). However, skill in identifying anomalies is likely also to require extended search and a willingness to avoid premature closure (Finke et al., 1992). Hunter et al. (2008) examined how various types of information—conceptual, associational, and case based—were related to the production of creative solutions to a social innovation problem where problem solutions were appraised by judges for quality, originality, and elegance. They found that the most creative problem solutions emerged when case-based, experiential knowledge was employed, along with either conceptual or associational knowledge. Accordingly, information gathering may also require skill in integrating facts and anomalies with personal experience gained in working on other, relevant creative problems.

Concept Selection

Not only must information be integrated with experience to guide information gathering, but also the information obtained must be organized. In an initial study of information organization, or concept selection, on creative thinking, Mumford, Supinski, Threlfall, and Baughman (1996) asked 135 undergraduates to produce solutions to a creative problem-solving task where judges appraised solutions for quality and originality. Prior to working on this task, however, participants were presented with a series of novel, ill-defined problems and a set of concepts that might be used in problem-solving, where concepts differed with respect to content. It was found that the most creative problem solutions were produced by those who preferred to employ long-range, macro organizing concepts when working on creative problems.

Of course, concepts are not isolated entities. Rather, concepts come in integrated sets. These integrated sets of concept outcome linkages are referred to as mental models (Goldvarg & Johnson-Laird, 2001; Ward, Patterson, & Sifonis, 2004). Mumford et al. (2012) devised a set of procedures where people were taught how to illustrate their mental models. Two studies were conducted: one where undergraduates were asked to provide solutions to a creative educational problem, and one where undergraduates were asked to provide solutions to a creative marketing problem. In both studies, judges appraised solutions for quality, originality, and elegance. Prior to providing their problem solutions, participants were asked to illustrate their mental model for understanding the problem. Objective features (e.g., number of concepts, number of content linkages) and subjective features (e.g., coherence, complexity) of these mental models were appraised by judges. It was found that the most creative problem solutions emerged when people illustrated coherent, workable, mental models which took into account both important concepts and moderators/mediators which conditioned the impact of these variables on problem outcomes. Thus skill in concept selection may depend not only on having viable mental models and base concepts, but also on skill in taking into account and working with complex relationships among concepts.

Conceptual Combination

The concepts embedded in mental models must be combined and/ or reorganized to provide a basis for generating *new* ideas. Mumford, Baughman, et al. (1997) asked 110 undergraduates to work on Mobley et al. (1992) conceptual combination problems where three concepts (e.g., birds, sporting equipment) were defined by four concept exemplars (e.g., owls, balls). Participants were asked in solving these problems to label their new category, list additional exemplars of this new category, and provide as many exemplars of this new category as they could think of, with judges evaluating these products for quality and originality. Subsequently, participants were asked to provide marketing campaigns for the 3D holographic television where judges appraised solution quality and originality. It was found that production of high quality and original features on these conceptual combination problems were strongly, positively, related to production of creative solutions to the marketing problem. Thus skill in identifying common features of concepts, a skill we would refer to as commonality identification, is apparently critical to conceptual combination.

Conceptual combination, however, not only depends on commonality identification, it also appears to require elaboration of identified commonalities. Scott et al. (2005) asked some 200 undergraduates to prepare plans for leading an experimental secondary school—plans appraised by judges for quality, originality, and elegance. Participants were presented with key concepts involved in various instructional techniques—up to 28 in all depending on the features of the instructional programs under consideration. Participants were then asked to identify shared and non-shared features of these concepts. After formulating these new concepts, participants were asked to elaborate on the implications of them. These elaborative responses were coded by judges for effectiveness. It was found that effectiveness of these elaborations was strongly related, as strongly positively related as commonality identification, to the quality, originality, and elegance of creative problem solutions. Thus conceptual combination depends not only on commonality identification skill, but also on elaborative skill in exploring and refining new concepts with respect to their implications for problem-solving.

Idea Generation

Idea generation, in part as a result of divergent thinking tests, has been among the most heavily investigated of the creative thinking processes (Acar & Runco, 2012). For example, extended time in idea generation has been found to contribute to generation of more original ideas (Mumford & Gustafson, 1988). Idea generation, the number and quality of the ideas generated, has been found to be related to certain personality variables such as openness (McCrae, 1987). Moreover, idea generation moreover has been found to depend on expertise (Vincent et al., 2002). Although many studies have examined influences on idea generation, less effort has been devoted to identifying skills underlying idea generation.

Initial evidence pertaining to the nature of the skills underlying idea generation has been provided in a study by Mumford, Marks, Connelly, Zaccaro, and Johnson (1998). In this study, a large sample of Army officers were asked to complete Christensen, Merrifield, and Guilford's (1953) Consequences test, where people are asked to generate ideas bearing on unlikely events such as "what might happen if gravity was cut in half." In addition, creative problem-solving in a military context was assessed along with critical incident performance and indices of achievement as a military leader (e.g., medals won). Skills were assessed by rating the ideas generated on the consequences measure with respect to whether they reflected about positive consequences, negative consequences, the time frame over which ideas unfolded, the realism of ideas, the complexity of ideas, and the use of principles (e.g., mass) in generating ideas.

It was found that these varied criteria—creative problem-solving, critical incident performance, leader achievement—were strongly, positively related to use of principles, or features, arising from conceptual combination in idea generation. Thus principle-based idea generation appears to represent one skill underlying idea generation, with those who employ a wider range of richer principles generating more creative problem solutions and evidencing better performance on tasks calling for creative thought. In addition, however, it was found that generation of more complex ideas was also strongly, positively related to creative problem-solving. As such, idea elaboration vis-à-vis context also appears to represent a skill contributing to idea generation. Principle-based generation and contextual elaboration thus appear to represent two key skills contributing to idea generation.

Idea Evaluation

Many ideas may be produced in idea generation. However, people cannot act, or solve, problems using a large number of ideas. Thus idea evaluation, the screening and appraisal of ideas generated, is a critical creative thinking process (Runco & Acar, 2012). In fact, people are not always good at idea evaluation due in part to a failure to recognize the unique, creative properties of ideas (Licuanan et al., 2007). However, when people have domain expertise and intend to take actions based on these ideas, their evaluation of ideas becomes far more accurate.

Gibson and Mumford (2013) conducted a study bearing on idea evaluation skills. They asked 197 undergraduates to provide advertising campaigns for a clothing firm, where campaigns provided were appraised by judges for quality, originality, and elegance. Prior to preparing these campaigns, participants were presented with a set of candidate ideas and asked to provide written criticisms of each idea. These criticisms of ideas were appraised with respect to a number of attributes, including amount, number, depth, usefulness, range, complexity, isolation, risk sensitivity, operational relevance, and specificity. It was found the highest quality, most original, and most elegant creative problem solutions emerged when people focused on a limited number of deep criticisms. Therefore it appears that depth of evaluation is one key skill contributing to effective execution of the idea evaluation process.

Idea evaluation, however, is not a passive process. In idea evaluation, people work with ideas to improve them. Lonergan et al. (2004), in another study of idea evaluation, asked 148 undergraduates to formulate advertising campaigns for Redmond et al.'s (1993) 3D holographic television task. In this study, however, participants were asked to assume the role of a manager evaluating ideas from teams they were responsible for prior to preparing their final campaign. Participants' final campaigns were evaluated by judges for quality, originality, and elegance. Teams' ideas, drawn from Redmond et al. (1993), were either of high quality or high originality. Participants were instructed to appraise these ideas with respect to either innovative potential or operating efficiency. It was found the most creative advertising campaigns were obtained when highly original ideas were appraised with respect to operating efficiency *and* when high-quality ideas were appraised with respect to innovation potential. Thus idea evaluation seeks not only to identify the best idea, but also to compensate for deficiencies in ideas. As a result, compensatory skill, a skill likely dependent of expertise, contributes to idea evaluation. Therefore idea evaluation appears to depend on both depth appraisal skill and skill in formulating strategies for compensating for deficiencies in candidates ideas.

Implementation Planning

To solve problems, it is not enough to have an idea. People must formulate plans for acting on and implementing these ideas (Latham & Arshoff, 2015). As a result, it seems reasonable to expect that implementation planning will also contribute to peoples' success in creative problem-solving.

Osburn and Mumford (2006) asked undergraduates to solve a social innovation problem calling for formulating a plan for leading an experimental secondary school—plans appraised by judges for quality and originality. Prior to preparing the plans, however, participants were asked to complete a set of self-paced instructional modules illustrating skills that might contribute to planning creative work—such as penetration, identification of key causes. Not only was it found that training in these planning skills contributed to the production of creative problem solutions, but that they were especially valuable for more creative people as defined by high scores on measures of divergent thinking ability.

Marta, Leritz, and Mumford (2005) conducted a study intended to examine the impact of planning skills on creative problem-solving. In this study, 55 teams of undergraduates were asked to work on a business restructuring task calling for formation of a plan to "turn around" a failing automotive firm. The quality and originality of the resulting plans was appraised by judges. Prior to starting work on the task, however, all participants were asked to complete a measure of planning skills as measured through performance on a set of business cases. This measure provided scores assessing identification of key causes, identification of emergent restrictions, identification of downstream consequences, opportunistic implementation, and environmental scanning. It was found teams led by leaders possessing these skills produced the most original and highest quality plans for turning around this firm. Moreover, these planning skills were found to exert their strongest effects when the task was made more complex and the task work environment was subject to change or turbulence—both conditions characterizing real-world creative problem-solving.

Planning, however, is a complex activity (Mumford, Schultz, & Van Doorn, 2001)—thus the rather large number of skills apparently contributing to implementation planning. In creative efforts, however, plans do not always work out as expected. New opportunities arise calling for opportunistic exploration (Patalano & Seifert, 1997), and failures occur requiring execution of backup plans (Xiao, Milgram, & Doyle, 1997). As a result, it seems reasonable to expect that both skill in opportunistic exploration and backup planning would also contribute to creative problem-solving.

Solution Monitoring

As noted previously, creative problem-solving efforts in the "real world" occur in a dynamic, turbulent environment. Moreover, new ideas and new problem solutions must be adapted and refined to allow potential problem solutions to be effective. One implication of this observation is that creative problem-solving will require substantial adaptability. Adaptability allows people to adjust or shift approaches to a problem as new or unexpected events are executed. In fact, Mumford, Baughman,

Threlfall, Costanza, and Uhlman (1993) have provided evidence indicating adaptability skill, skill in adjusting or rearranging solution elements does, positively relate to performance on complex, novel tasks.

Although solution monitoring may call for adaptation skill, this observation poses a key question with regard to solution monitoring: How do people know when, and how, to adapt creative problem solutions? An initial answer to this question has been provided in a study by Caughron and Mumford (2008). They asked 219 undergraduates to formulate plans for resolving three educational problems requiring creative problem solutions. The resulting solution plans were appraised by judges for quality, originality, and elegance. Prior to preparing these plans, however, participants were trained in various planning techniques used to appraise progress in projects: (1) Gantt charts, (2) case-based planning, and (3) critical path analysis. It is of note that critical path analysis requires identification of disruptive influences and specification of markers for monitoring of disruptive influences on task performance. Caughron and Mumford (2008) found that instruction in critical path analysis resulted in the most creative solutions to these educational problems. Apparently, skill in identifying descriptive events to be monitored during solution implementation contributes to effective execution of the solution monitoring process, especially when accompanied by requisite adaptive capacity.

CROSS-PROCESS SKILLS

Our foregoing observations indicate that effective execution of each of the processes involved in creative thought depends on acquisition of multiple creative thinking skills. Although the available evidence indicates that each of these skills is of some importance, the skills discussed to this point appear to be process specific. Thus elaboration is important in conceptual combination, while constraint analysis is important in problem definition. The specificity of these skills, however, broaches another question: Are there skills that generalize across a number of processes? In fact, it appears at least five skills exist that contribute to creative problem-solving across a number of processes and a number of different domains: (1) causal analysis, (2) forecasting, (3) error analysis, (4) applications analysis, and (5) wisdom.

CAUSAL ANALYSIS

When people seek to generate creative problem solutions, they must know what variables, or attributes, of the problem to think about. And, they must frame action with respect to these variables. Thus one would expect that identification of critical causes, and organization of key causal operatives, would prove critical to creative thought. Some initial evidence pointing to the importance of causal analysis skills has been provided in a set of studies by Marcy and Mumford (2007, 2010).

Marcy and Mumford (2007) asked 180 undergraduates to provide solutions to six social innovation problems, three drawn from the business domain and three drawn from the educational domain, where judges appraised the quality and originality of the solutions provided. Prior to starting work on these problems, however, participants were, or were not, asked to complete a set of self-paced instructional modules. These instructional modules taught people to employ various strategies for thinking about causes on tasks drawn from various domains. Specifically, instruction encouraged them to (1) think about causes that can be manipulated, (2) influence multiple outcomes, (3) have large effects, (4) can be controlled, (5) have synergistic effects, (6) work together, and (7) have direct effects. It was found that training in these causal analysis skills resulted in production of both higher quality and more original solutions across both business and educational social innovation problems.

In another study, Marcy and Mumford (2010) asked undergraduates to work on a university leadership simulation exercise with the goal of improving research performance. This novel, complex, ill-defined task—a task calling for creativity—allowed performance to be assessed in terms of objective outcomes. Again, participants either were, or were not, given training in causal analysis skills. It was found that stronger performance in this simulation exercise occurred when participants completed causal analysis training.

In a more recent study, Hester et al. (2012) asked participants to provide solutions to a creative marketing problem (to provide advertising campaigns for a high-energy root beer), where judges appraised solutions for quality, originality, and elegance. Prior to starting work on this problem, however, 232 undergraduate participants were provided with two forms of instruction: (1) techniques for illustrating their mental model for understanding marketing problems and (2) training in strategies for causal analysis. It was found that training in strategies for causal analysis resulted in the production of higher quality, more original, and more elegant problem solutions. Causal analysis training, however, also contributed to acquisition of stronger mental models for understanding the problem at hand. Thus causal analysis skills, by strengthening peoples' basic understanding of problems—their mental models—contributed to production of creative problem solutions.

Forecasting

In creative problem-solving, the outcomes of potential actions to be taken are inherently uncertain, especially as outcomes unfold over time.

The uncertainty of the outcomes associated with any creative effort, of course, implies that forecasting is also likely to prove a critical skill in creative problem-solving (Mumford, 2001). However, execution of any given creative thinking process serves as an input, or feed, into subsequent processing activities. Thus in process execution people must be able to forecast, or anticipate, the outcomes of process execution with respect to later, subsequent, processing activities. Finally, forecasting outcomes of process execution provides a basis for systematic refinement of the products flowing from process execution. These three observations all lead to the conclusion that forecasting might be a critical, cross-process creative thinking skill (Mumford, 2003).

Some support for this conclusion has been provided in a set of studies by Byrne, Shipman, and Mumford (2010) and Shipman, Byrne, and Mumford (2010). In the Byrne et al. (2010) study, undergraduates were asked to formulate a marketing campaign for a new high-energy root beer. In the Shipman et al. (2010) study, they were asked to formulate plans for leading a new, experimental, secondary school. In both studies, judges appraised the resulting products for quality, originality, and elegance. In both of these low fidelity simulation studies, participants received emails from a consulting firm asking them to forecast anticipated outcomes of their plans. The responses to these emails were then coded by judges for 27 attributes, such as forecasting negative outcomes, forecasting positive outcomes, forecasting obstacles, and forecasting restrictions. These ratings were then factored with four dimensions emerging: (1) forecasting extensiveness, (2) forecasting timeframe, (3) forecasting negative outcomes, and (4) forecasting constraints. When these factors were correlated with the quality, originality, and elegance of obtained problem solutions, they were found to evidence a strong, positive, relationship ($r = 0.40$) with evaluations of solution quality, originality, and elegance. And, in fact, they produced stronger relationships with these indices of creative problem-solving performance than traditional ability measures such as intelligence and divergent thinking.

The impact of forecasting skill on peoples' creative problem-solving performance may at first glance appear surprising given the widespread belief that people are poor at forecasting (Pant & Starbuck, 1990). Dailey and Mumford (2006), however, have provided evidence indicating this assumption does not hold. They asked undergraduates to assume the role of a member of a proposal review panel with proposals being drawn from prior work in the educational and public policy domains. Participants were asked to forecast outcomes of the proposed effort and resources needed for execution. These proposals, however, were drawn from real-world cases, allowing the accuracy of forecasts to be assessed. It was found that when people intended to act based on forecasts and had domain expertise, their forecasts could, in fact, prove quite accurate—to within a fifth of a standard deviation. Thus the forecasts of experts, experts who intend to act on these forecasts, can be quite accurate. And, accurate forecasts in turn contribute to creative problem-solving.

Error Analysis

One value of forecasts is that they allow people to anticipate errors—potentially errors in process execution. Identification of potential errors in process execution allows people to cycle back through processes and produce more viable products in process execution. Thus one might expect error analysis skills would contribute to the execution of multiple processes involved in creative thought, and, thus creative problem-solving performance. In fact, this observation is not truly unique. Both Cropley (2006) and Parnes and Noller (1972) have argued convergent thinking ability, an ability found to contribute to idea evaluation, contributes to creative problem-solving.

Some initial evidence pointing to the value of error analysis skills has been provided in a study by Robledo et al. (2012). They asked 225 undergraduates to formulate a plan for leading a new, experimental secondary school with judges being asked to appraise the resulting plans for quality, originality, and elegance. In this study, participants were provided with training in how to illustrate their mental model for understanding problems, and, subsequently, they were provided, or not provided, training in various error analysis techniques. Specifically, participants were asked to complete none or up to four self-paced instructional modules where viable techniques for error analysis were illustrated. These self-paced instructional modules illustrated the value of (1) identifying critical errors that might arise, (2) identifying chains of errors, (3) identifying potential errors under personal control, and (4) thinking about the impact of errors on different stakeholders. It was found that this error management training resulted in the production of higher quality, more original, and more elegant solutions to this creative problem, while allowing participants to formulate stronger mental models for understanding the problem at hand. Thus error analysis skill appears to contribute to creative problem-solving.

Traditionally, error analysis skill has received scant attention in studies of creative thinking due in part to the assumption that creative efforts are fraught with error. However, it is precisely because creative efforts are fraught with error that error analysis skills may prove crucial to creative problem-solving and effective execution of the various processes contributing to creative thought. Indeed, qualitative studies of eminent achievement in the sciences indicate that thoughtful analysis of errors was central to eventual production of a creative product (Bird & Sherwin, 2005). Given these qualitative observations, and the findings obtained in the Robledo et al. (2012) study, more needs to be done in appraising the impact of error analysis skill in both execution of creative thinking processes and appraisal of creative problem-solving performance.

Wisdom

A common assumption made in studies of creativity is the creative act unto itself is of interest in its own right. Creative ideas, however, must be developed and implemented within a social system to be of any value. This point implies that in creative problem-solving, people must take into account both their environment and the people within it, such as relevant stakeholders who will be impacted by the creative problem solution. Therefore creative problem solutions and execution of creative thinking processes must be embedded in context. Embedding problem solutions in context has traditionally been subsumed under the rubric of wisdom (McKenna, Rooney, & Boal, 2009; Orwoll & Perlmutter, 1990; Sternberg, 1985, 1990).

Embedding process execution, however, is not an easy task. It implies skills such as self-reflection, systems perception, and judgment under uncertainty: all of which fall under the skill of wisdom (McKenna et al., 2009). Therefore wisdom should contribute to creative problem-solving and effective execution of creative thinking processes. Evidence pointing to the importance of wisdom has been provided in a study by Zaccaro, Mumford, Connelly, Marks, and Gilbert (2000). In this study, 1818 Army officers were asked to complete a measure of wisdom, or social judgment, skills where they were presented with two scenarios describing failed efforts arising from unwillingness to attend to complex conflicting social cues. After reading through these scenarios, officers were asked to answer three questions: (1) why did this situation occur, (2) what was the central mistake made, and (3) what would you do in this situation. Judges rated written responses to these questions with respect to key attributes of wisdom, such as solution fit to context. In addition, however, participants' skill in executing each of the creative thinking processes was assessed, using a think-aloud method, and creative problem-solving, critical incident performance, and military achievement were assessed.

Connelly et al. (2000) and Mumford, Marks, Connelly, Zaccaro, and Reiter-Palmon (2000), in separate studies, examined the substantive implications of wisdom for officer creative problem-solving. In these studies, three critical conclusions emerged. First, it was found that wisdom increased as a function of experience. Second, it was found that wisdom was positively related to both creative problem-solving performance and indices of officer performance (e.g., critical incident performance). Third, it was found that these attributes of wisdom were positively related to effective execution of all of the creative thinking processes—problem definition, information gathering, concept selection, conceptual combination, idea generation, idea evaluation, implementation planning, and monitoring. Thus wisdom does appear to contribute to effective execution of multiple creative thinking processes as well as creative problem-solving.

Scholars often object to the importance of wisdom as a skill supporting process execution because it is "messy." However, wisdom is not always a "messy" construct. Wisdom involves addressing process outputs in context. One key output of process application in most fields of creative work is whether the outputs proposed will prove of practical value. Barrett et al. (2013) asked participants, 248 in all, to formulate an advertising campaign for a new line of athletic shoes being marketed by an extreme sports firm. Judges evaluated the resulting marketing plans for quality, originality, and elegance. Prior to providing these advertising plans, participants were trained in strategies that might help them think about idea application in context. More specifically, participants were asked to complete none to four self-paced instructional models where they were instructed to think about (1) the impact of plans on different user groups, (2) the setting needed for plan execution, (3) the preparation user groups had for implementing the plan, and (4) how sustainable the marketing plan would be. It was found that training these approaches for thinking about applications, a component of wisdom, contributed to the production of higher quality, more original, and more elegant marketing plans. Indeed, other research by Finke et al. (1992) indicates that thinking about applications contributes to creative problem-solving on tool design tasks. Thus wisdom, thinking about socially viable applications, does appear to contribute to creative thought.

DISCUSSION

Before turning to the broader implications of the present effort, certain limitations should be noted. To begin, although evidence is available for the existence of causal analysis, forecasting, error analysis, and wisdom, these four skills likely do not represent the only skills of value in facilitating effective execution of multiple creative thinking processes. For example, perhaps parsimony, or appropriate simplification, is a viable cross-process skill (Partlow, Medeiros, & Mumford, 2015). Similarly, one might argue attentional allocation is of some importance in effective execution of multiple creative thinking processes (Bink & Marsh, 2000). Thus this list of general cross-process skills should not be viewed as complete.

Along related lines, certain cross-process skills need more study. Clearly, as noted earlier, this holds true for error analysis skill. However, one might also make the case that research regarding the interplay of cross-process skills should be conducted. For example, we need to know the nature of the material that must be forecasted, or how people select the material to be forecasted, in execution of different creative thinking processes. Although more research is needed, it does seem that certain skills do exist that contribute to effective execution of multiple processing operations held to contribute to creative problem-solving.

Along similar lines, it should be recognized that some process-specific skills have been reasonably well established. For example, the value of elaboration in conceptual combination has been given substantial attention in studies by Baughman and Mumford (1995), Finke et al. (1992), and Scott et al. (2005). Similarly, the importance of constraint analysis in problem definition has received more attention in recent years (Medeiros et al., 2014; Stokes, 2008). However, more research is needed examining the extent to which in-depth analysis is needed in idea evaluation, including the merits of concept flexibility, or context adaptability, in concept selection. Moreover, in keeping with our observations about cross-process skills, it should be evident that we likely have not identified all the skills contributing to effective execution of each and every creative thinking process.

With this said, another key conclusion comes to fore—a conclusion nicely illustrated in the Byrne et al. (2010), the Connelly et al. (2000), and the Marta et al. (2005) studies. These skills are exceptionally good predictors of performance on creative problem-solving tasks, producing validity coefficients far larger than those obtained from traditional ability measures. Indeed, the findings obtained by Mumford, Supinski, et al. (1997) indicate that when multiple skills are examined it is reasonable to expect multiple correlations in the .50s or .60s with appraisals of the quality, originality, and elegance of creative problem solutions—a finding that is especially impressive when one bears in mind the reliability of these measures of creative performance ($r_{tt} \cong 0.80$).

The strong positive relationship between creative problem-solving and creative thinking skills, both within-process and cross-process skills, is not surprising. This relationship is not surprising, in particular, if one assumes abilities (e.g., intelligence or divergent thinking) give rise to skills, and that these skills in turn have a direct impact on peoples' creative problem-solving performance. The strong direct impact of these creative problem-solving skills on creative performance, however, brings to fore a question: what do studies of creative problem-solving skills tell us about how we should go about appraising creative potential?

Traditionally, assessments of creative potential have been based on divergent thinking measures (Acar & Runco, 2012). And, if one is interested in assessing creative potential without respect to domain, or expertise, this approach is appropriate. When, however, one is interested in assessing creative potential in a population which has education and/or experience working in a domain, then a skills-based approach opens up a number of new, potentially quite valuable, techniques for the assessment of creative potential.

Consider, for example, the elaborative skill found to be important for conceptual combination. To assess this skill, one might provide new, unfamiliar, concepts and ask people to elaborate the implications of each concept for the domain at hand with judges being asked to appraise the extensiveness, or depth, of elaboration. Earlier, we argued that constraint analysis skills are important in problem definition. To assess this skill, one might present problem statements and a list of 15 to 20 constraints that might impact creative problem-solving where people are asked to select the 3 or 4 constraints they believe to be most important. Scoring might occur based on convergence of constraints selected, with those selected by creative experts working in the field. Still another example may be found in the compensatory skill found to be important in idea evaluation. Here people might be presented with ideas and the context in which each idea is to be implemented. People would then be asked to list the three to five changes they would make in each idea to improve its impact with judges scoring for the viability of these compensatory changes.

Not only do the process-specific skills suggest some new ways for assessing creative potential, the cross-process skills also point to some potentially useful new ways for the assessment of creative potential. To begin, consider error analysis skill. One might present both good and bad products flowing from various processes as people work within a domain. Subsequently, people would be asked to select the most critical errors evident in these process outputs from a list of 10 to 20 potential errors. Casual analysis skill might be assessed quite directly by presenting people with a list of 20 to 30 concepts applying in a domain. They would be asked to illustrate their understanding of problems by selecting critical concepts, or indicating critical linkages among concepts, with scoring being based on convergence of these appraisals with those of creative experts. In forecasting one might provide both good and poor creative problem solutions and ask people to project the downstream outcomes of implementing this solution with the resulting forecasts being scored for attributes such as extensiveness and time frame.

With regard to these measures for skill assessment, however, it is important to bear in mind a key point about complex problem-solving skills. Complex problem-solving skills are applied in the context of domain-specific knowledge (Mumford, Todd, Higgs, & McIntosh, 2017). In fact, the same principle holds for creative problem-solving skills (Mumford, Marks, et al., 1998). As a result, development of these, or other, potential measures of key creative problem-solving skills should be framed in terms of problems likely to be encountered with a given domain of creative work.

Our foregoing observations about the role of knowledge in skill application point to a noteworthy conclusion with regard to the development of creative thinking skills. The acquisition of creative both process-specific and cross-process creative thinking skills will depend on acquisition of requisite expertise (Ericsson, 2009). This observation is of some importance because, at present, we lack evidence as to when in a cycle of expertise acquisition attempts to develop any given process-specific or cross-process creative thinking skill should begin. Moreover, we lack evidence bearing on the sequencing of skill development and the particular types of exercises most likely to prove useful in skill development.

By the same token, prior research has shown that a focus on key creative thinking skills provides the basis for successful educational and training interventions (Scott, Leritz, & Mumford, 2004), and many of the studies examined in the present effort have explicitly pointed to the feasibility of developing these skills if adequate expertise is already in place. Thus the Marcy and Mumford (2007, 2010) studies point to the feasibility of developing causal analysis skills, while the Robledo et al. (2012) study points to the feasibility of developing error analysis skill. Although more evidence is needed with respect to the feasibility of developing within process skills, the evidence available at this juncture does point to the feasibility of training to ensure requisite within-process skills can also be developed through appropriate training interventions (Mumford, Mecca, Gibson, & Giorgini, 2012).

Our observations with regard to both within-process and cross-process creative thinking skills, however, point to another issue that needs to be addressed in the assessment and development of creative thinking skills. Put directly, there are simply a large—potentially very large—number of skills that people need for creative problem-solving. People must have process-specific skills such as constraints analysis (problem definition), concept relationship specification (concept selection), elaboration (conceptual combination), principle-based production (idea generation), compensation (idea evaluation), and backup planning (implementation planning) to mention a few. To complicate matters further, a number of cross-process skills—causal analysis, forecasting, error analysis, and wisdom—also appear to contribute to create problem-solving.

It is unlikely any assessment program or any development program will attempt, or could appraise and/or seek to develop, all these skills. By the same token, prior research has shown that certain processes are particularly important to performance in certain domains of creative work. Thus Mumford et al. (2010) found that conceptual combination was particularly important to creative performance in the social sciences, while implementation planning was particularly important to creative performance in the health sciences. This observation is noteworthy because it suggests that application of systematic task, on work analysis, procedures might be used to identify those creative thinking skills that should be assessed and/or developed in particular work domains.

At one level, students of creativity may find our foregoing observations a bit disconcerting. Students of creativity have long sought a single construct, for example, divergent thinking, that might provide the basis for all attempts to assess creative potential and all attempts to develop creative potential. Creative thinking skills, however, are too numerous, and too complex, to allow the "one size fits all" approach to prove workable in the assessment and development of creative potential. Rather, we need to conceive of creative problem-solving depending on an array of skills as these skills are applied to domain-specific knowledge. By formulating models that take into account the inherent complexity of creative thought, however, we may well be able to formulate new, more effective approaches for the assessment and development of creative potential. We hope the present effort serves as an impetus for further work that recognizes not only the value of creative thought but also its complexity.

Acknowledgments

We would like to think Roni Reiter-Palmon, Gina Ligon, Sam Hunter, Rich Marcy, Amanda Shepherd, Christina Byrne, and Kelsey Mederios for their contributions to the present effort. Correspondence should be addressed to Dr. Michael D. Mumford, Department of Psychology, The University of Oklahoma, Norman, Oklahoma 73,019 or mmumford@ou.edu.

References

Acar, S., & Runco, M. A. (2012). Psychoticism and creativity: a meta-analytic review. *Psychology of Aesthetics, Creativity, and the Arts, 6*, 341–350.

Baer, J. (1998). The case for domain specificity of creativity. *Creativity Research Journal, 11*, 173–177.

Barrett, J. D., Peterson, D. R., Hester, K. S., Robledo, I. C., Day, E. A., Hougen, D. P., et al. (2013). Thinking about applications: effects on mental models and creative problem-solving. *Creativity Research Journal, 25*, 199–212.

Baughman, W. A., & Mumford, M. D. (1995). Process analytic models of creative capacities: operations involved in the combination and reorganization process. *Creativity Research Journal, 9*, 63–76.

Besemer, S. P., & O'Quin, K. (1999). Confirming the three-factor creative product analysis matrix model in an American sample. *Creativity Research Journal, 12*, 287–296.

Bink, M. L., & Marsh, R. L. (2000). Cognitive regularities in creative activity. *Review of General Psychology, 4*, 59–78.

Bird, K., & Sherwin, M. J. (2005). *American Prometheus: The triumph and tragedy of J. Robert Oppenheimer*. New York: Knopf.

Byrne, C. L., Shipman, A. S., & Mumford, M. D. (2010). The effects of forecasting on creative problem-solving: an experimental study. *Creativity Research Journal, 22*, 119–138.

Caughron, J. J., & Mumford, M. D. (2008). Project planning: the effects of using formal planning techniques on creative problem-solving. *Creativity and Innovation Management, 17*, 204–215.

Christensen, P. R., Merrifield, P. R., & Guilford, J. P. (1953). *Consequences form A-I*. Beverley Hills, CA: Sage.

Christiaans, H. H. (2002). Creativity as a design criterion. *Communication Research Journal, 14*, 41–54.

Connelly, M. S., Gilbert, J. A., Zaccaro, S. J., Threlfall, K. V., Marks, M. A., & Mumford, M. D. (2000). Exploring the relationship of leadership skills and knowledge to leader performance. *The Leadership Quarterly, 11*, 65–86.

Cropley, A. (2006). In praise of convergent thinking. *Creativity Research Journal*, *18*, 391–404.

Dailey, L., & Mumford, M. D. (2006). Evaluative aspects of creative thought: errors in appraising the implications of new ideas. *Creativity Research Journal*, *18*, 385–390.

Dewey, J. (1910). *How we think*. Lexington, MA: D.C. Heath.

Ericsson, K. A. (2009). *Development of professional expertise: Toward measurement of expert performance and design of optimal learning environments*. Cambridge: Cambridge University Press.

Estes, Z., & Ward, T. B. (2002). The emergence of novel attributes in concept modification. *Creativity Research Journal*, *14*, 149–156.

Eubanks, D. L., Murphy, S. T., & Mumford, M. D. (2010). Intuition as an influence on creative problem-solving: the effects of intuition, positive affect, and training. *Creativity Research Journal*, *22*, 170–184.

Feist, G. J., & Gorman, M. E. (1998). The psychology of science: review and integration of a nascent discipline. *Review of General Psychology*, *2*, 3–47.

Finke, R. A., Ward, T. B., & Smith, S. M. (1992). *Creative cognition: Theory, research, and applications*. Cambridge, MA: MIT Press.

Friedrich, T. L., & Mumford, M. D. (2009). The effects of conflicting information on creative thought: a source of performance improvements or decrements? *Creativity Research Journal*, *21*, 265–281.

Gibson, C., & Mumford, M. D. (2013). Evaluation, criticism, and creativity: criticism content and effects on creative problem solving. *Psychology of Aesthetics, Creativity, and the Arts*, *7*, 314–331.

Goldvarg, E., & Johnson-Laird, P. N. (2001). Naive causality: a mental model theory of causal meaning and reasoning. *Cognitive Science*, *25*, 565–610.

Hester, K. S., Robledo, I. C., Barrett, J. D., Peterson, D. R., Hougen, D. P., Day, E. A., et al. (2012). Causal analysis to enhance creative problem-solving: performance and effects on mental models. *Creativity Research Journal*, *24*, 115–133.

Hunter, S. T., Bedell-Avers, K. E., Hunsicker, C. M., Mumford, M. D., & Ligon, G. S. (2008). Applying multiple knowledge structures in creative thought: effects on idea generation and problem-solving. *Creativity Research Journal*, *20*, 137–154.

Latham, G. P., & Arshoff, A. S. (2015). Planning: a mediator in goal setting theory. In M. D. Mumford & M. Frese (Eds.), *The psychology of planning in organizations: Research and applications*. New York: Routledge.

Licuanan, B. F., Dailey, L. R., & Mumford, M. D. (2007). Idea evaluation: error in evaluating highly original ideas. *The Journal of Creative Behavior*, *41*, 1–27.

Lonergan, D. C., Scott, G. M., & Mumford, M. D. (2004). Evaluative aspects of creative thought: effects of idea appraisal and revision standards. *Creativity Research Journal*, *16*, 231–246.

Marcy, R. T., & Mumford, M. D. (2007). Social innovation: enhancing creative performance through causal analysis. *Creativity Research Journal*, *19*, 123–140.

Marcy, R. T., & Mumford, M. D. (2010). Leader cognition: improving leader performance through causal analysis. *The Leadership Quarterly*, *21*, 1–19.

Marta, S., Leritz, L. E., & Mumford, M. D. (2005). Leadership skills and group performance: situational demands, behavioral requirements, and planning. *The Leadership Quarterly*, *16*, 97–120.

McCrae, R. R. (1987). Creativity, divergent thinking, and openness to experience. *Journal of Personality and Social Psychology*, *52*, 1258–1265.

McKenna, B., Rooney, D., & Boal, K. B. (2009). Wisdom principles as a meta-theoretical basis for evaluating leadership. *The Leadership Quarterly*, *20*, 177–190.

Medeiros, K. (2016). *Assembling the box: Investigating the role of constraints and creative problem solving*. [ProQuest Dissertation and Theses].

Medeiros, K. E., Partlow, P. J., & Mumford, M. D. (2014). Not too much, not too little: the influence of constraints on creative problem solving. *Psychology of Aesthetics, Creativity, and the Arts*, *8*, 198–210.

Mobley, M. I., Doares, L. M., & Mumford, M. D. (1992). Process analytic models of creative capacities: evidence for the combination and reorganization process. *Creativity Research Journal, 5*, 125–155.

Mumford, M. D. (2001). Something old, something new: revisiting Guilford's conception of creative problem solving. *Creativity Research Journal, 13*, 267–276.

Mumford, M. D. (2003). Where have we been, where are we going? Taking stock in creativity research. *Creativity Research Journal, 14*, 107–120.

Mumford, M. D., Antes, A. L., Caughron, J. J., Connelly, S., & Beeler, C. (2010). Cross-field differences in creative problem-solving skills: a comparison of health, biological, and social sciences. *Creativity Research Journal, 22*, 14–26.

Mumford, M. D., Baughman, W. A., Maher, M. A., Costanza, D. P., & Supinski, E. P. (1997). Process-based measures of creative problem-solving skills: IV. Category combination. *Creativity Research Journal, 10*, 59–71.

Mumford, M. D., Baughman, W. A., Supinski, E. P., & Anderson, L. E. (1998). A construct approach to skill assessment: procedures for assessing complex cognitive skills. In M. D. Hakel (Ed.), *Beyond multiple choice: Evaluating alternatives to traditional testing for selection* (pp. 75–112). Hillsdale, NJ: Lawrence Earlbaum Associates, Inc.

Mumford, M. D., Baughman, W. A., Supinski, E. P., & Maher, M. A. (1996). Process-based measures of creative problem-solving skills: II. Information encoding. *Creativity Research Journal, 9*, 77–88.

Mumford, M. D., Baughman, W. A., Threlfall, K. V., Costanza, D. P., & Uhlman, C. E. (1993). Personality, adaptability and performance: performance on well-defined and ill-defined problem solving tasks. *Human Performance, 5*, 241–285.

Mumford, M. D., Baughman, W. A., Threlfall, K. V., Supinski, M., & Costanza, M. (1996). Process-based measures of creative problem-solving skills: I. Problem construction. *Creativity Research Journal, 9*, 63–76.

Mumford, M. D., & Gustafson, S. B. (1988). Creativity syndrome: integration, application, and innovation. *Psychological Bulletin, 103*, 27–43.

Mumford, M. D., & Gustafson, S. B. (2007). Creative thought: cognition and problem solving in a dynamic system. *Creativity Research Handbook, 2*, 33–77.

Mumford, M. D., Hester, K. S., Robledo, I. C., Peterson, D. R., Day, E. A., Hougen, D. F., et al. (2012). Mental models and creative problem-solving: the relationship of objective and subjective model attributes. *Creativity Research Journal, 24*, 311–330.

Mumford, M. D., & Hunter, S. T. (2005). Innovation in organizations: a multi-level perspective on creativity. In F. J. Yammarino & F. Dansereau (Eds.), *Research in multi-level issues, Vol. 4* (pp. 11–74). Oxford: Elsevier.

Mumford, M. D., Marks, M. A., Connelly, M. S., Zaccaro, S. J., & Johnson, J. F. (1998). Domain-based scoring in divergent-thinking tests: validation evidence in an occupational sample. *Creativity Research Journal, 11*, 151–163.

Mumford, M. D., Marks, M. A., Connelly, M. S., Zaccaro, S. J., & Reiter-Palmon, R. (2000). Development of leadership skills: experience and timing. *The Leadership Quarterly, 11*, 87–114.

Mumford, M. D., Mecca, J., Gibson, C., & Giorgini, V. (2012). Strategy-based instruction for creativity: an incremental approach to education. In O. N. Saracho (Ed.), *Contemporary perspectives on research in creativity in early childhood education* (pp. 319–341). Charlotte, NC: Information Age Publishing.

Mumford, M. D., Medeiros, K. E., & Partlow, P. J. (2012). Creative thinking: processes, strategies, and knowledge. *The Journal of Creative Behavior, 46*, 30–47.

Mumford, M. D., Mobley, M. I., Uhlman, C. E., Reiter-Palmon, R., & Doares, L. (1991). Process analytic models of creative capacities. *Creativity Research Journal, 4*, 91–122.

Mumford, M. D., Reiter-Palmon, R., & Redmond, M. R. (1994). Problem construction and cognition: applying problem representations in ill-defined domains. In M. A. Runco (Ed.), *Problem finding, problem solving, and creativity* (pp. 3–39). Norwood, NJ: Ablex Publishing.

Mumford, M. D., Schultz, R. A., & Van Doorn, J. R. (2001). Performance in planning: processes, requirements, and errors. *Review of General Psychology*, 5, 213–240.

Mumford, M. D., Supinski, E. P., Baughman, W. A., Costanza, D. P., & Threlfall, K. V. (1997). Process-based measures of creative problem-solving skills: V. Overall prediction. *Creativity Research Journal*, 10, 73–85.

Mumford, M. D., Supinski, E. P., Threlfall, K. V., & Baughman, W. A. (1996). Process-based measures of creative problem solving skills: III. Category selection. *Creativity Research Journal*, 9, 395–406.

Mumford, M. D., Todd, E. M., Higgs, C., & McIntosh, T. (2017). Cognitive skills and leadership performance: the nine critical skills. *The Leadership Quarterly*, 28, 24–39.

Orwoll, L., & Perlmutter, M. (1990). The study of wise persons: integrating a personality perspective. In R. J. Sternberg (Ed.), *Wisdom: Its nature, origins, and development* (pp. 160–177). New York: Cambridge University Press.

Osburn, H. K., & Mumford, M. D. (2006). Creativity and planning: training interventions to develop creative problem-solving skills. *Creativity Research Journal*, 18, 173–190.

Pant, P. N., & Starbuck, W. H. (1990). Innocents in the forest: forecasting and research methods. *Journal of Management*, 16, 433–460.

Parnes, S. J., & Noller, R. B. (1972). Applied creativity: the creative studies project. *The Journal of Creative Behavior*, 6, 164–186.

Partlow, P. J., Medeiros, K. E., & Mumford, M. D. (2015). Leader cognition in vision formation: simplicity and negativity. *The Leadership Quarterly*, 26, 448–469.

Patalano, A. L., & Seifert, C. M. (1997). Opportunistic planning: being reminded of pending goals. *Cognitive Psychology*, 34, 1–36.

Redmond, M. R., Mumford, M. D., & Teach, R. (1993). Putting creativity to work: effects of leader behavior on subordinate creativity. *Organizational Behavior and Human Decision Processes*, 55, 120–151.

Reiter-Palmon, R., Mumford, M. D., O'Connor Boes, J., & Runco, M. A. (1997). Problem construction and creativity: the role of ability, cue consistency, and active processing. *Creativity Research Journal*, 10, 9–23.

Robledo, I. C., Hester, K. S., Peterson, D. R., Barrett, J. D., Day, E. A., Hougen, D. P., et al. (2012). Errors and understanding: the effects of error-management training on creative problem-solving. *Creativity Research Journal*, 24, 220–234.

Runco, M. A., & Acar, S. (2012). Divergent thinking as an indicator of creative potential. *Creativity Research Journal*, 24, 66–75.

Scott, G., Leritz, L. E., & Mumford, M. D. (2004). The effectiveness of creativity training: a quantitative review. *Creativity Research Journal*, 16, 361–388.

Scott, G. M., Lonergan, D. C., & Mumford, M. D. (2005). Conceptual combination: alternative knowledge structures, alternative heuristics. *Creativity Research Journal*, 17, 79–98.

Shipman, A. S., Byrne, C. L., & Mumford, M. D. (2010). Leader vision formation and forecasting: the effects of forecasting extent, resources, and timeframe. *The Leadership Quarterly*, 21, 439–456.

Sternberg, R. J. (1985). Implicit theories of intelligence, creativity, and wisdom. *Journal of Personality and Social Psychology*, 49, 607–627.

Sternberg, R. J. (1990). *Metaphors of mind: Conceptions of the nature of intelligence*. New York: Cambridge University Press.

Sternberg, R. J., & O'Hara, L. A. (1999). Creativity and intelligence. In R. J. Sternberg (Ed.), *Handbook of creativity* (pp. 251–272). New York, NY: Cambridge University Press.

Stokes, P. D. (2008). Creativity from constraints: what can we learn from Motherwell? From Modrian? From Klee? *The Journal of Creative Behavior*, 42, 223–236.

Vincent, A. S., Decker, B. P., & Mumford, M. D. (2002). Divergent thinking, intelligence, and expertise: a test of alternative models. *Creativity Research Journal*, 14, 163–178.

Wallas, G. (1928). *The art of thought*. New York: Harcourt-Brace.

Ward, T. B., Patterson, M. J., & Sifonis, C. M. (2004). The role of specificity and abstraction in creative idea generation. *Creativity Research Journal, 16,* 1–9.

Weisberg, R. W. (2011). Frank Lloyd Wright's Fallingwater: a case study of inside-the-box creativity. *Creativity Research Journal, 23,* 296–312.

Xiao, Y., Milgram, P., & Doyle, D. J. (1997). Capturing and modeling planning expertise in anesthesiology: results of a field study. In C. E. Zsambok & G. Klein (Eds.), *Naturalistic decision making* (pp. 197–205). Hillsdale, NJ: Lawrence Erlbaum Associates, Inc.

Zaccaro, S. J., Mumford, M. D., Connelly, M. S., Marks, M. A., & Gilbert, J. A. (2000). Assessment of leader problem-solving capabilities. *Leadership Quarterly, 11,* 37–64.

Zhang, X., & Bartol, K. M. (2010). Linking empowering leadership and employee creativity: the influence of psychological empowerment, intrinsic motivation, and creative process engagement. *Academy of Management Journal, 53,* 107–128.

The Intellectual Structure and Outlooks for Individual Creativity Research: A Bibliometric Analysis for the Period 1950–2016

Sabina Bogilović*, Matej Černe[†]

*Faculty of Administration, University of Ljubljana, Ljubljana, Slovenia,
[†]Faculty of Economics, University of Ljubljana, Ljubljana, Slovenia

INTRODUCTION

Creativity within an organizational context is part of organizational innovation, and together they form a part of a much broader domain—organizational change (Harrison, Price, Gavin, & Florey, 2002; Woodman, Sawyer, & Griffin, 1993). Organizational change has been recognized as a building block for organizational effectiveness and survival. Creativity is "the cornerstone of organizational change, the foundation of innovation, and a key to organizational effectiveness" (Gilson, Mathieu, Shalley, & Ruddy, 2005, p. 521). Organizations can respond to opportunities, adapt, grow, and compete if they use and implement creative ideas from their employees (Amabile, 1996; Oldham & Cummings, 1996). Therefore it is not surprising that creativity and innovation have seen considerable attention in academic research, especially in social sciences, and particularly by organizational psychologists and management scholars (Zhou & Hoever, 2014).

As part of organizational change, creativity and innovation are closely related processes in organizations; what is more, they are part of almost the same process (Anderson, Potočnik, & Zhou, 2014). Some scholars even used the terms interchangeably (Ford, 1996), as individual creativity represents the most important starting point for innovation (Amabile, Conti, Coon, Lazenby, & Herron, 1996), and both constructs are related to the same criteria of novelty and usefulness (Nijstad, Berger-Selman, & De Dreu, 2014). Although scholars (Amabile, 1988; Ford, 1996; Oldham & Cummings, 1996; Woodman et al., 1993) make a distinction between creativity and innovation, there is still a need for clear distinctions regarding where creativity ends and innovation begins. For example, Anderson et al. (2014) make a distinction between creativity and innovation, yet in their review paper, they present comprehensively key research findings of creativity and innovation together.

As such, we need to stress that in this chapter we will focus only on the creativity literature, as innovation is a broader concept than creativity (Axtell, Holman, Unsworth, Wall, & Waterson, 2000) and involves the generation, adoption, and implementation phases of the idea journey (Perry-Smith & Mannucci, 2017; Van de Ven, Angle, & Poole, 1989). Creativity mainly encompasses the generation phase, in which employees develop novel and useful ideas that can be successfully implemented as innovations within an organization (Amabile, 1996; Shalley, Gilson, & Blum, 2009; Shalley, Zhou, & Oldham, 2004; Zhou & Shalley, 2003). Generally, scholars define creativity as the production of ideas that are both novel and useful (Amabile, 1996), and by itself, it does not automatically guarantee organizational change through innovation (Amabile, 1988) because only some creative ideas from employees are selected for further development and implementation in organizations (Litchfield, Gilson, & Gilson, 2015). Moreover, predictors that can trigger employees' creativity may not enhance innovation processes in organizations (West, 2002; Zhou & Hoever, 2014); therefore in this paper we will focus only on creativity.

To the best of our knowledge, thus far there has not been a study that would show the developmental path of creativity research or reveal an intellectual structure of the field, and do so in an objective, all-inclusive and comprehensive manner, looking at the development of the field, current state and make informed prognoses about its future outlook. As such the interpretation of the definition of creativity from different domains and the underlying structure of how the creativity field has evolved, and how researchers have built their work on each other still remain vague.

In recent years, scholars have embraced a method of science mapping, which aims to create a representation of a structure of a specific research area and is used to examine how scientific disciplines are related one to another (Zupic & Čater, 2015). Bibliometric methods, although not new (Small, 1973), started to attract a more widespread attention in recent years with easy accessible online databases with citation data and the development of new software and tools for conducting bibliometric analyses (Zupic & Čater, 2015). Reviews based on bibliometrics can provide a more objective, aerial view on the examined field of research, as well as map the social structure presenting the development and current state of the research area, suggesting that the use of this techniques complement

traditional narrative reviews. Using bibliometric techniques, we can identify the most influential topics, understand the evolution and underlying
structure of the field and finally, recognize emerging topics that have potential to develop in the future. Therefore our aim is to fill this gap by
exploring the building blocks of the creativity literature with bibliometric
cocitation meta-analysis and development patterns of creativity research
with help of bibliographic coupling. With our research, we aim to investigate how creativity field evolved through years by providing the cocitation analysis with five distinct periods (i.e., 1949–70, 1971–85, 1986–2000,
2001–10, 2011–17). More recent time frames are shorter because of the ex-
ponential growth of scholarly work in this field, making the results for a
specific period comparable in terms of the number of analyzed publications, and easier to interpret. Based on the cocitation analyses, we present
the development patterns of creativity research from 1949 until 2017. We
take a step forward and additionally provide bibliographic coupling analysis of the individual creativity field for 2011–16, presenting its current
state of the art and comparing it with the creativity field in general, based
of which we suggest the future outlooks for both individual creativity and
creativity research in general.

   We complement existing qualitative creativity reviews (e.g., Anderson
et al., 2014; Zhou & Hoever, 2014) with a quantitative one based on bibliometrics, using a combination of two different bibliometric techniques:
document cocitation analysis and bibliographic coupling. From a methodological point of view, this approach provides us a more comprehensive
view of the creativity research development, as well as enables us to identify promising avenues for future research. Document cocitation analysis
reflects the state and the development of the field in a certain period in the
past (Nerur, Rasheed, & Natarajan, 2008; Vogel & Güttel, 2013) and adds to
understanding of the underlying structure and evolution of the field. This
technique uses a matrix of cocitation frequencies between scientific outputs as its input (McCain, 1990). The relatedness of two publications (i.e.,
strength of a cocitation) is defined as the number of times two documents
have been cited together (White, 2003); that is, the number of times they
have appeared together on the reference lists of other outputs. By using
cocitation ties between scientific contributions as the basic unit of analysis,
we are able to identify the most important clusters of related publications.

   Bibliographic coupling links documents that reference the same set of
cited documents (Kessler, 1963); the more the bibliographies of two articles overlap, the stronger their connection. This technique is suitable for
detecting current trends and future priorities as they are reflected in the
most recent publications (documents that include citations are de facto
more recent than those cited papers). Such an approach thereby enables
us to identify emergent topics and potential future avenues of the development of the literature. The use of a combination of bibliometric techniques complements and expands other qualitative and meta-analytical

reviews, offering a more comprehensive, inclusive and objective review study (Zupic & Čater, 2015).

Furthermore, by building on the conceptual framework of "invisible colleges" (cf., Vogel, 2012) used to metaphorically portray the sub streams within the literature, this study aims to add to the creativity literature by showing the dynamic perspective of evolving colleges of literatures that creativity studies have cited in a certain time period. The key outcome of such an approach is to map the field, discuss similarities and differences with findings offered by existing qualitative reviews of the creativity literature, and propose most promising developmental areas for the future evolution of the field. Furthermore, with this paper we provide a valuable reference guide (i.e., overview of the definitions and research history) for interdisciplinary researchers, business consultants, managers, and leaders who want to become familiar with the creativity literature.

FOUNDATIONS OF (INDIVIDUAL) CREATIVITY

Creativity, from Guilford's (1950) psychometric perspective, is the expression of divergent thinking, and from Amabile's (1983a, 1983b, 1983c) componential theory, it is a dynamic relationship between an individual's motivation and his or her relevant skills. In contrast, Pinheiro and Cruz (2014, p. 263), in their latest work on mapping creativity measurements, summarize, "It is no joke saying that creativity exists only in people's minds." Nevertheless, creativity "can be viewed as the first stage of an innovation process" (Baer, 2012, p. 1102), and thus considerable research has built up over the last 40 years in the field of creativity in organizations (Anderson et al., 2014).

Creativity, prior to 1970, has mostly been researched in perspectives of the discussion of inventions (Royce, 1898), Freudian accounts (e.g., Freud, 1908) to Guilford's call for creativity research in 1950, cognitive accounts (Mednick, 1962), and sociological accounts (Stein, 1967). Therefore it is no surprise that in the Rothenberg and Greenberg (1976) research, there were nearly 7000 citations in a bibliography dating from 1566 to 1974 in the field of creativity, yet only 138 included the social or environmental characteristics, and many of those documents researched the "social variable" that influences creativity, simply social class. Amabile (1983c, p. 357), in her article "The Social Psychology of Creativity: A Componential Conceptualization," stresses that prior "research ha[s] focused almost exclusively on a personality approach to creativity and, to a lesser extent, a cognitive-abilities approach." Specifically, the aim of empirical research in the field of creativity before 1980 was to identify what the personality differences are between creative and noncreative individuals (Nicholls, 1972).

Departing from the traditional approach to creativity, which focused on the individual characteristics of creative persons, Simonton's (e.g., Simonton, 1975, 1977a, 1977b, 1979) experimental studies of social influences on creativity were some of the first attempts to research creativity from the social psychology point of view. However, there was no research that explored how the working environment can contribute to the creative process in an organization. Hence, the foundation of the research on how organizational characteristics affect individual creativity at work started in the late 1980s and through the 1990s. The most influential and important works in that period are from Amabile (1988), Shalley (1991), Staw (1990), and Amabile et al. (1996). During that period, scholars (Amabile, 1987; Oldham & Cummings, 1996; Staw, 1984; Woodman et al., 1993) also started to provide more in-depth insight into the combined effect of personal and contextual factors on individual creativity at work.

Building on that seminal work, scholars (Amabile, 1988; Ford, 1996; Woodman et al., 1993) started to theorize and elaborate on the importance of distinguishing between organizational innovation and creativity in the organizational context. These were the foundations for researchers (see (Shalley et al., 2004; Zhou & Shalley, 2003) to focus more on personal or contextual factors that can enhance or stifle employee creativity in the workplace during the late 1990s and through the 2000s. Yet Shalley et al. (2004, pp. 952–953), in their review on creativity in organizations, stress that questions like "Will boosting creativity at work necessarily result in more innovative organizations?" or "What are the benefits and costs of creativity for the organization and its employees?" still remain.

From 2002 to 2014, the body of research of creativity in the field rapidly grew (Anderson et al., 2014). In Anderson et al.'s (2014) latest review on creativity in organizations, the scholars provide an in-depth summary of research findings in the creativity field from 2002 to 2011. More precisely, they summarize that at the individual level, scholars mostly researched the effect of individual differences (e.g., personality, goal orientation, values, thinking styles, self-concepts), individual factors (e.g., psychological states, motivation, strain/psychological contract, trust), task contexts (e.g., job complexity, goals and job requirements, time pressure, rewards), and social contexts (e.g., leadership and supervision, coworker influences, customer influences, feedback, social network, resources for creativity) on creativity. At the team level, the researchers analyzed the influence of team structure (e.g., task and goal interdependence), composition (e.g., heterogeneity (diversity)/cognitive style), climate (e.g., participative safety, conflict), processes (e.g., information exchange, problem solving style/team participation, conflict management, and minority dissent), leadership (e.g., transformational leadership, participative leadership), and other factors (e.g., information privacy) on creativity (see Anderson et al., 2014).

Moreover, some of the researchers even started to analyze creativity as a multilevel phenomenon—a summary of this logic is compiled in a handbook Multi-level Issues in Creativity and Innovation (2008; edited by M. Mumford, S.T. Hunter, and K.E. Bedell-Avers), as part of the Research in Multi-level Issues series. Chapters in this handbook review research on creativity and social influence (e.g., Dionne, 2008), and creativity and cognitive processes (e.g., Reiter-Palmon, Herman, & Yammarino, 2008) within a multilevel domain, and call for further cross-level (bottom-up and top-down) research on creativity. Following these calls, several studies then looked at the context of creativity with regards to team structure (Hirst, Van Knippenberg, Chen, & Sacramento, 2011), team climate (Černe, Nerstad, Dysvik, & Škerlavaj, 2014; Pirola-Merlo & Mann, 2004), team composition (Hirst, Van Knippenberg, & Zhou, 2009; Shin, Kim, Lee, & Bian, 2012), transformational leadership (Shin et al., 2012; Wang & Rode, 2010), and leader–member exchange—LMX (Liao, Liu, & Loi, 2010).

Although the research on creativity in an organizational context is quite spread out, the foundation of creativity still remains the same and thus has been mostly researched from the perspective of three different theories: componential theory of organizational creativity (Amabile, 1997), interactionist theory of organizational creativity (Woodman et al., 1993), and theory of individual creative action (Ford, 1996). Thus following we provide a summary of the definitions of creativity from the main authors in the field from an organizational context, the level of analysis or base for the conceptualization of creativity, and some of the most relevant authors in the field of creativity at work who adopted those definitions in Tables 1 and 2.

From these two tables, we can see that at the individual level, creativity was first defined as individual ability (Guilford, 1950), then later the definition of individual creativity evolved into the generation of novel and useful ideas, processes, or solutions (Amabile, 1996). These ideas are based on individual subjective judgment (Ford, 1996) and have to be also potentially relevant for the organization (Oldham & Cummings, 1996). Thus scholars in the last 60 years revealed that individual creativity is not only an individual characteristic, yet it is a generation process that is stimulated by individual factors, task contexts, and social contexts. The brief summary of the research in the creativity field in Tables 1 and 2 provided foundations for our bibliometric cocitation analysis of the creativity field, implemented in the following section of the Chapter. First, we provide brief cocitation analysis from 1900 until 2017, after which we implement five different cocitation analyses based on different time periods in order to obtain a more detailed insight for patterns of the evolution of "invisible colleges" within the creativity literature.

TABLE 1   A Brief Summary of Definitions and Levels of Analysis as the Basis for Conceptualization of Creativity (1)

Authors	Definition	Level of analysis	Adopted by some of the most relevant authors in the field of creativity at work
Shin and Zhou (2007, p. 1715)	"… the production of novel and useful ideas concerning products, services, processes, and procedures by a team of employees working together"	Team creativity	Farh, Lee, and Farh (2010)
Zhou and Shalley (2003)	"… the production of novel and useful ideas concerning products, services, processes, and procedures by an employee"	Individual level	Shin et al. (2012) and Madjar (2005)
Ford (1996, p. 1115)	"… as a domain-specific, subjective judgment of the novelty and value of an outcome of a particular action"	Individual level	Zhou, Shin, Brass, Choi, and Zhang (2009), Shalley and Gilson (2004), and Tierney and Farmer (2004)
Amabile (1996)	"… generation of novel and useful ideas, processes, or solutions"	Individual level	Baer (2010, 2012), Baer, Leenders, Oldham, and Vadera (2010), Gong, Huang, and Farh (2009), Zhou et al. (2009), Shin and Zhou (2007), Madjar (2005), Baer, Oldham, and Cummings (2003), Drazin, Glynn, and Kazanjian (1999), Tierney, Farmer, and Graen (1999), Perry-Smith and Shalley (2003), Zhou and Shalley (2003), Shalley and Gilson (2004), Gilson and Shalley (2004), Tierney and Farmer (2004), Grant and Berry (2011), and Černe et al. (2014)
Amabile et al. (1996, p. 1155)	"… as the production of novel and useful ideas in any domain"	Individual level	Shin and Zhou (2003, 2007)

TABLE 2   A Brief Summary of Definitions and Levels of Analysis as the Basis for Conceptualization of Creativity (2)

Authors	Definition	Level of analysis	Adopted by some of the most relevant author in the field of creativity at work
Oldham and Cummings (1996, p. 608)	"… as production, of ideas, or procedures that satisfy two conditions: (1) they are novel or original, and (2) they are potentially relevant for, or useful to, an organization"	Individual level	Baer (2010, 2012), De Stobbeleir, Ashford, and Buyens (2011), Baer et al. (2010, 2003), Zhou et al. (2009), Hirst et al. (2009), George and Zhou (2007), Shin and Zhou (2007), Shalley and Gilson (2004), Zhou and Shalley (2003), and Madjar and Oldham (2002)
Woodman, Sawyer, and Griffin (1993, p. 293)	"… is the creation of a valuable, useful new product, service, idea, procedure, or process by individuals working together in a complex social system"	Organizational level	Jia, Shaw, Tsui, and Park (2014), Shin and Zhou (2007), Gilson and Shalley (2004), Tierney and Farmer (2004), and Zhou and George (2001)
Mumford and Gustafson (1988, p. 28)	"… as a syndrome involving a number of elements: (a) the processes underlying the individual's capacity to generate new ideas or understandings, (b) the characteristics of the individual facilitating process operation, (c) the characteristics of the individual facilitating the translation of these ideas into action, (d) the attributes of the situation conditioning the individual's willingness to engage in creative behavior, and (e) the attributes of the situation influencing evaluation of the individual's productive efforts"		Unsworth (2001)

(Continued)

TABLE 2   A Brief Summary of Definitions and Levels of Analysis as the Basis for Conceptualization of Creativity (2)—cont'd

Authors	Definition	Level of analysis	Adopted by some of the most relevant author in the field of creativity at work
Koestler (1964)	"Creativity involves a 'bisociative process'— the connecting of two previously unrelated 'matrices of thought' to produce a new insight or invention"	Creativity as a process	
Guilford (1950, p. 444)	"… creativity refers to the abilities that are most characteristic of creative people"	Individual level	

METHODS AND RESULTS

Cocitation Analysis

We used ISI Web of Science in order to obtain secondary data for bibliometric cocitation analysis since the majority of researchers in bibliometric studies (e.g., Nerur et al., 2008) use this database. We searched all citation databases offered by ISI: SCI-EXPANDED (Science Citation Index Expanded), SSCI (Social Sciences Citation Index), and A&HCI (Arts & Humanities Citation Index) using the search term "OR." The following keywords were used: "creativity" or "creative." At this point, we would like to stress that our aim was to explore the field of creativity, thus we intentionally did not put "innovation" or "innovative" or "idea implementation" as keywords in the research. The research obtained a database containing 76,989 units of literature (documents) in June 2017. We then refined the search by key areas (Web of Science categories): Management, Psychology Multidisciplinary, Business, Psychology Educational, Social Sciences Interdisciplinary, Psychology Applied, Psychology Experimental, Psychology Social, Psychology, Operations Research Management Science, Social Issues, Public Administration, and Behavioral science. From this search, we obtained a database containing 19,420 units of literature (documents). Focusing only on the articles (excluding books, book chapters, conference proceedings etc.), Fig. 1 presents the distribution of the primary published items per year during the 1920–2017 period. The articles published on the topic of creativity exponentially increased throughout the years.

Fig. 2 reveals the citations in each year (period 1996–2015) for 2435 units of documents that Web of Science generated. In line with the publication

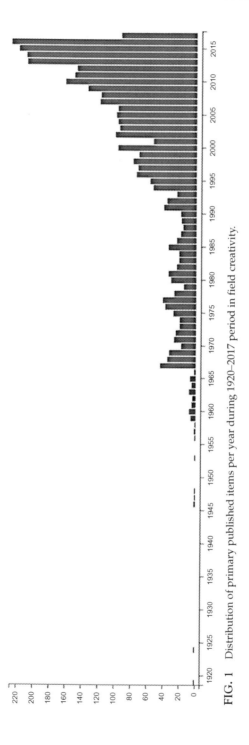

FIG. 1   Distribution of primary published items per year during 1920–2017 period in field creativity.

FIG. 2 Number of citations of creativity documents in each year.

of documents, the citations also exponentially increased throughout the years. The highest number of citations of documents in the field of creativity was in the years 2015 and 2014. The most cited article in this search is paper from Amabile, Conti, Coon, Lazenby, and Herron with tittle "Assessing the work environment for creativity" published in the Academy of Management (i.e., total of 1326 citations; 60.27 per year).

As we wanted to obtain a more detailed view of the creativity research development in the organizational behavior domain, we divided the field of creativity on five distinct periods (i.e., 1949–70, 1971–85, 1986–2000, 2001–10, 2011–16). From Figs. 1 and 2 we can see that until 1970 there are not as many publications and citations in the creativity field, thus we wanted to first see what the foundations of the creativity field are and which patterns of creativity research can be found from 1949 to 1970. The Web of Science research obtained a database containing 2403 units of documents, 850 units of literature after the refinement by key areas, and 469 units after manual exclusion of irrelevant articles. The most cited article from that period is Mednick (1962) article "The associate basis of the creative process" that was published in Psychological review (i.e., total of 1138 citations; 20.69 per year). In order to conduct cocitation bibliometric analysis, we exported the database of the chosen articles into VOS viewer. Due to a large number of unique secondary documents a cutoff point, which refers to a minimum number of citations of a document, was applied to the reference list. We applied a cutoff point at a minimum of 10 citations of a document.[1] The visualization was created in VOS viewer and revealed four different clusters (Fig. 3).

From Fig. 3, we can see that there are two main islands that are very well connected with each other and two peripheral islands. The works of Mednick (1962), Barron (1955, 1957), and Stein and Heinze (1960) represent one island that is more central to the network. The authors in this island focus their research of creative process and how intelligence can stimulate individual originality. On the other hand, the island that includes works from Torrance (1962, 1965), Getzels and Jackson (1962), Wallach and Kogan (1965), and Taylor and Barron (1963) is more focused on how to spot the creative talent in a child and how creative thinking can be trained in schools. Although the research in these two islands is not directly related to each other, both represent the core of the cocitation network, indicating that these mentioned authors are the most important in the field in period from 1949 until 1970.

---

[1] According to expert advice (Zupic & Čater, 2015), the exact cutoff points for specific time periods depend on researchers and should be done in a way to enable as much visual information and potential for interpretation as possible. Nonetheless, this is a somewhat iterative process, subjective to the interpretation by researchers, which is one of the key limitations of bibliometric methods.

FIG. 3 Cocitation analysis of the creativity field, 1949–70.

The third island includes authors like Mackinnon (1962), Golann (1963), Cattell and Drevdahl (1955), Drevdahl (1956), Barron (1953), and Barron and Welsh (1952), in which authors focus on measures of creativity (e.g., intelligence, originality, preference) and how to nurture individual creative talent. Therefore it is no surprise that this island actually connects the previously two mentioned islands. However, the dots in this island are smaller than in the previous two, thus this island is less important. Authors such as Osborn (1957) and Meadow, Parnes, and Reese (1959) focus their research on imagination and brainstorming. Since they are not connected as much to research topics in previous islands, it is no surprise that this island is more outside of the cocitation network. As such, it is not as important in the creativity field in the period from 1949 until 1970.

We continued our research for the period from 1971 until 1985. The research obtained a database containing 5026 units of documents, which after refinement of key areas obtained a database containing 1163 units of literature, and after manual exclusion 465 units. We applied a cutoff point at minimum of five citations of a document. The visualization revealed four different clusters (Fig. 4).

In this cocitation network, we can see that there are two main islands that are very well connected with each other and tree periphery islands. The main island includes authors such as Kogan (Wallach & Kogan, 1965), Mednick (1962), Welsh (1959), Winer (1962), Gordon (1961), and Maier (1970). The authors in the island focus their research on the creative process, problem solving, and how modes of thinking can influence individual creativity. The second largest island in Fig. 4 includes authors such as MacKinnon (1962), Guilford (1950, 1959), Torrance (1962), and Glover (Glover & Gary, 1976), and the main aim of their research is linking creativity with individual personality, traits, and intelligence. The authors

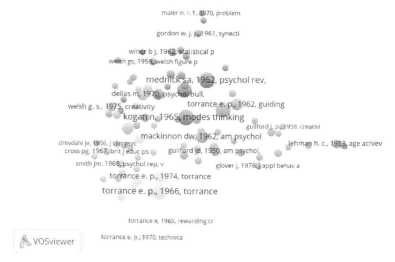

maier n. r. f., 1970, problem

gordon w. j. j, 1961, synecti

winer b j, 1962, statistical p
welsh gs, 1959, welsh figure p

mednick sa, 1962, psychol rev,
delias m, 1970, psychol bull,
welsh g. s., 1975, creativity   torrance e. p., 1962, guiding
kogan n, 1965, modes thinking
guilford j, p. 1959, creativi
mackinnon dw, 1962, am psychol
drevdahl je, 1956, j clin psyc   lehman h. c., 1953, age achiev
cross pg, 1967, brit j educ ps   guilford jp, 1950, am psychol,
smith jm, 1969, psychol rep, v   glover j, 1976, j appl behav a
torrance e. p., 1974, torrance
torrance e. p., 1966, torrance

torrance e, 1965, rewarding cr

VOSviewer   torrance e. p., 1970, technica

FIG. 4   Cocitation analysis of the creativity field, 1971–85.

Welch (1975), Dellas (Dellas & Gaier, 1970), Cross, Cattell, and Butcher (1967), and Smith and Schaefer (1969) form their own island, yet it is much smaller than the previous ones. This island includes research on how to stimulate individual creativity and how we can measure it by providing creativity scales for the Adjective Check List (ACL) (Smith & Schaefer, 1969). The work of Smith and Schaefer (1969) is related to another Torrance (1966, 1974) island which is focused on how to measure individual creativity by introducing Torrance Tests of Creative Thinking (TTCT) (1966, 1974).

The cocitation network of the creativity field for the period 1971–85 differs from the previous network such that this network is denser and has more authors, which is no surprise since the published items per year in the period from 1971 until 1985 had increased (see Fig. 1). We can see that in the period 1971–85, in the center of the cocitation network there are authors such as Wallach and Kogan (1965), Torrance (1962), and MacKinnon (1962) that were on the periphery in the prior network. Moreover, we can find new authors that were not in the prior network, such as Guilford (1950, 1959), Glover and Gary (1976), Welsh (1975, 1959), and Dellas and Gaier (1975). Yet, the position of the authors such as Mednick (1962) and Drevdahl (1956) stayed the same as in the cocitation network for the period 1949–70.

The Web of Science search for the period 1986–2000 obtained an initial database containing 9754 units of documents. We then refined the search by key areas (resulting in 3292 documents after refinement) and were left off with 453 units after manual exclusion. We applied a cutoff point at minimum of three citations of a document. The visualization revealed four different clusters (Fig. 5) that form three main islands that are very well connected with each other and two periphery islands. The most dense island includes authors such as Guilford (1950, 1967), MacKinnon

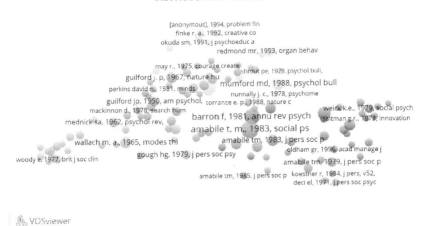

FIG. 5   Cocitation analysis of the creativity field, 1986–2000.

(1978), Perkins (1981), and Torrance (1988) that research creative thinking and intelligence. Moreover, this island is well related to the island on the periphery that includes authors such as Mednick (1962), Wallach and Kogan (1965), Woddy (Woody & Claridge, 1977), and Gough (1979).

Fig. 5 also identifies a new stream of authors that emerges in the cocitation network of the creativity field 1986–2000. The most important is the Amabile (1979, 1983a, 1983b, 1983c, 1985) island that also includes authors such as Deci (1971) and Koestner (Koestner, Ryan, Bernieri, & Holt, 1984). This island is crucial for future development of individual creativity in the working environment, while the researchers started to explore how individual motivation is related to creativity (e.g., the impact of extrinsic or intrinsic motivation on individual creativity) and how working environment is related to individual creativity (e.g., job complexity and supervisor supporting behavior). As such, we argue that this island mostly examines the social psychology side of creativity and is connected with the island that includes authors such as Barron (Barron & Harrington, 1981) and Weick (1979). Their research focus is on personality and social psychology of organizations; therefore is no surprise that these two islands are close in the cocitation network and connected. The island that is the smallest and most on the periphery includes authors such as Mumford (Mumford & Gustafson, 1988), Redmond (Redmond, Mumford, & Teach, 1993), and Finke, Ward, and Smith (1992). The primary research focus of this island is innovative achievement, originality, and creative invention, thus it is no surprise that it is not so related with the Amabile (1983a, 1983b, 1983c) island and her research on individual creativity or Mednick (1962) creative process and thinking modes island.

The cocitation network of the creativity field for the period 1986–2000 differs from the cocitation network of the previous period 1971–85 such that the more recent network is even denser and has more authors. From Fig. 5 (in comparison with Fig. 4) we can see that in the period 1986–2000, a new line of research emerges in the creativity literature that provides an insight into the social side of creativity psychology at work. More precisely, it reveals how employees' personal characteristics, organizational context, cognitive abilities, and social factors might contribute to the individual creative process. The Torrance (1966, 1974) island (see Fig. 4) is no longer visible in the cocitation network of the creativity field for the period 1986–2000. However, there are still islands characterized by pieces such as Mednick (1962)—following the creative process and thinking modes stream of research, MacKinnon (1978) and Guilford (1950)—exploring the cognitive aspect of creativity related to thinking modes.

The cocitation analyses for the period 2000–10 reveal 16,240 units of documents in the initial search, 3077 units after refinement for key areas. We applied a cutoff point at minimum of 10 citations of a document. The visualization revealed only three different clusters (see Fig. 6). There are two main islands and one smaller, emerging island. The largest islands include authors such as Barron and Harrington (1981), Guilford (1950), Mednick (1962), Torrance (1974), Kirton (1976), Amabile (1983a, 1983b, 1983c), and Runco (1991). In this island, we can find the authors that could be found also in the cocitation network from the prior period (see Figs. 4 and 5) and thus represent the foundation of the new creative research stream. The second largest island in the cocitation network for period 2001–10 includes authors such as Zhou (Zhou & George, 2001), Tierney (Tierney & Farmer, 2002), Oldham (Oldham & Cummings, 1996), Shin and Zhou (2003), George (George & Zhou, 2002), Shalley (1991), and Shalley et al. (2004). The authors in this island research how different aspects (i.e.,

FIG. 6   Cocitation analysis of the creativity field, 2001–10.

personal context, leadership, organizational environment) can stimulate or hide creativity at work and how creativity is related to innovation.

The smallest island on the periphery that includes authors such as Woodman et al. (1993), Drazin et al. (1999), and Amabile (1996) mostly define organizational creativity and examine how organizational creativity is related to innovation literature. We wanted to see whether these islands will be divided and how the creativity literature will involve in the final period of 2010–16, thus we conducted another cocitation analysis.

This revealed an initial database containing 19,608 units of documents, 1775 after refinement for key areas, after which we put 500 of the most cited units into further analyses. We applied a cutoff point at minimum of 10 citations of a document. The visualization revealed only three different clusters (see Fig. 7).

We can see that authors such as Amabile (1988, 1996), Woodman et al. (1993), West (2002), Perry-Smith (2006), and Hülsheger (Hülsheger, Anderson, & Salgado, 2009) form a cluster that is mostly research on creativity at organizational and team levels, and its linkages with innovations in organizations. Authors Scott (Scott & Bruce, 1994), Shalley (Shalley & Gilson, 2004), Bass (1985), and Bliese (2000) form another cluster that focuses more on leadership and methodological approaches. From Fig. 7, we can see that authors Zhou and George (2001), George and Zhou (2002, 2007), Shalley, Gilson, and Blum (2000), Shalley and Perry-Smith (2001), Amabile (1996), and Amabile, Barsade, Mueller, and Staw (2005) form their own cluster. This cluster is focused on how we can simulate individual

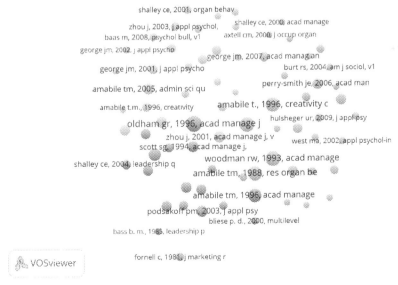

FIG. 7 Cocitation analysis of the creativity field, 2010–16.

creativity at work. Taken together, these cocitation networks (see Figs. 3–7) represent the foundation for the development of patterns of the evolution of "invisible colleges" within the creativity literature. Therefore in the next section, we connect the described cocitation networks and explain the development patterns of the creativity literature from 1949 until 2017.

Patterns of the Evolution of "Invisible Colleges" Within the Creativity Literature

The results of the network analysis presented in the previous section surfaced the nested, sociocognitive structure of creativity development where different clusters were identified. In this section we present the evolutionary patterns of dynamic change in creativity research over five time intervals. We use an evolutionary framework proposed by Vogel (2012) and used in other fields like organizational socialization (Batistic & Kase, 2015) and leadership (Batistič, Černe, & Vogel, 2017). The evolution path of creativity shows that four main different colleges were identified in the initial time stamp (1949–70): creativity training and development, developmental psychology, creative process and intelligence, originality and personality. Comprehensive summary results are presented in Fig. 8.

Turning to specific (trans)formations of colleges in the creativity field, we describe each developmental pattern with different occurrences and examples in the creativity field. The emergence of a new college is college appearance, where there is no predecessor in the same field, even though its foundations may be long standing. While examining the development of the creativity field, we can actually not observe such an occurrence. It seems that all the dominant clusters have evolved from their predecessors in previous time frames.

College transformation is a slow or sudden change of an existing college, which can result in the formation of a new college (Vogel, 2012). For example, we can observe college transformation of the cluster on *creative process and intelligence* (with Guilford and Mednick as exemplar scholars) in the first time period, which transformed into the cluster on *creativity vs intelligence* (Guilford and Getzels) in the second time period. Cluster of *creative process and thinking modes* from the second time period (Mednick) transformed into a cluster with the same label in the third one (Mednic, Wallach). *Organizational creativity* cluster from the third period (Woodman, Barron) transformed into *organizational creativity* (Woodman, Ford, Drazin) in the fourth period and finally into *organizational and social creativity and innovation* (Woodman, Perry-Smith, Hulsheger) in the final time stamp. *Social psychology of creativity* (Amabile) in the third period transformed into *creativity at work* (Oldham, Tierney, Zhou, Shalley) in the fourth period.

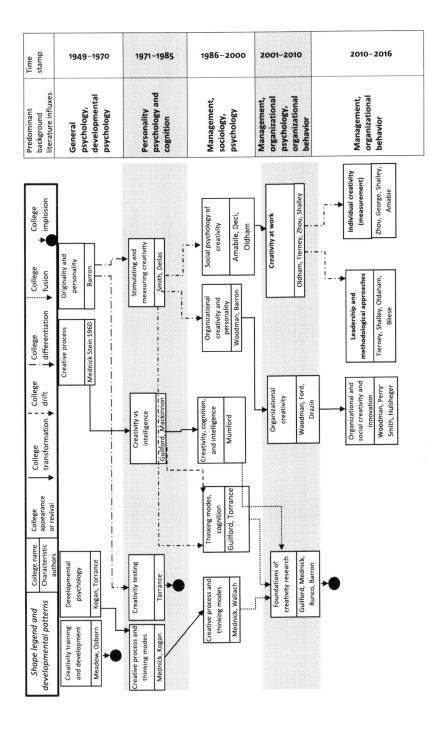

FIG. 8 Development patterns of creativity research.

College drift is described as a process by which parts of a college become incorporated into another, preexisting college (Vogel, 2012). One example of such drift can be seen between time stamps two and three, where part of the *creativity* vs *intelligence* cluster drifted into the *thinking modes and cognition cluster* (Runco, Guilford); another one in the same time period when he cluster on *cognitive aspects of creativity* (Kogan, Torrance) drifted into *social psychology of creativity*.

College differentiation describes a process by which a broadly defined college splits up into several new colleges, each with a more specialized focus and indicates a pattern of divergent evolution (Vogel, 2012). The creativity field development has an abundance of such examples; *originality and personality* cluster from the first time stamp (Barron) has differentiated into *creativity testing* (Torrance), *cognitive aspects of creativity* (Kogan, Torrance), and *personality and creativity* (Barron, Welsch) in the second period; the *developmental psychology cluster* (Kogan, Torrance) from the first period has differentiated into *creative process and thinking modes* (Mednick) and *cognitive aspects of creativity* in the second period; the *personality and creativity* cluster from the second period (Barron, Welsch) has differentiated into *organizational creativity* (Woodman, Barron) and *social psychology of creativity* in the third period; and the *creativity at work* (Oldham, Tierney, Zhou, Shalley) cluster from the fourth period has differentiated into *leadership and methodological approaches* (Tierney, Bass, Bliese) and *individual creativity (measurement*; Tierney, Zhou, George) in the final time stamp. These examples suggest that the differentiation of college is accompanied by growth in the number of publications. On the other hand, despite the growth of the college the differentiation may not occur, but maintain coherence of specific college (Vogel, 2012).

College fusion happens when two or more previously independent colleges merge into a single college (Vogel, 2012). An example of this pattern of convergent evolution can be seen in the integration of clusters on *creative process and thinking modes, thinking modes and cognition,* and *creativity, cognition, and intelligence* in the third period into a cluster of *foundations of creativity research* (Guilford, Mednick, Runco, Barron) in the fourth one.

College implosion is when a college disappears without successor. The disappearance of present colleges is a common phenomenon in the evolution of a field (Batistic & Kase, 2015; Vogel, 2012). It was suggested that only few colleges survive longer than a decade; this mortality is particularly high among more peripheral colleges and in some cases, even core colleges are not immune (Batistič et al., 2017; Vogel, 2012). In our case, results show several such instances, such as the *creativity training and development* cluster (Meadow, Osborn) after the first time stamp, *creativity testing* after the second period, and even the cluster on the aforementioned *foundations of creativity research* after the fourth time frame, which is not a common foundation of cocitations for research in the final examined period any more.

College revival refers to the reappearance of a certain college that has temporarily disappeared. Our analysis shows no such instance, although it needs to be recognized that the ideas from, for instance, imploded clusters on creativity training and development were applied in later clusters on organizational creativity, ideas from creativity testing in later clusters on creativity measurement, and foundations of creativity research in all recent clusters in the field.

Taken together, as an overview of theoretical foundations of creativity research, predominant background literature influxes across the time periods include general and developmental psychology (1949–70); personality psychology and cognition (1971–85); management, sociology, and psychology (1986–2000); management organizational psychology and organizational behavior (2001–10); and management and organizational behavior in the final time stamp (2010–16).

Bibliographic Coupling

Bibliographic coupling is used for analyzing the citing documents; those that cite the same references. It uses the number of references shared by two documents as a measure of the similarity between them. The more the bibliographies of two articles overlap, the stronger their connection. It differs from cocitation analysis in a sense that bibliographic coupling represents a permanent relationship, because of the dependence on the references contained in the coupled document, whereas cocitation varies over time (Cobo, López-Herrera, Herrera-Viedma, & Herrera, 2011; Zupic & Čater, 2015). Thus the main point of this analysis is to obtain the current state of the art in the field.

The same dataset was used for bibliographic coupling as in the document cocitation analysis. For this analysis, we defined the time period 2010–16 and exported the database of target articles into VOSviewer. We applied a cutoff point at minimum of 10 citations of a document. The visualization was again created in VOSviewer and revealed four different clusters (Fig. 9).

The analysis shows a cluster centered around studies of Miron-Spektor, Gino, and Argote (2011) and Grant and Berry (2011) focused on *framing and complex motivations for creativity*; the next one centered around Baer (2012) concentrated on the *implementation of creative ideas* and the link between creativity and innovation; another one revolving around Madjar, Greenberg, and Chen (2011) and Sosa (2011) focused on *creative interactions and cocreation*; and the final one revolving around Somech and Drach-Zahavy (2013) and Gong, Kim, Lee, and Zhu (2013) narrowing in on *group creativity*; there is an additional cluster on the periphery, revolving around studies of Rego, Sousa, Marques, and de Pina E Cunha (2012) focusing on *positive psychological capital, leadership and creativity*. These seem to be

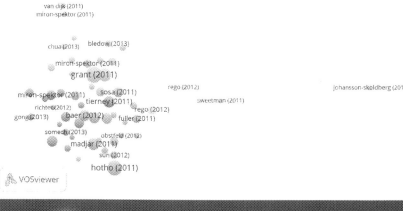

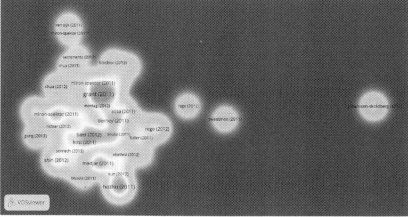

FIG. 9   Bibliographic coupling of the creativity field, 2011–16.

currently (in the final time stamp of our examined field development) the most popular topics of research that are being the most heavily cited.

Briefly comparing and contrasting these bibliographic coupling results of general creativity field with the current state of the art of research focused specifically on individual creativity, Fig. 10 reveals results of a similar analysis for individual creativity. Indeed, the situation is quite different, as almost none of the most influential studies in the general creativity field can be found in research specifically targeting individual creativity. Here, the analysis revealed six clusters, which are spread more; we cannot really describe the core–periphery pattern, as clusters seem to be more equally represented. The highest density is found around Anderson et al. (2014) and Zhou and Hoever (2014) *review papers on creativity and innovation* (yellow cluster); another cluster revolves around studies of Agnihotri, Rapp, Andzulis, and Gabler (2014) and Harrison and Rouse (2014) on *creative group work and boundary spanning*; the next cluster includes studies of Černe

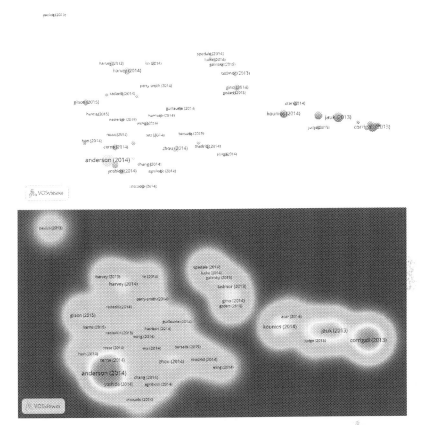

FIG. 10 Bibliographic coupling of the individual creativity field, 2011–16.

et al. (2014), Gilson, Maynard, Jones Young, Vartiainen, and Hakonen (2015), and Wang, Tsai, and Tsai (2014) on *obstacles and boundary conditions of creativity*; another cluster revolves around studies of Perry-Smith and Shalley (2014), Radaelli, Lettieri, Mura, and Spiller (2014), and Gino and Wiltermuth (2014) on *team processes and composition, dishonesty, and creativity*; another one includes studies of Harvey (2013, 2014) and Paulus, Kohn, Arditti, and Korde (2013) and deals with *group creativity*; and the final one consists of studies of Jauk, Benedek, Dunst, and Neubauer (2013), Corrigall, Schellenberg, and Misura (2013), and Kounios and Beeman (2014) and deals with *cognition, intelligence, and neuroscience for creativity*.

In order to provide a better explanation where this research is headed, we also composed a word cloud in an online free tool called word cloud based on the paper abstracts from the research papers that were identified in the bibliographic coupling of the individual creativity field, 2011–16. The aim was to provide and give greater prominence to words that appear more frequently in the research papers. The word cloud is presented in

FIG. 11 Words cloud based on abstracts from papers derived from the bibliographic coupling of the individual creativity field, 2011–16.

Fig. 11, and we can see that the most common used word form in all of these researchers was creativity and creative (80 authors used this term) followed by research (results, studies, study, and authors), a team (teams, group, and members), ideas, diversity, knowledge, and process. This indicates that the studies in the last research period (2011–16) have linked individual creativity with different ideas, diversity, knowledge, stressing that individual creativity is the ongoing process. Moreover, the term innovation (20 authors used this term) is not so commonly used in these abstracts; we can thus conclude that organizational researchers have started to make a distinction between creativity and innovation. We can further see that researchers have linked individual creativity to sharing, ties, traits, roles, critical processes, intuition, personality, and leadership. We can therefore conclude that organizational research moved from initial start connecting creativity with intelligence and started to explore how state-like, trait-like, and environment factors stimulate individual creativity

DISCUSSION

Cocitation network analysis provided us with insights about the origins of creativity and how the field itself has evolved through the years from 1949 until 2017 (see Figs. 1–7). From the cocitations networks we can see that the main authors are well connected to each other and that the field itself has involved through years. With the help of cocitation networks, we portrayed the development of the evolution path of creativity, identified the "invisible colleges" and their evolution over the years. Moreover, we conducted bibliographic coupling of both the creativity field and the individual creativity subfield for the period 2011–16, portraying the state of the art of the field, based on which we further provide recommendations for future researchers.

Contributions and Implications

This paper goes beyond traditional qualitative reviews of like Gilson and Shalley (2004), Shalley et al. (2004), Anderson et al. (2014), and Zhou and Hoever (2014) to provide a more detailed insight into the most important and influential papers and authors in the creativity field. First, we complement existing qualitative (e.g., Anderson et al., 2014; Zhou & Hoever, 2014) reviews of the creativity field and provide a more objective, comprehensive, and all-inclusive portrayal of its historical development based on bibliometric indicators. This analysis narrowed in on five distinctive periods (i.e., 1949–70, 1971–85, 1986–2000, 2001–10, 2011–17). The foundation of individual creativity has between 1949 until 1985 mostly based on research streams such as originality (Barron, 1955, 1957), creative thinking (Torrance, 1962, 1965), imagination (Osborn, 1957), invention (Finke et al., 1992), innovation (Mumford and Gustafson, 1988), creative process (Mednick, 1962).

However, in the period of 1985–2000, new lines of research emerged in the creativity literature, such as the social side of creativity, the psychology of creativity and organizational creativity. These two research streams represent a new point of view on how to approach creativity at work at the individual and organizational levels. Moreover, the social side of creativity psychology stream of research provides an insight into how employees' personal characteristics, organizational context, cognitive abilities, and social factors might stimulate individual creativity. In the following years (e.g., period 2001–10), the individual creativity subdomain emerged from the social psychology of creativity research stream via creativity at work and representative authors such as Zhou and George (2001), Tierney and Farmer (2002), Oldham (1996), Shin and Zhou (2003), George and Zhou (2002), Shalley (1991), Shalley et al. (2004). Thus with the help of cocitation analysis, we provide objectively grounded evidence into the foundations of individual creativity at work and how it emerged.

Second, this study adds to previous reviews by presenting evolutionary development of creativity using a framework of "invisible colleges" (Vogel, 2012). This approach enabled us to identify and describe clusters of colleges of the intellectual foundations, that is, studies that the creativity field has cited. Based on this methodology, we were able to combine different streams of research and identified influxes that are based on an all-inclusive portrayal of the development of the field. Specifically, we provided evidence into how a specific research stream evolved and is connected with other subdomains in different periods on the basis of cocitations. Although we provide evidence for the whole creativity field, our aim was to explore how the individual creativity at work subfield emerged and what are its main patterns of foundations.

Thirdly, using a combination of two different bibliometric techniques: document cocitation analysis and bibliographic coupling, this approach provides us a more comprehensive view of the development of the field. The use of bibliometrics as a quantitative approach offers an objective and non-predetermined examination (Zupic & Čater, 2015) of the evolution of the creativity field. Bibliometric techniques are more data grounded and thus less biased as they allow us to include a large scale of textual resources (Batistič et al., 2017). Our extensive review based on an objective, quantifiable approach reveals the roots of evolution of creativity field and potential future research directions. Cocitation analysis examines scientific communication through formal publication channels and enables us to operationalize "invisible colleges." By using these methods, bibliometric mapping served as an effective technique for identifying the existence of "invisible colleges" through detected clusters of highly cited works and including the dynamic aspect of their evolution over time (Vogel, 2012).

Looking into the future of creativity research, we based our suggestions on bibliographic coupling. The advantage of this technique is a use of newer publications that are not cited yet or with less citations. The analysis is best performed within a limited time frame, as the connection is established by the authors of the articles in focus. Although it is known a decade more than cocitation, it has been used less frequently. Since there are only few studies applying this technique, it has a great potential for further use in the management leadership domain (Zupic & Čater, 2015).

In terms of the differences between the fields of general creativity and individual creativity, content-wise, there are many, as described in the previous section. In terms of research analysis levels, the differences seem to be semantical, as both identified literatures examine both individual and group levels of analysis. A clear opportunity for future research includes multilevel clusters that would include the logic of individual-level creativity research while still including contextual ideas from the field of creativity in general, which could become central to this field of research. This initial suggestion opens up many specific future research avenues opened up by our bibliometric analyses; we describe these later.

Future Research Suggestions

From the bibliographic coupling, it seems that several avenues for future research are particularly promising. In addition to lately an ever-present plea for research embrace a multilevel paradigm to a larger extent and offer a more complex account of theoretical ideas that span across several levels of analysis, a key avenue of research in particular for individual creativity lies in its linkage with prosocial motivation and behavior. In particular, linking prosocial motivation with personal values, and potentially tapping into the dark side of otherwise positive concepts, such as creativity and prosocial behavior, could be a promising way to drive the field forward, in particular by connecting these ideas to expanding research on ethics and (un)ethical behavior. Creative bootlegging (Criscuolo, Salter, & Ter Wal, 2013), for example, represents such an interesting line of investigation that lies on the intersection of these phenomena, as does the connection of creativity with knowledge hiding, a recently popular research stream (Bogilović, Černe, & Škerlavaj, 2017; Černe et al., 2014) that also emerged in our bibliographic coupling analyses.

Bibliographic coupling also revealed that there is density around the Shin et al. (2012) paper, exploring team diversity and its relationship with individual team member creativity. Although some studies have shown that creativity is indeed linked with cultural diversity at work (Chua, 2013; Chua, Morris, & Mor, 2012; Cox, Lobel, & McLeod, 1991; Giambatista & Bhappu, 2010; Stahl, Maznevski, Voigt, & Jonsen, 2010), the research has not yielded equally consistent evidence that cultural diversity definitely triggers individual or team creativity (Hülsheger et al., 2009; Jackson & Joshi, 2011). Reviewing a growing body of research on creativity, Anderson et al. (2014, p. 1301) explained that "significant research-practice gap has led to repeated calls for greater research attention on cultural differences and creativity." Moreover, Erez and colleagues (Erez, Van de Ven, & Lee, 2015, p. 1) in the special issue of the Journal of Organizational Behavior on "Contextualizing Creativity and Innovation Across Cultures" stressed that: "there has been ongoing research on the effects of culture on creativity and innovation, leading to inconsistent findings." Thus in line with repeated calls (Anderson et al., 2014; Gilson & Shalley, 2004; Shalley & Gilson, 2004), we suggest that future research should explore individual creativity within the diversity setting in organizations.

Further, the very definition of creativity and its two dimensions (novelty and usefulness) also represent a promising way to drive the field forward, in particular by examining how these two facets of creativity could share similar (or not) antecedents and outcomes. Reinvigorating research into the creative process of ideation, illumination, etc., and how it each stage is linked with the two criteria of creativity also seems a promising avenue for future research. Linking creativity with subsequent stages of the (micro-)innovation process is also relevant, and examining differentiating predictors of idea generation vs implementation, and the boundary conditions influencing this (curvilinear; Škerlavaj, Černe, & Dysvik, 2014) relationship also require further investigation.

Future research could also delve into different types of creativity, such as radical vs incremental creativity (Madjar et al., 2011). Doing so, researchers can find their logic on the existing knowledge on the scope of innovations from the broader innovation field, but also include domain-specific insights into the processes of idea generation that are more grounded in psychology as opposed to those more grounded in business and economics that are characteristic for innovation research.

Additionally, the Johansson-Sköldberg, Woodilla, and Çetinkaya (2013) article that emerged from our bibliographic coupling analysis explores the design thinking concept, and although the cluster around it was not deemed as very dense and is not connected to other research of creativity, it represents a new stream of research that may provide us with a more detailed insight into the individual creative process at work, while offering potential linkages with research of innovation and entrepreneurship at the organizational level of research. There are a few studies that have already linked the design-thinking method with creativity (Ulibarri, Cravens, Cornelius, Royalty, & Nabergoj, 2014) and creative idea implementation (Bogilović, Škerlavaj, & Wong, 2016); however, more research is needed to examine the relationship between creativity and design thinking.

Limitations and Conclusion

The contributions presented in this chapter should be interpreted in light of several limitations. First, it needs to be acknowledged that cocitation and bibliographic coupling networks include an interpretation of the obtained results and are thus even though they are based on objective indicators (citations, cocitations), to some degree subjective and left in the hands of the interpreter. Thus we propose that future bibliometric findings should be interpreted with the help of experts in the organizational creativity field in order to objectify the results and implications. Second, a limitation of our bibliometric analysis for the creativity field deals with the foundation of analysis itself. While a number of citations cannot always be the most appropriate representation of a document's influence on the whole research field, we nevertheless used this criterion based on its advantages (Kim, Morse, & Zingales, 2006), such as being widely used in the academic research field and being more objective than personal opinions of researchers. Third, in line with Fetscherin and Heinrich (2015), we did not exclude self-citations by authors themselves in the bibliometric analyses. Nevertheless, we propose that future research could exclude self-citations in order to arrive at perhaps an even more accurate cocitation network in the creativity field.

Despite these limitations, this study provided a relatively objective, aerial view of the intellectual structure providing the foundation of the creativity field, the interpretation of its patterns of development based on the framework of "invisible colleges," its current state of the art and comparison with the subfield of individual creativity, and informed suggestions for future outlooks based on bibliographic coupling. Taken together, it behooves us to further understand the development and evolution of the creativity field.

References

Agnihotri, R., Rapp, A. A., Andzulis, J. M., & Gabler, C. B. (2014). Examining the drivers and performance implications of boundary spanner creativity. *Journal of Service Research*, *17*(2), 164–181.

Amabile, T. M. (1979). Effects of external evaluation on artistic creativity. *Journal of personality and Social Psychology*, *37*(2), 221.

Amabile, T. M. (1983a). Brilliant but cruel: perceptions of negative evaluators. *Journal of Experimental Social Psychology*, *19*(2), 146–156.

Amabile, T. M. (1983b). *The social psychology of creativity*. New York: Springer.

Amabile, T. M. (1983c). The social psychology of creativity: a componential conceptualization. *Journal of Personality and Social Psychology*, *45*(2), 357–376.

Amabile, T. M. (1985). Motivation and creativity: effects of motivational orientation on creative writers. *Journal of Personality and Social Psychology*, *48*(2), 393.

Amabile, T. M. (1987). The motivation to be creative. In S. Isaken (Ed.), *Frontiers of creativity research: Beyond the basics* (pp. 223–254). Buffalo, NY: Bearley Limited.

Amabile, T. M. (1988). A model of creativity and innovation in organizations. In B. M. Staw & L. L. Cummings (Eds.), *Research in organizational behavior*: 10. (pp. 123–167). Greenwich, CT: JAI.

Amabile, T. M. (1996). *Creativity in context: Update "to the social psychology of creativity"*. Boulder, CO, US: Westview Press.

Amabile, T. M. (1997). Motivating creativity in organizations: on doing what you love and loving what you do. *California Management Review*, *40*(1), 39–58.

Amabile, T. M., Barsade, S. G., Mueller, J. S., & Staw, B. M. (2005). Affect and creativity at work. *Administrative Science Quarterly*, *50*(3), 367–403.

Amabile, T. M., Conti, R., Coon, H., Lazenby, J., & Herron, M. (1996). Assessing the work environment for creativity. *Academy of Management Journal*, *39*(5), 1154–1184.

Anderson, N., Potočnik, K., & Zhou, J. (2014). Innovation and creativity in organizations: a state-of-the-science review, prospective commentary, and guiding framework. *Journal of Management*, *40*(5), 1297–1333.

Axtell, C. M., Holman, D. J., Unsworth, K. L., Wall, T. D., & Waterson, P. E. (2000). Shopfloor innovation: facilitating the suggestion and implementation of ideas. *Journal of Occupational and Organizational Psychology*, *73*, 265–285.

Baer, M. (2010). The strength of weak ties perspective on creativity: A comprehensive examination and extension. *Journal of Applied Psychology*, *95*(3), 592–601.

Baer, M. (2012). Putting creativity to work: the implementation of creative ideas in organizations. *Academy of Management Journal*, *55*(5), 1102–1119.

Baer, M., Leenders, R., Oldham, G. R., & Vadera, A. K. (2010). Win or lose the battle for creativity: the power and perils of intergroup competition. *Academy of Management Journal*, *53*(4), 827–845.

Baer, M., Oldham, G. R., & Cummings, A. (2003). Rewarding creativity: when does it really matter? *Leadership Quarterly*, *14*(4–5), 569–586.

Barron, F. (1953). Complexity-simplicity as a personality dimension. *The Journal of Abnormal and Social Psychology*, *48*(2), 163.

Barron, F. (1955). The disposition toward originality. *The Journal of Abnormal and Social Psychology*, *51*(3), 478.

Barron, F. (1957). Originality in relation to personality and intellect. *Journal of Personality*, *25*(6), 730–742.

Barron, F., & Harrington, D. M. (1981). Creativity, intelligence, and personality. *Annual Review of Psychology*, *32*(1), 439–476.

Barron, F., & Welsh, G. S. (1952). Artistic perception as a possible factor in personality style: its measurement by a figure preference test. *The Journal of Psychology*, *33*(2), 199–203.

Bass, B. M. (1985). Leadership: good, better, best. *Organizational Dynamics*, *13*(3), 26–40.

Batistič, S., Černe, M., & Vogel, B. (2017). Just how multi-level is leadership research? A document co-citation analysis 1980–2013 on leadership constructs and outcomes. *The Leadership Quarterly, 28*(1), 86–103.

Batistic, S., & Kase, R. (2015). The organizational socialization field fragmentation: a bibliometric review. *Scientometrics, 104*(1), 121–146.

Bliese, P. D. (2000). Within-group agreement, non-independence, and reliability: implications for data aggregation and analysis. In K. J. Klein & S. W. J. Kozlowski (Eds.), *Multilevel theory, research, and methods in organizations* (pp. 349–381). San Francisco: Jossey-Bass.

Bogilović, S., Černe, M., & Škerlavaj, M. (2017). Hiding behind a mask? Cultural intelligence, knowledge hiding, and individual and team creativity. *European Journal of Work and Organizational Psychology, 26*(5), 710–723.

Bogilović, S., Škerlavaj, M., & Wong, S. I. (2016). *Idea implementation and cultural intelligence.* In *Capitalizing on creativity at work: Fostering the implementation of creative ideas in organizations* (pp. 39–50). Edward Elgar.

Cattell, R. B., & Drevdahl, J. E. (1955). A comparison of personality profile (16 PF) of eminent researchers with that of eminent teachers and administrators, and of general population. *British Journal of Psychology, 46*(4), 248–261.

Černe, M., Nerstad, C., Dysvik, A., & Škerlavaj, M. (2014). What goes around comes around: knowledge hiding, perceived motivational climate, and creativity. *Academy of Management Journal, 57*(1), 172–192.

Chua, R. Y. (2013). The costs of ambient cultural disharmony: indirect intercultural conflicts in social environment undermine creativity. *Academy of Management Journal, 56*(6), 1545–1577.

Chua, R. Y., Morris, M. W., & Mor, S. (2012). Collaborating across cultures: cultural metacognition and affect-based trust in creative collaboration. *Organizational Behavior and Human Decision Processes, 118*(2), 116–131.

Cobo, M. J., López-Herrera, A. G., Herrera-Viedma, E., & Herrera, F. (2011). Science mapping software tools: review, analysis, and cooperative study among tools. *Journal of the Association for Information Science and Technology, 62*(7), 1382–1402.

Corrigall, K. A., Schellenberg, E. G., & Misura, N. M. (2013). Music training, cognition, and personality. *Frontiers in Psychology, 4*, 222.

Cox, T. H., Lobel, S. A., & McLeod, P. L. (1991). Effects of ethnic group cultural differences on cooperative and competitive behavior on a group task. *Academy of Management Journal, 34*(4), 827–847.

Criscuolo, P., Salter, A., & Ter Wal, A. L. (2013). Going underground: bootlegging and individual innovative performance. *Organization Science, 25*(5), 1287–1305.

Cross, P. G., Cattell, R. B., & Butcher, H. J. (1967). The personality pattern of creative artists. *British Journal of Educational Psychology, 37*(3), 292–299.

De Stobbeleir, K. E., Ashford, S. J., & Buyens, D. (2011). Self-regulation of creativity at work: the role of feedback-seeking behavior in creative performance. *Academy of Management Journal, 54*(4), 811–831.

Deci, E. L. (1971). Effects of externally mediated rewards on intrinsic motivation. *Journal of Personality and Social Psychology, 18*(1), 105–115.

Dellas, M., & Gaier, E. L. (1970). Identification of creativity: the individual. *Psychological Bulletin, 73*(1), 55.

Dellas, M., & Gaier, E. L. (1975). The self and adolescent identity in women: options and implications. *Adolescence, 10*(39), 399–407.

Dionne, S. S. (2008). Social influence, creativity, and innovation: boundaries, brackets, and non-linearity. In M. D. Mumford, S. T. Hunter, & K. E. Bedell-Avers (Eds.), *Multi-level issues in creativity and innovation* 7 (pp. 63–73). London, UK: JAI Press.

Drazin, R., Glynn, M. A., & Kazanjian, R. K. (1999). Multilevel theorizing about creativity in organizations: a sense making perspective. *Academy of Management Review, 24*(2), 286–307.

Drevdahl, J. E. (1956). Factors of importance for creativity. *Journal of Clinical Psychology, 12*(1), 21–26.

Erez, M., Van de Ven, A. H., & Lee, C. (Eds.). (2015). Contextualizing creativity and innovation across cultures. *Journal of Organizational Behavior, 36*(7), 895–898.

Farh, J. L., Lee, C., & Farh, C. I. C. (2010). Task conflict and team creativity: a question of how much and when. *Journal of Applied Psychology, 95*(6), 1173–1180.

Fetscherin, M., & Heinrich, D. (2015). Consumer brand relationships research: a bibliometric citation meta-analysis. *Journal of Business Research, 68*(2), 380–390.

Finke, R. A., Ward, T. B., & Smith, S. M. (1992). *Creative cognition: Theory, research, and applications.* Cambridge, MA: MIT Press.

Ford, C. M. (1996). Theory of individual creative action in multiple social domains. *Academy of Management Review, 21*(4), 1112–1142.

Freud, S. (1908). The relation of the poet to day-dreaming. *Collected papers*: Vol. 4. (pp. 173–183). London: Hogarth Press.

George, J. M., & Zhou, J. (2002). Understanding when bad moods foster creativity and good ones don't: the role of context and clarity of feelings. *Journal of Applied Psychology, 87*(4), 687–697.

George, J. M., & Zhou, J. (2007). Dual tuning in a supportive context: joint contributions of positive mood, negative mood, and supervisory behaviors to employee creativity. *Academy of Management Journal, 50*(3), 605–622.

Getzels, J. W., & Jackson, P. W. (1962). *Creativity and intelligence: Explorations with gifted students.*

Giambatista, R. C., & Bhappu, A. D. (2010). Diversity's harvest: interactions of diversity sources and communication technology on creative group performance. *Organizational Behavior and Human Decision Processes, 111*(2), 116–126.

Gilson, L. L., Mathieu, J. E., Shalley, C. E., & Ruddy, T. M. (2005). Creativity and standardization: complementary or conflicting drivers of team effectiveness? *Academy of Management Journal, 48*(3), 521–531.

Gilson, L. L., Maynard, M. T., Jones Young, N. C., Vartiainen, M., & Hakonen, M. (2015). Virtual teams research: 10 years, 10 themes, and 10 opportunities. *Journal of Management, 41*(5), 1313–1337.

Gilson, L. L., & Shalley, C. E. (2004). A little creativity goes a long way: an examination of teams' engagement in creative processes. *Journal of Management, 30*(4), 453–470.

Gino, F., & Wiltermuth, S. S. (2014). Evil genius? How dishonesty can lead to greater creativity. *Psychological Science, 25*(4), 973–981.

Glover, J., & Gary, A. L. (1976). Procedures to increase some aspects of creativity. *Journal of Applied Behavior Analysis, 9*(1), 79–84.

Golann, S. E. (1963). Psychological study of creativity. *Psychological Bulletin, 60*(6), 548.

Gong, Y. P., Huang, J. C., & Farh, J. L. (2009). Employee learning orientation, transformational leadership, and employee creativity: the mediating role of employee creativity self-confidence. *Academy of Management Journal, 52*(4), 765–778.

Gong, Y., Kim, T. Y., Lee, D. R., & Zhu, J. (2013). A multilevel model of team goal orientation, information exchange, and creativity. *Academy of Management Journal, 56*(3), 827–851.

Gordon, W. J. (1961). *Synectics: The development of creative capacity.* England: Oxford.

Gough, H. G. (1979). A creative personality scale for the adjective check list. *Journal of Personality and Social Psychology, 37*(8), 1398.

Grant, A. M., & Berry, J. W. (2011). The necessity of others is the mother of invention: intrinsic and prosocial motivations, perspective taking, and creativity. *Academy of Management Journal, 54*(1), 73–96.

Guilford, J. (1950). Creativity. *American Psychologist, 5*, 444–454.

Guilford, J. P. (1967). Creativity: yesterday, today and tomorrow. *The Journal of Creative Behavior, 1*(1), 3–14.

Guilford, J. P. (1959). Traits of creativity. In H. H. Anderson (Ed.), *Creativity and its cultivation* (pp. 142–161). New York: Harper & Row.

Harrison, D. A., Price, K. H., Gavin, J. H., & Florey, A. T. (2002). Time, teams, and task performance: changing effects of surface-and deep-level diversity on group functioning. *Academy of Management Journal, 45*(5), 1029–1045.

Harrison, S. H., & Rouse, E. D. (2014). Let's dance! Elastic coordination in creative group work: a qualitative study of modern dancers. *Academy of Management Journal, 57*(5), 1256–1283.

Harvey, S. (2013). A different perspective: the multiple effects of deep level diversity on group creativity. *Journal of Experimental Social Psychology, 49*(5), 822–832.

Harvey, S. (2014). Creative synthesis: exploring the process of extraordinary group creativity. *Academy of Management Review, 39*(3), 324–343.

Hirst, G., Van Knippenberg, D., Chen, C. H., & Sacramento, C. A. (2011). How does bureaucracy impact individual creativity? A cross-level investigation of team contextual influences on goal orientation-creativity relationships. *Academy of Management Journal, 54*(3), 624–641.

Hirst, G., Van Knippenberg, D., & Zhou, J. (2009). A cross-level perspective on employee creativity: goal orientation, team learining, behavior, and individual creativity. *Academy of Management Journal, 52*(2), 280–293.

Hülsheger, U. R., Anderson, N., & Salgado, J. F. (2009). Team-level predictors of innovation at work: a comprehensive meta-analysis spanning three decades of research. *Journal of Applied Psychology, 94*(5), 1128–1145.

Jackson, S. E., & Joshi, A. (2011). Work team diversity. In S. Zedeck (Ed.), *APA Handbooks in Psychology. APA handbook of industrial and organizational psychology, Vol. 1. Building and developing the organization* (pp. 651–686). Washington, DC: American Psychological Association.

Jauk, E., Benedek, M., Dunst, B., & Neubauer, A. C. (2013). The relationship between intelligence and creativity: new support for the threshold hypothesis by means of empirical breakpoint detection. *Intelligence, 41*(4), 212–221.

Jia, L., Shaw, J. D., Tsui, A. S., & Park, T.-Y. (2014). A social-structural perspective on employee-organization relationships and team creativity. *Academy of Management Journal, 57*(3), 869–891.

Johansson-Sköldberg, U., Woodilla, J., & Çetinkaya, M. (2013). Design thinking: past, present and possible futures. *Creativity and Innovation Management, 22*(2), 121–146.

Kessler, M. M. (1963). Bibliographic coupling between scientific papers. *Journal of the Association for Information Science and Technology, 14*(1), 10–25.

Kim, E. H., Morse, A., & Zingales, L. (2006). What has mattered to economics since 1970. *Journal of Economic Perspectives, 20*(4), 189–202.

Kirton, M. (1976). Adaptors and innovators: a description and measure. *Journal of Applied Psychology, 61*(5), 622–629.

Koestler, A. (1964). *The act of creation.* New York: Dell.

Koestner, R., Ryan, R. M., Bernieri, F., & Holt, K. (1984). Setting limits on children's behavior: the differential effects of controlling vs. informational styles on intrinsic motivation and creativity. *Journal of Personality, 52*(3), 233–248.

Kounios, J., & Beeman, M. (2014). The cognitive neuroscience of insight. *Annual Review of Psychology, 65,* 71–93.

Liao, H., Liu, D., & Loi, R. (2010). Looking at both sides of the social exchange coin: a social cognitive perspective on the joint effects of relationship quality and differentiation on creativity. *Academy of Management Journal, 53*(5), 1090–1109.

Litchfield, R. C., Gilson, L. L., & Gilson, P. W. (2015). Defining creative ideas toward a more nuanced approach. *Group & Organization Management, 40*(2), 238–265.

MacKinnon, D. W. (1962). The nature and nature of creative talent. *American Psychologist, 17*(7), 484–495.

MacKinnon, D. W. (1978). *In search of human effectiveness. Creative Education Foundation.* Buffalo, NY: Bearly.

Madjar, N. (2005). The contributions of different groups of individuals to employees' creativity. *Advances in Developing Human Resources*, 7(2), 182–206.

Madjar, N., Greenberg, E., & Chen, Z. (2011). Factors for radical creativity, incremental creativity, and routine, noncreative performance. *Journal of Applied Psychology*, 96(4), 730–743.

Madjar, N., & Oldham, G. R. (2002). Preliminary tasks and creative performance on a subsequent task: effects of time on preliminary tasks and amount of information about the subsequent task. *Creativity Research Journal*, 14(2), 239–251.

Maier, N. R. (1970). *Problem solving and creativity in individuals and groups*. Belmont, CA: Brooks/Cole.

McCain, K. W. (1990). Mapping authors in intellectual space: a technical overview. *Journal of the American Society for Information Science*, 41(6), 433–443.

Meadow, A., Parnes, S. J., & Reese, H. (1959). Influence of brainstorming instructions and problem sequence on a creative problem solving test. *Journal of Applied Psychology*, 43(6), 413.

Mednick, S. (1962). The associative basis of the creative process. *Psychological Review*, 69(3), 220–232.

Miron-Spektor, E., Gino, F., & Argote, L. (2011). Paradoxical frames and creative sparks: enhancing individual creativity through conflict and integration. *Organizational Behavior and Human Decision Processes*, 116(2), 229–240.

Mumford, M. D., & Gustafson, S. B. (1988). Creativity syndrome: integration, application, and innovation. *Psychological Bulletin*, 103(1), 27–43.

Nerur, S. P., Rasheed, A. A., & Natarajan, V. (2008). The intellectual structure of the strategic management field: an author co-citation analysis. *Strategic Management Journal*, 29(3), 319–336.

Nicholls, J. G. (1972). Creativity in the person who will never produce anything original and useful: the concept of creativity as a normally distributed trait. *American Psychologist*, 27(8), 517–527.

Nijstad, B. A., Berger-Selman, F., & De Dreu, C. K. W. (2014). Innovation in top management teams: minority dissent, transformational leadership, and radical innovations. *European Journal of Work and Organizational Psychology*, 23(2), 310–322.

Oldham, G. R., & Cummings, A. (1996). Employee creativity: personal and contextual factors at work. *Academy of Management Journal*, 39(3), 607–634.

Osborn, A. F. (1957). *Applied imagination*. (p. 1957). New York: Scribners's.

Paulus, P. B., Kohn, N. W., Arditti, L. E., & Korde, R. M. (2013). Understanding the group size effect in electronic brainstorming. *Small Group Research*, 44(3), 332–352.

Perkins, D. N. (1981). *The mind's best work: A new psychology of creative thinking*. Cambridge: Harvard University Press.

Perry-Smith, J. E. (2006). Social yet creative: the role of social relationships in facilitating individual creativity. *Academy of Management Journal*, 49(1), 85–101.

Perry-Smith, J. E., & Mannucci, P. V. (2017). From creativity to innovation: the social network drivers of the four phases of the idea journey. *Academy of Management Review*, 42(1), 53–79.

Perry-Smith, J. E., & Shalley, C. E. (2003). The social side of creativity: a static and dynamic social network perspective. *Academy of Management Review*, 28(1), 89–106.

Perry-Smith, J. E., & Shalley, C. E. (2014). A social composition view of team creativity: the role of member nationality-heterogeneous ties outside of the team. *Organization Science*, 25(5), 1434–1452.

Pinheiro, I. R., & Cruz, R. M. (2014). Mapping creativity: creativity measurements network analysis. *Creativity Research Journal*, 26(3), 263–275.

Pirola-Merlo, A., & Mann, L. (2004). The relationship between individual creativity and team creativity: aggregating across people and time. *Journal of Organizational Behavior*, 25(2), 235–257.

Radaelli, G., Lettieri, E., Mura, M., & Spiller, N. (2014). Knowledge sharing and innovative work behaviour in healthcare: a micro-level investigation of direct and indirect effects. *Creativity and Innovation Management*, 23(4), 400–414.

Redmond, M. R., Mumford, M. D., & Teach, R. (1993). Putting creativity to work: effects of leader behavior on subordinate creativity. *Organizational Behavior and Human Decision Processes*, 55(1), 120–151.

Rego, A., Sousa, F., Marques, C., & de Pina E Cunha, M. (2012). Authentic leadership promoting employees' psychological capital and creativity. *Journal of Business Research*, 65(3), 429–437.

Reiter-Palmon, R., Herman, A. E., & Yammarino, F. J. (2008). Creativity and cognitive processes: a multi-level linkage between individual and team cognition. In M. D. Mumford, S. T. Hunter, & K. E. Bedell-Avers (Eds.), *Multi-level issues in creativity and innovation*. Amsterdam, NL: JAI Press.

Rothenberg, A., & Greenberg, B. (1976). *The index of scientific writings on creativity: General, 1566–1974*. Hamden, CT: Archon Books.

Royce, J. (1898). The psychology of invention. *Psychological Review*, 5(2), 113–144.

Runco, M. A. (1991). *Divergent thinking*. Norwood, NJ: Ablex.

Scott, S. G., & Bruce, R. A. (1994). Determinants of innovative behavior: a path model of individual innovation in the workplace. *Academy of Management Journal*, 37(3), 580–607.

Shalley, C. E. (1991). Effects of productivity goals, creativity goals, and personal discretion on individual creativity. *Journal of Applied Psychology*, 76(2), 179–185.

Shalley, C. E., & Gilson, L. L. (2004). What leaders need to know: a review of social and contextual factors that can foster or hinder creativity. *The Leadership Quarterly*, 15(1), 33–53.

Shalley, C. E., Gilson, L. L., & Blum, T. C. (2000). Matching creativity requirements and the work environment: effects on satisfaction and intentions to leave. *Academy of Management Journal*, 43(2), 215–223.

Shalley, C. E., Gilson, L. L., & Blum, T. C. (2009). Interactive effects of growth need strength, work context, and job complexity on self-reported creative performance. *The Academy of Management Journal*, 52(3), 489–505.

Shalley, C. E., & Perry-Smith, J. E. (2001). Effects of social-psychological factors on creative performance: the role of informational and controlling expected evaluation and modeling experience. *Organizational Behavior and Human Decision Processes*, 84(1), 1–22.

Shalley, C. E., Zhou, J., & Oldham, G. R. (2004). The effects of personal and contextual characteristics on creativity: where should we go from here? *Journal of Management*, 30(6), 933–958.

Shin, S. J., Kim, T. Y., Lee, J. Y., & Bian, L. (2012). Cognitive team diversity and individual team member creativity: a cross-level interaction. *Academy of Management Journal*, 55(1), 197–212.

Shin, S. J., & Zhou, J. (2003). Transformational leadership, conservation, and creativity: evidence from Korea. *Academy of Management Journal*, 46(6), 703–714.

Shin, S. J., & Zhou, J. (2007). When is educational specialization heterogeneity related to creativity in research and development teams? Transformational leadership as a moderator. *Journal of Applied Psychology*, 92(6), 1709–1721.

Simonton, D. K. (1975). Sociocultural context of individual creativity: a trans-historical time-series analysis. *Journal of Personality and Social Psychology*, 32(6), 1119–1133.

Simonton, D. K. (1977a). Creative productivity, age, and stress: a biographical time-series analysis of 10 classical composers. *Journal of Personality and Social Psychology*, 35(11), 791–804. a.

Simonton, D. K. (1977b). Eminence, creativity, and geographical marginality: a recursive structural equation model. *Journal of Personality and Social Psychology*, 35(11), 805–816. b.

Simonton, D. K. (1979). Multiple discovery and invention: zeitgeist, genius, or chance? *Journal of Personality and Social Psychology*, 37, 1603–1616.

Škerlavaj, M., Černe, M., & Dysvik, A. (2014). I get by with a little help from my supervisor: creative-idea generation, idea implementation, and perceived supervisor support. *The Leadership Quarterly*, 25(5), 987–1000.

Small, H. (1973). Co-citation in the scientific literature: a new measure of the relationship between two documents. *Journal of the American Society for Information Science*, 24, 265–269.

Smith, J. M., & Schaefer, C. E. (1969). Development of a creativity scale for the adjective check list. *Psychological Reports*, 25(1), 87–92.

Somech, A., & Drach-Zahavy, A. (2013). Translating team creativity to innovation implementation: the role of team composition and climate for innovation. *Journal of Management*, 39(3), 684–708.

Sosa, M. E. (2011). Where do creative interactions come from? The role of tie content and social networks. *Organization Science*, 22(1), 1–21.

Stahl, G. K., Maznevski, M. L., Voigt, A., & Jonsen, K. (2010). Unraveling the effects of cultural diversity in teams: a meta-analysis of research on multicultural work groups. *Journal of International Business Studies*, 41(4), 690–709.

Staw, B. M. (1984). Organizational behavior: a review and reformulation of the field's outcome variables. *Annual Review of Psychology*, 35(1), 627–666.

Staw, B. M. (1990). An evolutionary approach to creativity and innovation. In M. West & J. L. Farr (Eds.), *Innovationa and creativity at work* (pp. 287–308). Chichester, UK: Wiley.

Stein, K. B. (1967). Correlates of the ideational preference dimension among prison inmates. *Psychological Reports*, 21(2), 553–562.

Stein, M. I., & Heinze, S. J. (1960). *Creativity and the individual*. Glencoe, IL: Free Press.

Taylor, C. W., & Barron, F. E. (1963). *Scientific creativity: Its recognition and development*. New York, NY: John Wiley and Sons, Inc.

Tierney, P., & Farmer, S. M. (2002). Creative self-efficacy: its potential antecedents and relationship to creative performance. *Academy of Management Journal*, 45(6), 1137–1148.

Tierney, P., & Farmer, S. M. (2004). The Pygmalion process and employee creativity. *Journal of Management*, 30(3), 413–432.

Tierney, P., Farmer, S. M., & Graen, G. B. (1999). An examination of leadership and employee creativity: the relevance of traits and relationships. *Personnel Psychology*, 52(3), 591–620.

Torrance, E. P. (1962). *Guiding creative talent*. Englewood Cliffs, NJ: Prentice-Hall.

Torrance, E. P. (1965). *Rewarding creative behavior: Experiments in classroom creativity*. Englewood Cliffs, NJ: Prentice-Hall.

Torrance, E. P. (1966). *The torrance tests of creative thinking–norms—technical manual research edition—verbal tests, forms A and B—figural tests, forms A and B*. Princeton, NJ: Personnel Press.

Torrance, E. P. (1974). *The torrance tests of creative thinking–norms—technical manual research edition—verbal tests, forms A and B—figural tests, forms A and B*. Princeton, NJ: Personnel Press.

Torrance, E. P. (1988). The nature of creativity as manifest in its testing. In R. J. Sternberg (Ed.), *The nature of creativity* (pp. 43–75). Cambridge: Cambridge University Press.

Ulibarri, N., Cravens, A. E., Cornelius, M., Royalty, A., & Nabergoj, A. S. (2014). Research as design: developing creative confidence in doctoral students through design thinking. *International Journal of Doctoral Studies*, 9, 249–270.

Unsworth, K. (2001). Unpacking creativity. *Academy of Management Review*, 26(2), 289–297.

Van de Ven, A., Angle, H., & Poole, M. (Eds.), (1989). *Research on the management of innovation: The Minnesota studies*. New York: Harper and Row.

Vogel, R. (2012). The visible colleges of management and organization studies: a bibliometric analysis of academic journals. *Organization Studies*, 33(8), 1015–1043.

Vogel, R., & Güttel, W. H. (2013). The dynamic capability view in strategic management: a bibliometric review. *International Journal of Management Reviews*, 15(4), 426–446.

Wallach, M. A., & Kogan, N. (1965). *Modes of thinking in young children*. New York: Holt, Rinehart and Winston.

Wang, P., & Rode, J. C. (2010). Transformational leadership and follower creativity: the moderating effects of identification with leader and organizational climate. *Human Relations*, 63(8), 1105–1128.

Wang, C. J., Tsai, H. T., & Tsai, M. T. (2014). Linking transformational leadership and employee creativity in the hospitality industry: the influences of creative role identity, J. (1962). *Statistical problems in experimental* creative self-efficacy, and job complexity. *Tourism Management*, 40, 79–89.

Weick, K. (1979). *The social psychology of organizations*. Reading, MA: Addison-Wesley.

2. INTELLIGENCE AND COGNITION

Welch, G. S. (1975). *Creativity and intelligence: A personality approach.* Chapel Hill, NC: University of North Institute for Research in Social Science, University of North Carolina.

Welsh, G. S. (1959). *Preliminary manual for the Welsh figure preference test.* Palo Alto, CA: Consulting Psychologists Press.

Welsh, G. S. (1975). *Creativity and intelligence: a personality approach.* Chapel Hill, NC: Institute for Research in Social Science at the University of North Carolina.

West, M. A. (2002). Sparkling fountains or stagnant ponds: an integrative model of creativity and innovation implementation in work groups. *Applied Psychology, 51*(3), 355–387.

White, H. D. (2003). Pathfinder networks and author cocitation analysis: a remapping of paradigmatic information scientists. *Journal of the American Society for Information Science and Technology, 54*(5), 423–434.

Winer, B. J. (1962). *Statistical problems in experimental design.* (p. 319–337). New York: McGraw-Hill.

Woodman, R. W., Sawyer, J. E., & Griffin, R. W. (1993). Toward a theory of organizational creativity. *Academy of Management Review, 18*(2), 293–321.

Woody, E., & Claridge, G. (1977). Psychoticism and thinking. *British Journal of Clinical Psychology, 16*(3), 241–248.

Zhou, J., & George, J. M. (2001). When job dissatisfaction leads to creativity: encouraging the expression of voice. *Academy of Management Journal, 44*(4), 682–696.

Zhou, J., & Hoever, I. J. (2014). Research on workplace creativity: a review and redirection. *The Annual Review of Organizational Psychology and Organizational Behavior, 1*(1), 333–359.

Zhou, J., & Shalley, C. E. (2003). Research on employee creativity: a critical review and directions for future research. In J. Martocchio (Ed.), *Research in personnel and human resources management* (pp. 165–217). Oxford, UK: Elsevier.

Zhou, J., Shin, S. J., Brass, D. J., Choi, J., & Zhang, Z. X. (2009). Social networks, personal values, and creativity: evidence for curvilinear and interaction effects. *Journal of Applied Psychology, 94*(6), 1544–1552.

Zupic, I., & Čater, T. (2015). Bibliometric methods in management and organization. *Organizational Research Methods, 18*(3), 429–472.

Further Reading

George, J. M., & Zhou, J. (2001). When openness to experience and conscientiousness are related to creative behavior: an interactional approach. *Journal of Applied Psychology, 86*(3), 513–524.

Harvey, S., & Kou, C. Y. (2013). Collective engagement in creative tasks: the role of evaluation in the creative process in groups. *Administrative Science Quarterly, 58*(3), 346–386.

MOTIVATION/ AFFECT/ PREFERENCES

8

Creative Styles in the Workplace: New vs Different

Roni Reiter-Palmon*, James C. Kaufman†

*University of Nebraska at Omaha, Omaha, NE, United States, †University of Connecticut, Storrs, CT, United States

In education, learning styles have fallen out of favor with researchers. The idea that people can be categorized according to how they learn best has been called a myth (Newton & Miah, 2017) to the point of being included in a popular compendium of psychological myths (Lilienfeld, Lynn, Ruscio, & Beyerstein, 2011). Learning styles do not predict school achievement (e.g., Massa & Mayer, 2006; Price, 2004) and are accused of pigeonholing students (Kirschner & van Merriënboer, 2013), leading several scholars to argue for alternate approaches (An & Carr, 2017).

Learning styles were not helped by extreme advocates with extensive and often conflicting models; the idea that everyone needed a specific, tailored learning style seemed ripe for parody—and, indeed, at one point, *The Onion* wrote a satire piece about how nasal learners needed a special odor-based curriculum ("Parents of nasal learners demand odor-based curriculum," 2000). Learning styles are often criticized and seen of less importance (although, it is important to note, this opinion is not universal; see Sternberg, Grigorenko, & Zhang, 2008). However, it is important to note that many of the criticisms are directed at studies involving educational outcomes and are primarily critiquing the concept of visual, auditory, and kinesthetic learning styles (Kirschner, 2017; Newton, 2015). Most of the problems that are discussed with learning styles in the schools do not transfer to more general discussion of styles or preferences in other settings (such as the workplace).

A consistent critique of styles in general (beyond the specifics of the current attacks on learning styles) is that that there are so many theories and typologies that it is difficult to keep track of which ones may or may not work (Kirschner & van Merriënboer, 2013). In this chapter, we will attempt to synthesize multiple perspectives, models, and theories of creative styles into two broad dimensions that encompass many different approaches: New and Different. Instead of (as with learning styles in the classroom) making the group be dependent on the needs of the individual, we suggest that creative styles be used for two distinct purposes: to help the personnel selection process find creative individuals (Hunter, Cushenbery, & Freidrich, 2012) and to then to form groups that would be effective for the specific task—generation, implementation, or both (Reiter-Palmon, de Vreede, & de Vreede, 2013).

CREATIVE STYLES: NEW VS DIFFERENT

One way of increasing an organization's creativity is to hire creative people. But, of course, it is not that simple. If creative people are put in situations that do not maximize their abilities, then the company loses many of the possible benefits. How can an organization maximize employee creativity? Much of the research focusing on improving organizational creativity has focused on the role of the leader or supervisor or organizational climate (Reiter-Palmon, Mitchell, and Royston, n.d.). Another way, however, is to make sure that groups are comprised of well-matched creativity styles.

It is not enough to think of employees as "more creative" or "less creative." A better approach is to consider how they are creative. For instance, people can be creative across domains (Kaufman & Baer, 2002; Kaufman, Glăveanu, & Baer, 2017), but most organizations implicitly understand this concept and act accordingly. For example, few accounting departments would seek out accomplished sculptors. There are also variations in an employee's creative ability, such as whether it is more personal, everyday, or professional (Kaufman & Beghetto, 2009). Again, the importance of such knowledge is intuitive; most companies know enough to send highly creative types to marketing or management and not the stockroom.

Creative styles are more complex. These cover both people's preferences for how they choose to be creative (such as in which domain or situation it is expressed) as well as a person's specific creative strengths (such as thinking of many ideas or being able to decide which idea is the most creative). Just as learning styles are not the same as intelligence, creative styles are not the same as creativity. They can be used to match a worker to a particular job or to construct a team with creators whose strengths will be complementary.

However, with so many theories and models of creativity, an organization or employer may be overwhelmed and have no idea of how these different conceptions overlap or can best be used. To simplify this question—and offer a potential measurement—we have integrated many approaches to propose a central dichotomy: New vs Different. This dichotomy is rooted in the work of many different people, dating back to creativity scholar Guilford (1950), who famously proposed multiple mental operations as part of the Structure of Intellect model. People with a New thinking style are more likely to have many diverse ideas, embrace large-level change, and seek out opportunities. People with a Different thinking style are more likely to focus on evaluation and implementation of ideas, seek more incremental and adaptational change, and be aware of potential constraints. We will now discuss these ideas in greater detail.

Divergent vs Convergent

Guilford's work represents a good starting point to consider differences in how someone is creative. In the larger framework of Guilford's (1967) model of intelligence, the ideas of divergent and convergent thinking are most relevant for creativity. Divergent thinkers tend to generate solutions and brainstorm, whereas convergent thinkers are more prone to evaluate and select the best idea to continue to pursue. A similar model is the Geneplore model (Finke, Ward, & Smith, 1992). In the generative phase, many possible creative solutions can be imagined. Next, in the exploratory phase, each solution is considered in terms of the constraint of the final goal.

Divergent and convergent thinking, of course, are not mutually exclusive. Many workers will use both types of thought, often as part of the same project. They may shift between divergent to convergent thinking and then back on multiple occasions. But regardless of ability, people tend to also have a preference (even if unconscious) for a type of thinking (Basadur, Wakabayashi, & Graen, 1990). Does a person want to generate something New? Come up with wild ideas and unleash a stream of multiple solutions? Perhaps someone else enjoys evaluating, judging, and weighing each possible idea to select the one that is the most exciting and the most possible. This distinction between divergent and convergent thinking is the first piece of our synthesis, with divergent thinkers being New and convergent being Different. Specifically, those that prefer a divergent thinking style prefer to generate something New. Those with a more convergent thinking style prefer, in the context of creativity, to think in different ways about the current situation and ways to solve the problem. It is important to note that we consider both divergent and convergent thinking as creative styles. They may represent preferences (some people may enjoy generating ideas more than evaluating them) as well as potential strengths (some people are simply better at one than the other). We will continue to expand on the different theories that contribute to our approach.

RADICAL VS INCREMENTAL

Another theory of creativity examines how a particular contribution changes the field. The Propulsion Model (Sternberg, 1999; Sternberg, Kaufman, & Pretz, 2002, 2004) highlights many ways that a product can have an impact. The stereotypical approach to creativity focuses on products or ideas that move the domain in a completely New direction. This can occur by redirection, synthesizing two different fields or pieces of information, or reinitiation, which redraws the boundaries of the field (Mumford, Mobley, Reiter-Palmon, Uhlman, & Doares, 1991; Sternberg & Kaufman, 2012). Such contributions, like Kirton's (1976) Innovators and Gilson and Madjar's (2011) radical creativity, seek to be strikingly New. The people who choose to innovate at the paradigm-bending level are akin to our New thinkers.

However, some creative products are primarily an adaption of something that already exists. These can include the Propulsion categories of replications (which try to recreate past successes with comparatively little New ideas) or redirections (which seek alternate used for existing concepts of tools). These types of contributions are similar to Kirton's (1976) Adapters and what Gilson and Madjar (2011) dubbed incremental creativity. The people who prefer to adapt and make incremental contributions are akin to our Different thinkers.

OPPORTUNITY VS CONSTRAINTS

Another perspective is provided by theories that focus on how people interact with their environment. Some individuals view situations as opportunities to achieve, learn, and succeed (Scholer & Higgins, 2013). In this context, obstacles for this achievement are viewed as challenges, and individuals will look for a way to exploit this New opportunity, therefore resulting in New ideas. On the other hand, some individuals will view the same situation by focusing on constraints and limiting factors (Stokes, 2008). However, it is important to note that in this case the constraints can give rise to creative ideas by evaluating how these constraints can be overcome, typically in creative ways (Haught, 2015). This approach results in alternative ways of thinking about the current situation and ways to solve the problem. Similar to the previously discussed constructs, the focus on opportunities or constraints can both result in creative ideas or products. These two approaches provide different paths to creativity. A focus on opportunity would be linked to New ways of thinking, whereas a focus on constraints would be linked to Different ways of thinking about the problem.

TABLE 1 Comparison of New vs. Different Styles

Style	New	Different
Preferred thinking	Preference for divergent thinking	Preference for convergent thinking
Preferred type of creative contribution	Radical	Incremental
Preferred work mode	Innovation	Adaptation
Preferred interaction with environment	Opportunity	Constraint

All of these different approaches help us consider the complexity of how an employee can be creative. In merging these ideas together, our aim to simplify and synthesize; we do not claim that the New-Different dichotomy does a better job of expressing these ideas but rather may offer an easier way to explain different potential creative styles to organizations. For example, the New creative style is associated with thinking of radically novel ideas, of a larger variety of ideas, and how to overcoming potential constraints by viewing these as opportunities. In contrast, the Different creative style is associated with adapting and improving existing concepts, highlighting optimal ideas to pursue, and working within constraints (see Table 1).

Is there a better or preferred style for organizational creativity? The research suggests that both styles, New and Different can play a role in creativity. Recent research suggests that organizational ambidexterity, or the ability to focus on both exploration and exploitation, is key to organizational creativity and innovation (Gupta, Smith, & Shalley, 2006). In fact, the highest level of creativity and innovation are observed in organizations that can do both. Exploration refers to creating something New (New product, New solution) whereas exploitation refers to exploiting current knowledge in a Different way (Different use for an existing product). As such, both styles are essential to a company's success.

Teams provide an opportunity to intentionally create a mix of individuals in terms of creative thinking style. While it is possible that one individual would not have a preference, and be good at both styles, the number of these individuals is relatively small. Diversity in group composition in terms of functional characteristics, such as education, personality, and style has been found to be predictive of creative problem solving in teams (Hulsheger, Anderson, & Salgado, 2009; Karwowski & Lebuda, 2013; Reiter-Palmon et al., 2013). The New creative thinking style is necessary for the development of New ideas, but a Different creative thinking style is needed to identify potential obstacles for development and implementations and how to address those.

APPLICATION OF NEW AND DIFFERENT CREATIVE STYLES

The previous sections detailed a synthesis of previous constructs related to preferences of creativity styles. Some of these constructs have many measures (such as divergent vs convergent thinking), whereas others are not as commonly tested (such as radical vs incremental contributions). In order to allow organizations to assess all of these constructs in a single, straightforward way, we have developed a measure to assess these two creativity styles that would allow organizations to take advantage of these styles. In the next sections we will detail the development of this measure and potential benefits of using such a measure in an organizational context.

CREATIVE RESPONSE EVALUATION AT WORK (CRE-W)

The Creative Response Evaluation at Work (CRE-W; Kaufman & Reiter-Palmon, 2017) was designed to help with employee selection, development, and team formation. To this end, the CRE-W provides different scores for each person. One score is for overall creative initiative, which is less relevant for the purpose of this chapter. In addition, two creative styles scores—for New and Different—are also calculated. Our choice to focus in part on creative styles stemmed from the growing concern that many organizations have regarding the use of various creativity measures—namely, that they seem unrelated to work and organizational practices. For example, how can we relate one's interest in creative activities such as writing poetry or painting, or being able to think of many uses for a brick, to creativity in the workplace?

The test used scenarios to relate directly to actual workplace issues and, therefore offer more face validity than a more general measure. These scenarios were developed to depict real-life work situations that would be similar to what many workers encounter directly or indirectly. Each scenario posed a problem that the test-taker would need to address in some way. For each scenario, several possible responses were offered that represented many potential ways of solving the problem—from taking drastic action to doing almost nothing in response. The test taker is asked to rate each solution on a 1–6 scale indicating the likelihood that he/she would choose this course of action. Initially, 28 scenarios were developed with six potential responses. Two responses were designed to reflect the New creative style, two responses were designed to reflect the Different creative style, and two responses reflected neither style (but were used for the third score, creative initiative). Scenarios and responses that possessed limited psychometric properties (such as being equally associated with both the New and Different styles) were removed. An example scenario is provided in Fig. 1—this scenario was removed from the final test version due to lack of psychometric properties, but is included to provide an example of the nature of the items.

The original set of scenarios and response options was reviewed by a set of internationally renowned creativity experts. They were asked to provide feedback and suggestions on the viability of the situations, potential cultural bias, clarity of the scenario, and the exact wording. The test was revised based on their collective input. The revised test was then evaluated by a diverse panel assembled by the test publisher that represented multiple countries (primarily European). Our goal was to identify scenarios that may not apply (or have different meanings) across cultures. Again, these reviewers were asked to provide feedback and suggestions for the viability of the situations, specifically taking into account cultural context.

Additional analyses were conducted using a large data set collected from MTurk to ensure that items loaded on the appropriate dimensions and discriminated between the dimensions and to evaluate relationships with traditional creativity measures and are described in Kaufman and Reiter-Palmon (2017). The final measure included 20 scenarios, with 4–6 response options, resulting in a total of 93 items to be rated. Of these 29 items were classified as Different (alpha = 0.87) and 23 items were classified as New (alpha = 0.84), showing good reliability. The rest of the items were used in the creation of the creative initiative score (which is not described in this chapter).

POTENTIAL BENEFITS

How could this measure be used in any applied setting? Certainly, creativity and innovation are concepts that organizations understand are related to productivity and success, and in order to achieve such outcomes, they need to be able to hire creative people and enable them to work in teams that can propose and test creative ideas (Anderson, Potočnik, & Zhou, 2014). However, current measures of creativity are a poor fit for this need. Using self-report measures are of limited use. Many focus on participation in creative activities in everyday life (e.g., Kaufman, 2012), which do not transfer to measuring creativity in a work setting. Self-report measures are often fine for low-stakes or research-based situations (Reiter-Palmon, Robinson-Morral, Kaufman, & Santo, 2012; Silvia, Wigert, Reiter-Palmon, & Kaufman, 2012), they are less likely to work in high-stakes situations. They often ask test-takers to estimate their own creativity and thus may be prone to response bias and social desirability (Kyllonen, Walters, & Kaufman, 2005). Further, given that most self-assessments are transparent, there is also the risk of someone simply lying or faking (Kaufman, 2016).

Although there are many other established measures in educational (Torrance, 2008) or research (Amabile, 1996; Baer & Kaufman, 2012) settings, they are less commonly used in organizations. Most have core flaws (in this context) that make them less useful to companies, such as the need for complex scoring, the need for extensive time investment by the employee, or addressing domains that may not be relevant to the scope of the company. Often an organization may use a commercial or in-house assessment with limited (if any) evidence of validity or accuracy.

APPLICATIONS OF NEW AND DIFFERENT STYLES TO ORGANIZATIONAL ISSUES

The New and Different scores generated by the CRE-W have a number of applications for human resources and managing employees. Specifically, the test can be used for training, development, and coaching as well as project team creation and composition.

TRAINING, DEVELOPMENT, AND COACHING

The two preference or creativity style scores can be used for training development and coaching. As shown by Scott, Leritz, and Mumford (2004) in their meta-analysis, creativity can be trained effectively. Individuals can be trained to increase awareness of their dominant style and the effects this preference may have on creativity. Previous research suggests that how problems are framed have an important effect on creativity, and creativity styles such as New and Different can influence how a problem is structured and framed (Reiter-Palmon, Mumford, O'Connor Boes, & Runco, 1997; Reiter-Palmon & Robinson, 2009). By increasing awareness to the importance of problem framing, and that framing is in part based on one's creativity style, training may facilitate increasing the various ways in which the problem is framed. Framing the problem in multiple and different ways has been shown to relate to creativity of the solutions (Arreola & Reiter-Palmon, 2016; Reiter-Palmon, Mumford, & Threlfall, 1998).

In addition, research suggests that adopting a thinking style that is less preferred can lead to greater creativity, suggesting that training may focus on the less dominant style (Dane, Baer, Pratt, & Oldham, 2011). This would indicate that awareness of one's preferred style may allow for training or coaching to focus on the less dominant style, potentially improving creativity.

PROJECT TEAM CREATION AND COMPOSITION

One important strength of the CRE-W creativity styles is the ability to use them for team composition. Research suggests that team diversity, particularly diversity that is related to the task at hand, facilitates creativity (Hulsheger et al., 2009; Somech & Drach-Zahavy, 2013). This type of diversity is based on education, knowledge, job function, as well as ways of thinking, or thinking style. In addition, organizations are not only interested in developing New ideas or products, but also in their implementation (Bledow, Frese, Anderson, Erez, & Farr, 2009). As such, teams composed of individuals from the two styles are more likely to not only develop New ideas, but also allow for effective implementation. Additionally, teams that include members that have Different levels of both styles are more likely to come up with ideas that span both radical and incremental creativity (Rosing, Frese, & Bausch, 2011). Therefore one use for the styles measure is to identify potential team members that are diverse in their styles to allow for strength in generation and implementation of creative ideas.

CONCLUSION

In this chapter we have synthesized previous models and theories on the various ways individuals can be creative. We see the New and Different model as a simplification and synthesis of a great deal of past theories and models. The chapter also provides some information on our development of a measure for these constructs in a way that is more appropriate to organizations, and uses a more subtle approach to evaluate preferences. The initial measure, the CRE-W, is specifically designed to be used in organizations in a multitude of ways. However, we hope that these ideas can be applied to other avenues of creativity, such as everyday creativity as expressed in hobbies, daily life, or weekend pursuits.

As part of your job, you are responsible for leading weekly project meetings with a group of your peers. In a recent meeting you notice that Jay and John were having petty arguments and making everyone uncomfortable. What is the best way to address this problem before the meeting takes place?

a. Contact their respective managers and find out what is going on
b. Meet with John and Jay for the purpose of brainstorming different ideas to solve this problem
c. Request that one of them assigned to a different project so they are not present at the same meeting
d. Meet with John and Jay for the purpose of determining the cause of the problem
e. Let Jay and John know that this behavior will not be tolerated in the meeting
f. Find a way to get Jay and John to use their competitiveness to the benefit of the project

Note: This item was eliminated from the test in tryouts. Responses a and e were not designed to measure a particular style. Responses b and f were intended to measure "New," and responses c and d were intended to measure "Different."

References

Amabile, T. M. (1996). *Creativity in context: Update to the social psychology of creativity.* Boulder, CO: Westview Press.

An, D., & Carr, M. (2017). Learning styles theory fails to explain learning and achievement: recommendations for alternative approaches. *Personality and Individual Differences, 116,* 410–416.

Anderson, N., Potočnik, K., & Zhou, J. (2014). Innovation and creativity in organizations: a state-of-the-science review, prospective commentary, and guiding framework. *Journal of Management, 40,* 1297–1333.

Arreola, N. J., & Reiter-Palmon, R. (2016). The effect of problem construction creativity on solution creativity across multiple everyday problems. *Psychology of Aesthetics, Creativity, and the Arts, 10,* 287–295.

Baer, J., & Kaufman, J. C. (2012). *Being creative inside and outside the classroom: How to boost your students' creativity—And your own.* Boston, MA: Sense Publishers.

Basadur, M., Wakabayashi, M., & Graen, G. B. (1990). Individual problem-solving styles and attitudes toward divergent thinking before and after training. *Creativity Research Journal, 3,* 22–32.

Bledow, R., Frese, M., Anderson, N., Erez, M., & Farr, J. (2009). A dialectic perspective on innovation: conflicting demands, multiple pathways, and ambidexterity. *Industrial and Organizational Psychology, 2,* 305–337.

Dane, E., Baer, M., Pratt, M. G., & Oldham, G. R. (2011). Rational versus intuitive problem solving: how thinking "off the beaten path" can stimulate creativity. *Psychology of Aesthetics, Creativity, and the Arts, 5,* 3–12.

Finke, R. A., Ward, T. B., & Smith, S. M. (1992). *Creative cognition: Theory, research, and applications*. Cambridge, MA: The MIT Press.

Gilson, L. L., & Madjar, N. (2011). Radical and incremental creativity: antecedents and processes. *Psychology of Aesthetics, Creativity, and the Arts*, 5, 21–28.

Guilford, J. P. (1950). Creativity. *American Psychologist*, 5, 444–454.

Guilford, J. P. (1967). *The nature of human intelligence*. New York: McGraw-Hill.

Gupta, A. K., Smith, K. E., & Shalley, C. E. (2006). The interplay between exploration and exploitation. *Academy of Management Journal*, 49, 693–706.

Haught, C. (2015). The role of constraints in creative sentence production. *Creativity Research Journal*, 27, 160–166.

Hulsheger, U., Anderson, N., & Salgado, J. (2009). Team-level predictors of innovations at work: a comprehensive meta-analysis spanning three decades of research. *Journal of Applied Psychology*, 94, 1128–1145.

Hunter, S. T., Cushenbery, L., & Freidrich, T. M. (2012). Hiring an innovative workforce: a necessary yet uniquely challenging endeavor. *Human Resource Management Review*, 22, 303–322.

Karwowski, M., & Lebuda, I. (2013). Extending climato-economic theory: when, how, and why it explains differences in nations' creativity. *Behavioral and Brain Sciences*, 36, 493–494.

Kaufman, J. C. (2012). Counting the muses: development of the Kaufman-domains of creativity scale (K-DOCS). *Psychology of Aesthetics, Creativity, and the Arts*, 6, 298–308.

Kaufman, J. C. (2016). *Creativity 101* (2nd ed.). New York: Springer.

Kaufman, J. C., & Baer, J. (2002). Could Steven Spielberg manage the Yankees?: creative thinking in different domains. *Korean Journal of Thinking & Problem Solving*, 12, 5–15.

Kaufman, J. C., & Beghetto, R. A. (2009). Beyond big and little: the four C model of creativity. *Review of General Psychology*, 13, 1–12.

Kaufman, J. C., Glăveanu, V., & Baer, J. (2017). *Cambridge handbook of creativity across domains*. New York: Cambridge University Press.

Kaufman, J. C., & Reiter-Palmon, R. (2017). *The creative response evaluation at work test manual*. Amsterdam: Hogrefe.

Kirschner, P. A. (2017). Stop propagating the learning styles myth. *Computers & Education*, 106, 166–171.

Kirschner, P. A., & van Merriënboer, J. J. (2013). Do learners really know best? Urban legends in education. *Educational Psychologist*, 48, 169–183.

Kirton, M. (1976). Adaptors and innovators: a description and measure. *Journal of Applied Psychology*, 61, 622–629.

Kyllonen, P. C., Walters, A. M., & Kaufman, J. C. (2005). Noncognitive constructs and their assessment in graduate education. *Educational Assessment*, 10, 153–184.

Lilienfeld, S. O., Lynn, S. J., Ruscio, J., & Beyerstein, B. L. (2011). *50 Great myths of popular psychology: Shattering widespread misconceptions about human behavior*. Hoboken, NJ: John Wiley & Sons.

Massa, L. J., & Mayer, R. E. (2006). Testing the ATI hypothesis: should multimedia instruction accommodate verbalizer-visualizer cognitive style. *Learning and Individual Differences*, 16, 321–335.

Mumford, M. D., Mobley, M. I., Reiter-Palmon, R., Uhlman, C. E., & Doares, L. M. (1991). Process analytic models of creative capacities. *Creativity Research Journal*, 4, 91–122.

Newton, P. M. (2015). The learning styles myth is thriving in higher education. *Frontiers in Psychology*, 6, 1908.

Newton, P. M., & Miah, M. (2017). Evidence-based higher education—is the learning styles 'myth' important? *Frontiers in Psychology*, 8, 444–464.

"Parents of nasal learners demand odor-based curriculum". (March 2000). *The onion*. Retrieved from http://www.theonion.com/article/parents-of-nasal-learners-demand-odor-based-curric-396.

Price, L. (2004). Individual differences in learning: cognitive control, cognitive style, and learning style. *Educational Psychology*, 24, 681–698.

Reiter-Palmon, R., de Vreede, T., & de Vreede, G. J. (2013). Leading creative interdisciplinary teams: challenges and solutions. In S. Hemlin, C. M. Allwood, B. Martin, & M. D. Mumford (Eds.), *Creativity and leadership in science, technology and innovation* (pp. 240–267). New York: Routledge.

Reiter-Palmon, R., Mitchell, K., & Royston, R. (n.d.). Improving creativity in organizational settings: applying research on creativity to organizations. In J. C. Kaufman and R. J. Sternberg (Eds.), Cambridge handbook of creativity (2nd ed.) (in press).

Reiter-Palmon, R., Mumford, M. D., O'Connor Boes, J., & Runco, M. A. (1997). Problem construction and creativity: the role of ability, cue consistency and active processing. *Creativity Research Journal, 10*, 9–23.

Reiter-Palmon, R., Mumford, M. D., & Threlfall, K. V. (1998). Solving everyday problems creatively: the role of problem construction and personality type. *Creativity Research Journal, 11*, 187–197.

Reiter-Palmon, R., & Robinson, E. J. (2009). Problem identification and construction: what do we know, what is the future? *Psychology of Aesthetics, Creativity, and the Arts, 3*, 43–47.

Reiter-Palmon, R., Robinson-Morral, E., Kaufman, J. C., & Santo, J. (2012). Evaluation of self-perceptions of creativity: is it a useful criterion? *Creativity Research Journal, 24*, 107–114.

Rosing, K., Frese, M., & Bausch, A. (2011). Explaining the heterogeneity of the leadership-innovation relationship: ambidextrous leadership. *The Leadership Quarterly, 22*, 956–974.

Scholer, A. A., & Higgins, E. T. (2013). Dodging monsters and dancing with dreams: success and failure at different levels of approach and avoidance. *Emotion Review, 5*, 254–258.

Scott, G., Leritz, L., & Mumford, M. D. (2004). The effectiveness of creativity training: a quantitative review. *Creativity Research Journal, 16*, 361–388.

Silvia, P. J., Wigert, B., Reiter-Palmon, R., & Kaufman, J. C. (2012). Assessing creativity with self-report scales: a review and empirical evaluation. *Psychology of Aesthetics, Creativity, and the Arts, 6*, 19–34.

Somech, A., & Drach-Zahavy, A. (2013). Translating team creativity to innovation implementation: the role of team composition and climate for innovation. *Journal of Management, 39*, 684–708.

Sternberg, R. J. (1999). A propulsion model of types of creative contributions. *Review of General Psychology, 3*, 83–100.

Sternberg, R. J., Grigorenko, E. L., & Zhang, L. (2008). A reply to two stylish critiques: response to Hunt (2008) and Mayer (2008). *Perspectives on Psychological Science, 3*, 516–517.

Sternberg, R. J., & Kaufman, S. B. (2012). Trends in intelligence research. *Intelligence, 40*, 235–236.

Sternberg, R. J., Kaufman, J. C., & Pretz, J. E. (2002). *The creativity conundrum: A propulsion model of kinds of creative contributions.* New York: Psychology Press.

Sternberg, R. J., Kaufman, J. C., & Pretz, J. E. (2004). A propulsion model of creative leadership. *Creativity and Innovation Management, 13*, 145–153.

Stokes, P. D. (2008). Creativity from constraints: what can we learn from Motherwell? From Modrian? From Klee? *The Journal of Creative Behavior, 42*, 223–236.

Torrance, E. P. (2008). *The Torrance tests of creative thinking norms-technical manual.* Bensenville, IL: Scholastic Testing Service.

9

Freedom, Structure, and Creativity

Eric F. Rietzschel

Department of Psychology, University of Groningen, Groningen,
Netherlands

FREEDOM, STRUCTURE, AND CREATIVITY

There is no lack of advice on how to stimulate individual creativity, either in the workplace or the personal domain, and there are many techniques to help people generate more creative ideas or insights. The underlying message of many techniques and recommendations seems to be that everybody can be creative; one simply needs to learn the right techniques, tricks, or shortcuts. At the same time, however, there seems to be a pervasive belief that creativity cannot really be directed, and that spontaneity and a lack of rules are key to performing truly creatively. In fact, many highly creative individuals are characterized by their disregard for rules and procedures and their fierce individuality (Feist, 1998). Thus, there seems to be something of a paradox: If creativity is best achieved through freedom and a disregard for "the rules," how can creativity be stimulated or taught by giving people procedures to use?

In this chapter I will summarize much of the literature on the dynamic tension between freedom and structure within the context of creativity. In the first section, I will address the role of autonomy in creativity, and outline how its effects may partly depend on individual differences. Next, I will go into the possible benefits of constraints and structure, looking at the role of individual differences there as well. Finally, I will attempt to integrate the findings and theories discussed so far into some practical recommendations for organizations interested in stimulating creativity by optimally arranging autonomy and structure.

CREATIVITY AND FREEDOM

Of all our knowledge on organizational creativity, the importance of autonomy and a lack of external control may be the best known. Autonomy here is defined as the degree to which people (employees, research participants) can decide for themselves what to do, and how and when to do it (e.g., Breaugh, 1985; Hackman & Oldham, 1976; Humphrey, Nahrgang, & Morgeson, 2007; Langfred & Moye, 2004; Spector, 1986). The theme of external control and its detrimental influence on creativity was extensively studied in the second half of the 20th century, often in the context of self-determination theory (SDT; e.g., Deci & Ryan, 2002). A basic tenet of SDT is that (work) motivation and creative performance depend on the fulfillment of three basic human needs: the need for autonomy, the need for competence, and the need for relatedness. Situations (such as work environments) that contribute to need fulfillment are motivating; situations that thwart need fulfillment lead to lower motivation and hence lower performance. Since external control (or the feeling of external control) thwarts the fulfillment of people's need for autonomy, controlling situations are demotivating and hence should lead to lower creativity.

The notion that autonomy is important for motivation and performance is not unique to the creativity literature or SDT. For example, within the broader literature on organizational behavior and work performance, an influential model that also addresses the importance of autonomy is Hackman and Oldham's (1976) job characteristics model (JCM). According to the JCM, job characteristics such as autonomy, task variety, and challenge increase a job's motivating potential and hence are expected to lead to more favorable outcomes, such as motivation and performance. Empirical research has largely supported these propositions, and the JCM remains influential (see, e.g., Morgeson & Humphrey, 2006; Oldham & Cummings, 1996).

An extensive research program has yielded substantial support for the hypothesis that creativity suffers when people's sense of autonomy is threatened. This research has mostly focused on the role of rewards, evaluation, and supervisory behavior (see, e.g., Amabile, 1996; Hennessey & Amabile, 2010; Shalley, Zhou, & Oldham, 2004; Zhou & Shalley, 2008, for overviews). For example, an early study on evaluation and creativity was done by Amabile (1979), who found that college students performed less creatively when they expected their creative artworks to be evaluated by experts (as compared to a condition where participants were told their artworks would not be evaluated at all), except when they also received detailed instructions on how to make their artworks more creative. Similar results were obtained in subsequent studies. For example, Amabile, Hennessey, and Grossman (1986) conducted three studies on the relation between rewards and creativity, finding that both children and adults were less creative when they did a creative task in order to obtain a reward.

While much of the work on autonomy and creativity has focused on rewards and evaluation, the importance of autonomy has been supported by a wide range of studies. In a recent field study, for example, Joo, Yang, and McLean (2014) found that autonomy positively predicted employee creativity. In another field study, Mathisen (2011) found that autonomy positively predicted employees' creative self-efficacy (the degree to which they felt capable of generating creative ideas).

On the whole, then, the notion that autonomy is important for creativity, and that factors that may reduce autonomy, such as rewards and evaluations, can be a threat to creativity has been solidly supported. However, it is certainly not the case that *all* rewards or evaluations kill creativity. One important factor is the contingency of the reward: are people rewarded for doing a task, for high performance, or for creative performance? Research by Eisenberger and colleagues (e.g., Eisenberger & Rhoades, 2001) showed that creativity-contingent rewards can actually increase creativity, and that this effect may even be mediated by self-determination (because people are given the information they need in order to perform well and attain desired outcomes, their needs for autonomy and competence are supported). A recent meta-analysis by Byron and Khazanchi (2012) confirms that reward contingency is a crucial moderator for the relation between rewards and creativity.

Another relevant factor is the way in which a reward or evaluation is delivered. For example, Shalley and Perry-Smith (2001) showed that creativity was inhibited by *controlling* evaluation (where people were told that the evaluation would revolve around whether they performed as they should), but not by *informational* evaluation (where people were told the evaluation could help them develop themselves). Byron and Khazanchi's (2012) meta-analysis also confirms that creativity-contingent rewards are more effective when employees perceive more choice and freedom. Thus, while the importance of autonomy for creativity has been—and continues to be—solidly demonstrated, this does not mean that the effect is unconditional and independent of other factors.

Autonomy and Individual Differences

SDT takes the perspective that the need for autonomy is a basic and fundamental need shared by all people, and hence has addressed variability in need fulfillment by looking at differences between environments (i.e., more or less autonomy-supporting environments). Another approach is to look at interindividual differences in *need strength*, and to see whether these differences predict how people respond to different kinds of environments (e.g., Van Yperen, Rietzschel, & De Jonge, 2014).

In their influential analysis of task autonomy and its effects, Langfred and Moye (2004, also see Lawler, Hackman, & Kaufman, 1973) stress that the effects of autonomy will depend on its "overall utility": "Giving autonomy to an employee who perceives great benefit and little cost to autonomy is likely to be motivating, just as giving autonomy to the employee who perceives little benefit but great cost to autonomy is likely to harm motivation" (p. 936). While the benefits of autonomy have been emphasized extensively in the research literature, especially in the creativity literature, the potential costs have remained somewhat neglected. As an example, Langfred and Moye mention "the perception that more autonomy in the job can result in more work, involving more difficult and uncomfortable decisions and greater stress" (p. 936). Autonomy means that employees get control over how to perform their work tasks, how to schedule and plan them, or even over which tasks they want to do. Thus, working under high autonomy requires more information processing, especially in terms of choosing, planning, and monitoring one's tasks. Not everybody will respond to these extra demands in the same way, suggesting that the effects of autonomy on motivation and (creative) performance are probably moderated by relevant individual differences (also see Langfred, 2004, for an example of moderated team-level effects of autonomy).

Growth Need Strength

A classic example of this "need strength" approach is the research on the role of "growth need strength" in the job characteristics literature (Hackman & Oldham, 1976). Although the JCM states that some jobs have a higher motivating potential than others, this effect is proposed to be more pronounced for some employees than for others: some employees are not that interested in self-development and hence will not react as strongly to challenge or job autonomy as employees who find self-development very important and have a high *growth need strength* (Hackman & Lawler, 1971). Growth need strength has been found to moderate the motivational effects of job design (e.g., Hackman & Oldham, 1976; also see Beehr, Walsh, & Taber, 1976), and Shalley, Gilson, and Blum (2009) applied the concept to creative performance at work. In a survey study among employees they found, among other things, that a creativity-supporting climate in the organization was especially strongly related to (self-reported) creativity when growth need strength was high.

Need for Autonomy

An obvious candidate trait to moderate the effects of job or task autonomy is, of course, need for autonomy itself (also sometimes called need for control or need for independence; see Langfred & Moye, 2004). Generally, highly creative people tend to have more "independent" personalities; that is, they are less influenced by social norms and peer influence, and more likely to follow their own preferences and initiatives (e.g., Feist, 1998, 1999). However, these traits show considerably interindividual variance in the general population, and as such may well moderate people's response to different contexts or situation. Some studies have found that autonomy relates more strongly to outcomes such as job satisfaction among people who have a strong need for autonomy or independence. In an early study on this topic, Vroom (1959) hypothesized and found that participation (i.e., the degree of influence employees had on their work tasks and work-related decisions) was more strongly related to performance and attitudes toward the job among employees with a high need for independence than among employees with a low need for independence. Further, Orpen (1985) conducted a study among managers in several industries and found that many job characteristics, including autonomy, correlated more strongly to performance and job satisfaction among managers with a high need for independence. However, several other studies have failed to find evidence for such moderation effects (see, e.g., Abdel-Halim & Rowland, 1976; De Rijk, Le Blanc, Schaufeli, & De Jonge, 1998; Strain, 1999).

Personality Traits

Barrick and Mount (1993) studied the relation between the Big Five personality traits and job performance as moderated by autonomy, with results (obtained in a field study among US Army training participants) showing that personality traits were more predictive of job performance when autonomy was high; however, these results can also be interpreted as evidence for a moderating role of personality on the relation between autonomy and performance, such that autonomy was especially related to performance among employees high on conscientiousness and extraversion, and low on agreeableness. With regard to the latter, this result is consistent with moderation effects found for need for autonomy, as people high in agreeableness tend to be more oriented toward cooperation and maintaining good relations than toward independence and individualism (e.g., McCrae & Costa, 1987; also see Feist, 1998).

Need for Structure

Given the ambiguity and complexity that may result from autonomy, people's general attitude toward ambiguity should also be expected to moderate its effects. Thus, for example, Slijkhuis, Rietzschel, and Van Yperen (2013) looked at the moderating role of personal need for structure (Neuberg & Newsom, 1993; Thompson, Naccarato, Parker, & Moskowitz, 2001). People with a high need for structure are chronically averse to ambiguity, and prefer situations and environments that are well ordered and predictable. Slijkhuis et al. argued that autonomy should be less important for people with a high need for structure, because a lack of autonomy often implies clarity and structure. Thus, while employees with a low need for structure should respond negatively to (i.e., be demotivated by) controlling environments, this should not be the case for employees with a high need for structure (also see Billing, Bhagat, & Babakus, 2013). In a field study, Slijkhuis et al. (2013) found support for this hypothesis; a follow-up experiment also showed that a controlling (as compared to informational) evaluation (cf. Shalley & Perry-Smith, 2001) only inhibited creative performance for participants low in need for structure. In a later study, Rietzschel, Slijkhuis, and Van Yperen (2014a) found that need for structure also moderated the effects of close monitoring (George & Zhou, 2001; Zhou, 2003) on employee motivation and satisfaction: whereas employees with a low need for structure were less motivated and satisfied when they perceived high levels of supervisory close monitoring (and this effect was mediated by perceived autonomy), the opposite was the case for employees with a high need for structure. Among the latter group, moreover, this effect was mediated by role clarity.

Motivation

A particularly interesting study was reported by Dysvik and Kuvaas (2011). Whereas most research approaches (intrinsic) motivation as a dependent variable (or a mediator) affected by autonomy, Dysvik and Kuvaas argued that "although perceived job autonomy provides an opportunity for employees to try out and master new tasks ... the extent to which they actually seize this opportunity depends on their intrinsic motivation" (p. 368). In two field studies, they found that the relation between job autonomy and performance indeed was only significant for employees who were highly intrinsically motivated. Intrinsic motivation is often linked to explorative behavior (Amabile, 1996), and as such appears to be a necessary precondition for employees to make use of their job autonomy.

Self-Control and Self-Efficacy

Beside people's preferences for high levels of autonomy, growth, or structure, or their level of intrinsic motivation, the positive effects of autonomy on creative performance will also depend on people's *ability* to effectively make use of the autonomy they have. For example, Chang, Huang, and Choi (2012) studied the role of self-control (Tangney, Baumeister, & Boone, 2004) in the relation between task autonomy and creative performance. In line with the analysis by Langfred and Moye (2004), Chang et al. argue that task autonomy can be cognitively distracting, and might therefore not be equally beneficial for everybody—people with low self-control might not be able to deal effectively with the ambiguity inherent in high task autonomy. Their results showed that participants with low self-control performed less creatively under conditions of high task autonomy. For participants with high self-control, task autonomy did not make much of a difference in terms of creative performance.

Orth and Volmer (2017) recently conducted a field study on the within-person relations between job autonomy and innovative behavior (i.e., the implementation of creative ideas in the work context), and found that employees reported higher levels of innovative behaviors on days when they experienced higher levels of job autonomy. Importantly, these relations were especially pronounced for employees who had high levels of creative self-efficacy (i.e., a strong belief in their creative abilities; Tierney & Farmer, 2002). In line with the argument put forward by Dysvik and Kuvaas (2011), Orth and Volmer argue that employees with high levels of CSE are "more inclined to translate perceived autonomy into desirable innovative outcomes" (p. 604).

Conclusion

All in all, then, autonomy does not seem to be equally motivating or helpful for everybody, and even its relation with creativity appears to depend on individual differences. Generally speaking, people are most likely to benefit from high levels of autonomy when they have a low need for structure, when they are highly intrinsically motivated, and when they have high levels of self-control, conscientiousness, or creative self-efficacy. However, the results with regard to actual need for autonomy are inconclusive. Several other studies have approached the issue from the perspective of possible positive consequences of a *lack* of autonomy. In the next section, I will explore this in some more depth.

CONSTRAINTS AND CREATIVITY

External control and a lack of autonomy are often considered "constraints" (also see Caniëls & Rietzschel, 2015), because they limit a person's range of behavioral options and sense of self-determination. However, an increasing amount of research suggests that these kinds of limits can in fact be beneficial for creativity. In other words, reducing autonomy (in the sense of restricting a person's range of behavioral options) may stimulate creative performance. The underlying reason is the *complexity* inherent in autonomy. Autonomy, while motivating, also implies an *absence of information*, either regarding desired outcomes (what one is expected to do or achieve) or regarding procedures (how one is expected to do it). This requires the individual employee to explore and find his or her own way within the job. Of course, this room for exploration is why autonomy is generally thought to be beneficial for creativity, but the question is whether people are always likely to actually *use* the leeway they have (cf. Dysvik & Kuvaas, 2011) and hence to arrive at creative performance. In fact, theory and research suggest that a *lack* of autonomy may sometimes be more helpful for creativity.

The Path of Least Resistance

Ward (1994) and Finke, Ward, and Smith (1995) stipulated that creativity tends to follow the *path of least resistance*, in that people usually come up with whatever ideas are easiest to generate. This means that ideas tend to be based on highly accessible knowledge and schemas (also see Nijstad & Stroebe, 2006). This reliance on highly accessible knowledge can be considered a heuristic: it helps people deal with an ill-structured task. However, it does not help creativity, since high accessibility usually means that people generate mostly "obvious" ideas of low originality (but presumably high feasibility). Thus, for example, Ward, Patterson, Sifonis, Dodds, and Saunders (2002) found that participants who were instructed to come up with novel ideas regarding hypothetical extraterrestrial animals, fruits, or tools, tended to use highly accessible (and hence common) exemplars as starting points for creative idea generation, even when explicitly instructed to generate imaginary or highly creative exemplars.

Problematically, there are reasons to assume that people are especially likely to follow the path of least resistance when faced with a total lack of constraints. When problems are completely open and ill structured, and "anything goes," the number of possible approaches, strategies, and solutions can be cognitively overwhelming. The tendency to use mental shortcuts is especially strong when faced with complex and ill-structured problems (Branscombe & Cohen, 1991; Simon, 1955) and under conditions of high cognitive load (e.g., Ford & Kuglanski, 2005; Van Prooijen & Van de Veer, 2010). Since research suggests that this indeed carries over into people's ability to come up with creative ideas, Finke, Ward, and Smith (1992) suggested that "Restricting the ways in which creative cognitions are interpreted encourages creative exploration and discovery and further reduces the likelihood that a person will fall back on conventional lines of thought" (p. 32). In other words, people could—paradoxically—be forced off the path of least resistance (cf. Moreau & Dahl, 2005; Rietzschel, Nijstad, & Stroebe, 2007) by restricting their room for exploration, because this limits the complexity of the task and thereby decreases people's reliance on heuristics. Another positive consequence of constraints could be that, by diminishing task complexity, they reduce the load on working memory (Baddeley, 1996), which several studies have also linked to creativity (Benedek, Jauk, Sommer, Arendasy, & Neubauer, 2014; De Dreu, Nijstad, Baas, Wolsink, & Roskes, 2012; Lee & Therriault, 2013).

The Benefits of Constraints

The notion that constraints can stimulate creative performance has found substantial empirical support. For example, several studies showed that participants generated more ideas when they were instructed to address subcategories of a brainstorming topic sequentially, rather than simultaneously (Coskun, Paulus, Brown, & Sherwood, 2000; Dennis, Aronson, Heninger, & Walker, 1999; Dennis, Valacich, Conolly, & Wynne, 1996). Addressing only one subtopic at a time apparently enabled participants to go deeper into each subcategory than they would otherwise have done. Following similar logic, Rietzschel et al. (2007) used a priming procedure to activate participants' domain knowledge about certain subcategories of a brainstorming problem, and found that this caused participants to be more productive and more original within the primed subcategories. In a later study, Rietzschel, Nijstad, and Stroebe (2014) had participants generate ideas about a broad or a more narrow problem (improving education at a university vs improving the lectures at that university), and found that participants generated ideas of higher originality with the narrow problem. In a design study, Moreau and Dahl (2005) found that participants who were instructed to use a preselected set of elements made more creative designs than participants who were instructed to make their own selection of which elements to use. Further, Goldenberg, Mazursky, and Solomon (1999) identified creativity "templates," sets of operations that can be used to come up with novel designs or ideas (such as "displacement," where a core element or feature of an existing product is removed, and people get to explore the possibilities that this opens up), and found that use of these templates indeed contributed to the generation of more creative ideas.

Another way in which creative tasks can be constrained is by giving people explicit instructions on the kinds of ideas they are expected to generate. Thus, for example, participants may be given specific criteria to use or targets to strive toward (e.g., "generate original ideas"). Often, such instructions are already embedded in the general instructions for the creativity task, but the degree to which specific outcome dimensions are emphasized or elaborated upon may differ. Giving people such instructions generally seems to be helpful (e.g., Evans & Forbach, 1983; Harrington, 1975; Parnes & Meadow, 1959; Rietzschel, Nijstad, & Stroebe, 2014; Runco, Illies, & Reiter-Palmon, 2005). Arguably, these kinds of instructions are "weaker" constraints than some of the examples mentioned previously, because participants are not forced to follow or use any particular procedure. In a sense, participants' behavior is not so much constrained as calibrated. Nevertheless, information about the kinds of ideas that one is expected to produce can reduce the ambiguity and complexity of the task.

Task Structure

Some studies have addressed the issue of constraints by looking at the potential benefits of *task structure*, or procedural information about how to perform a (creative) task. Like the previously discussed constraints, task structure has two interrelated consequences: it limits the degrees of freedom people have in executing the task and thereby reduces task complexity and cognitive load. The studies on sequentially addressing subcategories in a brainstorming task (e.g., Dennis et al., 1996) are good examples of this approach. A somewhat different, but related approach to the benefits of structure was taken by Binyamin and Carmeli (2010), who found that the degree to which organizational HRM practices were structured positively predicted employee creativity, and that these effects were partly mediated by a reduction in uncertainty.

Although little theory exists on the nature or consequences of task structure, some older theories have addressed its role and importance. For example, House's (1971, 1996) path-goal theory of leadership states that a leader's role is to clarify which outcomes are desired and how these should (or can) be attained. Specifying these desired outcomes and the way toward them reduces ambiguity for employees, and hence is expected to lead to higher performance. A similar notion is found in Fiedler's (1965) contingency theory of leadership, which states that increasing task structure is a core task for supervisors. According to Fiedler, task structure has four dimensions: (1) decision verifiability (is there a demonstrably "correct" solution or outcome?), (2) goal clarity (are there clear requirements regarding task execution?), (3) goal-path multiplicity (can the task be performed in only one way, or in several ways?), and (4) solution specificity (is there one possible or permissible outcome, or are multiple solutions possible?). Thus, task structure is highest when it is unambiguously clear which outcomes are expected and how these are supposed to be attained.

Although the research discussed previously suggests that task structure can enhance creative performance, it also seems clear that this is not necessarily the case. Taking Fiedler's dimensions of task structure, for example, it seems plausible that high levels of decision verifiability and solution specificity actually *decrease* the opportunity for creative performance, because there is little room for novel responses. In contrast, low levels of goal-path multiplicity and high levels of goal clarity have the potential to "free up" cognitive resources without limiting the opportunity for creative behavior. In terms of the motivational research discussed earlier in this chapter, one could speculate that the former would be more "constraining" in the sense of reducing autonomy and the opportunity for exploration (also see Onarheim, 2012), whereas the latter would be considered helpful in the sense of reducing task complexity and ambiguity (also see Runco et al., 2005, for similar arguments and results).

A Model of Constraints and Creativity

In line with the reasoning earlier, Roskes (2015) proposed a model of constraints and creativity, distinguishing between constraints that *limit* cognitive resources and constraints that *channel* cognitive resources. Examples of the former are time pressure, environmental noise, and dual-task demands; examples of the latter are clear procedural instructions and restricted goal definitions. Moreover, Roskes argues that the effects of these constraints are contingent on individual differences in approach and avoidance motivation; that is, the degree to which people strive to attain positive outcomes or to avoid negative outcomes (Elliot, 1999). Approach and avoidance motivation have been linked to creative performance: Approach motivation positively predicts creativity because it is associated with greater flexibility and exploration, whereas avoidance motivation negatively predicts creativity because it is associated with a narrower focus and feelings of threat (e.g., Elliot, 2006; Friedman & Förster, 2002). Roskes' model posits that constraints will differentially affect creativity depending on people's approach and avoidance motivation. For example, according to the model, people with a strong avoidance motivation are likely to benefit from channeling constraints, because these fit with their focused and systematic thinking style.

Individual Differences and Constraints

Roskes' hypothesis that different types of constraints may not have the same effects on everybody is in line with several studies. For example, Sagiv, Arieli, Goldenberg, and Goldschmidt (2010) found that the effects of task structure were moderated by participants' cognitive style: Whereas participants with a more intuitive thinking style were more creative than participants with a systematic thinking style under unstructured conditions, this difference disappeared when the creative task was presented in a more structured way. Similar results were obtained by Rietzschel, Slijkhuis, and Van Yperen (2014b), who found that the effects of task structure on creative performance were moderated by participants' need for structure, such that participants with a high need for structure performed less creatively, except under conditions of high task structure.

Importantly, however, the positive effects of task structure found by Rietzschel et al. also depended on the way in which task structure was operationalized. As explained previously, task structure may contain both procedural- and outcome-related information. Although both kinds of information reduce ambiguity and complexity, only procedural information leaves room for creative outcomes. This would imply that a form of task structure where outcomes are specified or implied should kill creative performance, but might still be attractive to people with a high need for structure, and indeed this is what Rietzschel, Slijkhuis, and Van Yperen (2014b) found. When participants were given structured task instructions accompanied by a highly typical example of what the outcome could look like (in this case, drawing an alien), participants tended to stick close to this example, and hence produced drawings of lower creativity than those who were not given task structure. This finding fits with earlier work on fixation effects in creative tasks (e.g., Jansson & Smith, 1991; Smith, Ward,

& Schumacher, 1993), which has shown that it can be very difficult *not* to use a given example in idea generation. However, despite this negative effect on creativity, people with a high need for structure were more satisfied than participants with a lower need for structure, suggesting that a lack of ambiguity was more important for them than the opportunity to perform creatively.

Conclusion

Constraints can be helpful for creativity, because they reduce the complexity of the task and hence nudge people off the path of least resistance. Giving employees the opportunity to do what they want can also mean that they are left to their own devices, and in those situations people will often tend to rely on the most accessible (and hence least creative) ideas. Individual differences seem to play an important moderating role here, as well as the way in which autonomy or constraints are operationalized or communicated.

PRACTICAL RECOMMENDATIONS

Given the paradoxes and the complexities surrounding the issue of autonomy and structure, is there any way organizations or supervisors can stimulate creative performance as broadly as possible? In this section, I will give some brief suggestions on how the existing research could be fruitfully applied in organizational settings.

Avoid External Control

Although autonomy is not equally helpful for everybody, and a lack of autonomy is not equally problematic for everybody, the sense of being externally controlled is never helpful for creativity. Even in a study like the one reported by Rietzschel, Slijkhuis, and Van Yperen (2014a), who found that employees with a higher need for structure felt more satisfied and motivated when they experienced high levels of supervisory close monitoring, this did not translate into higher levels of creative or innovative performance. The fact that the favorable effects of close monitoring for these employees were mediated by role clarity also suggests that what these people liked was not so much the absence of autonomy, as the presence of information regarding what was expected of them. The large body of literature on external control, intrinsic motivation, and creativity has amply demonstrated the risks of external control; the more recent findings by Dysvik and Kuvaas (2011) add to this by showing that lower levels of intrinsic motivation may not only predict lower levels of creativity per se, but may also inhibit employees' tendency to make creative use of the job autonomy they have. Thus, a sense of self-determination remains important, and recognizing the possible pitfalls of autonomy or the benefits of task structure should not be an excuse to impose external control. Similarly to the literature on goal setting (see, e.g., Locke & Latham, 2002), it is likely that high levels of task structure will only motivate people to perform creatively if the structure allows for a sense of responsibility, ownership, and commitment (also see De Treville & Antonakis, 2006); simply giving people a procedure they have to follow may not work so well.

Provide Procedural Information

In contrast to the popular stereotype of creativity as spontaneous and undirected (e.g., Ritter & Rietzschel, 2017), total freedom often makes creative tasks overwhelming. In the absence of any information about how to do a task, people will rely on highly accessible knowledge and schemas, and hence fail to produce creative work. Procedural information (e.g., decomposing a problem into subcategories) can reduce the cognitive load of the task and hence help people explore less accessible "areas" of problem space. Importantly, this procedural information need not take the form of specific task instructions; Goldenberg et al.'s (1999) innovation templates are good examples as well. These templates provide people with a series of operations they can perform on a problem or an object, many of which are counterintuitive and therefore likely to push people off the path of least resistance. These templates may also have the advantage that they are less likely to be seen as actual "instructions" that could make people feel controlled. Rather than giving people detailed information on how to come up with creative ideas, Goldenberg et al.'s inventive templates are easily presented as *tools* that can help people come up with novel ideas. The unexpected nature of the templates (since most people would not spontaneously come up with the kinds of operations and transformations specified in the templates) probably also aligns with people's expectations and stereotypes regarding creativity and creative tasks (e.g., Baas, Koch, Nijstad, & De Dreu, 2015; Ritter & Rietzschel, 2017), and as such could lead to "fit" effects (cf. Cesario, Grant, & Higgins, 2004), which in turn could serve intrinsic motivation and creativity (however, also see Levine, Alexander, Wright, & Higgins, 2016).

Avoid Outcome Information

Although reducing autonomy somewhat by providing people with task-relevant information can be helpful, not all such information will have positive effects on creativity (Onarheim, 2012). Creative performance depends on the possibility to deviate from the norm and to produce work that is unexpected. The more salient the "standard" is made, the more difficult it becomes to deviate from it. This is not just because such outcome standards set a norm for what is allowed (e.g., Ruscio & Amabile, 1999) but also because of fixation effects: When presented with a typical example of task execution, people can easily get cognitively fixated on this example and keep generating new ideas along the lines of the example (Jansson & Smith, 1991; Smith et al., 1993). Of course, there may be beneficial effects of providing people with highly creative examples or role models (e.g., Shalley & Perry-Smith, 2001), for example, because these can give an idea of the kinds of highly novel performance that apparently are allowed or expected (in the absence of such information, people may perhaps assume that only moderately original ideas are valued); nevertheless, even highly creative examples may come with the risk of fixation effects. Therefore, procedural information is probably to be preferred.

Take Individual Differences Into Account

Research on organizational creativity has long recognized the need for an *interactionist* perspective (e.g., Woodman, Sawyer, & Griffin, 1993). Because creative performance is interactively predicted by contextual and personal characteristics, practical recommendations on how to stimulate creativity must involve both. The effects of autonomy and task structure clearly depend on individual differences in personality, needs and preferences, and abilities, and so will the effects of interventions in this area. Not every employee will be equally overwhelmed by high levels of autonomy, and not every employee will benefit equally strongly from procedural instructions. Some of these individual differences are "given" in that they reflect more or less stable traits that may be difficult to change substantially in an organizational context, but others, such as intrinsic motivation or creative self-efficacy, may lend themselves more readily to development on the job. For example, Tierney and Farmer (2011) found that creative self-efficacy at work could be developed over a 6-month period, and that this development was positively predicted by increases in employee creative role identity and supervisor creative expectations. As employees develop higher levels of creative self-efficacy, their ability to turn job autonomy into creative or innovative performance might increase as well (Orth & Volmer, 2017). Thus, rather than merely training employees to become more creative (Scott, Leritz, & Mumford, 2004), or to change aspects of job design (like autonomy) that are expected to be conducive to creativity, organizations might want to invest in developing those states, traits and abilities that will allow employees to make the most out of the autonomy and structure that their job is able to provide.

CONCLUSION

The aim of this chapter was to give an overview of some of the literature on autonomy, structure, and creativity. Clearly, the relation between these variables is somewhat paradoxical, and some of the common beliefs we have about what stimulates creativity have been qualified by recent research, especially in the field of individual differences. The main paradox is that autonomy, crucially important though it remains, in itself poses a risk for creativity because of the complexity it implies. Limiting the cognitive demands of creative work by restricting the available (procedural) options may, as we have seen, be helpful here, but no intervention is without its risks. Hopefully, the principles and recommendations outlined previously will go some way toward helping organizations, supervisors, and employees resolve the paradox of freedom, structure, and creativity.

References

Abdel-Halim, A. A., & Rowland, K. M. (1976). Some personality determinants of the effects of participation: a further investigation. *Personnel Psychology*, 29, 41–55. https://doi.org/10.1111/j.1744-6570.1976.tb00400.x.

Amabile, T. M. (1979). Effects of external evaluation on artistic creativity. *Journal of Personality and Social Psychology*, 37, 221–233. https://doi.org/10.1037/0022-3514.37.2.221.

Amabile, T. M. (1996). *Creativity in context*. Boulder, CO: Westview Press.

Amabile, T. M., Hennessey, B. A., & Grossman, B. S. (1986). Social influences on creativity: the effects of contracted-for reward. *Journal of Personality and Social Psychology*, 50, 14–23. https://doi.org/10.1037/0022-3514.50.1.14.

Baas, M., Koch, S., Nijstad, B. A., & De Dreu, C. W. (2015). Conceiving creativity: the nature and consequences of laypeople's beliefs about the realization of creativity. *Psychology of Aesthetics, Creativity, and the Arts*, 9, 340–354. https://doi.org/10.1037/a0039420.

Baddeley, A. (1996). Exploring the central executive. *The Quarterly Journal of Experimental Psychology*, 49, 5–28. https://doi.org/10.1080/027249896392784.

Barrick, M. R., & Mount, M. K. (1993). Autonomy as a moderator of the relationships between the Big Five personality dimensions and job performance. *Journal of Applied Psychology*, 78, 111–118. https://doi.org/10.1037/0021-9010.78.1.111.

Beehr, T. A., Walsh, J. T., & Taber, T. D. (1976). Relationships of stress to individually and organizationally valued states: higher order needs as a moderator. *Journal of Applied Psychology*, 61, 41–47. https://doi.org/10.1037/0021-9010.61.1.41.

Benedek, M., Jauk, E., Sommer, M., Arendasy, M., & Neubauer, A. C. (2014). Intelligence, creativity, and cognitive control: the common and differential involvement of executive functions on intelligence and creativity. *Intelligence*, 46, 73–83. https://doi.org/10.1016/j.intell.2014.05.007.

Billing, T. K., Bhagat, R. S., & Babakus, E. (2013). Task structure and work outcomes: exploring the moderating role of emphasis on scheduling. *Management Research Review*, 36, 136–152. https://doi.org/10.1108/01409171311292243.

Binyamin, G., & Carmeli, A. (2010). Does structuring of human resource management processes enhance employee creativity? The mediating role of psychological availability. *Human Resource Management*, 49, 999–1024. https://doi.org/10.1002/hrm.20397.

Branscombe, N. R., & Cohen, B. M. (1991). Motivation and complexity levels as determinants of heuristic use in social judgment. In J. Forgas (Ed.), *Emotion and social judgments* (pp. 145–160). Oxford: Pergamon Press.

Breaugh, J. A. (1985). The measurement of work autonomy. *Human Relations, 38*, 551–570. https://doi.org/10.1177/001872678503800604.

Byron, K., & Khazanchi, R. (2012). Rewards and creative performance: a meta-analytic test of theoretically derived hypotheses. *Psychological Bulletin, 138*, 809–830. https://doi.org/10.1037/a0027652.

Caniëls, M. J., & Rietzschel, E. F. (2015). Organizing creativity: creativity and innovation under constraints. *Creativity and Innovation Management, 24*, 184–196. https://doi.org/10.1111/caim.12123.

Cesario, J., Grant, H., & Higgins, E. T. (2004). Regulatory fit and persuasion: transfer from 'Feeling Right'. *Journal of Personality and Social Psychology, 86*, 388–404. https://doi.org/10.1037/0022-3514.86.3.388.

Chang, J. W., Huang, D. W., & Choi, J. N. (2012). Is task autonomy beneficial for creativity? Prior task experience and self-control as boundary conditions. *Social Behavior and Personality, 40*, 705–724. https://doi.org/10.2224/sbp.2012.40.5.705.

Coskun, H., Paulus, P. B., Brown, V., & Sherwood, J. J. (2000). Cognitive stimulation and problem presentation in idea-generating groups. *Group Dynamics, 4*, 307–329. https://doi.org/10.1037/1089-2699.4.4.307.

De Dreu, C. K. W., Nijstad, B. A., Baas, M., Wolsink, I., & Roskes, M. (2012). Working memory benefits creative insight, musical improvisation and original ideation through maintained task-focused attention. *Personality and Social Psychology Bulletin, 38*, 656–669. https://doi.org/10.1177/0146167211435795.

De Rijk, A. E., Le Blanc, P. M., Schaufeli, W. B., & de Jonge, J. (1998). Active coping and need for control as moderators of the job demand–control model: effects on burnout. *Journal of Occupational and Organizational Psychology, 71*, 1–18. https://doi.org/10.1111/j.2044-8325.1998.tb00658.x.

De Treville, S., & Antonakis, J. (2006). Could lean production job design be intrinsically motivating? Contextual, configurational, and levels-of-analysis issues. *Journal of Operations Management, 24*, 99–123. https://doi.org/10.1016/j.jom.2005.04.001.

Deci, E. L. & Ryan, R. M. (Eds.), (2002). *Handbook of self-determination research*. Rochester, NY: University of Rochester Press.

Dennis, A. R., Aronson, J. E., Heninger, W. G., & Walker, E. D. (1999). Structuring time and task in electronic brainstorming. *MIS Quarterly, 23*, 95–108. https://doi.org/10.2307/249411.

Dennis, A. R., Valacich, J. S., Conolly, T., & Wynne, B. E. (1996). Process structuring in electronic brainstorming. *Information Systems Research, 7*, 268–277. https://doi.org/10.1287/isre.7.2.268.

Dysvik, A., & Kuvaas, B. (2011). Intrinsic motivation as a moderator on the relationship between perceived job autonomy and work performance. *European Journal of Work and Organizational Psychology, 20*, 367–387. https://doi.org/10.1080/13594321003590630.

Eisenberger, R., & Rhoades, L. (2001). Incremental effects of reward on creativity. *Journal of Personality and Social Psychology, 81*, 728–741. https://doi.org/10.1037/0022-3514.81.4.728.

Elliot, A. J. (1999). Approach and avoidance motivation and achievement goals. *Educational Psychologist, 34*, 169–189. https://doi.org/10.1207/s15326985ep3403_3.

Elliot, A. J. (2006). The hierarchical model of approach-avoidance motivation. *Motivation and Emotion, 30*, 111–116. https://doi.org/10.1007/s11031-006-9028-7.

Evans, R. G., & Forbach, G. B. (1983). Facilitation of performance on a divergent measure of creativity: a closer look at instructions to 'be creative'. *Applied Psychological Measurement, 7*, 181–187. https://doi.org/10.1177/014662168300700206.

Feist, G. J. (1998). A meta-analysis of personality in scientific and artistic creativity. *Personality and Social Psychology Review, 2*, 290–309. https://doi.org/10.1207/s15327957pspr0204_5.

Feist, G. J. (1999). The influence of personality on artistic and scientific creativity. In R. J. Sternberg & R. J. Sternberg (Eds.), *Handbook of creativity* (pp. 273–296). New York, NY: Cambridge University Press.

Fiedler, F. E. (1965). The contingency model: a theory of leadership effectiveness. In H. Proshansky & B. Seidenberg (Eds.), *Basic studies in social psychology* (pp. 538–551). New York, NY: Holt, Rinehart, and Winston.

Finke, R. A., Ward, T. B., & Smith, S. M. (1992). *Creative cognition: Theory, research, and applications.* Cambridge, MA: The MIT Press.

Finke, R. A., Ward, T. B., & Smith, S. M. (1995). *The creative cognition approach.* Boston, MA: MIT Press.

Ford, T. E., & Kuglanski, A. W. (2005). Effects of epistemic motivations on the use of accessible constructs in social judgment. *Personality and Social Psychology Bulletin, 21,* 950–962. https://doi.org/10.1177/0146167295219009.

Friedman, R. S., & Förster, J. (2002). The influence of approach and avoidance motor actions on creative cognition. *Journal of Experimental Social Psychology, 38,* 41–55. https://doi.org/10.1006/jesp.2001.1488.

George, J. M., & Zhou, J. (2001). When openness to experience and conscientiousness are related to creative behavior: an interactional approach. *Journal of Applied Psychology, 86,* 513–524. https://doi.org/10.1037/0021-9010.86.3.513.

Goldenberg, J., Mazursky, D., & Solomon, S. (1999). Toward identifying the inventive templates of new products: a channeled ideation approach. *Journal of Marketing Research, 36,* 200–210. https://doi.org/10.2307/3152093.

Hackman, J. R., & Lawler, E. E. (1971). Employee reactions to job characteristics. *Journal of Applied Psychology, 55,* 259–286. https://doi.org/10.1037/h0031152.

Hackman, J. R., & Oldham, G. R. (1976). Motivation through the design of work: test of a theory. *Organizational Behavior and Human Performance, 16,* 250–279. https://doi.org/10.1016/0030-5073(76)90016-7.

Harrington, D. M. (1975). Effects of explicit instructions to 'be creative' on the psychological meaning of divergent thinking test scores. *Journal of Personality, 43,* 434–454. https://doi.org/10.1111/j.1467-6494.1975.tb00715.x.

Hennessey, B. A., & Amabile, T. M. (2010). Creativity. *Annual Review of Psychology, 61,* 569–598. https://doi.org/10.1146/annurev.psych.093008.100416.

House, R. J. (1971). A path goal theory of leader effectiveness. *Administrative Science Quarterly, 16,* 321–338. https://doi.org/10.2307/2391905.

House, R. J. (1996). Path-goal theory of leadership: lessons, legacy, and a reformulated theory. *Leadership Quarterly, 7,* 323–352. https://doi.org/10.1016/S1048-9843(96)90024-7.

Humphrey, S. E., Nahrgang, J. D., & Morgeson, F. P. (2007). Integrating motivational, social, and contextual work design features: a meta-analytic summary and theoretical extension of the work design literature. *Journal of Applied Psychology, 92,* 1332–1356. https://doi.org/10.1037/0021-9010.92.5.1332.

Jansson, D. G., & Smith, S. M. (1991). Design fixation. *Design Studies, 12,* 3–11.

Joo, B.-K., Yang, B., & McLean, G. (2014). Employee creativity: the effects of perceived learning culture, leader–member exchange quality, job autonomy, and proactivity. *Human Resource Development International, 17,* 297–317. https://doi.org/10.1080/13678868.2014.896126.

Langfred, C. W. (2004). Too much of a good thing? Negative effects of high trust and individual autonomy in self-managing teams. *Academy of Management Journal, 47,* 385–399. https://doi.org/10.2307/20159588.

Langfred, C. L., & Moye, N. A. (2004). Effects of task autonomy on performance: an extended model considering motivational, informational, and structural mechanisms. *Journal of Applied Psychology, 89,* 934–945. https://doi.org/10.1037/0021-9010.89.6.934.

Lawler, E. E., Hackman, J. R., & Kaufman, S. (1973). Effects of job redesign: a field experiment. *Journal of Applied Social Psychology, 3,* 49–62. https://doi.org/10.1111/j.1559-1816.1973.tb01294.x.

Lee, C. S., & Therriault, D. J. (2013). The cognitive underpinnings of creative thought: a latent variable analysis exploring the roles of intelligence and working memory in three creative thinking processes. *Intelligence, 41*, 306–320. https://doi.org/10.1016/j.intell.2013.04.008.

Levine, J. M., Alexander, K. M., Wright, A. C., & Higgins, E. T. (2016). Group brainstorming: when regulatory nonfit enhances performance. *Group Processes & Intergroup Relations, 19*, 257–271. https://doi.org/10.1177/1368430215577226.

Locke, E. A., & Latham, G. P. (2002). Building a practically useful theory of goal setting and task motivation: a 35-year odyssey. *American Psychologist, 57*, 705–717. https://doi.org/10.1037/0003-066X.57.9.705.

Mathisen, G. E. (2011). Organizational antecedents of creative self-efficacy. *Creativity and Innovation Management, 20*, 185–195.

McCrae, R. R., & Costa, P. T. (1987). Validation of the five-factor model of personality across instruments and observers. *Journal of Personality and Social Psychology, 52*, 81–90. https://doi.org/10.1037/0022-3514.52.1.81.

Moreau, C. P., & Dahl, D. W. (2005). Designing the solution: the impact of constraints on consumers' creativity. *Journal of Consumer Research, 32*, 13–22. https://doi.org/10.1086/429597.

Morgeson, F. P., & Humphrey, S. E. (2006). The Work Design Questionnaire (WDQ): developing and validating a comprehensive measure for assessing job design and the nature of work. *Journal of Applied Psychology, 91*, 1321–1339. https://doi.org/10.1037/0021-9010.91.6.1321.

Neuberg, S. L., & Newsom, J. T. (1993). Personal need for structure: individual differences in the desire for simpler structure. *Journal of Personality and Social Psychology, 65*, 113–131. https://doi.org/10.1037/0022-3514.65.1.113.

Nijstad, B. A., & Stroebe, W. (2006). How the group affects the mind: a cognitive model of idea generation in groups. *Personality and Social Psychology Review, 10*, 186–213. https://doi.org/10.1207/s15327957pspr1003_1.

Oldham, G. R., & Cummings, A. (1996). Employee creativity: personal and contextual factors at work. *Academy of Management Journal, 39*, 607–634. https://doi.org/10.2307/256657.

Onarheim, B. (2012). Creativity from constraints in engineering design: lessons learned at Coloplast. *Journal of Engineering Design, 23*, 323–336. https://doi.org/10.1080/09544828.2011.631904.

Orpen, C. (1985). The effects of need for achievement and need for independence on the relationship between perceived job attributes and managerial satisfaction and performance. *International Journal of Psychology, 20*, 207–219. https://doi.org/10.1080/00207598508247733.

Orth, M., & Volmer, J. (2017). Daily within-person effects of job autonomy and work engagement on innovative behaviour: the cross-level moderating role of creative self-efficacy. *European Journal of Work and Organizational Psychology, 26*, 601–612. https://doi.org/10.1080/1359432X.2017.1332042.

Parnes, S. J., & Meadow, A. (1959). Effects of 'brainstorming' instructions on creative problem solving by trained and untrained subjects. *Journal of Educational Psychology, 50*, 171–176. https://doi.org/10.1037/h0047223.

Rietzschel, E. F., Nijstad, B. A., & Stroebe, W. (2007). Relative accessibility of domain knowledge and creativity: the effects of knowledge activation on the quantity and originality of generated ideas. *Journal of Experimental Social Psychology, 43*, 933–946. https://doi.org/10.1016/j.jesp.2006.10.014.

Rietzschel, E. F., Nijstad, B. A., & Stroebe, W. (2014). Effects of problem scope and creativity instructions on idea generation and selection. *Creativity Research Journal, 26*, 185–191. https://doi.org/10.1080/10400419.2014.901084.

Rietzschel, E. F., Slijkhuis, J. M., & Van Yperen, N. W. (2014a). Close monitoring as a contextual stimulator: how need for structure affects the relation between close monitoring and work outcomes. *European Journal of Work and Organizational Psychology, 23*, 394–404. https://doi.org/10.1080/1359432X.2012.752897.

Rietzschel, E. F., Slijkhuis, J. M., & Van Yperen, N. W. (2014b). Task structure, need for structure, and creativity. *European Journal of Social Psychology, 44,* 386–399. https://doi.org/10.1002/ejsp.2024.

Ritter, S. M., & Rietzschel, E. F. (2017). Lay theories of creativity. In C. M. Zedelius, B. C. N. Müller, & J. W. Schooler (Eds.), *The science of lay theories* (pp. 95–126). New York, USA: Springer.

Roskes, M. (2015). Constraints that help or hinder creative performance: a motivational approach. *Creativity and Innovation Management, 24,* 197–206. https://doi.org/10.1111/caim.12086.

Runco, M. A., Illies, J. J., & Reiter-Palmon, R. (2005). Explicit instructions to be creative: a comparison of strategies and criteria as targets with three types of divergent thinking tests. *Korean Journal of Thinking and Problem Solving, 15,* 5–15.

Ruscio, A. M., & Amabile, T. M. (1999). Effects of instructional style on problem-solving creativity. *Creativity Research Journal, 12,* 251–266. https://doi.org/10.1207/s15326934crj1204_3.

Sagiv, L., Arieli, S., Goldenberg, J., & Goldschmidt, A. (2010). Structure and freedom in creativity: the interplay between externally imposed structure and personal cognitive style. *Journal of Organizational Behavior, 31,* 1086–1110. https://doi.org/10.1002/job.664.

Scott, G., Leritz, L. E., & Mumford, M. D. (2004). The effectiveness of creativity training: a quantitative review. *Creativity Research Journal, 16,* 361–388. https://doi.org/10.1207/s15326934crj1604_1.

Shalley, C. E., Gilson, L. L., & Blum, T. C. (2009). Interactive effects of growth need strength, work context, and job complexity on self-reported creative performance. *Academy of Management Journal, 52,* 489–505. https://doi.org/10.5465/AMJ.2009.41330806.

Shalley, C. E., & Perry-Smith, J. E. (2001). Effects of social-psychological factors on creative performance: the role of informational and controlling expected evaluation and modeling experience. *Organizational Behavior and Human Decision Processes, 84,* 1–22. https://doi.org/10.1006/obhd.2000.2918.

Shalley, C. E., Zhou, J., & Oldham, G. R. (2004). Effects of personal and contextual characteristics on creativity: where should we go from here? *Journal of Management, 30,* 933–958. https://doi.org/10.1016/j.jm.2004.06.007.

Simon, H. A. (1955). A behavioral model of rational choice. *Quarterly Journal of Economics, 69,* 99–118. https://doi.org/10.2307/1884852.

Slijkhuis, J. M., Rietzschel, E. F., & Van Yperen, N. W. (2013). How evaluation and need for structure affect motivation and creativity. *European Journal of Work and Organizational Psychology, 22,* 15–25. https://doi.org/10.1080/1359432X.2011.626244.

Smith, S. M., Ward, T. B., & Schumacher, J. S. (1993). Constraining effects of examples in a creative generation task. *Memory & Cognition, 21,* 837–845. https://doi.org/10.3758/BF03202751.

Spector, P. E. (1986). Perceived control by employees: a meta-analysis of studies concerning autonomy and participation at work. *Human Relations, 39,* 1005–1016. https://doi.org/10.1177/001872678603901104.

Strain, C. J. (1999). Perceived autonomy, need for autonomy, and job performance in retail salespeople. *Journal of Social Behavior & Personality, 14,* 259–265.

Tangney, J. P., Baumeister, R. F., & Boone, A. L. (2004). High self-control predicts good adjustment, less pathology, better grades, and interpersonal success. *Journal of Personality, 72,* 271–324. https://doi.org/10.1111/j.0022-3506.2004.00263.x.

Thompson, M. M., Naccarato, M. E., Parker, K. C. H., & Moskowitz, G. B. (2001). The personal need for structure and personal fear of invalidity measures: historical perspectives, current applications, and future directions. In G. B. Moskowitz (Ed.), *Cognitive social psychology: the Princeton symposium on the legacy and future of social cognition* (pp. 19–39). Mahwah, NJ: Lawrence Erlbaum.

Tierney, P., & Farmer, S. M. (2002). Creative self-efficacy: its potential antecedents and relationship to creative performance. *Academy of Management Journal, 45,* 1137–1148. https://doi.org/10.2307/3069429.

Tierney, P., & Farmer, S. M. (2011). Creative self-efficacy development and creative performance over time. *Journal of Applied Psychology, 96*, 277–293. https://doi.org/10.1037/
a0020952.

Van Prooijen, J.-W., & Van De Veer, E. (2010). Perceiving pure evil: the influence of cognitive load and prototypical evilness on demonizing. *Social Justice Research, 23*, 259–271.
https://doi.org/10.1007/s11211-010-0119-y.

Van Yperen, N. W., Rietzschel, E. F., & De Jonge, K. M. M. (2014). Blended working: for whom
it may (not) work. *PLos One, 9*, e102921https://doi.org/10.1371/journal.pone.0102921.

Vroom, V. H. (1959). Some personality determinants of the effects of participation. *The Journal
of Abnormal and Social Psychology, 59*, 322–327. https://doi.org/10.1037/h0049057.

Ward, T. B. (1994). Structured imagination: the role of category structure in exemplar generation. *Cognitive Psychology, 27*, 1–40. https://doi.org/10.1006/cogp.1994.1010.

Ward, T. B., Patterson, M. J., Sifonis, C. M., Dodds, R. A., & Saunders, K. N. (2002). The role
of graded category structure in imaginative thought. *Memory & Cognition, 30*, 199–216.
https://doi.org/10.3758/BF03195281.

Woodman, R. W., Sawyer, J. E., & Griffin, R. W. (1993). Toward a theory of organizational
creativity. *Academy of Management Review, 18*, 293–321. https://doi.org/10.2307/258761.

Zhou, J. (2003). When the presence of creative coworkers is related to creativity: role of supervisor close monitoring, developmental feedback, and creative personality. *Journal of
Applied Psychology, 88*, 413–422. https://doi.org/10.1037/0021-9010.88.3.413.

Zhou, J. & Shalley, C. E. (Eds.), (2008). *Handbook of organizational creativity.* New York:
Erlbaum.

The Heart of Innovation: Antecedents and Consequences of Creative Self-Efficacy in Organizations

Alexander S. McKay, *Jeffrey B. Lovelace†, Matt C. Howard‡*

*Virginia Commonwealth University, Richmond, VA, United States, †University of Virginia, Charlottesville, VA, United States, ‡University of South Alabama, Mobile, AL, United States

Belief in your creative capacity lies at the heart of innovation. *Tom Kelley and David Kelley (2013, p. 2), IDEO*

Achieving creative outcomes is difficult. Navigating the many stages of the creative process, from obtaining information, to generating ideas, and finally to implementing specific plans, can prove to be quite arduous (e.g., Anderson, Potocnik, & Zhou, 2014; Hennessey & Amabile, 2010). Yet, as the Kelley brothers indicate, having confidence in one's creative abilities is critical to conquering the stages of creativity. Creative self-efficacy (CSE), defined as "the belief one has the ability to produce creative outcomes" (Tierney & Farmer, 2002, p. 1138), is viewed as one of the most important antecedents for creativity in organizational and educational settings (Beghetto, 2006; Beghetto, Kaufman, & Baxter, 2011; Karwowski & Lebuda, 2015; Puente-Díaz, 2016).

The present chapter reviews the literature on CSE in organizational settings to highlight and integrate key findings and to identify next steps for future research. We split our review into five sections: (a) a brief overview of the theoretical background underlying CSE, (b) antecedents of CSE, (c) outcomes (i.e., creativity) of CSE, (d) measurement of CSE, and

(e) directions for future research. To expand on recent reviews (Farmer & Tierney, 2017; Puente-Díaz, 2016) and metaanalyses focusing on creative self-beliefs and CSE (Karwowski & Lebuda, 2015; Liu, Jiang, Shalley, Keem, & Zhou, 2016), we also include our own metaanalytic review of CSE, published for the first time in this chapter. Our metaanalytic investigation overlaps with several aspects of Liu et al.'s (2016) metaanalysis of CSE in organizational settings. Thus our metaanalytic results are only meant to supplement the findings of Liu et al. (2016) and Karwowski and Lebuda (2015) by examining factors and moderators not included in either metaanalysis. We report results from all three metaanalytic efforts to provide a comprehensive overview in an effort to help focus future efforts in this domain. Table 1 provides a summary of factors examined with CSE in the literature while indicating which metaanalysis explored each relationship.

TABLE 1   Factors and the Corresponding Metaanalysis Examining Those Factors With CSE

Variables examined	Metaanalysis examining relationship
Antecedents of CSE	
PERSONAL SOURCES	
Job-self efficacy	Current chapter
Job knowledge	
Education	Current chapter
Job tenure	Current chapter
Task expertise	Current chapter
Training	Current chapter
Personality	
Openness to experience	Karwowski and Lebuda (2015) and Liu et al. (2016)
Conscientiousness	Karwowski and Lebuda (2015) and Liu et al. (2016)
Extraversion	Karwowski and Lebuda (2015)
Emotional stability/ neuroticism	Karwowski and Lebuda (2015)
Agreeableness	Karwowski and Lebuda (2015)
Motivational factors	
Intrinsic motivation	Liu et al. (2016)
Prosocial motivation	Liu et al. (2016)

Continued

TABLE 1 Factors and the Corresponding Metaanalysis Examining Those Factors With CSE—cont'd

Variables examined	Metaanalysis examining relationship
CONTEXTUAL SOURCES	
Leadership	Liu et al. (2016)
Job characteristics	
Job complexity	Liu et al. (2016)
Job autonomy	Liu et al. (2016)
Job requirements for creativity	Current chapter
MODERATORS OF ANTECEDENT AND CSE RELATIONSHIPS	
Culture	Current chapter
Job type	Current chapter
Outcomes of CSE	
Creativity	Liu et al. (2016)
MODERATORS OF CSE AND CREATIVITY RELATIONSHIP	
Environmental moderators	
Culture	Liu et al. (2016)
Job type	Current chapter
Methodological moderators	
Self- vs other-reported creativity	Liu et al. (2016)
Cross sectional vs longitudinal design	Current chapter
Type of self-efficacy measure used (general vs creativity specific)	Liu et al. (2016)

Note. Samples from Karwowski and Lebuda (2015) included high school and college students and working adults. Samples from Liu et al. (2016) included working adults.

METAANALYTIC METHODS

In our review of the literature for this chapter we recognized several important relationships between CSE and other factors (i.e., job self-efficacy, job knowledge, and moderators of antecedents and outcomes of CSE) that were not systematically reviewed by previous metaanalyses. To supplement the findings of these previous efforts (and to reinforce their findings) we decided to supplement their findings with our own metaanalytic effort for this chapter. To identify articles to include in our metaanalysis, we conducted a literature search to find articles meeting the following criteria: (a) used an organizational sample, (b) included relationships between CSE and other constructs at the individual level, (c) included a measure of CSE, (d) was published in English, and (e) included the necessary information to calculate an effect size. As a starting point, we searched for articles citing Tierney and Farmer (2002) using Google Scholar. We manually searched these articles to identify those meeting our criteria. We then conducted an additional search in PsycINFO between 1995 and 2016 using the term "creative self-efficacy," with and without the hyphen and manually searched the references in a recent review of CSE (Puente-Díaz, 2016). This search yielded 42 usable samples from 40 published articles and theses/dissertations.

Metaanalytic results were calculated with a program developed by Bosco and Aguinis (2013) to calculate sample-size-weighted mean correlations and unreliability-corrected correlations. Multiple effect sizes for the same relationship in a single study were averaged together. Further, all results were corrected for unreliability using the individual correction method, as reliability statistics were available for most studies. For articles that did not report reliability coefficients, a mean replacement method was applied. We corrected for unreliability in both variables for each correlation.

Moderator analyses were performed for relationships that consisted of three or more effect sizes for each category of the moderator. The same metaanalytic methods described previously were applied to calculate the mean correlations within moderator categories. To determine whether a significant difference existed between the correlations across moderator categories, the Q_B statistic and z-scores were used. The Q_B statistic tests the null hypothesis that the category mean effect sizes are equal and are analogous to the F-test in ANOVA (Hedges & Pigott, 2004). We used the formula provided by Quiñones, Ford, and Teachout (1995, p. 896) to calculate z-scores for comparing the corrected effect sizes across levels of the moderators. We only calculate z-scores when the Q_B statistic was statistically significant and P values for the z-scores were based on a two-tailed hypothesis test. A detailed summary of our metaanalysis is available from the first author upon request.

THEORETICAL BACKGROUND OF CREATIVE SELF-EFFICACY

The study of self-efficacy was popularized by the social cognitive theory of motivation (Bandura, 1997). This theory argues that a person's knowledge and abilities are developed through personal experiences and observing others. Thus self-efficacy is a sociomotivational mechanism underlying performance across domains. Because another review has provided a thorough overview of the theoretical basis for self-efficacy and CSE (see Puente-Díaz, 2016), we provide only a brief review of these foundations.

In general, four sources have been identified and proposed to develop self-efficacy (Bandura, 1997; Mathisen, 2011; Tierney & Farmer, 2002): (a) mastery experiences, (b) vicarious experiences, (c) verbal persuasion, and (d) physiological and affective states. Mastery experiences are the most influential source and involve a person achieving successful performance outcomes, which helps them believe they can succeed on similar future tasks. Vicarious experiences, or role modeling, involve an observer watching another person experience a successful performance outcome and learning from this observation. This vicarious experience boosts the observer's efficacy because they believe that if others can accomplish the task, they can too. Verbal persuasion involves someone convincing another person that they have the capability to perform a task successfully. This positive feedback boosts energy focused toward the task, which increases task persistence and effort. Last, physiological and affect states revolve around the arousal one feels while working on a task. For example, high arousal results in large energy expenditures and indicates someone is working too hard and struggling to complete the task, which can reduce efficacy. This also encompasses the influence of mood and affect on creative performance (Baas, De Dreu, & Nijstad, 2008). We turn next to discuss the antecedents that influence CSE through these four mechanisms.

ANTECEDENTS OF CREATIVE SELF-EFFICACY

We utilize Woodman, Sawyer, and Griffin's (1993) framework of personal sources, contextual sources, and social sources to organize our review of CSE's antecedents. Personal sources are characteristics of the person, contextual sources are job characteristics/factors operating outside of the person, and social sources are interpersonal relationships. Our metaanalytic and conceptual review of CSE antecedents is thorough but not exhaustive. To review the various antecedents, we draw on two metaanalyses: one focusing on personality and creative self-beliefs (Karwowski & Lebuda, 2015) and another focusing on motivational mechanisms of individual creativity in organizational settings (Liu et al., 2016). We supplement the results from these two previous metaanalyses with our metaanalytic findings.

Personal Sources of Creative Self-Efficacy

Job Self-Efficacy

Job self-efficacy refers to the belief in oneself to complete their general work duties (Chen, Gully, & Eden, 2001). General types of efficacy, like job self-efficacy, shape more specific types of efficacy like CSE (Bandura, 1997; Tierney & Farmer, 2002). The previous metaanalyses did not examine the relationship between job self-efficacy and CSE, which was surprising because Tierney and Farmer (2002) proposed job self-efficacy as a core antecedent of CSE. Although few studies have examined the relationship between job self-efficacy and CSE, in our metaanalytic effort we found that the two were positively correlated ($k=4$, $N=890$, $r=0.37$ [95% CIs $=0.27$–0.48], $\rho=0.47$). Due to the limited number examining this relationship, it is important for future research to examine both types of self-efficacy. By including measures of each self-efficacy, researchers can determine the incremental validity of CSE beyond general, job self-efficacy.

Job Knowledge

Like job self-efficacy, Tierney and Farmer (2002) proposed job knowledge as a core antecedent of CSE, but job knowledge was not examined in previous metaanalyses. Job knowledge includes (a) prior education, (b) job tenure, (c) task expertise, and (d) training. Education and tenure have not been the primary focus of research on antecedents of CSE, but are regularly included as control variables resulting in a large number of studies reporting the correlations among these factors. Although Tierney and Farmer (2002) proposed and found two aspects of job knowledge (education and tenure) to positively predict CSE, additional research has been less consistent for job tenure. Specifically, in our effort we found a nonsignificant metaanalytic effect between job tenure and CSE ($k=24$, $N=6042$, $r=0.02$ [95% CIs $=-0.02$–0.05], $\rho=0.02$). The remaining job knowledge factors had effect sizes that were either small in magnitude or lacking enough research to produce reliable results. Education had a significant, albeit weak, positive relationship with CSE ($k=21$, $N=5061$, $r=0.11$ [95% CIs $=0.07$–0.16], $\rho=0.13$). Task expertise ($k=2$, $N=259$, $r=0.23$ [95% CIs $=0.15$–0.31], $\rho=0.28$) and training ($k=2$, $N=1061$, $r=0.18$ [95% CIs $=0.18$–0.18], $\rho=0.23$) were positively related to CSE, but only two studies examined each of these factors.

This pattern of results for job knowledge indicates a couple of potential interpretations. First, more passive forms of acquiring job knowledge (e.g., tenure) are unrelated to CSE, whereas more active forms of acquiring job knowledge (e.g., education, training) are positively related to CSE. Second, education, task expertise, and training more accurately capture the dimensions of mastery experiences, which are not captured with tenure. Overall, job knowledge aids in some development of CSE and is a potential area for future research, especially the possibility of training indirectly affecting creativity through CSE.

Personality

Researchers have also examined the relationships between CSE and the Big Five (openness to experience, extraversion, conscientiousness, agreeableness, neuroticism). Currently, two metaanalyses have examined these relationships. First, Karwowski and Lebuda (2015) metaanalyzed research on the relationship between all Big Five factors and creative self-beliefs broadly, which are a person's belief of their own creativity, as well as specific creative self-belief dimensions (i.e., self-rated creativity, creative personal identity, and CSE). The samples included in their metaanalysis were college students, working adults, and high school students. Of the Big Five facets, openness to experience has the strongest relationship with CSE. Karwowski and Lebuda (2015) found a corrected correlation of 0.69 between openness to experience and CSE. After controlling for the other Big Five facets in a regression analysis, the corrected relationship remained large at 0.64. The remaining Big Five facets were differentially related to CSE. Extraversion had a significant, positive corrected correlation of 0.37 with CSE (Karwowski & Lebuda, 2015). However, the corrected effect size reduced to 0.07 after controlling for the other Big Five facets. This reduction was likely due to the positive correlation between openness to experience and extraversion. Conscientiousness had a moderate relationship of 0.31 with CSE and after controlling for the other Big Five facets, the corrected effect size reduced to 0.19. Both agreeableness and neuroticism had weaker corrected relationships with CSE (0.18 and −0.16, respectively). In a regression analysis, they found these corrected effect sizes were small and reversed directions: agreeableness was −0.05 and neuroticism was 0.01.

Second, Liu et al. (2016) metaanalyzed organizational research measuring CSE and two Big Five factors: openness to experience and conscientiousness. For openness to experience and CSE, they found a relationship of 0.23 ($\rho = 0.30$). After controlling for job autonomy, job complexity, conscientiousness, and supportive leadership in a regression analysis, the relationship remained similar in strength at 0.18. The relationship between conscientiousness and CSE was moderate in strength ($r = 0.30$, $\rho = 0.38$). The corrected effect size remained at 0.33 in a regression analysis when controlling for job autonomy, job complexity, openness to experience, and supportive leadership.

Overall, openness to experience, extraversion, and conscientiousness are positively correlated with CSE. The strongest relationship with CSE has been observed with openness to experience. However, the relationship between openness to experience and CSE was different across the two metaanalyses. This difference might be due to the different types of samples and contexts included. The relationship between extraversion and CSE is likely due to the shared relationship between extraversion and openness to experience. The relationships between conscientiousness and CSE were similar across the two metaanalyses. Overall, openness to experience and conscientiousness appear to predict CSE across domains and are important Big Five personality traits for CSE.

Contextual Sources of Creative Self-Efficacy

A number of contextual sources have been examined as antecedents of CSE. These include (a) leadership, (b) job complexity, (c) job autonomy, and (d) job requirements for creativity. First, supportive supervision and leadership has been identified as an important antecedent of CSE (Tierney & Farmer, 2002).[1] Tierney and Farmer (2002) argued leaders influence subordinate efficacy in three ways. First, leaders serve as role models to subordinates. Leaders overseeing creative projects often demonstrate creative problem-solving abilities, take risks, and empower their subordinates on creative tasks, which aids subordinates learning novel approaches to solve problems (Gong, Huang, & Farh, 2009; Mumford, Hunter, Eubanks, Bedell, & Murphy, 2007; Shin & Zhou, 2003; Wang, Tsai, & Tsai, 2014). Second, leaders provide their subordinates with tasks that challenge them, creating mastery experiences (Tierney & Farmer, 2002). Third, leaders can persuade subordinates that they have the capacity to engage in creative activities. Leaders are uniquely positioned to influence subordinates' perceptions with positive feedback, which can increase subordinate's efficacy. Indeed, Redmond, Mumford, & Teach (1993) found that subordinate creativity was increased when leader's behaviors focused on increasing subordinate's self-efficacy. In their metaanalysis, Liu et al. (2016) found that supportive leadership was correlated with CSE at 0.32 ($\rho = 0.37$). Of the contextual sources examined in their metaanalysis, supportive leadership was the strongest predictor of CSE.

Relatedly, supervisor-subordinate tenure (i.e., how long a subordinate and supervisor have worked together) is an additional contextual leadership factor examined with CSE. Three studies have examined the relationship between supervisor–subordinate tenure and CSE and found conflicting results. Specifically, Strickland and Towler (2011) found a significant, positive relationship between subordinate–supervisor tenure and CSE ($r = 0.28$). However, Huang, Krasikova, and Liu (2016) found a significant, negative relationship ($r = -0.14$), and Yang and Mossholder

---

[1] Although leadership could be considered by some to be a social source for creativity, we believe it fits best as a contextual source. This rationale is due to leadership often being measured as the type of leadership (e.g., transformational, LMX) and its relationship with CSE and creativity.

(2010) found a nonsignificant relationship ($r = 0.06$). Thus the relationship between supervisor–subordinate tenure and CSE might be more complex and be influenced by other personal, contextual, and leader–subordinate dyadic factors. Future research is needed to better understand and explain why these studies found conflicting results.

A second set of contextual factors deal with the work tasks themselves. Three job characteristics that influence CSE development are as follows: (a) job complexity, (b) job autonomy, and (c) job requirements for creativity (Amabile, 1998; Mathisen, 2011; Tierney & Farmer, 2002). These work-related tasks allow people to master creativity-related skills and observe role models in similar jobs within the organization. Jobs high in complexity are often more challenging and provide opportunities for people to work in less routinized positions and develop mastery experiences (Oldham & Cummings, 1996; Tierney & Farmer, 2002). Since Tierney and Farmer's (2002) initial study, job autonomy and job requirements for creativity have also been proposed as antecedents of CSE (Mathisen, 2011). Like job complexity, these factors provide mastery experiences allowing a person freedom to engage in creative activities. Liu et al. (2016) found that job complexity was correlated with CSE at 0.15 ($\rho = 0.19$) and job autonomy was correlated at 0.28 ($\rho = 0.34$). We found in our metaanalysis that job requirements for creativity was positively correlated with CSE at 0.24 ($k = 7$, $N = 1533$, [95% CIs $= 0.20$–0.29], $\rho = 0.28$). In their metaanalysis, Liu et al. (2016) also regressed CSE on two personal sources (openness to experience and conscientiousness) and three contextual sources (job complexity, job autonomy, and job requirements for creativity) and found that all five antecedents were significantly, positively related to CSE. Thus these different sources each appear to exert a unique influence on CSE.

Social Sources of Creative Self-Efficacy

Personal and contextual sources have received the most attention in empirical research studying CSE while social sources have received less attention. For social sources, we focus our effort on studies examining CSE from a social network perspective, which emphasizes the role of interpersonal relationships. To our knowledge, there are only two studies utilizing social network methodology that measure CSE. First, Yang and Cheng (2009) examined two social network factors and their relationship to CSE in a sample of software developers: network strength (i.e., the strength of interaction between a person and the people in their network) and degree centrality (i.e., the number of contacts in a person's network). The bivariate correlations between CSE with network strength and degree centrality were nonsignificant (rs $= 0.12$ and -0.14, respectively). In a regression analysis controlling for computer self-efficacy and domain-specific IT skills, both network strength and degree centrality were significantly related to CSE, although the effect sizes were small to moderate (ßs = 0.23 and −0.25, respectively). We found these results to be surprising given the importance of role modeling for self-efficacy development. That is, a person's social network includes people that a person can observe and imitate to build their own efficacy. It is possible these factors interact with personal and contextual sources for predicting CSE. Thus these relationships might be more complex than the simple main effects examined.

Indeed, in a second study using social network methodology, Grosser, Venkataramani, and Labianca (2017) examined the relationship between an employee's innovative behavior and their problem-solving network contacts' (i.e., alters) average CSE and innovative behavior. They found that alters' average CSE was positively related to the employee's innovative behavior and this relationship was mediated by the alters' average innovative behavior. They also found that the positive relationship between alters' average innovative behavior and employee's innovative behavior was moderated by average alter personal network density. Specifically, the relationship between alters' average innovative behavior and the employee's innovative behavior was significant and positive when alters had sparse personal networks, whereas the relationship was nonsignificant when alters had dense personal networks. In a post hoc analysis, they found that alters' average CSE at time 1 was significantly related to the employee's CSE measured at time 2 (1 year later) when the employee's CSE was low at time 1. When the employee's CSE at time 1 was high, there was no relationship between alters' average CSE at time 1 and employee's CSE measured at time 2. The results of this study indicate that one's social network connections play a role in shaping one's CSE and creativity, but in more complex ways than examining the number and strength of contacts.

Moderators of the Relationship Between Antecedents With CSE

In our metaanalysis, we examined various moderators for the relationships between antecedents and CSE. The antecedents not examined were those with a limited number of studies (i.e., less than three studies in each moderator category). We examined two moderators: job type and culture. Job type, which distinguishes between blue and white jobs, was included because of differences Tierney and Farmer (2002) originally observed. Culture, distinguished as Western and Eastern countries, was included as previous research has found differing results for the relationship between CSE and other factors across cultures (Shin, Kim, Lee, & Bian, 2012; Zhang & Zhou, 2014). Overall, we found one effect size was moderated by job type and no effect sizes moderated by culture. Specifically, job type significantly moderated the relationship between education and CSE, $Q_B = 14.71$,

$P < .001$. The relationship between education and CSE was significantly stronger in blue-collar jobs ($\rho = 0.21$) than in white-collar jobs ($\rho = 0.08$), $z = 13.43$, $P < .001$. This result was surprising, but likely indicates range restriction in white-collar jobs given most white-collar jobs require some level of higher education. For example, Huang et al. (2016) reported that 62% of their employee sample and 46% of their leader sample had some graduate education in a white-collar sample. Tierney and Farmer (2002) reported their white-collar sample had, on average, 2.79 years of education beyond high school, whereas their blue-collar sample had 1.31 years on average. Thus these results might be influenced more by sample characteristics (i.e., most employees having more education) than by those jobs requiring less education for CSE. Future efforts should deliberately collect and report relevant information about these potential moderating variables to facilitate more in-depth examination of these relationships moving forward.

CREATIVE SELF-EFFICACY'S RELATIONSHIP WITH OTHER MOTIVATIONAL FACTORS

Although CSE is a key motivational force for creativity, it is not the only motivational force underlying creativity. Amabile and colleagues (Amabile, 1983, 1996; Amabile & Pratt, 2016) argued intrinsic motivation is another important motivational factor. Grant (2008; see also Grant & Berry, 2011) also argued that prosocial motivation is an important motivational factor. These motivational factors are distinguished by CSE serving as the "can do," intrinsic motivation as the "want to do," and prosocial motivation as the "usefulness" (Liu et al., 2016). These factors are neither antecedents nor outcomes of CSE, but mediate the relationship between various antecedents and creativity like CSE.

Liu and colleagues examined whether these three motivational factors were distinct from each other, finding they moderately to strongly correlate with each other. Specifically, CSE and intrinsic motivation were correlated at 0.44 ($\rho = 0.53$) and CSE and prosocial motivation were correlated at 0.22 ($\rho = 0.25$). Additionally, Liu and colleagues predicted that each motivational factor would uniquely predict creativity after controlling for the other factors. In terms of rank ordering, they found that CSE was the strongest predictor of creativity ($r = 0.35$, $\rho = 0.40$), followed by intrinsic motivation ($r = 0.28$, $\rho = 0.34$), and then prosocial motivation ($r = 0.20$, $\rho = 0.21$). In a regression analysis, they found that CSE positively predicted creativity after controlling for intrinsic and prosocial motivation. Thus although the three motivational forces relate to one another, they are each distinct motivational forces underlying creativity.

OUTCOMES OF CREATIVE SELF-EFFICACY

When examining outcomes of CSE, creativity has been the primary outcome examined. In fact, we were unable to identify studies including outcomes other than creativity. In general, these studies have demonstrated that CSE is an important predictor of creativity across multiple contexts. As mentioned, Liu et al. (2016) found a moderate relationship between CSE and creativity ($r = 0.35$, $\rho = 0.40$) in their metaanalysis and this relationship remained after controlling for intrinsic and prosocial motivation.

Moderators of the CSE-Outcome Relationship

Notably, the studies examining CSE's relationship with creativity come from different environments (e.g., culture, job types) and utilize different methodological approaches (e.g., creativity was self- vs other-reported). For example, studies have been conducted across various cultures like Pakistan (Malik, Butt, & Choi, 2015), China (e.g., Zhang, Long, & Zhang, 2015), Taiwan (e.g., Hsu, Hou, & Fan, 2011), Europe (e.g., Caniëls & Rietzschel, 2015), and the United States (e.g., Tierney & Farmer, 2002, 2011). They have also utilized either self-reported creativity (e.g., Baumann, 2011; Vinarski-Peretz, Binyamin, & Carmeli, 2011) or other-report creativity (e.g., Gong et al., 2009; Zhang & Zhou, 2014). To determine whether the relationship is similar across environments and using different methodological approaches, we report results from Liu et al.'s (2016) metaanalysis and supplement with our metaanalytic results.

Although the relationship between CSE and creativity is strong, a number of factors moderate the strength of this relationship. The first group of moderators involves environmental factors, which includes culture. Liu et al. (2016) explored how individualism and cultural tightness moderated the relationship between CSE and creativity. Cultural tightness is defined as, "the strength of social norms, or how clear and pervasive norms are within societies, and the strength of sanctioning, or how much tolerance there is for deviance from norms within societies" (Gelfand, Nishii, & Raver, 2006, p. 1226). Liu and colleagues found a significant interaction between individualism and cultural tightness. Specifically, the relationship between CSE and creativity was more likely to be positively affected by individualistic cultures in countries with a tight culture rather than in countries with a loose culture. Thus evidence suggests that culture has an influence on the relationship between CSE and creativity.

A second environmental factor is job type (blue- vs white-collar jobs). Tierney and Farmer (2002) found the relationship between CSE and creativity differed between their blue- and white-collar samples. Specifically, CSE accounted for only 1% of the variance after controlling for the five proposed antecedents (job self-efficacy, education, job tenure, supervisor support, and job complexity) in their blue-collar sample, whereas CSE accounted for 6% of the variance in their white-collar sample. Based on these results, they stated, "…creative performance among white-collar employees may be largely efficacy driven" (p. 1146). Although they observed this difference, we did not find a significant difference in the relationship between CSE and creativity in blue-collar jobs ($k=8$, $N=2144$, $r=0.41$ [95% CIs $=0.27$–0.55], $\rho=0.47$) compared to white-collar jobs ($k=16$, $N=5187$, $r=0.33$ [95% CIs $=0.24$–0.42], $\rho=0.40$), $z=1.06$, $P=290$. Thus creative performance appears to be driven, in part, by CSE in both blue- and white-collar jobs.

Four methodological factors represent the second group of moderators. First, Liu et al. (2016) examined whether creativity measured using self-report vs other-report influenced the relationship between CSE and creativity. They found that the relationship between CSE and creativity was stronger when creativity was self-report ($r=0.50$, $\rho=0.59$) than when it was not self-report ($r=0.27$, $\rho=0.31$). Second, in our metaanalytic investigation, we examined whether a cross-sectional vs time-lagged research design moderated the relationship between CSE and creativity. We found a stronger relationship between CSE and creativity when a cross-sectional design was used ($k=25$, $N=7189$, $r=0.36$ [95% CIs $=0.29$–0.44], $\rho=0.43$) than when a time-lagged design was used ($k=7$, $N=1828$, $r=0.29$ [95% CIs $=0.18$–0.39], $\rho=0.35$), $z=2.01$, $P=.044$. Based on the results of rating source and research design, common method bias appears to be a problem with CSE and creativity measurement. Thus future researchers should try to utilize an other-rated creativity measure or an objective source to ensure the accuracy of results. If this is not possible, including a time lag can also reduce some common method bias.

Third, the type of self-efficacy measure moderates the relationship between CSE and creativity. Liu et al. (2016) found that the relationship between CSE and creativity was stronger when a specific CSE measure was used ($r=0.36$, $\rho=0.29$) compared to when a general self-efficacy measure was used ($r=0.29$, $\rho=0.32$). Last, Liu et al. (2016) also examined whether publication status (published vs unpublished) influenced the relationship between CSE and creativity. They found that published studies ($r=0.39$, $\rho=0.45$) had significantly stronger relationships than did unpublished studies ($r=0.23$, $\rho=0.37$).

The relationship between CSE and creativity might also differ depending on the type of creativity examined. Specifically, Jaussi and Randel (2014) examined the relationship between CSE with incremental and radical creativity rated by a colleague they frequently interacted with at work. They found a nonsignificant relationship between CSE and incremental creativity ($r=0.06$), but found a significant relationship between CSE and radical creativity ($r=0.17$). Although this is the only study to our knowledge that investigated different types of creativity, examining how CSE relates to various types of creativity might be a fruitful area for future research.

MEASUREMENT OF CREATIVE SELF-EFFICACY

As mentioned, the definition of CSE is the self-perception that one has the ability to generate creative outcomes (Tierney & Farmer, 2002). Thus CSE measures should focus on self-perceptions of one's creative ability. In organizational research, two approaches have been used: (a) applying scales specifically developed to measure CSE or (b) adapting measures of general self-efficacy to creativity. The second approach is often problematic because many researchers assume that the psychometric properties and validity information regarding the original scale are necessarily replicated in the adapted scale. This is not always the case. On the other hand, the first approach is often preferred, because authors most often conduct several studies to ensure the psychometric properties and validity information for their newly developed scale. Table 2 provides a summary of the measures discussed in this chapter.

TABLE 2 Summary Table of Measures of CSE

Author(s)	Source	Notes
Tierney (1997)	Journal of Behavioral and Social Psychology	
Tierney and Farmer (2002)	Academy of Management Journal	Further establishes the scale introduced by Tierney (1997)
Carmeli and Schaubroeck (2007)	The Leadership Quarterly	Adapted from Chen et al.'s (2001) GSE Scale
DiLiello, Houghton, and Dawley (2011)	Journal of Psychology	Added two items to Tierney and Farmer (2002)
Yang and Cheng (2009)	Computers in Human Behavior	Adapted from Zhou and George's (2001) creative performance measure
Malik et al. (2015)	Journal of Organizational Behavior	Adapted from Schwarzer's (1999) GSE scale
Wang and Lin (2012)	Journal of Engineering and Technology Management	Innovation self-efficacy scale
Beeftink, Eerde, Rutte, and Bertrand (2012)	Journal of Business and Psychology	Adapted from Schwarzer's (1999) GSE Scale
Akinlade (2014)	Unpublished Dissertation	Adapted Tierney and Farmer's (2002) scale to the team level
Karwowski, Lebuda, and Wisniewska (in press)	Psychology of Aesthetics, Creativity, and the Arts	

The first popularized CSE measure was originally developed by Tierney (1997) with Tierney and Farmer (2002) elaborating further on the development of the scale. The authors developed an overrepresentative item list, before reducing the list to 13 items, and further reducing to the final three-item CSE scale. In their study, the authors distinguished CSE from job self-efficacy using confirmatory factor analysis and found that a two-factor model (CSE and job self-efficacy) fit the data better than did a one-factor model (self-efficacy). They also found that the measure was invariant across two organizational samples (manufacturing and operations sample). Given its sound psychometric foundation, this measure is the most often used CSE scale, and it consistently demonstrates a strong internal consistency (e.g., Cronbach $\alpha > 0.90$; see Zhang & Zhou, 2014).

Still, several alternative scales have been used to measure CSE. First, Carmeli and Schaubroeck (2007) adapted Chen et al.'s (2001) measure of general self-efficacy to focus specifically on creativity. This measure has been used in a number of studies that further reinforced its construct validity (e.g., Dayan, Zacca, & Benedetto, 2013; Shin et al., 2012; Vinarski-Peretz et al., 2011), and it also demonstrates a strong internal consistency (e.g., Cronbach $\alpha > 0.90$). Second, others have added items to Tierney and Farmer's (2002) original scale (DiLiello et al., 2011; Slåtten, 2014). For example, DiLiello et al. (2011) added two items: one focusing on whether people believe they have the ability to do well in their work and the other focusing on whether they believe they possess the ability to take chances when trying out new ideas. These additional items appear to go beyond the scope of CSE with one item measuring job self-efficacy and the other measuring risk taking. Last, Yang and Cheng's (2009) scale was adapted from a measure of creative performance (i.e., Zhou & George, 2001) by adding an additional stem to each item ("The belief that..."). Little psychometric or validity information has been obtained for some of these scales, leaving it unclear whether these scales adequately gauge CSE, further investigation of these modified scale's factor reliability and validity is necessary.

As another example, Malik et al. (2015) adapted Schwarzer's (1999) general self-efficacy scale to measure creativity. It is important to note that Schwarzer's conceptualization and operationalization of self-efficacy differs from the perspective of Bandura (1997) and Tierney and Farmer (2002). Specifically, Schwarzer's measure focuses on whether one is optimistic and believes they are capable of handling various stressors, which extends beyond Bandura's (1997) conceptualization of self-efficacy because it focuses on a broader construct than what self-efficacy represents.

There are also a number of scales to measure constructs similar to CSE. Wang and Lin (2012) developed a measure of innovation self-efficacy. However, the psychometric properties of this measure have yet to be examined, and the items reflected overall performance rather than one's confidence in their abilities to implement creative ideas. Beeftink et al. (2012) used a measure adapted from Schwarzer's (1999) to examine design self-efficacy, but it suffers from the same conceptualization issues as the general measure (detailed previously). Additionally, the psychometric properties of this measure were not examined.

Although CSE is primarily studied as an individual-level construct, some studies have examined CSE at the team level (Akinlade, 2014) or within team settings (Hirst, Knippenberg, Zhou, Zhu, & Tsai, 2018; Richter, Hirst, Knippenberg, & Baer, 2012; Shin et al., 2012). Akinlade (2014) utilized a referent shift model to examine CSE at the team level, and the words "my team" were added to each item of Tierney and Farmer's scale (e.g., "I have confidence in *my team's* ability to solve problems creatively"). The measure showed good internal consistency with a Cronbach's alpha of 0.84. The remaining team-level studies utilized multilevel modeling and examined the interaction between individual- and team-level constructs on creativity. In those studies, CSE was included as an individual-level predictor. These studies utilized well-established and validated measures of CSE, specifically Tierney and Farmer's (2002) or Carmeli and Schaubroeck's (2007) scales.

In sum, although multiple CSE measures exist, not all of them have been properly established psychometrically and others utilize different operational definitions of self-efficacy. The most reliable and psychometrically sound measures are those developed by Tierney and Farmer (2002) and by Carmeli and Schaubroeck (2007). Recently, Karwowski et al. (in press) developed a six-item CSE measure that is reliable. They demonstrated the measure was distinct from creative-role identity and provided additional evidence of convergent and discriminant validity. As such, this new measure shows potential as a viable tool for measuring CSE moving forward. Future effort should explore the strength of the relationships between these validated measures of CSE.

FUTURE RESEARCH DIRECTIONS

Although there is an established body of literature on CSE, there is still much to study. When discussing areas for future research, we avoid suggestions of prior reviews and metaanalyses (see Farmer & Tierney, 2017; Liu et al., 2016; Puente-Díaz, 2016). We highlight four potential areas for future research. First, the majority of the research on the nomological network of CSE focuses on facilitating factors and rarely considers constraining factors (Zhou & Hoever, 2014). That is, research focuses on what positively predicts CSE and what strengthens the relationship between CSE and creativity. Although this research is valuable and has important theoretical and practical implications, research has not examined antecedents that might negatively predict CSE or attenuate the relationship between CSE and creativity. A notable exception is that when people were assigned work requiring more creativity, they reported decreases in CSE across time (Tierney & Farmer, 2011). To build theory and inform practice, research would benefit from examining the relationship between CSE and factors like work-task changes (Tierney & Farmer, 2011), abusive supervision (Liu, Liao, & Loi, 2012), or biases against creativity (Mueller, Melwani, & Goncalo, 2012). This research can be facilitated by qualitative methods in which employees discuss how both facilitating and constraining factors influence their efficacy and subsequent creativity. Additionally, quantitative longitudinal studies would also help identify personal and contextual sources that decrease CSE.

Second, researchers should give greater attention to examining CSE as a team-level construct. As mentioned, only one study has measured CSE as a team-level construct (Akinlade, 2014), though others have examined individual CSE in a team context (Hirst et al., 2018; Richter et al., 2012; Shin et al., 2012). Because of the important role of CSE for individual creativity, it would be a fruitful endeavor to identify antecedents and consequences of CSE at the team level. There will likely be overlap between antecedents as well as unique team-level factors that relate to team CSE and moderate the relationship between team CSE and team creativity.

Third, along with research on CSE at the team level, examining social sources underlying CSE would also be beneficial. As mentioned, limited research has been conducted on the social sources of CSE. This lack of research is surprising given that social cognitive theory proposes that a person's knowledge and ability are developed based on observing others and through experience, and two of the factors that shape self-efficacy are role modeling and verbal persuasion (Bandura, 1997). This research could apply a variety of methodological approaches including social network methodology. For example, researchers could study how different centrality measures (e.g., degree centrality, betweenness centrality) relate to CSE or whether different network factors moderate the relationship between CSE and creativity. We believe developing a deeper understanding of the social side of CSE is a critical avenue for future research to explore.

Last, there are currently no organizational studies measuring CSE and creativity using objective creativity measures (e.g., patents or research reports). Previous research has relied on leader-reported creativity, self-reported creativity, colleague-reported creativity (Jaussi & Randel, 2014; Jaussi, Randel, & Dionne, 2007), or a divergent thinking-type task where participants listed problems they experience in their work (Mathisen & Bronnick, 2009). Although there is often a small to moderate correlation between leader-reported creativity and objective measures, such as patents or research reports (Oldham & Cummings, 1996; Tierney, Farmer, & Graen, 1999), it is important to distinguish between these measures.

Montag, Maertz, and Baer (2012) argued that creativity as a criterion should be distinguished into performance behaviors and outcome effectiveness. Performance behaviors reflect "the set of interdependent observable and unobservable activities that occur in response to a nonalgorithmic task or project and that purportedly constitute the creative process," whereas outcome effectiveness reflects "the extent to which the outcomes (idea, prototype, product, etc.) of nonalgorithmic task or project completion are judged by relevant stakeholders to be both novel and useful" (Montag et al., 2012, p. 1365). Thus self- and leader-report measures focus primarily on performance behaviors, whereas objective measures like patents and research reports focus primarily on outcome effectiveness. Future research should examine the relationship between CSE and outcome effectiveness to obtain a more accurate understanding of the true influence of CSE in the workplace.

CONCLUSION

Overall, research supports the notion that having a belief in one's creative ability is an important driver of creativity and innovation. Although CSE has been studied for nearly 15 years, it has continued to gain increasing attention, especially over the last several years. Indeed, over 80% of the studies we metaanalyzed were published since 2010. In this review, we aimed to provide a broad overview of the CSE literature by summarizing and evaluating research on the antecedents and consequences of CSE, measurement approaches to CSE, and to identify future research efforts that will further facilitate our understanding of CSE in organizational settings. Given the results of several large-scale metaanalyses on the motivational drivers for creativity including CSE, we see great opportunity for CSE research moving forward.

References

Akinlade, E. (2014). *The dual effect of transformational leadership on individual- and team-level creativity.* Chicago, IL: University of Illinois at Chicago.

Amabile, T. M. (1983). The social psychology of creativity: a componential conceptualization. *Journal of Personality and Social Psychology, 45,* 357–376. https://doi.org/10.1037/0022-3514.45.2.357.

Amabile, T. M. (1996). *Creativity in context: Update to the social psychology of creativity.* Boulder, CO: Westview Press.

Amabile, T. M. (1998). How to kill creativity. *Harvard Business Review, 76,* 77–87.

Amabile, T. M., & Pratt, M. G. (2016). The dynamic componential model of creativity and innovation in organizations: making progress, making meaning. *Research in Organizational Behavior, 36,* 157–183. https://doi.org/10.1016/j.riob.2016.10.001.

Anderson, N., Potocnik, K., & Zhou, J. (2014). Innovation and creativity in organizations: a state-of-the-science review, prospective commentary, and guiding framework. *Journal of Management, 40,* 1297–1333. https://doi.org/10.1177/0149206314527128.

Baas, M., De Dreu, C. K. W., & Nijstad, B. A. (2008). A meta-analysis of 25 years of mood-creativity research: hedonic tone, activation, or regulatory focus? *Psychological Bulletin, 134*, 779–806. https://doi.org/10.1037/a0012815.

Bandura, A. (1997). *Self-efficacy: The exercise of control.* New York, NY: Freeman.

Baumann, P. K. (2011). *The relationship between individual and organizational characteristics and nurse innovation behavior.* Bloomington, IN: Indiana University.

Beeftink, F., van Eerde, W., Rutte, C. G., & Bertrand, J. W. M. (2012). Being successful in a creative profession: the role of innovative cognitive style, self-regulation, and self-efficacy. *Journal of Business and Psychology, 27*, 71–81. https://doi.org/10.1007/s10869-011-9214-9.

Beghetto, R. (2006). Creative self-efficacy: correlates in middle and secondary students. *Creativity Research Journal, 18*, 447–457. https://doi.org/10.1207/s15326934crj1804_4.

Beghetto, R. A., Kaufman, J. C., & Baxter, J. (2011). Answering the unexpected questions: exploring the relationship between students' creative self-efficacy and teacher ratings of creativity. *Psychology of Aesthetics, Creativity, and the Arts, 5*, 342–349. https://doi.org/10.1037/a0022834.

Bosco, F. A., & Aguinis, H. (2013). *MPMA: Multi-purpose meta-analysis (Version 4.20.09) [Software].* Retrieved from http://www.frankbosco.com/.

Caniëls, M. C. J., & Rietzschel, E. F. (2015). Organizing creativity: creativity and innovation under constraints. *Creativity and Innovation Management, 24*, 184–196. https://doi.org/10.1111/caim.12123.

Carmeli, A., & Schaubroeck, J. (2007). The influence of leaders' and other referents' normative expectations on individual involvement in creative work. *The Leadership Quarterly, 18*, 35–48. https://doi.org/10.1016/j.leaqua.2006.11.001.

Chen, G., Gully, S. M., & Eden, D. (2001). Validation of a new general self-efficacy scale. *Organizational Research Methods, 4*, 62–83. https://doi.org/10.1177/109442810141004.

Dayan, M., Zacca, R., & Di Benedetto, A. (2013). An exploratory study of entrepreneurial creativity: its antecedents and mediators in the context of UAE firms. *Creativity and Innovation Management, 22*, 223–240. https://doi.org/10.1111/caim.12036.

DiLiello, T. C., Houghton, J. D., & Dawley, D. (2011). Narrowing the creativity gap: the moderating effects of perceived support for creativity. *The Journal of Psychology, 145*, 151–172. https://doi.org/10.1080/00223980.2010.548412.

Farmer, S. M., & Tierney, P. (2017). Considering creative self-efficacy: its current state and ideas for future inquiry. In M. Karwowski & J. C. Kaufman (Eds.), *The creative self: Effects of beliefs, self-efficacy, mindset, and identity* (pp. 23–47). London: Academic Press. https://doi.org/10.1016/B978-0-12-809790-8.00002-9.

Gelfand, M. J., Nishii, L. H., & Raver, J. L. (2006). On the nature and importance of cultural tightness-looseness. *Journal of Applied Psychology, 91*, 1225–1244. https://doi.org/10.1037/0021-9010.91.6.1225.

Gong, Y., Huang, J., & Farh, J. (2009). Employee learning orientation, transformational leadership, and employee creativity: the mediating role of employee creative self-efficacy. *Academy of Management Journal, 52*, 765–778. https://doi.org/10.5465/AMJ.2009.43670890.

Grant, A. M. (2008). Does intrinsic motivation fuel the prosocial fire? Motivational synergy in predicting persistence, performance, and productivity. *Journal of Applied Psychology, 93*, 48–58. https://doi.org/10.1037/0021-9010.93.1.48.

Grant, A. M., & Berry, J. W. (2011). The necessity of others is the mother of invention: intrinsic and prosocial motivations, perspective taking, and creativity. *Academy of Management Journal, 54*, 73–96.

Grosser, T. J., Venkataramani, V., & Labianca, G. (2017). An alter-centric perspective on employee innovation: the importance of alters' creative self-efficacy and network structure. *Journal of Applied Psychology, 102*, 1360–1374. https://doi.org/10.1037/apl0000220.

Hedges, L. V., & Pigott, T. D. (2004). The power of statistical tests for moderators in meta-analysis. *Psychological Methods, 9*, 426–445. https://doi.org/10.1037/1082-989X.9.4.426.

Hennessey, B. A., & Amabile, T. M. (2010). Creativity. *Annual Review of Psychology, 61,* 569–598. https://doi.org/10.1146/annurev.psych.093008.100416.

Hirst, G., Van Knippenberg, D., Zhou, Q., Zhu, C. J., & Tsai, P.C.-F. (2018). Exploitation and exploration climates' influence on performance and creativity: diminishing returns as function of self-efficacy. *Journal of Management, 44,* 870–891. https://doi.org/10.1177/0149206315596814.

Hsu, M. L. A., Hou, S. T., & Fan, H. L. (2011). Creative self-efficacy and innovative behavior in a service setting: optimism as a moderator. *Journal of Creative Behavior, 45,* 258–272. https://doi.org/10.1002/j.2162-6057.2011.tb01430.x.

Huang, L., Krasikova, D. V., & Liu, D. (2016). I can do it, so can you: the role of leader creative self-efficacy in facilitating follower creativity. *Organizational Behavior and Human Decision Processes, 132,* 49–62. https://doi.org/10.1016/j.obhdp.2015.12.002.

Jaussi, K. S., & Randel, A. E. (2014). Where to look? Creative self-efficacy, knowledge retrieval, and incremental and radical creativity. *Creativity Research Journal, 26,* 400–410. https://doi.org/10.1080/10400419.2014.961772.

Jaussi, K. S., Randel, A. E., & Dionne, S. D. (2007). I am, I think I can, and I do: the role of personal identity, self-efficacy, and cross-application of experiences in creativity at work. *Creativity Research Journal, 19,* 247–258. https://doi.org/10.1080/10400410701397339.

Karwowski, M., & Lebuda, I. (2015). The Big Five, the Huge Two, and creative self-beliefs: a meta-analysis. *Psychology of Aesthetics, Creativity, and the Arts, 10,* 214–232. https://doi.org/10.1037/aca0000035.

Karwowski M., Lebuda I. and Wisniewska E. (in press). Measurement of creative self-efficacy and creative role-identity, High Ability Studies.

Kelley, T., & Kelley, D. (2013). *Creative confidence: unleashing the creative potential within us all.* New York, NY: Crown Business.

Liu, D., Jiang, K., Shalley, C. E., Keem, S., & Zhou, J. (2016). Motivational mechanisms of employee creativity: a meta-analytic examination and theoretical extension of the creativity literature. *Organizational Behavior and Human Decision Processes, 137,* 236–263. https://doi.org/10.1016/j.obhdp.2016.08.001.

Liu, D., Liao, H., & Loi, R. (2012). The dark side of leadership: a three-level investigation of the cascading effect of abusive supervision on employee creativity. *Academy of Management Journal, 55,* 1187–1212. https://doi.org/10.5465/amj.2010.0400.

Malik, M. A. R., Butt, A. N., & Choi, J. N. (2015). Rewards and employee creative performance: moderating effects of creative self-efficacy, reward importance, and locus of control. *Journal of Organizational Behavior, 36,* 59–74. https://doi.org/10.1002/job.1943.

Mathisen, G. E. (2011). Organizational antecedents of creative self-efficacy. *Creativity and Innovation Management, 20,* 185–195. https://doi.org/10.1111/j.1467-8691.2011.00606.x.

Mathisen, G. E., & Bronnick, K. S. (2009). Creative self-efficacy: an intervention study. *International Journal of Educational Research, 48,* 21–29. https://doi.org/10.1016/j.ijer.2009.02.009.

Montag, T., Maertz, C. P., & Baer, M. (2012). A critical analysis of the workplace creativity criterion space. *Journal of Management, 38,* 1362–1386. https://doi.org/10.1177/0149206312441835.

Mueller, J. S., Melwani, S., & Goncalo, J. A. (2012). The bias against creativity: why people desire but reject creative ideas. *Psychological Science, 23,* 13–17. https://doi.org/10.1177/0956797611421018.

Mumford, M. D., Hunter, S. T., Eubanks, D. L., Bedell, K. E., & Murphy, S. T. (2007). Developing leaders for creative efforts: a domain-based approach to leadership development. *Human Resource Management Review, 17,* 402–417. https://doi.org/10.1016/j.hrmr.2007.08.002.

Oldham, G. R., & Cummings, A. (1996). Employee creativity: personal and contextual factors at work. *Academy of Management Journal, 39,* 607–634. https://doi.org/10.2307/256657.

Puente-Díaz, R. (2016). Creative self-efficacy: an exploration of its antecedents, consequences, and applied implications. *The Journal of Psychology, 150*, 175–195. https://doi.org/10.108 0/00223980.2015.1051498.

Quiñones, M. A., Ford, J. K., & Teachout, M. S. (1995). The relationship between work experience and job performance: a conceptual and meta-analytic review. *Personnel Psychology, 48*, 887–910. https://doi.org/10.1111/j.1744-6570.1995.tb01785.x.

Redmond, M. R., Mumford, M. D., & Teach, R. (1993). Putting creativity to work: effects of leader behavior on subordinate creativity. *Organizational Behavior and Human Decision Processes, 55*, 120–151. https://doi.org/10.1006/obhd.1993.1027.

Richter, A. W., Hirst, G., van Knippenberg, D., & Baer, M. (2012). Creative self-efficacy and individual creativity in team contexts: cross-level interactions with team informational resources. *Journal of Applied Psychology, 97*, 1282–1290. https://doi.org/10.1037/a0029359.

Schwarzer, R. A. (1999). *General perceived self-efficacy in 14 cultures*. Retrieved May 8, 2017, from http://userpage.fu-berlin.de/~gesund/publicat/ehps_cd/health/world14.htm.

Shin, S. J., Kim, T. Y., Lee, J. Y., & Bian, L. (2012). Cognitive team diversity and individual team member creativity: a cross-level interaction. *Academy of Management Journal, 55*, 197–212. https://doi.org/10.5465/amj.2010.0270.

Shin, S. J., & Zhou, J. (2003). Transformational leadership, conservation, and creativity: evidence from Korea. *Academy of Management Journal, 46*, 703–714. https://doi.org/10.2307/30040662.

Slåtten, T. (2014). Determinants and effects of employee's creative self-efficacy on innovative activities. *International Journal of Quality and Service Sciences, 6*, 326–347. https://doi.org/10.1108/IJQSS-03-2013-0013.

Strickland, S., & Towler, A. (2011). Correlates of creative behaviour: the role of leadership and personal factors. *Canadian Journal of Administrative Sciences, 28*, 41–51. https://doi.org/10.1002/cjas.157.

Tierney, P. (1997). The influence of cognitive climate on job satisfaction and creative efficacy. *Journal of Social Behavior and Personality, 12*, 831–847.

Tierney, P., & Farmer, S. M. (2002). Creative self-efficacy: its potential antecedents and relationship to creative performance. *Academy of Management Journal, 45*, 1137–1148. https://doi.org/10.2307/3069429.

Tierney, P., & Farmer, S. M. (2011). Creative self-efficacy development and creative performance over time. *Journal of Applied Psychology, 96*, 277–293. https://doi.org/10.1037/a0020952.

Tierney, P., Farmer, S. M., & Graen, G. B. (1999). An examination of leadership and employee creativity: the relevance of traits and relationships. *Personnel Psychology, 52*, 591–620. https://doi.org/10.1111/j.1744-6570.1999.tb00173.x.

Vinarski-Peretz, H., Binyamin, G., & Carmeli, A. (2011). Subjective relational experiences and employee innovative behaviors in the workplace. *Journal of Vocational Behavior, 78*, 290–304. https://doi.org/10.1016/j.jvb.2010.09.005.

Wang, R. T., & Lin, C. P. (2012). Understanding innovation performance and its antecedents: a socio-cognitive model. *Journal of Engineering and Technology Management, 29*, 210–225. https://doi.org/10.1016/j.jengtecman.2012.01.001.

Wang, C.-J., Tsai, H.-T., & Tsai, M.-T. (2014). Linking transformational leadership and employee creativity in the hospitality industry: the influences of creative role identity, creative self-efficacy, and job complexity. *Tourism Management, 40*, 79–89. https://doi.org/10.1016/j.tourman.2013.05.008.

Woodman, R. W., Sawyer, J. E., & Griffin, R. W. (1993). Toward a theory of organizational creativity. *Academy of Management Review, 18*, 293–321. https://doi.org/10.5465/AMR.1993.3997517.

Yang, H. L., & Cheng, H. H. (2009). Creative self-efficacy and its factors: an empirical study of information system analysts and programmers. *Computers in Human Behavior, 25*, 429–438. https://doi.org/10.1016/j.chb.2008.10.005.

Yang, J., & Mossholder, K. W. (2010). Examining the effects of trust in leaders: a bases-and-foci approach. *The Leadership Quarterly, 21*, 50–63. https://doi.org/10.1016/j.leaqua.2009.10.004.

Zhang, Y., Long, L., & Zhang, J. (2015). Pay for performance and employee creativity. *Management Decision, 53*, 1378–1397. https://doi.org/10.1108/MD-11-2013-0596.

Zhang, X., & Zhou, J. (2014). Empowering leadership, uncertainty avoidance, trust, and employee creativity: interaction effects and a mediating mechanism. *Organizational Behavior and Human Decision Processes, 124*, 150–164. https://doi.org/10.1016/j.obhdp.2014.02.002.

Zhou, J., & George, J. M. (2001). When job dissatisfaction leads to creativity: encouraging the expression of voice. *Academy of Management Journal, 44*, 682–696. https://doi.org/10.2307/3069410.

Zhou, J., & Hoever, I. J. (2014). Research on workplace creativity: a review and redirection. *Annual Review of Organizational Psychology and Organizational Behavior, 1*, 333–359. https://doi.org/10.1146/annurev-orgpsych-031413-091226.

Affect and Creativity

Hector P. Madrid, Malcolm G. Patterson†*

*School of Management, Pontificia Universidad Católica de Chile, Santiago, Chile, †Institute of Work Psychology, Management School, University of Sheffield, Sheffield, United Kingdom

AFFECT AND CREATIVITY

In his seminal paper entitled "The motivational basis of organizational behavior," Katz (1964) highlighted that given the increasing uncertainty and dynamism of organizational environments, organizations that depend solely upon the blueprints of prescribed behavior represent very fragile social systems; therefore *creative and innovative behavior*, defined as less formalized actions oriented to deal with unforeseen contingencies or opportunities, was essential for effective organizational functioning. More than 50 years after, Katz's diagnosis is a fact for many, if not most, organizations. Innovation and creativity in the workplace have become increasingly important determinants of organizational survival and success.

Today, the most adopted definition of creativity at work is "the production of novel and useful ideas by an individual or small group of individuals working together" (Amabile & Pratt, 2016, p. 158). This involves the identification of incongruences and discontinuities in the work environment, such as things that do not behave as originally prescribed, or opportunities to develop new approaches that enhance effectiveness. These discontinuities lead to the *generation* of new ideas in order to benefit from solutions to problems or opportunities. Once ideas have been generated, individuals *voice* them to other relevant people in the workplace (e.g., coworkers, supervisors, team leaders, and managers) (Madrid, Patterson, Birdi, Leiva, & Kausel, 2014; Madrid, Patterson, & Leiva, 2015; Madrid, Totterdell, & Niven, 2016; Zhou & George, 2001), with the aim of enriching these ideas and gaining support for their adoption (Kanter, 1988).

Given the relevance of creativity to, for example, developing new products, services, and work procedures and promoting individual and organizational effectiveness (Anderson, Potočnik, & Zhou, 2014), a weight of research has aimed to identify and understand what drives creative performance, under the assumption that creativity involves a complex set of cognitions and behavior (Anderson et al., 2014; George, 2007; Hennessey & Amabile, 2010; Zhou & Hoever, 2014). Generating and voicing novel ideas demands thinking in an unconventional way and challenging the status quo, together with impetus for the adoption of novel ideas (Kanter, 1988; West & Farr, 1990; Yuan & Woodman, 2010). Therefore a major stream of research has also been dedicated to understanding the affective experience as a driver of creative performance because of its profound and pervasive influences on cognition and behavior (Ashkanasy & Dorris, 2017; Brief & Weiss, 2002; Elfenbein, 2007; Totterdell & Niven, 2014).

Affect refers to constructs such as emotions and moods. Emotions represent momentary, limited to seconds or minutes, affective reactions toward specific objects, being intense enough to interrupt conscious thought processes (Frijda, 1986). Thus emotions unfold quickly into specific cognitive and behavioral processes, such as approaching when feeling joy or fleeing when feeling fear (Davidson, 1994; Ekman, 1992; Frijda, 1994). In turn, moods denote long-lasting affective states experienced within a day or over a few days/weeks (Ekman, 1994; Kagan, 1994). Moods are mild feelings experienced as diffuse psychological states, with no clear causal factor, which often are not intense enough to disturb conscious processes of thought and behavior (Thayer, 1996; Watson, 2000). However, moods have substantial implications for processing information and conducting a wide array of actions over their duration (Forgas, 1995; Forgas & George, 2001; Schwarz & Clore, 2003). For example, moods influence memory, styles of thinking, and behavioral tendencies. These psychological implications have led researchers to focus on moods when approaching the study of affect relative to creativity. In creativity research affect and moods are mostly used interchangeably.

In structural terms, studies on affect and creativity have relied on the model of positive and negative affect (Watson & Clark, 1992; Watson & Tellegen, 1985; Watson, Wiese, Vaidya, & Tellegen, 1999), along with most research on affect in work and organizational psychology and organizational behavior (Seo, Barrett, & Sirkwoo, 2008). According to this, feelings are grouped according to two dimensions labeled as positive affect and negative affect, represented by, for example, enthusiasm, excitement and activation or nervousness, upset and distress, respectively. The focus here is on positive and negative valence. Valence represents the extent to which individuals experience pleasant and unpleasant feelings, or, in other words, "feeling good" vs "feeling bad." Positive and negative affect categories are not ends of the same continuum, but they are two independent affective dimensions; thus feeling positive or negative may involve different cognitive and behavioral correlates. The same independence, furthermore, makes possible the parallel experience of positive and negative feelings, for instance, when concomitantly feeling excitement and nervousness over short periods of time (George, 2011).

Based on the earlier understanding of affect, studies on creativity applied in organizational environments indicate that positive affect is a positive predictor of creativity (Amabile, Barsade, Mueller, & Staw, 2005; Binnewies & Woernlein, 2011; George & Zhou, 2007; Madjar, Oldham, & Pratt, 2002; Madrid et al., 2014). This means that increments in experiencing positive feelings are associated with increases in generating ideas considered novel and useful. The explanation for this relationship has relied on theories that highlight the informational function of affect and their cognitive implications (Forgas & George, 2001; Fredrickson, 2001; Martin & Stoner, 1996). So, creativity increases as a function of positive affect because the latter signals to individuals that there are opportunities to explore and test alternative courses of action and the same positive feelings also lead to broadened cognition expressed in wider attentional focus and divergent thinking. A defocused attention enlarges the amount of available information and knowledge that are the rudiments of ideas, while divergent thinking facilitates the organization of this information and knowledge in an unconventional way, all of which are critical for novel ideas.

Regarding negative affect, from a theoretical point of view, this should decrease creativity as it entails narrowing cognition in terms of a closed attentional focus and also convergent thinking (George & Zhou, 2007; Nijstad, De Dreu, Rietzschel, & Baas, 2010). These cognitive processes are adaptive because they warn individuals that possible risks are present in the environment, such that managing possible threats would be serviced by focused attention and an analytic way of thinking about them (Fredrickson, 2004). Therefore because this sort of cognition is not helpful for producing unconventional thoughts and ideas, a negative relationship between negative affect and creativity is expected. However, evidence does not support this proposition. Most studies conducted in organizational settings have not shown a direct correlation between both constructs (Binnewies & Woernlein, 2011; Bledow, Rosing, & Frese, 2013; George & Zhou, 2002, 2007; Madrid et al., 2014; To, Fisher, & Ashkanasy, 2015), which has led researchers to propose that the implications of negative affect for creative performance might involve greater complexity, underpinned by interactive and dynamic psychological processes.

George and Zhou (2007) propose a dual-tuning model to address this complexity. They propose that creativity results from a joint function between negative and positive feelings, such that the optimal generation of novel ideas unfolds when individuals experience both affective experiences. This involves understanding creativity as a two-stage process, namely, problem identification and creative ideation, where negative affect is related to the former and positive affect with the latter. The mechanisms that explain the association of both these affective experiences with creativity are the same as that proposed for their direct effects, but combined as a synergetic process. Thereby, negative affect promotes systematic problem identification (Schwarz & Skurnik, 2003), aided by the cognitive correlates of negative feelings manifested in focused attention and analytic thinking based on simplifying heuristics (Kaufmann, 2003; Schwarz & Clore, 2003). On the other hand positive affect facilitates ideation of unconventional thoughts that are helpful for solving the problem at hand, assisted by expansive and divergent thinking (Clore, Gaspar, & Garvin, 2001; Fiedler, 1988; Kaufmann, 2003; Schwarz, 2002; Schwarz & Clore, 2003). As such, the dual-tuning process highlights routes by which negative affect may link to creativity and also, through the joint function described, it challenges the propositions that creativity is a simple product of positive or negative affect.

Expanding the dual-tuning model, Bledow et al. (2013) proposes the Affective Shift Model to disentangle the possible link between negative affect and creativity. According to this, creativity results from the dynamic and longitudinal interplay between negative and positive feelings, which develops as an initial experience of negative affect that decreases over time, while positive affect increases concomitantly. This shift causes negative affect to exert an effect on creativity, because this affective experience builds the foundation of a creative process by helping to target and delineate the problems to be dealt with (problem identification), while the subsequent positive feelings facilitate solving these problems with novel thoughts (creative ideation). Thus as a starting point, problems or failures at work are conducive to negative affect, which acts as information that performance might be impaired and, therefore cognitive processes that are oriented to dealing with possible drawbacks are activated. Specifically, negative feelings narrow attention to elements that are threatening, leading individuals to analyze them in a bottom-up information processing manner, for example, in an isolated and sequential way (Baumann & Kuhl, 2002; Bless et al., 1996; Gasper, 2003; Spering, Wagener, & Funke, 2005). As a result of these processes, a clear understanding about what problems are faced is developed and possible courses of action start to being incubated (Sio & Ormerod, 2009). Then, the shift process follows with a decrease of the initial experience of negative affect and the parallel increase of positive affect. This change facilitates processing of information about the challenges in a broader and top-down way of thinking (Baumann & Kuhl, 2005; Derryberry & Tucker, 1994). At this stage, the defocused attention and flexible reorganization of the available information associated with positive affect increases the number of unconventional associations. Consequently, the likelihood of coming up with novel ideas specifically linked to the issues confronted is increased, leading to closing the creative process.

Taken together, the dual-tuning and the affective shift process share the notion that the greatest creative performance is promoted by both negative and positive affect and their respective narrow and broadened cognition, relative to problem identification and creative ideation. However, the affective shift departs from the dual-tuning model regarding the dynamism of the psychological mechanisms involved. Dual tuning is a static process that entails both high levels of positive and negative feelings, whereas an affective shift approach describes a longitudinal process in which creativity unfolds as a function of the reduction of negative affect and increments of positive affect over the task execution. In any case, the current state of play is that much more research is needed to determine if these models are robust enough for their proposals to be generalized, as supporting evidence comes only from a handful of empirical studies (Bledow et al., 2013; George & Zhou, 2007).

Thus far, the variety of advances in research on affect and creativity are extensive and have enhanced our understanding of how these relationships play out in the workplace. However, an important opportunity to expand this stream of research is to go beyond just distinguishing between positive and negative feelings in general. The affective experience is not limited to the pleasure dimension but also involves energy expenditure, namely, activation (Russell, 1980). Thus, for example, positive affective states such as enthusiasm and comfort are both pleasant experiences, but the former involves high activation, whereas the latter embodies low activation. A similar rationale applies to negative affect. Anxiety and depression are unpleasant feelings but are distinguished by their level of energy expenditure. Therefore accounting for both affective valence and activation offers the opportunity to study how a more diverse array of feelings might, or might not, be directly relevant to understanding creativity.

Another opportunity to further knowledge on affect and creativity is to consider also voice behavior (advocating changes to make things better) that creative performance entails in organizational settings (Madrid et al., 2014, 2015, 2016; Zhou & George, 2001). Much of the research presented previously has focused on the psychological processes underlying idea generation (problem identification and creative ideation), paying less attention to those cognitive and behavioral underpinnings entailed in communicating novel ideas. These psychological processes are likely to be different for idea generation and for voice, because the first denotes an intrapersonal phenomenon, while the latter is an interpersonal behavior (Madrid et al., 2014). In order to more fully address the role of affect in creativity, we adopt an affective valence and activation approach to discuss and delineate a finer-grained understanding to the affective experience and creativity, expressed in idea generation and voice behavior, in the workplace.

CORE AFFECT, AFFECTIVE VALENCE, AND ACTIVATION

An alternative approach to the model of positive and negative affect to understanding the affective experience, that recognizes the importance of activation, is provided by Core Affect Theory (Russell, 2003; Russell & Barrett, 1999; Yik, Russell, & Steiger, 2011). According to this, affect represents "a neurophysiological state that is consciously accessible as a simple, non-reflective feeling that is an integral blend of hedonic (pleasure– displeasure) and arousal (sleepy–activated) values" (p. 147), which "is primitive, universal, and simple (irreducible on the mental plane)" (p. 148) (Russell, 2003). As such, two basic bipolar dimensions, namely, valence and activation, structurally describe affect. While valence refers to the extent to which feelings are experienced as positive or negative in hedonic tone (pleasure-displeasure), the activation dimension denotes the state of readiness (activation-deactivation) provided by the same feelings (Russell, 1980). The linear combination of bipolar dimensions of valence and activation can be depicted as a circumplex representation describing at least four affective quadrants (Fig. 1) (Remington, Fabrigar, & Visser, 2000), which work and organizational psychology and organizational behavior researchers have labeled

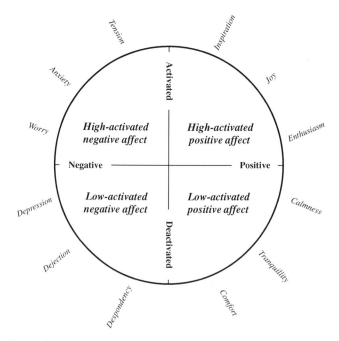

FIG. 1   Circumplex representation of affect.

as high-activated positive affect, low-activated negative affect, high-activated negative affect, and low-activated positive affect (Bindl, Parker, Totterdell, & Hagger-Johnson, 2012; Madrid et al., 2014). Regarding psychological and experiential denominations, these affective categories are manifested in states of, for example, enthusiasm, comfort, anxiety, and depression (Warr, 2007).

Therefore the core affect approach offers an expanded understanding of both the affective experience and the implications of affect for important work concepts such as motivation, task performance, proactivity, citizenship, and counterproductive work behaviors in organizations (Bindl et al., 2012; Seo, Barrett, & Bartunek, 2004; Seo, Bartunek, & Barrett, 2010; Warr, Bindl, Parker, & Inceoglu, 2014). This is because existing research predicated on the positive and negative valence model of affect, which is predominant in work and organizational psychology, cover positive and negative feelings involving high activation only, such as enthusiasm, joy, fear, and anxiety, neglecting those low in activation (Watson & Clark, 1994). Thus whether low activation affective experiences involve discrete cognitive and behavioral processes that influence creativity by means other than those associated with feelings high in activation, remains mostly neglected in theory and empirical studies in organizations (cf. Seo et al., 2008). We next draw on the core affect conceptualization of affect to provide a more complete approach to describe the interplay between affect and creativity.

Core affect is a structural model that helps to define diverse possible affective experiences in the phenomenological domain. However, a structural description itself does not involve explanations about how these affective experiences influence other psychological processes, such as cognition and behavior. Thus additional theoretical proposals are needed to disentangle the processes of thinking and behaving that may be possible explanations for the relationship between affect and creativity. In this regard, with a focus on the psychological function of affective activation, basic psychology research has proposed that activation explains cognitive performance. Specifically, energy expenditure of feelings is described as an antecedent of cognitive processes regarding working memory and psychological engagement (Bledow et al., 2013; De Dreu, Baas, & Nijstad, 2008; Nijstad et al., 2010). Accordingly, working memory manages information processing in terms of retrieval of memories, and thinking and planning courses of action based on the information available. In turn, psychological engagement refers to the level of cognitive involvement and attachment to the tasks carried out and the persistence shown in dealing with the challenges of those activities. As such, very low affective activation relates to a tendency to neglect information in the environment together with cognitive detachment expressed in limited psychological persistence. On the other hand, very high activation could overload the psychological system and, thereby, impair cognition by reducing perception, memory, and evaluation and integration of information to execute the tasks in hand. However, moderate to high levels involve optimal psychological functioning by triggering alertness and integration of information about tasks being performed.

Supporting this function of activation, De Dreu et al. (2008) conducted a series of laboratory studies with university students, showing that affective activation was associated with creative fluency and originality, namely, the number of novel ideas generated in a creative task and the extent to which these ideas were unique relative to the total number of ideas produced (Nijstad et al., 2010). In these studies, results indicated that, in general, feelings high in activation (e.g., happiness, elation, anger, fear), but not those low in activation (e.g., relaxation, calmness, sadness, depression), lead to greater creative fluency and originality when performing tasks involving brainstorming and gestalt completion. Based on this, these researchers proposed the "dual pathway to creativity model" arguing that while high-activated positive affect was positively related to creative performance due to cognitive flexibility, high-activated negative affect has a positive link to the same outcome due to increased cognitive perseverance. Nevertheless, a metaanalytical review only provided partial support for this model (Baas, De Dreu, & Nijstad, 2008), finding that high-activated positive affect was positively linked to creativity over and beyond low-activated positive affect; but the same pattern of results was not observed for negative affect. Indeed, results indicated that high-activated negative affect (i.e., fear and anxiety) was, in contrast to expectations from the model, negatively related to creative flexibility.

This mixed evidence challenges proposals about the general effect of affective activation on creativity, that activation should enhance cognitive performance for both positive and negative feelings, increasing the likelihood of coming up with novel problem solutions. The evidence suggests that cognitive performance might not be a mere function of affective activation but a possible combination of valence and activation. This is aligned with a central proposition of core affect theory stressing that valence and activation can be treated in a separate way for heuristic and analytical purposes only, because the affective experience is one of integral blends of pleasure and energy, in which they are embedded in each other (Russell, 2003). Based on this, it may be argued that different amalgams of valence and activation may exert different effects on creativity because these blends involve diverse cognitive and behavioral correlates.

In general terms, psychological correlates of affect can be conceptualized in the extent to which they represent broadening and narrowing psychological processes, the former denoting a set of flexible psychological properties and the latter a restricted set of the same processes to perform a task. Specifically, these correlates are attention, information processing, and behavioral tendencies. Attention refers to the focus on the task and environment, which defines the degree of information available to perform the task. Attention is broadened when focus is wider and narrow when focus is restricted (Fredrickson, 2001; Gable & Harmon-Jones, 2008, 2010). Information processing denotes whether information attended to is treated using top-down flexible cognitive strategies (broaden) or bottom-up systematic and effortful way of thinking (narrow) (Baumann & Kuhl, 2002, 2005; Clore et al., 2001; Fiedler, 1988; Kaufmann, 2003; Schwarz, 2002; Schwarz & Clore, 2003). Behavioral tendencies refer to the degree of responsiveness to the task and their environment, energy expenditure, perseverance, approach vs avoidant orientation, and disengaged vs acquiescent behavior (Brehm, 1999; Elliot, 2008; Frijda, 1986) (Table 1).

In the following section, we analyze, argue, and make a series of proposals about how different affective states molded by diverse blends of affective valence and activation should relate to creative performance, by means of cognitive and behavioral processes.

TABLE 1   Cognitive and Behavioral Correlates of Affect

		Valence	
		Negative	**Positive**
Activation	High	Attention • Narrow focus of attention Information processing • Bottom-up cognitive processing • Systematic and effortful thinking Behavioral tendencies • Energy, effort, and perseverance • Avoidant or approach behavior depending on sense of control	Attention • Broaden focus of attention Information processing • Top-down cognitive processing • Divergent and less effortful thinking Behavioral tendencies • Energy, effort, and perseverance • Approach behavior
	Low	Attention • Narrow focus of attention Information processing • Bottom-up cognitive processing • Systematic and effortful thinking Behavioral tendencies • Passiveness • Disengaged behavior	Attention • Broaden focus of attention Information processing • Top-down cognitive processing • Divergent and less effortful thinking Behavioral tendencies • Passiveness • Acquiescent behavior

Valence, Activation, and Creativity

To analyze and argue possible associations of affect with creativity based on core affect theory, we adopt a four-quadrant approach to affective valence and activation (Yik et al., 2011). The respective blends of valence and activation of these quadrants refer to high-activated positive affect, low-activated positive affect, high-activated negative affect, and low-activated negative affect (Bindl et al., 2012; Warr et al., 2014). Drawing on this, we first discuss negative affective states and then positive states, following research on the dual-tuning model of affect and affective shift that places negative feelings as possible initial precursors of creativity (Bledow et al., 2013; George & Zhou, 2007). Furthermore, we use the distinction between problem identification, creative ideation, and creative voice as references of creative performance. Problem identification refers to the psychological process oriented to delineate the issues to be dealt with and solved associated with the task at hand, creative ideation is the production of ideas, with novel potential, to solve the problem identified, and creative voice is the communication of these ideas in the interpersonal realm, within the organizational setting. Creative voice expands on typical conceptualization of creativity in experimental psychology but is an important consideration for creative performance in organizational settings (Zhou & George, 2001).

High-activated negative affect involves unpleasant and energized feelings, such as anxiety, tension, and worry. These feelings are associated with appraisals about hazards and problems to be solved in the environment relative to the tasks executed, such as, in the organizational context, threats to work performance (Martin & Stoner, 1996; Watson, 2000). These appraisals narrow cognition in the performance situation, such that a closer attentional focus unfolds around the threats and tasks, together with bottom-up cognitive processing involving systematic and effortful ways of thinking (Clore, Schwartz, & Conway, 1994; Loewenstein & Lerner, 2003; Schwarz, 1990; Schwarz & Clore, 2003). These psychological processes are helpful to clearly delineate the issues to be solved and determining courses of action to manage these threats and their eventual consequences. Thus in terms of creativity, high-activated negative affect should facilitate problem identification. These feelings signal that there is a problem to be dealt with; therefore gathering specific information about the tasks and their environment is triggered in order to build an understanding of the issues at hand. This evaluation is also served by narrowing cognition that allows a closer understanding of the problematic etiology of the negative affective experience (Bledow et al., 2013; George, 2011).

The same narrowing processes, however, should hinder creative ideation. This stage of the creative process is essentially described by a kaleidoscopic way of thinking, which allows unconventional organizing of information and knowledge about the problems and ways to deal with them (Kanter, 1988). As such, creative ideation should lead to novel ideas based on the flexible integration of problem and solution-relevant material. Conversely, the restricted attention and controlled thinking approach embedded in activated negative feelings would not facilitate the production of novel ideas and may actually stifle it. This may explain the negative relationship observed between this activated negative affect and the flexibility component of creativity observed in metaanalytical research (Baas et al., 2008).

In turn, the influence of high-activated negative effect on creative voice behavior should depend of whether this affective experience is accompanied, or not, with a sense of control and consequently, avoidant or approach behavior (Elliot, 2008; Gable, Reis, & Elliot, 2000). As described at the beginning of this chapter, creativity in organizations is not only a matter of generating novel ideas because it also requires advocating these ideas to relevant others in the work setting. With no voice behavior, novel ideas are limited to the individual's intrapersonal realm, so they are not available in the work environment, preventing evaluation of their usefulness and suitability for adoption. Thus in contrast to the simple idea generation, creative voice is the interpersonal behavior of communicating novel ideas in the work environment (Madrid et al., 2016), which involves challenging the status quo and possibly facing skepticism from coworkers and managers (Yuan & Woodman, 2010). As such, creative voice is sensitive to high-activated negative affect in two ways. If the affective state involves concerns about possible threats (e.g., resistance to change) and the individual has a low sense of control, feelings of anxiety, tension, and worry would reduce voice behavior, because perceptions of threats are enhanced and energy and effort is used to avoid this adverse situation (cf. Lazarus & Folkman, 1984). In contrast, if the same feelings are complemented by a sense of control, individuals would appraise the situation as challenging and thereby utilize energy and perseverance to communicate their novel ideas (Lazarus, 2001). Thus in this case, negative affect, high in activation would be positively related to creative voice by means of approach behavior.

Low-activated negative affect, characterized by feelings such as depression, dejection, and despondency, signal that something is wrong in the environment and with relevant tasks, and is typically associated with the experience of loss or failing to achieve a desired outcome (Gable & Harmon-Jones, 2010; Treynor, Gonzalez, & Nolen-Hoeksema, 2003). In this scenario, narrowing cognition is prevalent, expressed in limited attentional focus and bottom-up cognitive processing Introspection and cognitive rumination, which is deep repetitive thinking about negative events and losses in one's own life, accompany this experience (Nolen-Hoeksema, 2000; Nolenhoeksema, Parker, & Larson, 1994). This psychological configuration should have the potential to benefit problem identification with closer attention facilitating concentration on relevant information. Furthermore, depressive feelings may be positively related to creative ideation by means of narrowing cognition conveyed by rumination (Lyubomirsky & Nolenhoeksema, 1993, 1995). Specifically, this kind of affect could lead to repetitive and systematic, but deep thinking about negative events in one's own life, which in turn facilitates the production of novel ideas to cope with these events. In other words, feelings of low-activated negative affect may lead to creativity by failure or loss. In support of this, laboratory studies showed that depressive feelings are positively related to creative fluency and originality through cognitive rumination (Verhaeghen, Joorman, & Khan, 2005; Verhaeghen, Joormann, & Aikman, 2014), and a study with large samples of employees indicated that similar feelings increase problem identification in the workplace (Bindl et al., 2012).

In contrast, low-activated negative affect has the potential to reduce the likelihood of creative voice. The limited activation embedded in these feelings leads to disengagement with the environment, social apathy, and passiveness (Verhaeghen et al., 2005). This therefore makes individuals orientate to their intrapersonal domain and, concomitantly, detach from interpersonal behavior, such as speaking out with novel ideas. Specifically, feelings of depression, dejection, and despondency make individuals prone to think rather than behave. This way of thinking involves a lack of confidence, hesitation, and cynicism about the relevance and usefulness of our own behaviors (Nolen-Hoeksema, 2000; Nolen-Hoeksema, Larson, & Grayson, 1999), all of which exacerbates passiveness. Accordingly, this psychological configuration is opposite to that needed for creative voice, because this behavior demands energy to face possible resistance in the environment, together with social engagement to make this communication process happen. Supporting this, emerging research in organizations has found that negative affect low in activation is positively related to employee silence, namely, the extent to which individuals in the workplace withhold and do not communicate information and ideas for improvements (Madrid et al., 2015; Warr et al., 2014).

Thus far, we have argued that negative affect's influence on creativity should depend on the level of activation and the specific dimension of creative performance. According to this line of argumentation, high-activated negative affect may increase problem identification but reduce creative ideation due to narrowing cognition, together with increasing or decreasing creative voice depending on the individual's sense of control and attendant avoidant or approach tendencies. In a different way, low-activated negative affect, by means of narrowing cognition, should enhance problem identification and creative ideation, but reduce communicating novel ideas due to behavioral and interpersonal disengagement. The next step is to perform a similar analysis relative to positive affect with different degrees of activation, which is developed as follows.

Low-activated positive affect is expressed, for instance, in feelings like comfort, tranquility, and calm, which inform individuals that the environment is free of threats or hazards that might compromise task performance (cf. Martin & Stoner, 1996). In concordance with this appraisal, broadening cognition is predominantly expressed in an open attentional focus and top-down flexible and divergent ways of thinking (Clore et al., 1994; Fredrickson, 2001). These psychological processes should be less associated with problem identification, because even when an increased amount of information is available due to wider attention, this might be more about retrieval of knowledge to solve the problem rather than to define it. Furthermore, in this case, information processing is less effortful, thus it might be more open to reconfiguration of knowledge than building a systematic diagnosis of the problem faced. In contrast, these broadening cognitive correlates should be positively related to creative ideation (Isen, Daubman, & Nowicki, 1987). As previously discussed, ideation is the seminal component of idea generation, for which an extended pool of information and flexible processing is essential. Novel thoughts, ideas, and solutions by definition emerge from larger amounts of information about the task, the environment and previous experiences of them, together with plasticity on how to treat these pieces of information in an unconventional way.

In the case of creative voice, the reduced affective activation plays an important explanatory role. The same as low-activated negative affect, feelings like comfort make individuals prone to their intrapersonal realm, involving primarily behavioral passiveness expressed in tendencies to reflect rather than behave. However, the difference between these affective states is that low-activated negative affect entails apathy based on the appraisal of failures and losses, while low-activated positive feelings comprise acquiescent behavioral tendencies due to appraisals of lack of threats (cf. Frijda, 1986). As such, passiveness associated with deactivated positive affect should be more about compliance with the current state of affairs and not challenging this safe situation with ideas that threaten regular practices, even when individuals might have generated novel ideas to solve problems in the environment. A study focused on generation, promotion, and implementation of novel ideas in organizations provided support for this, by showing a lack of association between feelings of comfort with these outcomes when other experiences such as enthusiasm, anxiety, and depression were controlled (Madrid et al., 2014). These results are consistent with a metaanalysis study that showed that feelings of relaxation—which is a kind of low-activated negative affect—was not correlated with creative performance (Baas et al., 2008).

Finally, high-activated positive affect entails feelings such as enthusiasm, joy, and inspiration, which are linked to the perception of opportunities for successful task performance. This sort of affect has been widely supported as a positive predictor of creativity (Amabile et al., 2005; Binnewies & Woernlein, 2011; Madjar et al., 2002, 2014; To, Fisher, Ashkanasy, & Rowe, 2011), and cognitive correlates proposed to explain this relationship are broadening processes such as expanded attentional focus and flexible information processing manifested in divergent thinking (De Dreu et al., 2008; George & Zhou, 2007). However, in light of our analysis provided here, we put forward some nuances. With regards to problem identification, activated positive feelings should be less related to it because cognitive flexibility, dispersion, and divergence are less functional to the analytical and effortful psychological configuration that helps to delineate task issues. In contrast, the same flexibility should be central to facilitating creative ideation to tackle emerging problems. Activation of feelings is also relevant to ideation because it facilitates psychological dedication to, and perseverance in, generating novel solutions. This activation also participates in creative voice, because it energizes approach behavior in relation to getting involved in the task, sustaining effort in challenging possible resistance to change, and generating enthusiasm in other relevant individuals.

In relation to attentional focus and high-activated positive affect, researchers agree that attention is expanded under this affective state. This should facilitate creativity through gathering increased amounts of information to be then flexibly processed in the next stage of creative ideation (Amabile et al., 2005; Fredrickson, 2001). However, this becomes problematic when proposals about the influence of affective activation are taken into account. As discussed previously, affective activation mobilizes the cognitive system which is expressed in narrowing cognition such that, for instance in the case of high-activated negative affect, attentional focus is narrowed to pay attention in detail to tasks and their concomitant issues (Baas et al., 2008; Bledow et al., 2013; De Dreu et al., 2008; Nijstad et al., 2010). Thus in this case, while negative valence would explain bottom-up information processing, manifested in systematic and effortful thinking, activation would contribute to closing the cognitive functions to provide specific information for such processing actions. If a similar rationale is applied to high-activated positive affect, there may be the case that positive valence would primarily be associated with top-down and flexible information processing strategies, while activation should be linked to a *narrower attentional* focus, but not to broader attention as most research has proposed. The idea that affective activation narrows instead of broadens cognition is long lasting (Easterbrook, 1959), but it has not generally percolated through to studies on creativity in organizations. One possible explanation to this possible contradictory scenario is that affect and attention involves much more complexity than scholars have believed (Gable & Harmon-Jones, 2008, 2010; Harmon-Jones & Gable, 2008), such that complex configurations of expanded and restricted attention might coexist in a certain period of time.

If that is correct, in the case of positive affect, an expanded attentional focus might be associated with flexibility offered by positive valence, whereas restricted attention is offered by affective activation. In such a case, broadened attention would be functional when having a greater amount of information and knowledge to be processed, while narrow attention would be helpful to maintaining focus on tasks and persistence in coming up with a creative solution. Nevertheless, this is only speculation and much more theory development and empirical evidence is needed.

In general, for positive affect, we are proposing that low-activated positive feelings should be less helpful to problem identification and creative voice due to the broadening processes of dispersion and behavioral passiveness, but it should aid creative ideation by means of increased reflectivity. In turn, high-activated positive affect should be less related to problem identification due to the broadening processes oriented to generate rather than analyze information. The same feelings, however, are beneficial to creative ideation and voice, because they enhance broad and flexible information processing together with energy to persist and strive for creative ideas and their advocacy.

In this section we appeal to a wider understanding of the relation between affect and creativity, adopting a core affect approach to affect and a multidimensional understanding of creative performance. This involves complexity regarding the psychological explanations, expressed in cognition and behavioral tendencies, that acts as means by which blends of affective valence and activation influence problem identification, creative ideation, and creative voice. A summary of the psychological processes described is in Table 2. At this point, some proposed arguments are at an early stage of development, so these ideas may be used as a starting point for further research in terms of theorization and empirical studies.

SUMMARY AND FINAL REMARKS

In this chapter, we addressed the question of how the affective experience relates to creativity. The strong finding in extant research is that creativity is a function of positive affect, such that feelings entailed in this experience broaden cognition increasing the likelihood of producing unconventional thoughts and thereby novel solutions to problems. With regards to negative affect, the findings are less straightforward. In general, negative affect has not shown a direct effect on creativity. In order to address this, alternative models describing interactive and longitudinal processes have indicated that negative feelings might lead to creativity when they interact with positive affect. However, these models involve greater complexity and supporting evidence still comes from a handful of studies.

TABLE 2   Summary of Psychological Processes

		Valence	
		Negative	Positive
Activation	High	Attention: narrow Information processing: bottom-up and systematic Behavioral tendencies: avoidance or approach depending on level of control Creative performance: • Increased problem identification • Decreased ideation • Increased/decreased voice depending on level of control	Attention: broadened/narrow depending on valence and activation Information processing: top-down and divergent Behavioral tendencies: approach. Creative performance: • Decreased problem identification • Increased ideation • Increased voice
	Low	Attention: narrow Information processing: bottom-up and systematic Behavioral tendencies: passiveness. Creative performance: • Increased problem identification • Increased ideation • Decreased voice	Attention: broadened Information processing: top-down and divergent Behavioral tendencies: acquiescence Creative performance: • Decreased problem identification • Increased creative ideation • Decreased voice

We argue and propose that adopting core affect theory may provide an alternative understanding of the direct effect of diverse positive and negative affective experiences on creative performance. This approach relies on the idea that affect is described not only by affective valence but also by affective activation. Based on this, we propose that influences of positive and negative affect should depend on their level of activation through diverse correlates associated with broadening vs narrowing cognition together with active or passive behavioral tendencies.

We trust that the theory and evidence presented and discussed in this chapter will contribute to the literature on affect and creativity and that future research develops the knowledge presented here to benefit creativity and innovation in organizations.

References

Amabile, T. M., Barsade, S. G., Mueller, J. S., & Staw, B. M. (2005). Affect and creativity at work. *Administrative Science Quarterly, 50*(3), 367–403. https://doi.org/10.2189/asqu.2005.50.3.367.

Amabile, T. M., & Pratt, M. G. (2016). The dynamic componential model of creativity and innovation in organizations: Making progress, making meaning. *Research in Organizational Behavior, 36*, 157–183. https://doi.org/10.1016/j.riob.2016.10.001.

Anderson, N., Potočnik, K., & Zhou, J. (2014). Innovation and creativity in organizations. *Journal of Management, 40*(5), 1297–1333. https://doi.org/10.1177/0149206314527128.

Ashkanasy, N. M., & Dorris, A. D. (2017). Emotions in the workplace. *Annual Review of Organizational Psychology and Organizational Behavior, 4*(1), 67–90. https://doi.org/10.1146/annurev-orgpsych-032516-113231.

Baas, M., De Dreu, C. K. W., & Nijstad, B. A. (2008). A meta-analysis of 25 years of mood-creativity research: Hedonic tone, activation, or regulatory focus? *Psychological Bulletin, 134*(6), 779–806. https://doi.org/10.1037/a0012815.

Baumann, N., & Kuhl, J. (2002). Intuition, affect, and personality: Unconscious coherence judgments and self-regulation of negative affect. *Journal of Personality and Social Psychology, 83*(5), 1213–1223. https://doi.org/10.1037/0022-3514.83.5.1213.

Baumann, N., & Kuhl, J. (2005). Positive affect and flexibility: Overcoming the precedence of global over local processing of visual information. *Motivation and Emotion, 29*(2), 123–134. https://doi.org/10.1007/s11031-005-7957-1.

Bindl, U., Parker, S. K., Totterdell, P., & Hagger-Johnson, G. (2012). Fuel of the self-starter: How mood relates to proactive goal regulation. *Journal of Applied Psychology, 97*(1), 134–150. https://doi.org/10.1037/a0024368.

Binnewies, C., & Woernlein, S. C. (2011). What makes a creative day? A diary study on the interplay between affect, job stressors, and job control. *Journal of Organizational Behavior, 32*(4), 589–607. https://doi.org/10.1002/job.731.

Bledow, R., Rosing, K., & Frese, M. (2013). A dynamic perspective on affect and creativity. *Academy of Management Journal, 56*(2), 432–450. https://doi.org/10.5465/amj.2010.0894.

Bless, H., Schwarz, N., Clore, G. L., Golisano, V., Rabe, C., & Wölk, M. (1996). Mood and the use of scripts: Does a happy mood really lead to mindlessness? *Journal of Personality and Social Psychology, 71*(4), 665–679. https://doi.org/10.1037/0022-3514.71.4.665.

Brehm, J. W. (1999). The intensity of emotion. *Personality and Social Psychology Review, 3*(1), 2–22. https://doi.org/10.1207/s15327957pspr0301_1.

Brief, A. P., & Weiss, H. M. (2002). Organizational behavior: Affect in the workplace. *Annual Review of Psychology, 53*, 279–307. https://doi.org/10.1146/annurev.psych.53.100901.135156.

Clore, G. L., Gaspar, K., & Garvin, E. (2001). Affect as information. In J. P. Forgas (Ed.), *Handbook of affect and social cognition* (pp. 121–144). Mahwah, NJ: Erlbaum.

Clore, G. L., Schwartz, N., & Conway, N. (1994). Affective causes and consequences of social interaction processing. In R. S. Wyer & T. K. Srull (Eds.), *Handbook of social cognition*: Vol. 1. (pp. 323–417). Hillsdale, NJ: Lawrence Erlbaum.

Davidson, R. J. (1994). On emotion, mood, and related affective constructs. In P. Ekman & R. J. Davidson (Eds.), *The nature of emotion. Fundamental questions* (pp. 51–55). New York: Oxford University Press.

De Dreu, C. K. W., Baas, M., & Nijstad, B. A. (2008). Hedonic tone and activation level in the mood-creativity link: Toward a dual pathway to creativity model. *Journal of Personality and Social Psychology, 94*(5), 739–756. https://doi.org/10.1037/0022-3514.94.5.739.

Derryberry, D., & Tucker, D. M. (1994). *Motivating the focus of attention*. San Diego, CA: Academic Press.

Easterbrook, J. A. (1959). The effect of emotion on cue utilization and the organization of behavior. *Psychological Review, 66*, 183–201. https://doi.org/10.1037/h0047707.

Ekman, P. (1992). An argument for basic emotions. *Cognition & Emotion, 6*, 169–200. https://doi.org/10.1080/02699939208411068.

Ekman, P. (1994). Moods, emotions and traits. In P. Ekman & R. J. Davidson (Eds.), *The nature of emotion. Fundamental questions* (pp. 56–58). New York: Oxford University Press.

Elfenbein, H. A. (2007). Emotion in organizations. A review and theoretical integration. *Academy of Management Annals*, *1*, 315–386. https://doi.org/10.1080/078559812.

Elliot, A. J. (2008). In A. J. Elliot (Ed.), *Handbook of approach and avoidance motivation*. New York: Taylor & Francis Group.

Fiedler, K. (1988). Emotional mood, cognitive style, and behavior regulation. In K. Fiedler & J. P. Forgas (Eds.), *Affect, cognition and social behavior* (pp. 101–119). Toronto: J. Hogrefe.

Forgas, J. P. (1995). Mood and judgment: The affect infusion model (AIM). *Psychological Bulletin*, *116*, 39–66. https://doi.org/10.1037/0033-2909.117.1.39.

Forgas, J. P., & George, J. M. (2001). Affective influences on judgments and behavior in organizations: An information processing perspective. *Organizational Behavior and Human Decision Processes*, *86*(1), 3–34. https://doi.org/10.1006/obhd.2001.2971.

Fredrickson, B. L. (2001). The role of positive emotions in positive psychology: The broaden-and-build theory of positive emotions. *American Psychologist*, *56*, 218–226. https://doi.org/10.1037/0003-066X.56.3.218.

Fredrickson, B. L. (2004). The broaden-and-build theory of positive emotions. *Philosophical Transactions of the Royal Society of London Series B-Biological Sciences*, *359*(1449), 1367–1377. https://doi.org/10.1098/rstb.2004.1512.

Frijda, N. H. (1986). *The emotions*. Cambridge: Cambridge University Press.

Frijda, N. H. (1994). Varieties of affect: Emotions and episodes, moods and sentiments. In P. Ekman & R. J. Davidson (Eds.), *The nature of emotion. Fundamental questions* (pp. 59–67). New York: Oxford University Press.

Gable, P. A., & Harmon-Jones, E. (2008). Approach-motivated positive affect reduces breadth of attention. *Psychological Science*, *19*(5), 476–482. https://doi.org/10.1111/j.1467-9280.2008.02112.x.

Gable, P. A., & Harmon-Jones, E. (2010). The blues broaden, but the nasty narrows: Attentional consequences of negative affects low and high in motivational intensity. *Psychological Science*, *21*(2), 211–215. https://doi.org/10.1177/0956797609359622.

Gable, S. L., Reis, H. T., & Elliot, A. J. (2000). Behavioral activation and inhibition in everyday life. *Journal of Personality and Social Psychology*, *78*(6), 1135–1149. https://doi.org/10.1037//0022-3514.78.6.1135.

Gasper, K. (2003). When necessity is the mother of invention: Mood and problem solving. *Journal of Experimental Social Psychology*, *39*(3), 248–262. https://doi.org/10.1016/S0022-1031(03)00023-4.

George, J. M. (2007). Creativity in organizations. *Academy of Management Annals*, *1*, 439–477. https://doi.org/10.1080/078559814.

George, J. M. (2011). Dual tuning: A minimum condition for understanding affect in organizations? *Organizational Psychology Review*, *1*(2), 147–164. https://doi.org/10.1177/2041386610390257.

George, J. M., & Zhou, J. (2002). Understanding when bad moods foster creativity and good ones don't: The role of context and clarity of feelings. *Journal of Applied Psychology*, *87*(4), 687–697. https://doi.org/10.1177/2041386610390257.

George, J. M., & Zhou, J. (2007). Dual tuning in a supportive context: Joint contributions of positive mood, negative mood, and supervisory behaviors to employee creativity. *Academy of Management Journal*, *50*, 605–622. https://doi.org/10.5465/AMJ.2007.25525934.

Harmon-Jones, E., & Gable, P. A. (2008). Incorporating motivational intensity and direction into the study of emotions: Implications for brain mechanisms of emotion and cognition-emotion interactions. *Netherlands Journal of Psychology*, *64*, 132–142. https://doi.org/10.1007/BF03076416.

Hennessey, B. A., & Amabile, T. M. (2010). Creativity. In S. T. Fiske, D. L. Schachter, & R. J. Sternberg (Eds.), *Annual review of psychology*: Vol. 61. (pp. 569–598). Palo Alto, CA: Annual Reviews. https://doi.org/10.1146/annurev.psych.093008.100416.

Isen, A. M., Daubman, K. A., & Nowicki, G. P. (1987). Positive affect facilitates creative problem solving. *Journal of Personality and Social Psychology*, *51*, 1122–1131. https://doi.org/10.1037/0022-3514.52.6.1122.

Kagan, J. (1994). Distinctions among emotions, moods, and temperament qualities. In P. Ekman & R. J. Davidson (Eds.), *The nature of emotion. Fundamental questions* (pp. 74–78). New York: Oxford University Press.

Kanter, R. M. (1988). When a thousand flowers bloom—Structural, collective, and social conditions for innovation in organization. *Research in Organizational Behavior, 10*, 169–211. https://doi.org/10.1016/B978-0-7506-9749-1.50010-7.

Katz, D. (1964). The motivational basis of organizational-behavior. *Behavioral Science, 9*(2), 131–146. https://doi.org/10.1002/bs.3830090206.

Kaufmann, G. (2003). The effect of mood on creativity in the innovative process. In L. Shavinina (Ed.), *The international handbook on innovation* (pp. 191–203). Oxford, UK: Elsevier Science.

Lazarus, R. S. (2001). Relational meaning and discrete emotions. In *Appraisal processes in emotion. Theory, methods, research*. New York: Oxford University Press.

Lazarus, R. S., & Folkman, S. (1984). *Stress, appraisal and coping*. New York: Springer.

Loewenstein, G., & Lerner, J. S. (2003). The role of affect in decision making. In R. J. Davidson, K. R. Scherer, & H. H. Goldsmith (Eds.), *Handbook of affective sciences* (pp. 619–642). Oxford, UK: Oxford University Press.

Lyubomirsky, S., & Nolenhoeksema, S. (1993). Self-perpetuating properties of dysphoric rumination. *Journal of Personality and Social Psychology, 65*(2), 339–349. https://doi.org/10.1037/0022-3514.65.2.339.

Lyubomirsky, S., & Nolenhoeksema, S. (1995). Effects of self-focused rumination on negative thinking and interpersonal problem-solving. *Journal of Personality and Social Psychology, 69*(1), 176–190. https://doi.org/10.1037//0022-3514.69.1.176.

Madjar, N., Oldham, G. R., & Pratt, M. G. (2002). There's no place like home? The contributions of work and nonwork creativity support to employees' creative performance. *Academy of Management Journal, 45*, 757–767. https://doi.org/10.2307/3069309.

Madrid, H. P., Patterson, M. G., Birdi, K. S., Leiva, P. I., & Kausel, E. E. (2014). The role of weekly high-activated positive mood, context, and personality in innovative work behavior: A multilevel and interactional model. *Journal of Organizational Behavior, 35*(2), https://doi.org/10.1002/job.1867.

Madrid, H. P., Patterson, M. G., & Leiva, P. I. (2015). Negative core affect and employee silence: How differences in activation, cognitive rumination, and problem-solving demands matter. *Journal of Applied Psychology, 100*(6). https://doi.org/10.1037/a0039380.

Madrid, H. P., Totterdell, P., & Niven, K. (2016). Does leader-affective presence influence communication of creative ideas within work teams? *Emotion, 16*(6), https://doi.org/10.1037/emo0000183.

Martin, L. L., & Stoner, P. (1996). Mood as input: What we think about how we feel determines how we think. In L. L. Martin & A. Tesser (Eds.), *Striving and feeling: Interactions among goals, affect, and self-regulation* (pp. 279–301). Mahwah, NJ: Erlbaum.

Nijstad, B. A., De Dreu, C. K. W., Rietzschel, E. F., & Baas, M. (2010). The dual pathway to creativity model: Creative ideation as a function of flexibility and persistence. *European Review of Social Psychology, 21*, 34–77. https://doi.org/10.1080/10463281003765323.

Nolen-Hoeksema, S. (2000). The role of rumination in depressive disorders and mixed anxiety/depressive symptoms. *Journal of Abnormal Psychology, 109*(3), 504–511. https://doi.org/10.1037/0021-843x.109.3.504.

Nolen-Hoeksema, S., Larson, J., & Grayson, C. (1999). Explaining the gender difference in depressive symptoms. *Journal of Personality and Social Psychology, 77*(5), 1061–1072. https://doi.org/10.1037//0022-3514.77.5.1061.

Nolenhoeksema, S., Parker, L. E., & Larson, J. (1994). Ruminative coping with depressed mood following loss. *Journal of Personality and Social Psychology, 67*(1), 92–104. https://doi.org/10.1037/0022-3514.67.1.92.

Remington, N. A., Fabrigar, L. R., & Visser, P. S. (2000). Reexamining the circumplex model of affect. *Journal of Personality and Social Psychology, 79*(2), 286–300. https://doi.org/10.1037//0022-3514.79.2.286.

Russell, J. A. (1980). A circumplex model of affect. *Journal of Personality and Social Psychology, 39*(6), 1161–1178. https://doi.org/10.1037/h0077714.

Russell, J. A. (2003). Core affect and the psychological construction of emotion. *Psychological Review, 110*(1), 145–172. https://doi.org/10.1037/0033-295x.110.1.145.

Russell, J. A., & Barrett, L. F. (1999). Core affect, prototypical emotional episodes, and other things called emotion: Dissecting the elephant. *Journal of Personality and Social Psychology, 76*, 805–819. https://doi.org/10.1037/0022-3514.76.5.805.

Schwarz, N. (1990). Feeling as information: Informational and motivational functions of affective states. In E. T. Higgins & R. Sorentino (Eds.), *Handbook of motivation and cognition: Foundations of social behavior*: Vol. 2. (pp. 527–561). New York: Guilford.

Schwarz, N. (2002). Situated cognition and the wisdom of feelings: Cognitive tuning. In L. Feldman Barrett & P. Salovey (Eds.), *The wisdom in feelings* (pp. 144–166). New York, NY: Guilford.

Schwarz, N., & Clore, G. L. (2003). Mood as information: 20 years later. *Psychological Inquiry, 14*(3–4), 296–303. https://doi.org/10.1080/1047840X.2003.9682896.

Schwarz, N., & Skurnik, I. (2003). Feeling and thinking: Implications for problem solving. In J. E. Davidson & R. J. Sternberg (Eds.), *The psychology of problem solving* (pp. 263–290). Cambridge, UK: Cambridge University Press.

Seo, M. G., Barrett, L. F., & Bartunek, J. M. (2004). The role of affective experience in work motivation. *Academy of Management Review, 29*(3), 423–439. https://doi.org/10.2307/20159052.

Seo, M. G., Barrett, L. F., & Sirkwoo, J. (2008). The structure of affect: History, theory, and implications for emotion research in organizations. In N. Ashkanasy & C. D. Cooper (Eds.), *Research companion to emotion in organizations*. Cheltenham: Edward Elgar Publishing.

Seo, M. G., Bartunek, J. M., & Barrett, L. F. (2010). The role of affective experience in work motivation: Test of a conceptual model. *Journal of Organizational Behavior, 31*(7), 951–968. https://doi.org/10.1002/job.655.

Sio, U. N., & Ormerod, T. C. (2009). Does incubation enhance problem solving? A meta-analytic review. *Psychological Bulletin, 135*(1), 94–120. https://doi.org/10.1037/a0014212.

Spering, M., Wagener, D., & Funke, J. (2005). The role of emotions in complex problem-solving. *Cognition & Emotion, 19*(8), 1252–1261. https://doi.org/10.1080/02699930500304886.

Thayer, R. E. (1996). *The origin of everyday moods: Managing energy, tension, and stress*. New York: Oxford University Press.

To, M. L., Fisher, C. D., & Ashkanasy, N. M. (2015). Unleashing angst: Negative mood, learning goal orientation, psychological empowerment and creative behaviour. *Human Relations, 68*(10), 1601–1622. https://doi.org/10.1177/0018726714562235.

To, M. L., Fisher, C. D., Ashkanasy, N. M., & Rowe, P. A. (2011). Within-person relationships between mood and creativity. *Journal of Applied Psychology, 97*(3), 599–612. https://doi.org/10.1037/a0026097.

Totterdell, P., & Niven, K. (2014). *Workplace moods and emotions: A review of research*. Charleston, SC: CreateSpace Independent Publishing.

Treynor, W., Gonzalez, R., & Nolen-Hoeksema, S. (2003). Rumination reconsidered: A psychometric analysis. *Cognitive Therapy and Research, 27*(3), https://doi.org/10.1023/A:1023910315561.

Verhaeghen, P., Joorman, J., & Khan, R. (2005). Why we sing the blues: The relation between self-reflective rumination, mood, and creativity. *Emotion, 5*, 226–232. https://doi.org/10.1037/1528-3542.5.2.226.

Verhaeghen, P., Joormann, J., & Aikman, S. N. (2014). Creativity, mood, and the examined life: Self-reflective rumination boosts creativity, brooding breeds dysphoria. *Psychology of Aesthetics, Creativity, and the Arts, 8*(2), 211–218. https://doi.org/10.1037/a0035594.

Warr, P. B. (2007). *Work, happiness and unhappiness*. New Jersey: Lawrence Erlbaum Associates.

Warr, P. B., Bindl, U., Parker, S. K., & Inceoglu, I. (2014). Job-related affects and behaviors: Activation as well as valence. *European Journal of Work and Organizational Psychology, 23*(3), 342–363. https://doi.org/10.1080/1359432X.2012.744449.

Watson, D. (2000). *Mood and temperament*. New York: Guilford Press.

Watson, D., & Clark, L. A. (1992). On traits and temperament—General and specific factors of emotional experience and their relation to the 5-factor model. *Journal of Personality, 60*(2), 441–476. https://doi.org/10.1111/j.1467-6494.1992.tb00980.x.

Watson, D., & Clark, L. A. (1994). *The PANAS-X: Manual for the positive and negative affect schedule-expanded form*. Unpublished manuscriptUniversity of Iowa.

Watson, D., & Tellegen, A. (1985). Toward a consensual structure of mood. *Psychological Bulletin, 98*(2), 219–235. https://doi.org/10.1037/0033-2909.98.2.219.

Watson, D., Wiese, D., Vaidya, J., & Tellegen, A. (1999). The two general activation systems of affect: Structural findings, evolutionary considerations, and psychobiological evidence. *Journal of Personality and Social Psychology, 76*(5), 820–838. https://doi.org/10.1037/0022-3514.76.5.820.

West, M. A., & Farr, J. (1990). *Innovation and creativity at work. Psychological and organizational strategies*. Chichester: John Wiley and Sons.

Yik, M. S. M., Russell, J. A., & Steiger, J. H. (2011). A 12-point circumplex structure of core affect. *Emotion, 11*(4), 705–731. https://doi.org/10.1037/a0023980.

Yuan, F. R., & Woodman, R. W. (2010). Innovative behavior in the workplace: The role of performance and image outcome expectations. *Academy of Management Journal, 53*(2), 323–342. https://doi.org/10.5465/AMJ.2010.49388995.

Zhou, J., & George, J. M. (2001). When job dissatisfaction leads to creativity: Encouraging the expression of voice. *Academy of Management Journal, 44*, 682–696. https://doi.org/10.2307/3069410.

Zhou, J., & Hoever, I. J. (2014). Research on workplace creativity: A review and redirection. *Annual Review of Organizational Psychology and Organizational Behavior, 1*(1), 333–359. https://doi.org/10.1146/annurev-orgpsych-031413-091226.

LEADERSHIP AND TEAMS

12

Proposing a Multiple Pathway Approach to Leading Innovation: Single and Dual Leader Approaches

Samuel Hunter*, Julian B. Allen*, Rachel Heinen*, Lily Cushenbery†

*Penn State University, University Park, PA, United States, †Stony Brook University, Stony Brook, NY, United States

> "Now, the most important thing that goes into creative success is having the people who can come up with the great ideas. But the next most important thing is often overlooked: having people who will enable those great ideas, and support those creative people – manage the creativity with real economic foresight… That leader alongside me, that coach and that cheerleader at Disney, was Frank [Wells]." **CEO of Disney's Michael Eisner on his partnership with Disney president Frank Wells**

In a recent set of independent global surveys, consulting groups asked organizations to list the assets needed to succeed both now and into the future (Andrew, Manget, Michael, Taylor, & Zablit, 2010; Boatman & Wellins, 2011; IBM, 2010). Across more than 20,000 leaders and HR professionals surveyed, one of the top assets reported was leading and encouraging innovative performance—a sentiment echoed in the academic literature as well (e.g., Alegre & Chiva, 2008; Anderson, Potocnik, & Zhou, 2014). However, personnel in these same organizations simultaneously described a perceived *inability* to lead and manage sustained innovative output. That is, across a sizable sample of global organizations and sources, leading for innovation was listed as an essential asset, but also one most lacking.

Scholars have considered two general approaches to resolve the need for more innovative leadership: a single leader with flexible skills, or a pair of leaders that work well together. In the first, an ambidextrous approach, a single individual manages the difficult and often disparate leadership roles comprising innovation (Rosing, Frese, & Bausch, 2011; Rosing, Rosenbusch, & Austin, 2010; Zacher, Robinson, & Rosing, 2016; Zacher & Rosing, 2015). Ambidextrous leadership theories propose that a single leader is capable of successfully engaging in both "opening" behaviors that support idea exploration and "closing" behaviors that support idea exploitation. Other organizations, however, have chosen to engage in a seemingly more unconventional leadership practice. Conceding that many single or unitary leaders lack the capacity, on their own, to meet the demanding requirements of sustained innovation, shared leadership has emerged as a viable option (Arena, Ferris, & Unlu, 2011; Davis & Eisenhardt, 2011; O'Toole, Galbraith, & Lawler, 2002). Specifically, a small but growing number of organizations distribute leadership roles between *two* individuals and embrace a dual leadership approach to encourage and instantiate creative ideas. Thus the aim of this effort is to showcase the notion that there are multiple pathways to successfully managing the paradoxes of innovation with a particular emphasis on the less researched approach of dual leadership (Hunter, Cushenbery, & Jayne, 2017; Mainemelis, Kark, & Epitropaki, 2015). Before turning to a discussion of these approaches, however, we must begin with a case for why there are conflicting demands in the pursuit of innovation.

DEMANDS OF LEADING FOR INNOVATION

Consistent with innovation scholars (e.g., Amabile, 1996; Baer, 2012; Mumford & Gustafson, 1988), we define creativity as the generation of ideas that are both novel and useful and define innovation as the implementation of those ideas. Central to our argument that leading for innovation requires unique approaches is the premise that these processes are difficult to manage with a single individual possessing a more static or rigid skillset. Specifically, we draw on role conflict and role identity literature (e.g., Stryker & Burke, 2000) to argue that innovation places a severe set of role demands on those tasked with its facilitation. As a means to convince the reader of this core premise, we suggest that innovation demands be most accurately viewed as (a) a complex, multiactivity process; (b) an iterative and nonlinear process; (c) a process that is perpetually challenging; and at times, (d) a phenomenon with nearly paradoxical antecedents.

Such characterizations are also true of general performance requirements for leaders in many, if not most, organizations (Byrne et al., 2014). However, there are a number of distinguishing characteristics unique to innovation, as well (e.g., paradoxical antecedents, frequent failure). Moreover, there is not a single factor but a combination of innovation demands that create a complex environment requiring a unique approach to leadership.

Innovation as a Complex Process

Although there has been some variability in the specificity of the models and theoretical frameworks put forth (see Lubart, 2001 for a review), process perspectives of innovation contain a common theme. Namely, they depict creative and innovative achievement as the result of a series of activities rather than a single event or outcome (Baer, 2012). Stated another way, innovation requires success across a *range* of behaviors and actions rather than simply a single activity, such as idea generation. Conceding some degree of variability on the level of specificity, most models depict creativity and innovation as beginning with the framing and understanding of a problem, continuing through to idea generation and evaluation, and then reaching more formalized stages of implementation planning and execution (Basadur, Runco, & Vega, 2000). Implicit within a process perspective of innovation and core to this paper is that leaders must manage a *range of activities*—activities that may, given their disparate nature, be at odds with one another (Bledow, Frese, Anderson, Erez, & Farr, 2009; Bledow, Frese, & Mueller, 2011; March, 1991).

By viewing creativity and innovation as a successful outcome of a series of interrelated events, the list of requirements for *each* activity must be acknowledged, thereby adding to a larger and more complex composition of overall antecedents. Facilitators of idea generation activities, for example, include cognitive resources as primary drivers, such as divergent thinking (e.g., Davis, Peterson, & Farley, 1974). For idea evaluation, however, team dynamics, such as psychological safety, become more critical (Baer & Frese, 2003; Gong, Cheung, Wang, & Huang, 2012; West, 2002). Along related lines, there is growing neuroscience evidence that cognitive requirements for idea generation are distinct from those in idea evaluation (Ellamil, Dobson, Beeman, & Christoff, 2012). Finally, implementing and monitoring ideas requires resources from an organization or larger business unit (Baer, 2012). Several other examples exist (e.g., Rosing et al., 2011), yet the above should suffice to illustrate that demands and requirements come from individuals, teams, and wider business units, thereby adding to the complexity of what it takes to successfully lead for innovation.

Innovation as a Nonlinear Process

Despite process models often describing the activities comprising innovation in such a way that they may *appear* linear, they are most certainly not, nor do the majority of innovation scholars view their models as such. Instead, as a number of researchers have emphasized in their own work (e.g., Finke, Ward, & Smith, 1992; Li, Maggitti, Smith, Tesluk, & Katila, 2013; Ward, Smith, & Finke, 1999), the innovation process is a dynamic and iterative set of interrelated events. For example, although a product may be prototyped and approved to move onto focus group testing, feedback from early consumers may result in the product being pulled back in and completely revised (i.e., move back to the generative stages of the innovation process) rather than moving onto production in a more linear fashion. This sentiment is well illustrated by the Geneplore model, which depicts the creative process as having two primary activities: generation and exploration, with creative output occurring from the iteration between these processes (Finke et al., 1992). From a leadership standpoint, this means that managing innovation requires oscillating between a set of demands and requirements in a way that is oftentimes quite unpredictable and nearly always ongoing in a cyclical, dynamic fashion.

Innovation and Frequent Failure

Most organizations that rely on innovation as a driver of growth understand that the overwhelming majority of creative ideas do not succeed, with estimates of failure rates ranging from 60% to 90% (Blank, 2013; Brown & Anthony, 2011; Crawford, 1977; DiMasi, 1995; Nobel, 2011). There are several implications flowing from this observation. The first is that successful leaders of innovation cannot lock onto a single idea. Instead, recurrent and sometimes unpredictable failure requires leaders to maintain a project portfolio comprised of multiple ongoing and interrelated projects with the aim of producing a single or subset of successful outputs. Thus leaders must maintain a near perpetual body of innovative work to have sustained success in innovation. The second is that complexity increases, as the nonlinear process of innovation becomes confounded with the management of varying phases of innovation both across and within multiple projects. Stated more directly, for as long as innovation remains a key strategic theme for an organization, managing innovation is both an ongoing and demanding process.

Innovation and Paradox

The premise of conflicting demands in the pursuit of innovation is well documented by scholars who explored the tensions (Lewis, Welsh, Dehler, & Green, 2002), contradictions (King, Anderson, & West, 1991), paradoxes (Miron, Erez, & Naveh, 2004), and dilemmas (Benner & Tushman, 2003) that characterize the innovation process (see Bledow et al., 2009 for summary). Perhaps the most well known is the exploitation/exploration dilemma first outlined by March (1991) building on earlier work by Shumpeter (1934). To put it simply, exploration activities include those that are more generative, for example, while exploitation includes activities that are focused on implementation. Core to our argument is the premise that successful engagement in some innovation activities creates challenges for other innovation activities. In the case of exploration and exploitation (March, 1991), for example, it is difficult for decision-makers to allocate resources equally to both processes—choices must often be made as to which receive the lion's share of attention and support.

Along these lines, Hunter, Thoroughgood, Myer, and Ligon (2011) outlined several paradoxes or tensions faced by leaders, explicitly, in the pursuit of innovation. As an illustration, the authors describe the generation-evaluation paradox whereby a leader is tasked with facilitating high psychological safety necessary for radical idea generation while also being charged with making pragmatic evaluative decisions about which ideas are likely to be most fruitful for a departmental or organizational portfolio and cutting those that are not. Similar tension is evident in the restriction-freedom paradox, where creative idea generation requires leaders to offer freedom and latitude to subordinates but simultaneously provide structure to progress more amorphous ideas. Lastly, the vision-autonomy paradox further requires leaders push in two alternate paths, as they must establish a direction for subordinates while at the same time provide sufficient freedom to support creative thought. Although an overview of each paradox is beyond the scope of this paper, the central premise is agreed upon by a growing number of scholars: innovation places demands on a leader that are not only challenging and complex but also—at times—at odds with one another.

ROLE CONFLICT AND INNOVATION

Having established that innovation produces conflicting demands, we may now turn to how these demands and related conflicts impact innovation. As indicated by the literature on identity, we attach meaning to the various roles we play in our lives (Stryker & Burke, 2000), helping to define who we are as individuals (Burke, 1991). Our identities can be derived from a range of factors, though broadly speaking, are viewed as the result of social and contextual expectations including but not limited to group membership (Mead, 1934). In somewhat oversimplified terms, contextual demands result in individuals taking on various roles that, in turn, shape their identity, which then shapes subsequent cognition and behavior. This approach has been applied directly to the leadership and subordinate arena, helping to provide conceptual guidance on the mechanisms of leader emergence and recognition (DeRue & Ashford, 2010).

There are several extensions flowing from an identity perspective. The first is that our changing contextual demands can dictate our roles, and in turn shape our identity. In fact, maintaining a singular identity across situations is challenging and can result in significant stress (Sluss, van Dick, & Thompson, 2011; Wiley, 1991). To this point, scholars have proposed that we develop various subidentities that comprise our larger total identity (Hall, 1972; Miller, 1963) as a means to cope with the various demands dictated by context. Taken a step further, and central to the chapter, is evidence suggesting that taking on distal or disparate identities may result in greater strain on an individual. For example, Wiley (1991) proposed that workingwomen take on identities and subidentities that have less overlap than those taken on by men, whose various work, family, and social roles are more closely linked. The predicted result was greater overall stress for workingwomen than for workingmen due to the disparity in identities and role demands. The point is well summarized by Sluss et al. (2011) who stated, "Sometimes, those multiple role identities may be in conflict…[and] these conflicting aspects of an individuals' roles and attached role identities can be a source of great strain" (p. 514).

In leading for innovation, leader identity may be conflicted because of the inherent complexity of the innovation process (Benner & Tushman, 2003, 2015). Innovation processes require success across a *range* of behaviors and actions rather than simply a single activity such as idea generation (Baer, 2012). Extending such arguments to the present effort, we contend that innovation demands result in leaders having to take on multiple roles that are often quite disparate and may even conflict with one another (Bledow et al., 2009, 2011). The result is cognitive resource depletion and associated strain impacting both the leader's own cognition and decision-making directly, as well as having more indirect influences on innovation through subordinate interactions.

HOW LEADER ROLE CONFLICT AFFECTS INNOVATION OUTCOMES

Having discussed that innovation demands are difficult for one leader to manage, we may now turn to a description of the mechanisms by which role conflict may hamper creative and innovative achievement. As outlined previously, innovation demands are predicted to produce leader role conflict, largely manifested as identity conflict and resource demand conflict. These impacts, however, are theorized to influence innovation through mechanisms operating at the leader level, but also more indirectly through subordinates. That is, whereas most research on leadership and innovation has justifiably focused on how leaders shape subordinate creative and innovative output, we draw on work by Daft (1978) and Hunter and Cushenbery (2011) to suggest that leaders themselves are members of the innovative ecosystem, having the capacity to propose, edit, implement, and sustain ideas themselves.

As a means to illustrate this assertion, consider directing a film as a metaphor for leading innovation. A director can have a direct influence on the creative work in the film through specific editing choices (e.g., what scenes to cut, what score to include over a series of shots), changing scripts or dialog, or even by appearing in the film itself. In contrast, a director can also impact the creativity of the film through more indirect mechanisms such as casting and hiring, as well as through motivational or supportive mechanisms with the actors and crew. The point here is that as a facilitator of innovation, the means by which leaders shape creative output can vary from a very direct path to more of a "setting of the stage" approach, with most leaders employing a range of tactics to "direct" complex projects into success.

Following from this model, we propose that leader role conflict will impact innovative achievement in two primary ways. First, role conflict will hamper innovative achievement directly (i.e., impact the leader's ability to contribute creative ideas) by causing stress and strain to the leader themselves. Second, leader role conflict will have a more indirect impact on innovative achievement by placing strain and stress on subordinates as well as producing a lack of clarity regarding project direction and predictability in interacting with the leader. Finally, it is also of note that leader stress and strain will have a harmful influence on subordinates as well, further hampering innovative achievement. That is, as leaders feel and emote stress it will be transferred to subordinates through emotional contagion effects (Gump & Kulik, 1997; Johnson, 2008). Each of these mechanisms is described in greater detail as follows.

Direct Leader Influences

Daft (1978) and others (e.g., Hunter & Cushenbery, 2011) suggested that in addition to encouraging subordinate creative efforts leaders are part of the innovation ecosystem themselves. As such, not only leaders are shepherds, shapers, and supporters of creative ideas but also generators of ideas and planners of implementation. As an illustration, consider some of the most influential innovative leaders of the recent creative era. Steve Jobs of Apple, Bill Gates of Microsoft, Walt Disney of Disney, and Sergey Brin of Google all founded organizations aimed at supporting innovation, yet each had a hand in shaping the innovation process directly through their own ideas and input.

By acknowledging that leaders serve as both marshals of subordinate creativity and drivers of creative production, we must also concede that they are likely to be susceptible to the barriers of innovation, often faced by other members of the organization. Specifically, we suggest that leader stress, strain, and distress is caused by leader role conflict flowing from the demands of innovation and, as a result, creative production will subsequently be hampered.

Consistent with distraction arousal theory (Teichner, Arees, & Reilly, 1963) we contend that stressors constrain the cognitive resources available for creative performance and in turn, limit original output. There is some support for this contention, most recently in a meta-analysis conducted by Byron, Khazanchi, and Nazarian (2010). It must be noted that the authors predicted and observed a curvilinear effect for stressors and creativity, yet the nature of this relationship was such that high levels of stress were strongly associated with decreases in creative performance, particularly when individuals felt that they had limited control in managing stressors. Along similar lines, a meta-analysis on mood and creativity revealed that reported higher levels of anxiety were associated with lower levels of creativity and lower cognitive flexibility in particular (Baas, De Dreu, & Nijstad, 2008). Thus it is important to acknowledge the inherent complexity between role conflict and creative performance but overall it appears that high levels of stress, strain, and anxiety are harmful for creative performance.

Indirect Leader Influences

Turning now to the role that subordinates play in innovative achievement, we suggest that leader role conflict hampers performance in two primary ways. First, when leaders experience conflict in managing various roles and identities, subordinates may be unsure of how to engage with their leader. For example, as leaders oscillate between operating as supporters and evaluators of original ideas, the overall message from the leader may lack clarity. As a number of scholars have suggested and observed, clarity in vision is essential for creative and innovative output (Anderson & West, 1998). Borrill, West, Shapiro, and Rees (2000), for example, found that clarity of vision was associated with high levels of team innovation in primary health care teams. Similar results were also observed for top management teams (West & Anderson, 1996). Thus to the degree that role demands force a single leader to offer differing and likely conflicting messages about behavioral expectations, creative and innovative output will suffer.

Moreover, to the extent that subordinates are unclear as to how they might be interacting with their leader in a given exchange, we predict that stress will be increased and therefore, creative performance hindered. Put another way, the need for leaders to manage multiple roles, often in an erratic fashion, translates to a lack of clarity in what "hat" their leader might be wearing that day, which in turn may result in anxiety and stress when interacting with that leader. Further, as leaders begin to lack clarity in their own role, subordinates may also begin to question the clarity of their roles in innovative efforts. Some peripheral evidence along these lines may be seen in a study examining organizations in both the United States and

New Zealand, where O'Driscoll and Beehr (1994) found that supervisor behaviors such as a lack of structure and unclear goals predicted role ambiguity, role conflict, and uncertainty, which in turn were significantly associated with subordinate psychological strain and turnover intentions.

In addition to effects derived from leader role conflict, we suggest that leaders who experience stress and strain will transfer similar affective reactions via mechanisms akin to emotional contagion (Hatfield, Cacioppo, & Rapson, 1994). That is, as leaders experience stress, we predict that this will have a trickle-down effect on subordinate stress. In a study of supervisors and subordinates, Bono and Illies (2006) found evidence of a link between leader emotion and follower mood, although it must be acknowledged that the study focused on positive affective states rather than more negative affective states. Similar evidence was found in a study of health care workers (Bono, Foldes, Vinson, & Muros, 2007), as well as in a laboratory setting (Lyons & Schneider, 2009). Thus although research is limited in demonstrating a link between negative leader affect and subordinate affect, available data do suggest that there is a link between leader affect and subordinate affect. Moreover, work by Miner, Glomb, and Hulin (2005) found that when negative interactions occurred with a leader, these effects were five times stronger than the effects observed through positive interactions. In addition, consistent with the job demands-resources model, job characteristics can vastly impact employee strain, burnout, and engagement (Bakker & Demerouti, 2007). However, more central to our argument, leaders can have an indirect effect on followers' well-being as they can both reduce job demands and increase the availability of resources (Schaufeli, 2017). As such, we predict that leaders will transfer their stress to their subordinates via contagion effects or through the unsuccessful management of their follower's demands and resources. Thus leaders who experience stress due to role conflict will transfer that stress to their subordinates, which will consequently harm creative and innovative performance.

A MULTIPLE PATHWAY APPROACH

Summarizing the above, it is clear that there is an increasing desire for innovative output and leaders are a key force in driving that output. Yet problematically, leading for innovation is wrought with challenges and requires unique forms of leadership to address the paradoxical demands that characterize the innovation process. In our chapter, we propose that there are several ways that these challenges can be resolved and innovation enhanced in organizations. Specifically, we argue that there are multiple *pathways* to leading for innovation. To be clear, we do not contend that either pathway is inherently more viable than the other. Instead, we argue that organizations and researchers must consider both the context and qualities of the leaders to understand which pathway will best lead to innovative achievement. Most importantly, we encourage embracing the notion that an expanded view of leadership pathways (Mumford, 2006) can lead to the richest understanding of leading innovative endeavors.

PATHWAY ONE: AMBIDEXTROUS LEADERSHIP

As March (1991) laid out in his discussion on exploration and exploitation, organizations must deal with the inherent tension between such pursuits characterizing innovative efforts. An ambidextrous leadership approach proposes that a single leader can best manage these tensions by engaging in cognitions and behaviors that support both exploration and exploitation outcomes. Specifically, Rosing et al. (2011, 2010) suggest that ambidextrous leaders engage in "opening" behaviors that encourage a wider array of thinking and experimentation, leading to a greater variety of ideas produced. Leader behaviors include providing support for challenging conventional ideas, rewarding experimentation, and providing autonomy for independent thinking. In contrast, "closing" behaviors are those that tighten and narrow thinking allowing for idea refinement and production. Leader behaviors include making corrections, setting clear and specific goals, and monitoring goal achievement.

Defining Ambidextrous Leadership

Leader ambidexterity is grounded in the notion that flexibility is required across a range of potentially paradoxical and taxing behaviors. The central case for leader ambidexterity enhancing innovative performance is that if a leader can successfully engage in both opening and closing behaviors, innovation is maximized. Indeed, in two recent studies, there has been support for this prediction. In a sample of 388 working adults, the researchers found that leader opening behaviors led to employee exploration, that leader closing behavior led to employee exploitation and, most central to our discussion here, that innovation was highest when both exploration and exploitation behaviors were high (Zacher et al., 2016). Similarly, in a sample of 33 team leaders and 90 employees gathered in design firms and architecture fields, Zacher and Rosing (2015) found that innovation was greatest when leaders engaged in both opening and closing behaviors. Thus the core aspects of the model have received strong, albeit preliminary, support.

As outlined previously, engaging in both opening and closing behaviors is the first defining characteristic of ambidextrous leadership. The second characteristic defining this form of leading is having the "temporal flexibility to switch between both as the situation requires" (Rosing et al., 2011, p. 966). Successful and flexible engagement in both activities, then, requires a number of leadership capabilities. First, a leader must be able to recognize when each set of behaviors is most appropriate. This capacity requires skill in both relationship-oriented behaviors and social engagement, as well as task-oriented behaviors such as forecasting, planning, and organizing (Mumford, Scott, Gaddis, & Strange, 2002). Second, a leader must have the capacity to engage in both sets of behaviors, effectively. Put another way, in successful ambidextrous leadership scenarios, a single leader must possess a broad set of skills as a precursor to engaging in that range of behaviors. Third and along related lines, a leader must possess the flexibility to oscillate between these varied behaviors. This flexibility is, perhaps, one of the greatest challenges for leaders given the demands associated with engaging in potentially conflicting roles. Finally, as noted by Rosing et al. (2011), a leader must integrate these potentially contradictory sets of behaviors in a systematic and effortful fashion. A leader cannot, for example, simply utilize one role or set of behaviors (e.g., engage in opening behaviors) without foresight for channeling that output into a subsequent set of potentially contradictory situational demands (e.g., closing behaviors).

Challenges of Ambidextrous Leadership

Turning again to the role conflict and role identity literature (e.g., Stryker & Burke, 2000), we made the argument earlier in the chapter that oscillating between such demanding behaviors is taxing for a single leader to engage in. A key component to successfully leading through ambidexterity, then, is to be able to manage these potentially conflicting behaviors and associated roles. More specifically, we have proposed in recent work (Hunter et al., 2017) that these conflicting roles place a number of burdens on leaders, including high cognitive demands, emotional tensions, and demands related to time as a resource. Because of such demands, leaders feel greater stress and strain, thereby impeding the creative output of themselves and their subordinates.

Leaders who are able to successfully utilize ambidexterity to balance the aforementioned demands of innovation will possess several distinctive characteristics that permit meeting the challenges of generating and implementing novel ideas. Such qualities include, but are not limited to, higher levels of stress tolerance, expertise that is both broad and diverse, high levels of leadership skills across both task- and relationship-oriented behaviors, high physical energy to pursue potentially conflicting goals characterizing opening and closing outcomes, and perhaps most critically, comfort and skill in flexibility. Although such qualities are useful for leaders, broadly, ambidextrous leaders must possess all of these qualities at particularly high levels.

Given the unique demands and impressive skillset required to engage in ambidexterity, it is unlikely that all leaders are capable of leading for innovation, ambidextrously. To put a sharper point on the argument, it is unlikely that many, if not most, leaders will be able to successfully utilize ambidextrous leadership in the pursuit of innovation. Certainly, a number of leaders possess outstanding ambidextrous qualities and such exemplars are notable. Elon Musk of Tesla and Space X, Mary Barra of General Motors, Jeff Bezos of Amazon, and Satya Nadella of Microsoft all represent remarkable examples and highlight the outstanding capabilities and achievements of ambidextrous leaders. These leaders, however, represent an uncommon form of achievement and due to this rarity, are an even more impressive class of leaders.

Benefits of Ambidextrous Leadership

In light of the challenges surrounding both innovation broadly and ambidextrous leadership more narrowly, it is open to question if the approach is viable as a pathway to innovation. The benefits of a single leader utilizing ambidexterity are numerous and, in the aggregate, help to illustrate the viability of this pathway. The broadest benefit has ties back to Fayol's (1949) conceptualization of the unity of command philosophy. According to the unity of command view, by having a single leader operating and managing key processes, organizational efficiency is maximized. As a result of such efficiency, decisions are made more quickly, subordinate action is taken at a more rapid pace, communication is improved relative to shared leadership scenarios where it may be unclear which leader should have or has received information. To illustrate, Chipotle recently transitioned from a Co-CEO structure to unity of command model in an effort to streamline communication, with CEO Ells becoming the sole CEO of the organization. A second key benefit of utilizing a single, highly flexible leader, is the improved clarity of vision. A single leader is able to provide a clearer path forward relative to two or more leaders who will inherently have different though not necessarily conflicting goals.

In addition to performance and efficiency arguments, there are several additional and highly practical advantages associated with using a single, highly flexible leader. Namely, for a given leadership need, organizations must concern themselves with acquiring one, and only one, individual. In contrast, shared leadership requires considering both the qualities of each individual leader as well as the fit between the two. Relatedly, compensating a single leader is most cost effective than compensating two leaders. Given the costs at the highest levels of organizations for compensating leaders, this is not a trivial benefit (Shue & Townsend, 2017).

PATHWAY TWO: DUAL LEADERSHIP

Although a single leader or unity of command ambidextrous approach to leadership is a viable pathway to leading innovation, we have suggested in other efforts that finding an individual that possesses the qualities needed to meet the paradoxical demands of innovation is, in and of itself, a challenge. This challenge is perhaps reflected in the discussion at the outset of the chapter where we noted that leading for innovation was both desired by organizations but also noted as a weakness by most (e.g., Boatman & Wellins, 2011). In short, an ambidextrous leader is certainly capable of leading for innovation, but such leaders are hard to find. Instead, we have begun exploring the possibility of a second pathway to leading innovation, termed "dual leadership."

Defining Dual Leadership

Extending process definitions of leadership (Bass & Bass, 2009; Dansereau, Seitz, Chiu, Shaughnessy, & Yammarino, 2013; Northouse, 2001) to dual leadership, we define the phenomenon as a collective approach where two individuals share the leadership workload and through coordinated efforts, engage subordinates toward the accomplishment of a set of the often-disparate goals characterizing the generation and implementation of novel ideas (Bledow et al., 2009). In the case of innovation, the nature of those goals is of particular importance because their antecedents will vary by the stage of the creativity and innovation process (Anderson et al., 2014; Caniëls, De Stobbeleir, & De Clippeleer, 2014).

A growing body of literature suggests that the interest and application of shared leadership and leader dyads, in particular, is increasing. In an investigation of coprincipals in schools, for example, Eckman (2007) found that dual leadership was linked to increased satisfaction, also observing "many of the respondents noted that they experienced less role conflict because they had a partner" (p. 11). Such trends were similarly observed in a comparison sample of 51 dual leaders and 51 single female leaders (Eckman & Kelber, 2010). Further, a study by Arena et al. (2011) found that dual leadership was positively associated with firm value and positive market reactions. Arnone and Stumpf (2010) interviewed 19 dual leaders and found that dual leaders were well suited to innovative endeavors, concluding that "one leader might focus on new business opportunities requiring innovation and creativity, while the other ensured proper control and risk management of current operations" (p. 15). Their interviews also highlighted the challenges of dual-leader parings, underscoring the importance of matching pairs appropriately.

Along similar lines, a recent study of 71 leaders also indicated that leader pairings are complex social endeavors and that boundary conditions (e.g., power gaps among pairs) play an important role in shaping performance (Krause, Priem, & Love, 2014). Alvarez, Svejenova, and Vives (2007) also note, explicitly, the utility of dual leadership in innovation as well as indicating a growing use of this type of leadership structure. Finally, as predicted by the Hay Group (2011) in their 2030 Leadership Forecast, these types of shared leadership structures, or matrix structures, will become increasingly utilized as workplace demands and complexity increase. Although other examples exist both in research (e.g., De Voogt, 2006; Fosberg & Nelson, 1999; Gronn, 2008) and anecdotal cases (e.g., Sergey Brin and Larry Page founding Google, Leslie Groves and Robert Oppenheimer in managing the Manhattan Project), the previous discussion should serve to illustrate increasing interest and use of dual leadership approaches, with a particular emphasis on application in innovative environments.

Having introduced the notion of dual leadership, broadly, we argue that dual leaders are further defined in several unique ways. First, leader dyads must be comprised of two individuals who share influence with one another. This influence may be due to formal power structures or more personalized power bases such as charisma or expertise. What is critical is that the influence process is substantively bidirectional. In other words, dual leadership is not merely a form, type, or subset of a leader and key-lieutenant relationship. Instead, each member of the dyad has latitude in deciding when and how to influence the other, rather than being called upon for advice or input. Task conflict and debate are vital for developing ideas (Nemeth & Ormiston, 2007; Nemeth, Personnaz, Personnaz, & Goncalo, 2004), and status differences may prevent a follower in a leader-follower pair from expressing dissent.

Second, subordinates must recognize both individuals as leaders. That is, both individual leaders must have influence over subordinates in addition to each other. Finally, individuals outside of the dyad (subordinates, clients, customers, upper-level leaders) must recognize that exchanges with one leader also carry the weight and influence of the second leader. This is not to suggest that a contradiction among leaders in a dyad precludes them from our definition, this will of course happen from time to time. Rather, when one partner in the dyad speaks, the assumption made by others is that the leader speaks, on some level, for both members of the dyad. Moreover, this assumption also brings with it an implicit argument that dual leaders communicate to develop an agreed-upon vision, with responsibilities divvied and shared between them.

Challenges of Dual Leadership

The growth of shared leadership broadly and dual leadership specifically suggests the viability of this pathway to leading for innovation. However, such a pathway is not without its own set of challenges. Such challenges fall along two broad lines. The first is the increased coordination requirements of having two leaders that must reach consensus on key decisions, which impact both leader's processes. Also, leaders will need to coordinate to provide further clarity for subordinates on the individual roles of each member of the leadership dyad. This increase in coordination is witnessed at both practical levels where leaders must set aside time to discuss emerging issues at hand, as well as more strategically where both leaders must assess current objectives against each leaders' own set of priorities. The complex process of innovation further augments these challenges, as multiple innovative projects in multiple phases of innovation are often at play. As an illustration, in a sample of CEOs that shared responsibilities with a COO, organizational performance suffered (Hambrick & Cannella, 2004).

The second key challenge dual leaders face is the difficulty in finding an appropriate and suitable pairing. That is, a pair of leaders must both possess qualities and attributes that overlap to ensure common ground can be found on finding a way forward, but also possess distinct enough qualities that there is a diversity benefit to having two leaders. Further, the effectiveness of the pair may develop over time by both parties actively shaping and negotiating the relationship. This negotiation is especially important to establish role clarity and identity of each leader and fully mitigate role conflict. It may not even be readily apparent that two leaders would work well together at the inception of their pairing. As an analogy, a single leader is a puzzle piece that must fit within the broader organizational puzzle whereas a dual leader approach requires leaders to first fit two pieces together with that connected piece, then fitting within a broader framework.

Benefits of Dual Leadership

Despite such challenges, there are a number of benefits for a dual leadership approach. Recall the observation that innovation demands result in leaders having to take on multiple roles on a frequent and unpredictable basis. These roles, moreover, are often quite disparate and may even conflict with one another (Bledow et al., 2009, 2011). The result is greater stress and strain on the leader which may impact both the leader's own cognition and decision-making directly, as well as having more indirect influences on innovation through subordinate interactions. A dual leader approach allows leaders to divvy up such conflicting roles, thereby reducing stress and strain and ultimately enhancing leader and subordinate creative output.

Contrasting the type of conflict that emerges from managing multiple identities is a more pragmatic view on why two leaders are useful to the management of innovation. Namely, the complex and disparate nature of innovation demands makes it cognitively difficult for a single leader to engage in multiple tasks simultaneously (Osman, 2010). Notably, a neuroscience study by Ellamil et al. (2012) placed participants in a fMRI machine and asked them to engage in generative and evaluative activities. Results show that creative idea generation and idea evaluation utilize different neural processes, indicating that these stages of the innovative process have unique cognitive demands. This suggests that from a biological perspective, it may be difficult for leaders to either engage in disparate tasks simultaneously or, more commonly, to quickly alternate back and forth between differing processes.

At an even more basic level, by dividing the disparate and often conflicting aspects of the innovation process among members of a leadership pair, each member of the leader dyad is allowed to leverage their primary skill-set, while allowing the other leader to manage those aspects that may be a weakness (Arena et al., 2011). In a study of eight technology collaborations, Davis and Eisenhardt (2011) found that a rotating leadership approach (i.e., shifting decision control and objectives between partners) was most beneficial to facilitating innovation, noting that for pairs of leaders "alternating decision control is likely to improve innovation performance because it facilitates partners' access to their complimentary capabilities" (p. 179). Moreover, the authors found that the unique networks resulting from dual leadership were also beneficial to enhancing innovation. In contrast, single leader approaches were found to be associated with the lowest levels of innovation, particularly when that single leader was inflexible and insistent on control of the entire innovation process. This process requires not only knowledge of the other leader's unique skillset, but also trust in their ability to follow through on their roles. Thus each leader requires both competence in technical aspects of their jobs as well as insight within that unique relationship to manage the processes. In other words, successful dual leaders should thoroughly understand not only their partner's strengths but also their limitations and foster unique ways of managing each other. Thus dual leaders' complementary skillsets are likely to develop and become more distinct over time.

Along similar lines, cognitive resource models and conservation of resource theories (e.g., Hobfoll, 1989; Kanfer & Ackerman, 1989; Kanfer, Ackerman, Murtha, Dugdale, & Nelson, 1994; Wood & Bandura, 1989) propose that as task demands increase in complexity, there are fewer cognitive resources available for additional tasks and overall performance can suffer. In a study of 172 leaders and direct reports, for example, Byrne et al. (2014) found that high task demand resulted in leader resource depletion that, in turn, was associated with lower forms of positive leadership (i.e., transformational behaviors) and higher levels of harmful behaviors (e.g., abusive supervision). In the case of innovation, we contend that managing the innovation process represents a severe form of task complexity and task demand. Thus not only do leaders perceive stress and strain from managing disparate roles, but are also heavily taxed cognitively, making it difficult to tackle the burdens of the innovation process.

Finally, given the severe demands innovation can place on a leader (Shaw & Weekley, 1985), a dyadic approach may also afford a unique form of social and emotional support. Single leaders can often feel stranded and alone in their roles, unable to share their concerns with superiors for fear they will be seen as weak, but also unwilling to seek support from subordinates who might hold them in high regard. A second leader can reduce stress directly, as a confidant and a resource, and indirectly, as a buffer for negative experiences (Cohen & Wills, 1985). Furthermore, having a partner that believes in the pursuit of innovation can reinforce a difficult goal even after repeated failures. Thus the uniquely equalized power structure in a dyadic leader pair can provide fertile ground for sharing the emotional and social burdens of leadership.

DECIDING WHICH PATH TO TAKE

To summarize, we argue that innovation is a unique form of performance that often places conflicting and paradoxical demands on leaders attempting to enhance it. Meeting these demands is challenging for leaders and many organizations report an inability to do it well. To manage such paradoxes, we suggested there are several pathways to leadership that organizations may take. The first is a single leader, ambidextrous pathway that requires a leader capable of engaging in a range of behaviors in a resilient fashion. The second is a shared leader approach, where two leaders help distribute the unique and conflicting demands of innovation. Conceding that there are mixed approaches that blend these two exemplar pathways (e.g., in a shared leadership scenario, the leaders themselves may be ambidextrous), the question that emerges is how to decide which pathway is most viable for a given organization or circumstance. Acknowledging the inherent complexity and nuance of such a decision, we aim to offer some guidance—albeit imperfect—on helping make that decision. Specifically, we propose three components to consider when choosing such pathways.

Decision Consideration One: Rapid Decision-Making Demands

One of the benefits that distinguish unity of command (i.e., single leader) from shared leadership is efficiency. Single leaders are generally more capable of making rapid decisions and responding to pressing requests than dual leaders who must often confer with each other before making a final collective choice. Thus organizations that have high efficiency demands are often better suited for a flexible, single leader. Consider, for example, the army captain who requests air support in a firefight. Such a situation would be better suited for the single army colonel to approve the request rather than two colonels who have to confer with one another before rendering a decision. Extending to creativity domains, consider a development team engaging in rapid prototyping where efficient decision making is central to testing and refining ideas (Rayna & Striukova, 2016).

Despite the inherent efficiency of a single leader relative to dual leaders, it is possible to be efficient as a dual leader pair. This efficiency is contingent, however, on how clearly distributed roles might be. That is, if in a shared leadership scenario each leader has clearly prescribed roles and responsibilities—along with authority to make decisions within such roles—efficiency is possible and indeed, potentially superior to a single leader approach given that more leaders are thereby available for support. As such, we consider role clarity a second key consideration, as follows.

Decision Consideration Two: Clarity of Roles

In the early days of Apple, Steve Wozniak managed the technical side of the business and Steve Jobs handled the broader strategic thinking and sales. The partnership worked, in part, due to clarity on which leader was handling which task. Subordinates knew whom to ask when a question arose and the leaders knew they had the authority to answer it. Similar relationships existed with co-CEOs of Oracle, who stepped in after Larry Ellison took a narrower role of chief technology officer. Mark Hurd and Safra Catz balance each other with Hurd handling external facing demands such as sales and service, while Catz handles internal issues such as finance, manufacturing, and legal. Contrast these scenarios with a failed leadership pairing at Martha Stewart Living Omnimedia company who appointed co-CEOs Wenda Millard and Robin Marino. Although the partnership failed for a number of reasons, chief among them was a lack of role division and clarity. Both CEOs conflicted with one another over the same duties and responsibilities. Thus unless an organization is able to divvy up roles in a clear fashion, a single leader will likely be the superior pathway.

Decision Consideration Three: Diversity of Demands

As noted throughout the chapter, innovation is unique in its demands on leaders. When a single leader can meet those demands, several potential conflicts can be avoided and in many cases, efficiency improved. However, as the diversity of demands increases, it becomes more and more difficult for a single leader to manage the range of demands. Such situations are when dual leaders become most viable. Consider, as a hypothetical example, the bakery owner who produces creative confections. Imagine the bakery being visited by an online magazine critic who lauds the bakery for its novel products. The baker becomes inundated with demands and must expand into the online arena. Despite a strong skillset in one area (i.e., baking), the baker is lacking in another (i.e., technology). Such a scenario depicts when a leader pairing may perform particularly well. As the gap between diversity demands and leader skills increases, two leaders may be better able to cover the required tasks.

LIMITATIONS AND CLOSING COMMENTS

Limitations

Before turning to the final comments a number of limitations should be borne in mind. The first is that we have created an artificially distinct dichotomy between two forms of leadership that are more appropriately depicted as an overlapping set of approaches. In practice, shared leaders are often ambidextrous themselves (Rosing et al., 2011) and single leaders frequently form relationships with key lieutenants that are akin to shared leadership. Thus some form of reductionism is always necessary for a discussion of complex psychological phenomena, yet it is important to acknowledge the nuance that exists among the forms of leadership discussed in this chapter. Similarly, it is also important to note that while the focus of our argument is on innovation and innovation demands, a natural extension of a dual leader approach would flow to noninnovative contexts with similar performance requirements. That is, we do not suggest that the dual leadership approach would apply *only* to innovative endeavors, but rather that it is most applicable given the distinctive demands innovation places on leadership.

Second, we offered three points of consideration when making a choice about pursuing a single or dual leader approach to innovation. In reality, a number of supplemental decisions are also critical, including the age and history of the organization, the nature and type of the specific innovative product or process, and strategic goals of the organization itself. Perhaps the most substantial omission was one of fit. That is, although dual leadership is a viable pathway to innovation, two leaders must possess qualities that both supplement and complement each other. The sheer number of variations and combinations that exist preclude us from outlining a detailed discussion of fit in this chapter. Thus it must be conceded that we aimed to offer commentary on some of the key issues to consider, but space constraints dictate a level of reduction in the discussion.

Finally, although we acknowledged the complexity of the innovation process, we did not discuss dynamics of leading each of the various phases comprising innovation (see Stenmark, Shipman, & Mumford, 2011 for a more detailed consideration of the cognitive and social behaviors of leaders across the innovative process). Instead, we discussed leading at a more macro level with the primary contribution being an outline of a multiple pathway approach to managing innovation. We felt that more fine-grained discussion of leading each specific process would have resulted in a chapter that was overwhelming and overly detailed, yet it is important to note that the role of leadership in each of these processes is critical.

Closing Comments

In closing, we drew inspiration vis-à-vis the work of Mumford (2006) who took a notably novel approach to understanding and viewing leadership. Namely, rather than making the case for a single approach to leading, he proposed the notion that there are multiple ways to be successful, that there are multiple pathways to leader accomplishment. In keeping with that theme, we acknowledged the difficulty in managing the paradoxes of innovation and offered the broad sentiment that there are several ways to approach such challenges. Neither pathway is particularly easy nor is either pathway without its own unique difficulties. It is our hope, however, that this expanded and inclusive view of leadership may help inspire researchers aiming to understand the differing ways leaders can go about enhancing innovation and perhaps even more importantly, help guide decision makers who seek to choose those individuals who will instill their vision for novel pursuits.

References

Alegre, J., & Chiva, R. (2008). Assessing the impact of organizational learning capability on product innovation performance: An empirical test. *Technovation, 28*, 315–326.
Alvarez, J. L., Svejenova, S., & Vives, L. (2007). Leading in pairs. *MIT Sloan Management Review, Summer*, 9–14.
Amabile, T. M. (1996). *Creativity and innovation in organizations*. (Vol. 5). Boston: Harvard Business School.
Anderson, N., Potocnik, K., & Zhou, J. (2014). Innovation and creativity in organizations: A state of science review, prospective commentary, and guiding framework. *Journal of Management, 40*, 1297–1333.
Anderson, N. R., & West, M. A. (1998). Measuring climate for work group innovation: Development and validation of the team climate inventory. *Journal of Organizational Behavior, 19*, 235–258.
Andrew, J. P., Manget, J., Michael, D. C., Taylor, A., & Zablit, H. (2010). *Innovation 2010: A return to prominence—And the emergence of a new world order*. Boston, MA: Boston Consulting Group.
Arena, M. P., Ferris, S. P., & Unlu, E. (2011). It takes two: The incidence and effectiveness of co-CEOs. *The Financial Review, 46*, 385–412.
Arnone, M., & Stumpf, S. A. (2010). Shared leadership: From rivals to co-CEOs. *Strategy & Leadership, 38*(2), 15–21. https://doi.org/10.1108/10878571011029019.
Baas, M., De Dreu, C. K., & Nijstad, B. A. (2008). A meta-analysis of 25 years of mood-creativity research: Hedonic tone, activation, or regulatory focus? *Psychological Bulletin, 134*, 779–806.

Baer, M. (2012). Putting creativity to work: The implementation of creative ideas in organizations. *Academy of Management Journal*, *55*, 1102–1119.

Baer, M., & Frese, M. (2003). Innovation is not enough: Climates for initiative and psychological safety, process innovations, and firm performance. *Journal of Organizational Behavior*, *24*, 45–68.

Bakker, A. B., & Demerouti, E. (2007). The job demands-resources model: State of the art. *Journal of Managerial Psychology*, *22*(3), 309–328.

Basadur, M., Runco, M. A., & Vega, L. A. (2000). Understanding how creative thinking skills, attitudes and behaviors work together: A causal process model. *The Journal of Creative Behavior*, *34*, 77–100.

Bass, B. M., & Bass, R. (2009). *The bass handbook of leadership: Theory, research, and managerial applications*. Simon and Schuster.

Benner, M. J., & Tushman, M. L. (2003). Exploitation, exploration, and process management: The productivity dilemma revisited. *Academy of Management Review*, *28*, 238–256.

Benner, M. J., & Tushman, M. L. (2015). Reflections on the 2013 decade award: "Exploitation, exploration, and process management: The productivity dilemma revisited" ten years later. *Academy of Management Review*, *40*(4), 497–514.

Blank, S. (2013). Why the lean start-up changes everything. *Harvard Business Review*, *91*(5), 63–72.

Bledow, R., Frese, M., Anderson, N., Erez, M., & Farr, J. (2009). A dialectic perspective on innovation: Conflicting demands, multiple pathways, and ambidexterity. *Industrial and Organizational Psychology*, *2*, 305–337.

Bledow, R., Frese, M., & Mueller, V. (2011). Ambidextrous leadership for innovation: The influence of culture. *Advances in Global Leadership*, *6*, 41–69.

Boatman, J., & Wellins, R. S. (2011). *Global leadership forecast 2011: Time for a leadership revolution*. Bridgeville, PA: Development Dimensions International.

Bono, J. E., Foldes, H. J., Vinson, G., & Muros, J. P. (2007). Workplace emotions: The role of supervision and leadership. *Journal of Applied Psychology*, *92*, 1357–1367.

Bono, J. E., & Illies, R. (2006). Charisma, positive emotions and mood contagion. *The Leadership Quarterly*, *17*, 317–334.

Borrill, C., West, M., Shapiro, D., & Rees, A. (2000). Team working and effectiveness in health care. *British Journal of Healthcare Management*, *6*, 364–371.

Brown, B., & Anthony, S. D. (2011). How P&G tripled its innovation success rate. *Harvard Business Review*, *89*(6), 64–72.

Burke, P. J. (1991). Identity processes and social stress. *American Sociological Review*, *56*, 836–849.

Byrne, A., Dionisi, A. M., Barling, J., Akers, A., Robertson, J., Lys, R., et al. (2014). The depleted leader: The influence of leaders' diminished psychological resources on leadership behaviors. *The Leadership Quarterly*, *25*, 344–357.

Byron, K., Khazanchi, S., & Nazarian, D. (2010). The relationship between stressors and creativity: A meta-analysis examining competing theoretical models. *Journal of Applied Psychology*, *95*, 201.

Caniëls, M. C., De Stobbeleir, K., & De Clippeleer, I. (2014). The antecedents of creativity revisited: A process perspective. *Creativity and Innovation Management*, *23*(2), 96–110.

Cohen, S., & Wills, T. A. (1985). Stress, social support, and the buffering hypothesis. *Psychological Bulletin*, *98*, 310–357.

Crawford, C. M. (1977). Marketing research and the new product failure rate. *The Journal of Marketing*, 51–61.

Daft, R. (1978). A dual-core model of organizational innovation. *Academy of Management Journal*, *21*, 193–210.

Dansereau, F., Seitz, S. R., Chiu, C. Y., Shaughnessy, B., & Yammarino, F. J. (2013). What makes leadership, leadership? Using self-expansion theory to integrate traditional and contemporary approaches. *The Leadership Quarterly*, *24*, 798–821.

Davis, J. P., & Eisenhardt, K. M. (2011). Rotating leadership and collaborative innovation: Recombination processes in symbiotic relationships. *Administrative Science Quarterly*, *56*, 159–201.

Davis, G. A., Peterson, J. M., & Farley, F. H. (1974). Attitudes, motivation, sensation seeking, and belief in ESP as predictors of real creative behavior. *The Journal of Creative Behavior*, *8*, 31–39.

De Voogt, A. (2006). Dual leadership as a problem-solving tool in arts organizations. *International Journal of Arts Management*, *9*, 17–22.

DeRue, D. S., & Ashford, S. J. (2010). Who will lead and who will follow? A social process of leadership identity construction in organizations. *Academy of Management Review*, *35*, 627–647.

DiMasi, J. A. (1995). Success rates for new drugs entering clinical testing in the United States. *Clinical Pharmacology & Therapeutics*, *58*, 1–14.

Eckman, E. (2007). The co-principalship: It's not lonely at the top. *Journal of School Leadership*, *17*(3), 313–339.

Eckman, E. W., & Kelber, S. T. (2010). Female traditional principals and co-principals: Experiences of role conflict and job satisfaction. *Journal of Educational Change*, *11*(3), 205–219.

Ellamil, M., Dobson, C., Beeman, M., & Christoff, K. (2012). Evaluative and generative modes of thought during the creative process. *NeuroImage*, *59*, 1783–1794.

Fayol, H. (1949). *Industrial and general management*. London: Pitman.

Finke, R. A., Ward, T. B., & Smith, S. M. (1992). *Creative cognition: Theory, research, and applications*. Cambridge, MA: MIT Press.

Fosberg, R. H., & Nelson, M. R. (1999). Leadership structure and firm performance. *International Review of Financial Analysis*, *8*(1), 83–96.

Gong, Y., Cheung, S. Y., Wang, M., & Huang, J. C. (2012). Unfolding the proactive process for creativity integration of the employee proactivity, information exchange, and psychological safety perspectives. *Journal of Management*, *38*, 1611–1633.

Gronn, P. (2008). The future of distributed leadership. *Journal of Educational Administration*, *46*(2), 141–158.

Gump, B. B., & Kulik, J. A. (1997). Stress, affiliation, and emotional contagion. *Journal of Personality and Social Psychology*, *72*, 305–319.

Hall, D. T. (1972). A model of coping with role conflict: The role behavior of college educated women. *Administrative Science Quarterly*, 471–486.

Hambrick, D. C., & Cannella, A. A. (2004). CEOs who have COOs: Contingency analysis of an unexplored structural form. *Strategic Management Journal*, *25*(10), 959–979.

Hatfield, E., Cacioppo, J., & Rapson, R. (1994). *Emotional contagion*. New York: Cambridge University Press.

Hay Group. (2011). *Building the new leader: Leadership challenges of the future revealed*. Retrieved from http://www.haygroup.com/www/challenges/index.aspx?id=96.

Hobfoll, S. E. (1989). Conservation of resources: A new attempt at conceptualizing stress. *American Psychologist*, *44*, 513–524.

Hunter, S. T., & Cushenbery, L. (2011). Leading for innovation: Direct and indirect influences. *Advances in Developing Human Resources*, *13*, 248–265.

Hunter, S. T., Cushenbery, L. D., & Jayne, B. (2017). Why dual leaders will drive innovation: Resolving the exploration and exploitation dilemma with a conservation of resources solution. *Journal of Organizational Behavior*, *38*(8), 1183–1195.

Hunter, S. T., Thoroughgood, C. N., Myer, A. T., & Ligon, G. S. (2011). Paradoxes of leading innovative endeavors: Summary, solutions, and future directions. *Psychology of Aesthetics, Creativity, and the Arts*, *5*, 54.

IBM. (2010). *Capitalizing on complexity: Insights from the 2010 global CEO study*. Somers, NY: IBM.

Johnson, S. K. (2008). I second that emotion: Effects of emotional contagion and affect at work on leader and follower outcomes. The Leadership Quarterly, 19: 1–19.

Kanfer, R., & Ackerman, P. L. (1989). Motivation and cognitive abilities: An integrative/aptitude-treatment interaction approach to skill acquisition. *Journal of Applied Psychology*, *74*, 657.

Kanfer, R., Ackerman, P. L., Murtha, T. C., Dugdale, B., & Nelson, L. (1994). Goal setting, conditions of practice, and task performance: A resource allocation perspective. *Journal of Applied Psychology, 79*, 826.

King, N., Anderson, N., & West, M. A. (1991). Organizational innovation in the UK: A case study of perceptions and processes. *Work and Stress, 5*, 331–339.

Krause, R., Priem, R., & Love, L. (2014). Who's in charge here? Co-CEOs, power gaps, and firm performance. *Strategic Management Journal, 36*(13), 2099–2110. https://doi.org/10.1002/smj.2325.

Lewis, M. W., Welsh, M. A., Dehler, G. E., & Green, S. G. (2002). Product development tensions: Exploring contrasting styles of project management. *Academy of Management Journal, 45*, 546–564.

Li, Q., Maggitti, P. G., Smith, K. G., Tesluk, P. E., & Katila, R. (2013). Top management attention to innovation: The role of search selection and intensity in new product introductions. *Academy of Management Journal, 56*, 893–916.

Lubart, T. I. (2001). Models of the creative process: Past, present and future. *Creativity Research Journal, 13*, 295–308.

Lyons, J. B., & Schneider, T. R. (2009). The effects of leadership style on stress outcomes. *The Leadership Quarterly, 20*, 737–748.

Mainemelis, C., Kark, R., & Epitropaki, O. (2015). Creative leadership: A multi-context conceptualization. *The Academy of Management Annals, 9*(1), 393–482.

March, J. G. (1991). Exploration and exploitation in organizational learning. *Organization Science, 2*, 71–87.

Mead, G. H. (1934). *Mind, self and society*. Chicago: University of Chicago Press.

Miller, D. R. (1963). The study of social relationships: Situation, identity, and social interaction. In S. Koch (Ed.), *The process areas, the person, and some applied fields*: Vol. 5. Psychology: A study of a science (pp. 639–737). New York: McGraw Hill.

Miner, A., Glomb, T., & Hulin, C. (2005). Experience sampling mood and its correlates at work. *Journal of Occupational and Organizational Psychology, 78*, 171–193.

Miron, E., Erez, M., & Naveh, E. (2004). Do personal characteristics and cultural values that promote innovation, quality, and efficiency compete or complement each other? *Journal of Organizational Behavior, 25*, 175–199.

Mumford, M. D. (2006). *Pathways to outstanding leadership: A comparative analysis of charismatic, ideological, and pragmatic leaders*. Mahwah, NJ: Lawrence Erlbaum Associates.

Mumford, M. D., & Gustafson, S. B. (1988). Creativity syndrome: Integration, application, and innovation. *Psychological Bulletin, 103*, 27.

Mumford, M. D., Scott, G. M., Gaddis, B., & Strange, J. M. (2002). Leading creative people: Orchestrating expertise and relationships. *The Leadership Quarterly, 13*, 705–750.

Nemeth, C. J., & Ormiston, M. (2007). Creative idea generation: Harmony versus stimulation. *European Journal of Social Psychology, 37*(3), 524–535.

Nemeth, C. J., Personnaz, B., Personnaz, M., & Goncalo, J. A. (2004). The liberating role of conflict in group creativity: A study in two countries. *European Journal of Social Psychology, 34*(4), 365–374.

Nobel, A. (2011). *The empowerment paradigm*. Xlibris Corporation.

Northouse, P. G. (2001). *Leadership: Theory and practice*. Thousand Oaks, CA: Sage Publications.

O'Toole, J., Galbraith, J., & Lawler, E. E. (2002). When two (or more) heads are better than one: The promise and pitfalls of shared leadership. *California Management Review, 44*, 65–83.

O'Driscoll, M. P., & Beehr, T. A. (1994). Supervisor behaviors, role stressors and uncertainty as predictors of personal outcomes for subordinates. *Journal of Organizational Behavior, 15*, 141–155.

Osman, M. (2010). Controlling uncertainty: A review of human behavior in complex dynamic environments. *Psychological Bulletin, 136*, 65.

Rayna, T., & Striukova, L. (2016). From rapid prototyping to home fabrication: How 3D printing is changing business model innovation. *Technological Forecasting and Social Change, 102*, 214–224.

Rosing, K., Frese, M., & Bausch, A. (2011). Explaining the heterogeneity of the leadership-innovation relationship: Ambidextrous leadership. *The Leadership Quarterly, 22*, 956–974.

Rosing, K., Rosenbusch, N., & Austin, J. T. (2010). Ambidextrous leadership in the innovation process. In A. Gerybadze, U. Hommel, H. W. Reiners, & D. Thomaschewski (Eds.), *Innovation and international corporate growth* (pp. 191–204). Springer: Berlin.

Schaufeli, W. B. (2017). Applying the job demands-resources model. *Organizational Dynamics, 46*(2), 120–132.

Shaw, J. B., & Weekley, J. A. (1985). The effects of objective work-load variations of psychological strain and post-work-load performance. *Journal of Management, 11*, 87–98.

Shue, K., & Townsend, R. R. (2017). Growth through rigidity: An explanation for the rise in CEO pay. *Journal of Financial Economics, 123*(1), 1–21.

Shumpeter, J. A. (1934). *The theory of economic development.* Cambridge, MA: Harvard University Press.

Sluss, D., van Dick, R., & Thompson, B. (2011). Role theory in organizations: A relational perspective. In S. Zedeck (Ed.), Vol. 1. *Handbook of I/O-Psychology* (pp. 505–534). Washington, DC: American Psychological Association.

Stenmark, C. K., Shipman, A. S., & Mumford, M. D. (2011). Managing the innovative process: The dynamic role of leaders. *Psychology of Aesthetics, Creativity, and the Arts, 5*(1), 67.

Stryker, S., & Burke, P. J. (2000). The past, present, and future of an identity theory. *Social Psychology Quarterly*, 284–297.

Teichner, W. H., Arees, E., & Reilly, R. (1963). Noise and human performance, a psychophysiological approach. *Ergonomics, 6*, 83–97.

Ward, T. B., Smith, S. M., & Finke, R. A. (1999). Creative cognition. In R. J. Sternberg (Ed.), *Handbook of creativity* (pp. 189–212). New York, NY: Cambridge University Press.

West, M. A. (2002). Sparkling fountains or stagnant ponds: An integrative model of creativity and innovation implementation in work groups. *Applied Psychology, 51*, 355–387.

West, M. A., & Anderson, N. R. (1996). Innovation in top management teams. *Journal of Applied Psychology, 81*, 680.

Wiley, M. G. (1991). Gender, work, and stress: The potential impact of role-identity salience and commitment. *The Sociological Quarterly, 32*, 495–510.

Wood, R., & Bandura, A. (1989). Social cognitive theory of organizational management. *Academy of Management Review, 14*, 361–384.

Zacher, H., Robinson, A. J., & Rosing, K. (2016). Ambidextrous leadership and employees' self-reported innovative performance: The role of exploration and exploitation behaviors. *The Journal of Creative Behavior, 50*(1), 24–46.

Zacher, H., & Rosing, K. (2015). Ambidextrous leadership and team innovation. *Leadership and Organization Development Journal, 36*(1), 54–68.

13

Creative Leaders in Bureaucratic Organizations: Are Leaders More Innovative at Higher Levels of the Organizational Hierarchy?

Bo T. Christensen*, Peter V.W. Hartmann[†], Thomas Hedegaard Rasmussen[‡]

*Copenhagen Business School, Frederiksberg C, Denmark, [†]Performance, Analytics & HRIS, Getinge, Copenhagen, Denmark, [‡]National Australia Bank, Melbourne, VIC, Australia

INTRODUCTION

Research on creativity and innovation in large corporations has on the one hand indicated the crucial contribution and importance of creative employees to overall company innovation, but has on the other hand shown how a challenged creative work climate set by bureaucratic structures and lack of management support may stifle individual motivation and creativity (Amabile, 1997; Amabile, Conti, Coon, Lazenby, & Herron, 1996). Large organizations frequently employ bureaucratic structures characterized by functional departments, and clearly outlined hierarchy and job scope (Weber, 1946). Most often we think of creativity in bureaucratic organizations as belonging to specific functions (e.g., R&D or marketing), but that need not be the case—all jobs in bureaucratic organizations can in principle be carried out more or less creatively, although such creative activity may not (always) be valued positively in the organization. Life in bureaucratic

---

* Any details expressed in this article, including where the study was conducted, the sample, any conclusions and discussions, are unrelated to Getinge Group and does not represent Getinge, but is solely owned by the author(s).

organizations is replete with stories of good creative ideas killed by red tape and following-procedure, and of creative employees who struggle with narrow job boundaries and too many layers of management one needs to pass through in order to persuade the organization of the value in a new idea. The result can be motivation loss and companies carrying on in a business-as-usual manner as opposed to venturing into new innovative directions. Several organizational qualities of large corporations may be highlighted that potentially spur creative frustration: (A) long chains of command prohibit swift decision making and creative flexibility; (B) the pursuit of increased efficiency leads to exploitation at the expense of exploration (March, 1991); (C) job descriptions become increasingly clearly defined and specialized, leading to lowered job complexity, possibly with routine and uninteresting jobs resulting, especially at the lower levels in the organization (Dunne & Dougherty, 2012).

However, despite motivational struggles, pains and frustrations with bureaucratic organizing, an important unanswered question remains in the literature: are creative individuals actually more successful in organizational life (Jaussi & Benson, 2012)? "Success" may be measured in a variety of ways (e.g., performance, recognition and awards, salary level), but one important success factor in large corporations is that of leadership level and placement in the organizational hierarchy, which is the success dimension of interest in the present paper. We tested the relation between individual innovativeness to placement at a certain level in the organizational hierarchy in a large international corporation covering production, retailing, and distribution domains, with a distinctly hierarchical structure involving clear lines of command and well-defined job boundaries.

Bureaucratic organizations do need innovation, with support for innovation coming especially from supportive managers, weak ties, and increasing job complexity (Dunne & Dougherty, 2012). Thus it is possible that large corporations seek to place more creative employees higher in the hierarchy. On the other hand, it is also possible that individual creativity either does not matter for company advancement in bureaucratic organizations, or even that reduced individual creativity may be a distinct characteristic higher up in the organization. The latter might be the case if, for example, creative individuals choose more often to leave the company (i.e., a larger employee turnover for creative employees) based on self-deselection as when creative individuals leave in favor of other types of organizational structure favoring innovation. But it could also be due to individual creative virtues not being valued in the organization (e.g., if there is a trade-off between individual abilities needed in organizational exploitation vs. exploration; March, 1991). Such a trade-off would disfavor individuals with divergent capabilities to more convergent ones, leading possibly to increased layoff rates and/or lower promotion rates for creative individuals. An argument for why large companies might not value creativity in individuals is that creativity is inherently stochastic, wasteful, risky, and uncertain in nature (Simonton, 2003), which seem in sharp contrast with the logic of efficiency and exploitation driving bureaucratic organizing. An argument for the possible positive valuation of individual creativity would conversely be that while lower occupational levels in large corporations might be made up of primarily routine jobs, job complexity and thus the need for creative adaptation as well as intelligent behavior, would be increasingly needed at higher organizational levels. This, in turn, could (in so far as creative potential is recognized in the individual) create a situation where creative individuals are increasingly selected for promotion as the higher level of job complexity further up in the hierarchy may better match their creative capabilities. It thus remains an open question who actually gets selected into higher leadership levels of the organizational hierarchy: the divergent explorer vs. the efficient converger, and thus whether individual creativity is a help or a hindrance in organizational placement at higher levels. To our knowledge no past study has focused on the impact of leader innovativeness on internal company position placement in the organizational hierarchy. The present work aimed to help fill this research gap by examining whether individual innovativeness positively predicted placement into higher leadership levels in the organizational hierarchy. The general research question covered in the present study relates to the effects of IQ and leader innovativeness on leadership level in a large sample of leaders. The leader sample comes from one large international organization, tested for intelligence at recruitment and for innovativeness by their subordinates, thus offering ecological validity and suggesting practical relevance for the recruitment of leaders.

Creative Leadership

Organizational behavior research on employee creativity has examined mainly contextual or organizational factors that facilitate or inhibit creativity (Rego, Sousa, Cunha, Correia, & Saur-Amaral, 2007). In this line of research, leadership is typically regarded as a contextual factor either supporting or suppressing creativity among employees (e.g., Byrne, Mumford, Barrett, & Vessey, 2009; Koseoglu, Liu, & Shalley, 2017; Oldham & Cummings, 1996; Rickards & Moger, 2006; Zhou & George, 2003). However, the individual innovativeness of the leaders themselves should not be forgotten in the focus on employee creativity. Depending on the job function held, individual innovativeness may be crucial in order to be able to perform complex organizational tasks in a skilled and satisfactory manner, by suggesting and implementing novel and useful solutions. Individual innovativeness entails both generating novel and practical ideas or solutions in the early steps of innovation, but also includes activities related to idea development and implementation (Anderson, De Dreu, & Nijstad, 2004; Tierney & Farmer, 2011). Hülsheger, Anderson, and Salgado (2009) argued that it is important to conceptually distinguish among work innovation criteria, in order to clarify whether creativity (early stages, involving mainly idea generation or solution phases of innovation) or innovation (the whole innovation process, involving additionally idea development, support, and implementation) is studied. This study focuses on individual leader innovativeness, subsuming both managerial creativity skills, and skills relating to selection, development, and implementation of the ideas and concepts in the organization (Amabile, 1988, 1996; Randel, Jaussi, & Wu, 2011; Tierney & Farmer, 2011), in alignment with past studies of individual innovation among employees (e.g., Axtell et al., 2000; Axtell, Holman, & Wall, 2006; de Jong & den Hartog, 2010; Miron, Erez, & Naveh, 2004). The understanding of individual innovativeness among leaders is crucial to further develop the organizational capacity for creative performance at all organizational levels. Following we will briefly review the literature on innovativeness and intelligence in organizational settings.

Innovativeness and Creativity

Axtell et al. (2000) defined organizational innovation as a process involving the generation; adoption; implementation; and incorporation of new ideas, practices, or artifacts within the organization. Innovation may thus be regarded as a broader concept than creativity (which mainly refers to idea generation) and can be said to comprise two different phases involving an awareness or suggestion phase, and an implementation phase (e.g., Amabile, 1988; Axtell et al., 2000). Past research on individual creativity or innovativeness in organizations has tended to use leader ratings of subordinate creativity (e.g., Eisenberger & Aselage, 2009; George & Zhou, 2001; Tierney & Farmer, 2002, 2011) or subordinate innovativeness (e.g., Axtell et al., 2000, 2006). To assess leader (rather than employee) innovativeness, we aggregated subordinate ratings of their direct leader, arguing that subordinates should have direct access to both leader idea generation and idea implementation, as most often both the ideas and their implementations would involve and impact the subordinates directly.

The Relation Between Creativity and Intelligence

Most contemporary creativity research tends to view creativity and intelligence as distinct traits that are only modestly related (for reviews, see Batey & Furnham, 2006; Kim, Cramond, & Vantassel-Baska, 2011), with a meta-analytic study (Kim, 2005) yielding an average weighed r of 0.174 across 21 studies. The correlation may, however, not be of the same magnitude throughout the IQ spectrum, as suggested by threshold theory, which proposes that below a certain IQ level (approximately IQ 120), there is some (weak to moderate) correlation between IQ and creative potential and achievement, but above this cutoff point, there is no correlation (e.g., Barron, 1961; MacKinnon, 1962). Past research on threshold theory has shown somewhat mixed results, but some support was found in a previous study utilizing partly the same dataset as the current chapter (Christensen, Hartmann, & Rasmussen, 2017). The correlation between leader innovativeness and intelligence was small but positive and significant below an IQ cutoff point of IQ120, while there was no significant relation above this cutoff point, and the two correlations were significantly different. The results were fairly reliable across two samples collected in two distinct years, illustrating support for the theory, albeit the low effect sizes are notable as they render caution as to the practical utility of the results. For the present purposes, it is important to note the small albeit significant overall correlation ($r = 0.08$) between intelligence and individual innovativeness in the present sample, indicating the two constructs are effectively independent.

Intelligence, Individual Innovativeness, and Occupational Level

While many factors have been deemed important for managerial success in company advancement, intelligence remains one of best understood and arguably one of the most important factors. A meta-analysis of the relation between leadership and intelligence indicated a correlation of 0.27 (corrected for range restriction; Judge, Colbert, & Ilies, 2004), and longitudinal studies have corroborated that general mental ability is linked to extrinsic career success (Judge, Klinger, & Simon, 2010). Previous studies of a broad selection of jobs have found that when analyzing the central demands of those jobs, the complexity in the information processing emerges as the most dominant factor differentiating jobs, indicating that jobs can meaningfully be ranked according to their level of complexity (Gottfredson, 1997, 2002a, 2002b). As argued by Gottfredson (1997), organizational life is replete with uncertainty, change, confusion, and misinformation. An extremely important dimension distinguishing among jobs is the mental complexity of the work they require workers to perform. According to Arvey (1986) the most important factor in job complexity is the judgment and reasoning necessary when confronted with novelty, change, uncertainty, unpredictability, and the need to spot and master new information and emerging problems (as is the case in intellectual and innovative labor). Given these findings, it is of no surprise that when occupational level is determined and ranked according to level of complexity, the correlation between the occupational level and the average IQ for incumbents in the specific grade, amounts to 0.9–0.95 (Gottfredson,

1997, 2002a; Jensen, 1980, 1998; Schmidt & Hunter, 2004). However, on the individual level, the correlation between an individual's IQ and occupational level is typically between 0.5 and 0.7, with higher correlations later in life (Schmidt & Hunter, 2004), due to the influence of other factors like personality.

While the IQ literature has tended to examine how high IQ individuals are selected for jobs at higher leadership levels because they are capable of handling more complex information processing, research on creativity has conversely tended to regard job complexity as causal to individual levels of displayed creativity (see Shalley, Zhou, & Oldham, 2004 for a review). The argument is that contextual characteristics, such as the design of jobs (West & Farr, 1990), are of importance to the displayed level of creativity, in that more complex jobs are characterized by higher levels of autonomy, significance, identity, and skill variety, leading to higher levels of intrinsic motivation than simple or routine jobs (Amabile, 1996; Deci & Ryan, 1985). As such, more complex jobs should foster engagement with work tasks, leading to the development of more original and useful ideas. Furthermore, more complex jobs may actually demand creative outcomes by encouraging employees to focus simultaneously on multiple dimensions of their work, whereas simple or routine jobs may inhibit such a focus (Oldham & Cummings, 1996). Past correlational studies have tended to corroborate this hypothesized link between creativity and job complexity. Tierney and Farmer (2002, 2004) showed significant positive relations between supervisory ratings of creativity, and employee's job complexity, as measured from the Dictionary of Occupational Titles (Roos & Treiman, 1980). Using self-reported measures of complexity, Hatcher, Ross, and Collins (1989) also found significant positive relations between job complexity and the number of ideas suggested in an organizational setting. Amabile and Gryskiewicz (1989) illustrated the link between self-reported creativity and the level of freedom and challenge in work positions. Oldham and Cummings (1996) found that the interaction of individual creative skills and job complexity predicted contributions to individual suggestions made; employees produced the most creative work (made more suggestions) when they had appropriate creativity-relevant characteristics, and worked on complex, challenging jobs. Conversely, employees with low creativity-relevant skills did not benefit from enriching (more complex) jobs.

Given the cross-sectional nature of past research on the links between creativity and job complexity, the interpretation of causality between the two measures is debatable. As acknowledged by Oldham and Cummings (1996), it is possible that high creative performers are placed into more complex jobs, rather than job complexity leading to creative outcomes. The present study used data generated in two subsequent years to explore for longitudinal effects of stable individual innovativeness on leadership level, in order to try to tentatively estimate causality between the two constructs. It is possible that job complexity causes increased levels of innovative performance (through increased intrinsic motivation), but it is also possible that relatively stable levels of individual innovativeness is in part driving the placement of individuals into leadership positions with corresponding levels of complexity.

Further, individual innovativeness may prove a separate predictor of job complexity independent from intelligence, since complex jobs may demand creative skills (Oldham & Cummings, 1996) above and beyond intellectual capacity alone.

Finally, given individual creativity in part depends on domain expertise (Amabile, 1983; Weisberg, 1999), it is possible that the influence of individual innovativeness on leadership level increases with company tenure. Variability in domain expertise would be much higher at the lower level of company tenure (where a mix of novices and experts are being recruited), as opposed to the higher levels of company tenure (where, in effect, all leaders are experts). As such, domain experience would be an important predictor of leadership level for people new on the job, but as company tenure increases, experience would gradually be rendered less important. Similar findings have been shown in the IQ literature, where, for example, IQ becomes a better predictor of performance with higher levels of experience. The correlation between IQ and job performance ratings for incumbents increase with experience, in one study rising from 0.35 for people with 0–3 years experience going up to 0.59 for people with >12 years experience (McDaniel, 1985 quoted in Schmidt & Hunter, 2004). Conversely, the correlation between amount of experience and performance ratings for incumbents decrease with higher levels of job experience (McDaniel, Schmidt, & Hunter, 1988). Differences in experience are very important (0.49) among newly hired employees, but drops gradually to a low of 0.15 with 12+ years of experience.

In summary, the present study aimed to explore whether individual innovativeness and intelligence independently predict leadership level, and further whether the influence of individual innovativeness on leadership level increases with company tenure. Finally, following Oldham and Cummings (1996) and utilizing the longitudinal nature of the dataset, we explored whether an individual increase (or decrease) in leadership level led to an increase (or decrease) in perceived innovative behavior.

METHODS

Participants

Data were compiled from HR databases in a large international company with activities within multiple business segments, and in excess of 100.000 employees worldwide. All data were provided to the researchers for research purposes, provided the company could remain anonymous in any publication. Participants in this study were 4257 company leaders (1395 female, 2862 male), with a mean age of $M = 39.0$ ($SD = 8.4$; range: 22–68 years) representing 115 different nationalities, currently working in company branches in 117 different countries. They had a mean tenure in the company of $M = 10.8$ years ($SD = 7.7$; range: 0–45 years), and their occupational level, using the Mercer IPE (International Position Evaluation system; Mercer, 2017) scale reflecting job size and complexity, was $M = 54.6$ ($SD = 3.8$; range: 40–73).

Measures

Intelligence Test

All leaders were tested as a part of the recruitment procedure at the company using the in house intelligence test, developed by a leading global test developer. The test is similar to the Wonderlic (1961) test and is a 12-min test with 50 items: 25 verbal, 17 numerical, and 8 visual-spatial items. The tool is available in 68 different languages, and all employees take the test during recruitment following a standardized test procedure administered by HR professionals. Internal studies conducted by the organization show a test-retest correlation of 0.76, and find correlations to the commonly employed IQ test "Raven Advanced Progressive Matrices" ranging from 0.40 to 0.59. The test is applied globally by the organization, but only where it complies with local laws and regulations, and the test results are considered as one indicator together with other information about applicants. Hiring decisions are based on all information about applicants (CV, track record, education, performance, interview, references, etc.). Using intelligence measured at recruitment to test the present hypotheses is warranted, given that intelligence is considered a relatively stable construct across the lifespan, as indicated by both cohort-sequential analyses (e.g., Schaie & Hertzog, 1983), and longitudinal studies of differential stability (e.g., Larsen, Hartmann, & Nyborg, 2008).

Individual Innovativeness

Perception of leader innovativeness was scored using responses to the statement ("My leader is innovative and seeks out new ideas") from subordinates directly reporting to the leader on a 5-point Likert scale from "1" (strongly disagree) to "5" (strongly agree), as part of an employee satisfaction survey. The item denotes especially the innovative and ideational aspects of individual innovation. The use of a single item is less than optimal, but the large sample size renders it infeasible for the organization to include additional items in the survey. Construct validity and reliability tests are reported in the results section. The survey is conducted annually for the company by a global survey provider, and administered both online and in paper format, with employees responding anonymously and reports being generated when there is a minimum of five respondents per leader. The survey provider translated the survey for international use, with a subsequent translation check being carried out by bilingual company employees. By aggregating across subordinate ratings of leader innovativeness, it is possible to reduce the effect of outlier ratings, and test for the variance in ratings across subordinates. To reduce noise created from extreme cases where leaders were rated by only a single or few subordinates and in order to increase reliability of the innovativeness rating, we only included leaders who were rated by at least five subordinates. In 2009, the leaders were on average rated by 8.1 subordinate employees, for a total of 21,865 individual employees making innovativeness ratings of their direct leader, while in 2010, each leader was on average rated by 9.1 employees for a total of 26,769 employees rating their leader's innovativeness. The leaders were rated in 2009 and/or 2010, with 1303 leaders rated only in 2009, 1567 leaders rated only in 2010, and 1387 rated in both years. Both the combined sample and the subset rated in both 2009 and 2010 were utilized in the corresponding below analyses. Reliability, validity, and stability of the individual innovativeness measure are reported in the first part of the result section.

Leadership Level

Each leader's occupational level was collected by the company using the Mercer International Position Evaluation system (Mercer, 2017). This is widely used to assess the scope and complexity of jobs, to determine the appropriate compensation range, and gives an indication of the leader's hierarchical placement in the organization. Leaders are placed into occupational level bands with a corresponding title structure: Leaders below occupational level 53 are titled "Administrators," 53–55 are "Managers," 56–58 are "General Managers," 59–61 are "Directors," and 62 and above are "Executives." Higher level bands correspond to higher levels of job complexity. For the present analysis, these occupational level bands were assessed to be a valid aggregation of leadership levels, with similar levels of job complexity, and hence a useful grouping of occupational levels.

RESULTS

Reliability, Validity, and Stability of Individual Innovativeness

Validity tests displayed satisfactory construct validity of the individual innovativeness measure with Axtell et al.'s (2000, 2006) measure of individual innovativeness (reported in Christensen et al., 2017). Axtell et al.'s (2000, 2006) measure consists of two scales: *Suggestions* asks to which extent the respondent has proposed changes to various aspects of work, specifically (1) new targets or objectives, (2) new working methods or techniques, (3) new methods to achieve work targets, (4) new information or recording systems, (5) new products or product improvements, and (6) other aspects of their work ($r=0.78$ to individual innovativeness), and *implementations*, which cover the same aspects of work as the suggestions scale, but instead asks to which extent suggestions have been implemented ($r=0.69$ to individual innovativeness).

Reliability of the innovativeness ratings was assessed in two ways: While the employee satisfaction questionnaire was anonymous, a subset of the subordinates volunteered their identity, making it possible to estimate test-retest reliability across two sample years (see Christensen et al., 2017, for details). The test-retest reliability for leader innovativeness, where the same group of at least five subordinates rated the same leader for two consecutive years (2009 and 2010, respectively), was $r=0.68$. Overall, the subset of leaders who were rated in both 2009 and 2010 correlated $r=0.49$, but it should be noted that this estimate includes much more variability in the sample of raters, in that many of these leaders/subordinates would have changed position in the organization, or left (while new subordinates would have arrived). Overall, the average leader level of innovativeness was somewhat stable over a 1-year timespan.

Another reliability estimate was to identify leaders with multiple subordinates making ratings, and then randomly split the employees into two groups, making it possible to compare the average ratings of the two groups for the same leader. In effect this split-half measure constitutes a kind of interrater reliability for groups of raters, and it showed adequate reliability with at least five subordinates in each half $r=0.587$. With the criteria set to at least nine subordinates in each group (the approximate average number of direct reports from subordinates in our leader sample), the correlation was $r=0.72$, indicating a high level of agreement across subgroups.

Given the possibility that increased job complexity may influence creativity ratings positively, a number of tests were carried out to test whether a possible positive correlation between leadership level and innovativeness was caused by leadership level switches upwards (downwards) leading to higher (lower) innovativeness ratings (i.e., job complexity causing changes in individual innovativeness). We explored this using the subset of the leaders who switched position in the organization between 2009 and 2010, and noted whether this switch had been a move upwards or downwards in the organizational hierarchy. In so far as job complexity as an environmental factor has a positive effect on the judged level of innovativeness for leaders moving up in the hierarchy, but a negative effect on the innovativeness ratings of the leaders moving to a lower hierarchical level, that could support job complexity as a contextual factor affecting creative outcome in leader innovativeness perception scores. For leaders remaining in their position from 2009 to 2010, a paired t-test showed a slight increase in innovativeness scores over the 2 years $t(656) = 2.19$, $P < 0.03$ (mean 2009 = 3.99; mean 2010 = 4.03 on a 5-point scale). No significant differences could be detected for either leaders moving up, paired-$t(120) = 1.06$, $P = 0.29$ (mean 2009 = 3.97; mean 2010 = 3.92), or leaders moving down, paired-$t(56) = -0.32$, $P = 0.75$ (mean 2009 = 4.04; mean 2010 = 4.06) in the hierarchy over the 1-year time course. As such, no significant effect of changing job complexity was detected from 2009 to 2010 on leader innovativeness. This may in part be due to the reduced statistical power due to the small sample size, but tentatively it should be noted that if anything the directionality appears to be going in the opposing direction to that proposed by past research (Oldham & Cummings, 1996) which suggested that job complexity causes changes in creative output (i.e., slightly higher innovativeness scores when moving down in the hierarchy, and slightly lower innovativeness scores when moving up). In so far as job positions become less complex to perform by the leader with experience, it is counter to past research that innovativeness scores increase with leaders staying in their position. These results tentatively suggest that individual innovativeness is fairly stable over time, even in situations of contextual changes in job complexity.

Overall, the innovativeness measure used in the present study appears to be somewhat stable at the individual level across two distinct years and across samples of raters, making it suitable for predicting leadership level.

Intelligence, Innovativeness, and Leadership Level

To estimate the impact of innovativeness and intelligence on leadership level (job scope and complexity), multiple regression was carried out. Regressing occupational level onto innovativeness and intelligence with age and company tenure as covariates yielded the following results: Combined the four measures explained a significant proportion of the variance in manager occupational level, $R^2 = 0.37$, $F(4, 3921) = 585.58$, $P < 0.001$. Innovativeness significantly predicted leadership level ($\beta = 0.08$, $P < 0.001$), as did intelligence ($\beta = 0.36$, $P < 0.001$), age ($\beta = 0.45$, $P < 0.001$), and company tenure ($\beta = 0.07$, $P < 0.001$).

To examine whether the influence of intelligence and innovativeness on leadership level changes with company experience, we divided our sample into company tenure quartiles (see Table 1). We then ran individual regressions of age, intelligence, and innovativeness onto leadership level by tenure levels (see Table 2). Results indicated that for lower levels of tenure, age is an important predictor of leadership level (perhaps caused by recruitment of experienced leaders from outside the company), but this age effect diminishes for employees with more tenure. Intelligence and innovativeness significantly predict leadership level for all tenure levels, but with an increasing trend over tenure quartiles.

TABLE 1 Mean and SD for Intelligence, Innovativeness, and Age by Company Tenure Quartiles

Company Tenure	N	IQ Test Raw Score M (SD)	Innovativeness M (SD)	Age M (SD)
0–5 years	1119	24.85 (4.99)	3.94 (0.52)	37.04 (8.31)
6–9 years	1086	25.11 (5.34)	4.01 (0.49)	34.31 (5.88)
10–14 years	885	25.18 (5.21)	4.02 (0.50)	38.85 (6.03)
15+ years	900	25.61 (6.08)	3.98 (0.47)	47.60 (6.76)
Total	3990	25.14 (5.38)	3.98 (0.50)	39.00 (8.37)

TABLE 2 Regressing Occupational level onto Age, Intelligence, and Innovativeness by Company Tenure Quartiles

Company Tenure	F	R^2	Variable	B	β	t
0–5 years	$F(3,1063) = 346.30$	0.49	Age	0.29	0.64	29.45***
			Intelligence	0.20	0.27	12.40***
			Innovativeness	0.40	0.06	2.60**
6–9 years	$F(3,1079) = 167.62$	0.32	Age	0.25	0.44	17.47***
			Intelligence	0.23	0.36	14.42***
			Innovativeness	0.39	0.06	2.29*
10–14 years	$F(3,876) = 62.64$	0.18	Age	0.11	0.21	6.64***
			Intelligence	0.25	0.39	12.43***
			Innovativeness	0.74	0.11	3.69***
15+ years	$F(3,892) = 109.33$	0.27	Age	0.03	0.06	1.96
			Intelligence	0.33	0.49	16.90***
			Innovativeness	1.03	0.12	4.15***
Total	$F(4,3921) = 585.58$	0.37	Age	0.21	0.45	28.07***
			Intelligence	0.26	0.36	28.62***
			Innovativeness	0.65	0.08	6.62***
			Company tenure	0.03	0.07	4.17***

$*P < 0.05; **P < 0.01; ***P < 0.001.$

DISCUSSION

Combined, the results indicate that while many factors may influence the placement of individuals in a particular leadership level, two of the important factors are IQ and individual innovativeness. Individual innovativeness does, independently from IQ, predict leader placement into higher levels of the organizational hierarchy. This conclusion may help contextualize the predominantly negative stories of creative efforts in bureaucratic organizations: while creative frustration with bureaucratic structures with resulting motivation loss may predominate at lower levels, leaders placed into more complex jobs can make positive use of their individual capabilities. It may further comfort the creative individual currently stuck at the bottom of the pyramid, contemplating exit strategies: these results suggest that individual creativity is increasingly needed higher up in the organization, and these individual capabilities (together with intelligence) help predict at which leadership level leaders are positioned. With increasing company tenure, intelligence and innovativeness increase in their importance in predicting leadership level. Intelligence was the strongest predictor, but innovativeness was a separate and significant predictor as well, across all levels of company tenure. Interestingly, innovativeness displayed the strongest relation to leadership levels for the leaders with the most company tenure, suggesting that, like intelligence, the influence of innovativeness on leadership levels increases after significant company knowledge and experience is acquired—or perhaps that the higher IQ and innovativeness of the specific leader results in him/her acquiring the necessary content knowledge to increase in leadership level. The link between individual innovativeness and leadership level found in the present study tentatively challenges the assumption in past creativity research that high job complexity causes increased creative performance. Rather, the present study may be interpreted as tentative support to the converse explanation, that is, that individual innovativeness may be a fairly stable construct, where the correlation to job complexity (leadership level) could be a consequence of innovative individuals being placed into more complex jobs. Note, though, that it is also possible, that both causalities operate simultaneously. This would be the case if more complex jobs require increased individual creative capabilities to fulfill the position, and that the more complex job at the same time allow for increased display of these same creative capabilities.

The significant findings of individual innovativeness predicting leadership level hold promise for further examining the role of individual innovativeness in organizational behavior more generally. Further studies are needed to explore whether individual innovativeness predict promotions and career advancement more generally, and to what extent it is the skills involved in the early steps of innovation (such as idea generation, usually labeled creativity) or the later steps (such as idea development or implementation) that explains our findings. One important direction for future research is to look at the potential mediating role of personality in the relation between individual innovativeness and leadership level. The present analysis assumes that the documented link between innovativeness and leadership level is caused by innovative behavior in daily operations by the leaders. But past personality research has documented that leadership is associated with extraversion (Judge, Bono, Ilies & Gerhardt, 2002), that creative individuals (at least in some domains) are often more extraverted (Feist, 1998), and it has been documented that extraverted individuals more often get promoted (Ng, Eby, Sorensen, & Feldman, 2005). Therefore future research should consider whether (part of) the link between individual innovativeness and leadership level may be due to personality traits.

The present analysis was conducted in the context of a single international company working in multiple business segments. Given the case setting, it is not clear how the present findings will generalize to other companies in other business segments. It should be noted that the company business segments mainly cover typical production, distribution, and retailing domains. This is noteworthy because these domains are not considered typical creative industries in need of a high degree of innovation. Nonetheless, individual innovativeness as perceived by subordinates appeared as one factor predicting the placement in leadership levels. It may be hypothesized that the connection between innovativeness and leadership level could be even stronger (and the link between IQ and leadership level perhaps relatively weaker) in the so-called creative industries, or with jobs involving new product development. Naturally the present study has some limitations. The relationship between leadership level and IQ could possibly be confounded by the procedure used in the company for promotion. The company's knowledge of the importance of IQ in relationship to job performance and ability to handle increased complexity has resulted in increased attention to IQ and the use of IQ with respect to promotion. Part of the decision for promotion may sometimes be influenced by IQ level, thereby selecting higher IQ subjects into higher leadership levels. However, IQ is but one among many factors for promoting decisions, and other factors like past and current performance play a crucial role. For the present case, we have no reason to assume that a similar argument may be advanced for individual innovativeness, and thus it is possible that HR policies pushing for IQ estimates playing a part in matters of position filling could possibly act against effects of individual innovativeness in the present sample (thereby masking a potential larger true effect).

The current study does not contain an analysis of leaders leaving the company, but it can be expected that leaders leaving the company would be mixture of low performers (having their contracts terminated) and high performers (seeking new opportunities). It is unknown to which degree sample biases in these terminated or resigning leaders may confound some of our findings, although they are likely to cause a restriction of range. Future research should examine whether creative individuals more often leave bureaucratic organizations, and for what reason. Finally, given the single-company setting for the present sample, future research should examine whether these results generalize to other large bureaucratic corporations.

Implications

The present research suggests that leader individual innovativeness may be measured in a fairly simple manner, through subordinate ratings of their direct leader. Further, the results show that such a measure of individual innovativeness did have predictive value of placement in a real-life situation among leaders in a bureaucratic organization working within multiple (not usually termed creative) business domains. This would suggest that the level of individual innovativeness may be one important factor that organizations could attempt to measure, in matters of recruitment and placement into the organizational hierarchy. Furthermore, the present study documented that both intelligence and innovativeness predicted leadership level across various levels of tenure. It was not the case that individual innovativeness and intelligence was rendered irrelevant by company tenure. Rather, at all levels of tenure—even with 15 years company experience—individual innovativeness and intelligence predicted leadership level, evidencing the importance of the measures at all levels of experience.

References

Amabile, T. M. (1983). The social psychology of creativity: A componential conceptualization. *Journal of Personality and Social Psychology, 45*, 357–377.

Amabile, T. M. (1988). A model of creativity and innovation in organizations. In B. M. Staw & L. L. Cummings (Eds.), Vol. 10. *Research in organizational behavior* (pp. 123–167). Greenwich, CT: JAI Press.

Amabile, T. M. (1996). *Creativity in context*. Oxford: Westview Press.

Amabile, T. M. (1997). Motivating creativity in organizations: On doing what you love and loving what you do. *California Management Review, 40*(1), 39–58.

Amabile, T. M., Conti, R., Coon, H., Lazenby, J., & Herron, M. (1996). Assessing the work environment for creativity. *Academy of Management Journal, 39*(5), 1154–1184.

Amabile, T. M., & Gryskiewicz, N. D. (1989). The creative environment scales: Work environment inventory. *Creativity Research Journal, 2*, 231–252.

Anderson, N., De Dreu, C. K. W., & Nijstad, B. A. (2004). The routinization of innovation research: A constructively critical review of the state-of-the-science. *Journal of Organizational Behavior, 25*, 147–173.

Arvey, R. D. (1986). General ability in employment: A discussion. *Journal of Vocational Behavior, 29*, 415–420.

Axtell, C. M., Holman, D. J., Unsworth, K. L., Wall, T. D., Waterson, P. E., & Harrington, E. (2000). Shopfloor innovation: Facilitating the suggestion and implementation of ideas. *Journal of Occupational and Organizational Psychology, 73*, 265–285.

Axtell, C. M., Holman, D. J., & Wall, T. D. (2006). Promoting innovation: A change study. *Journal of Occupational and Organizational Psychology, 79*, 509–516.

Barron, F. (1961). Creative vision and expression in writing and painting. In D. W. MacKinnon (Ed.), *The creative person* (pp. 237–251). Berkeley: Institute of Personality Assessment Research, University of California.

Batey, M., & Furnham, A. (2006). Creativity, intelligence, and personality. A critical review of the scattered literature. *Genetic, Social, and General Psychology Monographs, 132*(4), 355–429.

Byrne, C. L., Mumford, M. D., Barrett, J. D., & Vessey, W. B. (2009). Examining the leaders of creative efforts: What do they do, and what do they think about? *Creativity and Innovation Management, 18*(4), 256–268.

Christensen, B. T., Hartmann, P., & Rasmussen, T. (2017). Threshold theory tested in an organizational setting: The relation between perceived innovativeness and intelligence in a large sample of leaders. *Creativity Research Journal, 29*(2), 188–193.

de Jong, J., & den Hartog, D. (2010). Measuring innovative work behavior. *Creativity and Innovation Management, 19*(1), 23–36.

Deci, E. L., & Ryan, R. M. (1985). *Intrinsic motivation and self-determination in human behavior.* New York: Plenum.

Dunne, D., & Dougherty, D. (2012). Organizing for change, innovation and creativity. In M. Mumford (Ed.), *Handbook of organizational creativity.* London: Academic Press.

Eisenberger, R., & Aselage, J. (2009). Incremental effects of reward on experienced performance pressure: Positive outcomes for intrinsic interest and creativity. *Journal of Organizational Behavior, 30*, 95–117.

Feist, G. J. (1998). A meta-analysis of personality in scientific and artistic creativity. *Personality and Social Psychology Review, 2*(4), 290–309.

George, J. M., & Zhou, J. (2001). When openness to experience and conscientiousness are related to creative behavior: An interactional approach. *Journal of Applied Psychology, 86*, 513–524.

Gottfredson, L. S. (1997). Why g matters: The complexity of everyday life. *Intelligence, 24*, 79–132.

Gottfredson, L. S. (2002a). Where and why g matters? Not a mystery. *Human Performance, 15*, 25–46.

Gottfredson, L. S. (2002b). G: Highly general and highly practical. In R. J. Sternberg & E. L. Grigorenko (Eds.), *The general factor of intelligence: How general is it?* Mahwah, NJ: Erlbaum.

Hatcher, L., Ross, T. L., & Collins, D. (1989). Prosocial behavior, job complexity, and suggestion contribution under gainsharing plans. *Journal of Applied Behavior Science, 25*, 231–248.

Hülsheger, U. R., Anderson, N., & Salgado, J. F. (2009). Team-level predictors of innovation at work: A comprehensive meta-analysis spanning three decades of research. *Journal of Applied Psychology, 94*, 1128–1145.

Jaussi, K. S., & Benson, G. (2012). Careers of the Creatives: Creating and managing the canvas. In M. Mumford (Ed.), *Handbook of organizational creativity.* London: Academic Press.

Jensen, A. R. (1980). *Bias in mental testing.* New York: Free Press.

Jensen, A. R. (1998). *The g factor: The science of mental ability.* Westport, CT: Praeger.

Judge, T. A., Bono, J. E., Ilies, R., & Gerhardt, M. W. (2002). Personality and leadership: a qualitative and quantitative review. *Journal of Applied Psychology, 87*(4), 765–780.

Judge, T. A., Colbert, A. E., & Ilies, R. (2004). Intelligence and leadership: A quantitative review and test of theoretical propositions. *Journal of Applied Psychology, 89*(3), 542–552.

Judge, T., Klinger, R. L., & Simon, L. S. (2010). Time is on my side: General mental ability, human capital, and extrinsic career success. *Journal of Applied Psychology, 95*(1), 92–107.

Kim, K. H. (2005). Can only intelligent people be creative? A meta-analysis. *Journal of Secondary Gifted Education, 16*, 57–66.

Kim, K. H., Cramond, B., & Vantassel-Baska, J. (2011). The relationship between creativity and intelligence. In J. C. Kaufman & R. J. Sternberg (Eds.), *The Cambridge handbook of creativity*. New York: Cambridge University Press.

Koseoglu, G., Liu, Y., & Shalley, C. E. (2017). Working with creative leaders: Exploring the relationship between supervisors' and subordinates' creativity. *The Leadership Quarterly, 28*(6), 798–811.

Larsen, L., Hartmann, P., & Nyborg, H. (2008). The stability of general intelligence from early adulthood to middle-age. *Intelligence, 36*(1), 29–34.

MacKinnon, D. W. (1962). The nature and nurture of creative talent. *American Psychologist, 17*, 484–495.

March, J. G. (1991). Exploration and exploitation in organizational learning. *Organization Science, 2*(1), 71–87.

McDaniel, M. A., Schmidt, F. L., & Hunter, J. E. (1988). Job experience correlates of job performance. *Journal of Applied Psychology, 73*, 327–330.

Mercer. (2017). *International Position Evaluation System (IPS)*. http://www.mercer.com/IPE (Accessed December 7, 2017).

Miron, E., Erez, M., & Naveh, E. (2004). Do personal characteristics and cultural values that promote innovation, quality, and efficiency compete or complement one another? *Journal of Organizational Behavior, 25*, 175–199.

Ng, T. W. H., Eby, L. T., Sorensen, K. L., & Feldman, D. C. (2005). Predictors of objective and subjective career success: A meta-analysis. *Personnel Psychology, 58*, 367–408.

Oldham, G. R., & Cummings, A. (1996). Employee creativity: Personal and contextual factors at work. *Academy of Management Journal, 39*(3), 607–634.

Randel, A. E., Jaussi, K. S., & Wu, A. (2011). When does being creative lead to being rated as creative? The moderating role of perceived probability of successfully bringing ideas to a Supervisor's attention. *Creativity Research Journal, 23*(1), 1–8.

Rego, A., Sousa, F., Cunha, M.P.e., Correia, A., & Saur-Amaral, I. (2007). Leder self-reported emotional intelligence and perceived employee creativity: An exploratory study. *Creativity and Innovation Management, 16*(3), 250–264.

Rickards, T., & Moger, S. (2006). Creative leaders: A decade of contributions from creativity and innovation management journal. *Creativity and Innovation Management, 15*(1), 4–18.

Roos, P. A., & Treiman, D. J. (1980). Worker functions and work traits for the 1970 U.S. census classification. In A. Miller (Ed.), *Work, jobs and occupations* (pp. 336–389). Washington, DC: National Academy Press.

Schaie, K. W., & Hertzog, C. (1983). Fourteen-year cohort-sequential analyses of adult intellectual development. *Developmental Psychology, 19*, 531–543.

Schmidt, F. L., & Hunter, J. E. (2004). General mental ability in the world of work: Occupational attainment and job performance. *Journal of Personality and Social Psychology, 86*(1), 162–173.

Shalley, C. E., Zhou, J., & Oldham, G. R. (2004). The effects of personal and contextual characteristics on creativity: Where should we go from here? *Journal of Management, 30*(6), 933–958.

Simonton, D. K. (2003). Scientific creativity as constrained stochastic behavior: The integration of product, person, and process perspectives. *Psychological Bulletin, 129*(4), 475.

Tierney, P., & Farmer, S. M. (2002). Creative self-efficacy: Potential antecedents and relationship to creative performance. *Academy of Management Journal, 45*, 1137–1148.

Tierney, P., & Farmer, S. M. (2004). The Pygmalion process and employee creativity. *Journal of Management, 30*, 413–432.

Tierney, P., & Farmer, S. M. (2011). Creative self-efficacy development and creative performance over time. *Journal of Applied Psychology, 96*(2), 277–293.

Weber, M. (1946). In H. H. Gerth & C. W. Mills (Eds.), *From Max Weber: Essays in sociology*. New York, NY: Oxford University Press.

Weisberg, R. W. (1999). Creativity and knowledge: A challenge to theories. In R. J. Sternberg (Ed.), *Handbook of creativity* (pp. 226–250). New York, NY: Cambridge University Press.

West, M. A., & Farr, J. L. (1990). Innovation at work. In M. West & J. Farr (Eds.), *Innovation and creativity at work: Psychological and organizational strategies* (pp. 3–13). Chichester: Wiley.

Wonderlic, E. F. (1961). *Wonderlic personnel test manual.* EF Wonderlic & Associates.

Zhou, J., & George, J. M. (2003). Awakening employee creativity: The role of leader emotional intelligence. *The Leadership Quarterly, 14,* 545–568.

Further Reading

Hennessey, B. A., Amabile, T. A., & Mueller, J. M. (2011). Consensual assessment. In M. A. Runco & S. R. Pritzker (Eds.), *Encyclopedia of creativity* (2nd ed.). Oxford: Elsevier.

14

The Role of Individual Differences in Group and Team Creativity

Lauren E. Coursey, Paul B. Paulus, Belinda C. Williams, Jared B. Kenworthy

University of Texas at Arlington, Arlington, TX, United States

INTRODUCTION

The vast majority of research in the domain of creativity has focused on the creativity of individuals and has uncovered many individual characteristics, tendencies, and personality traits related to creativity (see chapters in this volume). However, creativity also often occurs in social or group contexts (Paulus & Coskun, 2012; Paulus & Kenworthy, 2018; Reiter-Palmon, Wigert, & de Vreede, 2012). Most creative scholars, artists, and scientists develop their ideas based in part on prior intellectual contributions and interactions with their contemporaries (Farrell, 2001; John-Steiner, 2000; Snyder, 1989). Today the emphasis on teamwork and the need for a broad array of experts to solve challenging problems or develop new products has led to a reliance on creative activities in groups and teams. This literature has focused on a wide range of issues such as the processes involved in group creative activities and the conditions that predict, foster, or enhance group creativity. However, there has been only limited attention devoted to the role of individual differences in the collaborative creative process.

In this chapter, we will review this literature and develop a theoretical model for future research in this area. There are a variety of literatures that are relevant to our focus on individual creativity in group settings. There is a general literature on group creativity and team innovation that has focused on factors related to increased creativity (Paulus, Dzindolet, & Kohn, 2012; Reiter-Palmon et al., 2012). Research on diversity in groups and teams has examined the role of diversity of personal characteristics and abilities in enhancing performance (van Dijk, van Engen, & van Knippenberg, 2012). Research on small groups has examined the role of group composition and individual differences on performance (Levine & Moreland, 1998; Mann, 1959; Moreland, Levine, & Wingert, 1996; Moynihan & Peterson, 2004; Parks, 2012). Whereas many studies have examined the role of individual differences in individual creativity, relatively few have examined the role of individual differences in group and team creativity. We will touch on each of these literatures in developing a broad perspective on the role of individual differences in group creativity.

GROUP CREATIVITY

Much creative work is done by collaborative teams, and teamwork in general has been a steadily growing feature of modern organizations (Baer, Oldham, Jacobsohn, & Hollingshead, 2008; Paulus et al., 2012; Paulus & Kenworthy, 2018; Reiter-Palmon et al., 2012). Despite the general belief that group collaboration will lead to increased idea quantity and improved quality (Paulus, Dzindolet, Poletes, & Camacho, 1993; Stroebe, Diehl, & Abakoumkin, 1992), research has repeatedly shown that interactive groups produce fewer ideas overall, and fewer novel ideas, compared to similar numbers of noninteracting individuals, or nominal groups (Mullen, Johnson, & Salas, 1991). A number of social, cognitive, and motivational mechanisms may account for the productivity loss observed (Diehl & Stroebe, 1987; Paulus, Dugosh, Dzindolet, Coskun, & Putman, 2002). Social processes such as evaluation apprehension, social loafing, and downward comparison can impact creative motivation and decrease overall creative productivity (e.g., Diehl & Stroebe, 1987; Harari & Graham, 1975; Paulus & Dzindolet, 1993).

To reach high levels of creative performance, or synergy (exceeding the performance of the same number of solitary individuals—nominal groups), group members must overcome the motivational and social limitations inherent in collaborative work (see Bechtoldt, De Dreu, Nijstad, & Choi, 2010; Larson, 2009), which we discuss in greater detail later. If these limitations are overcome, idea sharing among group members can provide the cognitive stimulation necessary to realize the synergistic potential of group brainstorming (Nijstad & Stroebe, 2006; Paulus & Brown, 2003, 2007). Indeed, research has shown that when groups use effective interaction processes such as electronic brainstorming or brainwriting, group interaction can lead to higher creativity relative to nominal groups (Derosa, Smith, & Hantula, 2007; Korde & Paulus, 2017; Paulus & Yang, 2000).

One other way to more effectively tap group potential is to compose groups with members who have the ability and disposition to work effectively in creative groups. Creative employees have become an essential ingredient in any successful company (Puccio & Cabra, 2010). Creative synergy can be achieved, potentially, through the selection of team members with the skills and abilities necessary for the management of creative task work and teamwork (e.g., Tasa, Sears, & Schat, 2011). Various individual differences may drive behaviors directed toward accomplishing creative tasks and/or otherwise facilitating group social-emotional processes (Taggar, 2001). Further, overall group composition, or the specific cluster of individual differences within teams, may have a nonadditive impact on group performance through an influence on group processes. Group processes that enhance individual creative motivation promote open sharing of ideas, manage group conflict, and facilitate communication should lead to enhanced group creativity. In line with the input-process-output model (Hackman, 1987), individual group members' characteristics should contribute to the overall performance of the group through their impact on social-emotional and task-relevant group processes (Amabile, 1996; Mathisen, Martinsen, & Einarson, 2008; Taggar, 2002).

GROUP DIVERSITY AND CREATIVITY

The group composition issue is related to the topic of diversity in groups and teams. It is typically assumed that diversity in groups is beneficial for creativity and will lead to synergistic effects (Mannix & Neale, 2005; Paulus, van der Zee, & Kenworthy, 2018). Group homogeneity is cited as one reason interactive groups may fail to outperform nominal groups (Nijstad & De Dreu, 2002). Groups will likely find it difficult to achieve synergy when additional members do not contribute new knowledge or insight. Diversity is thought to increase group creativity through the introduction of nonoverlapping expertise, unique perspectives, and varied experiences. Thus group diversity is expected to produce enhanced cognitive stimulation and activate diverse semantic networks. However, there is only limited evidence for the synergistic benefits of demographic and functional diversity. For instance, in the research on diversity in teams, there is little evidence for the effects of demographic diversity but some evidence for the positive effects of functional or expertise diversity (Bell, Villado, Lukasik, Belau, & Briggs, 2011; Paulus & van der Zee, 2015; van Dijk et al., 2012). However, in the area of group creativity in particular, there has been some evidence that demographic diversity can indeed enhance creativity (cf., Paulus & van der Zee, 2015). The key may be the extent to which the diversity is relevant to the creative task. Obviously, a dimension of diversity that is not related to nonoverlapping knowledge and experience about a particular issue or problem is not likely to lead to enhanced creativity. For example, a group with diversity along the gender or sexual orientation dimensions may not be as creative as a group with strong ethnic diversity if the task is to generate creative solutions to community-police relations. In fact, Hülsheger, Anderson, and Salgado (2009) found that, across 10 studies included in a meta-analysis of innovation at work, job-relevant diversity was positively related to team innovation in the workplace. However, background diversity, or nonrelevant diversity, was not associated with team innovation.

Although group diversity has the potential to heighten cognitive flexibility, diversity is a double-edged sword and many groups struggle with the social costs incurred. Williams and O'Reilly (1998) offer two opposing perspectives on the relationship between diversity and group performance. The information/decision-making perspective represents the aforementioned belief that diverse groups lead to enhanced performance due to a broader range of available knowledge. The social categorization perspective, on the other hand, addresses the tendency for faultlines (Thatcher & Patel, 2011) and conflict (e.g., Pelled, Eisenhardt, & Xin, 1999) to emerge in diverse groups, in turn, leading to the deterioration of group member relations and disrupted performance (see De Dreu & Weingart, 2003). According to self-categorization theory (Turner, Hogg, Oakes, Reicher, & Wetherell, 1987), people naturally categorize the self and others into groups that create "us" and "them" distinctions, especially when situational cues make those categories meaningful and salient. Once salient, these distinctions form the basis for in-group-favoring norms, negative out-group attitudes and bias as individuals identify with and derive self-esteem from their in-group (Tajfel & Turner, 1986). Thus it is not surprising that much literature supports the benefit of demographic homogeneity on group performance (Levine & Moreland, 1998).

A major limitation of the diversity research is that it does not focus on how the creativity (or other traits) of individual group members influences the processes and outcomes of the collaborative creative process. Instead, the research questions typically center around demonstrating the effects of varying types and degrees of diversity. The research literatures we will review later provide a more focused picture on how individual differences in various characteristics may influence group creativity.

FACTORS INFLUENCING THE ROLE OF INDIVIDUAL DIFFERENCES IN GROUPS

Although there is an extensive literature on individual differences in group performance, the literature in the domain of group and team creativity is limited. Given the existing knowledge of the individual characteristics related to creativity, a straightforward assumption would be that these same characteristics would predict increased creativity in group settings. Obviously, the more creative people there are in a group, the more one would expect highly creative outcomes. However, this may not always be the case. In evaluating the potential contribution of research on individual differences in team creativity, it is important to consider a number of factors that will influence the role of individual differences in creative groups.

CONSTRAINT

One of the major factors that will limit the predictive power of individual differences is the extent to which the group or team interaction process constrains the ability of group members to freely contribute their ideas within the time provided. In many group creativity studies in which group members share ideas verbally in a short period of time, only one person can talk at one time. The inability to share ideas as they come to mind—*production blocking*—has been found to be a major factor in limiting group creativity in such contexts (Nijstad & Stroebe, 2006) and should also weaken the predictive power of individual differences. The impact of individual difference factors should be more evident in paradigms that do not constrain idea sharing, such as electronic brainstorming or brainwriting (Paulus & Kenworthy, 2018). Group or team interactions that occur asynchronously should also facilitate the impact of individual difference factors.

Social Context

Some individual difference factors may be particularly influential in group contexts. For example, social interaction anxiety (Leary & Kowalski, 1993) should have little impact on individual creativity (except in cases of creative performances in front of audiences) but a strong effect in groups (Camacho & Paulus, 1995). However, very few studies have compared the relative impact of individual differences on the performance of the same individuals (or groups of individuals with similar traits) in group settings versus alone. For example, Putman (2001) found no differential effects for the impact of a variety of personality traits on the performance of individuals compared to groups.

There are several factors that could potentially differentially influence the impact of individual differences on group performance. For example, on a simulated interaction task, teams composed of extraverted or agreeable members performed best under cooperative conditions. Under competitive conditions teams low in agreeableness and extraversion performed best (Beersma et al., 2003). Individual differences related to social interaction settings such as social anxiety and extraversion should be more strongly related to task performance in face-to-face settings than in computer-mediated interactions. However, we know of no studies that have examined this possibility.

Task Type

Group composition effects will also depend on the type of task (Levine & Moreland, 1998; Steiner, 1972). On simple additive tasks in which people can contribute independently, the group average may be a good predictor of the group's performance. For conjunctive tasks in which the performance of the least able person determines the outcome, only that person's performance will matter. For example, consider a group creativity task requiring that each member generate a certain number of ideas and pass them on to other group members. In such a case, if a group contains just one member with strong evaluation apprehension, who hesitates to share ideas out of fear of judgment, that group will have relatively poor performance.

By contrast, in the case of disjunctive tasks, in which the most capable person determines group success, only the performance of the best person predicts group success. If group members in this case generate creative ideas, and then select the best ideas from among those generated, then the presence of a group member with strong evaluation apprehension may not have much impact on the productivity and creativity of the group unless this happens to be the most creative group member. Of course, in real-world settings most tasks do not fall neatly in those categories, and for most group creativity tasks, the participation and interaction of the group members is a critical factor.

Creativity Phases

The different phases of the group creative process may be differentially affected by group composition. For example, Harvey (2013) found that deep-level diversity was related to more divergent contributions but that it hindered the convergent contributions (elaborations, building, combining). In a similar vein, groups that are diverse in personal characteristics related to creativity may be differentially effective in the divergent and convergent stages. Those who are good divergent thinkers should be most influential in the idea generation stage and those who are good "builders" should be most influential in the convergent phase of generating some final product from among the many shared ideas. For example, extraverts may be less inhibited in group contexts and make more contributions during the divergent phase. However, introverts may be more reserved and reflective during the divergent phase, but may make more effective contributions during the building and integration processes.

GROUP COMPOSITION EFFECTS

In their review of the literature concerning personality and groups, Moynihan and Peterson (2004) outline different frameworks for considering the impact of group composition. An additive approach assumes a general effect of the trait on performance without much concern for type of task and type of context. The contingent approach is concerned with examining the moderating effects of task type and context on the relationship between traits and performance outcomes. The configural approach considers the constellation of different traits and how some combinations might be more optimal than others. Simply having two highly creative and two low creative individuals in a group should lead to lower performance compared to a group with four creatives, presuming optimal group processes. However, if the group members differ in the task approaches, creativity styles, or interpersonal dispositions, more complex outcomes are possible, depending on the task.

Some research suggests that high performers will move in the direction of low performers (Paulus & Dzindolet, 1993). For example, there is evidence that low socially anxious individuals move their performance downward in the direction of high socially anxious individuals in brainstorming groups (Camacho & Paulus, 1995). This is most likely the case in situations in which there is not a high level of internal or external motivation for the task (Paulus & Dzindolet, 2008). As to interactive influences, the issue of primary interest is whether certain combinations will lead to higher levels of group creativity than others.

From our perspective, it is indeed important to assess the contingent and configural approaches. Our concern in this chapter is with creativity tasks. However, the literature on the effects of different traits on group performance, in general, is also of interest as it may help fill the gaps in the limited literature in the creativity domain. Thus in our review we will take a broad look at traits that affect group or team performance, highlighting studies with creativity measures. After the review we will suggest a broad model for the role of traits on group/team creativity.

GROUP COMPOSITION AND PROCESSES

There is an extensive literature on individual difference factors that are associated with individual creativity. Although there is also a literature on the role of individual differences in group or team creativity, it is much less extensive, as noted previously. A major focus of this research has been on the cognitive and social processes related to enhanced creativity.

However, it is recognized that individual differences will influence group and team creativity (e.g., De Dreu, Nijstad, & van Knippenberg, 2008). In a way, it would seem obvious that a group composed of individuals who are individually likely to be creative will demonstrate a high level of creativity. This would seem consistent with much research on group and team performance in which the average ability of the members predicts the group outcome (Devine & Philips, 2001).

According to Moreland et al. (1996), group composition effects depend on salience of the personal characteristics, the person's visibility in the group, and the degree of social integration (degree to which the group has environmental, cognitive, behavioral, and affective bonds) of the group. The effects of personal characteristics are expected to be stronger with high salience and visibility. With more integrated groups, more complex interactions among personal characteristics are likely. However, very few studies, other than those on demographic diversity, have allowed for an assessment of those factors in relation to personal characteristics and group creativity.

PERSONALITY

Personality, the relatively enduring characteristics of an individual, represents the unique and relatively stable patterns in affect, behavior, and cognitions (McCrae & Costa, 1995). We will focus on the Five Factor Model (Costa, McCrae, & Dye, 1991; Goldberg, 1999; McCrae and John, 1992)—Openness to Experience, Extraversion, Conscientiousness, Agreeableness, and Neuroticism—and its relationship with creative behaviors and performance. Those high in Openness can be described as curious, imaginative, and nonconforming, whereas those high in Conscientiousness are typically orderly, structured, and norm-abiding. Extraverts tend to be gregarious and outgoing, and those high in Agreeableness are trusting, warm, and cooperative. Finally, Neuroticism, compared to emotional stability, is characterized by chronic feelings of anxiety, impulsivity, and self-doubt. The five factors have been linked to job performance in general (primarily Conscientiousness) and creative performance specifically (primarily Openness), although the effects are somewhat inconsistent. Currently, there is little research on the relationship between neuroticism and group creativity. Some researchers have posited that the traits of neuroticism that mirror psychopathology (e.g., anxiety), might lead to improved creativity in individuals, pointing to the theories regarding creative geniuses (see Fürst and Lubart, 2017; Simonton, 2017). There is indeed some evidence that for a relationship between psychopathology and creativity (Baas, Nijstad, Boot, & De Dreu, 2016). However, this relationship has not been explored at the group level.

Personality at the group level poses somewhat of a measurement challenge. To determine a group's personality, should one use a combination or average of each of the five factors? Some researchers have discussed the measurement of group personality and its impact on creativity in greater depth (e.g., Litchfield, Gilson, & Shalley, 2017). Thus we will not focus on it here. Instead, we discuss the findings of the relevant personality factors on group creativity.

Openness to Experience

Openness is the trait most consistently associated with creativity (Batey, Chamorro-Premuzic, & Furnham, 2010; da Costa, Páez, Sánchez, Garaigordobil, & Gondim, 2015; Feist, 1998). In a meta-analysis of 83 studies, Feist (1998) found that artists were a full standard deviation higher in Openness, compared to nonartists, and that Openness also predicted creativity among scientists. Openness is related to performance on a variety of divergent thinking measures (Furnham & Bachtiar, 2008; King, McKee Walker, & Broyles, 1996). It is easy to see that Openness may reflect a more flexible cognitive style that allows one to overcome fixedness and generate unique solutions (Feist, 1998). Further, Openness may contribute to creativity through its potential to increase the variety and diversity of experiences and knowledge from which an individual draws inspiration (Baer et al., 2008; McCrae & Costa, 1995). Those open to new cultures, ideas, and experiences may have an enhanced ability to form novel connections. The relationship between aggregate, group-level Openness, and creative performance has not been extensively studied. If Openness is closely linked to creativity at the individual level, one may expect that those groups highest in aggregate Openness might be the most creative. As such, high mean and minimum levels of Openness should be associated with higher creative performance. However, some research suggests that heterogeneity of Openness is important, as low Openness facilitates the convergent innovation processes, such as combining, building, and selecting ideas. In a sample of 31 graduate project teams, Schilpzand, Herold, and Shalley (2011) found groups that were heterogeneous in Openness, with at least one member who was low on Openness, produced the most creative final projects. Low variability in group Openness, on the other hand, may reduce shared exchange within task groups (Bond & Shiu, 1997), thus possibly leading to decreased group creativity.

Extraversion

At the individual level, the level of Extraversion is often correlated with creative behaviors (Hoff, Carlsson, & Smith, 2012). Although introversion is often associated with creativity (Eysenck, 1995; Feist, 1998), mixed effects have been found, perhaps due to the various ways of measuring creativity (Batey & Furnham, 2006). Batey and Furnham (2006) concluded that Extraversion is positively related to divergent thinking (Martindale & Dailey, 1996), but that many creativity tasks would benefit from the sustained introspection that is typical of introverts. Feist (1998) found that Extraversion predicted creativity among scientists, but did not distinguish between artists and nonartists. Truly creative individuals may need to balance social stimulation and quiet reflection (Feist, 1998). Thus heterogeneity along the dimension of Extraversion may be optimal (Csikszentmihályi, 1997) in creative groups.

The overall proportion of various individual differences within the group may be particularly important, as well as member complementarity and diversity. For example, extraverts may facilitate communication, but too many extraverts may lead to low task focus. Thus it is not surprising that Extraversion can have a negative impact on group-level outcomes (Bolin & Neuman, 2006). However, Barry and Stewart (1997) found that a moderate number of extraverts predicted the best group problem-solving performance. A greater number of extraverts in problem-solving groups led to less task focus. High levels of off-task communication may be particularly detrimental in face-to-face brainstorming groups that are likely to suffer from production blocking (Dugosh, Paulus, Roland, & Yang, 2000). As noted, other research suggests that group-level heterogeneity or complementarity in Extraversion may be beneficial (Barrick, Stewart, Neubert, & Mount, 1998). Although Extraversion is related to preference for teamwork in general (Tekleab & Quigley, 2014), among MBA project teams, individual-team mismatch on Extraversion predicted self-rated attraction toward the team (Kristof-Brown, Barrick, & Stevens, 2005). Barrick et al. (1998) further report that team heterogeneity in Extraversion predicted increased social cohesion. van Vianen and De Dreu (2001), on the other hand, found that heterogeneity in Extraversion was unrelated to either social or task cohesion among student teams and drilling crews.

Agreeableness and Conscientiousness

Bell's (2007) meta-analytic review showed that mean-level Extraversion, Agreeableness, and Conscientiousness predicted team performance in field studies. Further, higher minimum-levels of Agreeableness and Conscientiousness were associated with higher team performance, suggesting that moderately high levels of Agreeableness and Conscientiousness are essential to group work. Halfhill, Nielsen, Sundstrom, and Weilbaecher (2005) found that both mean and minimum levels of Agreeableness and Conscientiousness predicted team performance among military service teams. van Vianen and De Dreu (2001) also found that minimum levels of Agreeableness and Conscientiousness were correlated with performance of student and drilling teams. Others have found that Agreeableness, Conscientiousness, and emotional stability (i.e., low Neuroticism) significantly predict team performance (Hough, 1992; Mount, Barrick, & Stewart, 1998). In order to meet task demands, groups may require the high levels of task-focus and socioemotional maintenance that conscientious, agreeable, and emotionally stable members provide.

At the group level, conscientious group members facilitate group performance primarily through task-related rather than social contributions (Stewart, Fulmer, & Barrick, 2005). In fact, highly conscientious individuals who lack interpersonal skills may have difficulty working collaboratively (Witt, Burke, Barrick, & Mount, 2002). On the other hand, conscientious group members may be particularly adept at assisting group members to complete tasks (Porter et al., 2003). For structured, routine tasks, the benefit of Conscientiousness is clear, but when it comes to creative tasks specifically, conscientious group members may inhibit performance (Batey et al., 2010). Because individuals high in Conscientiousness rigidly adhere to convention and norms, Conscientiousness is thought to reduce creative motivation and potential (Baer et al., 2008). Indeed, in Feist's (1998) analysis, artists were found to be significantly lower in Conscientiousness compared to nonartists. Despite the fact that Conscientiousness is positively related to a number of workplace performance measures (Barrick & Mount, 1991), the nature and demands of many creative tasks may be incompatible with the traits, tendencies, and behaviors of highly conscientious individuals. Although the achievement striving associated with Conscientiousness could enhance task focus, the structured and systematic tendencies of highly conscientious individuals could inhibit or preclude the cognitive flexibility that is necessary for idea generation and other divergent thinking activities (LePine, 2003; Reiter-Palmon, Illies, & Kobe-Cross, 2009; Robert & Cheung, 2010). Alternatively, due to heightened achievement motivation, groups high in Conscientiousness may be less likely to engage in social loafing, and thereby experience increased creative productivity. Groups that contain members low in Conscientiousness (Barrick et al., 1998) or which have high heterogeneity of Conscientiousness (Halfhill et al., 2005) may also see more group conflict. Group conflict may or may not increase creative performance, depending on the nature of the conflict (task vs relational; Paulus et al., 2018). Moderate amounts of conflict could facilitate the early creative process (Farh, Lee, & Farh, 2010; Kratzer, Leenders, & van Engelen, 2006). Unfortunately, few researchers have examined the relationship between group-level Conscientiousness and performance. However, some research suggests that social norms (e.g., creativity-promoting climate) and explicit task instructions may moderate the relationship between group creativity and group-level conscientiousness (Feist, 2010; George & Zhou, 2001; Robert & Cheung, 2010).

Agreeableness is thought to primarily influence social-emotional contributions to teamwork. At the individual level, the relationship between Agreeableness and creativity is inconsistent (da Costa et al., 2015). However, the link between Agreeableness and positive team processes is robust (Barrick et al., 1998; Neuman & Wright, 1999). Among a sample of military service teams, group-level Agreeableness and Conscientiousness interacted to predict performance, such that Conscientiousness predicted high performance only when Agreeableness was also high (Halfhill et al., 2005).

Much of the brainstorming research has focused on the extent to which group interaction enhances performance relative to the summed performance of individuals generating ideas alone (viz., nominal groups). These studies have found some evidence for such synergistic effects (see Paulus & Kenworthy, 2018, for a review). However, only a few studies have examined whether the interactive effects of personal dispositions in groups will produce an outcome different than that for nominal groups. Putman (2001) examined the role of interpersonal dominance (Ray, 1981) and the Big Five personality traits (Goldberg, 1999) in individual and group brainstorming. At the level of individuals, the number of ideas generated was positively correlated with Extraversion and intellect/imagination. At the group level, the number of high scorers (on Extraversion and intellect/imagination) in each group was related to number of ideas generated. To analyze the impact of variation in traits for both interactive and nominal groups, Putman calculated the extent to which particular deviations among trait scores in the groups (i.e., trait heterogeneity within the group) were related to the number of ideas from the overall mean for the sample. In no case was the impact of the deviations greater for the groups than for individuals. For example, the effects of deviations in Extraversion were the same for interactive groups and nominal groups. Thus there was no evidence of any special interactive effects in groups.

GROUP VERSUS INDIVIDUAL PERFORMANCE EFFECTS

Three other studies, however, have provided some evidence for interactive effects. Camacho and Paulus (1995) examined the performance of those high and low in interaction anxiety (Leary & Kowalski, 1993) for both nominal and interactive groups. Interactive groups low in interaction anxiety generated more ideas than those high on that trait. There was no difference in the performance of nominal groups that were low or high in interaction anxiety. Thus this is an example of a trait that is sensitive to the interaction context, not surprisingly. Larey and Paulus (1999) examined the role of preference for working in groups. Groups composed of individuals with a high preference for working in groups generated more ideas than those with a low preference. In the case of nominal groups, those composed of low preference for working in groups generated more ideas than those with a high preference. Nakui, Paulus, and van der Zee (2011) composed groups that varied in the extent to which they had a positive attitude to diversity. Groups that had a positive attitude to diversity performed better in groups that were diverse in language and ethnicity. Those who had a low preference performed better in homogeneous groups.

COGNITIVE ORIENTATIONS

In addition to personality characteristics, collaborative creativity is also influenced by various cognitive orientations or styles, self-beliefs, and differences in information processing. We now explore the potential role of these orientations in predicting group creative efforts and outputs.

Divergent versus Convergent Thinking Styles

Brown, Tumeo, Larey, and Paulus (1998) examined interactions between those with convergent and divergent thinking styles. Divergent thinkers tend to have increased flexibility (i.e., switching from one ideational category to another), whereas convergent thinkers tend to stay within categories and tap them more deeply before moving to another category. They conducted a number of simulations and found that pairs of divergent thinkers would indeed generate more ideas than two convergent thinkers. However, when a divergent thinker in the simulation was matched with a convergent partner, their idea generation increased. When a convergent brainstormer switched to a divergent partner, their performance declined. Thus in groups with different styles of interacting, some people may benefit, but others may be hindered. Such implications have yet to be tested empirically with real dyads or groups.

Need for Structure

Personal need for structure (PNS) is defined by Neuberg and Newsom (1993) as an individual's desire for simple structure or the chronic simplification of complex information in order to achieve a reduced cognitive load. Based on our previous discussion that Openness to Experience is a predictor of creative performance (Feist, 2010; Silvia, 2005), the need for structure might seem counterintuitive as a candidate for increasing creativity. There is also the general view that creative individuals are unencumbered or free and that creative tasks are unstructured.

However, recent research on PNS has shown that free, unstructured creative tasks are not the only ways of measuring creativity. Specifically, PNS has been shown to predict creative performance in specific situations; individuals high in PNS will benefit from a highly structured task, resulting in creative performance benefits. When high task structure involves a noncreative task, by contrast, creative performance decreased regardless of level of PNS (Rietzschel, Slijkhuis, & Van Yperen, 2014). Further, individuals that were high in PNS favored the high task structure and were more likely to self-select this approach when able. Rietzschel, De Dreu, and Nijstad (2007) studied the moderating role of personal fear of invalidity (PFI) on PNS and creativity. They found that PFI—which captures the extent to which an individual is worried about the consequences of a decision error—moderates the relationship between PNS and creative performance. When levels of PFI were low, PNS was positively related to creative performance, but PNS was negatively related to creative performance at high levels of PFI. The authors argue that if individuals are hindered by their own anxiety and self-doubt, this will lead to decreased performance. On the other hand, individuals low in PNS, when presented with social schema-inconsistent imagery, showed an increase in divergent thinking (Goclowska, Baas, Crisp, & De Dreu, 2014). These findings are potentially important when considering the impact of individual differences on group/team creativity. Specifically, if an individual high in PNS is presented with inconsistent information or is experiencing self-doubt, this can lead to decreased creative performance. Research has yet to explore the impact this might have on a collaborative outcome. One can deduce, however, that creative output might be decreased by the inclusion of group members who represent an interpersonal or ego threat. Research addressing PNS and creativity is not widespread, but its mixed findings and potential importance provide a basis for continued investigation.

Creative Self-Efficacy

Self-efficacy, or domain-specific capacity beliefs, are integral to self-motivation and task perseverance (Bandura, 1997; Bandura & Cervone, 1983). Creative self-efficacy, specifically, is the belief that one has the capacity to perform creative work effectively (Tierney & Farmer, 2002). Given the challenges inherent in creative production, individuals must be driven and resilient in order to realize their creative potential. Creative self-efficacy beliefs have been shown to predict creative performance evaluations across industries, above and beyond more general work self-efficacy (Tierney & Farmer, 2002) and Openness to Experience (Jaussi, Randel, & Dionne, 2007). Creative self-efficacy should, likewise, help groups to overcome the factors that inhibit creative synergy (Taggar, 2018). Although groups should provide the increased informational resources and varied perspectives to promote creative stimulation, many groups fail to capitalize on these resources (De Dreu, Nijstad, Bechtoldt, & Baas, 2011). Richter, Hirst, van Knippenberg, and Baer (2012) found that membership in a functionally diverse group predicted higher individual creativity only among members with high creative self-efficacy. The authors argue that creative self-efficacy predicts one's propensity to benefit from the group's informational resources. High creative self-efficacy may increase the likelihood that group members possess the confidence to openly share unusual ideas.

The link between creative self-efficacy beliefs and idea sharing or evaluation apprehension has not been tested. However, narcissists—those who tend to have very high confidence—pitched their ideas with more enthusiasm, leading to higher *perceptions* of creativity among evaluators (Goncalo, Flynn, & Kim, 2010). In a follow-up study, Goncalo et al. (2010) found that narcissists may facilitate group creativity up to a point, but groups with too high a group narcissism score showed diminishing creativity.

At the group level, collective creative self-efficacy is the belief that the *group* is capable of accomplishing creative goals (Shin & Zhou, 2007). Collective creative self-efficacy is distinct from individual creative efficacy; an individual with high individual creative efficacy may not believe that the group is capable of creative performance. Collective creative efficacy may influence the degree to which cross-fertilization of ideas occurs (Shin & Zhou, 2007). Group members must have the motivation to overcome social loafing tendencies and evaluation apprehension in order to share, combine, and elaborate on ideas. Such motivations are likely enhanced by group efficacy beliefs. Further, efficacy beliefs interaction with personality to predict team performance. Group personality composition interacted with collective creative efficacy to predict team creativity among student management teams (Baer et al., 2008). Group level Extraversion (high), Openness (high), and Conscientiousness (low) predicted team creative performance only when collective creative efficacy was high. Although not specific to creativity, Tasa et al. (2011) found that collective efficacy promoted team performance primarily through its relationship with teamwork, rather than performance management behavior. Collective efficacy predicted team-level interpersonal support, which in turn, predicted team performance. The relationship between collective creative efficacy and task work has not been examined. Shin and Zhou (2007) argue that collective creative efficacy promotes open sharing of ideas. However, teamwork versus task work behaviors were not explicitly measured.

Information Processing and Motivation

Individual difference factors in information processing in groups have been emphasized by the Motivated Information Processing model (MIP-G, De Dreu et al., 2008; Nijstad, Bechtoldt, & Choi, 2018; Nijstad & De Dreu,

2012). This model highlights the differing impacts of epistemic motivation (motivation to process information) and social motivation. Epistemic motivation is presumably influenced both by external conditions, such as accountability and time pressure, and by personal characteristics, such as need for cognition or Openness to Experience. In regard to social motivation, a distinction is made between the extent to which group members prioritize group outcomes over individual outcomes (pro-social) or individual outcomes over group outcomes (pro-self). Social motivation can also be influenced both by individual inclinations (e.g., Agreeableness) and external factors, such as a cooperative task structure. Group performance on cognitive or creativity tasks should be best when both epistemic and social motivation are high. Moreover, benefits are most likely when the task requires input from all members and provides sufficient time for such efforts. Bechtoldt et al. (2010) also demonstrated that a combination of high epistemic motivation and prosocial orientation led to the highest level of individual creativity in groups.

The research on need for closure is consistent with this perspective since high need for closure should be related to reduced willingness to carefully process information in groups. Indeed, it has been found to be related to reduced creativity in groups (Chirumbolo, Livi, Mannetti, Pierro, & Kruglanski, 2004; Chirumbolo, Mannetti, Pierro, Areni, & Kruglanski, 2005). Research on the positive impact of cohesion and psychological safety on team innovation is also consistent with this model (e.g., Hülsheger, Anderson, & Salgado, 2009).

Finally, need for cognition (NfC; Cacioppo & Petty, 1982) refers to individual differences in the preference for deep effortful cognitive processing. Those high in NfC are intrinsically motivated to seek out and analyze information, and to enjoy reasoning and complex problem solving (Cacioppo, Petty, Feinstein, & Jarvis, 1996). Past research has demonstrated a positive relationship between high NfC and creative performance, particularly in unconstrained tasks (Butler, Scherer, & Reiter-Palmon, 2003; Dollinger, 2003; Wu, Parker, & de Jong, 2014). However, results are mixed with some researchers finding that NfC is related to certain indices of creativity (e.g., quality of ideas) but not to others (e.g., originality; Hunter, Bedell-Avers, Hunsicker, Mumford, & Ligon, 2008; Watts, Steele, & Song, 2017). Task constraints may explain some of these inconsistencies. For instance, Butler et al. (2003) found that task objectives, or constraints, diminished the effect of NfC on flexibility and fluency, suggesting that task structure may compensate for low-NfC brainstormers. To our knowledge, no research has examined the link between NfC and creativity within a group context. It seems likely that those high in NfC would possess the intrinsic motivation to carefully process group members' ideas, perhaps enhancing cross-fertilization and idea combination. Further, those high in NfC may be less likely to engage in social loafing. More work is needed to examine the effects of NfC on creative group processes.

INDIVIDUAL DIFFERENCES DURING THE CONVERGENT PHASE

Creativity is commonly defined as the generation of ideas that are both novel and useful (Amabile, 1996; Runco, 2004), with innovation described as the successful implementation of creative ideas or solutions (West & Richter, 2008). It has been long recognized that the innovative process involves a number of stages moving from divergent idea generation to idea evaluation, selection, and eventual implementation (Basadur, Basadur, & Licina, 2012; Rietzschel, Nijstad, & Stroebe, 2006, 2018; Wallas, 1976). Thus it is important to understand the role of individual differences at the level of each of the stages. Most laboratory studies of group creativity have focused on the divergent ideation stage and thus have been unable to examine this issue. Studies of team innovation may deal with outcomes that are the result of interactions over multiple stages, but they have not examined the unique role of individual differences on the different stages. There has, however, been some research on the impact of individual differences on the idea selection process. A study by Silvia (2008) found that Openness to Experience enhanced both idea generation and the selection of the most creative ideas. Several other studies have also found that people who generate the most ideas tend to be good at judging which ideas are most creative (Basadur, Runco, & Vega, 2000; Runco & Dow, 2004; Runco & Smith, 1992). Thus it seems likely that any personal characteristic that enhances idea generation also enhances the ability to discern which ideas are most creative. However, it is also important to discern the extent to which ideas are feasible. A study by Fürst, Ghisletta, and Lubart (2016) found that individuals who were high on Agreeableness were better at the process of critically evaluating ideas. Therefore it may be important for a group to have a mixture of members so that some excel in selecting creative ideas and others in making them more feasible (Rietzschel et al., 2018). Putman (2001) also examined a decision phase in which participants/groups selected the top ideas. Those who were high on Agreeableness had ideas that were more feasible and which occurred with a higher frequency.

Another personal characteristic that has been shown to influence both the generation and evaluation process is regulatory focus (Higgins, 1997). Individuals with a promotion focus (concerned with goal attainment) tend to be more creative, and take greater risks, than those with a prevention focus (concerned with attaining security, nonlosses; see Bittner, Bruena, & Rietzschel, 2016; Friedman & Förster, 2001; Herman & Reiter-Palmon, 2011). However, those with a prevention focus appear to be better at recognizing the feasibility of ideas (Herman & Reiter-Palmon, 2011). When the regulatory focus of the group does not match that of the task strategy (eager or vigilant), groups can experience regulatory nonfit. Groups generate more nonredundant ideas and spend longer working when they experience nonfit (Levine, Alexander, Wright, & Higgins, 2016).

Emotional intelligence (EI) may also have a positive impact on convergent group creativity. EI has been defined as the "ability to monitor one's own and others' feelings and emotions, to discriminate among them, and to use this information to guide one's thinking and actions" (Salovey & Mayer, 1989, p. 189). This type of ability could be beneficial for collaborative creativity as it may increase attention to ideas shared by others, especially in diverse environments. However, most research on EI has focused on success in the workplace (Joseph, Jin, Newman, & O'Boyle, 2015). There is considerable controversy about its predictive power in this domain. An analysis of the literature by Joseph et al. (2015) finds that EI ability does not predict career success very well, but a measure of EI that includes other measures such as personality (mixed EI) does predict.

In regard to group and team performance, the story appears to be more positive for EI ability. A number of studies have demonstrated that the average EI ability of group members is related to enhanced group or team outcomes (Bell, 2007; Chang, Sy, & Choi, 2012; Hjertø & Paulsen, 2016). However, thus far there have been no studies examining EI in the context of group creativity. One study has examined the role of EI on elaboration processes in informationally diverse groups (viz., those having diverse perspectives or knowledge stores; Wang, 2015). Wang proposed that EI enhances performance of informational diverse teams in part through its moderating effect on information elaboration and found support for this prediction for a survival problem-solving task. Given the importance of information diversity and elaboration processes in collaborative creativity, this research suggests the potential for a similar positive outcome in this setting. The interesting issue for research will be how variance in group composition on this dimension will influence outcomes, and whether longer term groups can develop some degree of collective EI that goes beyond a simple additive model, similar to findings on collective intelligence (Woolley, Chabris, Pentland, Hashmi, & Malone, 2010).

A CONTINGENCY/CONFIGURAL MODEL OF THE EFFECTS OF TRAITS ON GROUP CREATIVITY

We have provided an overview of how individual difference factors may influence group creativity. Much of this is based on the literature concerning individual differences in individual creativity. It is presumed that there will be some degree of similarity between the effects observed for individuals and groups. However, we have highlighted a number of ways in which the effects of individual differences may not be simply additive. Only a small number of studies have examined these possibilities. Since most groups in real-world settings are likely to be diverse in their creative dispositions, it is important to develop a more sophisticated understanding of the role of this diversity factor in various phases of the group creative process. Research is impeded to some extent by the limitations in analytical techniques for examining such diversity. Thus we need more studies to examine the diversity of creativity potential in groups and the development of sophisticated methods for analysis.

Based on our review of the literature, we propose a model to predict the effects of group composition on creativity. Group creativity requires attention to the ideas of others, the cognitive processing of shared ideas, and building on the ideas of others. Traits that will generally facilitate creativity are ones that facilitate these processes. Openness to Experience should dispose one to be attentive to ideas from others, especially novel ones. Creative groups also need productive members who share a lot of ideas so that there is an increased exchange of great ideas flowing to the top. Individuals who are divergent thinkers, who are comfortable sharing ideas in groups (low social anxiety, high extraversion), are likely to be productive in creative groups. In the early stages of the creative process, group members who are high generators and who reply to each other's ideas and build on them should be the most influential. However, in the evaluation stage an entirely different set of characteristics are needed. At this point, groups need members who are willing to consider the potential of very novel ideas and are able to modify them to increase their feasibility and likelihood of implementation. Presumably, those who are open to experience are more likely to accept highly novel ideas for further consideration. Those who have a promotion focus are more likely to recognize novel ideas (Herman & Reiter-Palmon, 2011). Convergent thinkers may be useful in this phase since they may be able to build more effectively on ideas of others. Those who are high on Agreeableness may also be more willing to consider radical ideas and to facilitate the selection and decision processes that are part of the convergent stages of creativity—development and implementation. Although Conscientiousness is typically not highly related to creativity (Reiter-Palmon et al., 2009), people high in this trait may be more motivated to persist in the difficult and potentially less exciting phases of idea selection, development, and implementation.

Thus in agreement with the configural perspective of Moynihan and Peterson (2004), certain team compositions may be ideal for groups that go through the full phases of the creative process. One strategy would be to compose a team that had the "right mixture" for the multiple phases or one could compose separate teams specifically for different phases. The advantage of the diverse mix approach is that all phases of the group creative process may involve some degree of each type of skill. Furthermore, over time, this team may develop increasing facility in using their complementary skills to optimize group outcomes. However, in large organizations with multiple teams there may be an advantage to have teams that excel in different aspects of the creative process focus on different phases.

The choice of strategy will also depend on the type of task. In the case of a general planning or problem-solving process, a mixed team may be optimal. However, if the different phases require distinctly different skill sets such as strategic thinking, manufacturing, and marketing, different teams will be needed. However, communication among the teams throughout the process is likely to be important to the eventual success of an initiative such as the launch of a new product by a high technology company. A broad range of studies in both controlled and work settings will be required to shed light on this issue.

Some research has found that equality of contributions is an important factor in enabling groups to perform at a high level across a range of tasks (Woolley et al., 2010). Although this has not been examined systematically for creative groups, one might presume that it would be beneficial to have full involvement of all group members in order to tap the group's creative potential. This would be particularly important for groups in which the diversity of background and expertise is relevant to the task (Paulus et al., 2018). However, variations in individual difference factors within the group that are related to productivity (e.g., number of ideas generated) may reduce the equality of contributions. The importance of quality of contributions may vary with type of task. For creativity tasks, having the most creative people dominate the interaction may be more beneficial, especially if there is competition for speaking time in face-to-face settings. However, if the task requires different task skills such as generating, building, and evaluating to come up with a final innovative product or solution, equality of contributions may not be very predictive. Rather, for optimal outcomes those who excel in these different domains of performance should dominate the interaction in the appropriate phases. However, in short-term ad hoc groups it is not likely that such a sophisticated distribution will occur. This would require experience as a group over a series of creative sessions in which participants become aware of each other's unique capabilities.

Acknowledgments

The preparation of this paper was supported by collaborative grant INSPIRE BCS 1247971 to the second and fourth authors from the National Science Foundation. Any opinions, findings, and conclusions or recommendations expressed in this material are those of the authors and do not necessarily reflect the views of the National Science Foundation.

References

Amabile, T. M. (1996). *Creativity in context*. Boulder, CO: West-view Press.
Baas, M., Nijstad, B. A., Boot, N. C., & De Dreu, C. K. W. (2016). Mad genius revisited: Vulnerability to psychopathology, biobehavioral approach-avoidance, and creativity. *Psychological Bulletin, 142*(6), 668–692.

Baer, M., Oldham, G. R., Jacobsohn, G. C., & Hollingshead, A. B. (2008). The personality composition of teams and creativity: The moderating role of team creative confidence. *The Journal of Creative Behavior, 42*, 255–282.

Bandura, A. (1997). *Self-efficacy: The exercise of control.* New York: W H Freeman/Times Books/Henry Holt & Co.

Bandura, A., & Cervone, D. (1983). Self-evaluative and self-efficacy mechanisms governing the motivational effects of goal systems. *Journal of Personality and Social Psychology, 45*, 1017–1028.

Barrick, M. R., & Mount, M. K. (1991). The Big Five personality dimensions and job performance: a meta-analysis. *Personnel Psychology, 44*(1), 1–26. https://doi.org/10.1111/j.1744-6570.1991.tb00688.x.

Barrick, M. R., Stewart, G. L., Neubert, M. J., & Mount, M. K. (1998). Relating member ability and personality to work-team processes and team effectiveness. *Journal of Applied Psychology, 83*, 377–391.

Barry, B., & Stewart, G. L. (1997). Composition, process, and performance in self-managed groups: The role of personality. *Journal of Applied Psychology, 82*, 62–78.

Basadur, M., Basadur, T., & Licina, G. (2012). Organizational development. In M. D. Mumford (Ed.), *Handbook of organizational creativity* (pp. 668–703). Amsterdam: Elsevier.

Basadur, M., Runco, M. A., & Vega, L. A. (2000). Understanding how creative thinking skills, attitudes and behaviors work together: A causal process model. *The Journal of Creative Behavior, 34*, 77–100. https://doi.org/10.1002/j.2162-6057.2000.tb01203.x.

Batey, M., Chamorro-Premuzic, T., & Furnham, A. (2010). Individual differences in ideational behavior: Can the big five and psychometric intelligence predict creativity scores? *Creativity Research Journal, 22*, 90–97.

Batey, M., & Furnham, A. (2006). Creativity, intelligence, and personality: A critical review of the scattered literature. *Genetic, Social, and General Psychology Monographs, 132*, 355–429. https://doi.org/10.3200/MONO.132.4.355-430.

Bechtoldt, M. N., De Dreu, C. W., Nijstad, B. A., & Choi, H. (2010). Motivated information processing, social tuning, and group creativity. *Journal of Personality and Social Psychology, 99*, 622–637. https://doi.org/10.1037/a0019386.

Beersma, B., Hollenbeck, J. R., Humphrey, S. E., Moon, H., Conlon, D. E., & Ilgen, D. R. (2003). Cooperation, competition, and team performance: Toward a contingency approach. *Academy of Management Journal, 46*, 572–590. https://doi.org/10.2307/30040650.

Bell, S. T. (2007). Deep-level composition variables as predictors of team performance: A meta-analysis. *Journal of Applied Psychology, 92*, 595–615.

Bell, S. T., Villado, A. J., Lukasik, M. A., Belau, L., & Briggs, A. (2011). Getting specific about demographic diversity variable and team performance relationships: A meta-analysis. *Journal of Management, 37*, 709–743.

Bittner, J. V., Bruena, M., & Rietzschel, E. F. (2016). Cooperation goals, regulatory focus, and their combined effects on creativity. *Thinking Skills and Creativity, 19*, 260–268.

Bolin, A. U., & Neuman, G. A. (2006). Personality, process, and performance in interactive brainstorming groups. *Journal of Business and Psychology, 20*, 565–585.

Bond, M. H., & Shiu, W. Y. (1997). The relationship between a group's personality resources and the two dimensions of its group process. *Small Group Research, 28*, 194–217.

Brown, V., Tumeo, M., Larey, T. S., & Paulus, P. B. (1998). Modeling cognitive interactions during group brainstorming. *Small Group Research, 29*, 495–526.

Butler, A. B., Scherer, L. L., & Reiter-Palmon, R. (2003). Effects of solution elicitation aids and need for cognition on the generation of solutions to ill-structured problems. *Creativity Research Journal, 15*, 235–244. https://doi.org/10.1207/S15326934CRJ152&3_13.

Cacioppo, J. T., & Petty, R. E. (1982). The need for cognition. *Journal of Personality and Social Psychology, 42*(1), 116–131. https://doi.org/10.1037/0022-3514.42.1.116.

Cacioppo, J. T., Petty, R. E., Feinstein, J. A., & Jarvis, W. G. (1996). Dispositional differences in cognitive motivation: The life and times of individuals varying in need for cognition. *Psychological Bulletin, 119*, 197–253. https://doi.org/10.1037/0033-2909.119.2.197.

Camacho, L. M., & Paulus, P. B. (1995). The role of social anxiousness in group brainstorming. *Journal of Personality and Social Psychology*, *68*, 1071–1080.

Chang, J. W., Sy, T., & Choi, J. N. (2012). Team emotional intelligence and performance: Interactive dynamics between leaders and members. *Small Group Research*, *43*, 75–104. https://doi.org/10.1177/1046496411415692.

Chirumbolo, A., Livi, S., Mannetti, L., Pierro, A., & Kruglanski, A. W. (2004). Effects of need for closure on creativity in small group interactions. *European Journal of Personality*, *18*, 265–278. https://doi.org/10.1002/per.518.

Chirumbolo, A., Mannetti, L., Pierro, A., Areni, A., & Kruglanski, A. W. (2005). Motivated closed-mindedness and creativity in small groups. *Small Group Research*, *36*, 59–82. https://doi.org/10.1177/1046496404268535.

Costa, P. T., McCrae, R. R., & Dye, D. A. (1991). Facet scales for agreeableness and conscientiousness: A revision of the NEO personality inventory. *Personality and Individual Differences*, *12*, 887–898. https://doi.org/10.1016/0191-8869(91)90177-D.

Csikszentmihályi, M. (1997). *Creativity: Flow and the psychology of discovery and invention*. New York, NY: Harper Perennial.

da Costa, S., Páez, D., Sánchez, F., Garaigordobil, M., & Gondim, S. (2015). Personal factors of creativity: A second order meta-analysis. *Revista de Psicología del Trabajo y de las Organizaciones*, *31*, 165–173. https://doi.org/10.1016/j.rpto.2015.06.002.

De Dreu, C. K. W., Nijstad, B. A., Bechtoldt, M. N., & Baas, M. (2011). Group creativity and innovation: A motivated information processing perspective. *Psychology of Aesthetics, Creativity, and the Arts*, *5*, 81–89. https://doi.org/10.1037/a0017986.

De Dreu, C. W., Nijstad, B. A., & van Knippenberg, D. (2008). Motivated information processing in group judgment and decision making. *Personality and Social Psychology Review*, *12*, 22–49. https://doi.org/10.1177/1088868307304092.

De Dreu, C. W., & Weingart, L. R. (2003). Task versus relationship conflict, team performance, and team member satisfaction: A meta-analysis. *Journal of Applied Psychology*, *88*, 741–749. https://doi.org/10.1037/0021-9010.88.4.741.

Derosa, D. M., Smith, C. L., & Hantula, D. A. (2007). The medium matters: Mining the long-promised merit of group interaction in creative idea generation tasks in a meta-analysis of the electronic group brainstorming literature. *Computers in Human Behavior*, *23*, 1549–1581.

Devine, D. J., & Philips, J. L. (2001). Do smarter teams do better: A meta-analysis of cognitive ability and team performance. *Small Group Research*, *32*, 507–532.

Diehl, M., & Stroebe, W. (1987). Productivity loss in brainstorming groups: Toward the solution of riddle. *Journal of Personality and Social Psychology*, *53*, 497–509.

Dollinger, S. J. (2003). Need for uniqueness, need for cognition and creativity. *The Journal of Creative Behavior*, *37*, 99–116. https://doi.org/10.1002/j.2162-6057.2003.tb00828.x.

Dugosh, K. L., Paulus, P. B., Roland, E. J., & Yang, H. (2000). Cognitive stimulation in brainstorming. *Journal of Personality and Social Psychology*, *79*, 722–735.

Eysenck, H. J. (1995). Genius: The natural history of creativity. In L. A. Pervin (Ed.), *Problems in the behavioral sciences, 12. Monograph*. Cambridge, UK: Cambridge University Press.

Farh, J., Lee, C., & Farh, C. C. (2010). Task conflict and team creativity: A question of how much and when. *Journal of Applied Psychology*, *95*, 1173–1180.

Farrell, M. P. (2001). *Collaborative circles: Friendship dynamics and creative work*. Chicago, IL: University of Chicago Press.

Feist, G. J. (1998). A meta-analysis of personality in scientific and artistic creativity. *Personality and Social Psychology Review*, *2*, 290–309.

Feist, G. J. (2010). The function of personality in creativity: The nature and nurture of the creative personality. In J. C. Kaufman, R. J. Sternberg, J. C. Kaufman, & R. J. Sternberg (Eds.), *The Cambridge handbook of creativity* (pp. 113–130). New York, USA: Cambridge University Press. https://doi.org/10.1017/CBO9780511763205.009.

Friedman, R. S., & Förster, J. (2001). The effects of promotion and prevention cues on creativity. *Journal of Personality and Social Psychology*, *81*, 1001–1013. https://doi.org/10.1037/0022-3514.81.6.1001.

Furnham, A., & Bachtiar, V. (2008). Personality and intelligence as predictors of creativity. *Personality and Individual Differences, 45*, 613–617. https://doi.org/10.1016/j.paid.2008.06.023.

Fürst, G., Ghisletta, P., & Lubart, T. (2016). Toward an integrative model of creativity and personality: Theoretical suggestions and preliminary empirical testing. *The Journal of Creative Behavior, 50*, 87–108. https://doi.org/10.1002/jocb.71.

Fürst, G., & Lubart, T. (2017). An integrative approach to the creative personality: Beyond the big five paradigm. In G. J. Feist, R. Reiter-Palmon, & J. C. Kaufman (Eds.), *The Cambridge handbook of creativity and personality research* (pp. 140–164). New York: Cambridge University Press.

George, J. M., & Zhou, J. (2001). When openness to experience and conscientiousness are related to creative behavior: An interactional approach. *Journal of Applied Psychology, 86*, 513–524. https://doi.org/10.1037/0021-9010.86.3.513.

Goclowska, M. A., Baas, M., Crisp, R. J., & De Dreu, C. K. W. (2014). Whether social schema violations help or hurt creativity depends on need for structure. *Personality and Social Psychology Bulletin, 40*, 959–971. https://doi.org/10.1177/0146167214533132.

Goldberg, L. R. (1999). A broad-bandwidth, public domain, personality inventory measuring the lower-level facets of several five-factor models. *Personality Psychology in Europe, 7*, 7–28.

Goncalo, J. A., Flynn, F. J., & Kim, S. H. (2010). Are two narcissists better than one? The link between narcissism, perceived creativity, and creative performance. *Personality and Social Psychology Bulletin, 36*, 1484–1495. https://doi.org/10.1177/0146167210385109.

Hackman, R. J. (1987). The design of work teams. In W. Lorsch (Ed.), *Handbook of organizational behavior* (pp. 315–342). Englewood Cliffs, NJ: Prentice Hall.

Halfhill, T., Nielsen, T. M., Sundstrom, E., & Weilbaecher, A. (2005). Group personality composition and performance in military service teams. *Military Psychology, 17*, 41–54. https://doi.org/10.1207/s15327876mp1701_4.

Harari, O., & Graham, W. K. (1975). Task and task consequences as factors in individual and group brainstorming. *Journal of Social Psychology, 95*, 61–65.

Harvey, S. (2013). A different perspective: The multiple effects of deep level diversity of group creativity. *Journal of Experimental Social Psychology, 49*, 822–832. https://doi.org/10.1016/j.jesp.2013.04.004.

Herman, A., & Reiter-Palmon, R. (2011). The effect of regulatory focus on idea generation and idea evaluation. *Psychology of Aesthetics, Creativity, and the Arts, 5*, 13–20. https://doi.org/10.1037/a0018587.

Higgins, E. T. (1997). Beyond pleasure and pain. *American Psychologist, 52*, 1280–1300. https://doi.org/10.1037/0003-066X.52.12.1280.

Hjertø, K. B., & Paulsen, J. M. (2016). Beyond collective beliefs: Predicting team academic performance from collective emotional intelligence. *Small Group Research, 47*, 510–541. https://doi.org/10.1177/1046496416661236.

Hoff, E. V., Carlsson, I. M., & Smith, G. J. W. (2012). Personality. In M. D. Mumford (Ed.), *Handbook of organizational creativity* (pp. 241–270). London: Elsevier.

Hough, L. M. (1992). The "Big Five" personality variables—Construct confusion: Description versus prediction. *Human Performance, 5*, 139–155. https://doi.org/10.1207/s15327043hup0501&2_8.

Hülsheger, U. R., Anderson, N., & Salgado, J. F. (2009). Team-level predictors of innovation at work: A comprehensive meta-analysis spanning three decades of research. *Journal of Applied Psychology, 94*, 1128–1145. https://doi.org/10.1037/a0015978.

Hunter, S. T., Bedell-Avers, K. E., Hunsicker, C. M., Mumford, M. D., & Ligon, G. S. (2008). Applying multiple knowledge structures in creative thought: Effects on idea generation and problem-solving. *Creativity Research Journal, 20*, 137–154. https://doi.org/10.1080/10400410802088779.

Jaussi, K. S., Randel, A. E., & Dionne, S. D. (2007). I am, I think I can, and I do: The role of personal identity, self-efficacy and cross-application of experiences in creativity at work. *Creativity Research Journal, 19*, 247–258. https://doi.org/10.1080/10400410701397339.

John-Steiner, V. (2000). *Creative collaboration*. New York: Oxford University Press.

Joseph, D. L., Jin, J., Newman, D. A., & O'Boyle, E. H. (2015). Why does self-reported emotional intelligence predict job performance? A meta-analytic investigation of mixed EI. *Journal of Applied Psychology, 100*, 298–342. https://doi.org/10.1037/a0037681.

King, L. A., McKee Walker, L., & Broyles, S. J. (1996). Creativity and the five-factor model. *Journal of Research in Personality, 30*, 189–203. https://doi.org/10.1006/jrpe.1996.0013.

Korde, R., & Paulus, P. B. (2017). Alternating individual and group idea generation: Finding the elusive synergy. *Journal of Experimental Social Psychology, 70*, 177–190.

Kratzer, J., Leenders, R. J., & van Engelen, J. L. (2006). Team polarity and creative performance in innovation teams. *Creativity and Innovation Management, 15*, 96–104. https://doi.org/10.1111/j.1467-8691.2006.00372.x.

Kristof-Brown, A., Barrick, M. R., & Stevens, C. K. (2005). When opposites attract: A multi-sample demonstration of complementary person-team fit on extraversion. *Journal of Personality, 73*, 935–958. https://doi.org/10.1111/j.1467-6494.2005.00334.x.

Larey, T. S., & Paulus, P. B. (1999). Group preference and convergent tendencies in groups: A content analysis of group brainstorming performance. *Creativity Research Journal, 12*, 175–184.

Larson, J. R. (2009). *In search of synergy in small group performance*. New York: Psychology Press.

Leary, M. R., & Kowalski, R. M. (1993). The interaction anxiousness scale: Construct and criterion-related validity. *Journal of Personality Assessment, 61*, 136–146.

LePine, J. A. (2003). Team adaptation and postchange performance: Effects of team composition in terms of members' cognitive ability and personality. *Journal of Applied Psychology, 88*, 27–39. https://doi.org/10.1037/0021-9010.88.1.27.

Levine, J. M., Alexander, K. M., Wright, A. G. C., & Higgins, E. T. (2016). Group brainstorming: When regulatory nonfit enhances performance. *Group Processes & Intergroup Relations, 19*, 257–271. https://doi.org/10.1177/1368430215577226.

Levine, J. M., & Moreland, R. L. (1998). Small groups. In D. T. Gilbert, S. T. Fiske, & G. Lindzey (Eds.), *The handbook of social psychology*. (4th ed.)(pp. 415–469). New York: McGraw-Hill.

Litchfield, R. C., Gilson, L. L., & Shalley, C. E. (2017). Can teams have a creative personality? In G. J. Feist, R. Reiter-Palmon, & J. C. Kaufman (Eds.), *The Cambridge handbook of creativity and personality research* (pp. 354–371). New York: Cambridge University Press.

Mann, R. D. (1959). A review of the relationships between personality and performance in small groups. *Psychological Bulletin, 56*, 241–270.

Mannix, E. A., & Neale, M. A. (2005). What difference makes a difference: The promise and reality of diverse groups in organizations. *Psychological Science in the Public Interest, 6*, 31–55.

Martindale, C., & Dailey, A. (1996). Creativity, primary process cognition and personality. *Personality and Individual Differences, 20*, 409–414. https://doi.org/10.1016/0191-8869(95)00202-2.

Mathisen, G. V., Martinsen, O., & Einarson, S. (2008). The relationship between creative personality composition, innovative team climate, and team innovativeness: An input-process output perspective. *Journal of Creative Behavior, 42*, 13–31.

McCrae, R. R., & Costa, P. T. (1995). Trait explanations in personality psychology. *European Journal of Personality, 9*, 231–252. https://doi.org/10.1002/per.2410090402.

McCrae, R. R., & John, O. P. (1992). An introduction to the five-factor model and its applications. *Journal of Personality, 60*, 175–215. https://doi.org/10.1111/j.1467-6494.1992.tb00970.x.

Moreland, R. L., Levine, J. M., & Wingert, M. L. (1996). Creating the ideal group: Composition effects at work. In E. H. Witte, J. H. Davis, E. H. Witte, & J. H. Davis (Eds.), *Understanding group behavior: Small group processes and interpersonal relations* Vol. 2. (pp. 11–35). Hillsdale, NJ, US: Lawrence Erlbaum Associates, Inc.

Mount, M. K., Barrick, M. R., & Stewart, G. L. (1998). Five-factor model of personality and performance in jobs involving interpersonal interactions. *Human Performance, 11*, 145–165. https://doi.org/10.1207/s15327043hup1102&3_3.

Moynihan, L. M., & Peterson, R. S. (2004). The role of personality in group processes. In B. Schneider & D. B. Smith (Eds.), *Personality and organizations* (pp. 317–345). Mahwah, NJ: Lawrence Erlbaum Associates Publishers.

Mullen, B., Johnson, C., & Salas, E. (1991). Productivity loss in brainstorming groups: A meta-analytic integration. *Basic and Applied Social Psychology*, 12, 3–24.

Nakui, T., Paulus, P. B., & van der Zee, K. I. (2011). The role of attitudes in reactions to diversity in work groups. *Journal of Applied Social Psychology*, 41, 2327–2351.

Neuberg, S. L., & Newsom, J. T. (1993). Personal need for structure: Individual differences in the desire for simple structure. *Journal of Personality and Social Psychology*, 65, 113–131.

Neuman, G. A., & Wright, J. (1999). Team effectiveness: Beyond skills and cognitive ability. *Journal of Applied Psychology*, 84, 376–389. https://doi.org/10.1037/0021-9010.84.3.376.

Nijstad, B. A., Bechtoldt, M., & Choi, H.-S. (2018). Information processing, motivation, and group creativity. In P. B. Paulus & B. A. Nijstad (Eds.), *Handbook of group creativity: Innovation through collaboration*. New York: Oxford University Press.

Nijstad, B. A., & De Dreu, C. W. (2002). Creativity and group innovation. *Applied Psychology: An International Review*, 51, 400–406. https://doi.org/10.1111/1464-0597.00984.

Nijstad, B. A., & De Dreu, C. K. W. (2012). Motivated information processing in organizational teams: Progress, puzzles, and prospects. *Research in Organizational Behavior*, 32, 87–111.

Nijstad, B. A., & Stroebe, W. (2006). How the group affects the mind: A cognitive model of idea generation in groups. *Personality and Social Psychology Review*, 10, 186–213.

Parks, C. D. (2012). Personality influences on group processes: The past, present, and future. In K. Deaux & M. Snyder (Eds.), *The Oxford handbook of personality and social psychology: 2012* (pp. 517–544). New York: Oxford University Press.

Paulus, P. B., & Brown, V. (2003). Enhancing ideational creativity in groups: Lessons from research on brainstorming. In P. B. Paulus & B. A. Nijstad (Eds.), *Group creativity: Innovation through collaboration* (pp. 110–136). New York, NY: Oxford University Press.

Paulus, P. B., & Brown, V. R. (2007). Toward more creative and innovative group idea generation: A cognitive-social-motivational perspective of group brainstorming. *Social and Personality Psychology Compass*, 1, 248–265.

Paulus, P. B., & Coskun, H. (2012). Group creativity. In J. M. Levine (Ed.), *Group processes* (pp. 215–239). Amsterdam: Elsevier.

Paulus, P. B., Dugosh, K. L., Dzindolet, M. T., Coskun, H., & Putman, V. L. (2002). Social and cognitive influences in group brainstorming. Predicting production gains and losses. *European Review of Social Psychology*, 12, 299–325. https://doi.org/10.1080/14792772143000094.

Paulus, P. B., & Dzindolet, M. T. (1993). Social influence processes in group brainstorming. *Journal of Personality and Social Psychology*, 64, 575–586.

Paulus, P. B., & Dzindolet, M. T. (2008). Social influence, creativity and innovation. *Social Influence*, 3, 228–247.

Paulus, P. B., Dzindolet, M. T., & Kohn, N. (2012). Collaborative creativity—Group creativity and team innovation. In M. D. Mumford (Ed.), *Handbook of organizational creativity* (pp. 327–357). London: Elsevier.

Paulus, P. B., Dzindolet, M. T., Poletes, G. W., & Camacho, L. M. (1993). Perception of performance in group brainstorming: The illusion of group productivity. *Personality and Social Psychology Bulletin*, 19, 78–89.

Paulus, P. B., & Kenworthy, J. B. (2018). Overview of team creativity and innovation. In R. Reiter-Palmon (Ed.), *Team creativity*. Oxford University Press.

Paulus, P. B., & van der Zee, K. I. (2015). Creative processes in culturally diverse teams. In S. Otten, K. I. van der Zee, & M. Brewer (Eds.), *Towards inclusive organizations: Determinants of successful diversity management at work* (pp. 108–131). New York: Psychology Press.

Paulus, P. B., van der Zee, K. I., & Kenworthy, J. (2018). Diversity and group creativity. In P. B. Paulus & B. A. Nijstad (Eds.), *Handbook of group creativity: Innovation through collaboration*. New York: Oxford University Press.

Paulus, P. B., & Yang, H. (2000). Idea generation in groups: A basis for creativity in organizations. *Organizational Behavior and Human Decision Processes*, *82*, 76–87.

Pelled, L. H., Eisenhardt, K. M., & Xin, K. R. (1999). Exploring the black box: An analysis of work group diversity, conflict, and performance. *Administrative Science Quarterly*, *44*, 1–28. https://doi.org/10.2307/2667029.

Porter, C. H., Hollenbeck, J. R., Ilgen, D. R., Ellis, A. J., West, B. J., & Moon, H. (2003). Backing up behaviors in teams: The role of personality and legitimacy of need. *Journal of Applied Psychology*, *88*, 391–403. https://doi.org/10.1037/0021-9010.88.3.391.

Puccio, G. J., & Cabra, J. F. (2010). Organizational creativity: A systems approach. In J. C. Kaufman, R. J. Sternberg, J. C. Kaufman, & R. J. Sternberg (Eds.), *The Cambridge handbook of creativity* (pp. 145–173). New York, NY, US: Cambridge University Press. https://doi.org/10.1017/CBO9780511763205.011.

Putman, V. L. (2001). *Effects of additional rules and dominance on brainstorming and decision making*. Unpublished doctoral dissertation University of Texas at Arlington.

Ray, J. J. (1981). Authoritarianism, dominance and assertiveness. *Journal of Personality Assessment*, *45*, 390–397.

Reiter-Palmon, R., Illies, J. J., & Kobe-Cross, L. M. (2009). Conscientiousness is not always a good predictor of performance: The case of creativity. *The International Journal of Creativity & Problem Solving*, *19*, 27–45.

Reiter-Palmon, R., Wigert, B., & de Vreede, T. (2012). Team creativity and innovation: The effect of group composition, social processes, and cognition. In M. D. Mumford (Ed.), *Handbook of organizational creativity* (pp. 295–326). London: Elsevier.

Richter, A. W., Hirst, G., van Knippenberg, D., & Baer, M. (2012). Creative self-efficacy and individual creativity in team contexts: Cross-level interactions with team informational resources. *Journal of Applied Psychology*, *97*, 1282–1290. https://doi.org/10.1037/a0029359.

Rietzschel, E. F., De Dreu, C. K. W., & Nijstad, B. A. (2007). Personal need for structure and creative performance: The moderating influence of fear invalidity. *Personality and Social Psychology Bulletin*, *33*, 855–866. https://doi.org/10.1177/0146167207301017.

Rietzschel, E. F., Nijstad, B. A., & Stroebe, W. (2006). Productivity is not enough: A comparison of interactive and nominal brainstorming groups on idea generation and selection. *Journal of Experimental Social Psychology*, *42*, 244–251.

Rietzschel, E. F., Nijstad, B. A., & Stroebe, W. (2018). Idea evaluation and selection. In P. B. Paulus & B. A. Nijstad (Eds.), *Handbook of group creativity: Innovation through collaboration*. New York: Oxford University Press.

Rietzschel, E. F., Slijkhuis, J. M., & Van Yperen, N. W. (2014). Task structure, need for structure, and creativity. *European Journal of Social Psychology*, *44*, 386–399. https://doi.org/10.1002/ejsp.2024.

Robert, C., & Cheung, Y. H. (2010). An examination of the relationship between conscientiousness and group performance on a creative task. *Journal of Research in Personality*, *44*, 222–231. https://doi.org/10.1016/j.jrp.2010.01.005.

Runco, M. A. (2004). Creativity. *Annual Review of Psychology*, *55*, 657–687. https://doi.org/10.1146/annurev.psych.55.090902.141502.

Runco, M. A., & Dow, G. T. (2004). Assessing the Accuracy of Judgments of Originality on Three Divergent Thinking Tests. *Korean Journal of Thinking & Problem Solving*, *14*(2), 5–14.

Runco, M. A., & Smith, W. R. (1992). Interpersonal and intrapersonal evaluations of creative ideas. *Personality and Individual Differences*, *13*, 295–302. https://doi.org/10.1016/0191-8869(92)90105-X.

Salovey, P., & Mayer, J. D. (1989). Emotional intelligence. *Imagination, Cognition and Personality*, *9*, 185–211. https://doi.org/10.2190/DUGG-P24E-52WK-6CDG.

Schilpzand, M. C., Herold, D. M., & Shalley, C. E. (2011). Members' openness to experience and teams' creative performance. *Small Group Research*, *42*, 55–76. https://doi.org/10.1177/1046496410377509.

Shin, S. J., & Zhou, J. (2007). When is educational specialization heterogeneity related to creativity in research and development teams? Transformational leadership as a moderator. *Journal of Applied Psychology*, *92*, 1709–1721. https://doi.org/10.1037/0021-9010.92.6.1709.

Silvia, P. J. (2005). Cognitive appraisals and interest in visual art: exploring an appraisal theory of aesthetic emotions. *Empirical Studies of the Arts*, *23*, 119–133.

Silvia, P. J. (2008). Discernment and creativity: How well can people identify their most creative ideas? *Psychology of Aesthetics, Creativity, and the Arts*, *2*, 139–146. https://doi.org/10.1037/1931-3896.2.3.139.

Simonton, D. K. (2017). Creative genius and psychopathology: Creativity as a positive and negative personality. In G. J. Feist, R. Reiter-Palmon, & J. C. Kaufman (Eds.), *The Cambridge handbook of creativity and personality research* (pp. 235–250). New York: Cambridge University Press.

Snyder, S. H. (1989). *Brainstorming: The science and politics of opiate research*. Cambridge: Harvard University Press.

Steiner, L. D. (1972). *Group process and productivity*. New York: Academic.

Stewart, G. L., Fulmer, I. S., & Barrick, M. R. (2005). An exploration of member roles as a multilevel linking mechanism for individual traits and team outcomes. *Personnel Psychology*, *58*, 343–365. https://doi.org/10.1111/j.1744-6570.2005.00480.x.

Stroebe, W., Diehl, M., & Abakoumkin, G. (1992). The illusion of group effectivity. *Personality and Social Psychology Bulletin*, *18*, 643–650.

Taggar, S. (2001). Group composition, creative synergy, and group performance. *The Journal of Creative Behavior*, *35*, 261–286. https://doi.org/10.1002/j.2162-6057.2001.tb01050.x.

Taggar, S. (2002). Individual creativity and group ability to utilize individual creative resources: A multilevel model. *Academy of Management Journal*, *45*, 315–330. https://doi.org/10.2307/3069349.

Taggar, S. (2018). The distal and proximal antecedents of creativity in teams. In P. B. Paulus & B. A. Nijstad (Eds.), *Handbook of group creativity: Innovation through collaboration*. New York: Oxford University Press.

Tajfel, H., & Turner, J. C. (1986). The social identity theory of intergroup behavior. In S. Worchel & W. G. Austin (Eds.), *Psychology of intergroup relations* (pp. 7–24). Chicago: Nelson-Hall.

Tasa, K., Sears, G. J., & Schat, A. H. (2011). Personality and teamwork behavior in context: The cross-level moderating role of collective efficacy. *Journal of Organizational Behavior*, *32*, 65–85. https://doi.org/10.1002/job.680.

Tekleab, A. G., & Quigley, N. R. (2014). Team deep-level diversity, relationship conflict, and team members' affective reactions: A cross-level investigation. *Journal of Business Research*, *67*, 394–402. https://doi.org/10.1016/j.jbusres.2012.12.022.

Thatcher, S. B., & Patel, P. C. (2011). Demographic faultlines: A meta-analysis of the literature. *Journal of Applied Psychology*, *96*, 1119–1139.

Tierney, P., & Farmer, S. M. (2002). Creative self-efficacy: Its potential antecedents and relationship to creative performance. *Academy of Management Journal*, *45*, 1137–1148. https://doi.org/10.2307/3069429.

Turner, J. C., Hogg, M. A., Oakes, P. J., Reicher, S. D., & Wetherell, M. S. (1987). *Rediscovering the social group: A self-categorization theory*. Oxford, England: Blackwell.

van Dijk, H., van Engen, M. L., & van Knippenberg, D. (2012). Defying conventional wisdom: A meta-analytical examination of the differences between demographic and job-related diversity relationships with performance. *Organizational Behavior and Human Decision Processes*, *119*, 38–53.

van Vianen, A. M., & De Dreu, C. W. (2001). Personality in teams: Its relationship to social cohesion, task cohesion, and team performance. *European Journal of Work and Organizational Psychology*, *10*, 97–120. https://doi.org/10.1080/13594320143000573.

Wallas, G. (1976). Stages in the creative process. In A. Rothenberg & C. R. Hausman (Eds.), *The creativity question* (pp. 69–73). Durham, NC: Duke University.

Wang, S. (2015). Emotional intelligence, information elaboration, and performance: The moderating role of informational diversity. *Small Group Research*, *46*, 324–351. https://doi.org/10.1177/1046496415578010.

Watts, L. L., Steele, L. M., & Song, H. (2017). Re-examining the relationship between need for cognition and creativity: predicting creative problem solving across multiple domains. *Creativity Research Journal, 29*(1), 21–28. https://doi.org/10.1080/10400419.2017.1263505.

West, M. A., & Richter, A. W. (2008). Climates and cultures for innovation and creativity at work. In J. Zhou & C. E. Shalley (Eds.), *Handbook of organizational creativity* (pp. 211–236). New York: Psychology Press.

Williams, K. Y., & O'Reilly, C. A. (1998). Demography and diversity in organizations: A review of 40 years of research. *Research in Organizational Behavior, 20,* 77–140.

Witt, L. A., Burke, L. A., Barrick, M. R., & Mount, M. K. (2002). The interactive effects of conscientiousness and agreeableness on job performance. *Journal of Applied Psychology, 87,* 164–169. https://doi.org/10.1037/0021-9010.87.1.164.

Woolley, A. W., Chabris, C. F., Pentland, A., Hashmi, N., & Malone, T. W. (2010). Evidence for a collective intelligence factor in the performance of human groups. *Science, 330*(6004), 686–688. https://doi.org/10.1080/10400410903579494.

Wu, C., Parker, S. K., & de Jong, J. J. (2014). Need for cognition as an antecedent of individual innovation behavior. *Journal of Management, 40,* 1511–1534. https://doi.org/10.1177/0149206311429862.

Further Reading

Karau, S. J., & Williams, K. D. (1993). Social loafing: A meta-analytic review and theoretical integration. *Journal of Personality and Social Psychology, 65,* 681.

Paulus, P. B., van der Zee, K. I., & Kenworthy, J. (2016). Cultural diversity and team creativity. In V. P. Glăveanu & V. P. Glăveanu (Eds.), *The Palgrave handbook of creativity and culture research* (pp. 57–76). New York, NY: Palgrave Macmillan. https://doi.org/10.1057/978-1-137-46344-9_4.

Waung, M., & Brice, T. S. (1998). The effects of conscientiousness and opportunity to caucus on group performance. *Small Group Research, 29,* 624–634.

Constructing an Evidence-Based Model for Managing Creative Performance

Ben Wigert

The Gallup Organization, Omaha, NE, United States

Creativity is essential to the success and evolution of organizations. It is the critical element that allows organizations to adapt to the changing marketplace, to survive, and to thrive (Mumford, Whetzel, & Reiter-Palmon, 1997; Reiter-Palmon, 2011; Shalley & Zhou, 2008; Zhou & Hoever, 2014). Many organizations emphasize the importance of creativity as a "cultural value" or seek to create an environment where creativity is "encouraged," but few truly treat creativity like an expectation that must be supported by their performance management philosophies and systems (Gallup, 2017). In order for creativity to be embedded in the daily work of employees, research-based practices known to increase creativity must become an important part of how performance is approached and managed.

As such, this chapter provides a practical, evidence-based framework for cultivating the creativity of individual employees through improved management strategies. Managers seeking to foster a culture of creativity must become more adept at setting expectations to be creative, providing opportunities for creativity to flourish, and supporting the creative process.

The chapter begins by painting a picture of how employees are experiencing these key elements of the creative process in relation to best practices for driving creativity. Only through an understanding of how employees view creativity in their job can we truly make progress in changing how they approach it. Circumstances in which it may be more or less difficult to nurture a creative environment are also identified and addressed. After discussing the fundamentals of setting up employees for

Individual Creativity in the Workplace
https://doi.org/10.1016/B978-0-12-813238-8.00015-2

success, the remainder of the chapter addresses how these fundamentals can be reinforced and built upon.

Notably, a strong distinction is not made between creativity and innovation. Creativity is the generation of creative ideas and solutions; whereas, innovation extends to the implementation of creative concepts into an outcome that is utilized and supported by the organization (Runco & Jaeger, 2012). Innovation typically includes dedication of resources beyond the individual, such as cross-functional teamwork, money, communication, and logistical considerations. Creativity may not lead to innovation, but innovation requires creativity. As such, because this chapter is about applied creativity, innovation research will be cited and assumed to include creativity unless demonstrated otherwise.

More specifically, the focus of the chapter is on "creative performance" of individual employees and how it can be enhanced. Creative performance occurs relative to the expectations set for an employee and how effectively those expectations are achieved. For instance, creative performance may be expected to occur in the form of behavior, ideas, processes, service, or work produced. It may be judged relative to standards such as performance ratings of creativity, metrics, goals, process improvements, or successful innovations.

Finally, meta-analytic and longitudinal studies were prioritized when determining what key predictors of creative performance managers should emphasize. Established best practices from the broader management literature are also integrated into advice for managers, especially in areas where creativity-specific research was lighter. Recommendations for managing creativity are based on generalizable factors that can be individualized and are sequenced to start with the basics of performance management and evolve into subsequent actions that naturally become more sophisticated.

CONSTRUCTING AN EVIDENCE-BASED MODEL FOR MANAGING CREATIVE PERFORMANCE

This chapter aims to help managers foster the creativity of individual employees in organizations by:

1. examining the extent to which employees believe they are expected and empowered to be creative at work,
2. describing circumstances in which a creative environment may be more or less difficult to create, and
3. providing a practical, evidence-based framework for managers to cultivate creativity.

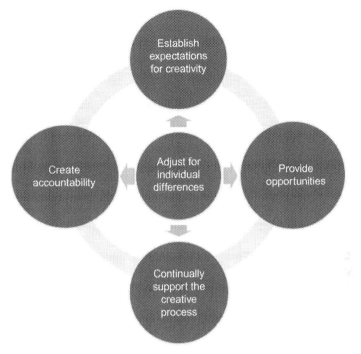

FIG. 1   Evidence-based model for managing creative performance.

The chapter is organized by a framework of key principles that are scientifically linked to individual creativity in organizations and provide managers with practical advice for fostering creativity (Fig. 1).

LAYING A FOUNDATION FOR CREATIVITY AND BUILDING UPON IT

Creativity in organizations fundamentally requires expectations to be creative, opportunities to act, and freedom to take risks (Hammond, Neff, Farr, Schwall, & Zhao, 2011; Hunter, Bedell, & Mumford, 2007; Ma, 2009). These three requirements for creative performance are like a stool with three legs—if one is weak, the other two will struggle to compensate (Gallup, 2017; Woodman & Schoenfeldt, 1990; Zhang & Bartol, 2010). The following sections describe what it takes to lay a strong foundation for fostering individual-level creativity in organizations and how to apply these principles as intentionally and effectively as possible.

Creativity is also a dynamic, iterative process (Reiter-Palmon & Illies, 2004; Woodman & Schoenfeldt, 1990). Managers must learn to build upon basic requirements for creativity and make the creative process an engaging part of each employee's job (Zhang & Bartol, 2010). Through a better understanding of how the average employee tends to experience these pillars of creative performance and how they are interconnected, opportunities for improvement can be quickly identified.

ESTABLISH EXPECTATIONS FOR CREATIVITY

Expectations mark the starting and ending points of performance. When they are clearly defined, understood by all parties responsible for them, and aligned with the needs of the organization, a roadmap and criterion for success are established. Gallup finds that when employees know what is expected of them at work, they tend to be more productive, more satisfied with their job, safer, less likely to leave the organization, and more likely to deliver exceptional customer service (Harter, Schmidt, & Hayes, 2002).

Extensive research has been conducted on the art of setting expectations. Multiple high quality meta-analyses spanning decades of studies, across a wide range of situations have demonstrated the positive effects of expectation setting interventions on performance (e.g., Harkin et al., 2016; Locke & Latham, 2002; McEwan et al., 2016). Locke and Latham's *Goal Setting Theory*, Drucker's *Management by Objectives* (MBO) strategy, *SMART goals*, and *Balanced Scorecards* (BSC) are some of the most renowned philosophies and methods organizations have used for decades to improve their expectation-setting practices. While the fundamental mechanisms that make them effective are similar across all of these methods, each method makes its own unique contribution to how expectation setting and accountability can influence performance in the workplace.

Locke and Latham have authored arguably the most prolific pipeline of research on performance expectations as their decades of seminal research provide insights into what makes goals effective and why. Their *Goal Setting Theory* posits that goals affect performance through four causal mechanisms (Locke & Latham, 2002, 2006):

- *Directive function*: Goals have a directive function that focuses attention on what is to be achieved and steers attention away from other activities.
- *Energizing function*: Goals motivate people to act and signal the amount of effort that should be applied.
- *Persistence function*: Challenging goals tend to result in more prolonged effort.
- *Discovery and use of task-relevant knowledge and strategies function*: Goals indirectly affect performance by encouraging people to explore information and strategize before taking action.

In addition to being supported by a long stream of research by Locke and Latham (2002, 2006), a large body of research (e.g., DeWalt et al., 2009; Mento, Steel, & Karren, 1987; Parker, Jimmieson, & Amiot, 2009; Tubbs, 1986; Wehmeyer & Shogren, 2017) indicates that the effectiveness of goal setting is largely determined by: (1) goal clarity and specificity, (2) appropriateness of goal difficulty, (3) involvement of employees in the goal-setting process, and (4) feedback and progress monitoring as performance toward goals occurs. By mastering these key principles, performance expectations can be better leveraged by managers and co-owned by employees.

Unfortunately, Gallup has found that only 50% of employees strongly agree they "know what is expected" of them at work (Wigert & Harter, 2017). Thus one-half of the workforce shows up to their jobs each day not fully knowing what they are supposed to do. This statistic is very concerning given that it is difficult to address sophisticated aspects of performance like leveraging your strengths, collaborating effectively, advancing an organization's mission, and growing developmentally at work if employees do not fully understand their basic performance expectations (Gallup, 2017; Wigert & Harter, 2017). Confusion around performance expectations is also not surprising given how rapidly the marketplace and workplace are changing. Businesses are trying to respond to the speed of an increasingly global and digital marketplace by making changes in how teams are structured, how they can do more with less, how they respond to customer demands, and how they build their talent pipeline.

As a result, employees are left with a laundry list of expectations to fulfill. For instance, they are often charged with living the values, vision, mission, and objectives of the organization, in addition to their own personal job descriptions, role competencies, performance ratings, metrics, and goals. Not to mention, there are also the critical responsibilities that are actually required of them during daily work, but are not written on paper. Unsurprisingly, only 34% of employees strongly agree that their job description aligns with the work they actually do (Wigert & Harter, 2017).

How can we expect employees to align their performance with the needs of their organization and drive business outcomes if they do not fully understand what is expected of them when they come to work every day?

Expectations for creative performance are riddled with the same lack of clarity and alignment to organizational priorities that plague traditional work responsibilities and goals. And worse, expectations for creativity get lost in the mix of other seemingly more important performance expectations that can be easily translated to business results (Ensley, Pearson, & Amason, 2002; Mumford, 2000; Porter & Lilly, 1996; Shalley & Gilson, 2004; Tierney & Farmer, 2011). Instead of pursuing creative performance, employees tend to see their job responsibilities as the more concrete, routine things they do every day to tangibly contribute to the organization. Whereas, they see creative performance as something that could happen, but struggle to conceptualize what those actions would look like and how they might tangibly help the business. Further, there are systems and management issues that deprioritize expectations for creativity (Amabile, 1988; Gupta & Singhal, 1993; Mumford, 2000). Leaders, managers, and individual contributors are held accountable to and often paid incentives based on the key performance metrics recorded on their performance reviews that reflect behaviors and outcomes that help organizations today rather than creatively improve performance in the future.

Overall, a major problem with unsatisfactory creativity from individual employees stems from organizations often seeking creative production from their employees, but rarely setting expectations to be creative in a manner that is clearly understood, supported, or evaluated. To better understand exactly how pronounced this issue is across the US workforce and various types of roles and industries, Gallup conducted a study in 2017 of how employees are experiencing expectations and opportunities to be creative in their jobs. The study found that 29% of employees strongly agree that they are "expected to be creative or think of new ways to do things at work." That is, 71% of employees do not fully believe that creativity is an important part of their job. And if the vast majority of employees do not think they're supposed to be creative, how can organizations expect to evolve with the speed of business?

Notably, Gallup focuses on "strongly agree" responses because the organization's research shows that these responses are more predictive of behavioral change and business outcomes than combining the top two or three response options together. In their research and practice, they generally interpret "agree" responses as ranging from a "yes, but…" to a "maybe"; whereas, "neutral" responses tend to be a "soft no." The chart below illustrates the full distribution of responses for the item showing that even when "agree" and "strongly agree" responses are combined, just over half of employees (61%) think their job requires some level of creativity.

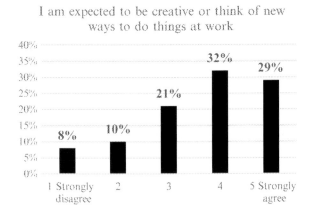

I am expected to be creative or think of new ways to do things at work

Given the importance of goal clarity and commitment to creative performance, this statistic shows that the majority of employees do not view expectations to be creative as a critical part of their job, and therefore are not likely to give their best effort to be creative (Klein, Wesson, Hollenbeck, & Alge, 1999). Having less than one-third of employees in an organization entirely clear on their expectations to be creative will not result in a culture of innovation.

Organizations must reexamine the expectations they are setting for creative production from their employees and envision what is needed for the future. Setting expectations for creativity is a powerful motivator of creative self-efficacy, behavior, and outcomes (Hammond et al., 2011; Ma, 2009; Tierney & Farmer, 2004, 2011). It is important that organizations and managers are careful to set the right expectations in a manner that makes the most sense for individual employees, their team, and the organization at large.

But What Exactly Do We Mean by Expectations for "Creative Performance"?

If employees, managers, and organizations do not start with this question, how can they ever agree on whether they are being more creative? While there is no single, universally accepted definition for "creativity" most studies operationalize creativity as being "original," "high quality," and "useful" ideas or solutions (Amabile, 1991; Mumford & Gustafson, 1988; Mumford, Reiter-Palmon, & Redmond, 1994). Creativity is also contextual. It occurs in response to an "ill-defined" problem that can be ambiguous, unstructured, have missing information, and/or be solved in multiple ways, rather than one correct way.

Defining Creativity for Employees

"Originality" is the quintessential characteristic of creativity, but it is important to unpack exactly what that means in an employee's role. In general, originality refers to the novelty or uniqueness of an idea or solution (Hennessey & Amabile, 2010; Runco, 2004). However, when defining originality in a work setting, the key question to ask is "original compared to what?". Originality can be relative to a task, role, organization, or industry, to name a few comparisons. In the context of applied creativity, "original" does not necessarily mean the idea has never been thought of before. Rather, an idea can be original relative to how it is being applied. For instance, when *Airbnb* was created, online vacation rental sites already existed, but *Airbnb* came up with the creative idea of building an online marketplace that operates with the efficiencies of a brick-and-mortar hotel chain and novelty of consumer direct lodging supplied by people willing to rent their dwelling. Similarly, gamification aimed at improving well-being existed before *Pokemon Go*, but it had not previously been applied by popular smart phone games using location-based augmented reality.

It is also important to understand that originality alone does not lead to creativity if it is not accompanied by quality and usefulness. For instance, eating soup with a fork and knife might be original, but it is certainly not useful. In business, there is also often the risk of doing something differently, but the outcome is not actually better than the current way of doing things—these ideas lack quality. Further, creativity can be incremental (Gilson, Lim, D'Innocenzo, & Moye, 2012; Madjar, Greenberg, & Chen, 2011). When a support staff employee improves a process in a way that is novel and improves how work gets done, the employee should be recognized for a substantial creative contribution. When organizations produce major innovations, there are likely many creative acts that made the final outcome possible. Opportunities to be creative vary in size and nature, just as the ambiguity of a problem or one's autonomy to act varies.

Thus creativity in organizations is largely dependent on the context and goals of performance. By adopting a definition of creative performance that can be understood relative to an employee's role and brings clarity to expectations, it is likely employees will be able to see creativity as part of their day and understand how it will be evaluated (Unsworth, Wall, & Carter, 2005). Given that the vast majority of employees do not fully believe creativity is a primary expectation for them (Gallup, 2017), most roles will likely benefit from a definition that is simple and broad. Rather than focusing on precise descriptions of originally, quality, and usefulness, a good starting point for jobs that have fewer requirements for creativity might be simply defining creativity as "New ideas and ways to do things that make us better."

Determining how to calibrate a definition for creativity and performance expectations largely depends on the responsibilities of the employee, complexity of the task, and readiness of the employee and organization.

Role Responsibilities

Role responsibilities suitable for creativity can range from helping think of new ideas, to helping implement them, to being involved throughout the idea generation and implementation processes. In roles with minimal creativity requirements, such as support functions or compliance focused-roles, employees need to first understand the aspects of their job that have the most potential for creativity. Creativity in these roles could be an improvement to a process, customer service, or way of helping colleagues perform better. At times, distinctions between creativity and continuous improvement may seem small, but when minimal opportunity for creativity exists, a "do your best to be creative" expectation can lead to substantial increases in creativity (Shalley, 1995). When setting expectations for creativity is new or seems difficult, discussing how small contributions to the team's creative process can also be a safe starting place and learning opportunity for employees to increase their confidence (i.e., creative self-efficacy) (Mathisen, 2011).

Conversely, for roles with greater requirements for applying creativity, progress toward expectations tends to be more precisely defined and measureable. Such roles may require successful completion of certain phases of creative work, tangible deliverables, timelines, and ownership of the implementation process. Working with a manager to openly discuss these responsibilities is an important starting point before specific performance goals are set.

Problem Discovery and Definition

Setting expectations to be creative can be challenging because by definition ill-defined problems that require creativity are unlikely to have a clear solution. Often, setting expectations to be creative starts with setting expectations to discover when and where there are opportunities to be creative. For some roles the opportunities and parameters for being creative will already be outlined by management, job descriptions, and/ or performance goals. However, even when guidelines for creativity are provided, revisiting how business problems are defined can enhance creativity (Mumford & Gustafson, 1988; Mumford et al., 1994).

Commonly recognized models for the creative thought process describe creative cognition as starting with a *problem construction* (i.e., discovery and definition) stage, which leads to subsequent *idea generation, idea evaluation*, and *idea selection* phases (Dewey, 1910; Guilford, 1967; Mumford, Mobley, Reiter-Palmon, Uhlman, & Doares, 1991). These phases are not necessarily linear and likely have multiple feedback loops between them. Nonetheless, *problem construction* is particularly important to the process because it influences all subsequent processes. In fact, studies show that prompts for reconstructing problems using different assumptions about the parameters, goals, constraints, and other conceptualizations of a problem are a particularly effective method for improving creative problem solving (Csikszentmihalyi & Getzels, 1971, 1988; Getzels & Csikszentmihalyi, 1976; Mumford, Baughman, Threlfall, Supinski, & Costanza, 1996; Reiter-Palmon, 2011). Thus when expectations to be creative are first being defined or are unclear, starting with problem discovery and definition goals may be necessary before determining what problems deserve further ideation and consideration.

Task Difficulty, Readiness, and Goal Specificity

Expectation setting is most effective when expectations are challenging but realistic for employees to achieve (Brown, Lent, Telander, & Tramayne, 2011; Hunter et al., 2007; Locke & Latham, 2002, 2006; Rahyuda, Syed, & Soltani, 2014; Shalley, 1995). Both sides of this equation must work in harmony as more *challenging expectations* can be set when *employee readiness* to meet those expectations is also high. The level of challenge inherent to creativity expectations includes the complexity of the task, time pressure, and shear difficulty of the creativity requirements (Farr, Sin, & Tesluk, 2003; Hammond et al., 2011). *Readiness* includes having the necessary knowledge, skills, ability, experience, and confidence to approach a creativity task (Brown & Latham, 2002; Mone & Shalley, 1995).

Challenging expectations tend to be detrimental to performance when employees have not first acquired the necessary knowledge, skills, or experience to perform the task. As such, the nature of creativity goals should differ depending on task difficulty and readiness. When readiness for a task is low, a more general goal or learning goal (e.g., "do your best," "determine a strategy," "achieve these steps in the process") tends to be more effective than a specific outcome goal focused on results (Brown et al., 2011; Latham & Brown, 2006; Locke & Latham, 2002, 2006; Rahyuda et al., 2014; Shalley, 1995). Similarly, when a task is difficult because it is complex—not just set at a high standard—a learning goal (e.g., try a certain number of different strategies for solving the problem) tends to be more effective. Conversely, when a task is less complex, more specific goals focused on results tend to be associated with higher performance than general goals.

Determining what expectations to set for employees who have high readiness and complex tasks takes careful consideration (Hunter, Thoroughgood, Myer, & Ligon, 2011). It is important to challenge these employees but not overwhelm or handcuff them. Shalley (1995) found that both "do your best" and "high difficulty creativity goals" were effective at eliciting high levels of creativity when expectations to be productive were high (i.e., complete many tasks).

Creativity goals should also take into account other role expectations. Creativity is not a linear process and does not occur in a vacuum. Conflicting demands, time pressures, and stretching of limited cognitive resources can inhibit the creative process (Amabile, 1998; Amabile, Hadley, & Kramer, 2002; Baer & Oldham, 2006; Koppel & Storm, 2014). Employees who have multiple creativity and productivity goals must be able to balance and prioritize. Madjar and Shalley (2008) found that creativity is highest when multiple creativity and productivity goals are set and discretion is given to switch back and forth between goals. That is, having multiple creativity goals has a positive effect on creative production as long as employees have some control over what they work on and when.

Evidence-Based Recommendations for Integrating Creativity and General Performance Goals

Expectations for creativity must become a part of everyday performance conversations, otherwise creativity will continue to be viewed as separate from an employee's primary role expectations. Therefore, creative performance expectations must be set in conjunction with other performance expectations. Fortunately, best practices in general goal-setting research closely align with research specific to creativity goals. Using the four best practices previously identified as top predictors of general goal-setting effectiveness (Locke & Latham, 2002, 2006), key considerations and recommendations unique to creativity goals are overlaid in Table 1.

TABLE 1   Principles and advice for setting creativity goals.

---

1. **Set clear and specific goals**
   - Define creativity for each employee in a manner that is relevant to their role (e.g., "New ideas and ways to do things that make us better")
   - Define broad role responsibilities, including areas where they should or should not explore creativity
   - Set specific goals for creativity, including how success will be measured (e.g., timelines vs progress milestones)
   - Ensure creativity goals are clearly understood by asking the employee to explain their expectations and what success may look like
   - Consider assigning problem discovery and definition goals when creativity needs are unclear
2. **Ensure goals are appropriately difficult**
   - Make creativity goals challenging but realistic
   - Identify the difficulty of the task, starting with complexity and standards for achievement
   - Identify the readiness of the employee to fulfill the creativity goal, including knowledge, skills, ability, confidence, and experience with the issue at hand
   - Consider setting more general goals (e.g., learning, strategy, process completion, or discovery goals) when tasks are complex and/or readiness is lower
   - Consider setting more specific, results-oriented goals when tasks are less complex
3. **Involve employees in the goal-setting process**
   - Ask employees to help set goals that will stretch them but are appropriately difficult, as they should know the challenges they will face, their aspirations, and their readiness as well as anyone
   - Ensure employees feel like they have a voice in the process that is heard and understood so that they feel a sense of increased empowerment and goal commitment
   - Articulate how goal pursuit will be supported so that co-ownership of creativity is established between the employee and manager
4. **Monitor progress and provide feedback**
   - Be prepared to adjust creativity goals as circumstances change
   - Provide feedback on progress and explain why any necessary creativity goal changes are made
   - Strategies for progress monitoring and providing effective feedback are further discussed in the following sections of the chapter with special emphasis in the section about continually supporting the creative process.

By mastering these key principles, creativity, like other performance outcomes, can be better managed and owned by employees. Naturally, setting expectations for creativity and recalibrating them as circumstances change is a learning process. It is important to start slow, small, and simple as expectations for creativity should increase with preparation, practice, and experience. Consideration of how creative ideas will be used and implemented is also important to the expectation-setting process because when creative work does not result in action by the organization, employees become reluctant to take creativity seriously in the future.

PROVIDE OPPORTUNITIES TO BE CREATIVE

Expectations to be creative are only valuable if employees have sufficient opportunities to freely explore problems and work through multiple iterations of ideas. Creativity cannot simply be integrated into a busy work schedule without planning and commitment to the creative process (Hargadon & Bechky, 2006; Sio & Ormerod, 2009). Creativity is not a linear process that can be put on a strict schedule. Rather, opportunities to explore problems, skills, strategies, and ideas requiring creativity should be made available for employees to address at their discretion (Basadur, 2004).

In order to align expectations and opportunities for creativity, managers must set clear and appropriate goals for an employee while allowing the employee flexibility in determining how and when to approach the goal (Amabile, 1998; Hammond et al., 2011; Hunter et al., 2007). That is, managers should control what problems are being approached and how success is evaluated, but employees must be empowered to determine the approach.

Unfortunately, only 30% of employees report even having time to "think creatively or discuss new ideas" on a daily basis (Gallup, 2017). Another 18% are allotted time to be creative a few times a week, which means approximately one in two employees (52%) are limited to being creative a few times a month or less. Given the importance of dedicating substantial time and cognitive resources to the creative process, organizations have a long way to go when it comes to creating meaningful opportunities for creativity.

Even more alarming is that when employees strongly agree that they are expected to be creative at work, only 52% of them are also allotted time to think creatively on a daily basis. Thus if an employee is required to be creative in their job, there is only a 50/50 chance that employee will have time to make creativity a part of their workday. This raises the question of when and how to best provide opportunities for creativity given an employee's expectations for creative performance.

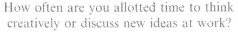

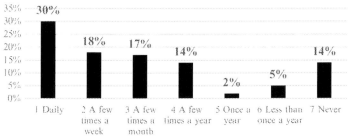

While finding time for creativity is the first step in making it a regular part of performance expectations, there are a multitude of factors that influence the effectiveness of opportunities to be creative (Amabile, Conti, Coon, Lazenby, & Herron, 1996; Hammond et al., 2011; Hunter et al., 2007; Ma, 2009). Organizations and managers must be mindful that everyone approaches creativity differently, but by providing a variety of creativity boosting opportunities, employees can explore what works best for them. The following factors should be given careful consideration when creating an environment conducive to creativity.

Time Pressure and Scheduling Flexibility

The most creative ideas are rarely a product of deciding to be creative during a single brainstorming session. Highly creative ideas tend to benefit from "incubation" which is the process of setting aside problems or ideas and coming back to them after a person is allowed time for ideas to percolate and naturally let thoughts come to them. The unconscious mind can have a substantial impact on creative thinking, as illustrated by studies showing the benefits of sleep, mind wandering, relaxation, and mental set shifting (Dodds, Ward, & Smith, 2003; Orlet, 2008; Sio & Ormerod, 2009). These studies show that highly creative thought is difficult to force. Creative thought tends to benefit from letting the mind wonder and automatically form loose associations between concepts that are not usually observed as working together within the same context.

The challenge with creativity in organizations is that unlike the unconscious mind, organizations run on a schedule and have important deadlines. Fortunately, while time pressure is clearly detrimental to creativity in many situations (Amabile, Hadley, et al., 2002; Amabile, Mueller, et al., 2002; Andrews & Smith, 1996; Baer & Oldham, 2006), there are also situations where time pressure leads to enhanced creativity (Andrews & Farris, 1972) or has no clear effect on creativity (Amabile et al., 1996;

Madjar & Oldham, 2006). Thus the influence of time pressure on creativity seems to somewhat depend on contextual factors.

Further insights into how time pressure affects creativity can be gleaned from a 2006 study by Baer and Oldham that indicates a moderate amount of time pressure boosts creativity in an environment where the manager and coworkers are supportive of creativity, but as time pressure continues to increase, creativity decreases. They also found a similar curvilinear relationship when employees had high openness to experience and were in a supportive environment. In this situation, again, a moderate amount of time pressure was beneficial but too much was destructive to creative solutions. However, in an environment that was not supportive of creativity, the researchers found that as time pressure increased, creativity decreased, even when pressure was small to moderate.

In practice, organizations often kill creativity with fake deadlines and unrealistic timelines (Amabile, 1998). Fake deadlines may cause trust and motivation issues, while unrealistic timelines may cause burnout and substandard work. Creativity is a time-consuming process and the more ill-defined the problem, the longer it will take to construct a way forward. Managers who do not authentically support and carefully plan for exploration and incubation will likely hinder present and future creative efforts. Nonetheless, projects must move forward, less promising ideas must be discarded, and a moderate amount of time pressure can inspire creative action if applied in a reasonable and supportive manner. Thoughtful and adjustable timelines can promote a sense of focus and importance that can inspire creativity and unstick individuals when they are having difficulty making progress. Setting process or stage-based milestones can also reduce pressure on individuals responsible for creativity by giving stakeholders the progress checks they need to justify their investment in a project while allowing flexibility in what the outcome looks like at each milestone.

Additionally, providing flexibility in work schedules and location where work is conducted can help alleviate time pressure challenges (Gallup, 2017; Heunks, 1998; Malone, 2004; Mumford, 2000). For instance, a 2017 study conducted by Gallup found that employees who have flexibility in choosing when they work and where they work (i.e., remote working) are more likely to have daily opportunities to be creative. And employees who are able to spend at least 20% of their time working remotely report having substantially more time to be creative (36% of remote workers are allotted daily vs 28% of nonremote workers are allotted time daily). These data indicate that when employees have more control over their work schedule and location, they can more easily find time to be creative. And because these work sessions are not "forced" by a rigid schedule, they have more latitude to choose creative work time when their thoughts are gathered, distractions are minimized, and they face less time pressure to quickly do the work before their next meeting.

Resources

Time to be creative is only productive if employees have the resources necessary to be creative and feel like their ideas can go somewhere beyond a brainstorming session and whiteboard. This starts with having the right information and supplies available to explore the problem and possible solutions (Hammond et al., 2011; Hunter et al., 2007). Necessary information includes access to organizational knowledge, processes, and people relevant to a task, and training necessary to understand the context of a problem and prior approaches. For instance, an employee might begin the discovery process by asking information gathering questions like: *How did this challenge or opportunity come about? What have others tried in this space? Who can I talk to if I want to bounce around ideas or learn more about other capabilities within the organization?* The information collection and filtering process naturally becomes more challenging as more specific insights are needed. Willingness to share information can be critical to creative performance, but unfortunately, information hoarding is common in organizations—both by accidental system limitations and intentional protection of ideas (Perry-Smith, 2006; Shalley & Gilson, 2004).

The idea generation process can benefit from a variety of physical "supplies" that help an individual conceptualize the problem and possible solutions. From basic supplies like white boards, computer monitors, and flip charts to advanced tools like computer animation and materials for prototyping, creativity benefits from the use of supplies that help conceptualize and animate thought. Further, as ideation moves into innovation, more physical resources will be needed to start testing and calibrating implementation mechanisms.

Evaluation, selection, and animation of creative ideas also activate the need for more people resources. As ideas move forward from suggestions to real possibilities to action, creative performance tends to require both more thought partnership and execution partnership. And the bigger the task, the more cross-functional support it requires, such as project planning, process implementation, technology, testing, and legal resources.

In all, if employees are not given resources that both facilitate ideation *and* inspire confidence that their top ideas will be animated and implemented, they are unlikely to take expectations to be creative seriously or be motivated to pursue them with high energy and persistence (Amabile et al., 1996; Zhou, 1998). As such, managers and organizations must identify what Amabile (1998) deems a "threshold of sufficient resources." She emphasizes that managers must learn to strike a balance between what the organization can afford to invest and what is required to support a project. Anything above the threshold of sufficiency will likely not accelerate creative performance. However, a greater danger lies in keeping resources too tight because this forces employees to expend their creative energy finding additional resources and creates doubt that the project will be successful.

Workspaces

Carefully engineered workspaces can create an environment that is conducive to creativity beyond just having the right resources on hand. A work environment that is quiet, natural, relaxed, and unrestrained tends to enhance individuals' creativity (Ma, 2009; McCoy & Evans, 2002). For instance, having a view of nature from a window and feelings of openness to the environment outside a small workspace is helpful (McCoy & Evans, 2002). The theoretical explanation for this effect is that it encourages a natural reorganization of knowledge, thoughts, cues, and parameters—key elements and processes of creative cognition.

Further, creativity—and certainly innovation—can benefit from more effective collaboration. Workspaces that make it easy to gather, interact freely, and break into small groups can facilitate collaboration. As open workspaces and collaboration areas become increasingly popular, future research should guide the design of creative workspaces. For instance, creativity and collaboration each bring their own unique challenges. As such, future workspaces may be more likely to include targeted collaboration aides like activities, workbooks, conversation starters, and coaching that help employees learn to think and work together more creatively. Until research-based workplace designs are better understood, intentionality in designing spaces that promote free thinking and interactivity is a step in the right direction.

However, strong caution should be taken when first reengineering a job, team, or organization to foster creativity. Managers often make the mistake of overly focusing on workspaces and collaboration at the expense of more critical requirements, like matching people with the assignments that best fit their capabilities, clarifying expectations, and giving them the freedom to work around traditional processes (Amabile, 1998; Hammond et al., 2011; Ma, 2009). Granted, workplaces, resources, and management can all be aligned simultaneously or at least in sequence. The lesson should be that managers should focus on work assignments, workflow, and support, first and foremost, while leadership or other organizational planning roles focus on the workspace.

Task Autonomy

Finally, task autonomy is one of the most important opportunities managers can provide to enable creative performance (Hammond et al., 2011; Hunter et al., 2007). Task autonomy is defined as the degree to which an individual is given freedom and discretion in carrying out a task (Hackman, 1980). By having the discretion to determine *how* to approach creativity and balance efforts with other work activities, employees can better navigate the slow, nonlinear, iterative nature of creative production. After all, if employees are told exactly *how* and *when* to work, and *what* to produce, they are by definition not being creative.

Once expectations for creativity are clearly defined, task autonomy enables key creative performance activities, such as:

- Information collection, problem construction, ideation, and sensemaking
- Calculated allocation of time and resources spent on the creative process vs general job demands and priorities
- Experimentation and freedom to fail early and often through trial and error
- Dedicated time for brainstorming and challenging conventional thinking
- Latitude to work around conventional processes

Conversely, when creativity is managed more rigidly or interrupted frequently, like other general work processes and timelines, the creative process is often hindered and difficult to resurrect (Janz, Colquitt, & Noe, 1997; Langfred, 2005; Langfred & Moye, 2004). Similarly, if task autonomy is not truly supported by the manager and organization, autonomy can transform into ambiguity and risk (Jungert, Koestner, Houlfort, & Schattke, 2013). That is, if employees are negatively evaluated or punished for trying something different and failing, they will begin to see autonomy as a job threat and avoid being truly creative. Choice without support can be paralyzing (Deci & Ryan, 1987, 2000; Furnham & Ribchester, 1995).

In all, jobs and teams must be structured in a manner that provides rich opportunities to act upon their expectations to be creative. Research indicates that time, resources, workspaces, and task autonomy all contribute to the quality of those opportunities (Hammond et al., 2011). As such, managers must be cognizant of all these factors and striking an appropriate balance. However, every action has an opportunity cost, so in a world of limited resources it is important to first focus disproportionately more effort into getting the basics of time and task autonomy right, because they have the greatest effect on creativity (Hammond et al., 2011). Complementary, but also important to the basics, are readily providing resource sufficiency and engaging workspaces as necessitated.

CONTINUALLY SUPPORT THE CREATIVE PROCESS

Effectively setting expectations and creating opportunities to be creative sets the stage for consistent, exceptional creative performance in organizations. However, as previously discussed, trying something new and different is risky to the careers of employees and investments of the organization. Attempts at innovation that do not result an increase to the organization's bottom-line often reflect poorly on the employees involved rather than breakdowns in the process, system, or market.

Not surprisingly, Gallup (2017) finds that a dismal 18% of employees strongly agree that they *can take risks at work that could lead to important new products, services, or solutions.* Thus while it is pretty disappointing that only 3 in 10 employees strongly agree *they are expected to be creative at work*, and 3 in 10 employees are *allotted time daily to be creative*, the number of employees who think they can actually take action on creative opportunities is much lower (30% expected to be creative vs 18% can take the risk). This gap is concerning because it highlights an incongruence between preparation and action that must be closed if organizations truly want to foster creativity.

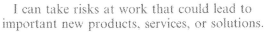

I can take risks at work that could lead to important new products, services, or solutions.

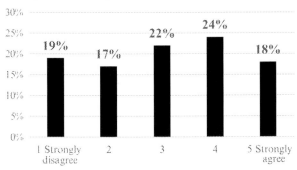

The good news is that confidence in taking risks increases with strong expectations and time allotted to be creative. Employees who strongly agree that they are expected to be creative *and* are allotted time daily are 3.4 times as likely to strongly agree they can take risks to be creative. While taking risks to be creative does not assure creative outcomes, these findings add color and insight to meta-analytic findings indicating that role expectations ($\rho = 0.44$), resources ($\rho = 0.27$), and job autonomy ($\rho = 0.32$) are among the highest correlates of creativity and innovation (Hammond et al., 2011).

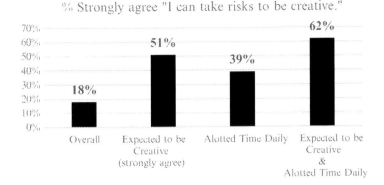

% Strongly agree "I can take risks to be creative."

Nonetheless, committing to the creative process only starts with expectation and opportunity. Creative performance is a dynamic series of events and employees will only fully commit to a challenging, time-consuming journey if they believe they have relentless support of those around them—starting with their manager.

Empowerment

Support goes beyond having a choice in how to approach work tasks. Autonomy in *how* and *when* creativity is approached leads to true *empowerment* only when employees trust that their manager will support their decision making and allow them to fail without repercussion. That does not mean employees have license to do whatever they want, rather they believe the manager will uphold their mutually agreed-upon expectations and parameters for specific opportunities. As a result, when employees' expectations for support throughout the creative process are upheld, they begin to feel secure in taking bigger risks without fear of negative consequences (Hammond et al., 2011; Hunter et al., 2007; Ma, 2009).

More specifically, there are key types of creativity enhancing support managers should monitor: psychological safety—*feeling accepted, respected, and able to act genuinely without negative consequences* (Carmeli, Reiter-Palmon, & Ziv, 2010), participative safety—*actively participating in decision making without fear of repercussion* (West, 1990), and sociopolitical support—*acting without fear of social or political consequences* (Seibert, Wang, & Courtright, 2011). When employees feel supported on all three levels, it is no surprise they tend to be more creative (Axtell et al., 2000; Baer & Frese, 2003; Spreitzer, 1995) because feeling supported increases confidence in their ability to succeed at higher stakes challenges. This is particularly important because raising the bar for creativity through high expectations, complex problems, and moderate time pressure can substantially boost creativity, but it can also diminish it if employees get overwhelmed. As such, manager support helps employees embrace these challenges to become more creative, rather than be hindered by them (Oldham & Cummings, 1996).

Empowering employees with task autonomy and managerial support also elevates intrinsic motivation, and subsequently, intensity of effort and persistence. By giving employees choice over how they approach creativity, they become more naturally motivated by the task itself (Deci & Ryan, 2000; Zhou, 1998). Additionally, support from the manager has an independent effect on intrinsic motivation, based on affirmation that the task is important and supported (Harackiewicz, 1979; Oldham & Cummings, 1996). Manager support may also activate motivation that stems from the interpersonal relationship between managers and employees.

Continual Coaching

For managerial support to actively and sustainably drive creativity, it must go beyond giving permission to be creative. Traditional approaches to performance management have largely failed to engage employees and substantially improve performance because they have been narrowly focused on the annual performance review and performance ratings (Wigert & Harter, 2017). That is, setting goals at the beginning of the year, only revisiting them a few times per year, and then, evaluating success at the end of the year is not an effective approach for inspiring or developing employees. Gallup finds that little managerial feedback occurs between these formal events as about $1/4^{th}$ of employees report receiving managerial feedback weekly, $1/4^{th}$ report receiving it a few times per month, and $1/2$ report receiving feedback a few times per year or less (Wigert & Harter, 2017).

If managers approach creative performance in the same manner, their efforts to improve creativity are likely to fail. Thus managers must fundamentally change how they are approaching performance and make creativity a central part of their approach if they want to foster creativity in their organizations. They must continually examine creativity expectations and progress, opportunities for creative production, and how employees are experiencing the process. As result, an ongoing dialog about expectations, progress, and development must emerge that makes the process dynamic and tailored to the unique needs of the work assignment and individuals involved.

This is a shift from task management to performance coaching. When managers become coaches they are regularly reexamining progress in relation to expectations and ensure the two are aligned. Continual coaching aligns with the iterative nature of creativity because it embraces that there are many stages and different types of activities involved in creative performance. When critical contextual factors—such as task complexity, autonomy, challenge, and time pressure—change, employees and managers should consider adjusting how they approach their work. Through a better understanding of the creative process, managers can help employees identify when their circumstances have changed and explore the proper adjustments.

In practice, this means recalibrating expectations, approaches to the work task, or both, as the creative process evolves. Managers may ask, *"Are we hitting the mark on current expectations and feel confident in achieving future expectations?,"* *"What circumstances or expectations have changed?,"* or *"Based on what we've learned, what should we start, stop, and continue doing?"* Answers to these types of conversation starting questions will reveal successes that should be celebrated and challenges that can be addressed. By celebrating progress and discussing approaches taken, creativity is further encouraged. However, well-meaning, investigative questions can quickly turn into premature evaluation and criticism which inhibit creativity. It is important that feedback about progress stays focused on priorities and outcomes, rather than micromanagement of how to approach the work.

Maintaining a positive, future-oriented dialog allows employees to safely voice challenges (Carmeli et al., 2010; Hunter et al., 2007; Seibert et al., 2011; West, 1990). When advice is given, it should be focused on using elements of the creative process discussed in this chapter to help employees think about how they can approach their work differently. For instance, managers may suggest revisiting the problem construction process, or identifying a coworker to ideate with who has had success approaching a similar issue. A change in work routine or space, as well as use of creativity-inducing exercises and skill-building activities can help employees get unstuck from mental hurdles. Not only is creative thinking facilitated by thought exercises and skills training, but these hands-on approaches also create opportunities for personal development during a natural workflow.

In short, it is through ongoing conversations about creative performance that employees will learn if their manager is truly supportive. For instance, if a manager says "you have the freedom to fail early-and-often through trial-and-error" or "feel free to share drafts of your ideas before they are fully baked" but quickly makes critical judgments about that early work, employees will not feel free to take those risks in the future. Similarly, when managers change their goals or criteria for success after performance has already occurred, trust in the process diminishes. However, when managers support the entire process, it is much easier for employees to commit to their goals and be highly confident in their abilities to be creative (Tierney & Farmer, 2004, 2011). Further, when managers are an active part of daily performance, they can more easily share learnings, make connections between coworkers, and align efforts—a benefit to both individual creativity and organizational alignment.

Supportive Team Climate

While this chapter focuses on individual-level creativity, it is important to acknowledge that the team environment impacts the creative performance of individuals. Meta-analytic research shows that fostering a team environment characterized by positivity and support for creativity is predictive of creative performance (Hammond et al., 2011; Hunter et al., 2007; Ma, 2009). Inspiring, challenging, and supporting employees throughout the creative process cannot fall solely on the shoulders of the manager. Managers must create a team environment where coworkers support and coach one another. In fact, a meta-analysis by Hunter et al. (2007) found that team climates characterized by high support and autonomy are especially effective at enabling creative performance under turbulent, high-pressure, competitive circumstances.

Deeper investigation into the effects of the team on individual-level creativity reveals that a multitude of factors, such as team information exchange, team goals, team support, and simply being on a more creative team, independently contribute to an individual's creativity (Gong, Kim, Lee, & Zhu, 2013; Scott & Bruce, 1994). Thus, managers can multiply their efforts by building a creative team environment. Starting with the basics, such as ensuring teammates are aware of one another's interests, expertise, and expectations for creativity, sets the stage for easier information exchange and support. Creative collaboration can be further enhanced by learning the creative process together and sharing experiences. Moreover, reminding teams of the resources and opportunities at their disposal will push teammates to interact and eventually challenge each other to be more creative.

CREATE ACCOUNTABILITY

Performing at a high level on a consistent basis requires accountability. Creative performance is no different. Expectations for creativity are more effective when employees know their work is being evaluated (Shalley, 1995). Thus, it is important to ensure expectations for creativity are both clearly defined and continually monitored. Accountability for creativity can be tricky because a detailed vision for a creative outcome may be difficult to conceptualize ahead of time. Nonetheless, clear progress criteria can be set that describe distinct aspects of creative performance, such as completion of key stages in the creative process, timelines, quality of collaboration, number of creative ideas, lessons learned, and quality of the effort.

Given that creative performance is novel and by definition can be approached different ways, it can also be difficult to know when a creative idea is "done" or "good enough" and ready for implementation.

Additionally, the market viability of a creative solution is dependent on a variety of factors, such as capacity and readiness of the organization for implementation, market opportunity, and anticipated return on investment. For this reason, accountability for generating creative ideas should be separated from accountability for implementation. Creative performance that requires implementation as part of the performance expectations can be approached in a more concrete manner after the creative solution has been approved for production because completion of implementation activities is much easier to track and evaluate objectively (e.g., speed, efficiency, timeliness, and quality measures).

Although there is no one-size-fits all way to measure creative performance, the important thing for managers to know is that they must follow-up on creativity expectations and formally evaluate progress— based on criteria defined during the expectation-setting process. If efforts for accomplishing creativity goals are not a core part of performance reviews, they will not be treated like a core aspect of performance by employees. Notably, more frequent performance progress checks tend to be more effective and engaging, in general (Wigert & Harter, 2017). Thus the iterative nature of creative performance is likely to especially benefit from more frequent monitoring and feedback (De Stobbeleir, Ashford, & Buyens, 2011).

Further, creative performance should be recognized and rewarded. While the creative process tends to be naturally intrinsically motivating, rewards also have a positive—albeit weaker—effect on individual creativity (Hammond et al., 2011). Rewards both signal the importance of creativity to the organization and extrinsically motivate employees through financial gain (Eisenberger, Armeli, Rexwinkel, Lynch, & Rhoades, 2001; Tesluk et al., 1997). Thus it is important to evaluate and reward creativity in a manner that motivates employees to take risks and pursue creativity, but in a way that does not punish failures or less original contributions (Shalley & Perry-Smith, 2001; Zhou & Shalley, 2003). For instance, bonuses paid on completion of creative expectations, or contests for generating solutions judged to be exceptionally creative relative to other ideas, can be structured to reward strong efforts and outstanding contributions without reflecting poorly on lesser efforts.

Rewards for creativity are not just about motivating intense short-term efforts; they also have lasting effects that are likely to affect later efforts. Gallup (2017) finds that when employees believe they are compensated fairly in general, understand how their performance affects their pay, or expect to get a raise or promotion soon, they are more likely to believe they can take risks to be creative. In addition to inspiring pursuit of short-term goals, being paid well for accomplishments creates the confidence needed to take calculated risks.

ADJUST FOR INDIVIDUAL DIFFERENCES

Managing creativity is not just about managing a process, it is about managing people. Employees' readiness to approach different types of creative assignments will vary with their knowledge, skills, and abilities. Meta-analytic research on individual differences shows that certain traits can affect employees' capacity for creativity. Traits that comprise a creative personality, like openness to experience and divergent thinking ability, are associated with being more creative across a variety of roles (Da Costa, Páez, Sánchez, Garaigordobil, & Gondim, 2015). Individual differences research is also riddled with mixed findings, suggesting that certain traits may situationally help, hinder, or have no effect on creative performance. Beyond natural abilities, expertise and experience matter, too, as education and tenure are positively correlated with creative performance (Ma, 2009).

As such, fit between employee capabilities and tasks requirements is an important foundation of performance (Kristof-Brown, Zimmerman, & Johnson, 2005). Amabile (1998) argues that diligently ensuring that the right people are assigned to the right task is more important to creative performance than many subsequent management actions. Research conducted from an "interactionist" perspective further describes how talent, task characteristics, manager characteristics, and management actions can work together to influence creative production. For instance, employees who have a highly creative personality and are tasked with a complex job tend to be more creative when their manager is supportive and noncontrolling (Oldham & Cummings, 1996). Similarly, individuals high on openness to experience are most creative when they receive positive feedback and job flexibility (George & Zhou, 2001). In all, research on interactionism and creativity indicates that management practices are often the key factor that moderates the relationship between individual differences and creative performance (Farmer, Tierney, & Kung-Mcintyre, 2003; George & Zhou, 2001; Oldham & Cummings, 1996; Shalley, Gilson, & Blum, 2009).

Practically speaking, managers have limited resources at their disposal and have to work with what's available to them—they "have to go to war with the army they have." As such, assigning expectations for creativity often cannot realistically entail a scientific alignment of knowledge, skills, and abilities with task requirements. Sometimes it is important to look beyond current capabilities and consider the employee's interests, aspirations, and career development plans.

Giving employees a developmental task that is interesting and excites them can trigger other factors correlated with creative performance, like intrinsic motivation and goal commitment. Assignments related to creativity goals can be exceptional developmental opportunities because they stretch employees to try new things, think differently, collaborate, and explore information. These developmental assignments can inspire a new passion for jobs that begin to feel mundane or spark ideas for exploring other jobs an employee might be interested in trying.

While there is no silver bullet when it comes to using individual differences to enhance creative performance, managers can and should do a much better job of individualizing their management approach to the unique abilities, needs, and aspirations of employees. By simply being more intentional about adapting expectations, opportunities, and support for creativity to each employee's respective situation, managers can begin to gradually make the creative process feel more natural and help employees play to their strengths.

SUMMARY AND CONCLUSION

Performance management approaches must be reengineered to foster creativity. Employees are not currently experiencing an environment where creativity is prioritized, with only 29% of employees strongly agreeing they are expected to be creative, 30% being allotted time to be creative on a daily basis, and 18% strongly agreeing that they can take the risks necessary to attempt creative performance (Gallup, 2017). If expectations and accountably for creative performance do not become a focus of performance review and recognition systems, employees will put all of their other work ahead of creativity.

Beyond expectations and opportunities to be creative, managers need to transform how they are approaching creativity on a daily basis. An ongoing dialog about the creative process must emerge whereby employees are continually exploring new ideas, sharing information, and recalibrating their efforts as circumstances change. This ongoing dialog creates many more opportunities to develop creative performance habits in a way that works best for each individual, and cultivates collaboration.

Teaching managers to coach for creativity can make up for a lot of deficiencies, from lack of employee talent to imperfect performance management and support systems. Continual coaching should be based on the premise that there is no one way to engineer creative performance. Rather, research supports a more holistic or interactionist approach requiring a multitude of factors to be brought into balance, including but not limited to expectations for creativity, individual differences, feedback, support, control, and characteristics of the supervisor (Baer & Oldham, 2006; George & Zhou, 2001; Madjar, Oldham, & Pratt, 2002; Oldham & Cummings, 1996; Zhou & Oldham, 2001; Zhou & Shalley, 2003). Only through acknowledgment of these factors and integration of them into the creative process can managers consistently foster creativity across a variety of situations.

Gallup (2017) research shows that as managers mature in their roles, they naturally get better at setting expectations, providing time to be creative, and empowering direct reports. Similarly, organizations will not become creativity factories overnight. Like any other organizational change initiative, programs aimed at elevating individual and organizational creativity should start small and manageable. Fostering creative performance is a learning process and an iterative process. Expectations for creativity should increase with preparation, practice, and experience. The key is to "meet people where they are at," meaning that everyone has a different level of readiness to be creative and readiness can change depending on the task at hand. Take time to understand where to start, be patient, try different approaches, and gradually increase expectations after basic tasks are mastered.

Beyond the readiness of individual employees to be creative, managers, teams, and organizations must be prepared to support creativity. If individuals escalate their creative performance, but their ideas are not used because they do not have the partners and resources to implement creative ideas, then innovation dies and individuals become discouraged from being creative in the future.

Finally, managers must be enabled to be a creativity coach. They require work conditions and support similar to what employees need to improve their creative performance. Without the proper expectations, time, resources, support, training, systems, and talent, it can feel nearly impossible for managers to foster the creative process for each of their employees. After all, creative performance is, and should be, a challenging journey. As such, organizations truly committed to innovation and growth must arm managers to navigate, adapt, and overcome hurdles in the creative process so employees can spend more time focused on the elements of the process that research shows are most likely to elevate creative performance (Fig. 2).

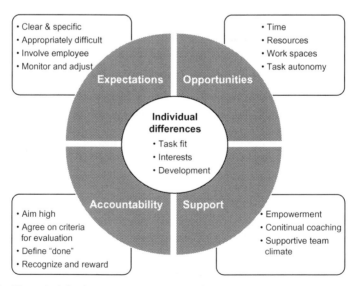

FIG. 2   Key principles for managing creative performance.

References

Amabile, T. M. (1988). A model of creativity and innovation in organizations. *Research in Organizational Behavior*, *10*, 123–167.

Amabile, T. M. (1991). Foundations of individual creativity. In B. M. Staw (Ed.), *Psychological dimensions of organizational behaviour* (pp. 537–558). New York: MacMillan.

Amabile, T. M. (1998). *How to kill creativity*. Vol. 87 Boston, MA: Harvard Business School Publishing.

Amabile, T. M., Conti, R., Coon, H., Lazenby, J., & Herron, M. (1996). Assessing the work environment for creativity. *Academy of Management Journal*, *39*, 1154–1184.

Amabile, T. M., Hadley, C. N., & Kramer, S. J. (2002). Creativity under the gun. *Harvard Business Review*, *80*, 52–63.

Amabile, T. M., Mueller, J. S., Simpson, W. B., Hadley, C. N., Kramer, S. J., & Fleming, L. (2002). *Time pressure and creativity in organizations: A longitudinal field study*. Harvard Business School Working Paper, No. 02-073.

Andrews, F. M., & Farris, G. F. (1972). Time pressure and performance of scientists and engineers: a five-year panel study. *Organizational Behavior and Human Performance*, *8*, 185–200.

Andrews, J., & Smith, D. C. (1996). In search of the marketing imagination: factors affecting the creativity of marketing programs for mature products. *Journal of Marketing Research*, *33*, 174–187. https://doi.org/10.2307/3152145.

Axtell, C. M., Holman, D. J., Unsworth, K. L., Wall, T. D., Waterson, P. E., & Harrington, E. (2000). Shopfloor innovation: facilitating the suggestion and implementation of ideas. *Journal of Occupational and Organizational Psychology*, *73*, 265–285.

Baer, M., & Frese, M. (2003). Innovation is not enough: climates for initiative and psychological safety, process innovations, and firm performance. *Journal of Organizational Behavior*, *24*, 45–68.

Baer, M., & Oldham, G. R. (2006). The curvilinear relation between experienced creative time pressure and creativity: moderating effects of openness to experience and support for creativity. *Journal of Applied Psychology*, *91*, 963–970.

Basadur, M. (2004). Leading others to think innovatively together: creative leadership. *The Leadership Quarterly*, *15*, 103–121.

Brown, T. C., & Latham, G. P. (2002). The effects of behavioural outcome goals, learning goals, and urging people to do their best on an individual's teamwork behaviour in a group problem-solving task. *Canadian Journal of Behavioural Science*, *34*, 276–285. https://doi.org/10.1037/h0087180.

Brown, S. D., Lent, R. W., Telander, K., & Tramayne, S. (2011). Social cognitive career theory, conscientiousness, and work performance: a meta-analytic path analysis. *Journal of Vocational Behavior*, *79*, 81–90.

Carmeli, A., Reiter-Palmon, R., & Ziv, E. (2010). Inclusive leadership and employee involvement in creative tasks in the workplace: the mediating role of psychological safety. *Creativity Research Journal*, *22*, 250–260.

Csiksientmihalyi, M., & Getzels, J. W. (1988). Creativity and problem finding in art. In F. H. Farley & R. W. Neperud (Eds.), *The foundations of aesthetics, art, and art education* (pp. 91–106). New York: Praeger.

Csikszentmihalyi, M., & Getzels, J. W. (1971). Discovery-oriented behavior and the originality of creative products: a study with artists. *Journal of Personality and Social Psychology*, *19*, 47–52.

Da Costa, S., Páez, D., Sánchez, F., Garaigordobil, M., & Gondim, S. (2015). Personal factors of creativity: a second order meta-analysis. *Journal of Work and Organizational Psychology*, *31*, 165–173.

De Stobbeleir, K. E., Ashford, S. J., & Buyens, D. (2011). Self-regulation of creativity at work: the role of feedback-seeking behavior in creative performance. *Academy of Management Journal*, *54*, 811–831.

Deci, E. L., & Ryan, R. M. (1987). The support of autonomy and the control of behavior. *Journal of Personality and Social Psychology, 53*, 1024.

Deci, E. L., & Ryan, R. M. (2000). The" what" and" why" of goal pursuits: human needs and the self-determination of behavior. *Psychological Inquiry, 11*, 227–268.

DeWalt, D. A., Davis, T. C., Wallace, A. S., Seligman, H. K., Bryant-Shilliday, B., Arnold, C. L., et al. (2009). Goal setting in diabetes self-management: taking the baby steps to success. *Patient Education and Counseling, 77*, 218–223.

Dewey, J. (1910). *How we think*. Boston, MA: D.C. Heath.

Dodds, R. A., Ward, T. B., & Smith, S. M. (2003). A review of the experimental literature on incubation in problem solving and creativity. *Creativity Research Handbook, 3*, 285–302.

Eisenberger, R., Armeli, S., Rexwinkel, B., Lynch, P. D., & Rhoades, L. (2001). Reciprocation of perceived organizational support. *Journal of Applied Psychology, 86*, 42–51.

Ensley, M. D., Pearson, A. W., & Amason, A. C. (2002). Understanding the dynamics of new venture top management teams: cohesion, conflict, and new venture performance. *Journal of Business Venturing, 17*, 365–386.

Farmer, S. M., Tierney, P., & Kung-Mcintyre, K. (2003). Employee creativity in Taiwan: an application of role identity theory. *Academy of Management Journal, 46*, 618–630.

Farr, J. L., Sin, H., & Tesluk, P. E. (2003). Knowledge management processes and work group innovation. In L. V. Shavinina & L. V. Shavinina (Eds.), *The international handbook on innovation* (pp. 574–586). New York: Elsevier Science. https://doi.org/10.1016/B978-008044198-6/50039-5.

Furnham, A., & Ribchester, T. (1995). Tolerance of ambiguity: a review of the concept, its measurement and applications. *Current Psychology, 14*, 179–199.

Gallup (2017). Workplace experience panel survey of 16,571 full and part time employees, aged 18 and older, conducted April 19th through May 7th 2017 [Data set]. The Gallup Organization [distributor].

George, J. M., & Zhou, J. (2001). When openness to experience and conscientiousness are related to creative behavior: an interactional approach. *Journal of Applied Psychology, 86*, 513.

Getzels, J. W., & Csikszentmihalyi, M. (1976). *Concern for discovery in the creative process*. In *The Creativity Question* (pp. 161–165). Durham, NC: Duke University Press.

Gilson, L. L., Lim, H. S., D'Innocenzo, L., & Moye, N. (2012). One size does not fit all: managing radical and incremental creativity. *The Journal of Creative Behavior, 46*, 168–191.

Gong, Y., Kim, T. Y., Lee, D. R., & Zhu, J. (2013). A multilevel model of team goal orientation, information exchange, and creativity. *Academy of Management Journal, 56*, 827–851.

Guilford, J. P. (1967). Creativity: yesterday, today and tomorrow. *The Journal of Creative Behavior, 1*, 3–14.

Gupta, A. K., & Singhal, A. (1993). Managing human resources for innovation and creativity. *Research Technology Management, 36*(3), 41–48.

Hackman, J. R. (1980). Work redesign and motivation. *Professional Psychology, 11*, 445–455.

Hammond, M. M., Neff, N. L., Farr, J. L., Schwall, A. R., & Zhao, X. (2011). Predictors of individual-level innovation at work: a meta-analysis. *Psychology of Aesthetics, Creativity, and the Arts, 5*, 90–105.

Harackiewicz, J. M. (1979). The effects of reward contingency and performance feedback on intrinsic motivation. *Journal of Personality and Social Psychology, 37*, 1352–1363.

Hargadon, A. B., & Bechky, B. A. (2006). When collections of creatives become creative collectives: a field study of problem solving at work. *Organization Science, 17*, 484–500.

Harkin, B., Webb, T. L., Chang, B. P., Prestwich, A., Conner, M., Kellar, I., et al. (2016). Does monitoring goal progress promote goal attainment? A meta-analysis of the experimental evidence. *Psychological Bulletin, 142*, 198–229.

Harter, J. K., Schmidt, F. L., & Hayes, T. L. (2002). Business-unit-level relationship between employee satisfaction, employee engagement, and business outcomes: a meta-analysis. *Journal of Applied Psychology, 87*, 268–279.

Hennessey, B. A., & Amabile, T. M. (2010). Creativity. *Annual Review of Psychology, 61*, 569–598.

Heunks, F. J. (1998). Innovation, creativity and success. *Small Business Economics*, *10*, 263–272.

Hunter, S. T., Bedell, K. E., & Mumford, M. D. (2007). Climate for creativity: a quantitative review. *Creativity Research Journal*, *19*, 69–90.

Hunter, S. T., Thoroughgood, C. N., Myer, A. T., & Ligon, G. S. (2011). Paradoxes of leading innovative endeavors: summary, solutions, and future directions. *Psychology of Aesthetics, Creativity, and the Arts*, *5*, 54.

Janz, B. D., Colquitt, J. A., & Noe, R. A. (1997). Knowledge worker team effectiveness: the role of autonomy, interdependence, team development, and contextual support variables. *Personnel Psychology*, *50*, 877–904.

Jungert, T., Koestner, R. F., Houlfort, N., & Schattke, K. (2013). Distinguishing source of autonomy support in relation to workers' motivation and self-efficacy. *The Journal of Social Psychology*, *153*, 651–666.

Klein, H. J., Wesson, M. J., Hollenbeck, J. R., & Alge, B. J. (1999). Goal commitment and the goal-setting process: conceptual clarification and empirical synthesis. *Journal of Applied Psychology*, *84*, 885–896.

Koppel, R. H., & Storm, B. C. (2014). Escaping mental fixation: incubation and inhibition in creative problem solving. *Memory*, *22*, 340–348.

Kristof-Brown, A. L., Zimmerman, R. D., & Johnson, E. C. (2005). Consequences of individual's fit at work: a meta-analysis of person-job, person-organization, person-group, and person-supervisor fit. *Personnel Psychology*, *58*, 281–342. https://doi.org/10.1111/j.1744-6570.2005.00672.x.

Langfred, C. W. (2005). Autonomy and performance in teams: the multilevel moderating effect of task interdependence. *Journal of Management*, *31*, 513–529.

Langfred, C. W., & Moye, N. A. (2004). Effects of task autonomy on performance: an extended model considering motivational, informational, and structural mechanisms. *Journal of Applied Psychology*, *89*, 934.

Latham, G. P., & Brown, T. C. (2006). The effect of learning vs. outcome goals on self-efficacy, satisfaction and performance in an MBA program. *Applied Psychology*, *55*, 606–623.

Locke, E. A., & Latham, G. P. (2002). Building a practically useful theory of goal setting and task motivation: a 35-year odyssey. *American Psychologist*, *57*, 705–717.

Locke, E. A., & Latham, G. P. (2006). New directions in goal-setting theory. *Current Directions in Psychological Science*, *15*, 265–268.

Ma, H. H. (2009). The effect size of variables associated with creativity: a meta-analysis. *Creativity Research Journal*, *21*, 30–42.

Madjar, N., Greenberg, E., & Chen, Z. (2011). Factors for radical creativity, incremental creativity, and routine, noncreative performance. *Journal of Applied Psychology*, *96*, 730.

Madjar, N., & Oldham, G. R. (2006). Task rotation and polychronicity: effects on individuals' creativity. *Human Performance*, *19*, 117–131.

Madjar, N., Oldham, G. R., & Pratt, M. G. (2002). There's no place like home? The contributions of work and nonwork creativity support to employees' creative performance. *Academy of Management Journal*, *45*, 757–767.

Madjar, N., & Shalley, C. E. (2008). Multiple tasks' and multiple goals' effect on creativity: forced incubation or just a distraction? *Journal of Management*, *34*, 786–805. https://doi.org/10.1177/0149206308318611.

Malone, T. W. (2004). *The future of work*. Audio-Tech Business Book Summaries, Incorporated.

Mathisen, G. E. (2011). Organizational antecedents of creative self-efficacy. *Creativity and Innovation Management*, *20*, 185–195.

McCoy, J. M., & Evans, G. W. (2002). The potential role of the physical environment in fostering creativity. *Creativity Research Journal*, *14*, 409–426.

McEwan, D., Harden, S. M., Zumbo, B. D., Sylvester, B. D., Kaulius, M., Ruissen, G. R., et al. (2016). The effectiveness of multi-component goal setting interventions for changing physical activity behaviour: a systematic review and meta-analysis. *Health Psychology Review*, *10*, 67–88.

Mento, A. J., Steel, R. P., & Karren, R. J. (1987). A meta-analytic study of the effects of goal setting on task performance: 1966-1984. *Organizational Behavior and Human Decision Processes, 39*, 52–83.

Mone, M. A., & Shalley, C. E. (1995). Effects of task complexity and goal specificity on change in strategy and performance over time. *Human Performance, 8*, 243–262. https://doi.org/10.1207/s15327043hup0804_1.

Mumford, M. D. (2000). Managing creative people: strategies and tactics for innovation. *Human Resource Management Review, 10*, 313–351.

Mumford, M. D., Baughman, W. A., Threlfall, K. V., Supinski, E. P., & Costanza, D. P. (1996). Process-based measures of creative problem-solving skills: I. Problem construction. *Creativity Research Journal, 9*, 63–76.

Mumford, M. D., & Gustafson, S. B. (1988). Creativity syndrome: integration, application, and innovation. *Psychological Bulletin, 103*, 27–43.

Mumford, M. D., Mobley, M. I., Reiter-Palmon, R., Uhlman, C. E., & Doares, L. M. (1991). Process analytic models of creative capacities. *Creativity Research Journal, 4*, 91–122.

Mumford, M. D., Reiter-Palmon, R., & Redmond, M. R. (1994). Problem construction and cognition: applying problem representations in ill-defined domains. In M. A. Runco (Ed.), 1994. *Problem finding, problem solving, and creativity* (pp. 3–39). Westport, CT: Ablex Publishing.

Mumford, M. D., Whetzel, D. L., & Reiter-Palmon, R. (1997). Thinking creatively at work: organization influences on creative problem solving. *Journal of Creative Behavior, 31*, 7–17.

Oldham, G. R., & Cummings, A. (1996). Employee creativity: personal and contextual factors at work. *Academy of Management Journal, 39*, 607–634.

Orlet, S. (2008). An expanding view on incubation. *Creativity Research Journal, 20*, 297–308.

Parker, S. L., Jimmieson, N. L., & Amiot, C. E. (2009). The stress-buffering effects of control on task satisfaction and perceived goal attainment: an experimental study of the moderating influence of desire for control. *Applied Psychology: An International Review, 58*, 622–652.

Perry-Smith, J. E. (2006). Social yet creative: the role of social relationships in facilitating individual creativity. *Academy of Management Journal, 49*, 85–101.

Porter, T. W., & Lilly, B. S. (1996). The effects of conflict, trust, and task commitment on project team performance. *International Journal of Conflict Management, 7*, 361–376.

Rahyuda, A., Syed, J., & Soltani, E. (2014). The role of relapse prevention and goal setting in training transfer enhancement. *Human Resource Development Review, 13*, 413–436.

Reiter-Palmon, R. (2011). Introduction to special issue: the psychology of creativity and innovation in the workplace. *Psychology of Aesthetics, Creativity, and the Arts, 5*, 1–2.

Reiter-Palmon, R., & Illies, J. J. (2004). Leadership and creativity: understanding leadership from a creative problem-solving perspective. *The Leadership Quarterly, 15*, 55–77.

Runco, M. (2004). Personal creativity and culture. In S. Lau, A. N. Hui, & G. Y. Ng (Eds.), *Creativity: When east meets west* (pp. 9–21). Singapore: World Scientific Publishing Co.

Runco, M. A., & Jaeger, G. J. (2012). The standard definition of creativity. *Creativity Research Journal, 24*, 92–96.

Scott, S. G., & Bruce, R. A. (1994). Determinants of innovative behavior: a path model of individual innovation in the workplace. *Academy of Management Journal, 37*, 580–607.

Seibert, S. E., Wang, G., & Courtright, S. H. (2011). Antecedents and consequences of psychological and team empowerment in organizations: A meta-analytic review. *Journal of Applied Psychology, 96*(5), 981–1003.

Shalley, C. E. (1995). Effects of coaction, expected evaluation, and goal setting on creativity and productivity. *Academy of Management Journal, 38*, 483–503.

Shalley, C. E., & Gilson, L. L. (2004). What leaders need to know: a review of social and contextual factors that can foster or hinder creativity. *The Leadership Quarterly, 15*, 33–53.

Shalley, C. E., Gilson, L. L., & Blum, T. C. (2009). Interactive effects of growth need strength, work context, and job complexity on self-reported creative performance. *Academy of Management Journal, 52*, 489–505.

Shalley, C. E., & Perry-Smith, J. E. (2001). Effects of social-psychological factors on creative performance: the role of informational and controlling expected evaluation and modeling experience. *Organizational Behavior and Human Decision Processes, 84*, 1–22.

Shalley, C. E., & Zhou, J. (2008). Organizational creativity research: a historical overview. In J. Zhou & C. E. Shalley (Eds.), *Handbook of organizational creativity* (pp. 3–32). New York: Erlbaum.

Sio, U. N., & Ormerod, T. C. (2009). Does incubation enhance problem solving? A meta-analytic review. *Psychological Bulletin, 135*, 94–120. https://doi.org/10.1037/a0014212.

Spreitzer, G. M. (1995). Psychological empowerment in the workplace: dimensions, measurement, and validation. *Academy of Management Journal, 38*, 1442–1465.

Tesluk, P. E., Farr, J. L., & Klein, S. R. (1997). Influences of organizational culture and climate on individual creativity. *The Journal of Creative Behavior, 31*, 27–41.

Tierney, P., & Farmer, S. M. (2004). The Pygmalion process and employee creativity. *Journal of Management, 30*, 413–432.

Tierney, P., & Farmer, S. M. (2011). Creative self-efficacy development and creative performance over time. *Journal of Applied Psychology, 96*, 277–293.

Tubbs, M. E. (1986). Goal-setting: a meta-analytic examination of the empirical evidence. *Journal of Applied Psychology, 71*, 474.

Unsworth, K. L., Wall, T. D., & Carter, A. (2005). Creative requirement: a neglected construct in the study of employee creativity? *Group & Organization Management, 30*, 541–560.

Wehmeyer, M. L., & Shogren, K. A. (2017). Goal setting and attainment and self-regulation. In K. Shogren, M. Wehmeyer, & N. Singh (Eds.), *Springer Series on Child and Family Studies*: Handbook of positive psychology in intellectual and developmental disabilities. Cham.: Springer. https://doi.org/10.1007/978-3-319-59066-0_16.

West, M. (1990). The social psychology of innovation in groups. In M. A. West & J. L. Farr (Eds.), *Innovation and creativity at work: psychological and organizational strategies* (pp. 309–333). Chichester: John Wiley & Sons, Ltd.

Wigert, B. G., & Harter, J. K. (2017). *Re-engineering performance management*. The Gallup Organization: Washington, DC.

Woodman, R. W., & Schoenfeldt, L. F. (1990). An interactionist model of creative behavior. *The Journal of Creative Behavior, 24*, 279–290.

Zhang, X., & Bartol, K. M. (2010). Linking empowering leadership and employee creativity: the influence of psychological empowerment, intrinsic motivation, and creative process engagement. *Academy of Management Journal, 53*, 107–128.

Zhou, J. (1998). Feedback valence, feedback style, task autonomy, and achievement orientation: interactive effects on creative performance. *Journal of Applied Psychology, 83*, 261–276.

Zhou, J., & Hoever, I. J. (2014). Research on workplace creativity: a review and redirection. *Annual Review of Organizational Psychology and Organizational Behavior, 1*, 333–359.

Zhou, J., & Oldham, G. R. (2001). Enhancing creative performance: effects of expected developmental assessment strategies and creative personality. *The Journal of Creative Behavior, 35*, 151–167.

Zhou, J., & Shalley, C. E. (2003). *Research on employee creativity: a critical review and directions for future research*. In *Research in personnel and human resources management* (pp. 165–217). Oxford, England: Emerald Group Publishing Limited.

Further Reading

Neubert, M. J. (1998). The value of feedback and goal setting over goal setting alone and potential moderators of this effect: a meta-analysis. *Human Performance, 11*, 321–335.

Zhou, J. (2008). *Promoting creativity through feedback*. In *Handbook of Organizational Creativity* (pp. 125–145). New York: Erlbaum.

16

The Role of Creative Capacity in the 21st Century Army[☆]

Gregory A. Ruark*, Nikki Blacksmith†,
Lee Spencer Wallace‡

*United States Army Research Institute for the Behavioral and Social Sciences, Fort Belvoir, VA, United States, †Consortium Research Fellows Program, Alexandria, VA, United States, ‡United States Army, The Pentagon, Washington, DC, United States

THE ROLE OF CREATIVE CAPACITY IN THE 21st CENTURY ARMY

When describing US Army operations or training, creativity is generally not the first term that comes to mind. Instead, images of the hierarchical structure, particularly chain of command, more often springs to the forefront of our thoughts. The very essence of the Army structure and system is often viewed in terms of conformity, parochialism, a stubborn adherence to process, and inherently task oriented. This view is commonly shared by those unfamiliar with the Army and associate creativity with the works of artists, philosophers, and musicians (Vego, 2013). However, nothing could be further from the truth—creativity is a valued skill and competitive advantage for the military. Success in military operations and training for those operations require considerable creativity. After all, Sun Tzu titled his famous work, "The *Art* of War" to emphasize the important of the application of creative skill to win wars.

In contrast to perception, commanders and their staff routinely employ creative processes when faced with any situation, whether in war or

---

☆ The views and opinions expressed in this article are those of the authors and do not necessarily reflect the views of the US Army Research Institute, Department of Defense, or the US government.

peacetime, to ensure the most effective solution is generated and implemented (Department of Army [DA], 2012). No overall process-oriented checklists exist for commander and staffs—or for the larger military enterprise—to reference and subsequently to execute when faced with a challenging or novel situation. Instead, the Soldier must quickly and expertly assess the situation and determine the appropriate type of decision—structured and routine versus creative—to execute. Ultimately, the Soldier must balance the need for creative thinking with the necessity for precise and compliant application of doctrine. The regimented processes and procedures of military doctrine and adherence to the chain of command (to generate, issue, and supervise specific orders) enable consistent facilitation of predictability and stability.

While adherence to doctrine and structured processes help to guide problem-solving, these alone are not enough for the Army to be successful in today's complex environment. The Army needs leaders who are flexible and grounded in the fundamentals of combat power to expertly utilize all decision means in generating solutions. The Army also needs leaders who can leverage creative capacity when drawing upon formal training and experience grounded in Army doctrine to achieve dominance over its operational environment (DA, 2012). Leaders must provide creative solutions to training and fighting when confronted with constrained resources, the constantly changing technological landscape, and an increasingly complex political environment (McClary, 2015). Leaders must understand how to provide the right training and education for our service personnel, but do so creatively focusing on the ever-changing needs of a new generation of Warriors (DA, 2012).

The purpose of this chapter is threefold. First, we review the scientific literature to present a brief overview of creativity and provide a framework for discussing creativity in the Army. While creativity can occur at the individual, team, and organizational level (Anderson, Potocnik, & Zhou, 2014), our focus in this chapter is at the individual creative capacity that can be cultivated and improved over time. Second, we describe the individual differences the Army values as a means to foster creativity among Soldiers. In this section, we draw on creativity research to assess the empirical relationships between individual differences and creative outcomes. Third, we describe interventions and future research that has the potential to increase the creative capacity of Army Soldiers.

WHAT IS CREATIVITY?

Creativity is a cognitive and behavioral process that results in novel and innovative outcomes (Mumford, Mobley, Uhlman, Reiter-Palmon, & Doares, 1991). Put simply, creativity refers to new or improved ways of doing things and entails change in behavior, processes, and outcomes (Carmelli, Gelbard, & Reiter-Palmon, 2013; Kandler et al., 2015; Mumford et al., 1991). It is dynamic, temporal, and influenced by person and environmental factors (Anderson et al., 2014). Scholars study creative processes in conjunction with cognitive processes to better understand the interaction and impact on problem-solving (e.g., Mumford et al., 1991). Cognitive processes associated with creativity include problem construction, information search, encoding and recalling information, convergent and divergent thinking, idea generation, and idea evaluation (Carmelli et al., 2013; McClary, 2015; Mumford et al., 1991; Reiter-Palmon & Illies, 2004). However, it is not enough to generate creative ideas; individuals must also translate those concepts into practice vis-à-vis behavioral processes (Mumford et al., 1991). Implementation of behavioral processes will likely vary based on the type of organization (e.g., small start-up technology company) with examples to include stakeholder buy-in, adoption of novel ideas, and production of innovative products.

Creative Capacity

Creative capacity represents individuals' capabilities to judiciously incorporate creative processes in a given situation. Creative competence is not a single, unitary construct nor does it occur in isolation; it is a broad, complex, domain-specific cognitive and behavioral, emergent phenomena (Anderson et al., 2014; Mumford et al., 1991; Sackett, Lievens, Van Iddekinge, & Kuncel, 2017; Woodman & Schoenfeldt, 1989). Fig. 1 provides a visual depiction of the phenomenon. Creative capacity can be best viewed as an aptitude for creativity that can be acquired and developed (Carmelli et al., 2013). Antecedents of creativity encompass characteristics of the individual to include personality and cognitive ability (Furnham & Bachtiar, 2008; Sackett et al., 2017). Environmental factors, such as the task characteristics or management support, are also antecedents and moderators that influence creative capacity. Outcomes of creativity can assume a range of forms to include products, services, work methods, or management processes (Zhou & Hoever, 2014). Thus creativity will manifest differently depending on the task and the environment (Kaufman et al., 2016; Reiter-Palmon & Robinson, 2009; Sackett et al., 2017). In the next section, we describe the military environment and its contextual factors that influence creative capacity.

CREATIVITY IN THE US ARMY

The Army views creativity as the essential skillset to prevail against the enemy; it is a core skill leaders need to possess, utilize, and foster in others. The Army defines creativity as the generation of new methods and

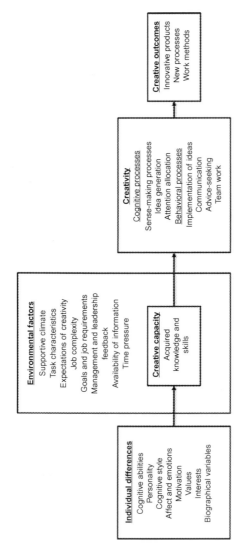

FIG. 1 Visual depiction of basic framework of creative capacity. This framework is not a comprehensive model of creativity's nomological network but rather a conceptual structure.

outcomes *unforeseen by the enemy*, that when executed properly, should *provide an unseen advantage* in war (DA, 2012, 2016). Unique to the Army is the approach that every Soldier is a leader, formal and informal, and is expected to exhibit the requisite attributes and behaviors that define Army leadership (see ADRP 6-22 Army Leadership, DA, 2012 for additional information). Thus every Soldier must possess, and express as appropriate, creative processes and behaviors. In this section, we describe the individual differences antecedents of creativity and environmental factors that affect Soldiers' creative capacity.

Individual Differences

The Army seeks *character*, *presence*, and *intellect* in their leaders and trusts these characteristics will enable creativity (DA, 2012). From a scientific perspective, these characteristics refer to an individual's personality and cognitive style, affective and emotional regulation, and intelligence. Relationships between individual differences variables and creative outcomes will vary based on task and environment (Reiter-Palmon & Illies, 2009; Woodman & Schoenfeldt, 1989; Zhou & Hoever, 2014); however, we describe general findings that support the significance of these characteristics in regards to creativity.

Personality and Cognitive Styles

Character, as the Army refers to it, represents a combination of an individual's cognitive styles and personality. Research has demonstrated an interesting and complex relationship between individual differences and creativity (Sackett et al., 2017; Sternberg, 2012). One particular type of individual difference, cognitive styles, has been found to be critical for creativity (Messick, 1976). Cognitive styles refer to an individual's preference or tendency to organize and process information in a specific manner (Messick, 1979). One type of style is divergent thinking, which is the tendency to think in new and abstract ways (Sternberg, 2012; Woodman & Schoenfeldt, 1989). Research has shown that those who possess higher levels of creative capacity tend to engage in more divergent thinking (McCrae, 1987; Sternberg, 2012). It is important to note, however, that while some argue that divergent thinking alone is the primary indicator of creative potential, others argue that it must also endure convergent thinking and manifest into a tangible outcome (Mumford et al., 1991).

Personality is also an important precursor to creative capacity (Anderson et al., 2014; Oleynick et al., 2017; Sternberg, 2012). The relationship between personality and creativity is not straightforward—it depends on the creative task and other contextual factors (Anderson et al., 2014; Furnham & Bachtiar, 2008). This dependency is consistent with the large body of employee testing literature that demonstrates personality-criterion relationships depend on the job task and thus should be conceptually matched (Ployhart, Schmitt, & Tippins, 2017; Sackett et al., 2017). Nevertheless, across the literature some consistencies have been found; individuals with high levels of openness to experience and willingness to take risks are more likely to be creative (e.g., Feist, 1998; Kaufman et al., 2016; McCrae, 1987; Oleynick et al., 2017; Sackett et al., 2017; Sternberg, 2012). Extraversion has also been found to reliably predict creative behaviors although correlations are weaker than those between openness and creativity (Oleynick et al., 2017). Motivational and achievement-oriented traits have also been identified as components of creative capacity (Anderson et al., 2014; Feist, 1998; Hirst, van Knippenberg, & Zhou, 2009; Oleynick et al., 2017; Sackett et al., 2017). Woo, Keith, Su, Saef, and Parrigon (2017) argue that in order to initiate a creative process, individuals must have sufficient motivation and desire to succeed.

Affective and Emotional Regulation

The second attribute, *presence*, refers to the outward appearance a leader impresses upon others such as subordinates, peers, and supervisors. That is, it represents one's ability to regulate affect and emotion in order to create positive impressions. Confidence—the projection of a feeling of certainty in competence—is a key aspect of impression formation. The importance of confidence in impression formation has repeatedly been demonstrated (e.g., Feist, 1998)—prior to implementing a creative idea, leaders need to help their team feel confident that they will succeed. The ability to regulate one's emotions is also important for managing the emotions that arise during the creative process (Ivcevic & Hoffmann, 2017). For example, if a leader receives negative feedback on her ideas they may lose motivation and willingness to continue the creative process.

Another aspect of presence is self-control (or self-regulation) as it speaks toward the leader's ability to control and harness emotions appropriately (DA, 2012); this ability is necessary for the implementation of creativity across a range of Army-specific contexts. The scientific literature supports the impact of one's ability to self-control on creative capacity (e.g., Rego, Sousa, Cunha, Correia, & Saur-Amaral, 2007; Runco, 2004). Leaders with lower self-control are not likely to take criticism well and therefore may be less likely to present or seek feedback on their original ideas and thus less likely to enhance their creative capacity (Rego et al., 2007). In contrast, higher self-control resulted in a greater likelihood of accepting others' ideas, providing helpful feedback, and fostering creativity without losing patience or getting frustrated.

Leaders who can harness emotions or moods that benefit the tasks they face are also more likely to generate creative ideas (Ivcevic & Hoffmann, 2017). For example, listening to upbeat music when brainstorming or sad music when working on analytical task can facilitate performance.

Prior research has demonstrated that negative moods can facilitate critical analysis and evaluation of situations (e.g., Gasper, 2003). Conversely, a positive mood can boost one's cognitive flexibility and originality. In other words, through the management of emotional regulation individuals can help a leader enable and transform their creative capacity.

Intelligence

The last characteristic the Army seeks in creative leaders is *intellect* or intelligence. Intelligence (i.e., intellect) allows leaders to quickly identify the problem space and work through alternative solutions if the current action is not producing effective results (Reeve & Bonaccio, 2011; Sternberg, 2012). Two main components make up intelligence: (1) the ability to learn, otherwise known as general mental ability (g), and (2) the outcomes of learning such as domain-specific knowledge and skills (Reeve & Bonaccio, 2011). Both g and knowledge are antecedents of creative capacity (Carroll, 1993; Kandler et al., 2015; Reiter-Palmon & Illies, 2009; Sternberg, 2012). Research has demonstrated that g predicts creativity and creative outcomes (e.g., Kuncel, Hezlett, & Ones, 2004). Individuals higher in g are more able to process, store, recall, and reason with information (Reeve & Bonaccio, 2011), which are important processes in idea generation and creative problem-solving.

Knowledge structures also have a significant impact on one's creative capacity (Benedek et al., 2017; Mumford et al., 1991). Knowledge can be defined as the fact or state of understanding information with familiarity (Cattell, 1943; Jensen, 1998; Reeve & Bonaccio, 2011); knowledge increases in understanding, coherence, and complexity through a combination of education, training, and experiences (Mumford, Marks, Connelly, Zaccaro, & Reiter-Palmon, 2000; Noe, Clarke, & Klein, 2014; Popper & Lipshitz, 2000). Knowledge in specific domains are important antecedents of creative processes and behaviors; in order to engage in creative behaviors (e.g., divergent thinking), individuals need to know what already exists in the domain in order to generate novel ideas (Carmelli et al., 2013). Individuals with extant knowledge can also reorganize or create new configurations of the information more readily that result in more creative solutions (Mumford et al., 1991). Army leaders begin their career with a basic understanding of their responsibilities and the organization; through education (e.g., Advanced Leader Course), training (e.g., Joint Readiness Training Center), and assignments (e.g., battalion commander), a leader begins to develop more complex knowledge structures needed to be successful (Mumford et al., 2000). This triad—education, training, and assignments—instills and develops military occupation specialty (MOS) specific skills that enable effective decisions and actions by accounting for complexity, realism, timeframe, and abstraction (Mumford et al., 2000; Mumford, Todd, Higgs, & McIntosh, 2017). For example, a brigade commander formulating a strategic order will leverage multiple, interwoven knowledge structures to include combat maneuvers, technology, and geographic characteristics (topography, weather, culture, etc.) to produce an accurate representation of the problem space and then to generate a strategic command that advances the Army's position in terms of force, constituencies, and long-term mission.

Environment Factors

The military environment and organizational culture are built on a unique set of shared values, professional standards, and military doctrine (DA, 2012, 2014, 2015, 2016). As leaders are educated and trained, individual perspectives are stripped away and they begin to adapt to the perspective of their service, and how they apply their resources on the field or place of battle. In other words, many of the trained values and standards serve to underscore the need for precise application of specific procedures and process, which may impede creative thought and application of creative solutions (McClary, 2015). Following we describe the espoused values, standards, doctrine, and commander's intent that guide behavior in the Army.

Values

The Army lives by seven core values that are taught to Soldiers in basic combat training (DA, 2015, 2016). Following basic combat training, Soldiers are expected to adhere to these values in everything that they do—both when on the job and off. The seven core values include Loyalty, Duty, Respect, Self-less service, Honor, Integrity, and Personal courage (see Table 1 for descriptions).

In addition to the core values that are inherent in every activity, the Army developed additional methods to instill the guiding principles in Soldiers to include ethos statements, creeds, songs, and oaths (DA, 2015). For example, following is the oath of enlistment (DA, 2015, p. B-1):

> I, _____, do solemnly swear (or affirm) that I will support and defend the Constitution of the United States against all enemies, foreign and domestic; that I will bear true faith and allegiance to the same; and that I will obey the orders of the President of the United States and the orders of the officers appointed over me, according to regulations and the Uniform Code of Military Justice. So help me God.

These espoused principles consistently highlight the importance of rule following and obedience to orders from authority, which can have the consequence of suppressing creative thinking across situations in the Army. As portrayed in this text, creative behaviors may be seen as deviating from rules or orders, which goes against the disciplined structure instituted by the Army; however, Army doctrine (e.g., DA, 2012) articulates

TABLE 1 The Army Values

Loyalty	Bear true faith and allegiance to the US Constitution, the Army, your unit, and other Soldiers. Bearing true faith and allegiance is a matter of believing in and devoting yourself to something or someone. A loyal Soldier is one who supports the leadership and stands up for fellow Soldiers. By wearing the uniform of the US Army you are expressing your loyalty. And by doing your share, you show your loyalty to your unit
Duty	Fulfill your obligations. Doing your duty means more than carrying out your assigned tasks. Duty means being able to accomplish tasks as part of a team. The work of the US Army is a complex combination of missions, tasks, and responsibilities—all in constant motion. Our work entails building one assignment onto another. You fulfill your obligations as a part of your unit every time you resist the temptation to take "shortcuts" that might undermine the integrity of the final product
Respect	Treat people as they should be treated. In the Soldier's Code, we pledge to "treat others with dignity and respect while expecting others to do the same." Respect is what allows us to appreciate the best in other people. Respect is trusting that all people have done their jobs and fulfilled their duty. And self-respect is a vital ingredient with the Army value of respect, which results from knowing you have put forth your best effort. The Army is one team and each of us has something to contribute
Self-less service	Put the welfare of the nation, the Army and your subordinates before your own. Selfless service is larger than just one person. In serving your country, you are doing your duty loyally without thought of recognition or gain. The basic building block of selfless service is the commitment of each team member to go a little further, endure a little longer, and look a little closer to see how he or she can add to the effort
Honor	Live up to Army values. The nation's highest military award is The Medal of Honor. This award goes to Soldiers who make honor a matter of daily living—Soldiers who develop the habit of being honorable, and solidify that habit with every value choice they make. Honor is a matter of carrying out, acting, and living the values of respect, duty, loyalty, selfless service, integrity, and personal courage in everything you do
Integrity	Do what's right, legally and morally. Integrity is a quality you develop by adhering to moral principles. It requires that you do and say nothing that deceives others. As your integrity grows, so does the trust others place in you. The more choices you make based on integrity, the more this highly prized value will affect your relationships with family and friends, and, finally, the fundamental acceptance of yourself
Personal courage	Face fear, danger, or adversity (physical or moral). Personal courage has long been associated with our Army. With physical courage, it is a matter of enduring physical duress and at times risking personal safety. Facing moral fear or adversity may be a long, slow process of continuing forward on the right path, especially if taking those actions is not popular with others. You can build your personal courage by daily standing up for and acting upon the things that you know are honorable

Note: These definitions were drawn DA (2015), p. B-5. The text of this article is a work of the US Government and is in the public domain pursuant to Sec. 105 of Title 17, the Copyright Act of 1976.

the importance of creativity. The inconsistency across Army narratives exemplifies the struggle between disciplined conformity and creativity thinking in Army processes, which has the potential to suppress creative thinking as they might be seen as deviating from the rules or orders.

Professional Standards

Within the Army, standards are formal, detailed instructions that provide a benchmark for assessing performance that leaders are required to train and enforce (DA, 2015). The Army believes that the enforcement of standards builds expertise and trust within squads, platoons, companies, etc. (DA, 2015). The Army requires Soldiers to continuously enact the Standards in every activity, which over time, may create the belief that being "inconsistent" in execution would be viewed poorly by subordinates, peers, and supervisors with the undesirable consequence of lost trust. As such, standards when followed "to a T" will potentially constrain and inhibit creative thinking. In other words, it is possible that some standards can act as behavioral constraints and inhibit creativity.

Military Doctrine

The Army doctrine represents the common operational concept for Soldiers to effectively perform across the range of military operations and domains (e.g., DA, 2012, 2016). Doctrine supports and enables the development of Soldier readiness for current and future operations by effectively providing guidelines on how the Army conducts operations. Doctrine, for instance, emphasizes synchronized action based on a thorough understanding of all dimensions of the operational environment. Further, doctrine supports and enables the development of Soldier readiness for current and future operations by effectively providing guidelines on how the Army conducts operations. It also provides guidance on Soldier development, from professionalism (i.e., what it means to a Soldier in the US Army) to specific MOS requirements. Together, doctrine provides Soldiers with guidance on development and conduct, which has the potential to impact creative capacity through afforded autonomy (more or less) regarding development and climate to support developmental activities such as exploration.

Commander's Intent

Mission command represents the Army's philosophy of comprehensive engagement for effective responsibility and decision making in support of unified land operations (DA, 2014). The Army defines mission command as "the creative and skillful exercise of authority through timely decision making and leadership" (DA, 2014, p. 5). A key principle of mission command that is associated with creativity is commander's intent. Commander's intent establishes the parameters for activities, which provides opportunity for creative processes in support of mission needs. Subordinates use discretionary autonomy scoped by their commander's intent to tackle these tasks. The commander's intent communicates the [science of] control to subordinates through information disseminated, communication style, structure of forces, and degree of control allocated. An effective command results in opportunities for subordinates to gain practical experience, and when appropriate, extend critical and creative thinking capacity.

Currently, however, a discrepancy appears to exist between the organization (i.e., the Army) and personnel, particularly junior officers (e.g., First Lieutenants), as to when creativity should be routinely integrated into activities (McClary, 2015). Creative processes are an integral component of command philosophy, which is a specific context controlled by a senior commander with staff over an area of operation. However, it is not uncommon for commanders to believe creative thinking should be reserved for mid-to-high level officers only (McClary, 2015). In contrast, Soldiers take the stance that creativity should be routinely integrated in carrying out tasks regardless of scope or context (McClary, 2015). This conflict in perceptions results in a mismatch in job expectations, which can have the unintended consequence of creative thinkers leaving the Army for other jobs that allow for immediate application of creative thinking (Kane, 2011; McClary, 2015).

In total, the training, education, and knowledge dissemination (e.g., values, doctrine) that occurs in the military are specific in function and require a high degree of repetition to master. This repetition coupled with the precise application of the doctrine can build a sense of belief that these specific functions are the only way to solve a given problem, which can stifle creative thinking. It, therefore, becomes important for the Army to balance specialization with opportunities that ensure creative capacity exists within ranks. Strategies include selecting those who possess creative capacity, developing a program to foster it, and establishing opportunities to apply the skill.

SELECTING, DEVELOPING, AND RETAINING THE CREATIVE SOLDIER

While the Army recognizes the importance of creativity as a key component to gain advantage over the enemy, it has experienced difficulties developing and fostering it throughout the organization. The frequency and force of creative behavior vary immensely within the organization. Leaders' application of doctrine influences the use of creative thinking. When enforced to the letter (i.e., strict adherence to rules and processes), creative thinking may be suppressed; in contrast, leaders who widen the aperture of doctrine enforcement likely promote creative exploration through increased autonomy and establishing a safe environment. In short, doctrine attempts to provide guidelines to balance adherence and creativity; the difficulty lies in finding the balance in large due to the magnitude of outcomes within the Army context. The structure and nature of tasks required of Soldiers typically involve a significant risk. Within the Army landscape, if a new idea or process is implemented consequences could amount to lives lost. Due to the severe consequences associated with creative change and processes, creativity may not always be fostered or supported. Following we discuss potential interventions that can help foster creativity in the unique Army environment.

Selection

In an ideal world, the Army would be able to select for creative capacity based on an easily identifiable and measurable set of individual differences. Measuring individual differences in creative capacity would also enable the Army to place the right Soldier in the right place at the right time (McClary, 2015). Yet, how creativity manifests from the interplay between multiple individual differences, the Army environment, and the specialized tasks is still unknown (National Research Council [NRC], 2015; Zhou & Hoever, 2014). Unearthing the necessary individual differences specific to the Army context will greatly expand the ability to foster creativity in the Army (McClary, 2015). Presently, no consensus exists for what constitutes a creative person (i.e., what is the profile of individual differences, skills, and experience). At the most basic level, creativity is a cognitive process driven by a need and utilizes a range of information—internal and external—to generate something novel. Given the need to access and manipulate a range of information, an individual's working memory capacity may be an important indicator of creative capacity. Working memory capacity reflects an individual's cognitive ability to temporarily store, recall, and make sense of information (Baddeley, 2012) and has been found to impact reasoning and decision making (Conway, Cowan, Bunting, Therriault, & Minkoff, 2002; Del Missier, Mäntyla, & Bruine de Bruin, 2012). This ability may facilitate divergent thinking, particularly fluency and originality, through active awareness of information to include resources, constraints, goals, and planning, and, combined with knowledge structures, results in more novel ideas. In addition, working memory capacity may impact the quality of the decision by maintaining temporary access to information required to evaluate its effectiveness.

Training

Given that the Army recognizes the importance of creativity, leaders would expect to see creativity capacities to be fostered and refined through continued development as provided by formal institutionalized learning, field experiences, and professional opportunities. However, the development and maintenance of creative capacity need to be understood within the Army process, which includes understanding how best to balance instilling disciplined understanding and initiative with judicious use of creative thinking as contexts dictate. Beyond just the initial training to instill creative capacity within individuals, the Army needs to consider the need for reinforcement (i.e., skill maintenance) to prevent deterioration in creative process. The bulk of scientific literature focuses on how to best train creative capacity (e.g., Memmert, 2007; Onarheim & Friis-Olivarius, 2013; Scott, Leritz, & Mumford, 2004); however, little attention is paid to maintenance and skill decay (Amabile, Barsade, Mueller, & Staw, 2005). Knowing this, skill maintenance and decay become extremely important, and yet a dearth (at best) of research exists on this topic. Further, creativity training may come in the guise of technical training; attainment of the appropriate knowledge enables a leaders' creative processes (Carmelli et al., 2013; Mumford et al., 1991). Ultimately, the development of creative capacity does not necessitate new curriculum per se but extension of current instruction with a focus on the different creative processes. For example, the Army could incorporate the red-yellow-green chart recently developed by Tannenbaum and associates, which provides the boundaries for exploration (e.g., trial-and-error learning) for a given learning situation where green represents full autonomy, yellow limits learning within supervision/collaboration with experienced personnel, and red restricts to procedures as described (Tannenbaum et al., 2018). The Army could utilize the system to maintain and develop creative thinking. For example, it could be modified such that red signals a focus on the development of doctrine-based knowledge and skills; yellow communicates the need to balance discipline with creative thinking; and green designates a safe zone for the learners to fully explore possibilities to include creative decisions and products to accomplish mission objectives but remaining within commander's intent and rules of engagement. Similarly, the Army could incorporate creative thinking and outcomes into the after action review. Specifically, the Army Observer-Controller-Trainer could dedicate a segment to discuss how creative thinking would have potentially achieved an operational advantage to include identifying when to think creatively and the generation, evaluation, and implementation of novel decisions.

Leadership and Performance Management

In order to foster creativity, an adept commander should promote critical and creative thinking throughout the warfighting functions in order to maximize mission success. In these incidences, it becomes important for the leader to create the appropriate climate that enforces standards and yet promotes creativity thinking in line with commander's intent and overall mission objectives. Commanders will need to establish flexible parameters that provide opportunity for creative processes in support of mission needs (Deci & Ryan, 1987; Mumford, Scott, Gaddis, & Strange, 2002). Subordinates can then use discretionary autonomy scoped by their commander's intent to tackle these tasks. Commanders can foster creative thinking by disseminating information, communicating the value of novel thinking and creative behaviors, and reducing the degree of control and structure (Amabile, Schatzel, Moneta, & Kramer, 2004; Madjar, Oldham, & Pratt, 2002; Mumford et al., 2002). An effective command should result in opportunities for subordinates to gain knowledge, practical experience, and when appropriate, extend critical and creative thinking capacity. While not even situation is appropriate to foster creativity, it is the commander's responsibility to identify and leverage those opportunities in an effort to develop their subordinates.

FUTURE RESEARCH

Selection, training, and performance management are all essential means to foster creativity. However, gaps exist in understanding best practices in particular within the Army context (NRC, 2015; Sackett et al., 2017). Even with the existing body of literature on creativity, the tension between developing and fostering creative thinking and adherence to rules and standards persist. One possible reason for this is that the research on creativity to date has been designed to inform businesses—profit and nonprofit—but unfortunately have limited generalizability to the Army. For instance, the typical organization identifies and accepts the risk involved with creativity, which can range from a "flop" (i.e., a loss of resources to include labor, time, and materials) to success such that it benefits the organization. However, the Army landscape is much different from other organizations primarily in consequences; a "flop" in the Army will likely result in lives lost. Although laboratory research has focused on constructs of importance to the Army (e.g., divergent thinking, personality, ability), this controlled environment may fail to adequately capture the complexities of the Army's operational environment, which results in large knowledge gaps impeding transition from theory to practice. Thus we believe that creativity research to be most beneficial to the Army will need to capture dynamic nature of the operational environment to include operational tempo and high-risk consequences. Following we describe future research that can aid in understanding how to best select, train, and manager individuals to foster creativity within the Army.

Construct Constellations

Individual creativity is a behavioral capacity that manifests from the interface between personality; conative factors, affective and emotional regulation; and intelligence (Mumford et al., 1991; Sackett et al., 2017). Thus to understand the individual differences related to creative capacity within the Army, researchers must study these fundamental precursors and their interactions with one another along with context (Corno et al., 2002; George & Zhou, 2001; McClary, 2015; Reeve, Scherbaum, & Goldstein, 2015). Researchers should draw on and integrate theories such as Snow's theory of aptitude (Corno et al., 2002; Snow, 1987, 1992); intelligence as process, personality, interests, and intelligence as knowledge (PPIK; Ackerman, 1996); and interactionalist perspectives such as interactionist perspective of organizational creativity (Woodman, Sawyer, & Griffin, 1993) or investment theories (e.g., Sternberg, 2012) when advancing theory of creative capacity. These theories underscore the importance of studying the relationship between abilities, affect, and intelligence. By taking this interactionist approach, we can start to understand human behavior by identifying the patterns of behavior(s) associated with creative outcomes. That is, we can no longer study performance by fragmenting single variables and looking at linear relationships (e.g., conscientiousness and job performance)—we must move beyond and study the complexity of the relationships between individual differences and their combined interaction with the environment. While we believe this shift is imperative in order to substantially move our understanding forward, we acknowledge that adoption comes with measurement challenges. As such, emphasis should also be placed on advancing psychometric theory and developing standard systems of measurement (Reeve et al., 2015).

Environmental Factors

The behavioral manifestation of creative capacity is influenced by task and environmental factors (Reiter-Palmon & Illies, 2009); Zhou & Hoever, 2014). As discussed earlier in the chapter, the Army introduces situational factors that may suppress creativity (McClary, 2015). Army doctrine and leadership practices emphasize compliance with standards and deference to authority that may conflict with creative expression and development. Therefore future research needs to look at how to effectively balance these two seemingly opposing needs by investigating creative processes (e.g., divergent thinking) in relation to command climate, supervisor support, leadership style, perceived organizational barriers, job characteristics (e.g., degree of autonomy), and organization culture to list a few (McClary, 2015). Although the Army has and is currently supporting research on creativity capacity (McClary, 2015; NRC, 2015), more research is needed to begin understanding the interaction of context on individual differences as it relates to creativity development and application.

CONCLUSION

Creativity is an integral component of the Army's operations process—plan, prepare, execute, and assess—with increased emphasis on execution to succeed in the evolving operational environment. Leaders must possess the capability to integrate emerging information, resources, and technology within the Army structure, requirements, and doctrine to effectively generate and enact novel plans to counter the adversaries' emerging advantages and continue advancement of the Army mission. Thus creative capacity is an essential capability for all leaders to possess.

Although the Army values creative thinkers, reports suggest creative thinkers are leaving the Army for organizations that develop and support creativity in its employees (e.g., Kane, 2011; McClary, 2015). Given the importance of creative capacity for Army strength, the challenge is to recruit, develop, and retain leaders possessing creative capabilities. Current literature touches on some strategies the Army could integrate into its programs; however, a reconceptualization of creativity is needed that is specific to the Army environment. New research incorporating unique aspects of the Army's context is required to understand the processes, boundaries, and ultimately measurement of the creative space.

References

Ackerman, P. L. (1996). A theory of adult intellectual development: process, personality, interests, and knowledge. *Intelligence, 22,* 227–257.

Amabile, T. M., Barsade, S. G., Mueller, J. S., & Staw, B. M. (2005). Affect and creativity at work. *Administrative Science Quarterly, 50,* 367–403.

Amabile, T. M., Schatzel, E. A., Moneta, G. B., & Kramer, S. J. (2004). Leader behaviors and the work environment for creativity: perceived leader support. *The Leadership Quarterly, 15,* 5–32.

Anderson, N., Potocnik, K., & Zhou, J. (2014). Innovation and creativity in organizations: a state-of-the-science review, prospective commentary, and guiding framework. *Journal of Management, 40,* 1297–1333.

Baddeley, A. (2012). Working memory: theories, models, and controversies. *Annual Review of Psychology, 63,* 1–29.

Benedek, M., Kenett, Y., Umdasch, K., Anaki, D., Faust, M., & Neubauer, A. (2017). How semantic memory structure and intelligence contribute to creative thought: a network science approach. *Thinking and Reasoning, 23,* 158–183.

Carmelli, A., Gelbard, R., & Reiter-Palmon, R. (2013). Leadership, creative problem-solving capacity, and creative performance: the importance of knowledge sharing. *Human Resource Management, 52,* 95–122.

Carroll, J. B. (1993). *Human cognitive abilities: a survey of factor analytic studies.* New York, NY: Cambridge University Press.

Cattell, R. B. (1943). The measurement of adult intelligence. *Psychological Bulletin*, *40*, 153–193.

Conway, A. R., Cowan, N., Bunting, M. F., Therriault, D. J., & Minkoff, S. R. (2002). A latent variable analysis of working memory capacity, short-term memory capacity, processing speed, and general fluid intelligence. *Intelligence*, *30*(2), 163–183.

Corno, L., Cronbach, L. J., Kupermintz, H., Lohman, D. F., Mandinach, E. B., Porteus, A. W., et al. (2002). *Remaking the concept of aptitude: Extending the legacy of Richard E. Snow*. Mahwah, NJ: Erlbaum.

Deci, E. L., & Ryan, R. M. (1987). The support of autonomy and the control of behavior. *Journal of Personality and Social Psychology*, *53*, 1024–1037.

Del Missier, F., Mäntyla, T., & Bruine de Bruin, W. (2012). Decision-making competence, executive functioning, and general cognitive abilities. *Journal of Behavioral Decision Making*, *25*, 331–351.

Department of the Army. (2012). *Army doctrine reference publication no. 6-22*. Army Leadership. Retrieved from http://cape.army.mil/repository/doctrine/adrp6-22.pdf.

Department of the Army. (2014). *Army doctrine reference publication no. 6-0. Mission Command*. Retrieved from https://fas.org/irp/doddir/army/adrp6_0.pdf.

Department of the Army. (2015). *Army doctrine reference No. 1.0. The Army profession*. Retrieved from http://data.cape.army.mil/web/repository/doctrine/adrp1.pdf.

Department of the Army. (2016). *Army doctrine reference publication no. 3-0. Operations*. Retrieved from http://www.apd.army.mil/epubs/DR_pubs/DR_a/pdf/web/ADRP%203-0%20FINAL%20WEB.pdf.

Feist, G. J. (1998). A meta-analysis of personality in scientific and artistic creativity. *Personality and Social Psychology Review*, *2*, 290–309.

Furnham, A., & Bachtiar, V. (2008). Personality and intelligence as predictors of creativity. *Personality and Individual Differences*, *45*, 613–617.

Gasper, K. (2003). When necessity is the mother of invention: mood and problem solving. *Journal of Experimental Social Psychology*, *39*, 248–262.

George, J. M., & Zhou, J. (2001). When openness to experience and conscientiousness are related to creative behavior: an interactional approach. *Journal of Applied Psychology*, *86*, 513–524.

Hirst, G., van Knippenberg, D., & Zhou, J. (2009). A cross-level perspective of employee creativity: goal orientation, team learning behavior, and individual creativity. *The Academy of Management Journal*, *52*, 280–293.

Ivcevic, Z., & Hoffmann, J. (2017). Emotions and creativity: from states to traits and emotion abilities. In G. J. Feist, R. Reiter-Palmon, & J. C. Kaufman (Eds.), *The Cambridge handbook of creativity and personality research*. New York, NY: Cambridge University Press.

Jensen, A. R. (1998). *The g factor: the science of mental ability*. Westport, CT: Praeger.

Kandler, C., Riemann, R., Angleitner, A., Spinath, F. M., Borkenau, P., & Penke, L. (2015). The nature of creativity: the roles of genetic factors, personality traits, cognitive abilities, and environmental sources. *Journal of Personality and Social Psychology*, *111*, 230–249.

Kane, T. (2011). Why our best officers are leaving. *The Atlantic*. Retrieved from: https://www.theatlantic.com/magazine/archive/2011/01/why-our-best-officers-are-leaving/308346/.

Kaufman, S. B., Quilty, L. C., Grazioplene, R. G., Hirsh, J. B., Gray, J. R., Peterson, J. B., et al. (2016). Openness to experience and intellect differentially predict achievement in the arts and sciences. *Journal of Personality*, *84*, 248–258.

Kuncel, N. R., Hezlett, S. A., & Ones, D. S. (2004). Academic performance, career potential, creativity, and job performance: can one construct predict them all? *Journal of Personality and Social Psychology*, *86*, 148–161.

Madjar, N., Oldham, G. R., & Pratt, M. G. (2002). There's no place like home? The contributions of work and nonwork creativity support to employees' creative performance. *The Academy of Management Journal*, *45*, 757–767.

McClary, R. (2015). *Creativity in the Army: Creative process, creative people, and the creative climate*. Ft. Leavenworth, KS: Mission Command - Capabilities Development and Integration Directorate.

McCrae, R. R. (1987). Creativity, divergent thinking, and openness to experience. *Journal of Personality and Social Psychology, 52*, 1258–1265.

Memmert, D. (2007). Can creativity be improved by an attention-broadening training program? An exploratory study focusing on sports teams. *Creativity Research Journal, 19*, 281–291.

Messick, S. (1976). Personality consistencies in cognition and creativity. In Messick, S. & Associates (Ed.), *Individuality in learning* (pp. 4–22). San Francisco, CA: Jossey-Bass.

Messick, S. (1979). Potential uses of noncognitive measurement in education. *Journal of Educational Psychology, 71*(3), 281–292.

Mumford, M. D., Marks, M. A., Connelly, M. S., Zaccaro, S. J., & Reiter-Palmon, R. (2000). Development of leadership skills: experience and timing. *The Leadership Quarterly, 11*, 87–114.

Mumford, M. D., Mobley, M. I., Uhlman, C. E., Reiter-Palmon, R., & Doares, L. M. (1991). Process analytic models of creative capacities. *Creativity Research Journal, 4*, 91–122.

Mumford, M. D., Scott, G. M., Gaddis, B., & Strange, J. M. (2002). Leading creative people: orchestrating expertise and relationships. *The Leadership Quarterly, 13*, 705–750.

Mumford, M. D., Todd, E. M., Higgs, C., & McIntosh, T. (2017). Cognitive skills and leadership performance: the nine critical skills. *The Leadership Quarterly, 28*, 24–39.

National Research Council. (2015). *Measuring human capabilities: An agenda for basic research on the assessment of individual and group performance potential for military accession.* Washington, DC: The National Academies Press.

Noe, R. A., Clarke, A. M., & Klein, H. J. (2014). Learning in the twenty-first-century workplace. *Annual Review of Organizational Psychology and Organizational Behavior, 1*, 245–275.

Oleynick, V. C., DeYoung, C. G., Hyde, E., Kaufman, S. B., Beaty, R. E., & Silvia, P. J. (2017). Openness/intellect: the core of the creative personality. In G. J. Feist, R. Reiter-Palmon, & J. C. Kaufman (Eds.), *The Cambridge handbook of creativity and personality research.* New York, NY: Cambridge University Press.

Onarheim, B., & Friis-Olivarius, M. (2013). Applying the neuroscience of creativity training. *Frontiers in Human Neuroscience, 7*, 1–10.

Ployhart, R. E., Schmitt, N., & Tippins, N. T. (2017). Solving the supreme problem: 100 years of selection and recruitment at the Journal of Applied Psychology. *Journal of Applied Psychology, 102*, 291–304.

Popper, M., & Lipshitz, R. (2000). Organizational learning: mechanisms, culture, and feasibility. *Management Learning, 31*, 181–196.

Reeve, C. L., & Bonaccio, S. (2011). The nature and structure of "intelligence". In T. Chamorro-Premuzic, S. von Stomm, & A. Furnham (Eds.), *The Wiley-Blackwell handbook of individual differences* (pp. 187–216). West Sussex, UK: John Wiley & Sons, Ltd.

Reeve, C. L., Scherbaum, C., & Goldstein, H. (2015). Manifestations of intelligence: expanding the measurement space to reconsider specific cognitive abilities. *Human Resource Management Review, 25*, 28–37.

Rego, A., Sousa, F., Cunha, M. P. E., Correia, A., & Saur-Amaral, I. (2007). Leader self-reported emotional intelligence and perceived employee creativity: an exploratory study. *Creativity and Innovation Management, 16*, 250–264.

Reiter-Palmon, R., & Illies, J. J. (2004). Leadership and creativity: understanding leadership from a creative problem-solving perspective. *The Leadership Quarterly, 15*(1), 55–77.

Reiter-Palmon, R., & Illies, J. J. (2009). Creativity and domain specificity: the effect of task type on multiple indexes of creative problem-solving. *Psychology of Aesthetics, Creativity, and the Arts, 3*, 73–80.

Reiter-Palmon, R., & Robinson, E. J. (2009). Problem identification and construction: what do we know, what is the future? *Psychology of Aesthetics, Creativity, and the Arts, 3*(1), 43.

Runco, M. A. (2004). Creativity. *Annual Review of Psychology, 55*, 657–687.

Sackett, P. R., Lievens, F., Van Iddekinge, C. H., & Kuncel, N. R. (2017). Individual differences and their measurement: a review of 100 years of research. *Journal of Applied Psychology.* Advance online publication https://doi.org/10.1037/apl0000151.

Scott, G., Leritz, L. E., & Mumford, M. D. (2004). The effectiveness of creativity training: a quantitative review. *Creativity Research Journal, 16,* 361–388.

Snow, R. E. (1987). Aptitude complexes. *Aptitude, Learning and Instruction, 3,* 11–34.

Snow, R. E. (1992). Aptitude theory: yesterday, today, and tomorrow. *Educational Psychologist, 27*(1), 5–32.

Sternberg, R. J. (2012). The assessment of creativity: an investment-based approach. *Creativity Research Journal, 24,* 3–12.

Tannenbaum, S. I., Mathieu, J. E., Donsbachk, J. S., Alliger, G. M., Cerasoli, C. P., & Beard, R. L. (2018). Training as a catalyst for field-based learning: An integrated theory, principles, and program of research (Technical Report). United States Army Research Institute for the Behavioral and Social Sciences, Fort Belvoir, VA.

Vego, M. (2013). On military creativity. *Joint Force Quarterly, 3*(70), 83–90.

Woo, S. E., Keith, M. G., Su, R., Saef, R., & Parrigon, S. (2017). The curious dynamic between openness and interests in creativity. In G. J. Feist, R. Reiter-Palmon, & J. C. Kaufman (Eds.), *The Cambridge handbook of creativity and personality research.* New York, NY: Cambridge University Press.

Woodman, R. W., Sawyer, J. E., & Griffin, R. W. (1993). Toward a theory of organizational creativity. *Academy of Management Review, 18,* 293–321.

Woodman, R. W., & Schoenfeldt, L. F. (1989). Individual differences in creativity: an interactionist perspective. In J. A. Glover, R. R. Ronning, & C. Reynolds (Eds.), *Handbook of creativity* (pp. 77–91). New York, NY: Springer Science and Business Media.

Zhou, J., & Hoever, I. J. (2014). Research on workplace creativity: a review and redirection. *Annual Review of Organizational Psychology and Organizational Behavior, 1,* 333–359.

Further Reading

Conway, A. R. A., Kane, M. J., Bunting, M. F., Hambrick, D. Z., Wilhelm, O., & Engle, R. W. (2005). Working memory span tasks: a methodological review and user's guide. *Psychonomic Bulletin & Review, 12,* 769–786.

Department of the Army. (2013). *Army doctrine reference publication no. 1.* Retrieved from http://cape.army.mil/adrp-1/repository/adrp-1-comes-alive-web.pdf.

Zaccaro, S. J., Connelly, S., Repchick, K. M., Daza, A. I., Young, M. C., Kilcullen, R. N., et al. (2015). The influence of higher order cognitive capacities on leader organizational continuance and retention: the mediating role of developmental experiences. *The Leadership Quarterly, 26,* 342–358.

Index

Note: Page numbers followed by *f* indicate figures and *t* indicate tables.

A

Affect
  activation, 250–259
  circumplex representation, 250*f*
  cognitive and behavioral correlates of, 253*t*
  core affect, 250–259
  and creativity, 245–249, 254–259
  valence, 250–259
Agreeableness, personality, 320–322
Ambidextrous leadership
  benefits of, 280
  challenges of, 279–280
  definition, 278–279
Autonomy and individual differences
  to avoid external control, 214–215
  to avoid outcome information, 215–216
  benefits of constraints, 210–214
    individual differences and, 213–214
    model of, 212–213
    task structure, 211–212
  growth need strength, 206
  interactionist perspective, 216
  motivation, 208
  need for, 206–207
  need for structure, 207–208
  personality traits, 207
  procedural information, 215
  recommendations, 214–216
  self-control and self-efficacy, 208–209

B

Behavior
  complex sets of, 245–246
  core affect, 251–252
  creativity, 247
  influences on, 245–246
Bibliographic coupling, 173–176
Bottom-up process
  categories, 98
  definition, 83–84
  studies of, 85

C

Change and uncertainty
  consumer consciousness, 37
  creativity defined, 35
  demographic factors, 36–37
  globalization, 37
  innovation
    change as driver of, 42
    creativity management, 46–48
    definition, 38–40
    and organization, 40–41
    phase model, 47*t*
    stages of, 42–43
  organizations engaging in, 36
Character, of soldiers, 375
Climate
  leadership and performance management, 383–384
  military doctrine, 380
Coaching, continue support, 358–359
Cocitation analysis, individual creativity, 161–170
Cognition
  broadening, 257
  complex set of, 245–246
  core affect, 251–252
  creativity, 247
  influences on, 245–246
  narrowing, 254
Cognitive orientations, 323–326
  creative self-efficacy, 324–325
  divergent *vs.* convergent thinking styles, 323
  information processing and motivation, 325–326
  personal need for structure (PNS), 323–324
Cognitive resources, 107–109
Cognitive styles, of soldiers, 375–376
Commander's intent, 380–381
Compilation emergence
  features of, 94–95
  prototype and exemplars of, 95–96

Printed in the United States
By Bookmasters